STUDIES IN EVANGELICAL HISTORY AND THOUGHT

God in our Nature

The Incarnational Theology of John McLeod Campbell

STUDIES IN EVANGELICAL HISTORY AND THOUGHT

*A complete listing of all titles in this series
will be found at the close of this book*

STUDIES IN EVANGELICAL HISTORY AND THOUGHT

God in our Nature

The Incarnational Theology of John McLeod Campbell

Peter Kenneth Stevenson

Foreword by Trevor Hart

Eugene, Oregon

Wipf and Stock Publishers
199 W 8th Ave, Suite 3
Eugene, OR 97401

God in our Nature
The Incarnational Theology of John McLeod Campbell
By Stevenson, Peter Kenneth
Copyright©2004 Paternoster
ISBN: 1-59752-735-1
Publication date 6/5/2006
Previously published by Paternoster, 2004

This Edition Published by Wipf and Stock Publishers
by arrangement with Paternoster

Paternoster
9 Holdom Avenue
Bletchley
Milton Keyes, MK1 1QR
Great Britain

*Stipple engraving of John McLeod Campbell,
by Charles Henry Jeens, National Portrait Gallery, London.*

STUDIES IN EVANGELICAL HISTORY AND THOUGHT

Series Preface

The Evangelical movement has been marked by its union of four emphases: on the Bible, on the cross of Christ, on conversion as the entry to the Christian life and on the responsibility of the believer to be active. The present series is designed to publish scholarly studies of any aspect of this movement in Britain or overseas. Its volumes include social analysis as well as exploration of Evangelical ideas. The books in the series consider aspects of the movement shaped by the Evangelical Revival of the eighteenth century, when the impetus to mission began to turn the popular Protestantism of the British Isles and North America into a global phenomenon. The series aims to reap some of the rich harvest of academic research about those who, over the centuries, have believed that they had a gospel to tell to the nations.

Series Editors

David Bebbington, Professor of History, University of Stirling, Stirling, Scotland, UK

John H.Y. Briggs, Senior Research Fellow in Ecclesiastical History and Director of the Centre for Baptist History and Heritage, Regent's Park College, Oxford, UK

Timothy Larsen, Associate Professor of Theology, Wheaton College, Illinois, USA

Mark A. Noll, McManis Professor of Christian Thought, Wheaton College, Wheaton, Illinois, USA

Ian M. Randall, Deputy Principal and Lecturer in Church History and Spirituality, Spurgeon's College, London, UK, and a Senior Research Fellow, International Baptist Theological Seminary, Prague, Czech Republic

*For my parents, Charles and Olive Stevenson,
with gratitude for their constant love and support.*

Contents

Foreword	xv
Preface and Acknowledgements	xix
Abbreviations	xxi
Introduction	1

Chapter 1
Campbell's Theological Journey 7
Criticisms of Campbell's Teaching 8
Campbell's Response to his Critics 15
    The Extent of the Atonement 15
    Universal Pardon through the Death of Christ . . . 17
    Assurance of the Essence of Faith 25
Campbell's Depositon from the Ministry
of the Kirk 30
Factors Contributing to his Dismissal 32
Campbell's Christological Orthodoxy
is Called into Question 41
From Row to *The Nature of the Atonement* 44
Journey to the Field of Peace 48
Conclusion 50

Chapter 2
The Nature of the Atonement 54
Theological Methods and Principles 55
    The Priority of Revelation 56
    An Experience-centred Approach? 59

An Objective Love	63
The Key to the Atonement	67
'No one knows the Father except the Son'	70
The Natural Development of the Incarnation	73
Retrospective and Prospective Aspects of the Atonement	74
Christ's Dealing with Humanity on the Part of God	74
Christ's Dealing with God on Behalf of Humanity	77
Christ's Witnessing for the Father to Humanity	84
Christ's Dealing with the Father on our Behalf	86
Further Elements of Campbell's Atonement Theology	89
Made Perfect Through Suffering	90
'My God, my God, why have you forsaken me?'	92
An Underdeveloped Doctrine of the Holy Spirit?	95
The Victory of Christ	96
Evaluating Campbell's Understanding of Atonement	97
Judging the Story of the Cross	97
Judging Campbell's Story of the Cross	101
Conclusion	109

Chapter 3
Campbell the Preacher — 114

The Row and Glasgow Sermons	114
The Row Sermons	114
The Glasgow Sermons	116
The Glasgow *Fragments* and *The Nature of the Atonement*	119
Fragments Added in 1861	119

Fragments Common to the 1843 and the 1861/1898 Editions	134
Fragments Unique to the 1843 Edition	136
The Row Sermons and *The Nature of the Atonement*	139
The Whole Counsel of God	139
Christ as 'The Great Confessor'	145
The Sufferings of Christ	147
An Objective Love	148
Christ the Revealer	149
Conclusion	150

Chapter 4
The Flesh of Christ Differed Not in One Particle from Mine — 152

The Subject of the Lord's Humanity	153
Christ Assumes our Sinful, Fallen Nature	153
The Flesh of Christ Differed Not in One Particle from Mine	155
He took Sinful Flesh	164
In the Likeness of Sinful Flesh	171
He Did Not Cease to be God	174
'He Became What We Are…'	176
The Union of Creature with the Creator	178
Glasgow Fragments	179
Jesus can Touch the Deep Stream of Pollution in Our Flesh	179
Campbell's Christology	182
The Sources of Campbell's Christology	183
A Distinguished Line of Thinkers	187
The Significance of the Subject of the Lord's Humanity	189

Chapter 5
Christ's Twofold Office — 192

The Priestly Office	195
An High Priest over the House of God	196

Past and Present Dimensions of Christ's Priestly Ministry	199
The Royal Office	203
'One from Among thy Brethren'	205
The Promised King	208
The Enthronement of Christ and its Consequences	211
'Man, as God, Reigning in Glory'	214
Conclusion	218

Chapter 6
Romanism, Revelation and Real Presence — 221

'The Present Occupation of Thought with Romanism'	222
Christ the Bread of Life	226
Exposing the Errors	227
The Self-Evidencing Light of Revelation	230
The Priority of Revelation	233
The Trinitarian Nature of Prayer and Worship	235
Advancing an Alternative Approach	237
From Simplicity to Mystery – the 'Development of the Mass of Romanism from the Sacred Institution of the Lord's Supper'	242
'Feeding upon Christ' – Campbell on Communion	244
The Real Presence of Christ	247
Conclusion	252

Chapter 7
Perfect Sonship Towards God: Campbell's Trinitarian Christology — 254

Campbell's Trinitarian Christology	256
The Son who Reveals the Father	257
The Son who Receives the Spirit	260
The Son who Gives the Spirit	264

Three Phases of Imparting the Spirit to the Son	266
The Soteriological Significance of Campbell's Christology	271
'A Perfect Confession of Our Sins'?	272
Conclusion	276

Appendix 1
Extract from a Preface written by John McLeod Campbell to Accompany the Publication of *Two Sermons* in 1830 — 279

Appendix 2
Extract of a Letter from the Rev. John McLeod Campbell, Minister of Row — 280

Appendix 3
LIBEL, &c. — 287

Appendix 4
Notes of Sermons 1.8. — Sermon on Galatians 2:20 'The Life of the Christian', preached at Row on Sunday 25 July 1830 — 294

Appendix 5
Notes of Sermons 3.31 — Sermon on Titus 2:11-14 (Second Sermon on the Text) — 312

Appendix 6
Notes of Sermons 2.13 — Sermon on 1 Peter 1:3-5 — 328

Appendix 7
Notes of Sermons 3.36 — Sermon on Hebrews 10:31 'It is a fearful thing to fall into the hands of the living God' — 352

Appendix 8
Notes of Sermons 3.34 — Sermon on Hebrews 2
'Therefore we ought...' 371

Appendix 9
Notes of Sermons 3.32 — Sermon on Titus 2:11-14
(Third Sermon on the Text) 387

Appendix 10
Notes of Sermons 1.9 — Notes of Fencing of the
Tables, Communion Service and Concluding
Address 21 July 1830 411

Bibliography 431

Index 453

Foreword

The real greatness of John McLeod Campbell did not lie in the work for which he is certainly best remembered, *The Nature of the Atonement* (1856). In a technical sense, of course, this was certainly his *magnum opus*, and has received due recognition in authoritative studies of the doctrine of the work of Christ ever since. Its prolix argument and use of idiosyncratic categories have secured for it criticism and plaudits in equal measure, often based on misunderstanding. At the core of its argument lies a distinction and a choice. The distinction is between understanding Christ's atoning death as, in its nature, 'either an equivalent punishment, or an equivalent sorrow and repentance' for the sins of the world. Campbell opts for the latter understanding, finding just too many unhelpful potential inferences in the image of the Father punishing the Son on the cross, both for Christology and Christian apprehension of the character of God. Instead, therefore, he opts for the admittedly unfamiliar language of 'vicarious penitence', and works out a model of Christ's atoning death in terms of it. The phrase 'vicarious penitence' has itself attracted criticism from Campbell's detractors as virtually meaningless. Yet he did not invent the category. The words cited above are not Campbell's own, but come from the eighteenth century New England theologian Jonathan Edwards' *Satisfaction for Sin*, and echo those of St Anselm some seven centuries earlier still: *aut poena, aut satisfactio*. In mounting his criticism of Edwards' model of atonement (and the criticism is a sustained and penetrating one), Campbell demonstrates that while their conclusions may be strikingly different, their starting point is certainly not. What he offers is a reading of the death of Jesus – as understood in Scripture – in terms of Edwards' unexplored alternative; in doing so, he attempts to show how such a reading is more consonant with the basic shape of Christology and God's character as revealed in the incarnate Son.

To some extent, the success or failure of Campbell's soteriological essay is less important than this unswerving focus on the character of God which motivated the intellectual effort represented in it. It is a great book. But Campbell's real greatness lay in his recognition of a malaise in the church of his day, and in the diagnosis and prescription which he made to relieve it. Remarkably, this 'theological wisdom' was not born of many years in the academy, but of very few months in the parish and a thorough familiarity with Scripture. Confronted with a congregation lacking in that joyous and confident trust in God which he believed to be of the essence of a living gospel faith, Campbell quickly reached the view that the root of the problem lay in a distorted understanding of who God is, and of God's disposition toward sinners (believers and unbelievers alike). Tracing the distortion to certain aspects of Puritan theology (ones which had already been the cause of considerable dispute in Scotland), Campbell began to emphasize in his weekly sermons some key themes: the universal scope of God's redemptive desire, the universal scope of Christ's atoning work, the revelation of God's essential character in that of the incarnate Son, and joyful assurance as the starting point and of the essence of Christian faith. It was his unashamed preaching of these gospel truths (as he insisted they were) from his pulpit which led to Campbell's notoriety on the west coast of Scotland. It was also these sermons, and not an esoteric sounding theology of 'vicarious penitence', which led to his deposition from the ministry of the Church in 1831.

Campbell was not, therefore, first and foremost a 'theologian', even though he has rightly been listed among Scotland's greatest. He never held an academic teaching post, though he was awarded an honorary doctorate by the University of Glasgow in recognition of his theological achievements. But Campbell was first and foremost a great pastor who recognised the impact which theology (whether adhered to explicitly or lurking in the subliminal background of faith) had on the practical living of Christian life. And the antidote to the sort of theology which, as he saw it, led straight back from a spirit of 'sonship' to one of slavery, is to be found in his sermons. Many of these were published, and one cannot help reflecting that if some of his more vociferous critics had paid more attention to them their criticisms would have been better targeted. In particular, interpretations of *The Nature of the Atonement* which lack this vital background are doomed to a certain level of misunderstanding. Much in that sustained essay takes for granted what Campbell had already worked out and insisted upon in his earlier wrestling with Scripture.

It is therefore a particular pleasure to write this foreword for Peter Stevenson's authoritative study of Campbell's theology which, in addition to redressing some imbalances of focus and exploring some hitherto neglected aspects of that theology, sees it as a whole, and offers a judicious reading of it.

Trevor Hart,
Professor of Divinity
Principal of St Mary's College
University of St Andrews

Preface and Acknowledgements

This book represents an expanded version of my PhD thesis submitted in 2001 which examined 'The Person and Work of Christ in the Preaching and Theology of John McLeod Campbell.' Labouring as the minister of an independent congregation in nineteenth century Glasgow, John McLeod Campbell wrote about 'the isolation of' his 'own position'. In contrast I can be grateful for the many people who have accompanied and encouraged me on this research journey.

Before returning to Scotland, Professor Alan Torrance supervised the early stages of research, arousing my interest in the subject and helping me to clarify the direction of my research. Throughout the whole process, Professor James B. Torrance was a constant source of encouragement and information. I was grateful not only for his infectious enthusiasm for McLeod Campbell's theology, but also for the generous way in which he allowed me to borrow some precious copies of McLeod Campbell's books. He strongly supported the publication of *God in our Nature*, and there is a tinge of sadness that he died just a few months before its publication. My hope is that in some way this book will bear witness to the Triune God of grace who was at the centre of James Torrance's life and teaching.

It is also a pleasure to acknowledge the significant role played by Dr Murray Rae at King's College, London who has been a most stimulating and helpful supervisor. Testing out this material in Postgraduate Seminars at the Research Institute in Systematic Theology at King's College has been another important and helpful part of the research process.

The research that lies behind this book was carried on alongside my responsibilities as a tutor at Spurgeon's College, and I value the support and encouragement that my colleagues have provided. The Academic Board of the College kindly granted me a semester's sabbatical during 1999 which made it possible to complete the main part of the research. Our college librarian, Mrs Judy Powles, provided sterling service by tracking down various books and articles with her characteristic efficiency.

From start to finish, friends at Chatsworth Baptist Church in West Norwood have taken an active interest in this project, and I hope that they will find the end result interesting.

Above all I am grateful to Susan, my partner in marriage and ministry, for her love and generosity which have sustained me throughout the long process of researching and writing.

Peter K. Stevenson,
Spurgeon's College,
London.
March 2004.

Abbreviations

Bread1	John McLeod Campbell, *Christ the Bread of Life: An attempt to give a profitable direction to the present occupation of thought with Romanism*, (Glasgow: Maurice Ogle and Son, 1851).
Bread2	John McLeod Campbell, *Christ the Bread of Life: An attempt to give a profitable direction to the present occupation of thought with Romanism*, (London: Macmillan and Co., 1869^2).
EG	*The Everlasting Gospel; Notes of a Sermon, by the Rev. J. M. Campbell, Minister of Row, Dumbartonshire; Preached in the Floating Chapel, at Greenock, 28th April, 1830*, (Greenock: R. B. Lusk, 1830).
FofE	*Fragments of Expositions of Scripture*, (London: J. Wright & Co, 1843). Originally published anonymously but mainly consisting of sermons by John McLeod Campbell.
FofTE	*Fragments of Truth: Being the Exposition of Several Passages of Scripture*, (Edinburgh: Edmoston and Douglas, 1861^3).
FofT	*Fragments of Truth: Being Expositions of Passages of Scripture chiefly from the teaching of John McLeod Campbell, D.D.* (Edinburgh: David Douglas, 1898^4).
GT	*Good Tidings of Great Joy to All People*, (Glasgow: Edward Khull, 1830). Originally published anonymously. At least 9 of the sermons were written by John McLeod Campbell.

Memorials	Donald Campbell, (ed.), *Memorials of John McLeod Campbell, D.D., Being selections from his correspondence*, 2 vols., (London: Macmillan:, 1877).
Nature	John McLeod Campbell, *The Nature of the Atonement*, (London: Macmillan, 1906^6).
NofS	John McLeod Campbell, *Notes of Sermons by the Rev. J. McL. Campbell*, Taken in Short Hand, 3 vols., lithographic reproduction, (Paisley: J. Vallance, 1831 & 1832).
Proceedings	*The Whole Proceedings before the Presbytery of Dumbarton, and Synod of Glasgow and Ayr, in the case of the Rev. John M'Leod Campbell, Minister of Row, including the libel, answers to the libel, evidence, and speeches*, (Greenock: R. B. Lusk, 1831).
Proceedings (GA)	*The Whole Proceedings in the case of the Rev. John M'Leod Campbell, late minister of Row, before the Presbytery of Dumbarton, the Synod of Glasgow and Ayr, and the General Assembly of the Church of Scotland; including besides all the documents, the speeches in all the different church courts*, (Greenock: R. B. Lusk, 1831).
Reminiscences	John McLeod Campbell, *Reminiscences and Reflections, Referring to his early ministry in the parish of Row, 1825-31*, edited with Introduction by Donald Campbell (London: Macmillan, 1873).
S&L	John McLeod Campbell, *Sermons and Lectures*, Vol. I, (Greenock: R. B. Lusk, 1831^3). John McLeod Campbell, *Sermons and Lectures*, Vol II, (Greenock: R. B. Lusk, 1832).

Abbreviations

TR   John McLeod Campbell, *Thoughts on Revelation*, (London: Macmillan, 1862).

TS   John McLeod Campbell, *Two Sermons*, (London: John Hatchard & Son, 1830).

Page references

References to *The Nature of the Atonement* primarily refer to the sixth edition, printed in 1906, which incorporates all the additional material which Campbell had added to the book originally published in 1856. The page numbers which follow in brackets refer to the paperback edition published by Eerdmans and Handsel Press in 1996.

Thus the footnote, *Nature*, 44 (65) refers to page 44 in the older edition, which corresponds to page 65 in the 1996 edition.

Memorials 1.71 represents *Memorials* volume 1 page 71.

NofS 1.3.6. represents *Notes of Sermons* Volume 1, Sermon 3, page 6. Each sermon in this edition is numbered separately

S&L 1.14.346 represents *Sermons and Lectures* Volume 1, Sermon 14, page 346.

The volume entitled, *The Whole Proceedings before the Presbytery of Dumbarton, and Synod of Glasgow and Ayr, in the case of the Rev. John M'Leod Campbell, Minister of Row, including the libel, answers to the libel, evidence, and speeches*, combines various speeches and reports which had been originally published separately. As a result it contains two sets of pages numbered 1 to 103! References to the second cycle of pages numbered 1- 103 appear in the form *51.

Introduction

Within a few years of being inducted to the picturesque parish of Row in Dumbartonshire in 1825, an inexperienced minister, John McLeod Campbell, was being tried for heresy. In May 1831 the Church of Scotland found him guilty of heresy and removed from its ministry someone regarded by Thomas F. Torrance as 'one of the profoundest theologians in the history of Scottish theology since the Reformation of the Church of Scotland.'[1] A quarter of a century after his deposition Campbell published his most influential work, *The Nature of the Atonement*. Its significance is reflected in the fact that many standard treatments of the doctrine of atonement continue to offer evaluations of Campbell's approach.

Now, as then, Campbell's theology provokes a wide range of responses, and this study argues that a reassessment of his approach is now appropriate. Previous accounts of his theology have been incomplete, and often inaccurate, for a number of reasons. In particular it appears that the theological significance of his sermons has been underestimated, sufficient attention has not been paid to his christology, and Campbell's understanding of the work of the Spirit has not been given adequate recognition. This last omission partly being the result of overlooking his association with the 'Gareloch pentecost' of 1830.

Whilst it is understandable that most scholarly attention has been concentrated upon Campbell's soteriology, this study argues that his christology is also significant. Considering that he published no systematic treatment of the person of Christ, it might initially appear that there is not enough material to justify a study of Campbell's christology. However, a number of factors suggest that sufficient resources are available to enable a serious consideration of his christology.

J. Moltmann observes that 'in the history of theology, the doctrine about the person of Christ has always provided the

---

[1] Thomas F. Torrance, *Scottish Theology from John Knox to John McLeod Campbell*, (Edinburgh: T & T Clark, 1996), 287.

inner premise for the soteriology which is to be substantiated; while soteriology is the outward result of the christology'.[2] Such an interdependence of the person and work of Christ would appear to be axiomatic in all doctrines of atonement, because it is the special nature of the person of Christ which makes his sufferings especially effective.[3] Conversely, the universal efficacy of his sufferings helps to reveal and confirm his special nature and status. If these central doctrines are so mutually interdependent then a study of Campbell's reflections on the work of Christ, set forth in *The Nature of the Atonement*, ought to yield considerable insights into his understanding of Christ's person.

However, any attempt to discern the contours of Campbell's christology must face the limitations indicated by Tuttle who observes that "while regarding the incarnation as a presupposition of the atonement, Campbell did not think it necessary to discuss the question as to how he is who he is — how the Son is related to the Father in the Godhead or how the Word is made flesh. These questions he set aside for the time being, along with a number of other matters surrounding the atonement.'[4] Bearing these limitations in mind, this study identifies those aspects of Campbell's christology which emerge from a detailed examination of *The Nature of the Atonement*.

A careful reappraisal of *The Nature of the Atonement* is also called for, because his approach to atonement is often misunderstood. To some extent Campbell's rather cumbersome style of writing may have contributed to misunderstandings of his position, by deterring some people from making the effort to read the book as a whole. It would be interesting to know how many readers have felt that they have done their duty, and have read no further, once they have reached the famous passage about Christ offering *'a perfect Amen in humanity to the judgement*

---

[2] J. Moltmann, *The Way of Jesus Christ*, (London: SCM Press, 1990), 44. Cf., Colin E. Gunton, *Yesterday and Today: A Study of Continuities in Christology*, (London: SPCK, 1997[2]), 182, 'The content of Christianity as a gospel about human forgiveness, reconciliation and flourishing is bound up with its Christology. Soteriology cannot be divorced from Christology...'
[3] E.g. In the classic work of Anselm where the life and death of the God-Man are of 'infinite value', so that He makes 'ample satisfaction for the sins of the whole world, and infinitely more'.
[4] George M. Tuttle, *John McLeod Campbell on Christian Atonement: So Rich a Soil* (Edinburgh: Handsel Press, 1986), 84.

of God on the sin of man.'[5] Readers yielding to this temptation miss out on a further two hundred pages of theological exploration, and when this material is taken into account it appears that Campbell was expressing a much more complex, and perhaps more satisfying, approach to atonement than many of his critics seem to realise. An important aim of this study, therefore, is to encourage further thought about Campbell's theology by offering a fresh reading of *The Nature of the Atonement*.

In addition to challenging some stereotypes of Campbell's theology, this reappraisal of his model of atonement contributes directly to the christological aims of this study. For the coinherence of soteriology and christology implies that a clear grasp of the soteriological heart of his theology is essential to any exploration of his understanding of the person of Christ.

If *The Nature of the Atonement* was the only resource available then the limited potential of such an inquiry would have to be conceded. However, another rich resource is available, because Campbell's legacy includes written scripts of sermons preached during his ministries at Row and at Glasgow. The printed record of his ministry at Row consists of over seventy sermons, many of which contain about nine thousand words. This represents a significant resource, amounting to over half a million words, which offers real insights into Campbell's thinking during that formative period of his ministry. Added to this are thirty four sermons and talks dating from the time of his ministry in Glasgow. Although many of these are briefer than the Row sermons, the two sets of sermons together create a substantial resource.

These sermons not only illustrate his distinctive approach to atonement but also offer valuable insights into Campbell's thinking about a variety of theological and pastoral topics. The young preacher of Row employed a wide range of biblical language and imagery to convey the ultimate significance of Christ. His preaching was shaped by a variety of biblical passages, and by the needs of his congregation, with the result that the sermons reflect something of the inevitable untidiness of pastoral ministry. Whilst these sermons do not supply a tidy, systematic definition of the person of Christ, it is possible to trace within them the contours of a coherent christology. These sermons, which have long been out of print, have not attracted the sort of attention devoted to *The Nature of the Atonement*, but

---

[5] *Nature*, 117 (118).

this study begins the process of redressing that imbalance by offering a close examination of some of these sermons. Hence chapters 3 to 5 devote considerable space to the exposition of key sermons.

Several substantial studies of Campbell's theology now exist which help to paint a more complete picture of his theology.[6] These studies vary in approach, and in the degree to which they draw upon the material in the Row sermons. The most comprehensive bibliography of works by and about Campbell is provided by James C. Goodloe, who makes substantial use of material from the sermons to support his particular reading of Campbell's view of atonement. He asserts that Campbell's understanding of Christian experience effectively determined his theory of atonement. This rather 'subjective' reading of Campbell's soteriology will be vigorously challenged by the material examined in this study. A contrasting approach is evident in Leanne Van Dyk's book which offers a more 'objective' reading of Campbell's theology, and highlights 'important and meaningful continuity between the atonement accounts of John Calvin and John McLeod Campbell.'[7] However, her appraisal of Campbell's soteriology is weakened by the absence of any reference to his sermons, which would have supplied further evidence of his debt to the Reformed tradition.

Previous studies have tended to see the Row sermons, either as useful background material for understanding the events leading up to his trial for heresy, or as the seedbed for his mature thinking about atonement. While both of these approaches are important, a different approach is adopted here which draws particular attention to the christology contained within those sermons. What appears to have gone largely unnoticed is that Campbell's sermons express a christology

---

[6] See for example, Leanne Van Dyk, *The Desire of Divine Love: John McLeod Campbell's Doctrine of the Atonement* (New York: P. Lang, 1995); George M. Tuttle, *So Rich a Soil*; James C. Goodloe, 'John McLeod Campbell, the Atonement and the Transformation of the Religious Consciousness', Unpublished PhD, University of Chicago, (1987); James C. Goodloe, *John McLeod Campbell: The Extent and Nature of the Atonement*, Studies in Reformed Theology and History (New Series 3), (Princeton Theological Seminary: Princeton, 1997); and Michael Jinkins, *A Comparative Study in the Theology of Atonement in Jonathan Edwards and John McLeod Campbell: Atonement and the Character of God*, (San Francisco: Mellen Research University Press, 1993).

[7] Van Dyk, *Desire of Divine Love*, 139.

which takes the humanity of Christ seriously, because it emphasises that the Son of God assumed fallen human nature, presenting it spotless to God in the power of the Holy Spirit. The discovery of this emphasis does not necessarily prove that Campbell was a theological innovator, because it is possible, even probable, that he derived this insight from his friend, Edward Irving. The identification of this element within Campbell's christology has potentially much greater significance for scholarly interpretation of *The Nature of the Atonement*. Given the interdependence of christology and soteriology, a fuller appreciation of his christology should lead to a more adequate understanding of his soteriology. This study offers a fresh perspective by arguing that an appreciation of Campbell's emphasis upon Christ as 'God in our nature' lends greater coherence and plausibility to his model of atonement. Campbell's portrayal of Christ making 'a perfect confession of our sins' has been deemed inadequate by a number of his critics. However, if Christ assumed sinful fallen nature, then it becomes more plausible to talk about Christ making such a confession on our behalf. A fuller understanding of the christology embedded in his sermons makes it possible, therefore, to view his model of atonement in a different light and, while not removing all the difficulties associated with Campbell's approach, this does permit a less distorted view of his theology.

To argue that material from his early sermons can assist our understanding of *The Nature of the Atonement* presupposes that Campbell was a consistent thinker, and so it is important to demonstrate the continuities between the thought of the young preacher in Row and the outlook of the mature author writing twenty five years later. Examination of material from different stages in his ministry indicates that the main characteristics of the theology 'written for the press' in 1856 were 'all present substantially very early' in his preaching.[8] If his theological approach did not change substantially during his ministry then it is important that the material within his early sermons is taken into account in any consideration of his theology.

Any evaluation of Campbell's christology requires an appreciation of the shape and texture of his theology as a whole. Similarly it is essential to see his theology against the background of the religious and social change taking place in nineteenth century Scotland. One of the contextual factors which is overlooked in most treatments of Campbell's trial for

---

[8] *Memorials* 2.159.

heresy, is, as we have mentioned, his association with an outbreak of charismatic phenomena in 1830, sometimes described as the Gareloch pentecost. One of the theological consequences of this omission is that the pneumatological dimensions of Campbell's christology and soteriology tend to be missed. A failure to take account of these events, with which Campbell and his circle were closely associated, also makes it more difficult, historically, to comprehend the way in which Moderates and Evangelicals were united in their drive to depose him. This study begins to remedy that situation by providing both a detailed account of the circumstances leading to his trial for heresy, and a briefer account of the rest of his life and thought.

The way in which the Evangelical party in the Kirk voted decisively to depose Campbell from the church's ministry raises questions about Campbell's theological orthodoxy. Now, as then, there are some who conclude that it is appropriate to describe him as a heretic.[9] This study argues that such criticisms are unjustified because when the material in Campbell's sermons is taken into account a much more rounded and evangelical picture of his theology begins to emerge. On the basis of his preaching and theology this study will contend that Campbell's theological development should be seen as a movement towards a larger evangelicalism, rather than a departure from mainstream evangelical truth.

---

[9] See for example, Robert Alexander Anderson, 'John McLeod Campbell: The Problem of Authority in Religion', Unpublished DPhil, University of Oxford (1978), chapter 4, who concludes that 'in terms of pure theology, it is concluded, finally that John McLeod Campbell's interpretation of the Christian revelation was heretical, both in relation to Reformed Orthodoxy, and in relation to a fair understanding of the total Hebrew-Christian revelation.'

Chapter 1

Campbell's Theological Journey

> The doctrines necessary to the full display of THE TRUTH are, that love is an essential attribute in Godhead, and manifested to all his creatures; while hatred is a property only of a sinful creature: in opposition to the false doctrine that God loves only a part of his creatures, and hates the remainder...[1]

The life of John McLeod Campbell (1800-72) represents a journey away from the federal theology[2] prevalent in Scotland at the beginning of the nineteenth century. He sought to lead people away from a theology which did not bring assurance and joy, towards a theology centred on the love of God revealed in the person of Christ. On this journey Campbell was influenced by a number of friends, and exerted his own influence on the wider church through his preaching and writing.

John McLeod Campbell was born near Kilninver in Argyllshire on 4 May 1800, the eldest son of Revd Donald Campbell, minister of the united parish of Kilninver and Kilmelford. As his mother died in April 1806, it was his father who had the main responsibility for his education and care. Along with his brother he went to Glasgow to begin studies at the University in November 1811, entering the Divinity Hall in 1817.[3] Completing his course of studies on 1 May 1820 he was

---

[1] *TS*, vi-vii. Appendix 1.
[2] James B. Torrance, 'The Concept of Federal Theology — Was Calvin a Federal Theologian?', in W. H. Neuser (ed.), *Calvinus Sacrae Scriptura Professor: Calvin as Confessor of Holy Scripture*, (Grand Rapids: Eerdmans, 1990), 16.
[3] Donald Leonard Faris, 'The Nature of Theological Inquiry as Raised by the Conflict of the Teaching of McLeod Campbell and Westminster Theology', Unpublished PhD, New College, University of Edinburgh, New College, (1967), 37. Faris considers the theological curriculum which Campbell was likely to have followed in Glasgow and concludes that 'In every regard then, it seems likely that McLeod Campbell received an extremely orthodox training in Westminster Theology.'

licensed to preach the Gospel by the Presbytery of Lorn. After preaching his first sermon, in Gaelic, in his father's church he spent a number of years awaiting the call to his first church. In May 1825 he was presented to the parish of Row[4] in Dumbartonshire by the Duke of Argyll and he was ordained minister of the parish in September of that year.

Criticisms of Campbell's Teaching

At the start of his ministry Campbell believed that there was nothing unusual about his theological approach,[5] but it was not long before a distinctive theology began to emerge. This arose partly out of his resolution to use nothing but the Bible and prayer in his sermon preparation,[6] and also from his desire to transform his pastoral visits into spiritual occasions which would help people to see that 'religion was a thing truly of all times, and of all seasons.' This immersion in parish life quickly made him aware of the negative effect of the prevailing theological orthodoxy upon his congregation. He was confronted by *'the want of living religion'*[7] one symptom of which was a shallow understanding of repentance. It appeared to him that most expressions of repentance were motivated by a fear of punishment rather than by any sincere desire for holiness and obedience to God. This discovery did not lead Campbell to condemn his parishioners, for he realised that all appeals for repentance were doomed to fail unless some way could be found to assure people of God's love.

> Meditating with prayer, on this painful ministerial experience, I was gradually taught to see that *so long as the individual is uncertain of being the object of love to his God, and is still without any sure hold of his personal* safety, in the prospect of eternity, it is in vain to attempt to induce him to serve God under the

---

[4] Pronounced *Roo*. The name of the village has now reverted to the Gaelic spelling, Rhu.

[5] In a letter written to his brother in India on 1 January 1831 Campbell describes how his views developed during the early stages of his ministry. This letter is an invaluable source of information about the ways Campbell's thinking developed during this crucial period in his ministry. Extracts from this letter can be found in *Reminiscences*, 10-11. A fuller version of this letter is printed at the beginning of *NofS* Volume 1, and is included here as Appendix 2.

[6] *Ibid.*, 11-12, Appendix 2.

[7] *Ibid.*, 10; Appendix 2.

power of any purer motive than the desire to win God's love for himself, and so to secure his own happiness: consequently, however high the standard, correspondence with it was sought under the influence of unmingled selfishness, making every apparent success a deeper deception. And thus I was gradually led to entertain the doctrine commonly expressed by the words, 'Assurance of Faith', having first seen the want of it precluded singleness of heart and eye in the service of God — and then having found in studying the Epistles to the first Christian Churches, that its existence, in those disciples, was *in them* taken for granted, and in every practical exhortation was presupposed, I accordingly began to urge on my people, that in order to their being free to serve God — in order to their being in a condition to act purely, under the influence of love to them, and delight in what he is, their first step in religion would require to be, *resting assured of his love in Christ to them as individuals*, and of their individually having eternal life given to them in Christ.[8]

These convictions about assurance developed towards the end of 1826 and by the summer of 1827 some people were expressing their disagreement with his teaching.[9] The result of encountering such opposition was to provoke further thought as to the grounds for assurance, and Campbell concluded that the only basis for genuine assurance would be found not, as the practical syllogism suggested, by searching within for evidences of election[10] but by looking to the cross where Christ died for the sins of all.[11] Years later his son, Donald, summed up this period in his father's ministry by saying that 'during 1827 the *nature* of faith had been the most prominent subject; during the two following years he dwelt rather on the *object* of faith, — namely, Christ's death for all men, forgiveness in Christ for all men.'[12]

However, some of those who heard Campbell talk about 'universal atonement and pardon through the blood of Christ' sensed that errors such as antinomianism and Arminianism were in the air. Around December 1828 a first attempt was made

---

[8] *Ibid.,* 18-19, Appendix 2.
[9] *Ibid.,* 19-21, Appendix 2.
[10] Daniel P. Thimell, 'Christ in Our place in the theology of John McLeod Campbell', in T. A. Hart and D. P. Thimell (eds.), *Christ In Our Place: The Humanity of God in Christ for the Reconciliation of the World,* (Exeter: Paternoster Press, 1989), 182-206.
[11] *Reminiscences,* 24, Appendix 2.
[12] *Reminiscences,* 27.

to bring the subject matter of Campbell's teaching under the consideration of the church courts.[13] Another similar petition signed by three or four individuals was presented to the Presbytery in March 1829. Only two petitioners appeared on the day, and one of them had his name withdrawn from the petition because he had been out of fellowship with the church for several years. The remaining petitioner was persuaded to withdraw the complaint for a time. 'This petition was never afterwards presented; nor did any of the same parties again appear before the Presbytery in any matter connected with the case.'[14]

The following year on 30 March 1830 a Memorial[15] was presented to the Presbytery, (signed 9 March 1830 by twelve parishioners) challenging his teaching on a number of issues. The complaint reminded the Presbytery of their earlier protests that 'certain unsound pernicious doctrines, contrary to the Scripture and the Standards of the National Church' had been propagated by Campbell in the church at Row. A twelve month cooling-off period had not had the desired effect, they argued, because 'not only have the original obnoxious tenets been inculcated by Mr. Campbell with increased earnestness ever since — it is with deep sorrow we say it — but a number of other "unprofitable questions" have been agitated, and doctrines, in our opinion, even more pernicious, have been introduced; for example, that of universal pardon.'[16] Around the same time a supportive Memorial, signed by about eighty householders and heads of families, was presented to, but not accepted by, the Presbytery.

The Presbytery appointed a committee to meet Campbell on 6 April 1830 but at that stage he decided, on procedural grounds,

---

[13] *Proceedings*, iv-v. 'About this time, a petition, signed by a few individuals, was lodged with the presbytery (*sic*) of Dumbarton, in which a variety of charges were brought against Mr. C., and among others his having taught that there was no occasion for repentance — no such thing as a good hope through grace — that Christ was no lawgiver, &c. &c. After this petition was received by the Presbytery, and, it is believed, after part of it was taken down in the Minutes, it was discovered to bear no date, an informality which made it necessary to return it to the petitioners.'
[14] *Ibid.*, v.
[15] 'Memorial' was the title for the official petitions sent to the Presbytery. It is interesting that after Campbell's death his son decided to entitle the two volumes of his father's correspondence *Memorials of John McLeod Campbell*. Was this play on words deliberate?
[16] *Proceedings*, v-vi.

Campbell's Theological Journey

not to co-operate. At the meeting of the Presbytery on the 4 May 1830, an Elder, Mr. Dunlop, persuaded them to accept the favourable memorial. The twelve petitioners were called to testify against him but only three appeared. As the case gathered momentum Campbell was still preaching what some must have felt to be rather provocative sermons. On the 9 June 1830 he preached at the Seaman's Chapel in Greenock about Elijah's battle with the prophets of Baal, leaving his hearers in no doubt as to who were the false prophets of their own day.

> I wish you to understand me, I have no desire but simply to carry home to your minds exactly my meaning, which is that the Baal — the false God worshipped in this land by so many of the people, is a God who only loves some men — whom men are encouraged to approach without being told whether their sins have been removed or not — in respect of whom it is said that if a Saviour has suffered for any one he cannot be punished whatever his sins afterwards may be.[17]

Such language on the lips of a ministerial novice was not likely to endear him to his more experienced colleagues who were soon to be passing judgement upon him. In the debates that were to follow it is possible to see signs of their resentment of what they felt to be Campbell's spiritual arrogance.

Following a judgement from the Kirk's General Assembly, the Presbytery meeting at Dumbarton decided that there should be a parochial visitation of the parish of Row on Thursday 8 July 1830. The committee duly turned up to hear Campbell preach a sermon based on Matthew 5:1-12. He suggested that he would need three hours to do justice to what he wanted to say, but after some debate it was agreed that the sermon and the service together should not exceed two hours. As it turned out this was more than enough time to inflame the situation. In preaching upon the Beatitudes he declared that the peacemakers, commended by Jesus, are those who seek to bring, not some, but *all* to faith. 'And who are those who shall be persecuted for righteousness' sake? They are those who will declare as the Apostle says, that Christ Jesus is the Saviour of all men, especially of those who believe.'[18] In a number of ways he left his critics in no doubt that in opposing the teaching of the

---

[17] *NofS*, 1.3.6.
[18] John McLeod Campbell, *Notes of a Sermon, Preached in the Parish Church of Row, on Thursday, 8th July 1830; Being the day of the visitation of that Parish by the Presbytery of Dumbarton,* (Greenock: R.B. Lusk, 1830), 25.

universal love of God they were in danger of rejecting God's voice. He concluded by insisting that he had spoken the truth and that 'for this truth I am ready to die.' Whilst his courage and sincerity cannot be doubted, questions can be raised about his diplomatic skills, for he ended the sermon in a very confrontational manner which could have left his opponents in no doubt about his meaning. 'If you refuse to hear what is of the glory of God, it matters not how little human authority may teach it, you will be condemned, because you do not believe.'[19]

Not surprisingly the disciplinary committee responded to this direct challenge and a meeting behind closed doors recommended that the Memorial should be converted into a Libel. It was reported that

> the Presbytery, by a great majority, recorded their detestation and abhorrence of the doctrine contained in two sentences of the sermon, which we believe are to the following purport — 'God loves every child of Adam with a love the measure of which is to be seen in the agonies of Christ' and that 'the person who knows that Christ died for every child of Adam, is the person who is in the condition to say to every human being, Let there be peace with you, peace between you and your God.'[20]

Campbell was informed of this by letter in the first week of September and responded in written form at the next meeting of the Presbytery later in September. He was duly summoned to appear before the Presbytery on the 21st September, and at that meeting both the Libel and Campbell's written answers were read out.

Once this disciplinary process had been set in motion the outcome was inevitable. For as Campbell admitted years later, in choosing to speak about universal atonement, pardon and assurance, he was teaching doctrines which he knew 'the living church in Scotland was *likely* — and, unless by some special grace of God, was *sure* — to reject.'[21] He and others would have known that such ideas were objectionable to many, because similar doctrines had been condemned a century earlier during the controversy surrounding the teaching of *The Marrow of*

---

[19] *Ibid.*, 26.
[20] *Proceedings*, xix-xx.
[21] *Memorials*, 2.34. Letter dated 13 November 1862.

Modern Divinity.²² This is made explicit in the wording of the Libel whose opening paragraph bluntly states that Campbell's teachings had been 'moreover condemned by the fifth Act of the General Assembly held in the year seventeen hundred and twenty, as being directly opposed to the word of God, and to the Confession of Faith and Catechisms of the Church of Scotland.'²³ As so many of his contemporaries insisted upon interpreting Campbell's case through the lenses provided by the *Marrow* controversy, it is necessary to consider what had been at stake in that earlier episode.

In 1717 the Presbytery of Auchterarder had suggested that new ministers should assent to the proposition, 'I believe it is not sound and orthodox to teach that we must forsake sin in order to our coming to Christ and instating us in covenant with God.' Intended to be an affirmation of the unconditional freeness of God's grace, its phrasing left it open to the charge of antinomianism and the proposition was duly condemned by the General Assembly as being 'unsound and most detestable.'²⁴

This precipitated considerable debate about the role of the law in the preaching of the gospel. T. F. Torrance explains how Thomas Boston of Ettrick 'was very troubled by the unevangelical and formalist tendencies in the presentation of salvation by grace due to the legalistic and contractual frame of contemporary Calvinism which resonated with what he called "a legal strain, a bias towards the first covenant (i.e. the covenant of works), running in the hearts of all men by nature."'²⁵ Similarly M. Charles Bell sees such a 'legal strain' in the earlier preaching of Federal theologians such as Samuel Rutherford, David Dickson and James Durham, and asserts that the result of this emphasis was to make law prior to grace.²⁶ If this was the case then these prominent Calvinists would have

---

22 Edward Fisher, *The Marrow of Modern Divinity*, originally published in 1645 and 1649, edited by C. G. M'Crie, (Glasgow: David Bryce, 1902).

23 *Proceedings*, 1-9. The full text of the Libel is included here as Appendix 3.

24 M. Charles Bell, *Calvin and Scottish Theology: The Doctrine of Assurance*, (Edinburgh: Handsel Press, 1985), 151.

25 Thomas F. Torrance, *Scottish Theology*, 204.

26 Bell, *Calvin and Scottish Theology*, 83 argues that Rutherford taught a conditional covenant of grace. 'This element of conditionality, and the use of contemporary mercantile language, combined with an active view of faith, led Rutherford to present faith more as a work of man, than as a gift of God's grace to man. This teaching was reinforced by his inversion of Calvin's *ordo salutis*, in placing law prior to grace.' See also 77-8. For a similar assessment of Dickson and Durham see chapter 4, e.g. 94, 105.

departed from the position of Calvin, who stated that 'it ought to be a fact beyond controversy that repentance not only constantly follows faith, but is also born of faith.'[27] Whether or not these theologians fell into the trap of proclaiming legal rather than evangelical repentance remains a matter of debate which cannot be resolved here.[28] However, what is clear is that people like Thomas Boston perceived that law was taking precedence over grace, and therefore feared that the freeness of the gospel was at risk. In seeking to steer a middle course between legalism and antinomianism he found help in the Puritan work, *The Marrow of Modern Divinity*, probably written by Edward Fisher, and published in England in 1645. Boston recommended the book to friends like James Hog of Carnock, who republished the book, with his own preface, in 1718.

Endorsing a federal approach recognising two covenants, the *Marrow* affirmed that Christian believers are dead to the law in Christ because they are no longer under the covenant of works. Entry to the covenant of grace is free because 'in this covenant there is not any condition or law to be performed on man's part by himself. No: there is no more for him to do, but only to know and believe that Christ hath done all for him.'[29] This does not mean, however, that the law is redundant because the Law of the Ten Commandments functions within the covenant of grace as the law of Christ, which 'is to be a perpetual rule of life to all mankind, yea to believers themselves.'[30] Although it seems clear from such statements that the Marrow had no desire to dispense with the importance of divine law, the dominant part of the Kirk reacted in horror to the possibility of antinomianism.

The so-called 'Marrow men', Boston, Hog along with Ralph and Ebenezer Erskine, vigorously defended the teaching of the *Marrow*; but all to no avail because the General Assembly of 1720, in what is known as the Black Act, condemned the book and instructed ministers to warn their congregations about it. Bell explains that 'the Assembly faulted the Marrow for teaching 1. that assurance of salvation is of the essence of faith, 2. universal or unlimited atonement, 3. that holiness is not

---

[27] Calvin, *Institutes*, III. iii. i. See also III. iii. 4.
[28] See for example, Paul Helm, *Calvin and the Calvinists*, (Edinburgh: Banner of Truth, 1982), 61-70 who explores 'the preaching of the law' and argues that an emphasis upon the preparatory preaching of the Law does not automatically lead to legal repentance, e.g. 70.
[29] Edward Fisher, *The Marrow of Modern Divinity*, 111.
[30] *Ibid.*, 244. See also 144ff and 182-3.

necessary for salvation, 4. that fear of punishment and hope of reward are not proper motives for Christian obedience, and 5. that believers are not under the law as a rule of life.'[31] This final judgement appears directly to contradict the *Marrow's* emphasis upon the law functioning as 'a perpetual rule of life,' and such misunderstandings lay behind the appeal to the Assembly to repeal the Black Act, which the 'Marrow men' made in 1722. Their appeal fell on deaf ears as the Assembly upheld its earlier decision and publicly rebuked the 'Marrow men'. A century later, as Campbell's trial unfolds many of these same accusations and misunderstandings were to come to the surface. From the moment the Libel was read out before the Presbytery of Dumbarton on 21 September 1830 one of the main concerns of Campbell's opponents was to prove that he was advocating errors which had already been condemned by the Act of 1720. Recognising that the Black Act would be used against him, Campbell sought to argue the technical point that, as the Act of 1720 had not formally been referred for discussion to the Presbyteries, it could not be regarded as part of the constitutional law of the Church of Scotland determining its doctrines.[32] Such technical niceties did not prevent his opponents from insisting that there was a similarity of doctrine which merited similar condemnation.

Responding to the Libel, the minister of Row concentrated on three main themes; the extent of atonement, universal pardon and the doctrine that assurance is of the essence of faith. These three themes contain the heart of the so-called 'Row Heresy' and they would be examined in detail by each of the church courts.

Campbell's Response to his Critics

The Extent of the Atonement

As to the extent of the atonement; I hold and teach that Christ died for all men — that the propitiation which he made for sin, was for all the sins of all mankind — that those for whom he gave himself an offering and a sacrifice unto God for a sweet smelling savour, were the children of men without

---

[31] Bell, *Calvin and Scottish Theology*, 152.
[32] *Proceedings* 12-14. *Proceedings (GA)*, 124-5 'What I hold is, that an act of Assembly is not a *law of the Church.*'

exception and without distinction. And this the Scriptures teach.[33]

In support of this he suggested that the Lord Jesus Christ came under the law of God 'as our brother'. As 'our brother' it was his duty to love his neighbour as himself. In that every man was his neighbour his final act of love should therefore be seen as 'a work for all'. After referring to some biblical passages whose natural interpretation supports the idea of universal atonement[34] Campbell went on to claim that he was not challenging the doctrine of election as such, because 'what the scriptures state on the subject of Election, distinctly teaches also the universal extent of the atonement'.[35]

Talk of a universal atonement immediately brought back echoes of the *Marrow* controversy, because the *Marrow* had claimed that Jesus Christ 'moved with nothing but with His free love to mankind lost hath made a deed of gift and grant unto them all, that whosoever of them all shall believe in this His Son shall not perish but have eternal life.'[36] For Thomas Boston such stress upon a universal atonement did not lead to universalism because he continued to believe in a limited atonement. However, the General Assembly rejected such teaching because it claimed that 'here is asserted an universal redemption as to purchase.'[37] Viewed from a penal understanding of atonement it seemed clear to them that if Christ has purchased redemption for all then salvation for all is not just an open possibility but a predetermined actuality. A century before the *Marrow* controversy, the same penal logic lay behind Samuel Rutherford's assertion that 'if Christ died for all, so that they may perchance suffer for their sins in hell, God shall be unjust in punishing Christ for their sins and in punishing those same sinners in hell.'[38] Against such a background it is not surprising that Campbell's attempt to proclaim universal atonement should meet with outright opposition, because the Scottish Reformed tradition regarded universal atonement as being synonymous with universal salvation.

---

[33] *Proceedings*, 16
[34] E.g. Jn. 3:16, 1 Jn. 2:2, Rom. 5:18, Lk.2:10, 1Tim. 2:1-6, Jn 4:32, 6:32, 33, 36.
[35] *Proceedings*, 30.
[36] Edward Fisher, *The Marrow of Modern Divinity*, 112. See also 115-6, 122-3.
[37] Extract from the Act of 1720, which was read out before Campbell's appearance before the General Assembly and printed in *Proceedings (GA)*, 5.
[38] T. F. Torrance, *Scottish Theology*, 109.

Standing before the bar of the General Assembly in May 1831 Campbell sought both to distance himself from the teaching of the *Marrow* and to counter the allegation that his teaching about universal atonement must imply universalism.

> I do honestly believe that it is not the doctrine I have taught that was taught in the Marrow...I am thankful to be reminded that it has been said that the doctrine which I teach tends to universal salvation. Moderator, I distinctly disclaim that doctrine, and distinctly disclaim having ever, either in public or in private given the slightest reason to any human being, who listened to me with any intelligence or attention, to suppose that I hold it. On the contrary. I have always held that the fact of the atonement did not infer the fact of ultimate salvation...But if I hold an universal atonement, I hold, also, that, in itself, it does not imply the exemption of a single soul from future misery. How, then, can my teaching be confounded with universal salvation?[39]

Sadly for Campbell, those who were accustomed to viewing everything in the light of the Westminster Confession found it all too easy to confound his teaching with universal salvation. As far as his opponents were concerned Campbell's teaching about universal atonement and pardon were not two separate doctrines but one erroneous teaching which tended inevitably towards universalism.

Universal Pardon through the Death of Christ

In responding to the Libel he also suggested that pardon could be understood in a number of ways.

> The pardon of sin may be understood to mean either an act of indemnity to the sinner, giving him security from all consequences of having sinned against God, irrespective of any condition as to moral character; or as the act of God in receiving back to the bosom of his love the returning sinner; or thirdly, as the removing the judicial barrier which guilt interposes between the sinner and God; so making the fact of being a sinner no hindrance to this coming to God, now, as to a reconciled Father.[40]

---

[39] *Proceedings (GA)*, 62-3.
[40] *Proceedings*, 32.

He firmly rejects *the indiscriminate pardon* of the first view which he bluntly says 'is distinct antinomianism'. The second outlook he feels to be uncontroversial and is happy to affirm that in practice it is only believers who enjoy what might be called *experienced pardon*. His distinctive understanding is found in the third position which might be seen as a form of *evangelical pardon*, with God removing the barriers to reconciliation. Conscious of the accusation that this might be seen as a form of Arminianism, he argues strongly that he is not advocating 'the Arminian doctrine of God's readiness to forgive and pardon all, on condition of their repenting and believing'.[41] It is God's work through and through because he both removes the judicial barrier which guilt puts between sinful people and God, and also seeks to help the sinner back through the gift of the Spirit. This is

> pardon, as the removal of the barrier in the way of our coming to God, which arises from personal guilt, and as the provision of actual strength, in the Spirit, to come to God, I hold to be the gift of God to all — in as much as it is contained in the gift of Christ; and is the justification of the statement that God has given to all eternal life in him.[42]

Whilst some have noted the limited number of references to the work of the Spirit in *The Nature of the Atonement*,[43] this comment alerts us to the fact that the work of the Spirit was an integral part of the approach Campbell advocated during his ministry at Row. The material examined in subsequent chapters indicates that a coherent doctrine of the Holy Spirit is present in Campbell's thought; and this evidence implies that *The Nature of the Atonement* will be more accurately interpreted when his pneumatology is taken into consideration.

Along with this emphasis upon universal pardon and forgiveness the sermons from this period echo with a call for people to repent and lay hold of the opportunity to approach God with confidence and faith. This regular call to commitment is clear evidence that for Campbell at least an emphasis upon universal pardon and atonement did not lead inevitably to universalism. Unlike his friend Thomas Erskine,[44] he did not

---

[41] *Proceedings*, 36.
[42] *Proceedings*, 44.
[43] Van Dyk, *Desire of Divine Love*, 169-170.
[44] William Hanna, (ed.), *Letters of Thomas Erskine of Linlathen*, (Edinburgh: David Douglas, 1884), 71, 'I trust that He who came to bruise the serpent's

believe that everybody would ultimately be saved.⁴⁵ Hence he warned those who rejected the opportunity to approach God during this time of grace, that the day was coming when they would face the wrath of God. This leads James Goodloe to assert that within Campbell's thought 'forgiveness is not limited to a predetermined number of persons, but it is limited in time. Now we live in a "Day of Grace", from the day of Pentecost to the Second Coming. The future will bring a "Day of Judgement". There will be no forgiveness then. Universal pardon is preliminary.'⁴⁶

The logic of Campbell's position, as far as Goodloe can see, is that while the atonement, pardon, and forgiveness are universal they are 'temporary.' So, by 'asserting that the atonement is universal in extent but limited in duration, Campbell denies the efficacy of grace. It remains possible that people can frustrate God's grace and disappoint God's love.'⁴⁷ Goodloe fears that the grace of God, as understood by Campbell, is not 'irresistible and invincible' and cannot therefore be guaranteed to be sufficient

---

head will not cease His work of compassion until He has expelled the fatal poison from every individual of our race', and 286, 'the hope of the final restoration, even of those who are now wandering farthest from God, is to me a most precious hope.' Thomas F. Torrance, *Scottish Theology*, 276-7. 'There is no doubt about the fact that Thomas Erskine's thought did move from *universal* pardon, understood unconditionally, to a universalist notion of the final salvation of all people, irrespective of faith...Erskine's move from universal pardon to universal salvation was a step that the Marrow men, and McLeod Campbell later, refused to take.' See also Geoffrey Rowell, *Hell and the Victorians*, (Oxford: Clarendon Press, 1974), 70-5.

⁴⁵ See *Memorials* 2.294-5. Hesitations about Erskine's eschatological conclusions surface in Campbell's letter to his eldest son in December 1870 where he says 'I still feel difficulties which did not weigh with him. I have never felt yet in a fulness of light which would enable me to teach on the subject; as I have felt on the Atonement — its extent — its nature – Revelation — the Lord's Supper.' However he does acknowledge that 'of the two directions of thought...in one or other of which men are going, I feel that both as a Scriptural question, and as one of Christian philosophy, the conception of *final restitution* commends itself incomparably more to me than that of *annihilation*; which I understand many Nonconformists, as well as some in the church are accepting.' Such words should not be seen as evidence of a firm decision in favour of universalism, but rather as a reflection upon the comparative merits of two options which were being vigorously debated.

⁴⁶ Goodloe, *Extent and Nature of the Atonement*, 12.
⁴⁷ Ibid., 12.

for anyone. Campbell's emphasis on the need for human response leaves Goodloe feeling that in Campbell's scheme of things 'belief merits salvation.'[48] It may indeed be the case that Campbell's understanding of grace does not neatly conform to Goodloe's notion of 'irresistible and invincible' grace. As becomes apparent in *The Nature of the Atonement*, Campbell's methodology involves seeing atonement in its own light. In this way he seeks to allow what God has done, to determine his understanding of atonement, and of all the other mysteries relating to God. This approach implies that our understanding of divine grace should be determined by what God has done in Christ, rather than by prior assumptions about the nature of grace. Allowing the event of the cross to shape our understanding of grace makes it difficult to accept Goodloe's description of grace as 'irresistible and invincible'. Such language tends to give the impression that grace is an automatic power, rather than seeing grace in more personal terms as an expression of the generous way in which God condescends to deal mercifully with people. The biblical narrative offers many examples which illustrate the ways 'that people can frustrate God's grace and disappoint God's love.'[49] The painful episode of the cross indicates a God who makes himself vulnerable by offering his love in the full knowledge that it may be resisted. Viewed from this perspective Campbell's approach seems more in tune with the notions of grace emerging from the biblical narrative.

Goodloe's critique is further weakened by the way in which his assertion that 'Campbell denies the efficacy of grace,'[50] is quickly contradicted by his acknowledgement that Campbell's emphasis on the gift of the Spirit in Christ which empowers human response 'would seem to be what others identify as efficacious grace, the will of God effecting the salvation of the hearers of the gospel.'[51] Whilst he appreciates that Campbell did not preach universal salvation, Goodloe cannot satisfactorily answer the question as to 'why, within Campbell's thought…some turn to God and some do not?'[52]

Within Federal Calvinism doctrines of election and limited atonement provided a ready explanation for the failure of some

---

[48] *Ibid.*, 13.
[49] For example, Ex. 32:9, Jer. 2:1-19, Hos. 11:8-9, Lk. 19:41-44, etc.
[50] *Ibid.*, 12.
[51] *Ibid.*, 16.
[52] *Ibid.*, 16.

to respond to the Gospel. However, such doctrines were incompatible with Campbell's stress upon universal pardon and could not be used to resolve the tension in his theology between the universal proclamation of pardon and a recognition that 'the number found in the true ark when the Lord comes will be small indeed.'[53] Campbell's rejection of the God of the double decree leaves Goodloe feeling uncertain about 'who determines who responds and who does not?'[54] Such comments express a typically Reformed concern that any weakening of God's role in determining who will be saved runs the risk of making human response more decisive than divine initiative. According to Goodloe this question about 'who determines who responds' to the Gospel is 'not ever settled'[55] within Campbell's early theology. It is hard, however, to see how Campbell could ever settle the matter to Goodloe's satisfaction because the question is phrased in such a way that only one right answer is permitted. A question enquiring about who *determines* human response, is so heavily freighted with Reformed notions of divine sovereignty, election and predestination that only strictly Reformed answers appear to be acceptable. As Campbell questioned conventional interpretations of the Calvinist tradition it is entirely predictable that he cannot, in Goodloe's eyes, supply an adequate answer to such a theologically loaded question. Although sympathetic to much in Campbell's thinking, Goodloe's doctrinal presuppositions distort his evaluation of Campbell's attempt to proclaim universal pardon without either lapsing into universal salvation or privileging human response over divine initiative. However, his comments usefully draw attention to a dimension of the theology of the Row sermons which deserves clarification.

In a sermon entitled 'The Nature and Necessity of Repentance',[56] Campbell asserts 'that the present condition of the human race is, that God has forgiven all men their sins — *not as a permanent and eternal condition of things*, but as a preliminary state — preliminary to a day in which he shall judge men according to the deeds done in the body, whether they have been good or whether they have been evil.'[57] There can be no doubting the young preacher's concern to urge his

---

[53] *NofS*, 3.28.9.
[54] Goodloe, *Extent and Nature of the Atonement*, 17.
[55] *Ibid.*, 17.
[56] *S&L*, 1.6.108ff.
[57] *Ibid.*, 119.

hearers to prepare for the coming judgement; but his comments about the preliminary nature of forgiveness provoke some important questions. If pardon is proclaimed to all, but is not ultimately enjoyed by all, does this imply that God's word of pardon is, as Goodloe suggests, temporary? If all are not finally saved, is this because God restricts the efficacy of his pardon by some form of election, or is it the case, eschatologically, that human response outweighs divine decision? Whilst it is possible that Campbell's theology is simply inconsistent at this point, it is worth considering alternative ways of resolving the apparent tensions in his thinking.

In spite of his best efforts before the Presbytery of Dumbarton, to distinguish between three forms of 'pardon', it is likely that opponents immersed in penal and legal ways of thinking about atonement, would understand universal pardon as a universal 'act of indemnity to the sinner, giving him security from all consequences of having sinned against God, irrespective of any condition as to moral character'[58] As Campbell worked without the limiting effects of a traditional doctrine of election, this would lead some critics to conclude that universal pardon must lead inexorably to universal salvation. However, this would be a distortion of his position because the biblical warning that 'except ye repent, ye shall all likewise perish'[59] led Campbell to state that 'the expressions used on the subject show, distinctly and decidedly that some shall be saved, and that some shall perish; and that *salvation* and *perishing* are the two opposite conditions of human beings throughout eternity.'[60] Maybe such distortions of his theology were inevitable when people insisted on evaluating a non-penal approach in the light of explicitly penal categories.

A further source of misunderstanding arises from a failure to recognise that there is a penal dimension undergirding the filial, personal soteriology already evident in the Row sermons. A penal dimension is visible when Campbell argues that there is no contradiction in proclaiming universal forgiveness and future judgement, because forgiveness is never at the expense of judgement.

> If it be an absurdity to conceive of God forgiving and afterwards judging those whom he has forgiven, then God cannot do. But if God cannot do it (and God cannot do an

---

[58] *Proceedings*, 32.
[59] Lk. 13:3, 5.
[60] S&L, 1.6.109.

absurdity,) God cannot forgive men at all, unless he be contented to give up the right of judging; that is to say, God, if he forgave us, would be giving up the reins of government, and saying that he would never afterwards judge. This would involve many awful consequences. Indeed, if God could never forgive freely, without involving such results, God would not forgive at all; for God will never give up the right of judging; so that saying that Christ cannot consistently judge men after he has forgiven them, is saying he can never forgive them freely, because he can never do a thing that would involve in it that he should cease to act as judge.[61]

If God had to cease judging sin in order to forgive sinners, he would, in Campbell's eyes, relinquish his essential role as the moral governor of the universe. Far from suspending judgement the divine judge has left intact the moral connection between sin and misery, for it is God who has decreed that 'misery is to arise as a *necessary consequence* from our sin — that God will not separate between sin and misery and therefore that there is no salvation from the lust of their evils but by being saved from the first — no way of escaping the wrath to come but by being renewed in the spirit of our minds.'[62] If the final judgement will reveal that God continues to oppose sin, then what God has done in Christ is not to remove the link between sin and judgement, but to provide a way of removing the sin which justly attracts divine judgement. Hence the work of Christ has not been 'for the purpose of making it possible for sinners to be taken out of his righteous judgement, but for the purpose of preparing them for judgement, by causing them to share in his estimate of sin, and so preparing them for being delivered from wrath in his righteousness.'[63] Within such a moral universe, pardon as an act of indemnity is an inadequate response to the underlying sin which brings misery and judgement in its train. For effective salvation a power is required which will wipe away the sin which brings misery and judgement in its train. The work of Christ has brought about such a dramatic change in human circumstances, and in Christ the power of the Spirit enables people to be holy.[64]

---

[61] *S&L*, 1.6.120.
[62] *NofS*, 3.30.5.
[63] *Proceedings*, 38.
[64] *NofS*, 3.30.7-8.

Campbell's comments about forgiveness being 'a preliminary state'[65] do not imply that in the future God will stop being forgiving and turn into a judgemental deity. Such thinking overlooks the way in which judgement and love are complementary, rather than contradictory, elements of the divine nature. It also fails to take account of the way in which Campbell is operating with relational, rather than with exclusively legal, presuppositions. Within his relational approach pardon is indeed preliminary, but in the sense that it is preliminary to, and for the purpose of, sinful people being reconciled to God. Thus, as he reflects upon the parable of the unmerciful servant,[66] and on Jesus' warning that 'if you forgive not men their trespasses, neither will your heavenly Father forgive you your trespasses', Campbell concludes that forgiveness is offered with the intention of transforming people so that they begin to offer forgiveness to others. 'Forgiveness is conferred for the purpose of teaching forgiveness; and where that object is not effected, judgement follows....Observe the harmony of the truth of God, that God in Christ forgives you that you should be taught forgiveness; but if you are not taught forgiveness; neither will you be acquitted on the great day of the Lord.'[67] Evidently forgiveness is being viewed as a preliminary stage in a process whereby God transforms sinful people and makes them holy, loving and forgiving.

Confusion arises when pardon is interpreted instead as being synonymous with reconciliation or salvation. If, however, pardon is regarded as something distinct from, but leading to, reconciliation, then Campbell's approach makes greater sense. The young preacher of Row sees God granting genuine pardon to all through Christ, with the hope that forgiven sinners will respond to this opportunity to be reconciled to God. However the universal character of this forgiveness does not lead to universalism, because people are not forced to be reconciled to God. The good news of universal atonement is not limited by the preaching of coming judgement, because the message of judgement merely underlines the inevitable consequences of refusing to be reconciled. Those who place themselves outside the salvation accomplished by Christ encounter the divine judgement upon sin which is the eternal shadow side of the divine love. As the wages of sin is death the problem is not that

---

[65] S&L, 1.6.108ff.
[66] Mt. 18:21-35.
[67] S&L, 1.6.122-3.

forgiveness is temporary, but that frail mortals are themselves temporary, and without God's aid they shall surely perish. So in affirming that the 'day of grace' will not go on for ever, Campbell is not imposing limits on forgiveness but is explaining that the coming judgement will expose the choices people have made.

Within some penal approaches to atonement universalism was avoided by employing a doctrine of limited atonement.[68] By contrast the minister of the parish of Row was developing a more personal model which steered clear of universalism by stressing that forgiveness does not eliminate the need for future judgement. Forgiveness is never given at the expense of judgement, because it is offered by the holy God who continues to be the divine judge of sin. This essential linkage between sin and judgement is part of what *The Nature of the Atonement* later describes as the 'fixed and necessary character of salvation.'[69]

Such considerations may not explain to everyone's satisfaction why some respond to God's offer and others do not, but they challenge Goodloe's assertion that within Campbell's approach human 'belief merits salvation.'[70] Within Campbell's preaching human decision does not dictate questions of salvation, because salvation depends from start to finish upon God. In terms of condemnation human responsibility plays a more active role, because refusal to accept the salvation accomplished by Christ inevitably leads to judgement. While human beings cannot save themselves it appears to be the case that God has granted them freedom to condemn themselves by opting out of the new humanity established through the work of Christ.

Assurance of the Essence of Faith

The doctrine that assurance is of the Essence of Faith and necessary for salvation was opposed by Campbell's critics as being contrary to the Holy Scriptures. In response he argued that advocates of limited atonement were clear that on the one hand believers had an assurance that God's testimony is true. In

---

[68] See for example John Owen who avoids the logical outcome of universalism by arguing for a limited atonement. John Owen, *The Works of John Owen*, vol. X, (ed.) W. H. Goold, (London: Banner of Truth, 1967) 247.
[69] *Nature*, chapter 8. This is explored more fully in Chapter 2. *An Objective Love*.
[70] *Ibid.*, 13.

terms of what God said there was no room for doubt. On the other hand when it came to questions about whether or not an individual had a personal interest in God's love then there was room for doubt, because how could anyone be really sure that she or he was one of the elect?

In contrast to this approach Campbell denied any such separation between the certainty of a truth of God's word, and the certainty of our own personal interest in his love. Anyone within the sound of the gospel who experiences a 'want of enjoyment of God' is therefore guilty of the sin of direct disbelief of God's word.

> And on this subject I hold and teach, that in believing the gospel, there is necessarily present in the mind, the certainty that the person believing is the object of God's love manifested to him in the gift of Christ — the certainty that he has remission of his sins, the gift of the Spirit, and all things pertaining to life and godliness, bestowed on him, by the free grace of God; so that he feels himself debtor to God for the gift of eternal life; and this I hold to be so of the essence of faith, that is to say, so necessarily implied in the existence of true faith, that no person can be regarded as in the belief of God's testimony who is not conscious to it.[71]

He claims that the scriptures surely assume that 'to believe God's expressed love and to be assured of it, are the same thing. He cannot accept the idea that whilst 'Christ is freely offered...it is kept secret for whom he died', believing that the person who trusts God's word finds in that word the grounds for personal assurance.

However, he does seek to distinguish between the assurance which is the essence of faith, and the assurance of being in the state of salvation, and concedes that trials and temptations may rob the believer of the enjoyment of living as a child of God. This distinction is important because

> whilst I hold assurance to be of the essence of faith, I do not hold that the converted person is necessarily always in a condition of assurance as to his being in a state of salvation; inasmuch as I do not hold it to be impossible for a converted person to be, at times, so overcome of the temptations of Satan, causing darkness, through the flesh, as it may be to stand in doubt of the first principles of the oracles of God; and it is manifest that if brought into such darkness, and such

---

[71] *Proceedings*, 45-6.

unbelief, there must be the interruption to the blessed consciousness of being a child of God, and an heir of glory.[72]

On arriving at Row, Campbell had struck up a friendship with the Revd Robert Story, who was minister of the parish of Rosneath, on the other shores of the Gareloch. Story was friendly with Dr Scott in Greenock and corresponded with Edward Irving. He had also been concerned about the topic of assurance and came to believe in universal atonement whilst recovering from illness in England. His son, Robert Herbert Story, suggests that his father came to see that the death of Christ for all, was the only basis for genuine assurance. For 'the individual could feel assured of *his own* salvation only through his belief in the *universal* offer and promise of it.'[73] Whether Story arrived at this conclusion independently or as a result of his contacts with Campbell and others is a matter of debate.[74] However, it is clear that he arrived at a similar position to Campbell, and in all the formal debates he was an energetic defender of his young ministerial colleague. At the end of this particular stage of the proceedings, however, 'in spite of Story's spirited defense of his friend, the Presbytery voted that the libel against Campbell was relevant, that is, they officially declared the views of John McLeod Campbell heretical. Only Robert Story and Elder Dunlop protested the vote.'[75] This decision was to be repeated as the case proceeded through the various church courts.

---

[72] *Proceedings*, 49.
[73] Robert Herbert Story, *Memoir of the Life of the Rev. Robert Story, Late Minister of Rosneath, Dumbartonshire. Including Passages of Scottish Religious and Ecclesiastical History During the Second Quarter of the Present Century*, (Cambridge: Macmillan and Co., 1862), 106.
[74] Robert Herbert Story suggests that his father arrived at the doctrine of universal atonement independently. 'Although in constant correspondence with Mr. Campbell, he does not seem to have been led to this by him, nor in his turn did he lead Mr. Campbell.' Story, *Memoir of the Life of the Rev. Robert Story*, 106. J. Philip Newell, 'A. J. Scott and His Circle', Unpublished PhD, University of Edinburgh (1981), 40, however, senses that the truth may have been rather more complex. 'In the light of the memoirs and biographies of those concerned, it can be clearly seen that there was, by this time, constant communication between Scott, Campbell, Ker and Story, in one form or another. To speak of any of these men, by this stage, "coming to a position alone" is inadequate.'
[75] Van Dyk, *Desire of Divine Love*, 15.

The next stage of the process was for these issues to be debated at the meetings of the Synod of Glasgow and Ayr held on the 13th and 14th April 1831. A similar pattern unfolds and includes Campbell making another major speech to defend his views. During his defence he argued that God did not need the cross in order to make him love people.

> Christ came not to change his Father, but to declare his Father's name; and when we see the work of God in Christ, and the love of God in Christ, we are not seeing some love in God, some mercy and tenderness, which had come forth in consequence of the work of Christ, but we are seeing a work springing from what was in the heart of our Creator who has become our Redeemer, and, in becoming our Redeemer, has declared unto us what our Creator is.[76]

Thus it is clear that he had realised, from an early stage of his ministry, that God's love is the cause, and not the consequence, of the atonement. Although his opponents accurately saw his theology as a direct challenge to Scottish Reformed orthodoxy, there is a case for saying that Campbell was himself being loyal to the Reformation heritage. In affirming that God did not have to be persuaded to be loving, Campbell was being loyal to the tradition of Calvin who stated that 'the work of the atonement derives from God's love; therefore it has not established the latter.'[77]

His affirmation of the priority of divine love means that for Campbell repentance is a response to the fact that God has forgiven us, and is not in itself the basis for that forgiveness. It is clear that he is not advocating a form of legal repentance where forgiveness is conditional upon repentance, but an *ordo salutis* where divine grace and forgiveness precede and enable faith.[78]

---

[76] *Proceedings*, *185.

[77] Calvin, *Institutes*, II. xvi. 4. Calvin quotes approvingly from Augustine. "God's love," says he, "is incomprehensible and unchangeable. For it was not after we were reconciled to him through the blood of his Son that he began to love us. Rather, he has loved us before the world was created, that we also might be his sons along with his only-begotten Son — before we became anything at all." Similarly II. xvi. 3. 'Therefore, by his love God the Father goes before and anticipates our reconciliation in Christ. Indeed, "because he first loved us" (1 John 4:19), he afterward reconciles us to himself.'

[78] Cf. Calvin, *Institutes*, III. iii. 4. See also III. iii. 1. 'Now it ought to be a fact beyond controversy that repentance not only constantly follows faith, but is also born of faith.'

Campbell's Theological Journey

> This, then, I say, that God every where invites sinners to repent — that God every where invites sinners to come back to him, whereby it is taught that God has forgiven sinners their departing from him, and so he invites them to return...And can any man repent — can any man turn to God — can any man receive God to reign in his heart, so long as he does not know that God has forgiven him?[79]

A further illustration of the way in which forgiveness is logically prior to repentance comes through in one of the sermons from this early phase of his ministry.

> The very invitation to come back, supposes that I have been forgiven the sin of going away. If I have offended my Father and hear that he has shown me kindness — inviting me to return — I would say that he has forgiven my going away and the preaching of repentance, has even been a preaching of the forgiving love of God, which is fully revealed in the preaching of Jesus Christ — and therefore it is that Christ is the Light — that 'lighteth every man that cometh into the world.'[80]

Thus within the very offer of forgiveness there is a note of judgement, because the decision to forgive implies the assessment that something has taken place which needs to be forgiven. Far from turning a blind eye to sin, the willingness to forgive implies both that sin exists and that it needs to be dealt with. Similarly, the genuine acceptance of forgiveness involves the tacit acceptance that the recipient has done something wrong which needs to be forgiven.

His speech to the Synod is unusual in the sense that it includes some quotations from Calvin's *Institutes* supporting his views on assurance.[81] In his response[82] to the libel of 7 September 1830 he had quoted from Calvin's *Catechism*, but in his later writings he seldom refers to Calvin directly. The extent of his direct knowledge of Calvin remains a matter of speculation, but at certain points in his trial a greater use of Calvin's teaching may have helped to support his case.[83]

---

[79] *Proceedings*, *186-7.
[80] *NofS*, 1.3.10.
[81] *Proceedings*, *223-4. After quoting from a number of Confessions of faith he quotes from Calvin's *Institutes*, III. ii. 16 and III. ii. 19.
[82] *Proceedings*, 63.
[83] Other passages in the *Institutes* which Campbell might have appealed to in defence of his understanding of assurance would be, II. xvi. 2-3, III. ii. 6-7, III. ii. 12, III. ii. 15-8, III. xiii. 4 and III. xvii. 1. In the light of this sort of evidence, Bell concludes that 'Calvin taught that assurance of salvation is

In his defence Campbell claimed that his teachings were faithful to the Word of God, and that it is upon this basis that he should be judged. However, his views were assessed on a rather different basis. Dr Fleming of Old Kilpatrick explained that it was the Standards of the national church which were the ultimate criterion of judgement on this occasion. 'Now, Sir, I think you must see very plainly, and at once, that the only fair and conclusive arguments that can be used are not so much to be drawn from the Scriptures, as from the interpretation given of these Scriptures by the Church, and ratified by the State.'[84]

Campbell's Deposition from the Ministry of the Kirk

The final act of the drama was acted out shortly after this at the meeting of the General Assembly of the Church of Scotland (24-25 May 1831). The arguments advanced were basically the same as those used in the debates in the other church courts. Echoes of the Marrow controversy are once again evident as Campbell defended himself before the General Assembly. In the speech where he tried to distance himself from the teaching of the *Marrow*,[85] he also argued that his doctrine of universal pardon had been misrepresented, because 'if any man say, that believers are persons who are pardoned in this sense, that they may do what they please, and that they will not be punished, I say there is no such pardon, and that to teach it is downright Antinomianism.'[86] His father, Revd Dr Donald Campbell, reminded the Assembly that his son 'has told you that he abhors what are called the Antinomian doctrines of "the Marrow;"' and that he 'never heard any preacher more earnestly and powerfully recommending holiness of heart and life.'[87]

Towards the end of the debate his father read out a petition signed by 420 individuals, 150 of whom were heads of families in the parish of Row. This represented 19/20ths of the whole population of the parish. The battle by then had been lost, but his father spoke movingly of his son's ministry and integrity.

> Moderator, I am not afraid for my son, though his brethren cast him out the Master whom he serves will not forsake him;

---

of the essence of faith.' Bell, *Calvin and Scottish Theology*, 32. For a different perspective see Paul Helm, *Calvin and the Calvinists*, 23-6.
[84] *Proceedings*, *251.
[85] *Proceedings (GA)*, 62. See Chapter 1. *The Extent of the Atonement.*
[86] *Ibid.*, 54.
[87] *Ibid.*, 177.

and, while I live, I will never be ashamed to be the father of so holy and blameless a son. Indeed, Sir, in these respects, I challenge any one in this house to bring forward any who can come into competition with him.[88]

In spite of such appeals the General Assembly confirmed the findings of the lower courts that Campbell's doctrines were contrary to Holy Scripture, the Westminster Confession of Faith and the Act of the General Assembly of 1720 which condemned the teaching of The *Marrow of Modern Divinity*. The motion to depose Campbell was carried by 119 to 6 and the Assembly adjourned at a quarter past six on the morning of 25 May 1831. In a slip of the tongue the Clerk of the General Assembly, is reported to have remarked that 'those doctrines of Mr. Campbell would remain and flourish after the Church of Scotland had perished and was forgotten'. On hearing this Campbell's friend Thomas Erskine whispered to a friend 'This spake he not of himself, being the High Priest – he prophesied'.[89]

Leanne Van Dyk describes this all-night session as 'nothing short of farcical' and goes on to assert that 'Campbell himself was not given the opportunity to speak.'[90] However, this particular criticism of the General Assembly is without foundation, because the Report of the Proceedings of the General Assembly clearly indicates that Campbell made two significant speeches in his own defence during the hearing.[91] In the event the speeches made little difference to the predictable outcome as Evangelicals and Moderates joined forces to remove him from the church's ministry. With the precedent of the Black Act of 1720 in mind the Assembly confirmed the verdict, outlined in the original Libel, that Campbell's teaching that assurance of salvation is of the essence of faith, and his preaching about universal atonement and pardon, were contrary to the word of God and to the doctrinal standards of the Kirk.

---

[88] *Ibid.*, 177-8.
[89] Hanna, (ed.), *Letters of Thomas Erskine*, 106.
[90] Van Dyk, *Desire of Divine Love*, 16.
[91] *Proceedings (GA)*, 37-63 and 119-128. This volume, documenting the procedures of the General Assembly is not included in Van Dyk's bibliography and this omission is the likely source of this misunderstanding.

Factors Contributing to his Dismissal

Three hundred and ten members had earlier voted at the election of the Procurator which implies that one hundred and eighty five of them did not vote for either of the motions. Some abstained, but a much larger number were absent. Did they think it a foregone conclusion or a matter of no great significance? It is significant that Campbell was deposed by the General Assembly in such a decisive way. Presuming that his father and his friend Robert Storey voted for him, only four others were willing to oppose his removal from the ministry of the Kirk. What was it that rallied both Moderates and Evangelicals to oppose him so strongly? J. H. S. Burleigh comments that,

> He did not directly reject the doctrine of Election, though he realised that it was in part responsible for the doubts and anxieties of earnest Christians, and more and more came to find it logically irreconcilable with active evangelicalism. But as his doctrine seemed implicitly to deny Election, Evangelicals were offended for they were strict Calvinists. On the other hand Moderates sensed 'fanaticism' in the word Assurance, which also smacked of Antinomianism for which The Marrow had been condemned in 1720.[92]

Another factor contributing to his downfall may have been his friendship with another controversial character, Edward Irving. The General Assembly which voted in 1831 to expel Campbell from its ministry also found his friend Edward Irving 'guilty' of heresy; and 'Campbell's condemnation provoked Irving to proclaim the assembly to have been "a wicked synagogue of Satan."'[93] Although the case against Irving was not completed until 1833 it may not have helped Campbell to have been considered alongside his controversial friend.

The relationship between Irving and Campbell was friendly, but it is unlikely that Irving directly shaped Campbell's outlook. Indeed there is evidence to suggest that, at least in some areas, it was Campbell who had a clearer influence upon his better known friend. During the week in May 1828 when the General Assembly was meeting, Campbell went to Edinburgh to hear Irving lecture on the Apocalypse to crowded congregations at

---

[92] J. H. S. Burleigh, *A Church History of Scotland*, (London: Oxford University Press, 1960), 333.
[93] *Ibid*, 331.

six o'clock in the morning.[94] Whilst in Edinburgh there was a private meeting between the two of them. However Campbell was later keen to make clear that he had not gone looking for guidance about any 'difficulties', but rather to discuss his conclusions about the doctrine of assurance. During their encounter Irving explained 'that assurance was a subject on which he needed more light.'[95]

Not long after this Irving preached at Rosneath on Sunday the 8th of June. He also visited Row where he expounded Matthew chapter 24.[96] His positive verdict on this visit being that, 'I was much delighted with Campbell and Sandy Scott'. Campbell was ready to leave to visit his sister in London and this prompted

---

[94] Iain Murray, *The Puritan Hope: A study in Revival and the Interpretation of Prophecy*, (Edinburgh: Banner of Truth, 1971), 187-206 sees Irving playing the major role in moving Evangelicalism from a post-millennial to a pre-millennial eschatology. Irving played a prominent part in the Albury Conferences on Prophecy which were held at the home of Henry Drummond from 1826 to 1830. Rev. Robert Story from Rosneath attended the second conference whilst convalescing in England in 1827. Although Campbell did not attend any of these conferences, his friendship with Story, and his contacts with Irving, meant that he was aware of the pre-millennial approach favoured by the Albury Conferences. D. W. Bebbington, *Evangelicalism in Modern Britain*, (London: Unwin Hyman 1989), 84, argues that the belief that Christ would come again in person was an innovation which 'was part of the Romantic inflow into Evangelicalism. Christ the coming King could readily be pictured by poetic imaginations fascinated by the strange, the awesome and the supernatural.'

[95] *Memorials*, 51-2. In a letter written in October 1862 Campbell explained 'The fact was…that I went to Edinburgh at that time to see Irving (and Dr. Chalmers also), in order to lay before them the conclusions at which I had arrived on the subject of Assurance of Faith, and the practical experience as a minister with which my arriving at these conclusions was connected. I did *not* go to *consult* them as one having "difficulties". I went in the hope that the grounds of my own convictions would commend themselves to them; and this latter form of my hope seemed to be realized as to both; though I cannot say that there was anything more as to either of them. But they both took the position of intending to weigh what I said; not…that of deciding at once that I was wrong, and setting themselves…to put me right.'

[96] Mrs M.O.W. Oliphant, *The Life of Edward Irving*, (London: Hurst and Blackett, 1864[5]), 233. Irving's letter dated 10 June 1828 reports on his visit to Rosneath and Row. It is not clear whether he preached at Row on Sunday evening, after preaching two sermons at Rosneath on June 8th or if his visit to Row came the following day.

Irving to ask him to preach for him in London.[97] At this point Campbell enigmatically observed that Irving's 'peculiar views were new to' him. He does not explain which views appeared peculiar or new, but as he had heard Irving speak about prophecy a few months earlier, it is probable that it was Irving's views on christology, rather than his eschatological speculations, which were 'new' to him. He was clearly happy to go ahead with the arrangement, and for at least the next three Sundays he occupied Irving's pulpit in London. At some point during his stay they had a significant discussion about the extent of the atonement. Whilst he could not be sure that this led to a change in Irving's view, Campbell noted with satisfaction that 'from that time he preached the Atonement as for all'.[98]

With such friendly links existing between them it would not be surprising if some people assumed that they held similar convictions about the gifts of the Holy Spirit.[99] An important link in this relationship was the Revd A. J. Scott who was for a time Irving's assistant in London.

> Son of Dr Scott of the Middle Church, Greenock, he preached his first sermon in Row, 'to the peculiar delight' of the minister there...In 1828 Scott was again in Row, where his sermons on I Corinthians 12, concerning spiritual gifts, led to manifestations of 'tongues' which played a part in the development of Edward Irving's pentecostal convictions, although Scott himself was doubtful of the spiritual value of the Row phenomena.[100]

Scott was to remain a close friend of Campbell's throughout his life and is one of those who may have contributed to

---

[97] *Reminiscences*, 28. In a letter Campbell said 'I have the prospect of preaching the glad tidings of free pardon in London... Mr. Irving has been with me and is away. I have had much pleasure in his short visit. His peculiar views are new to me, as to others, and too important to be suddenly taken up, but I feel much cause of thankfulness to be given me in possession of his most Christian friendship... Tell — of my going to London, and that I am to preach in Irving's pulpit.'

[98] *Memorials* 1.51-4, and *Reminiscences*, 28-9.

[99] See for example Sermon 15, on Haggai 2: 1-9, *NofS*, 2.15.

[100] George G. Cameron, *The Scots Kirk in London*, (Oxford: Becket Publications, 1979), 48 and 109. See also Alec R. Vidler, *The Church in an Age of Revolution*, (Harmondsworth: Penguin, 1961), 65-7; and Bebbington, *Evangelicalism*.

Campbell's theological development.[101] His father's ministry in Greenock had an emphasis upon the work of the Holy Spirit, at a time when this was unusual, and Scott may have imbibed from him a similar desire for the Spirit to bring the church into a deeper experience of communion with God.[102] In a letter to Thomas Chalmers written in April 1830, Campbell indicates that it was from Scott that he had learned that spiritual gifts were not just for the days of the early church.[103]

On a journey to Scotland late in 1829 Scott visited a lady called Mary Campbell who lived at Fernicarry in the neighbouring parish of Rosneath. Campbell's friend, Robert Story had recently published a memoir of Mary's saintly sister, Isabella, who had died after a long illness. This had aroused great interest and had attracted many visitors to Fernicarry, where Mary was apparently suffering from the same consumption. When Scott visited her he tried, unsuccessfully, to convince her of the distinction between regeneration and the baptism with the Holy Ghost, but before he left he urged her to read through the Acts of the Apostles. This may have prepared the way for an experience of healing which took place in March 1830.[104] As her sister and a friend prayed for the restoration to

---

[101] See Newell, 'A. J. Scott and His Circle', 38-39. Newell suggests that there is a connexion between the beginning of Scott's friendship with Campbell in September 1827 and Campbell's shift in emphasis to the universal extent of the atonement.

[102] *Ibid.*, 20.

[103] *Ibid.*, 37, 77-9, 92. Newell quotes from a letter Campbell wrote to Chalmers on 28 April 1830 (New College MS, CHA. 4.134.21). 'Personally it has been my faith in this department of truth for two years and upwards that the gifts enjoyed by the first Christians were *not characteristic of that time but of this present dispensation* and therefore possessed in right of God's gift by the church *all along and on until the second coming of Christ, however,* through lack of faith in that right, they have in point of fact been unsought and unenjoyed.' Newell argues that Campbell's language at various points echoes Scott's understanding of spiritual gifts as expressed in his book *Neglected Truths.*

[104] C. Gordon Strachan, *The Pentecostal Theology of Edward Irving*, (London: Darton, Longman & Todd, 1973), 64-5, suggests that an Irvingite understanding of the human nature of Christ also prepared the way for this charismatic experience. 'It was in December (1829) that she did read, not Acts, but John 14, 15, and 16, with Scott's distinction in mind and saw all that she read in a completely new light. She saw for the first time that the human nature of Christ was in itself the same as every man's, and that His holiness was not inherent but sustained by the Son of God acting faith

the church of the gifts of the Spirit, 'the Holy Ghost came with mighty power upon the sick woman as she lay in her weakness, and constrained her to speak at great length, and with superhuman strength, in an unknown tongue, to the astonishment of all who heard, and to her own great edification and enjoyment in God.'[105]

Around about the same time across the Clyde in Port Glasgow members of the MacDonald family began to experience the power of the Holy Spirit in surprising ways. One member of the family, Margaret, had been seriously ill for eighteen months and was believed to be close to death. An experience of the Holy Spirit brought healing and inspired her to predict a more widespread baptism of the Holy Spirit. Two weeks later, at a Friday night prayer meeting in their home, her brothers James and George began to speak in tongues. The MacDonald brothers had for a time been attending Campbell's church at Row[106] and the day after their initial experience of speaking in tongues their pastor paid a visit. 'On Saturday Mr. C. came over, and my mouth was again opened. He said, it is written "pray that ye may interpret"; he accordingly prayed. I was then made to speak in short sentences which George interpreted one by one. The first word of interpretation was "Behold he cometh – Jesus cometh."'[107] Some sources suggest that the MacDonald brothers began to speak in tongues on Friday 18th April, whereas the relevant Friday was the 16th April. This minor detail is of interest because one of Campbell's sermons about the Holy Spirit is specifically dated, Sunday 18 April 1830. In this sermon on Haggai 2:1, 9, preached at Row, Campbell argued that there is no reason for believing that the miraculous gifts of the Holy Spirit were intended only for the early church.[108] As Campbell's habit was to write out his sermons in full each Saturday,[109] it is possible that his sermon on Sunday 18 April represented an attempt to find some

---

on it by the Holy Spirit. This was what Irving had believed and taught in all his writings on the human nature of Christ since 1825.'

[105] Oliphant, *Life of Edward Irving*, 287. At this point Oliphant is quoting from R. H. Story, *Memoir of the Life of the Revd Robert Story*.

[106] Hanna, (ed.), *Letters of Thomas Erskine*, 130.

[107] Strachan, *Pentecostal Theology*, 68, quoting from R. Norton, *Memoirs of James and George MacDonald of Port Glasgow*, (London: John F. Shaw, 1840), 111.

[108] *NofS* 2.15. Sermon on Haggai 2:1 & 9.

[109] Appendix 2.

theological justification for the events witnessed in the MacDonald household the previous day.

Thus began the Gareloch pentecost which attracted visitors from all over the country. The wider significance of this revival was that it contributed to the development of a charismatic dimension in the increasingly controversial ministry of Edward Irving in London.[110] Up to this point Irving had been preaching that spiritual gifts were intended to be a normal part of the church's experience, but that these had been withdrawn as divine judgement upon the apostasy of the Gentile Church. This led him to believe that these gifts would not be restored until the second coming of Christ. However, the reports reaching him during the summer of 1830 convinced him that these gifts had not been withdrawn after all. In the light of this he was happy to support the meetings which were started in London to pray 'for the outpouring of the Holy Ghost.'[111] It is not necessary to describe these developments in detail here,[112] but they are relevant to a clearer understanding of the events contributing to Campbell's deposition. For it would appear to be the case that his close association with these episodes laid him open to charges of engaging in unseemly religious enthusiasm. Clear evidence of this unease surfaced at the Synod of Glasgow and Ayr on the 13th and 14th of April 1831, when the Revd Dr Graham referred to some 'charismatic' episodes which he

---

[110] N. R. Needham, *Thomas Erskine of Linlathen: His Life and Theology 1788-1837*, (Edinburgh: Rutherford House, 1990), 288-9, notes that the final Albury conference in July 1830 had collectively decided to pray for the revival of the spiritual gifts. 'Accordingly they sent a deputation composed of five Anglicans and one member of Irving's church to visit the Gareloch in September; the deputation brought back to London an entirely positive and favourable report of Mary Campbell, the MacDonalds and their gifts. This impelled groups of people to begin to meet in order to pray for the wider restoration of the charismata, and the way was thus paved for the appearance of these phenomena in Irving's own congregation and in others the following year.'

[111] Strachan, *Pentecostal Theology*, 55-60 and 70-84.

[112] Information about the Gareloch pentecost can be found in a number of sources. Hanna, (ed.), *Letters of Thomas Erskine*, 129-167; Oliphant, *Life of Edward Irving*, 274-341, 385-7; Strachan, *Pentecostal Theology*, 61-116; Needham, *Thomas Erskine*, 271-397; Columba Graham Flegg, *'Gathered Under Apostles': A Study of the Catholic Apostolic Church*, (Oxford: Clarendon Press, 1992), 41-6, 51-3. See also R. Norton, *Memoirs of James and George MacDonald of Port-Glasgow*.

suggested might cause 'mental derangement', especially in the case of impressionable youth.

> It is matter of notoriety the uneasy feelings that had been excited in the neighbourhood. Those who professed adherence to Mr. Campbell's opinions, seemed to intimate that they had received miraculous gifts from the Holy Ghost, for the purpose of confirming these opinions, and gaining proselytes. The rumours of signs and wonders which were spread abroad, were no doubt exaggerated; — but without entering minutely into the feelings of the time, because it is hardly possible to separate truth from falsehood, and though it were, it would be improper to enter minutely into them, as it would force me to give names that I would not like to mention. — But the agitation was extreme...[113]

In the light of Campbell's personal involvement in these dramatic events it is surprising that there are comparatively few references to them either in his autobiographical *Reminiscences and Reflections*, or in the two volumes of his correspondence. His close friend, Erskine of Linlathen, stayed with the MacDonalds in Port Glasgow for six weeks to investigate these phenomena. Initially convinced that he was witnessing an authentic move of the Holy Spirit, he wrote a supportive tract entitled 'On the Gifts of the Spirit', which was published towards the end of 1830. Within a couple of years, however, his initial enthusiasm appears to have waned.[114] Perhaps more surprisingly Scott, who had laid the theological foundations for these charismatic outbreaks, moved from a cautious silence to an outright rejection of these kinds of spiritual gifts.[115] The few hints that appear within Campbell's correspondence[116] leave the

---

[113] *Proceedings* *237-8. Dr Barr from Port Glasgow made similar allusions in a speech before the General Assembly of the Church of Scotland, *The Whole Proceedings (GA)* 106.

[114] This process can be followed in Erskine's correspondence from this period. See Hanna, (ed.), *Letters of Thomas Erskine*, 129-167. This is explored at some length in Needham, *Thomas Erskine*, 271-397.

[115] Newell, 'A. J. Scott and His Circle', 90-5.

[116] *Memorials* 2. 153-154. He retains the belief that the gifts of the Spirit are still available to the Church but expresses reservations about the authoritarian ways in which those gifts had been used within the Catholic Apostolic Church. See also *Memorials* 1.115-125. Mrs Oliphant notes Irving's disappointment that both Campbell and Scott drew back from active support for the movement of the Holy Spirit. Oliphant, *Life of Edward Irving*, 386.

impression that he similarly became increasingly cautious about this movement.

With the benefit of hindsight it is clear that the main thrust of Campbell's ministry was not an unhealthy preoccupation with the work of the Holy Spirit, but his involvement in these events left him vulnerable to criticism. Whilst this issue was not part of the formal accusations debated by the church courts, it is apparent that the controversy surrounding the Gareloch pentecost contributed to the passionate campaign for his exclusion from the ministry of the Church of Scotland. A survey of this period leads Nicholas Needham to conclude that 'the orthodox antipathy to the impious and absurd Gareloch pentecost thus probably contributed substantially to the strength of feeling against Campbell, and helps us a little better to understand the abrupt nature of the proceedings against him in the Church courts. It also helps us to understand the unity of the Moderates and Evangelicals in this matter since the former had even less time than the latter for religious mania of any sort.'[117] Whilst the labels 'impious' and 'absurd' may be harsh on some of those involved, they indicate something of the intensity of feelings generated by this period of spiritual renewal.

Another speaker at the Synod of Glasgow and Ayr felt that both Campbell's errors and Irving's eschatology were bringing the Kirk into disrepute.

> I have no particular interest in the question other than a Christian minister ought to have; but I am vexed to the bottom of my heart, that whilst in London we have an individual of our church searching after the millenium, (sic) and other extravagancies, and, in our own Synod, others uttering such doctrines as we have heard in this court, that our neighbours should have to say, that the Church of Scotland was going about with a fool's coat upon its back, and thus exposing our church to the scorn and contempt of all rational people.[118]

Alongside what might have been some elements of 'guilt by association' there were political factors to be borne in mind. At the meeting of the General Assembly one speaker, Dr Cook, expressed the view that if Campbell was permitted to question the Standards of the Established Church then this would undermine the whole relationship between church and state.

---

[117] Needham, *Thomas Erskine*, 359-360.
[118] Dr M'Lean reported in *Proceedings*, *341.

From the perspective of the politically conservative Moderates such dissent could not be tolerated.

> Our business is to uphold the doctrines of the Standards of our national Church. We have heard an open defiance given to these Standards — we have heard the defender state that he did not consider that they imposed upon him any obligation to teach the doctrines they inculcate — that he was at perfect liberty to state what he was led to consider the truth of God. If we were to permit this, we might relinquish the Established Church altogether.[119]

Whilst these sorts of considerations tend to suggest that Campbell's perceived 'fanaticism' and his disturbing of the religious *status quo* would not have endeared him to the Moderates, they do not fully explain his rejection by the Evangelicals of his day. In addition to these factors, his convictions about the universal extent of the atonement brought him into direct conflict with the view of limited atonement cherished by Scottish Evangelicals of his generation. Another bone of contention for some Calvinist Evangelicals would have been his friendship with Erskine of Linlathen, who was also questioning many traditional doctrines. Needham illustrates the way in which many contemporary critics saw Campbell as a follower of Erskine and observes that 'almost all the anti-Rowite literature of 1830 was directed specifically against Erskine. Orthodox Calvinists perceived him to be the particular fountainhead of the Gareloch heresy.[120] It is probably inaccurate to see Campbell as Erskine's disciple[121] but it may be the case that their close association attracted additional criticism to Campbell. As a layman Erskine was not subject to the disciplinary procedures of the Kirk[122] and it is tempting to wonder if some of his critics, frustrated by their inability to

---

[119] Dr Cook reported in *Proceedings (GA)*, 170.
[120] Needham, *Thomas Erskine*, 302.
[121] Campbell's relationship with Erskine is discussed in Chapter 2. *Conclusion*.
[122] Timothy C. F. Stunt, *From Awakening to Secession: Radical Evangelicals in Switzerland and Britain 1815-1835*, (Edinburgh: T & T Clark, 2000), 226. 'Erskine had been brought up in the Scottish Episcopal Church, but was a layman in the Congregationalist communion, so when his views began to diverge from the teaching of the Church of Scotland he did not become quite such a *cause célèbre* and was spared the harsh condemnation and penalties which the Assembly of the Kirk reserved for their own wayward ministers.'

silence him, found an outlet for their anger in a concerted effort to ensure that his close friend Campbell should be dismissed from the church's ministry. Evangelicals living through times of great social and political change, felt the need to defend what they perceived to be orthodoxy and this task took on added urgency in view of the growing numbers of Irish Roman Catholics in Scotland.[123] In such a defensive climate fundamental theological re-thinking would not be tolerated and so both Campbell and Scott were deposed and formal proceedings against Irving were set in motion.

It is tempting to speculate as to whether the outcome of the trial might have been different if Campbell had established greater links with other evangelicals at the outset of his ministry. However in a letter written to his brother in India on the 1st of January 1831 he explained that he had deliberately chosen not to align himself with either of the main groups within the Church.

> In September 1825 I was placed in the Parish of Row. I cannot say that there was anything then to mark my Theological Creed. As to Church politics I was distinguished, to my own mind, among the young Ministers, my contemporaries, by a deep conviction of the practical evils, which had arisen from party feelings, and by determined purpose to hold personally a perfect neutrality.[124]

From a human point of view this noble, but perhaps naïve, desire not to belong to any particular party was to result in his being extremely isolated.

Campbell's removal from his ministry at Row marks the end of the first phase of his ministry, which was dominated by arguments concerning the extent of the atonement. The conviction that Christ had accomplished a universal atonement never deserted him, as he went on to explore more fully *The Nature of the Atonement* that Christ had accomplished.

Campbell's Christological Orthodoxy is Called into Question

As the disciplinary procedures of the Kirk gathered momentum, Campbell wrote to his father in Kilninver on the 11 September 1830. It is obvious from the letter that his father had been expressing concerns that his son might also be called to account

---

[123] Needham, *Thomas Erskine*, 316-8.
[124] *Reminiscences*, 10. *NofS* volume 1, Appendix 2.

for christological heresy. For after outlining the charges contained in the libel, Campbell seeks to reassure his father with the words, 'You see your fears as to their putting the question of the humanity of our Lord into the libel are groundless.'[125] As events were to show, his father's fears were far from groundless, for he had accurately sensed that the Kirk was in no mood to permit any perceived deviation in teaching about the person of Christ. The General Assembly which deposed Campbell in May 1831 also disciplined three other ministers. In the case of Campbell's friend, A. J. Scott, the issue was clear cut, in that he freely admitted that he could not accept the Westminster Confession.[126] In the remaining two cases, however, the human nature of Christ was the point of contention.[127]

Having removed Campbell from office in the early hours of Wednesday 25 May, the next person on the General Assembly's list was the Revd Hugh Baillie MacLean. At MacLean's induction as minister of the Scottish congregation at London Wall in 1827, Edward Irving had preached the *Ordination Charge*, which was regarded as one of his finest sermons. In 1830 Mr. MacLean received a call to serve the parish of Dreghorn in Ayrshire where his 'heretical' opinions about 'the peccability of our Lord's human nature' were called into question.[128] On Thursday 26 May 1831 the General Assembly removed his licence to preach the gospel and referred his case to the local presbytery, who duly deposed him from the ministry.[129] Having

---

[125] *Memorials*, 1.71-2.

[126] Scott recalls that 'after that dreary night in the Assembly, the dawn breaking upon us, as we returned at length, alike condemned, to our lodgings in the New Town of Edinburgh, I turned round and looked upon my companion's face under the pale light and asked him, Could you sign the Confession now? His answer was No. The Assembly was right: our doctrine and the Confession are incompatible.' Hanna, (ed.), *Letters of Thomas Erskine*, 106.

[127] Newell, 'A. J. Scott and His Circle', 82-8, describes how Scott's ordination trials before the London Presbytery had explored his understanding of the human nature of Christ. He had accepted a christology similar to Irving but eventually a Presbytery committee produced a formula concerning Christ's humanity which Scott and Irving could agree to. 'Scott's orthodoxy on this particular doctrine was never again called into question. His language on the doctrine of Christ's humanity seems never to have been as extreme as was Irving's.' 88.

[128] Oliphant, *Life of Edward Irving*, 217, 283-5, 314.

[129] According to Irving the General Assembly disciplined MacLean 'because he maintained that the Son of God took our nature in its fallen,

dealt so firmly with MacLean, for holding what were perceived to be Irvingite views on the human nature of Christ, it is no surprise that the General Assembly also set in motion disciplinary procedures against Irving for teaching 'the sinfulness of Christ's humanity'. The Presbytery of Annan, who had ordained Irving, was instructed to bring him to trial on a charge of heresy, and they fulfilled their commission to remove him from the Church's ministry in March 1833.

Scott's case was processed on Friday 27 May, and so in the course of a few days a General Assembly, keen to assert its orthodoxy and authority, dealt decisively with the most significant dissenting voices within its ranks.[130] As Campbell was known to be friendly with Irving it would have been surprising if his christology was not also suspect. Evidence of this suspicion surfaces eighteen months after his deposition, and two months before Irving's removal from the ministry. In a letter to his sister, Campbell explains that the Presbytery of Lorn had issued a pastoral admonition, which ministers were required to read from their pulpits, setting forth the danger to which people exposed their souls by going to hear him preach. In the letter he says that

> The admonition in question my father represents as embodying a statement of the doctrines which they assume that I teach, and of which they express their abhorrence; and that statement is intended to include my teaching on other points besides the subject-matters of the libel. Of all my teaching it gives a very erroneous impression, and on the subject of the Lord's humanity it represents me as teaching what might justly be mentioned with abhorrence, viz., 'that our Lord's holiness was not immaculate.'[131]

Although not included in his disciplinary procedures, it is clear that questions were also being raised about his understanding of the person of Christ. The examination of some

---

and not in its unfallen state; and that its holiness was not necessary and essential, and inherent in its creature part, but derived from his union to it; and the unction of it by the Holy Ghost.' This extract from material from Irving's trial by the Presbytery of Annan is quoted in Strachan, *Pentecostal Theology*, 189.

[130] Andrew L. Drummond and James Bulloch, *The Scottish Church 1688-1843: The Age of the Moderates*, (Edinburgh: Saint Andrew Press, 1973), 203-5. They show how several others were deposed for related reasons over the next few years.

[131] *Memorials*, 1. 105. Letter written on the 19 January 1833.

of his Row sermons in chapter 4 will help to show why some people could argue that he was teaching 'that our Lord's holiness was not immaculate', and will also indicate the basis for Campbell's assertion that this was not an accurate description of his theology.

From Row to *The Nature of the Atonement*

The decision of the General Assembly to depose Campbell from his ministry at Row marked the end of the initial phase of his ministry. By arguing for the universal extent of the atonement he was calling into question the penal approach to atonement which was prevalent at the time. By taking such a decisive step away from the tradition he set in motion a process of theological exploration which was to lead him towards a very different understanding of the whole nature of the atonement.

Although the pulpits of the Kirk were now clearly out of bounds, Campbell was kept busy as an itinerant preacher for the first eighteen months after his deposition. Living with his father in Kilninver 'he generally preached at Oban on Sundays; sometimes in the Independent Chapel, and sometimes – when the congregation was very large and the weather fine – on the green hillside above the town. Many came in boats from the neighbouring islands; some from great distances; and on week days he often met them near their homes in Kerrera, Luing, and other islands.'[132] Correspondence from this period indicates that he preached in the open-air, in the barns of sympathetic friends and relatives, in the Methodist chapels in Dumfries and Greenock, to a crowd of two thousand gathered in a tent at Bonhill and to at least six thousand souls in the New Churchyard at Greenock.[133] That graveyard experience brought him some comfort for he thought it likely that 'all the ministers in Greenock together had not so many hearers.'[134]

In December 1832 he moved to Glasgow and in January he began a demanding style of ministry. Based initially at the Lyceum hall he preached three sermons in Glasgow each Sunday, and another on Monday evenings. Tuesday evenings found him preaching in Paisley and Friday night's destination was Greenock. Another evening each week he alternated between visits to Port Glasgow and Glentyan. This demanding

---

[132] *Ibid.*, 1. 88.
[133] *Ibid.*, chapter 4.
[134] *Ibid.*, 90.

Campbell's Theological Journey

schedule did not bring about spectacular results, but over the years a regular congregation was established and a new chapel in Blackfriars Street was opened as the permanent home of an Independent congregation on the 17 September 1837. Apart from some enforced absences due to illness Campbell served as the unpaid[135] pastor to this congregation from 1833 until his retirement due to ill-health in April 1859.

In a letter to his father dated 3 February 1834, he made it clear that he had no desire to join another denomination. 'Certainly there is no sect or denomination of Christians to which I would ever attach myself. As to forming a new sect, I have no wish to do so...'[136] Another letter the next day, addressed to a Mr. Carlyle, sought to explain his reluctance to join the movement which was developing out of the ministry of Edward Irving. A letter to his sister in May 1834 described his meeting with Henry Drummond and others who had been keen for Campbell to help to pioneer the work of the 'London Mission' in the West of Scotland. Although a certain Lady Harriet was moved twice to speak 'in the power' he remained unconvinced and decided not to join a movement which he feared was moving in an authoritarian direction.[137]

The outcome of all this was that for the next two decades Campbell served faithfully in Glasgow in the midst of considerable obscurity. Something of the painful nature of his situation emerges in a letter to his sister in September 1845 where he describes 'the isolation of my own position' and prays earnestly that God will 'deliver me from it'. He explains that the possibility, raised by a friend, that he might seek entrance to the Church of England, does not provide the answer to his prayer

---

[135] Tuttle, *So Rich a Soil*, 65, claims that 'Since his father had been able to supply a small income for him, he laboured without salary.' A letter written shortly after his father's death in 1843 seems to confirm that Campbell received generous support from his father. Writing to Mr Macnabb on 26 January 1843 he says, 'You will be thankful that our beloved father was enabled to realize what was so strong a wish of his heart, that my being put out of the Church of Scotland would not cause me to be worse provided for than an ordinary Scotch minister.' *Memorials*, 1.170-1.

[136] *Memorials*, 1.113. Before the trial he had written to his sister explaining that 'I have no wish to leave the Church of Scotland. I see no church theoretically better; and practically they are all on a level.' *Memorials* 1.64.

[137] *Ibid.*, 1.115-125.

for deliverance because he could not with integrity give full assent to the Thirty Nine Articles.[138]

The positive side of this comparative isolation is that it may have provided Campbell with more space for reading and reflection. In 1851 this started to bear some fruit with the publication of *Christ the Bread of Life*[139] and in 1856 he came to the attention of a much wider circle of readers with his best known work *The Nature of the Atonement*. Reflecting upon this twenty five year period of isolation and obscurity it is tempting to agree with Macquarrie in saying that 'during these years his theology took shape, for he had become convinced that one could only assert the universality of the atonement if one rethought the whole doctrine and broke out of the categories in which it had been for so long expressed.'[140] Whilst *The Nature of the Atonement* clearly represents his mature theology, and Campbell was happy to describe the way that his thoughts had been developing gradually over the years[141], it may still be somewhat misleading to say that it was during these years that his theology 'took shape'. The danger is that this kind of statement might be taken to imply that his later theology bore little or no resemblance to the theology he proclaimed during the early years of his ministry.[142]

---

[138] *Ibid.*, 1. 190-3.

[139] *Christ the Bread of Life* is examined in Chapter 6.

[140] J. Macquarrie, 'Campbell on Atonement' in *Thinking about God*, (London: SCM Press, 1975), 168.

[141] *Nature*, 342-3 (274-5). In a note added to the 1867 edition, Campbell explained that 'it is about forty years since the moral and spiritual nature of the atonement first dawned on my mind. What was then prominent in my faith and in my teaching was the Universality of the Atonement, and the assured peace with God which is quickened by the faith of the forgiveness of sins revealed in the Gospel. But my attention was drawn to *The Nature of the Atonement* and in tracing out the moral and spiritual power of faith in it, and in considering its immediate and direct object of bringing us to God. This element in my teaching, however, was not included when that teaching was called into question. But subsequently it more and more occupied my thoughts; gradually, through many years, taking the form which it presents in this book, viz., a moral and spiritual atonement.'

[142] Eugene Garrett Bewkes, *Legacy of a Christian mind; John M'Leod Campbell, Eminent Contributor to Theological Thought*, (Philadelphia: Judson Press, 1937), 35, 'The earlier and later views are poles apart from the standpoint of profound thought and depth of spiritual insight.'

Campbell's Theological Journey

However, it would be misleading to draw too sharp a contrast between his earlier and later thought because Campbell himself believed that there were real lines of continuity between the ideas he proclaimed from the pulpit at Row and the theology expressed in *The Nature of the Atonement*. Writing to his son in November 1866 he explained that...

> You have inverted the order of my own learning in reading the Row Sermons last. But what you have first read, as being last learned, ought to be more clear and thoroughly digested. I know, indeed, that what I have so laboured to illustrate in what I have written for the press was all present substantially very early in my preaching; but mixed with much that was called forth by the circumstances in which the light was dawning on me: circumstances, I mean, inward as well as outward; my own habits of thought as well as conditions of other minds. What, however, has most impressed a different character on my Row sermons as compared with my books, is the personal appeal incident to dealing with my people, and the constant endeavour to bring them to a point.[143]

Here is a frank admission that his Row sermons have a much more direct and personal style than his books, but also an insistence that in spite of the differences in style the theological heart of his approach 'was all present substantially very early' in his thinking and preaching. This claim, that what he had written for the press during 1855 was consistent with what he had been preaching twenty five years earlier, is potentially very significant. If his memory is reliable and there is such a consistency in his thinking throughout this period, then it is reasonable to look to his early sermons for material which will contribute to a fuller picture of his theology in general, and of his christology in particular.

In order to assess the degree of consistency in Campbell's thought across this period, it will be necessary first, in chapter 2, to identify and evaluate key elements in the mature theology of *The Nature of the Atonement*. Chapter 3 will build on this by illustrating some of the ways in which these ideas are present or anticipated in his early preaching. Around seventy sermons survive from his Row ministry and these are mainly contained in the collections, *Notes of Sermons* and *Sermons and Lectures*. It would appear that when Campbell was no longer headline news there was much less interest in recording his sermons,

---

[143] *Memorials* 2.159.

with the result that fewer sermons were published from his ministry in Glasgow. Nevertheless, the sermons from this period also offer helpful insights into his thinking at a strategic period in his ministry.

The material explored in chapter 3 demonstrates there are many lines of continuity which connect the views expressed in the Row sermons with the theology expressed in *The Nature of the Atonement*. What appears to have happened with the doctrines of atonement and revelation (explored in *Thoughts on Revelation* published in 1862), is that Campbell took ideas which were 'present substantially very early' and then wrote them out more fully and clearly for the press at a later date. In addition to these themes his early sermons touch on other areas of doctrine which for one reason or another Campbell did not write out for the press in the same way. Believing that it is plausible to regard him as a consistent thinker and theologian, chapters 4 and 5 draw upon material from his sermons in order to identify the central elements of Campbell's christology. The examination of his teaching about the Lord's Supper in Chapter 6 highlights further evidence of the ongoing coherence of his thinking.

Journey to the Field of Peace

In April 1859 Campbell's health meant that he had to retire from the pastorate of his congregation in Glasgow. Later that year one of his closest friends, Robert Story from Rosneath died. During the next decade a good deal of time was given over to writing, some of which led to the publication of *Thoughts on Revelation* in 1862. Campbell also wrote an introduction, and a number of endnotes, for a new edition of *The Nature of the Atonement* which appeared in 1867. He also provided some new material for the second edition of *Christ the Bread of Life*, published in 1869.

The closing stages on his life brought him a degree of recognition which would have been unthinkable during the tumultuous days at Row. On 1 May 1868 his old University at Glasgow conferred on him the degree of Doctor of Divinity. In the spring of 1870 Mr and Mrs Campbell were able to move from Glasgow to a house[144] in Rosneath where they could look across the Gareloch towards Row. The following year a meeting in his honour was held in Glasgow. His cousin and friend Revd

---

[144] The Gaelic name for the field where the house had been built sixty years earlier was Ach-na-sith, the 'Field of Peace'. To help people pronounce it properly Campbell modified the spelling to Achnashie.

Campbell's Theological Journey

Dr Norman Macleod made the presentations, and felt that as a former Moderator of the General Assembly, 'he could express the regret of himself and many others that Dr Campbell was no longer a minister of that Church. He felt sure that such an event as his deposition could not occur now.'[145] Soon afterwards he began to write his *Reminiscences and Reflections*, which were published shortly after his death. Living in Rosneath he was able to attend the church led by Robert H. Story, son of the man who had been such a firm supporter in earlier days. After a short illness John McLeod Campbell died on the 27 February 1872.

In a sermon preached at Rosneath on the Lord's Day following the funeral, Robert H. Story offered his verdict on Campbell's best known book.

> All books, that contain what are called theories or doctrines on the Atonement must at some point or other fail; for they deal with that "mystery of godliness", which was itself the outward expression of a divine love which "passes all understanding;" but those, who have, with the greatest reverence and keenest intelligence, studied the Christian doctrines that deal with the great question of man's reconciliation to God, through Jesus Christ, are the first to acknowledge that in Dr Campbell's book on the atonement — his chief book — they met with the most coherent, the most comprehensive, and the most exalted of all expositions of the atoning work of our Lord. Nowhere else do you find a more perfect candour and charity in dealing with an opponent's theories, a more anxious searching into all the conditions of an argument, a more intuitive perception of the divine counsel, and a more sustained flight of pure religious thought and feeling.[146]

It is not necessary to pass judgement on the accuracy of Story's assessment of Campbell's understanding of atonement, but having traced here the outline of Campbell's theological journey, chapter 2 will begin the process of examining and evaluating *The Nature of the Atonement*. A clear grasp of what represents the heart of Campbell's theology is essential preparation for the task of exploring his christology.

---

[145] *Memorials* 2. 297-300.
[146] Robert Herbert Story, *The Risen Christ: A Sermon preached in Rosneath Church on the Lord's Day after the death of John McLeod Campbell, D.D.*, (Glasgow: James Maclehose, 1872), 24.

Conclusion

What emerges from this account, and what will be demonstrated further in subsequent chapters, is that Campbell was a man of strong, evangelical convictions. Within the context of eighteenth and nineteenth century Scotland, loyalty to the Westminster Confession of Faith was a prerequisite of anyone claiming the title, Evangelical. Judged by that criterion it is clear that Campbell cannot be regarded as an Evangelical, or more accurately as that kind of evangelical. A different approach to defining evangelicalism however, is advanced by David Bebbington who argues that over the last two hundred and fifty years, the four persistent features which have characterised British Evangelicalism have been, *conversionism, activism, biblicism* and *crucicentrism*.[147] If these four characteristics are indeed indicative of evangelicalism, then there is a strong case for seeing Campbell as an evangelical preacher and theologian.

His sermons consistently culminated in a call for changed lives. Such preaching for a verdict, clearly indicates someone who passionately believed in the need for, and the possibility of, conversion. In terms of activism, the pattern of ministry he adopted in Row was a very active one, which involved regularly visiting and catechising his flock as well as regular preaching. Reflecting on Campbell's ministry in Glasgow leads Goodloe to conclude that 'the twenty-five long years of obscurity between his deposition and this major publication were not years of idleness. Instead, they were years of such extensive exertion that Campbell suffered some periods of protracted illness.'[148] Thus in his energetic pursuit of his ministerial duties he was much more akin to the perceived activism of the Evangelicals, than to the more leisured existence, rightly or wrongly attributed to the ministers of the Moderate camp.

At another level, in his particular regard for the Bible, Campbell was clearly evangelical. His sermons are overtly based upon biblical texts and they expound a biblical faith rather than the principles of human reason. In addition to the text in question, each sermon is replete with biblical quotations

---

[147] Bebbington, *Evangelicalism*, 3. 'There are the four qualities that have been the special marks of Evangelical religion: *conversionism*, the belief that lives need to be changed; *activism*, the expression of the gospel in effort; *biblicism*, a particular regard for the Bible; and what may be called *crucicentrism*, a stress on the sacrifice of Christ on the cross. Together they form a quadrilateral of priorities that is the basis of Evangelicalism'.
[148] Goodloe, *Extent and Nature of the Atonement*, 37.

and allusions. There can be little doubt that the sacrifice of Christ upon the cross was crucial to Campbell's theology. Whilst his doctrine of atonement has often been seen as a nineteenth century example of a purely subjective approach to the atonement, the following chapter will argue that this assessment is wide of the mark. It will be shown that a closer reading of Campbell's work supports Trevor Hart's conclusion that Campbell affirms 'the necessity for the accomplishment of an objective atonement between God and man in which the divine wrath over human sin is dealt with'.[149] Judged by such criteria Campbell can be viewed as standing firmly within an evangelical tradition.

In spite of such evidence, however, some would argue that Campbell should be seen more as the inspiration behind much of the liberal theology which developed during the nineteenth century. Goodloe, for example, asserts that the role played by experience in Campbell's theology 'relates him directly to the mainstream of nineteenth-century liberal Protestantism.'[150] Mark Hopkins shows how a direct line of influence can be traced between Campbell and the liberal Congregationalist minister, James Baldwin Brown.[151] It was whilst Brown was convalescing at the home of their mutual friend, A. J. Scott, that he first read *The Nature of the Atonement* and this contributed to a change of emphasis in his theology from the sovereignty to the fatherhood of God. Brown 'adopted Campbell's central idea that Christ made a perfect confession to the Father of man's sinfulness and guilt; this made it possible to claim that objective satisfaction for sin had been made without having recourse to the penal theory.'[152]

However, the fact that some liberal theologians found inspiration in Campbell's writings does not automatically undermine his evangelical credentials, for he cannot be held responsible for the ways in which other writers chose to develop his ideas. Part of the difficulty here arises from viewing *The*

---

[149] Trevor A. Hart, 'Anselm of Canterbury and John McLeod Campbell: Where Opposites Meet?' *Evangelical Quarterly* 62 (1990) 311-333.

[150] James C Goodloe, 'Transformation of the Religious Consciousness', 196. Goodloe's assessment of Campbell's theology is explored further in Chapter 2. *An experience-centred approach?*

[151] Mark Hopkins, *Nonconformity's Romantic Generation: Evangelical and Liberal Theologies in Victorian England: Nonconformity's Romantic Generation*, (Carlisle: Paternoster, 2004), 17-28.

[152] *Ibid.*, 26-7.

Nature of the Atonement in isolation, because when Campbell's preaching is taken into account there is sufficient material to support the claim that his theology is firmly rooted within the Reformed, evangelical tradition.

Instead of concluding that any move from penal to personal categories in soteriology implies a lurch to theological liberalism, it seems more appropriate to see this preference for the personal as a symptom of Romanticism's impact upon Evangelicalism during this period.[153] In reaction to rationalism and formalism, this new cultural mood looked for the supernatural significance of everyday things and placed a high value on direct personal experience. Edward Irving's friendship with Thomas Carlyle and Samuel Taylor Coleridge put him in touch with key figures in English Romanticism, and Bebbington argues that 'Irving was a Romantic' who 'owed his celebrity to a capacity for blending Evangelical religion with the latest intellectual fashions.'[154] The outbreak of speaking in tongues around the Gareloch and in Irving's church in London, as well as the interest in premillennial eschatology, all fit comfortably into a world view which was 'fascinated by the strange, the awesome and the supernatural.'[155] It is clear that Evangelicalism was being moulded to some extent by the Romantic spirit of the age; but this move towards the personal can also be seen as a movement to rescue Evangelical faith from a rationalist accommodation to Enlightenment thinking.

Campbell's friendship with Irving meant that he had direct knowledge of this movement which was having such a profound impact upon Evangelicalism. Confirmation of Romanticism's influence can be found in Campbell's correspondence which indicates his appreciation of Romantic writers such as Carlyle, Coleridge and Wordsworth.[156] His emphasis upon personal assurance, the work of the Spirit and his preference for filial approaches to atonement, all fit happily into the Romantic worldview which found the supernatural intriguing and encouraged personal experience of the truth. Seen against this backdrop, such emphases do not necessarily indicate a trend towards liberal theology but can be seen as a creative evangelical response to the cultural signs of the times. A

---

[153] Bebbington, *Evangelicalism*, 80-1, 84, 93, 103-4.
[154] *Ibid.*, 80.
[155] *Ibid.*, 84.
[156] *Memorials* 1.142, 144, 146, 237-240; 2.67, 174, 206, 259.

sympathy with Romanticism, a suspicion of Catholicism,[157] and an interest in premillennialism are reliable indicators that Campbell deserves to be seen within his historical context as an evangelical.

Campbell was reluctant to join any group within the Kirk, but in later life expressed his evangelical sympathies in a letter to one of his daughters which says that 'you know the extent and nature of my favourable feeling towards what are called Evangelicals. It is just a part of my feeling of a living bond with all who love the Lord Jesus.'[158] His language implies that he regarded himself as an outsider viewing evangelicalism from the outside; which is hardly surprising after the treatment he had received. Although it cannot, therefore, be claimed that he necessarily saw himself as an evangelical, the evidence suggests that he deserves to be seen within the evangelical family.[159] The weight of evidence points to the conclusion that although Campbell travelled away from what he perceived to be the restrictions of federal theology, this should be seen as a journey towards a larger evangelicalism, rather than a journey out of the evangelical fold.

---

[157] His hesitations about Roman Catholicism are evident in both editions of *Christ the Bread of Life*. See chapter 6 for further treatment of this topic.
[158] *Memorials* 2.111. Letter dated 18 December 1865.
[159] It is interesting that Stunt, *Awakening to Secession*, 228, sees Campbell, A. J. Scott and Hugh Baillie MacLean as 'some of the more prominent exponents of radical evangelicalism in Scotland.'

Chapter 2

The Nature of the Atonement

In 1847 Campbell wrote to his friend Thomas Erskine to explain that he had 'ventured to attempt to teach my people on the subject of the atonement. As respects the *extent* of the atonement — its bearing on the whole human race — the Calvinism of Scotland seems breaking up fast; but this in connection with teaching, which is not light but darkness as to its *nature*; and I feel that the work for this time, if it were so uttered as to command attention, is a word supplying this great want.'[1] It was this concern to supply the 'great want' for a more adequate expression of this subject which led to the publication in 1856 of *The Nature of the Atonement*.

Whereas his priority at the outset of his ministry had been to argue the case for the universal extent of the atonement, the challenge facing Campbell the author was much more to explore what the atonement was intended to accomplish. For him it was not enough to consider what Christ had saved people *from*, without also examining what Christ saves people *for*. The traditional emphasis upon what he termed the 'retrospective' aspect of atonement had to be seen alongside an equal concern for the 'prospective' aspect of God's redemptive work. This rethinking of the doctrine led to a substantial book which has provoked responses ranging from enthusiastic praise[2] to dismissive criticism.[3]

Campbell himself describes his approach as 'moral and spiritual' in contrast to prevailing penal approaches to the Cross. It is not surprising that some people have therefore concluded that he is advancing a moral influence model for

---

[1] *Memorials*, 1.207.
[2] James B. Torrance, 'The Contribution of McLeod Campbell to Scottish Theology', *Scottish Journal of Theology*, 26 (1973) 295-311, Trevor A. Hart, 'Where Opposites Meet?'
[3] John R. W. Stott, *The Cross of Christ*, (Leicester: IVP, 1986), 141-3, 'The attempt by these theologians (such as Campbell and Horace Bushnell) to retain the language of substitution and sin-bearing, while changing its meaning, must be pronounced a failure.'

interpreting the dynamics of atonement. Allied to this, some criticisms of *The Nature of the Atonement* focus upon Campbell's proposal that on the cross Christ made a perfect confession of sin. Having decided that the idea of 'vicarious repentance' is inadequate it seems a natural next step to conclude that Campbell's version of exemplarism must, therefore, be theologically deficient. The fact that Campbell did not actually use the term 'vicarious repentance' is one consideration which raises doubts as to the accuracy of this assessment. Alongside this must be placed the recognition that his proposal about Christ's confession on the cross is only one part of a more complex understanding of atonement. Taken in isolation the notion of Christ's 'perfect repentance' or 'perfect confession' does not provide a wholly adequate way of understanding Christian atonement. But Campbell never intended this idea to be separated off from the other three elements at the heart of his understanding of the retrospective and prospective aspects of atonement. This notion may be seen to merit more serious attention when it is viewed within this larger context of his approach to atonement.

Such considerations underline the need for a careful reading of *The Nature of the Atonement* which draws attention to the contours of Campbell's theology. The reappraisal of his soteriology outlined here argues that his approach is more varied and coherent than many of his critics have realized. It also begins to identify the implicit christology of *The Nature of the Atonement*, because the priestly soteriology articulated there implies a priestly christology. It is essential for Christ to be fully divine and fully human in order to function as an effective High Priest. Recognizing the priestly shape of Campbell's thinking helps to prepare the way for the exploration of the explicit christology of his Row sermons which begins in chapter 4.

Theological Methods and Principles

Reacting against the punitive images of atonement prevalent in the Calvinistic tradition familiar to him in nineteenth century Scotland, Campbell sought instead to develop a moral and spiritual understanding of atonement. An emphasis upon abstract principles of justice was replaced by a stress upon the filial dimensions of redemption for 'we have here to do with PERSONS, – the Father of spirits and His offspring.'[4] He

---

[4] *Nature*, 183 (163).

underlined the importance of both the retrospective and prospective aspects of redemption believing that 'the atonement is regarded as that by which God has bridged over the gulf which separated between what sin had made us, and what it was the desire of the divine love that we should become.'[5]

The Priority of Revelation

While such a summary may offer some insight into Campbell's thinking it does not, of course, do justice to the careful and complicated way in which Campbell outlines and supports his construal of the doctrine of atonement. It is vital at the outset to acknowledge the theological method which undergirds his theology. His methodological priority is to affirm that the atonement needs to be seen in its own light. For 'the grace which brings salvation is itself the light which reveals both our need of salvation, and what the salvation is which we need; explaining to us the mystery of our dark experience, and directing our aimless longings to the unknown hope which was for us in God.'[6]

By stressing that what God has done determines our understanding of both the need for and the nature of atonement Campbell was making a very important methodological statement. In terms of atonement this implied that its meaning should not be predetermined by legal principles which were foreign to the scriptural narrative. The opposite procedure was called for because a true understanding could only be gained by starting with reflection upon what God had actually done.

In the conclusion of *The Nature of the Atonement* Campbell recognizes that this approach has relevance to other doctrines as well. He admits that he has deliberately addressed the subject of atonement without first considering the mysteries which surround it. The mysteries he refers to appear to be some of the deeper questions about the inner being of God. However, he argues that even if his intention had been to explore those questions he would still have engaged in the study of atonement as an essential first step towards that larger exploration.

> Nay, what I have just said implies that I must have begun with this subject, had my ultimate purpose been to consider these mysteries; so that even with regard to those questions in

---

[5] *Ibid.*, 130 (127).
[6] *Nature*, 4 (37). See also xix, (21) 'Yet our "need" is to be measured, not by our own sense of need, but by what God has done to meet our need.'

relation to God and man, which take us most to the verge of light, the inquiry, which has now engaged us attaches to itself all the interest and importance which may be felt to belong to them.[7]

Thus what God has done, should determine human thinking, not only about atonement but about all aspects of theology. So 'whether we would ascend upwards to questions connected with the name of God the Father, the Son and the Holy Spirit, or meditate on the present or future of man, the due preparation for these regions of thought is the exercise of faith in the actual condition of things which the gospel reveals, and which, in the light of the kingdom of God within us, and in the measure in which we are taught of by God, we know as the truth.'[8] In choosing this style of theology Campbell sensed that he was following in the footsteps of Luther, whose understanding of atonement receives brief but sympathetic treatment in the second chapter of *The Nature of the Atonement*.[9] By adopting such a strategy he was also anticipating to some extent the *a posteriori* approach employed by Karl Barth during the following century.

Allowing what God has done to determine his thinking meant that Campbell sought to dispense with the legal and penal categories which had tended to dominate discussion about the work of Christ. In their place he decided to interpret the Christ event in a much more personal way by emphasizing the filial dimensions of atonement so that salvation in Christ is 'the experience of *orphans who have found their long-lost Father*. For, corresponding to the yearning of the Father's heart over us while yet in our sins, is the working of the misery of our orphan state as the *ultimate contradiction to the original law of our being*.'[10] The heart of salvation, therefore, is not about persuading the divine judge to give a favourable sentence but is much more to do with what God has done to enable us to participate in the life

---

[7] *Ibid.*, 328 (263).
[8] *Ibid.*, 328 (263).
[9] *Ibid.*, 37 (57). Campbell quotes with approval Luther's insistence upon the gospel determining our understanding of God. 'For "true Christian divinity setteth not God forth unto us in His majesty as Moses and other doctors do. It commandeth us not to search out the nature of God; but to know His will set out to us in Christ. (*Ibid.*).... Therefore begin thou there where Christ began, viz., in the womb of the virgin, in the manger and at His mother's breasts, &c."'
[10] *Ibid.*, 296 (241).

of sonship.[11] The invitation to participate in this life of sonship is clearly visible when Jesus taught people to pray to God as 'Our Father'.

Campbell is sure that human beings have a deep rooted awareness of God and that embedded within this fundamental dimension of existence is some kind of awareness that this God is the Father of our spirits.[12] This filial character of human experience is not, to Campbell's eyes, discovered through a philosophical analysis of human consciousness, but is to be found clearly revealed in the pages of scripture.

> Fatherliness in God originating our salvation: the Son of God accomplishing that salvation by the revelation of the Father; the life of sonship accomplished in us, the salvation contemplated; these are conceptions continually suggested by the language of Scripture if we yield our minds to its natural force; and they are conceptions which naturally shed light on each other, and which in their combined light, and contemplated together, so illustrate *The Nature of the Atonement*, as to impart a conviction like that produced by the eternal light of axiomatic truth.[13]

This raises some questions about the way in which Campbell used Scripture but it does point to his conviction that he was allowing Scripture to play an authoritative role in his theology. A desire to view the atonement in its own light, and an explicit acknowledgement of the authority of Scripture, would tend to suggest a theology where divine revelation takes precedence. However, such a reading of Campbell has recently been challenged by James Goodloe who argues that Campbell's concept of Christian experience tends to take priority over revelation in his thinking. Before moving further into an examination of *The Nature of the Atonement* it is appropriate to address this issue, because conclusions about the respective roles of revelation and experience in Campbell's thinking may influence the way in which his theology is read.

---

[11] *Ibid.*, 190 (167-8). Similarly 'If our redemption has its origin in the feelings with which God regards us as the Father of our spirits, if the Son of God accomplishes our salvation by revealing the Father to us, then is our salvation necessarily the truth of sonship.' 297 (242).
[12] *Ibid.*, 296-7 (242-3).
[13] *Ibid.*, 295(241).

An Experience-centred Approach?

Goodloe's monograph on Campbell does not overtly link him with the experience-centred theology of Schleiermacher, which emerged around the same time, but his analysis seems to point in that direction. Hence he claims that 'the entire theory of the atonement has been conceived to depict the atonement as that which is spiritually and morally necessary to generate the experience and consciousness of being children of God.'[14]

In a similar way, referring to sermons preached during the Glasgow phase of Campbell's ministry, Goodloe asserts that 'while all of these sermons are expositions of biblical texts and ostensibly based on the authority of the Scriptures, we find again an appeal to the authority of conscience as a way of knowing god (sic) which goes beyond the letter of Scripture.'[15] There appears to be the implication that Campbell's particular view of Christian experience may lead to unhealthy distortions in the way that he reads the Scriptures.

> Thus while he appeals to the Scripture as a norm and relates everything in his theory to the gospel story of Jesus Christ in a way that the penal theories do not, he reads the story from the perspective of his concept of Christian experience. Campbell, from his understanding of the consciousness of being a child of God and of being such because of the work of God in Christ, imposes upon the Scriptures a unified depiction of Christ as the perfect son and perfect elder brother, the unity of which depiction is not supported by the Scriptures themselves. A weakness of Campbell's theology lies in his handling of the very Scriptures to which he so eloquently and ardently appeals.[16]

To some extent Goodloe is simply stating the obvious, because all theologians inevitably read the gospel story from the perspective of a particular concept of Christian experience. David Kelsey suggests that

> at the root of a theological position there is an imaginative act in which a theologian tries to catch up in a single metaphorical judgement the full complexity of God's presence in, through, and over-against the activities comprising the church's common life and which, in turn, both provides the *discrimen* against which the theology criticizes the church's current

---

[14] Goodloe, *Extent and Nature of the Atonement*, 65.
[15] *Ibid.*, 45.
[16] *Ibid.*, 66.

forms of speech and life, and determines the peculiar "shape" of the position.[17]

Campbell makes plain the *discrimen* at the heart of his approach by pointing to the opening questions of the General Assembly's Shorter Catechism which affirm both that 'man's chief end is, to glorify God, and to enjoy Him for ever', and that 'the Word of God, which is contained in the Scriptures of the Old and New Testaments, is the only rule to direct us how we may glorify and enjoy Him.'[18] It is important to note that his recognition of the authority of the Bible is qualified to some extent by his insistence that this God-given revelation authenticates itself by provoking a response within the human conscience.[19] For Campbell there is no conflict between Revelation and Reason (or Conscience) because the conscience is divinely given and God chooses to speak through both channels. All of which leads George Tuttle to suggest that Campbell exemplified a much more revelation-oriented approach, within which the Bible functioned as 'his primary resource.'[20]

In addition to expressing the priority of the Bible within his theology, Campbell is careful to explain that human experience does not provide an independent authority within theology.

> Now this faith that these things are so comes entirely by receiving of what God has said. I cannot see in my own conscience that sin is forgiven: I do not find written anywhere in the heart of any man or in my own heart or in the practice of the world that my sins are forgiven. I cannot find it in men's notions about salvation, in men's endeavouring to escape wrath: there is no trace of it to be found in all the workings of the natural heart of man, in all the suggestions of the natural conscience of man. If I am to find any proof of it, it

---

[17] David H. Kelsey, *The Uses of Scripture in Recent Theology*, (London: SCM Press, 1975), 163.
[18] *Reminiscences*, 92-3; cf. 54, 126-7.
[19] Tuttle, *So Rich a Soil*, 15. 'God's word is authoritative because it carries its own evidence with it. And where are those evidences best recognized? – in the mind and heart, in the conscience of the believer where God is recognized for who he is and his commands are known to be true as issuing from him.'
[20] *Ibid.*, 66, 70-2, 14.

must be from some other quarter, and this makes it to be altogether a matter of faith.[21]

To some extent Campbell's theology was built upon the basis of Christian experience, because it was his reflection upon the experience of his parishioners' lack of Christian assurance which prompted him to rethink the theological tradition which they had been nurtured in. Goodloe builds too much on this when he asserts that from this point onwards it was the demands of Christian experience which dictated which parts of Scripture Campbell appealed to. Such an assertion underestimates the complexity of the interrelation of scripture and experience within Campbell's approach.

Campbell admits that 'the natural effect of having the mind fixed on the end of man's being as the glorifying of God and enjoying of Him, and the unquestioning acceptance of the Bible as a divine gift having its value in connection with this end, was to give special interest to those portions of Scripture, and those aspects of truth, which most obviously and unmistakably connected themselves with this end...Thus large portions of Scripture were left out of account in my teaching, both in preaching and in private intercourse...[22] This frank admission of a selective use of biblical material does not mean that Campbell's approach was not biblical. Although he clearly does not seek biblical verses to support every part of his argument, his approach can be seen as authentically biblical because he is constantly concerned to draw attention to the character of God as revealed in Scripture. It is clear that his relationship with his own father was very important to him, and that this relationship enhanced rather than hindered his faith in the heavenly Father.[23] However, it is equally clear that his emphasis upon God as the Father of our spirits, who longs for people to enjoy the life of sonship, is rooted not so much in his personal experience but in the biblical revelation of the divine Son who enjoys a constant communion with his heavenly Father.

One of the strengths of Goodloe's study is that it acknowledges the importance of Campbell's sermons both from

---

[21] *NofS*, 1.5.6. Sermon on 1 Pet. 1:7.
[22] *Reminiscences*, 126-7.
[23] *Ibid.*, 41. In a letter written in May 1871, Campbell commented on his relationship with his father. 'For no mere creature-gift of the "better Father" have I been so indebted and so grateful to Him as for the earthly father, whose being what he was filled that name with so much meaning for me.'

the period in Row and from the years of Campbell's ministry in Glasgow. It is not at all surprising that, in his sermons, Campbell was seeking to show the practical implications for Christian experience of the truths that he was discovering. However, this does not automatically imply that everything in his preaching and theology is driven to conform to a specific model of experience. More often than not within the sermons, it appears to be the case that the preacher is seeking to bring people's experience into line with ideas emerging from the scriptures, rather than the other way round.

The work of liberation theologians has served as a reminder of the importance of 'context' and 'contextualisation' within theology. Although an emphasis upon 'context' implies that present experience is a resource for theological construction, it does not mean that 'context' or 'experience' are adequate on their own. Christian theology which takes experience as its starting point, needs to engage in a serious dialogue with Christian Scriptures and with the Christian tradition. Without such a dialogue the process of theological reflection is in danger of veering off into relativism. A theology rooted in scripture and tradition which does not address contextual questions runs the equally serious risk of being irrelevant.

If Campbell's theology is assessed from this perspective then it could be seen as a healthy example of 'doing theology'. He begins by reflecting upon the experience of his church members, and the questions arising from their experience cause him to enter into a dialogue both with the prevalent theological tradition and with the scriptures. Arising from this interaction there begins to emerge that discrimen which motivates Campbell's understanding of the extent and *The Nature of the Atonement*. The preaching of this theory of the atonement generates fresh experiences which provoke further dialogues with Scripture and tradition.

If something of this dynamic is at work then it suggests that Goodloe's emphasis upon the priority of experience in Campbell's approach is important but incomplete. His emphasis upon the Christian experience of being a child of God clearly affects Campbell's reading of Scripture. However, if that emphasis derives from Scripture and is consonant with it, then it would be legitimate for Campbell to read Scriptures in its light. If all experience is interpreted experience then Campbell would not have come to his first parish free of all presuppositions but can only have viewed the experiences at Row through the lens of a mind already immersed in the Scriptures and the beliefs and catechisms of the Church. In addition it is important to note that Campbell makes his methodology clear by his insistence that his approach to questions of atonement is not determined by prior assumptions about Christian experience or anything else. The whole direction of his theology runs in the opposite direction from that suggested by Goodloe because, as has been shown already, Campbell explicitly states his desire 'that we should be in the position of learning from the atonement itself why it was needed, as well as how it has accomplished that for which it was needed.'[24]

An Objective Love

When atonement is seen in its own light it is clear that its origins lie in the God who so loved the world that he gave his Son. There is no question of an atonement being needed in order to make God gracious because 'the Scriptures do not speak of such an atonement; for they do not represent the love of God to man as the effect, and the atonement of Christ as the cause, but — just the contrary — they represent the love of God as the cause, and the atonement as the effect.'[25] Atonement originates in the 'fatherliness of God'[26] whose love and forgiveness precede any attempts to expiate sin. His costly, sacrificial love has an unparalleled power to save.

> It is that God is contemplated as manifesting clemency and goodness at a great cost, and not by a simple act of will that costs nothing, that gives the atonement its great power over the heart of man. For that is a deep, yea, the deepest spiritual instinct in man which affirms, that in proportion as any act manifests love it is to be believed as ascribed to God who is love. No manifestation of power meeting me can so assure me that I am meeting God as the manifestation of love does.[27]

If this was simply a costly display of love then it would not be of great value.

> Love cannot be conceived of as doing anything gratuitously, merely to show its own depth, for which thing there was no call in the circumstances of the case viewed in themselves. A man may love another so as to be willing to die for him; — but

---

[24] *Nature*, 197 (173).
[25] *Ibid.*, 17 (46).
[26] *Ibid.*, 290-1 (236).
[27] *Ibid.*, 21 (48-9).

he will not actually lay down his life merely to show his love, and without there being anything to render his doing so necessary in order to save the life for which he yields up his own.

...Self-sacrificing love does not sacrifice itself but for an end of gain to its object; otherwise it would be folly.[28]

The costly manifestation of God's love in Christ was not folly because it had the serious intention of saving sinners threatened by the divine wrath, who were in no position to save themselves. There is what Campbell calls the 'fixed and necessary character of salvation' which arises from the fixed and necessary character of God who must respond in loving wrath towards sin and injustice. A form of atonement had to be found which would vindicate the honour of the divine law. However, this does not mean that God's love and the law are somehow in conflict, because the law is an expression of God's love. The essential continuity between law and love is stated clearly in one of the Row sermons where Campbell says that *'God's law*, is God's own *heart come out in the shape of a law*; and when Christ magnified it and made it honourable, he proved it to be God's heart, and so he glorified the law. Do not feel, therefore, as if God's law and God's feelings were different things; and as if God commanded you to love, and yet was personally indifferent whether you loved or not; and God commanded you to be holy, and yet was personally indifferent whether you were holy or not.'[29]

The breaking of the law therefore is a rebellion against the love of God and this breaking of the law calls for a due expression of God's wrath against sin to take place in the history of redemption. Once again it is important to realize that wrath is not in conflict with love, but originates in the divine love.[30] Hence Campbell talks about the cross as the place where Christ 'dealt on behalf of man with the ultimate and absolute root of judgement in God.'[31] The withdrawal of the gift of life appears to be an important dimension of judgement. His ideas are expounded clearly in Principal Shairp's letter which explains that, '"The wages of sin is death." This is the Father's eternal irreversible way of looking at sin. He does not change his will. But Christ meets this will, says, "Thou art righteous O Father, in

---

[28] *Ibid.*, 22-3 (49-50).
[29] *S&L* 1.13.319.
[30] *Nature*, 127 (125).
[31] *Ibid.*, 199, 267 (174,221).

thus judging sin; and I accept Thy judgement of it; and meet it. I in my humanity say Amen to Thy judgement of sin."'³²

What Campbell seems to be saying is that there are certain unchanging laws which operate in the moral and spiritual universe created and sustained by the Father of our spirits. In the fixed and necessary nature of things, the wrath which originates in God's love, is not a temporary phenomenon but is the permanent shadow side of the divine love. It represents the way in which divine, holy love always reacts to sin.

> Now we cannot doubt the pain which the exposure of the unjust to suffering was to God, or the desire of His heart to save them from suffering; but we must not forget that the original reason for connecting sin and misery still continued, that the connexion was not arbitrary, that the wrath of God revealed against all unrighteousness of men was not a feeling that has passed, or could pass away: no revelation of the unchanging God could. Therefore when the just suffered for the unjust, it was with the direct purpose of bringing the unjust to God, — that is bringing the unjust to the obedience of the just, *leaving the connexion between suffering and injustice, or sin, undissolved, the righteousness of that connexion being unchanged.*³³

If there is something 'fixed and necessary' about the way things are then a redemption which simply consists of God lifting a legal penalty on sin would not be adequate because it does not seem to address the sin within people which continues to render them unacceptable to God. After the cross, as before, God continues to reject sin and injustice. So instead of issuing a legal pardon to sinners, which would not necessarily deal with their sinful essence, a way must be found to make people righteous, thus enabling them to enjoy living in the presence of God. In the same way in which the cross does not make God

---

³² *Memorials* 2.340-3. Although this letter was written after Campbell's death in 1872, it is based on detailed notes made by Shairp during a conversation with Campbell in Edinburgh on 11 March 1860. Whilst notes of a conversation may not supply the *ipsissima verba*, these comments resonate strongly with the language of Campbell's preaching and writing and probably provide access to the *ipsissima vox* of Campbell.

³³ *Nature*, 181 (161). See also 269 (223) 'Whatever be supposed to have been the nature of the link between Christ and our sins, it was needful that He should on our behalf deal with the righteous wrath of God against sin in that way which accorded with the eternal and unchanging truth of things.'

any more loving than he was before, it must also be the case that God is no less holy and righteous than he was before.

If the Father of our spirits is a God of holy love then an atonement originating in his fatherliness will be one which transforms sinful people and makes them righteous. This cannot be done by a legal fiction where Christ's righteousness is somehow credited to a person's account without necessarily making any difference to their behaviour. It can only come to pass if God provides in Christ 'everything we need for life and godliness.'[34] Through participation in 'the divine nature' believers begin to see themselves and their sin as God sees them and in the power of Christ's Spirit they are enabled to fulfil the command to love God and their neighbour. An atonement which is consistent with the fixed and necessary character of God will, therefore, need to address what God saves people for as well as what he saves them from.

Another dimension of the fixed and necessary character of salvation is bound up in the notion that Christ *is* the propitiation for our sins. For Campbell it is not that Christ at some distant time in the past provided a propitiation which was in some way separate from himself. The fact of the matter is that there is no other way to come back to God but in and through Christ, who here and now is and will continue to be the propitiation for our sins.[35]

Within such a moral universe the outlook for sinful people is bleak unless God acts to provide a way of atonement. A real gulf exists between what God had intended for human beings and what sin had made them. The message which Campbell advocated was that God himself had provided the means to cross this otherwise uncrossable gulf. 'Now the gospel declares, that the love of God has, not only desired to bridge over this gulf, but has actually bridged it over, and the atonement is presented to us as that in which this is accomplished.'[36] In all of this the initiative rests firmly in the hand of God.

> But let us be clear as to the elements of our consciousness when this is our conscious history. We have not by any movement of our own being caused this drawing of the Father; we have only yielded to it; — neither have we by any movement of our being brought the Son thus near to us. He was thus near to us even when we knew it not. Only under the

---

[34] 2 Pet. 1:3-4.
[35] *Ibid.*, 170-1 (153-4).
[36] *Ibid.*, 22 (49).

teaching of God we have Christ revealed in us the hope of glory. The mystery hid from the ages and generations is made known to us.[37]

Having observed that there is a tendency to see Anselm and Campbell as inhabiting opposite ends of the soteriological spectrum, Trevor Hart argues that in spite of differences in emphasis there are significant areas of theological convergence. He argues that in the work of Campbell, as well as in the work of Anselm, there is a clear sense that atonement is very much the objective accomplishment of God. 'Thus the atonement is something that God does, and not something that we do. It is the product of his prevenient love for sinful man, and not something which man brings to placate an angry and otherwise unforgiving deity.'[38]

The Key to the Atonement

On a number of occasions Campbell suggests that the key to the atonement is found in the phrase from Psalm 40 'Lo, I come to do Thy will, O God.'[39] This is not to be seen in terms of Christ coming to carry out some prearranged plan but much more along the lines that his life's work was to manifest the mind of God and to declare the name of the Father.[40] The climax of this work of revelation was on the cross where the Father was revealed by the Son in a number of ways.

In the light of his personal history it comes as no surprise to discover that Campbell takes issue in this book with various Calvinist writers who advocate a limited atonement. Part of his unease with John Owen and Jonathan Edwards is that 'while they set forth justice as a necessary attribute of the divine nature, so that God must deal with all men according to its

---

[37] *Ibid.*, 312 (253).
[38] Trevor A. Hart, *Where Opposites Meet*, 322. Faris, 'The Nature of Theological Inquiry', 288, argues that the background sources to Campbell's thinking share an objective emphasis, so that 'whether we look at Luther, Calvin, Henry Dorney, Fraser of Brae, Thomas Boston or Thomas Erskine, there is an emphasis on the objective nature of what has been done in Christ's work of Atonement. There is similarly, a common emphasis on the necessary relationship of the incarnation to the atonement.'
[39] *Nature*, 107, 272, 275 (111, 224, 227). See also *FofT* 19.237-240 and 20.241-2.
[40] Campbell refers here to Jn. 17:26 'I have declared They name, and will declare it.'

requirements, they represent mercy and love as not necessary, but arbitrary, and what, therefore, may find their expression in the history of only some men.'[41] If love is but an arbitrary attribute, then this must reduce the act of love on the cross, for the benefit of the elect, to the status of an arbitrary act. Such an arbitrary act cannot be a reliable guide to the divine nature for 'an arbitrary act cannot reveal character.'[42] Certain doctrines of election, therefore, may create the impression that God acts in one way to one group of people whilst acting in a totally different way with regard to another group. In the event of such different forms of behaviour which of God's actions should be taken as revealing the truth about him? Campbell feels that the logical conclusion of such a process of reflection is to leave us feeling that we are dealing with the unknown God. For these sorts of reasons he arrives at 'the conclusion, that the doctrine of an atonement for the elect only, destroys the claim of the work of Christ to be what fully reveals and illustrates the great foundation of all religion, that God is love.'[43] By contrast, he argues, that it is only a belief in the death of Christ for all, which is consistent with the core Christian convictions about God's loving character.

The depth and intensity of the Son's prayers to the Father in Gethsemane and at the Cross, help to reveal 'that God is the hearer and answerer of prayer.'[44] By trusting his Father in the midst of the agony of the cross the Son reveals that God is trustworthy. For 'in his last trying time, and while subjected to the hour and power of darkness, sustained by the simple faith of that original fatherliness of the Father's heart, which He had *come forth to reveal* and TO REVEAL IT BY TRUSTING IT.'[45] In the act of forgiving his enemies from the cross the Son reveals that the Father is a forgiving God.[46]

Some notions of revelation focus upon Jesus revealing truth about God through his teaching, by his love for others and in the way that he died. For a theologian like Karl Rahner[47] revelation does not involve God revealing propositional truths

---

[41] *Nature*, 54 (73).
[42] *Ibid.*, 55 (73).
[43] *Ibid.*, 56 (74).
[44] *Ibid.*, 202 (176).
[45] *Ibid.*, 244 (206).
[46] *Ibid.*, 247-8 (207-8).
[47] See Karl Rahner, *Foundations of Christian Faith*, (London: Darton, Longman & Todd, 1978), 117-133.

about himself, but consists rather in God offering himself to human beings through Christ. Campbell helpfully adds to ideas about revelation by pointing out that the truth about God's fatherliness has been revealed, not only through the words and actions of Jesus, but also by his inner attitude of trust towards God. The emphasis here is not so much upon Jesus as the supreme example of trust, but upon the supremely trustworthy God. Through the lens of trust we begin to see that the fatherliness of God is a vital aspect of what God is in himself. What comes to light through the trust of Jesus is the loving nature of the Father of our spirits who is graciously ready to hear and answer the prayers of all. The good news is not simply that the Son of God trusted God and was not disappointed, because it would be surprising for the divine Father to ignore the prayers of the divine Son. The gospel is that the trust of the fully human Jesus reveals a God who can be trusted by all human beings. The logic of Campbell's position implies that the Son of God has fully identified with fallen human beings, for only thus can his experience be of any relevance to us.

The cross also reveals God's holy condemnation of sin. For 'the condemnation of our sin in that expiatory confession of our sin which was perfected in the death of Christ is not less a part of the revelation of the Father by the Son than the trust in the depths of fatherliness in which life was asked and received for us.'[48] The upshot of this is that the sufferings of Christ upon the cross are '*not* the *measure* of what God *can inflict*, but the *revelation* of what God *feels*.'[49] It reveals a God who cannot be indifferent to sin and injustice.

So 'the Son of God saves us by a work whose essence and sum is the declaring of the Father's name... "We love Him because He first loved us." The power to quicken love in us is here ascribed to the love with which God regards us, considered simply as love.'[50] God does not use his miracle working power to force rebellious children to become loving children, but trusts that if the truth about his love is revealed fully then that love has an inherent power to convert and transform. Although the language is very different the ideas here are to some extent reminiscent of debates between Bernard of Clairvaux and Abelard as to whether the cross merely revealed love or had the

---

[48] *Nature*, 264 (219).
[49] *Ibid.*, 268 (222).
[50] *Ibid.*, 292 (238-9).

power to infuse love.⁵¹ Within the context of Campbell's thought it is clear that the love revealed through the Son's doing the will of the Father has the power to infuse divine love into human lives. It is not explained how this comes to pass but it is clear that the emphasis remains upon the divine initiative for 'our sanctification therefore is accomplished by the *will of God*, as *acting on our will*, by the *moral* and *spiritual power* of what that divine will *is in itself*. For the will of God, in order to be welcomed with that welcome which is holiness, i.e. *the free consecration of our will*, must be welcomed *just because* of WHAT IT IS.'⁵²

Although not the major feature in his approach these comments show that the revelation of the truth about God is a significant factor within the understanding of atonement which unfolds in *The Nature of the Atonement*. The success of the Son in his work of revealing God is also seen in the centurion's cry at the cross that 'Truly this was the Son of God'.⁵³

'No-one knows the Father except the Son'

In reflecting upon Romans 5:8 Campbell argues that the death of Christ can only be seen as a proof of God's love if Christ was indeed God.⁵⁴ Campbell affirms that 'of course this assumes that Christ is God', but does not, at that point, go on to explore the matter further. However, it would be legitimate to go on from there to say that it is only possible for the action of the Son to function as a full revelation of the Father if there is a real unity of essence between the Son and the Father. If the Son is the most exalted creature but not the divine Son then his love will be simply the love of a fellow creature. As such it will reveal some of the heights to which human love may reach but it cannot serve as a direct and full revelation of the love of God. 'A servant may make us acquainted with his master; a subject may make us to know the lawgiver and king to whom he owes allegiance; the Son alone could reveal the Father. "No one knoweth the Father save the Son, and he to whom the Son revealeth Him."'⁵⁵

---

⁵¹ Paul S. Fiddes, *Past Event and Present Salvation: The Christian Idea of Atonement*, (London: Darton, Longman and Todd, 1989), 144.
⁵² *Nature*, 292 (239).
⁵³ *Ibid.*, 218, 262 (188, 218).
⁵⁴ *Ibid.*, 23 (50).
⁵⁵ *Ibid.*, 63 (79). Campbell is here quoting from Mt. 11:27.

He was in no doubt that Christ should be seen as the one who reveals the truth about God because 'He that has seen me has seen the Father'.[56] The ultimate truth that is unveiled is that God is primarily 'the Father of our spirits' who longs for us to live as his children. In revealing such a God in the power of the Spirit, the Son is revealing a trinitarian understanding of God.

It is appropriate also to note that Campbell assumes some sort of pre-existence for Christ, because the perfection of sonship which had been manifested in humanity did *'not then come into existence.'*[57] Christ's power to enable us to participate in his life of sonship is another factor which leads people to recognise the divinity of Christ. There is something in his divinity which makes it possible for him to relate to all people so that what he does and accomplishes has relevance to all.

In a similar way Campbell believed that the Son of God also revealed the truth about humanity, '(for) the revealer of the Father is also the revealer of man, who was made in God's image.'[58] If the Son is thus able to reveal the full truth about humanity, then this implies a unity of essence between humanity and the revealer. One of the indications that Campbell takes the humanity of Christ very seriously is that he acknowledges a degree of development within 'our Lord's human consciousness.'[59]

Seeing Jesus Christ as the one who fully reveals the nature of God and the nature of humanity, implies and requires a theology which affirms both the divinity and humanity of the mediator of salvation. It is these sorts of consideration which lead Christian Kettler to assert that 'although he does not use the term, the Nicene doctrine of the *homoousion* between the Father and Son is very alive in the thought of Campbell.'[60]

---

[56] *Ibid.*, 62-63 (79), where Campbell is referring to Jn. 14:9. See also, Michael Jinkins, *Atonement and the Character of God*, 326-344.
[57] *Nature*, 287 (235).
[58] *Ibid.*, 138 (132).
[59] *Ibid.*, 248 (208). 'Adhering to the conception of a progressive development of the eternal life in our Lord's human consciousness, and looking at all that was appointed for Him by the Father as adapted by the divine wisdom for the end of forwarding this development, we indeed see abundant reason for that perfected personal experience of the enmity of the carnal mind to God, to which our Lord was subjected.' This is explored more fully in Chapter 2. *Made Perfect Through Suffering*.
[60] Christian D. Kettler, *The Vicarious Humanity of Christ and the Reality of Salvation*, (Lanham: University Press of America, 1991), 162.

This unity with God and with human beings is seen in Campbell's terminology as 'perfect sonship towards God and perfect Brotherhood towards men.'[61] Christ's participation in humanity makes possible human participation in the divine nature through Him.[62] Although there is no evidence of any direct literary dependence on Athanasius,[63] such talk of participation has resonances with his understanding of salvation in Christ in terms of re-creation or 'deification.' When Athanasius says that '*He became man that we might become god*' he is not suggesting that believers become gods, or sons of God, in the same sense that the Logos is the divine Son of God. Whereas he is Son in nature and in truth, believers are sons in a derivative way by appointment and grace. So if there is any kind of divinization, or participation in the divine nature, through the Logos, then this must be because he is by nature and substance true God of true God. Θεοποίησις (deification) could never obliterate the ontological distinction between God and his creatures, but the humanity of the Logos made participation in God possible through incorporation in him.'[64]

Leanne Van Dyk[65] notes how George Dion Dragas draws attention to the way that in the thought of Athanasius, Christ is related to all humanity by virtue of his being the Logos of all creation. In this respect the divinity of Christ does not distance him from ordinary human beings, but on the contrary provides a way in which what he does has implications for all.

> Thus the inner logic, as it were, of this substitutionary act is not to be traced to an abstract principle of forensic sacrificial transaction but to the headship of the Divine Logos in creation whereby he is related to all human beings and as such can act on their behalf as their true representative. Thus the substitutionary offering of one single body (humanity) for all rests on the fact that it is the 'Dominical body' [*to Kyriakon sōma*], that is to say, the body of him who is 'above all' [*ho epi pantōn*] and 'for all' [*ho epi pantas*] and, therefore, the one who

---

[61] *Nature*, xvii (19).

[62] *Ibid.*, 321 (259).

[63] At the end of the published report of Campbell's trial some quotations from Clement, Cyprian, Augustine and others were added by the publisher, to show that Campbell's views were not heretical. There is little explicit evidence that Campbell himself was knowledgeable in the theology of the early Church Fathers. *Proceedings (GA)*, 179-194.

[64] Frances Young, *From Nicea to Chalcedon*, (London: SCM Press, 1983), 75.

[65] Van Dyk, *Desire of Divine Love*, 119.

can also be 'instead of all' [*ho anti pantōn*], as the representative of all.⁶⁶

Study of the Row sermons, in chapters 4 and 5, will provide evidence that Campbell also believed in Christ as the head and the representative of the human race, whose actions have saving consequences for the whole of creation. The one who embodied perfect sonship towards God and perfect Brotherhood towards men and women was thus uniquely able to fulfil all the aspects at the heart of atonement as Campbell construes it. It is in the light of these factors that it is now possible to consider Campbell's distinctive understanding of the retrospective and prospective dimensions of atonement.

The Natural Development of the Incarnation

Campbell was critical of both earlier and later Calvinist writers for the way in which they viewed the relationship between christology and soteriology. For some writers the divinity of Christ made it possible for him to endure the infinite penal sufferings needed to balance the accounts of divine justice. Other later writers recoiled from this and suggested instead that the divinity of the Son of God gave infinite value to his finite sufferings. Within Campbell's moral and spiritual approach to atonement, the sufferings of Christ are seen very differently because they are seen as something arising naturally out of who he was.

At a number of points in *The Nature of the Atonement* Campbell affirms a link between incarnation and suffering by speaking of the atonement as 'the natural development of the incarnation.'⁶⁷ However, he does not pause to explain a phrase which is open to various interpretations. Leanne Van Dyk argues that 'this notion of the "natural" development of the atonement presents a challenge for the interpreter of Campbell. Campbell did not explain the content of the idea; he seems to consider it self-

---

⁶⁶ George Dion Dragas, 'St. Athanasius on Christ's Sacrifice', in S. W. Sykes (ed.), *Sacrifice and Redemption: Durham Essays in Theology*, (Cambridge: Cambridge University Press, 1991), 93.

⁶⁷ *Nature*, 277 (228). Cf., xvii (19). '(My) attempt to understand and illustrate *The Nature of the Atonement* has been made in the way of taking the subject to the light of the incarnation. Assuming the incarnation, I have sought to realise the divine mind in Christ as perfect Sonship towards God and perfect Brotherhood towards men, and doing so, the incarnation has appeared developing itself naturally and necessarily as the atonement.'

explanatory. He did not demonstrate how his theory is a natural interpretation in contrast to others which he sees as arbitrary. He just states that his atonement theology is "natural." It remains a bare assertion.' So she suggests that 'as a general rule, "natural" means an interpretation which starts from the facts of Christ's life on earth as recorded in the Scriptures rather than an interpretation which starts from an external point of inquiry such as the necessity, or possibility of the atonement.'[68]

If this is the case then atonement should be interpreted in the light of the actual story of Jesus and not as the mechanical outworking of some external laws of justice. Allowing the story of Jesus to provide the interpretative framework leads Campbell to believe that atonement should be understood in personal rather than penal terms. The coming of the incarnate Son leads naturally to atonement because such a mediator would sympathise both with God's anger at sin, and with the divine desire to create a way for sinful people to enter into a life of sonship.[69] Suffering is implied when atonement is seen as the natural development of the incarnation, because in a fallen world suffering inevitably arises when absolute holiness, in the perfection of divine sonship, is brought into close proximity with human sinfulness. So '...the truth is that the sufferings of Christ arose so naturally out of what He was, and the relation in which He stood to those for whose sins He suffered, that though His divine nature might be conceived of as giving them weight, however small in themselves, yet to that very divine nature must we refer their awful intensity, and, to us, immeasurable amount.'[70]

Retrospective and Prospective Aspects of the Atonement

Christ's Dealing with Humanity on the Part of God

This involved Christ's witnessing to the truth of God in the midst of a fallen world. Such perfect obedience to God in the midst of sinful people brought with it the inevitability of suffering as his perfect love was met with hatred. These

---

[68] Van Dyk, *Desire of Divine Love*, 41-2.
[69] Thomas F. Torrance, *Scottish Theology*, 313. 'As McLeod Campbell understood it, the atonement developed naturally and compellingly out of Christ's inner relation to men and women as the incarnate Son.'
[70] *Nature*, 99 (105-6).

sufferings were not penal in nature but represented the pain which God in our nature was bound to feel under the constant pressure from human sin. An important part of Christ's witnessing to the truth of God was his perfect sympathy with the Father's condemnation of sin. The Old Testament character of Phinehas is seen as a model for Christ in that his 'zeal for God, and sympathy in His condemnation of sin' helped to make atonement for the sins of Israel.

> There can be no uncertainty about the atoning element here. It was not the mere death of the subjects of the act of Phinehas. Had they died by the plague, their death would have been no atonement, — the death of the twenty-four thousand who so died was none. But the moral element in the transaction — the mind of Phinehas — his zeal for God — his sympathy in God's judgement on sin, this was the atonement, this its essence.[71]

In a much fuller way Christ's zeal for God has the power to arrest the course of judgement and contribute to making atonement for the sins of the world.

> If the principle of the divine procedure in that case can be recognised, we shall have no difficulty in seeing the place which the perfect zeal for the Father's honour, the living manifestation of perfect sympathy in the Father's condemnation of sin, the perfect vindication of the unselfish and righteous character of that condemnation as the mind of Him who is love, which were presented to men in the life of Christ, being perfected in His death, — we shall, I say, have no difficulty in seeing the place which this dealing of Christ with men on the part of God has in the work of redemption.[72]

This condemnation of sin does not occur simply on the cross but is a dimension of the whole incarnate life of Christ. This does not imply that he spent all his time going around condemning people. The emphasis here is upon Christ's life of absolute trust and obedience to God which reveals how God intends people to live and exposes the fact that men and women prefer to live in sinful independence of the Father of their spirits. The coming of the light of the world judges sin by revealing that people love darkness because their deeds are evil.

---

[71] *Ibid.*, 103f (108f). Referring to Num. 25:10-13.
[72] *Ibid.*, 113-4 (115-6).

Christ not only identifies with God's condemnation of sin but he also shares the Father's longing that his prodigal children should come to their senses and return. He also fulfilled the second great commandment by loving all human beings as himself. Such a love which longs for all humanity to share in the eternal life of God, inevitably brings upon itself the full burden of human sin, because it is painfully aware of all that stands in the way of men and women experiencing eternal life. The sufferings experienced by Christ therefore are not punishments inflicted by God but are the natural form which holiness and love take in the context of human sin and need.

Campbell's use of this unlikely Old Testament passage may seem strained to many Christian readers today. It is clear that the parallelism between Phinehas and Christ cannot be pressed too far, as Phinehas showed his zeal for God by killing others rather than by surrendering his own life. However, placing these two biblical characters side by side might have some value in pointing to an alternative approach to the understanding of justice? Might it be the case that the intervention of Phinehas implies a view of justice where God's justice represents, not divine punishment upon sinners, but a loving intervention whereby God seeks to prevent his creatures from destroying themselves? Might it be possible to see some similarity here with the approach of Anselm who regards justice, in part, as involving the loving intervention of God acting to prevent sinful human beings from destroying both themselves and creation? In this approach God acts justly by intervening to restore harmony to a moral universe disrupted by sin rather than acting to uphold an abstract, legal form of justice. This God is as much seeking to save people from themselves as he is seeking to uphold his own honour.[73]

If Campbell was feeling towards such an understanding of justice then why does he make such an effort in chapter IV of *The Nature of the Atonement* to attack the rectoral or public understanding of justice embodied in what he describes as 'recently modified' Calvinism? Part of the answer may lie in Campbell's unease with an approach which to his eyes creates

---

[73] 'What then is satisfaction? In large measure it has to do with the divine action in setting right that which has been thrown out of kilter by human sin...Satisfaction is therefore Anselm's way of speaking of that which took place as a result of the good God's being unwilling to allow his creatures to destroy themselves.' Colin E. Gunton, *The Actuality of Atonement*, (Edinburgh: T & T Clark, 1988), 91-2.

the impression that God was acting to uphold an abstract law rather than acting in a way to express his profound love for his creation.

Christ's Dealing with God on Behalf of Humanity

With reference to this aspect of atonement Campbell detects within the writings of Jonathan Edwards a hint that an alternative way of understanding atonement might be possible.

> In contending 'that sin must be punished with an infinite punishment', President Edwards says, that 'God could not be just to Himself without this vindication, unless there could be such a thing as a repentance, humiliation and sorrow for this (viz. sin) proportional to the greatness of the majesty despised,' for that there needs be, 'either an equivalent punishment or an equivalent sorrow and repentance' — 'so', he proceeds, 'sin must be punished with an infinite punishment,' thus assuming that the alternative of 'an equivalent sorrow and repentance' was out of the question.[74]

At the cross Campbell sees Christ offering such an equivalent repentance which acknowledges both the full horror of sin and the appropriateness of God meeting such sin with the full weight of judgement.

> That oneness of mind with the Father, which towards man took the form of condemnation of sin, would in the Son's dealing with the Father in relation to our sins, take the form of a perfect confession of our sins. This confession, as to its own nature, must have been *a perfect Amen in humanity to the judgement of God on the sin of man.* Such an Amen was due in the truth of things. He who was the Truth could not be in humanity and not utter it, — and it was necessarily a first step in dealing with the Father on our behalf. He who would intercede for us must begin with confessing our sins.[75]

It is his perfection of sonship which enables Christ to see the misery facing sinners in all its stark awfulness, and makes repentance possible in its absolute perfection. Such perfect confession includes all the major elements of repentance 'excepting the personal consciousness of sin'[76]

---

[74] *Nature*, 118 (118-9).
[75] *Ibid.*, 116-7 (118).
[76] *Ibid.*, 118 (118).

When Christ in his divine humanity was faced with the divine wrath he responded by saying '"Thou art righteous, O Lord, who judgest so,"...*and in that perfect response He absorbs it.*'[77] At this point Leanne Van Dyk brings out the implications of Campbell's statement by asking,

> what does it actually mean that Christ's repentance or contrition or sorrow 'absorbed' the wrath of God? Beyond this crucial and ambiguous word of explication, Campbell does not and cannot go much farther. It is the very core of the atonement mystery in Campbell's theology. Every atonement theory has its central mystery – the place where, finally, explanations of how God reconciled the world to Godself in the life and death of Jesus Christ end. For Campbell, the central mystery is the absorption of God's wrath in Christ's own perfect response to God's just judgement and his realization of sin in his own spirit. In this, somehow, is salvation. In this, somehow, God's justice is satisfied and human need is met.[78]

There may be some debate as to whether the boundary of mystery stands quite where Van Dyk suggests. In the comments made above, concerning the fixed and necessary character of salvation, it was noted that an important dimension of God's judgement upon sin consists in the fact that the wages of sin is death. If this is the case, then in accepting the sentence of death upon the cross is not Christ accepting the judgement and wrath of God? If judgement and wrath were understood by Campbell in this way then it may be appropriate to say with James B. Torrance that the response of the Son to the Father included a 'perfect submission on our behalf to the verdict of guilty'.[79] So although there is room for debate about what Campbell meant by talking about Christ absorbing the wrath of God it is hard to deny that he is seeking to take account of the reality of sin and wrath. This perfect response which absorbs the divine wrath is a perfect form of repentance which embodies a perfect sorrow and a perfect contrition for sin.

---

[77] *Ibid.*, 117 (118). See also 125 (124). 'absorbing and exhausting the divine wrath in that adequate confession and perfect response on the part of man, which was possible only to the infinite and eternal righteousness in humanity.'
[78] Van Dyk, *Desire of Divine Love*, 114.
[79] James B. Torrance, 'Contribution of McLeod Campbell', 309.

The Nature of the Atonement

This is one of the points where Campbell's implicit christology becomes visible, because, as Van Dyk observes, the idea of Christ's perfect response to God is undergirded by the conviction that Christ is fully human and fully divine. 'As fully human, Christ confesses human sin; as fully divine, Christ recognizes the weight and gravity and truth of God's verdict against human sin. Thus, it is only in the "divine humanity" of Christ that the Amen is possible.'[80]

Christ's expiatory confession was accompanied by his intercession for sinners. However, this priestly act of intercession was

> not an intercession which contemplated effecting a change in the heart of the Father, but a confession which combined with acknowledgement of the righteousness of the divine wrath against sin, hope for man from that love in God which is deeper than that wrath, — in truth originating it — determining also its nature, and justifying the confidence that, its righteousness being responded to, and the mind which it expresses shared in, that wrath must be appeased.[81]

It is appropriate to note in passing that this insistence upon seeing wrath as something which originates, not in divine justice, but in God's love, is a further reminder that love is not a secondary, arbitrary attribute of God. When Christ 'made intercession for the transgressors' in the midst of the suffering of the cross, this was the perfection of his life's work of retaliating with love. This move towards intercession provides a link towards the prospective dimension of atonement which will be treated in the next section.

From the outset this dimension of his theology has attracted criticism. Within a few months of the publication of *The Nature of the Atonement* a review by James Martineau, published in the *National Review*, had asked 'Is vicarious contrition at all more conceivable than vicarious retribution?'[82] It had appeared to be a strategic masterstroke to find the notion of an 'equivalent repentance' in a much respected Calvinist like Jonathan Edwards, but has that phrase in the end caused more harm than

---

[80] Van Dyk, *Desire of Divine Love*, 55.
[81] *Nature*, 127 (125).
[82] James Martineau, 'Mediatorial Religion', *National Review*, 2 (April 1856). Campbell responds to this question in a note added to the second edition of *The Nature of the Atonement* published in 1867. See *Nature*, 341 (273).

it was worth?⁸³ Whilst she observes that the controversial terms 'vicarious confession' or 'vicarious repentance' are not actually used by Campbell, nevertheless Leanne Van Dyk suggests that these terms 'can be usefully employed in a description of Campbell's own atonement theology in a representative sense rather than a substitutionary sense. Provided one understands that the vicarious aspect of Christ's confession is that Christ confessed on our behalf so that we too can confess, the term is legitimate.'⁸⁴

T. F. Torrance argues that this aspect of Campbell's thought was anticipated in the writings of the seventeenth century High Calvinist, Samuel Rutherford, who 'also thought of Christ as *repenting* for us in his passive obedience: "Christ weeped for my sinnes, and that is all the repentance required in me."'⁸⁵ From a similar perspective James B. Torrance suggests, in a number of articles, that the Old Testament symbolism associated with the work of the High Priest on the Day of Atonement provides the background for Campbell's thinking at this point. When the High Priest entered God's presence on behalf of the people 'all Israel entered *in his person*...Conversely, when he vicariously confessed their sins, and interceded for them before God, God accepted them as his forgiven people *in the person of their high priest*.'⁸⁶ Allied to this Old Testament perspective is the conviction derived from Calvin that 'our whole salvation and all

---

⁸³ B. A. Gerrish, *Tradition and the Modern World: Reformed Theology in the Nineteenth Century*, (Chicago: University of Chicago Press, 1978), 87. 'Plainly, Campbell believed he had made a shrewd move. He had demonstrated that his view of atonement was at least a theoretical possibility even within the limits of the older Calvinism. Even Edwards had recognized that a perfect repentance would be an adequate expiation, vindicating the justice of God in pardoning sin. With the wisdom of hindsight, however, we may suspect that Campbell fell into a conceptual discretion.'
⁸⁴ Van Dyk, *Desire of Divine Love*, 113.
⁸⁵ Thomas F Torrance, *Scottish Theology*, 305. Cf. 100. 'Rutherford went on to explain how he understood this vicarious soul-suffering of Christ in a passage in which he discussed the active and passive obedience of Christ, and spoke of Christ in his union with us in these words: "*Christ repenteth for us, and obeyeth for us, he being the end of the Law to everyone that believeth...Christ doth all for us, Christ* weeped for my sinnes, and that is all the repentance required for me."'
⁸⁶ James B. Torrance, 'The Vicarious Humanity of Christ', in T. F. Torrance (ed.), *The Incarnation*, (Edinburgh: Handsel Press, 1981)127-147, 139.

its parts are comprehended in Christ.'[87] If our salvation in all its parts is complete in Christ, and salvation includes the dimension of repentance, then in some way Christ must have performed the repentance required for salvation. The call to repentance, which the Christian gospel addresses to all people, is a call to evangelical repentance which is enabled by the prevenient repentance of Christ on our behalf.

Although the Old Testament contains regulations about many sacrifices, there is no precise explanation about how sacrifice works.[88] Whilst there is room for debate about the exact significance of the 'scapegoat' mentioned in Leviticus 16, it is clear that the High Priest functions in a representative role. This role involves confessing sins on behalf of others, because when the High Priest confesses the sins of the people, then the people's sins are transferred in some way to the goat, which 'will carry on itself all their sins to a solitary place.'[89] Exactly how this ritual brings about the removal of their sins may be shrouded in mystery, but it is hard to avoid the conclusion that the High Priest, as described in Leviticus, is engaging in an act of vicarious penitence which contributes to a renewal of God's covenant with Israel. Although the High Priest had to offer sacrifice for his own sin,[90] when it came to confessing the sins of the people, at that point he was confessing sins which he personally had not committed. Such vicarious confession or penitence appears to be acceptable to God, because it resulted in the wickedness, rebellion and sins of the people being taken away.

Similar vicarious dynamics appear to be at work in a number of other Old Testament passages. There may be an element of confessing the sins of others when Abraham pleads for Sodom,[91] because he both confesses God's right to judge and also prays that a way be found to avert the well deserved wrath. When the people of Israel incur divine displeasure by making a golden calf, Moses is moved to respond and goes to the Lord hoping to 'make atonement' for their sin. Whilst Moses' response includes the offer to allow God to blot out his life instead of the life of the nation, his basic atoning action is to confess the people's sin and

---

[87] Calvin, *Institutes*, II. xvi. 19.
[88] P. S. Fiddes, *Past Event and Present Salvation*, 61-82. F. Young, *Sacrifice and the Death of Christ*, (London: SCM Press, 1965).
[89] Lev. 16:22.
[90] Lev. 16:6, 11.
[91] Gen. 18:16-33.

to ask for forgiveness.[92] After yet another rebellion, Moses pleads once again for forgiveness basing his appeal not on sacrificial victims but solely 'in accordance with your great love.' The divine response is simple and direct; 'I have forgiven them, as you asked.'[93] The implication from such passages appears to be that the intercession of one person can somehow remove the sentence of judgement hanging over sinful people. A similar priestly principle seems to be at work in the case of various prophets who confess the sins of the people and plead with God for mercy.[94]

If the notion of vicarious penitence or confession is as empty of meaning as Campbell's critics suggest, then the same logic might suggest that Abraham, Moses and the prophets were engaged in meaningless gestures, and that the rites performed by the High Priest on the Day of Atonement were devoid of meaning. However, the New Testament does not reach such a negative assessment, because it sees the work of the High Priest being brought to its fulfilment in the work of Christ who is the great High Priest. Graham Redding argues that

> the notion of vicarious confession is carried through to the Epistle to the Hebrews in the New Testament, where in its application to the person and work of Christ it is intensified and deepened. There, confession is not in word or feeling or ritual act but in the actualised relations between God and humankind as the divine holiness in Christ is brought to bear upon the human condition at its deepest level. In Christ that human condition is opened up and offered to God in such a way that there results a clean conscience, a holy unity in knowing and living with God. Repentance is actualised in the submission of the sinner to the divine judgement and pardon — something that Christ the High Priest does in sinners' stead on their behalf.[95]

The fact that the book of Hebrews applies this complex of ideas about priesthood to Christ, may not answer all the questions about Campbell's depiction of Christ offering the

---

[92] Ex. 32:30-2. See also Ex. 34:6-10.
[93] Num. 14:10-25, especially verses 17-20.
[94] See for example Ezra 9:3-15; Neh. 9; Dan. 9:4-19; Amos 7:2-3, 5-6.
[95] Graham Redding, 'The Significance of the Priesthood of Christ for a Theology of Prayer in the Reformed tradition, with reference to T.F. and J.B. Torrance and the Eucharistic tradition of the Church of Scotland', Unpublished PhD, King's College, University of London (1999), 175-6.

perfect confession of sin. But it provides some biblical foundation for the notion that Christ, in some representative role, could confess wickedness, rebellion and sins which he himself had not committed. An extended treatment of this priestly theme is not appropriate at this point, but Christ's priestly office will be explored further in chapter 5.

However, in spite of this biblical background, some still ask how it is possible to talk meaningfully of Christ confessing and repenting of sins which he had not committed?[96] Responding to this line of thinking John Macquarrie suggests that

> the only way out of the difficulty seems to be to recognize that Christ's solidarity with the human race was such that he did indeed participate even in the sinfulness of humanity and so was able genuinely to repent of that sin and make an act of contrition. Campbell himself shrank from such a position, but the nettle has been grasped by several modern theologians... For if we accept that a true incarnation must have meant a full solidarity of Christ with humanity, a "joining himself to the company of the accursed", then it does become possible to think of Christ making a perfect confession and act of repentance for the sin which he had known from the inside, as it were.[97]

Macquarrie is correct in observing that this approach to atonement requires an affirmation of Christ's full solidarity with the human race in its fallenness. There is, however, much less evidence to support his contention that 'Campbell himself shrank from such a position'. Macquarrie tries to compensate for this deficiency in Campbell's outlook by referring to twentieth century discussions of corporate sin and suggesting that 'if Christ was truly man, then must he not, simply by living in human society, have in some ways participated in the disorientation of society which is corporate sin?'[98] This does not appear to resolve the problem because Christ's solidarity with

---

[96] Hart, 'Where Opposites Meet?' 329. In a footnote Hart observes that 'The oft made complaint that the notion of a sinless Christ 'repenting' for others is meaningless fails to see that for Campbell Christ's sinlessness, far from disqualifying him from such 'repentance', is actually that which enables him to confess the sins of the race, and that this 'repentance' culminates precisely in a oneness of mind with the divine judgment on sin, and a submission to the sentence of death.'
[97] J. Macquarrie, 'Campbell on Atonement', 172-4.
[98] *Ibid.*, 173. Cf., J. Macquarrie, *Jesus Christ in Modern Thought*, (London: SCM Press, 1990), 402-3.

the human race remains at an external level, with a perfect Christ coping with the disadvantages of living in an imperfect world. As chapter 4 will demonstrate, Campbell did not shrink from the idea that Christ participated in the sinfulness of humanity, because in his Row sermons he made explicit use of the idea that Christ had identified himself fully with fallen human nature.[99] In assuming sinful human nature Christ had thus to overcome, not just the external difficulties of his environment, but also the weaknesses inherent within the nature that had been assumed. Indeed such a complete identification with fallen human beings was essential so that he could function as a merciful High Priest. So if it can be shown that Campbell retained such an understanding of Christology when he was writing *The Nature of the Atonement*, then there are real grounds for reappraising his doctrine of atonement. If Christ has assumed sinful human nature, then he was not only in a position to confess that God was right to judge human sin, but he was also in a position to confess the sin affecting the human nature which he shared. This need not be in conflict with Campbell's emphasis that Christ's perfect repentance excludes 'the personal consciousness of sin,'[100] because there is no suggestion that he yielded to the temptations which the assumption of a fallen human nature had exposed him to. The recognition that Campbell's soteriology is undergirded by such christological assumptions may also suggest that he can be seen as another forerunner for the kind of approach, evident a century later in the work of Karl Barth, who portrays Christ assuming fallen human nature which brings with it guilt and the need to repent.[101]

Christ's Witnessing for the Father to Humanity

Many models of atonement appear to concentrate on the retrospective aspect to such an extent that it is difficult to see how that past event of salvation has any real connection with the present experience of salvation. In sharp contrast to that

---

[99] *NofS* 1.8.7. 'The flesh of Christ differed not in one particle from mine; but Christ did present his flesh, which was even my flesh, without spot to God through the eternal Spirit.'
[100] *Nature*, 118 (118).
[101] Karl Barth, *Church Dogmatics*, vol. I, part 2, (Edinburgh: T & T Clark, 1956), 40. See also, *Church Dogmatics*, vol. IV, part 1, (Edinburgh: T & T Clark, 1956), 258-9.

Campbell was deeply concerned to explore not only what human beings have been saved from but also what they have been saved for. 'I have said above, that the atonement is regarded as that by which God has bridged over the gulf which separated between what sin had made us, and what it was the desire of the divine love that we should become.'[102]

During his earthly ministry the Son of God bore witness to the nature of God and to what God intended for human beings. Now the risen Christ continues to witness that it is the desire of the divine love that we should become God's children and that we should enjoy communion with the Father now and thus share in eternal life.

> Let us not think of Christ, therefore, simply as revealing how kind and compassionate God is, and how forgiving to our sins, as those who have broken His righteous law. Let us think of Christ as the Son who reveals the Father, that we may know the Father's heart against which we have sinned, that we may see how sin, in making us godless, has made us as orphans, and understand that the grace of God, which is at once the remission of past sins, and the gift of eternal life, restores to our orphan spirits their Father and to the Father of spirits His lost children.[103]

The one 'who is the revealer of God to man is also the revealer of man to himself.'[104] In addition to revealing the depths into which sin had dragged people, Christ also revealed the otherwise hidden capacity for good within human beings, who are made in the image of God. This high capacity for good within humanity must not, however, be viewed as some faculty which operates independently of God. This capacity for good exists only within humanity as 'dwelt in by the Son of God'[105] and is the capacity for the life of sonship. The voice from heaven which marks out Jesus Christ as God's beloved Son, beckons people with the words 'hear ye Him', because it is only as people are drawn into union with the Son of God that they can begin to experience the life of sonship. The gift of eternal life is not some vague form of future blessedness which believers will experience in the distant future, but is the present experience of this life of sonship which is found exclusively in union with the

---

[102] *Nature*, 130 (127).
[103] *Ibid.*, 147-8 (139).
[104] *Ibid.*, 144, 138 (136, 132).
[105] *Ibid.*, 138 (132).

Son of God. The one who pervaded the life of humanity with the life of sonship invites others to enter into that form of relationship.

Christ's Dealing with the Father on our Behalf

In its retrospective dimension Christ's dealing with God on behalf of humanity involved offering a comprehensive confession of human sinfulness which expressed a genuine acknowledgment of God's righteousness in responding to such sin in wrath and judgement. The corresponding dynamic within the prospective aspect of atonement consists of Christ's intercession for our human participation in eternal life.

> And this is the right conception of Christ pleading His own merits on our behalf. Our capacity of that which He asked for us was so implied in these merits, and the Father's delight in these merits so implied His delight in their reproduction in us, that the prayer which proceeds on these grounds is manifestly according to the will of the Father — to offer it as a part of the doing of the Father's will — to offer it in the faith and hope of an answer is a part of the trust in the Father by which He declared the Father's name, and is to be contemplated as completing that response to the mind of the Father towards us in our sin and misery, which was present but in part in the retrospective confession of our sin.[106]

Campbell finds helpful the language and imagery of the High Priest praying for the people. He argues that the major function of Old Testament sacrifices was to cleanse people from the ritual uncleanness which prevented them from participating in the Temple worship. The sacrifice of Christ cleanses people now so that they can participate in the Son's worship of the Father. Such participation brings about a process of transformation because one goal of the intercession of Christ is that his attitude of genuine confession is 'reproduced in us', so that we begin to share in his expiatory confession of sin.

> As to our past sins, we not only see that the atonement presented to our faith is far more honouring to the righteous law of God against which we had sinned than any penal infliction for our sins, whether endured by another for us, or endured by ourselves in abiding misery, could have been; but are further able to accept, as a most welcome part of the gift of

---

[106] *Ibid.*, 150-1 (141).

The Nature of the Atonement

God in Christ, the power to confess our sins with an Amen to Christ's confession of them, true and deep in the measure in which we partake in His Spirit.[107]

Campbell is not reluctant to underline the contrast between his ideas about a 'moral and spiritual atonement'[108] and the penal views of both 'earlier' and 'latter' Calvinists. In the light of this kind of language, and in view of his emphasis upon the need for Jesus' confession of sin to be 'reproduced in us' it is not surprising that some people have concluded that Campbell portrayed Jesus as a righteous example who inspires people to reproduce a similar style of repentance. These sorts of factors lead George Carey to make the criticism

> that Campbell evacuates the atonement of any "objective" content. Christ did not die as "a substitute" or as a "punishment" but as a moral and spiritual sacrifice for sin. His sufferings were not the measure of what God can inflict, but the revelation of what God "feels". We have here, incidentally, a variation of the "moral influence" theory…The real atonement takes place when, with the same attitude and response of Christ's perfection, obedience is seen in us.[109]

A more detailed study of Campbell's work by Eugene Bewkes argues for a positive assessment of his theology, but the way in which he construes Campbell's understanding of atonement has an exemplarist ring to it.

> We can say without hesitation that in the development of his position, Campbell has ruled out the atonement as an objective transaction. The process of our being saved is a subjective one and we may call this moral and we may call it spiritual, for the two can mean the same thing. Campbell calls his theory moral and spiritual. He believed the atonement 'to be the most constraining moral power to make every man trust in God'…
>
> Is not the moral influence which comes from the Cross that which gives us the spiritual stimulus to commune with God? Does not the life of Christ and the Cross effect tremendously

---

[107] *Ibid.*, 153 (143).
[108] *Ibid.*, e.g., 251 (210).
[109] George Carey, *The Gate of Glory*, (London: Hodder and Stoughton, 1986) 125.

our moral nature, and awaken within us the well springs of the spiritual life which then flow out toward God?[110]

However, a closer look suggests that both friend and critic alike have reached an inadequate understanding of Campbell's approach. What is in view here is not some form of exemplarism or 'moral influence' theory, because this ability to confess is itself a gift of God in Christ. For Campbell it is clear that any genuine confession is 'reproduced in us' not as a result of human effort but by the power of the Spirit. If it is God who enables such a confession, by the power of his Spirit, then salvation is not the result of human effort but of divine grace.[111]

> In the faith of God's acceptance of that confession on our behalf, we receive strength to say Amen to it, — to join in it — and, joining in it, we find it a living way to God; and at the same time we feel certain that there is no other way, — that we get near to God just in the measure in which in the Spirit of Christ we thus livingly adopt His confession of our sins, — in this measure and no further.[112]

At this point it is clear that Campbell believes that something objective has taken place because Christ has offered a perfect confession which has been accepted by the Father. Whether human beings respond or not, something has taken place between the Son and the Father which changes the status of sinful people, who can now be drawn back to God through Christ in power of the Spirit. The purpose of Christ's offering is not to deal with an abstract rule of law, but to make it possible for people to return to the Father of their spirits, and to offer him the true and spiritual worship which is the essence of sonship. This being the case it is simply not possible to come close to God as Father without a realisation of the grief that human sin inflicts upon the heavenly Father. Therefore, to say that the expiatory confession of Christ is reproduced in the

---

[110] Eugene G. Bewkes, 'John McLeod Campbell – Theologian. His Theological Development and Trial, and a New Interpretation of His Theory of Atonement', Unpublished PhD, University of Edinburgh (1924), 252. See also Bewkes, *Legacy of a Christian mind*, 220.

[111] Van Dyk, *Desire of Divine Love*, 63. 'It can not fairly be said that Campbell is merely a theologian of inward experience or subjectivity. To characterize his theory as "a variation of the 'moral influence' theory" is to misunderstand thoroughly Campbell's atonement theology and his place in Reformed theology.'

[112] *Nature*, 156-7 (145).

believer by the Holy Spirit, may be a way of emphasising that the believer needs a personal recognition of the truth about humanity which has been revealed in and through the sufferings of Christ. These have revealed that human beings are fundamentally children in rebellion against their heavenly Father. The only basis for a new relationship of sonship with God the Father must therefore lie in a personal recognition that this is an accurate diagnosis of the human situation, and a personal response to what God in Christ has already done about it. Without such an admission or confession it is impossible for the relationship of sonship to exist. Faith is the glad acceptance of this situation, 'for our faith is, in truth, the Amen of our individual spirits to that deep, multiform, all-embracing, harmonious Amen of humanity, in the person of the Son of God, to the mind and heart of the Father in relation to man, − the divine wrath and the divine mercy, which is the atonement.'[113]

Campbell himself is aware of the potential dangers surrounding the use of the word 'example' and he is at pains to show that 'our participation in the atonement is radically a different thing from what the words "following an example" suggest.[114] To his eyes there is an absolute dependence upon God in Christ for salvation which is conveyed in the biblical image of Christ as the vine with believers as the branches. As the branch owes its existence to the vine and depends upon it for life so the believer is totally dependent on Christ for the gift of eternal life.[115]

If any one of these four dimensions, which form the core of Campbell's understanding of atonement, is taken in isolation then it can be seen to be inadequate. If, however, these four aspects are held together as he intended, the end result is a construal of the doctrine of atonement which does not easily fit into an 'exemplarist' category.

Further Elements of Campbell's Atonement Theology

Whilst the retrospective and prospective aspects represent the heart of Campbell's model of atonement, they do not exhaust his discussion of this topic because he explores it for a further nine chapters. This additional material helps to clarify some of his proposals and supplies some fresh insights. Before turning back

---

[113] Ibid., 194 (171).
[114] Ibid., 282-4 (232-3). See also 304 (247).
[115] Ibid., 311-2 (252).

to the Row sermons in search of anticipations of his mature theology, it is appropriate to draw attention to these other elements and to evaluate the adequacy of his approach overall.

Made Perfect Through Suffering

As the incarnation developed into atonement Christ was equipped to become the Captain of salvation by a process which plumbed the depths of suffering and death. In Campbell's eyes the suffering is real, but it does not consist of divinely inflicted punishment. He continues to break away from prevailing penal assumptions by arguing that the cup which Christ shrank from in Gethsemane was a cup of suffering filled with human enmity and opposition. It cannot be the cup of divine wrath because Jesus says that the disciples will have to drink this same cup for themselves.[116] 'Therefore was that hour and power of darkness permitted which the closing period of our Lord's course presents in which sonship towards the Father and brotherhood towards man have had their nature manifested and their power displayed to the utmost.'[117]

If Christ was to be able to confess human sin effectively, and to intercede on our behalf, then it seemed necessary to the divine wisdom to subject his love and trust in God and his patient forgiveness of sinners, 'to the trial of the hour and power of darkness'[118]. In this way the passion of Jesus represented the final stage in a process of development through which Christ was being made perfect through suffering to be a saviour. The danger of talk about the Son of God in humanity undergoing a process of development is that it may tend to imply that there was some imperfection in the Son which needed to be overcome. If there was any imperfection or lack in the Son then this would undermine any claim to be fully divine and would make it impossible for him to accomplish atonement. Campbell seems alert to this issue but sees grounds for such development in the growth that was needed in one who assumed real human nature. 'As our Lord "increased in wisdom and stature," so the elements of the atonement gradually developed themselves with the gradual development of His humanity, and corresponding development of the eternal life in His humanity. The sonship in

---

[116] Mk. 10:39

[117] *Nature*, 215 (186). Campbell is adapting the language of Lk. 22:53, 'this is your hour and the power of darkness.'

[118] *Ibid.*, 247 (207).

The Nature of the Atonement

Him was always perfect sonship.'[119] Further support for Campbell's approach at this point could be provided by the author of Hebrews who explains that although Jesus was a son, nevertheless, 'he learned obedience from what he suffered and, once made perfect, he became the source of eternal salvation for all who obey him.'[120]

This process of development involved Christ 'tasting' death in a way that no one else could. As one who was without sin he recognised and appreciated that life itself was God's gift. 'It was part of His sinless consciousness in humanity to possess life in the pure sense of it as God's gift; and therefore it was a part of this sinless consciousness in humanity to cleave to it — to desire to retain it. This desire was in Him a true and sinless utterance of humanity.'[121] As the sinless one he could see the true nature of sin in a way impossible to people whose moral perception was clouded by their own sinfulness. In a parallel fashion his sinless trust and obedience to God, the giver of life, meant that he would feel the withdrawal of life all the more intensely. For him the fact that 'the wages of sin is death' would be felt with supreme intensity. Therefore Christ has tasted' death in a way that no one else could.[122] His death assumed a saving power not simply because he tasted the wages of sin but because his death was filled with moral and spiritual meaning by virtue of his free offering of love and obedience in the power of the Holy Spirit. Might this reference to Christ tasting death as the wages of sin be another place where it is possible to see him submitting to the guilty verdict on behalf of others?

If Christ was to be fully equipped to function as a Saviour then he must pass through these fires of testing. 'The *peace-making* between God and man, which was perfected by our Lord on the cross, required to its reality the presence to the spirit of Christ of the *elements of alienation* as well as the possession by Him of that eternal righteousness in which was the virtue to make peace.'[123] He cannot accept that the God who said 'You are my Son, whom I love; with you I am well pleased', could ever turn the full weight of his wrath upon his beloved Son. How could God, even for a moment on the cross, cease to be well pleased with his Son? On the cross there would be a full

---

[119] *Ibid.*, 209-210 (182).
[120] Heb. 5:8-9.
[121] *Nature*, 259 (216).
[122] *Ibid.*, 258-261 (215-7).
[123] *Ibid.*, 249 (209).

appreciation by the Son of the divine wrath against sin, but never, thinks Campbell, a sense of that wrath being directed personally against him.

'My God, my God, why have you forsaken me?'

Throughout this process of development, as Christ's obedience and love for others is tested to the limit, there is a profound unity between the Father and the Son. This unbroken sense of the Father's favour is explicit in the way that Campbell interprets the cry ofderliction. He argues that this cry must be interpreted in the context of the whole of Psalm 22, believing that Christ would have had the whole of this passage in his mind as he was dying on the cross. If the psalm is taken as a whole he believes that it confirms his view that the cup Christ takes is a permitted trial of faith rather than an outpouring of wrath. The cry of derliction, therefore, should not be seen as the moment when the Son was cut off from the Father to endure the divine punishment upon sin but as the profoundest expression of faith and trust in God.[124] To portray the Father as withdrawing his presence from the Son so that he could be punished for sin is contradicted by the experience of the sufferer in Psalm 22 who celebrates God's presence with him in the words *'neither hath He hid His face from him'*.[125] Thus at no point during the passion is the fundamental unity between Father and Son broken.

By depicting Christ in this way Campbell has made some people wonder if he is in danger of depicting Christ in docetic colours?[126] There was no intention to move in a docetic direction

---

[124] *Ibid.*, 240 (203). 'But trust in God, personal trust, is that of which the trial is most conspicuous as pervading the psalm, — trust in utter weakness, — trust in the midst of enemies, — trust which the extremity of that weakness and the perfected enmity of those enemies tries to the uttermost, — trust which the Father permits to be thus tried; but trust the root of which in the Father's favour has not been cut off, nor even touched by any act of the Father or expression of His face as if He were turned into an enemy, — as if He looked on the suppliant in wrath, — as if He regarded him as a sinner, imputed sin to him. Not this, not the most distant approach to this.'

[125] Ps. 22:24.

[126] A. B. Macaulay, *The Death of Jesus in Three Aspects*, (London: n.p., 1938), 137-8, argued that 'the liberal Scottish theologian was unable to divest himself at this point of docetism.' Cited in M. Jinkins and Stephen Breck Reid, 'John McLeod Campbell on Christ's Cry of Derliction: A case study in Trinitarian Hermeneutics', *Evangelical Quarterly* LXX (1998) 135-149, 144.

but rather a concern not to revert to penal interpretations at the final stage of Christ's life. Leanne Van Dyk senses that at this point Campbell's interpretative assumptions had determined his reading of scripture and led to a smoothing out of some of the jagged edges of the cry of dereliction. The end result is not, as Campbell hoped, an example of trust in the midst of suffering which will inspire people to trust God in their own hour of need. By depicting Christ's unshakeable trust in this way may run the risk of distancing Christ from people who are currently experiencing abandonment and desolation. 'He seems not to consider the alternate idea that even if Christ experienced utter desolation and forsakenness in the cry of dereliction, God was still with him in a final, though hidden, sense. He seems not to realize that to deny the absolute loneliness of Christ's experience on the cross is, implicitly, to suggest that Christ cannot really be with us in our moments of absolute loneliness. For only a Christ who has experienced the darkest valley of the shadow of death can truly walk with us through our dark and forsaken valleys.'[127]

In response to this kind of criticism Michael Jinkins and Stephen Breck Reid offer a more positive reading of Campbell which seeks to incorporate some of these insights. In their eyes Campbell is not protesting about the passibility of God, but is advocating an insistence 'upon the communion of Father, Son and Holy Spirit, at the moment when Christ drank to its dregs the cup of passion, taking into the very heart of the Trinity the human alienation of Godforsakenness.'[128] This is an attractive and sympathetic reading of Campbell which is moving in a helpful direction, but the lingering suspicion is that it may represent what they would like Campbell to say, rather than what he himself would have been able to say. He manifests such reluctance to use the penal language of godforsakenness, that it is difficult to be sure that he would be happy with such a summary of his thought at this point.

What these comments do suggest is that Campbell's understanding at this point implies, and requires, the undergirding of a coherent doctrine of the Trinity. Tom Smail provides a helpful sketch of what this might look like. He notes the tension that exists between the bleak portrayal of godforsakenness in Mark's passion narrative with the undisturbed confidence of the Johannine Jesus who is convinced

---

[127] Van Dyk, *Desire of Divine Love* 106.
[128] Jinkins and Reid, 'Campbell on Christ's Cry of Dereliction', 144.

that if all else leave him his Father will not leave him alone, even on the cross.[129] Resisting the temptation to give one emphasis precedence over the other he suggests that both of these biblical insights need to be held together in a trinitarian context. Whilst he suspects that Campbell's treatment of the cry of dereliction 'looks suspiciously like an attempt to evade the awful implications of the Son's abandonment by the Father on the cross'[130] he is not entirely comfortable either with Moltmann's approach which portrays such a profound abandonment at the heart of the Father – Son relationship.[131] The way forward involves a more explicit recognition of the role of the Spirit at this crucial moment.

> I want to put it this way: on the cross the Son is not with the Father, but on the cross the Father is still with the Son. Jesus in the agony of his suffering and in his sharing of the separation from God that is the consequence of sin can no longer realise or affirm that togetherness with the Father that has been at the centre of his life…The Father in his own person, in the pursuit of his loving purpose, remains withdrawn from the Son and does nothing to relieve him. But the bond between Father and Son is the person of the Holy Spirit. The Spirit is the Father's presence on the Son's side of the relationship. In his own person the Father is distinct from the Son, but in the Spirit he gives himself to the Son in the way that is appropriate to the Son's situation at the different stages of his calling…On the cross, even when he has no sense of communion or communication with the Father, the Spirit of the Father is not withdrawn from the Son.[132]

Smail's Trinitarian portrayal of the cross offers one way of holding together the reality of Christ's godforsakenness with an emphasis upon Christ's trust in God. Without such Trinitarian supports Campbell's approach would be vulnerable at this point.

---

[129] Mk 15:34 and Jn 16:32.
[130] T. Smail, *Once and For All: A Confession of the Cross*, (London: Darton, Longman & Todd, 1998), 132.
[131] J. Moltmann, *The Crucified God*, (London: SCM, 1974), 151-2.
[132] Smail, *Once and For All*, 134.

An Underdeveloped Doctrine of the Holy Spirit?

A difficulty for reading Campbell in such a Trinitarian fashion, is the fact that within *The Nature of the Atonement* the Holy Spirit plays, what Leanne Van Dyk calls, a 'shadowy role'. She believes that so much attention is given over to the Father – Son relationship that the work of the Holy Spirit is rendered superfluous. If this pneumatological dimension is weakened then the coinherent doctrine of the Trinity would also be undermined. Van Dyk recognises, however, that within Campbell's theology as a whole the Trinity is not under threat because

> a fully developed Spirit doctrine is latent, or potential, in Campbell's work. For example, on Campbell's terms, it can be said that the Spirit is the divine actor that sustained Christ's trust and intimacy with the Father, that the Spirit links the believer to the mind of Christ, that the Spirit brings the believer to share in the confession of Christ and thus share in the sacrifice of Christ, that the Spirit is the natural bridge between the retrospective and the prospective, that the Spirit enlivens the believer's confidence of adoption into God's parental love, and that the Spirit actualized Christ's witness of the Father to humanity. These descriptions of the Holy Spirit's work are all implicit, or at least latent, in Campbell's atonement theology.[133]

Evidence for a more robust understanding of the work of the Holy Spirit is not plentiful within the pages of *The Nature of the Atonement*, but more explicit material about the Holy Spirit is evident within Campbell's sermons. The young preacher from Row regularly reminded his hearers that 'Christ has the Spirit for us.'[134] In practice this means that Christ enables people to come to faith, and to follow his example, by supplying the power of the Holy Spirit. The material examined in the following chapters will indicate that Campbell had a more coherent understanding of the work of the Spirit than is immediately apparent from reading *The Nature of the Atonement*. Chapter 3 will show that there is a strong link between his

---

[133] Van Dyk, *Desire of Divine Love* 170.
[134] *S&L*, 1.13.303. 'If Christ did present himself through the eternal Spirit without spot to God – if Christ was holy through the Holy Ghost – and if it be the sure truth of God, that Christ has the Spirit for us, then you see here is a perfect provision as well as a perfect example for us, that we should follow his steps.'

earlier preaching, and the theology written out much later for the press. This consistency of thought across the years suggests that it is legitimate to take his earlier teaching about the Holy Spirit into consideration; and when this is done the occasional references to the Spirit in *The Nature of the Atonement* take on greater significance. If a fuller doctrine of the Spirit undergirds his thinking then when Campbell says of Jesus that 'He ever through the Eternal Spirit offered Himself without spot to God,' he is not simply repeating familiar biblical phrases,[135] but is alluding to the vital role performed by the Spirit at every stage of the life and death of Jesus.

The Victory of Christ

The image of victory is another, perhaps unexpected, dimension to Campbell's approach to atonement. In the midst of the rejection and suffering of the cross Christ continued to love God wholeheartedly and persisted in loving his neighbours as himself. Remembering his endurance of suffering helps us 'to realise the trial to which forgiving love in the Son of God was put, and the mind of love in which He endured the trial, the manner of the victory of love.'[136] His death represents a triumph over the devil who had the power of death.[137] His prayer from the cross that his enemies might be forgiven is seen as a victory of love and forgiveness over hatred and evil.[138] The cross represents the ultimate trial of 'the faith of sonship' that characterises the earthly life of Christ. The 'victory of that faith' and trust in his heavenly Father is expressed in his dying words, 'Father, into thy hands I commend my spirit.'[139] Such loyalty to God represents a victory for obedience; the victory of sonship and brotherhood in a fallen world. Such a victory was not accomplished by exerting supernatural power, for 'it was not a might of power at all, but the might of *realized perfect weakness, whose only strength was the strength of faith.*'[140] This notion plays a much more shadowy role in *The Nature of the Atonement* than his comments about the Holy Spirit. This emphasis upon victory

---

[135] Heb. 9:14. *Nature*, 105, 136, 143, 147, 152, 156, 169, 256 (110, 131, 136, 138, 142, 144, 153, 213).
[136] *Ibid.*, 234 (199).
[137] *Ibid.*, 176-7, 225 (158, 193).
[138] *Ibid.*, 236 (200).
[139] Lk. 23:46. See *Nature*, 242-3, 236, 255-8 (204-5, 200, 213-5).
[140] *Ibid.*, 226 (194). See also 224-5, 234 (192-3, 199).

The Nature of the Atonement

through an obedience that is willing to suffer, to some extent anticipates more recent attempts to suggest ways of interpreting the *Christus Victor* image.[141] Might it be that Campbell was moving towards a realization that the cross not only reveals where God defeats evil, but that it also manifests God's way of overcoming evil through obedient, suffering love? Such love triumphs over evil by absorbing it at great personal cost. Indeed it may be possible to see something of this at work in Campbell's own ministry. To what extent did his gracious and loving absorption of his painful defeat in the General Assembly of 1831 contribute to the longer term 'success' of his ideas within the Church of Scotland?

It has been argued here that some criticisms of *The Nature of the Atonement* appear to address only parts of Campbell's thinking about atonement, this study has attempted to redress that imbalance, and to provide a more comprehensive view of the book. At a number of points already this examination of Campbell's proposals has raised questions about the strengths and weaknesses of his approach. It is necessary now to offer a fuller assessment of his expression of this core Christian doctrine.

Evaluating Campbell's Understanding of Atonement

Judging the Story of the Cross

For two millennia Christians have tried to put into words the power they experienced at the cross of Christ. These attempts to express the heart of their faith, carried out by believers in many different contexts, have created a fascinating range of images and theories about atonement. The variety of images within the biblical materials, and the ever-changing questions arising out of changes in the social and historical contexts facing the Church, help to explain why there are so many ideas about atonement. However, the recognition of this diversity of opinions does not necessarily offer assistance in the task of evaluating them.

In the absence of agreed criteria for evaluating atonement theories it is necessary to identify and justify the criteria employed in this evaluation of Campbell's work. Colin Gunton

---

[141] Gunton, *Actuality of Atonement*, 58. 'It is the refusal to succumb to temptation that is Jesus' victory.'

claimed that systematic theology, when rightly understood, is 'dedicated to thinking in as orderly a way as possible *from* the Christian gospel and to the situation in which it is set, rather than in the construction of systems.'[142] This suggests that a systematic attempt to express a doctrine of atonement should have secure roots within the biblical narrative which bears witness to the events at the heart of the Christian faith. Working *from* the Christian gospel implies that it is important to take into account the life and ministry of Jesus, as well as concentrating upon the climax of that life upon the cross. Some atonement theories focus upon the cross to such an extent that what went before, and what followed after, are effectively sidelined. Working *from* the Christian gospel would also suggest that a credible atonement theory will need to give due weight to the conquest of death through resurrection. This dynamic is more widely recognised within the Eastern Orthodox Christian tradition than in the Western version of Christianity, which has tended to be more fascinated by ideas of sin and guilt. An adequate acknowledgement of resurrection within atonement is essential to any theology which seeks to do justice to the biblical testimony about Jesus Christ. It is also essential to any approach which hopes to be relevant to contemporary people who, in Britain, appear to be more aware of their mortality than they are of their sin. A doctrine which seeks to do justice to the scriptural materials will also need to be faithful to the real offense and horror of the cross which, from the outset, scandalised Jews and Gentiles alike.

Implicit within many atonement models is an attempt to explain how the judgement which threatens sinful people has been overcome through the death of Christ. There is a sense in which judgement functions as a structural part of Christian doctrines, such as atonement, which are essential to Christian identity.[143] This suggests that credible construals of atonement will embody a real wrestling with judgement.

Most studies of Campbell's theology rightly pay attention to the ecclesiastical context that he emerged from, and to the

---

[142] Colin Gunton, 'A Rose by Any Other Name? From "Christian Doctrine" to "Systematic Theology"', *International Journal of Systematic Theology* 1 (1999) 4-23, 22. This article is included in Colin Gunton, *Intellect and Action: Elucidations on Christian Theology and the Life of Faith*, (Edinburgh: T & T Clark, 2000). Cf., chapter 2, 44.

[143] I have explored this idea elsewhere in P. K. Stevenson, 'Rehabilitating Judgement?', Unpublished MLitt thesis, University of Birmingham (1994).

The Nature of the Atonement

theological tradition of federal Calvinism which he reacted against. Much less attention has been paid to the wider social and historical context which also contributes to understanding of his thinking. Timothy Gorringe notes how the nineteenth century is being regarded by some as 'the age of atonement'; a time of seismic social change when the language of atonement was prominent in politics and literature as well as in the world of religion.[144] He suggests that the way in which Campbell questioned the penal assumptions underlying so much theological thinking provided, perhaps unconsciously, religious legitimation for the work of prison reformers like Mary Carpenter. The satisfaction theory implicit within the theology of vicarious suffering reinforces the view that sin deserves to be punished, and this in turn was used to justify punishing offenders without any attempt to work for their rehabilitation. If, however, the concept of vicarious suffering is called into question and is replaced by an emphasis upon vicarious penitence, then this lends credence to those who argue that 'the only form of punishment which is moral is that which is designed to produce penitence.'[145] Appreciation of this wider backdrop helps us to gain a fuller picture both of Campbell and his critics. It raises questions about the extent to which Campbell was reflecting the spirit of the age and the extent to which, in some small way, he may have contributed to a wider change of mood. Was his role to be one who sought to help the Church to interpret and respond to the changes which were underway in society as a whole? If Gorringe is correct that it was 'not until the very end of the century that theologians came out firmly in favour of rehabilitation',[146] then Campbell's questioning of penal views of atonement suggests that he may be regarded more as an original thinker than just a slavish follower of popular fashions.

The recognition that systematic theology moves 'from the Christian gospel and to the situation', alerts us to the role played by context in the formulation of doctrine. It suggests that an

---

[144] T. Gorringe, *God's Just Vengeance: Crime, violence and the rhetoric of salvation*, (Cambridge: Cambridge University Press, 1996), chapter 8, 193-219.
[145] *Ibid.*, 208. At this point Gorringe is referring to the work of R. C. Moberly *Atonement and Personality* (London: John Murray, 1901), 109-135, who developed Campbell's thinking by explicitly talking about 'vicarious penitence'.
[146] *Ibid.*, 225.

appreciation of the social, historical and religious contexts within which Campbell lived and worked will contribute to an understanding of his theology. This acknowledgement of the importance of context not only provokes questions as to how appropriate his theological formulations were within their original context, but it also raises questions as to their contemporary intelligibility and relevance.

Any viable theory of atonement needs to address the fundamental question as to how the death of a person two thousand years ago can make any difference to the situation and experience of people today. For as Colin Gunton points out, 'if there is to be human salvation, it must concern us as we live in the present, and that means that some account must be given of how we are related to the past events which we consider so crucial.'[147] It is difficult to envisage an effective response to this sort of question without some perception of the role of the Holy Spirit in taking the things of Christ and applying them to people through the ages and throughout the world. A neglect of this pneumatological dimension runs the risk of making the cross of Christ distant and irrelevant.

The movement *from* the gospel to the situation, similarly requires any credible doctrine of atonement to address the issues arising out of the contemporary context. Following the most violent century in human history, the major question for many people is about whether or not it is possible to believe in a loving God in the face of such widespread suffering and injustice. For, as Karl Rahner has observed, 'people today ... are more likely to have the impression that God has to be justified rather than that man himself is unjust and has to be justified by God and before God.'[148]

Jürgen Moltmann's theology of the cross[149] is probably the best known contemporary attempt to respond to these issues. In seeking to show how it might be possible to believe in a loving God after Auschwitz, Moltmann sees the cross more in terms of theodicy than in the traditional sense of delivering people from sin and guilt. His attempt to be sensitive and relevant to his German context after the Second World War was understandable and necessary. But in his desire to be pastorally relevant has he fallen into the trap of sacrificing faithfulness to the Scriptures, by neglecting those passages which focus on the

---

[147] Gunton, *Actuality of Atonement*, 7-8.
[148] Rahner, *Foundations of Christian Faith*, 92.
[149] Moltmann, *The Crucified God*.

removal of sin? Alert to this danger Smail argues that 'we must develop a theology of the cross that has room for both atonement and theodicy. The latter must never be presented as some sort of modern alternative to the atonement-type approach.'[150] Whilst this suggests that it would be unhelpful to make atonement synonymous with theodicy, any credible doctrine of atonement is likely to need to wrestle with, at least some aspects of, the question of theodicy. Consideration of larger scale questions of suffering and injustice also suggests that a purely individualistic understanding of sin is insufficient, and needs to be enlarged to take account of the sin and evil which seem to be woven into the large scale structures of human life.

Judging Campbell's Story of the Cross

> Although I should live a thousand years of Christian usefulness, I would die looking to the Cross of Christ as I did at first — as simply as I would ask one to do so who never looked to that Cross before. If then, you are looking to it, look steadfastly to it, and look simply to it, and let the love of God draw your heart to Him with cords of love. Look steadfastly to the Cross of Christ and freely; and yield your heart to all the comfort of it and all the hope; and remember that all true believers have just one and the same anchor for their souls, and no other, young or old in the Christ life, those who have longest trusted and those just beginning to trust...Look to God, and pray to God, who loves you, and wishes you to love Him, asking Him to enable you to understand His love. Fix your thoughts on Christ dying for your sins, and receive the teaching of the Spirit of God in your heart, enabling you to understand that blessed sight.[151]

It is clear that the Cross played a central role in Campbell's thinking, but how effective is his re-telling of the story of the cross? The approach adopted by Tuttle is to demonstrate Campbell's significance by tracing some of the ways in which

---

[150] Smail, *Once and For All*, 51.
[151] *Memorials*, 1.304-5, being an extract from a letter to his brother in law, Neil Campbell, who was seriously ill. The letter is dated, 8 December 1857.

his ideas influenced subsequent writers about atonement.[152] The aim here will be to evaluate the approach outlined in *The Nature of the Atonement* in the light of the criteria mentioned above.

It has already been shown that Campbell's methodology is one which works from the Christian gospel by seeking to see the atonement in its own light.[153] He seeks to interpret atonement in the light of the gospels rather than on the basis of some abstract legal principles. To this extent he can claim to be a theologian who is working from the gospel to his situation. Some commentators are content to acknowledge the biblical origins of his work but feel uncomfortable with the ways in which he handles the scriptures. Thus John Macquarrie asserts that

> what is most likely to turn away the modern reader is Campbell's use of the Bible in a way which is not possible for those who have been schooled in critical methods. The four gospels are quoted indiscriminately, and Campbell dwells especially on John's gospel which he accepts as accurately relating the words and deeds of Jesus. He sometimes ventures, in a way that few contemporary New Testament scholars would do, to reconstruct the intentions and inward life of Jesus on the basis of some reported utterances, such as the Lukan sayings from the cross, 'Father, forgive them for they know not what they do', and 'Into thy hands I commend my spirit' (Luke 23.34 and 46).[154]

The quarter of a century since that assessment was written has witnessed various developments in the realm of biblical hermeneutics, which raise questions about the assumptions expressed by Macquarrie. During that period the dominance of the historical critical method has been challenged by the emergence of literary approaches, and by the revival of interest in theological hermeneutics.[155] Seen against this background Campbell appears not as an early post-modern reader intent on

---

[152] Tuttle, *So Rich a Soil,* and George M. Tuttle, 'The place of John McLeod Campbell in British thought concerning the atonement', Unpublished PhD, Emmanuel College Victoria, University of Toronto (1961).
[153] See Chapter 2. *The Priority of Revelation.*
[154] Macquarrie, 'Campbell on Atonement', 168.
[155] Stephen E. Fowl, (ed.), *The Theological Interpretation of Scripture: Classic and Contemporary Readings,* (Oxford: Blackwell, 1997), xiii. 'I take theological interpretation of scripture to be that practice whereby theological concerns and interests inform and are informed by a reading of scripture. In this respect, throughout Christian history it has been the norm for Christians to read their scripture theologically.'

The Nature of the Atonement

forcing the text to say what he wants, but more as a pre-critical[156] reader engaged in a legitimate form of theological hermeneutics. If Campbell's views are questionable, simply because he did not use the tools of historical critical scholarship, this suggests that the views of all pre-Enlightenment Christians should be treated with equal scepticism. This would be a retrograde step which would cut the church off from the valuable insights of earlier generations. The use of historical critical methods does not automatically ensure the production of coherent theology, and the absence of such methods does not inevitably lead to incoherence.[157] Therefore it is important that the coherence of Campbell's theology should be assessed on its own merits, and not prejudged on the basis of an alleged failure to adopt an approved form of hermeneutics.

Although Campbell admitted that 'large portions of Scripture were left out of account'[158] in his teaching, a reading of *The Nature of the Atonement* reveals someone seeking to do theology in a way which allows the Bible to play a vital role. His plea for the filial to take precedence over the penal is firmly grounded in a range of biblical passages.[159] It is likely that any theology will leave some portions of Scripture out of account, but the weakness in Campbell's approach is that he seems to have smoothed away too many complexities from the gospel story. In Campbell's approach, suffering is an inevitable part of the Son's work of witnessing to people on behalf of the Father, but the way in which Jesus is portrayed lacks much of the drama and controversy apparent in the gospels. Some of the eschatological urgency apparent in the gospels, and also apparent in some of Campbell's early sermons, plays little part in Campbell's portrayal of the earthly ministry of the Son. The danger in apparently removing so much of the colour and controversy of

---

[156] David C. Steinmetz, 'The Superiority of Pre-Critical Exegesis', in Stephen E. Fowl, (ed.),*Theological Interpretation*, 26-38.

[157] *Ibid.*, 31. Steinmetz argues that a concern to identify the authorial intention behind a text does not conflict with a willingness to acknowledge other levels of meaning in biblical texts. 'Medieval exegetes admit that the words of scripture had a meaning in the historical situation in which they were first uttered or written, but they deny that the meaning of those words is restricted to what the human author thought he said or what his first audience thought they heard. The stories and sayings of scripture bear an implicit meaning only understood by a later audience...Yet the text cannot mean anything a later audience wants it to mean.'

[158] *Reminiscences*, 126-7.

[159] For example, Hos. 11:1-9, Lk. 11:1-13 and 15:11-32, Rom. 8:14-17.

the life of Jesus is that it could run the risk of making him seem less plausibly human. This concern has surfaced already in the comments of those who fear that Campbell's handling of the cry of dereliction suggests that he was shying away from the offense and horror of the cross. Macquarrie took this concern a step further by suggesting that there is not any final necessity for the death of Christ in Campbell's view of atonement. For 'the real suffering of Christ, the real bearing of our sins, was his act of confession and repentance...Gethsemane rather than Calvary was, for Campbell, the climactic moment of atonement.'[160] If Campbell's theory fails at this point then it would be very hard to view it as a credible doctrine of atonement.

His reworking of atonement does not unravel at this point, however, because of his emphasis that 'the wages of sin is death.' Calvary is necessary because the Son not only confesses the rightness of God's judgement upon humanity's sin, but he also freely accepts that judgement of death for himself, although it was a judgement that the obedient, loving Son did not personally deserve. In this sort of way the Son is depicted as accepting the guilty verdict on behalf of others. The cross also serves the purpose of revealing God's love and trustworthiness in their clearest hues, so that people will want to put their trust in such a God. Such a manifestation of the divine love is not a spectacular stunt, which looks good but actually accomplishes nothing. This purpose of revelation derives its meaning and significance from the objective accomplishment of Christ in freely accepting the judgement of God upon sin, and thus absorbing the wrath of God. It may perhaps be objected that these considerations merely suggest that the death of Christ was required within this scheme, but that they do not prove that it had to be this particular kind of death upon the cross. Seeking to see atonement in its own light meant beginning with the fact that Christ died on a cruel cross rather than arguing why this kind of death was the best way of equipping Jesus Christ to be the Captain of salvation.

Assessed on the basis of punitive views of justice and judgement alone, Campbell's treatment of the judgement theme will appear to be inadequate. However, it would be wrong to assume that all the biblical materials about judgement should be interpreted in a purely retributive fashion. Within some passages there appears to be a sense in which judgement is viewed as having a rehabilitating intention. This intention

---

[160] Macquarrie, 'Campbell on Atonement', 176.

surfaces in the book of Amos, where God's disappointment that his judgements on Israel have not had the desired effect, is expressed in the refrain, 'yet you have not returned to me'.[161] Something of the same rehabilitatory intention lies behind the cycle of judgements recorded in the Book of Revelation where it is sadly reported that the recipients of God's wrath 'refused to repent and glorify him'.[162] It is clear even from these passages that the rehabilitating purpose, embodied in divine judgement, does not automatically create an appropriate human response. In contrast to this, Campbell's portrayal of Christ offering a perfect Amen to the judgement of God, satisfies the divine intention underlying God's judgement.

The assumption that judgement always implies punishment is called into question by Stephen Travis' study of Pauline passages which appear to bring retributive ideas into relation with the death of Christ. As Paul understands sin as a relational concept, Travis argues that it is inappropriate to interpret divine judgement in terms of God imposing a penalty. Instead we should think of judgement along the lines of people experiencing the God-given consequences of their choices and actions.

> Paul's understanding of the death of Christ does not include the idea that he bore the retributive punishment for our sins which otherwise would have to be inflicted on us. To understand the atonement in those terms is to misunderstand what Paul means by "the wrath of God"... Rather than saying that in his death Christ experienced retributive punishment on behalf of humanity, Paul says that he entered into and bore on our behalf the destructive consequences of sin. Standing where we stand, he bore the consequences of our alienation from God. In so doing he absorbed and exhausted them, so that they should not fall on us. It is both true and important to say that he was "judged in our place" — that he experienced divine judgement on sin in the sense that he endured the God-ordained consequences of human sinfulness. But this is not the same as to say that he bore our punishment.[163]

---

[161] Amos 4:6, 8, 9, 10, 11.
[162] Rev. 16:9, 11.
[163] Stephen H. Travis, 'Christ as Bearer of Divine Judgement in Paul's Thought about the Atonement', in J. Goldingay (ed.), *Atonement Today* (London: SPCK, 1995) 37.

Whilst this is a summary of the views of Stephen Travis rather than of Campbell, such comments lend weight to the assertion that it is possible to take sin and divine judgement seriously without having to interpret judgement in a punitive, retributive nature. Observing the trend within the Old Testament for sacrifice to be spiritualized in terms of obedience, Travis also notes how Christ's obedience is another ingredient in Paul's understanding of the death of Christ. 'In obedience to the Father, Christ identified with Adam's race, shared in Adam's death, and attained to vindication and resurrection as the head of a new humanity. "The many" share in his vindication and new life by identification with him as their representative Head.'[164] The details of Travis' proposals are open to debate, but they are of interest here because they suggest ways in which it might be possible to defend and develop some of Campbell's ideas. Such a reading of Pauline theology is compatible with the ways in which Campbell understands the obedience of Christ and the participation of believers in his experience of sonship. Even if his handling of the scriptures is pre-critical, there are grounds for feeling that he had stumbled upon important biblical perspectives on sacrifice and atonement.

Recognizing that the conquest of death through resurrection is an important component of atonement, it has to be admitted that resurrection does not play a prominent role in *The Nature of the Atonement*. Campbell's understanding of the continuing ministry of Jesus as the great High Priest presupposes that Christ is risen from the dead, but the theme of resurrection tends to be assumed rather than explored. The resurrection is another occasion where the Father expresses his pleasure in the obedience of his beloved Son. The victory motif with Christ defeating the devil similarly assumes the reality of the resurrection without developing it fully.

These considerations suggest that Campbell's theology is rooted in the Christian gospel and seeks to do justice to essential elements within that gospel. Although his handling of central themes is open to question, it is clear that he was seeking to work from the gospel to the human situation rather than engaging in an experience driven kind of theology.

If Campbell is to move successfully from the Christian gospel to the situation, then his theology also needs to indicate how the present experience of salvation is connected with the Christ

---

[164] *Ibid.*, 35.

The Nature of the Atonement

event in the past. To some extent this concern is addressed by the theme of participation because Christ's participation in our humanity is seen as the thing which enables human participation in the divine nature.[165] It is assumed that Christ is somehow related to all people by virtue of his incarnation. One attractive way of explaining this has been through the concept of the vicarious humanity of Christ.[166] Kettler argues that T. F. Torrance's notion of "vicarious humanity" is influenced by emphases within the work of Athanasius, and that it provides a helpful framework for appreciating Campbell's theology.[167] 'Vicarious humanity' does not, however, appear to be a phrase which Campbell himself used, and Kettler's study reveals something of the complexity behind this idea.[168] The language which Campbell uses to describe Christ's nature is much less sophisticated, in that he speaks of Christ becoming the perfect elder brother who enters into a relationship of brotherhood with all people, by means of his identification with humanity in his incarnation.[169] At other times his talk of Christ as the Lord of our

---

[165] *Nature*, 321 (259).

[166] Christian Kettler, *Vicarious Humanity*, James B. Torrance, 'Vicarious Humanity of Christ', 127-147, and 'The Vicarious Humanity and Priesthood of Christ in the Theology of John Calvin', in W. H. Neuser (ed.), *Calvinus Ecclesiae Doctor: Die Referate des Congrès International de Recherches Calviniennes vom 25. bis 28. September, 1978 in Amsterdam*, (Kampen: J. H. Kok B.V., 1978) 69-84.

[167] Kettler, *Vicarious Humanity*, 123. 'If the Logos is of the "same essence" as the Father, this means that the very life of God is communicated into human flesh in the Incarnation. The true humanity, as well as the true divinity of Christ, falls into the very life of God. It was the theme of atonement as Christ communicating the life of God which was so dear to John McLeod Campbell, the nineteenth century theologian to whom Torrance is much in debt. In the doctrine of the *homoousion* we are dealing not just with a facade or a mask, but with the very life of divine Being himself.'

[168] Van Dyk, *Desire of Divine Love*, 120-1. 'Although "vicarious humanity" is clearly a term intended to be wide-ranging and evocative, it may be too rich, too dense. Indeed, Kettler lists nine theses which attempt to unpack the content of this laden expression. The term "vicarious humanity" is so multi-faceted and complex that it soon becomes clear it is a term which attempts to embrace the full reality of the Incarnation and the implications of the Incarnation for human redemption.'

[169] *Nature*, 109 (112). Alluding to Rom. 8:3, Campbell says 'To send Him in the likeness of sinful flesh was to make Him a sacrifice for sin, for it was to lay the burden of our sins upon Him. Thus related to us, while by love

spirits, suggests that it is a result of his divine nature as our Lord and Creator which makes his actions relevant and accessible to all. It is not possible at this point to prove whether or not the language of 'vicarious humanity' is the most helpful way of getting to the core of Campbell's theology, but it is enough to note that this is one way of showing how Christ is related to all people so that his representative actions can be seen to have consequences for all.

The Holy Spirit plays a vital part in linking the past Christ-event and bringing this alive in the experience of human beings today. For it is by the power of the Spirit that believers are enabled to share in the attitude of Christ, so that the confession of Christ is reproduced in us.[170] The Holy Spirit is part of God's gift to us in Christ, and it is in union with Christ that people experience the benefits of salvation.[171] An earlier section discussed the suggestion that the Spirit played only a shadowy role in Campbell's theology.[172] If Campbell's understanding of the Holy Spirit is weak then this would tend to undermine the ability of his atonement model to bridge the gap between past and present. However, when the evidence of the Row sermons is taken into account it can be seen that a more satisfying doctrine of the Spirit is available to link past event with present salvation.

One area where Campbell is much less effective in making an appropriate connection from the Christian gospel *to* the situation, is in relating to the tragic dimension of human life. An awareness of wider social issues does surface from time to time in his correspondence, but *The Nature of the Atonement* is so focused upon the filial relation which Christ came to restore, that there is no significant attempt to link the cross to larger scale questions about evil and suffering. Campbell's concern appears to be much more about encouraging people to respond

---

identified with us, the Son of God necessarily came under all our burdens, and especially our great burden — sin.'

[170] *Ibid.*, 153 (143).

[171] Faris, 'The Nature of Theological Inquiry', 258. 'The third "Row Companion", Henry Dorney (1613-1683) was not nearly as well known as Brainerd and Martyn, but in his book, Divine Contemplations and Spiritual Breathings, we may find a point of contact with a theological tradition which with its emphasis on the doctrine of "union with Christ", was much closer to Luther, Calvin and Scripture than was federal and Westminster theology.'

[172] See section Chapter 2. *An Underdeveloped Doctrine of the Holy Spirit?*

to suffering with something of the attitude of Christ, whom God made perfect through suffering. There is no sense here that God needs to be justified for the painful state of the world, but then it would be very surprising to have found Campbell asking such characteristically modern questions. Perhaps his insistence that love must be seen as the essential attribute of God is his most important contribution to those later debates?

In spite of this lack of connectedness with current questions about theodicy, however, there is a sense in which Campbell's theology may have a contemporary relevance. Although she charts out clearly a number of weaknesses within his approach, Leanne Van Dyk concludes that because

> Campbell's atonement theology is pastorally oriented to troubled and restless persons, it is also a uniquely modern, or thoroughly contemporary, theology. The religious and psychological markets of America are full of the latest remedies for the doubts, fears and struggles of searching people. But Campbell's atonement theology contains elements that meet the widespread hunger for acceptance and truth. Those elements include a consistent reassurance of God's love and mercy, a realistic appraisal of human lostness, a sturdy proclamation of the real salvific effects of Christ's life on earth, and a message of hope for present community and future wholeness. It is a message that can powerfully comfort those who search for authentic acceptance and genuine promise.[173]

Conclusion

This appraisal of *The Nature of the Atonement* argues that Campbell provides a valuable contribution to Christian thinking about atonement, even though his model is inevitably incomplete and in need of complementary insights from other approaches. A close reading of the text demonstrates that this book is more complex than many of its critics seem to allow. At the heart of his work lies an exploration of the retrospective and prospective aspects of atonement, which succeeds in restoring to the doctrine an emphasis upon what God saves people *for*. Implicit within this priestly soteriology is a priestly understanding of the person of Christ, because the one who reveals the truth about God and humanity needs to be fully divine and fully human.

---

[173] Van Dyk, *Desire of Divine Love*, 171.

With the publication of this book Campbell completed his move away from the limited atonement embodied in the federal theology treasured by Evangelicals in early nineteenth century Scotland. He proclaimed a God whose love brings about atonement, rather than a God who needed an act of atonement to enable him to be loving and merciful. Regarding love as an essential divine attribute rather than as an arbitrary one, Campbell placed love at the core of his thinking. In spite of his blind spots he is a theologian who adopted an *a posteriori* approach, moving from the Christian gospel with a revelation-centred approach to faith. Far from being at the subjective end of the theological spectrum, a strong case can be made for seeing Campbell's theology as testimony to what God has objectively done through the incarnation and crucifixion of Jesus Christ. Although the value of *The Nature of the Atonement* has been obscured by Campbell's cumbersome written style, the fresh ideas it introduced, and the discussion it still provokes, add weight to the proposal that this book deserves to be seen as a 'classic' treatment of this topic which merits continuing discussion and debate.

Whilst *The Nature of the Atonement* offers further evidence of Campbell's move away from the theology of the Westminster Confession, it also reveals his continued debt to the evangelical and Reformed traditions. Opinions vary as to the value of his critique of, what he calls, the earlier Calvinism[174] and modified Calvinism;[175] but it is nevertheless significant that his dialogue partners are exclusively chosen from the evangelical, Reformed stream.

Leanne Van Dyk questions the way in which Campbell groups John Owen, Jonathan Edwards and Thomas Chalmers together as representatives of a common point of view,[176] believing that this demonstrates a lack of awareness of the important theological differences between them.[177] Further questions relate to what Brian Gerrish suggests is one of the most curious features of *The Nature of the Atonement*, that although 'it contains some harsh (and penetrating) criticisms of

---

[174] In chapter 3 he engages with Owen and Edwards as representatives of earlier Calvinism. He sees Thomas Chalmers as a contemporary advocate of a similar approach.
[175] In chapter 4 he interacts with more recent writers, Jenkyn, Payne, Pye-Smith and Wardlaw.
[176] *Nature*, 44 (65).
[177] Van Dyk, *Desire of Divine Love*, 100-1.

Calvinism, it makes no attempt to deal with Calvin.'[178] In a letter to his sister written in 1829 Campbell had observed that 'as to the extent to which there is anything new in my views, I think I have a distinct conception of it, and when I go back to the writings of Luther and Calvin, I find it not great.'[179] The two occasions during his disciplinary hearings when Campbell quoted Calvin in support of his teaching about assurance,[180] indicate some familiarity with Calvin's teaching. That earlier familiarity makes the absence of any real reference to Calvin in *The Nature of the Atonement* all the more puzzling, for as Gerrish points out, there are several areas in Campbell's theology which could have been supported by an appeal to Calvin's teaching.[181] It is not possible here to resolve all the questions relating to Campbell's interaction with his Reformed inheritance. However, whilst he was clearly asking critical questions about aspects of this tradition, it is also obvious that he indwelt this tradition and found stimulus within it.[182]

Another topic meriting further exploration concerns the extent of Erskine of Linlathen's influence on Campbell's thinking about atonement. Needham implies that Campbell's views are dependent on *The Brazen Serpent* published by Erskine in 1831. He claims that

> the essence of the atonement according to Erskine...is that Christ suffered God's reformative penalties in the right spirit, a spirit of submission and acceptance, confessing the goodness of God in thus punishing sinful humanity of which He was head, so that it has become a righteous and honourable thing in God to restore sinful men — which is basically the doctrine of vicarious repentance, popularised by McLeod Campbell in his later book on the atonement in 1856.[183]

In his comprehensive reappraisal of Erskine's theology, Don Horrocks similarly argues that 'many of Campbell's later developed views were already evident in seed form in Erskine

---

[178] Gerrish, *Tradition and the Modern World*, 91.
[179] *Memorials*, 1.64. Letter dated Row, 6 March, 1829.
[180] See Chapter 1 *Assurance of the Essence of Faith*.
[181] Gerrish, *Tradition and the Modern World* 91-4.
[182] *Reminiscences*, 183. 'However affected by their views of the Atonement, I found in some Calvinists a higher standard both of faith and of the fruits of faith; and I have ever looked back with thankfulness on the intimate acquaintance which, in the beginning of my ministry, I made with such biographies as those of David Brainerd, Henry Martyn and H. Dorney.'
[183] N. R. Needham, *Thomas Erskine of Linlathen*, 332-3.

before they met in about 1827-28, Campbell having already read Erskine's early works.[184] As evidence for this, Horrocks points to the way in which Erskine introduced some ideas about the retrospective and prospective dimensions of the atonement over twenty years before the publication of *The Nature of the Atonement*.[185] However, rather than seeing Campbell as a 'popularizer', he argues that although 'the evidence supports Erskine as the earlier pioneer, visionary, and innovator, nobody would argue that out of the two, Campbell was not the true "theologian"'.[186]

Campbell readily admitted his indebtedness to Erskine who 'had a name in theology when I was yet a student of theology.'[187] However, this debt of gratitude does not necessarily imply dependence upon Erskine for his key ideas. In a letter to his father written in 1826, Campbell writes appreciatively about Erskine's *Internal Evidences*; but the comment about, 'his language, which you remember was mine',[188] tends to suggest that Campbell believed that Erskine's book contained confirmation of positions he had already arrived at independently.

One indication that the relationship might be better described in terms of mutuality, is that after hearing Campbell preach in an Edinburgh church in the Spring of 1828, Erskine said to a friend, 'I have heard today from that pulpit what I believe to be the true gospel.'[189] After Erskine's death, Campbell wrote about the way in which Erskine and their friend A. J. Scott had 'each and each separately — come to the same light of the divine love in which I was rejoicing.'[190] This coming together of like minded people marked the beginning of a mutually beneficial friendship which lasted over forty years. When it came to writing *The Nature of the Atonement*, Campbell explained to Erskine that 'in writing it you were mentally present with me…as one whose sympathy I could calculate.'[191] This leads Tuttle to conclude that Campbell

---

[184] Don Horrocks, *Laws of the Spiritual Order: Innovation and Reconstruction in the Soteriology of Thomas Erskine of Linlathen* (Carlisle: Paternoster, 2004), 14.
[185] Horrocks, *Laws of the Spiritual Order*, 108, note 65.
[186] Horrocks, *Laws of the Spiritual Order*, 15.
[187] *Memorials*, 2.208. Letter to Thomas Erskine, 2 May 1868.
[188] *Memorials*, 1.27. Letter dated 25 February 1826.
[189] Hanna, (ed.), *Letters of Thomas Erskine*, 102.
[190] *Memorials*, 2.273-4. Letter to his youngest daughter, 26th March, 1870.
[191] *Memorials*, 1.272. Letter to Mr. Erskine, 20 February, 1856.

found in his older friend corroborative support in all that mattered to him in both preaching and publication. If he had never read Erskine's works or entered into that friendship, Campbell would still no doubt have preached as he did at Row and written later on the atonement in much the same vein as he did in 1856. Yet Erskine's inspiration and support gave Campbell more confidence and helped to clarify his thought and lend a flavour to all his work.[192]

In the light of Horrocks' study it appears that Tuttle is underestimating Erskine's influence by suggesting that Campbell's preaching and writing would not have altered greatly if he had never encountered Erskine.[193] However Tuttle's description of Campbell as 'a comparatively independent mind' is much more appropriate than the assertion that he was just the popularizer of someone else's ideas.

This chapter has argued for a more positive reading of *The Nature of the Atonement*, and has drawn attention to some of the key elements within it. The next stage of this re-evaluation of Campbell's theology is to demonstrate the way in which many of these key ideas about atonement can be detected in the sermons dating from an early stage of his ministry. The next chapter will show that there are clear lines of continuity linking the views expressed in sermons from different stages in his ministry with the theology expressed at length in *The Nature of the Atonement*.

---

[192] Tuttle, *So Rich a Soil*, 68-9.
[193] Horrocks, *Laws of the Spiritual Order*, 260. 'In particular, there is scope for serious study of Erskine's relationship to John McLeod Campbell, who appeared to develop many of Erskine's soteriological ideas.'

Chapter 3

Campbell the Preacher

> ...what I have written for the press was all present substantially very early in my preaching.[1]

At this point it is appropriate to consider the evidence which supports the claim that there is an overall consistency in Campbell's theological output, from the early Row sermons to the later publications. The previous chapter identified key elements of his soteriology which are the better known features of his theology. If Campbell was a consistent thinker then it should be possible to see similar theological emphases appearing in sermons from earlier stages of his ministry. The evidence drawn from his sermons in Glasgow and in Row, supports Campbell's assertion that what he wrote for publication was substantially present in his earlier preaching. As several chapters will draw heavily upon these sermons, some preliminary comments about them are called for.

The Row and Glasgow Sermons

The Row Sermons

As controversy developed around Campbell at Row both friend and foe alike were interested in recording his sermons. The result of this interest is that a substantial body of material survives, consisting of over seventy sermons. This substantial resource has been largely neglected by scholars, and it is important to begin here the process of reclaiming material which offers valuable insights into a crucial stage in Campbell's life and ministry. Some sermons were initially published as separate tracts, before being re-issued as part of larger collections, and this causes some confusion because some sermons have appeared under a number of different titles.

---

[1] *Memorials* 2.159.

Campbell the Preacher 115

Access to the full range of material is possible by using three major collections of sermons, *Good Tidings*,[2] *Notes of Sermons*[3] and *Sermons and Lectures*,[4] supplemented by a small number of sermons which did not earn a place in the larger volumes.[5]

What appears to be the earliest of these sermons was given to a clerical society in Glasgow early in December 1828.[6] Most of

---

[2] *GT*. Originally published anonymously. At least nine sermons were by Campbell, and they had been published separately as numbered tracts, (*No. I, No. II, No. III, No. IV, No. V, No. VI, No. VII, No. VIII,* and *No. XIII*). A second edition was published in London by James Nisbet in 1873.

[3] *NofS*. This contains thirty six sermons and an extract from Campbell's letter to his brother dated 1 January 1831 which gives valuable information about this period. Seven sermons in this collection are also published in the two volume set, *Sermons and Lectures*. It also incorporates *Two Sermons*, (London: John Hatchard & Son, 1830), which are similarly reprinted in *Sermons and Lectures*. In the edition used for this study each sermon is numbered separately.

[4] *S&L*. This two volume set contains thirty five sermons, seven of which also appear in *NofS* with another one also appearing in *GT*. This collection has a complicated history. Initially nineteen sermons appeared in four short books, (*Notes of Sermons, Number One, Notes of Sermons, Number Two, Notes of Sermons, Number Three* and *Notes of Sermons, Number Four*) which were published by R. B. Lusk in 1830. These nineteen sermons were then combined into a volume, *Notes of Sermons* Vol. 1, (Greenock: R. B. Lusk, 1831). Presumably to avoid confusion with the three volume *Notes of Sermons* published in Paisley by J. Vallance, the third edition of R. B. Lusk's collection was renamed *Sermons and Lectures*, and a second volume was added. All references in this study to *Sermons and Lectures* will be to the two volume set published by R. B. Lusk. Some editions of *Sermons and Lectures* bear a title page with the shorter title, *Sermons*. Selections from these two volumes were later published under the title, *Responsibility for the Gift of Eternal Life*, (London: Macmillan, 1873). As this material has been heavily edited it is a less satisfactory source for information about Campbell's own thinking.

[5] *Notes and Recollections of Two Sermons, by the Rev. Mr. Campbell, delivered in the Parish Church of Row on Sunday, 6th September 1829*, (Greenock: R. B. Lusk, 1829).

Notes of a Sermon, preached in the Parish Church of Row, on Thursday, 8th July 1830; Being the day of the visitation of that Parish by the Presbytery of Dumbarton. By the Rev. J. M. Campbell, Minister of Row, (Greenock: R. B. Lusk, 1830).

The Everlasting Gospel; This sermon also appears as sermon 4 within *Good Tidings*.

[6] *GT*, chapter 5 'Confessing Christ'. Cf. *Memorials*, 1.61.

the published sermons cover a period from September 1829,[7] through to Monday 15 August 1831 when he preached his farewell address to his parishioners at Row.[8] These passionate sermons not only help to explain the content of the 'Row heresy', but they also provide direct evidence of Campbell's understanding of the person of Christ.

The Glasgow Sermons

In contrast to the abundance of tracts and books from his period at Row there are only three overlapping volumes of sermons dating from Campbell's ministry in Glasgow. *Fragments of Expositions of Scripture* was published anonymously in 1843. Campbell appears to be the author of all but two of the sermons which were by his close friend A.J. Scott. The preface to the third edition, renamed *Fragments of Truth: Being the Exposition of Several Passages of Scripture*, refers to a second edition, but no copies of this seem to survive. Nine of Campbell's sermons from 1843 were not reprinted in the 1861 edition, but seventeen others were added. One sermon is divided into two parts, with the result that there are thirty sermon fragments. The two sermons from A. J. Scott are repeated and a further two from Thomas Erskine of Linlathen are added to the book.[9] The same combination of sermons is duplicated in the 1898 edition, where an enlarged title[10] makes explicit that the book is predominantly Campbell's work. Nine of Campbell's sermons appear only in the 1843 edition, eight appear in all editions, and seventeen appear in the 1861 and 1898 versions of the book. The title *Fragments* was a deliberate allusion to the fact that these did not represent the full text of the sermons, but were instead 'recollections noted down by different individuals, of Sermons

---

[7] *Notes and Recollections of Two Sermons*,

[8] S&L 2.29 Sermon on Lk. 8:4-15 'The parable of the Sower', preached in a field near Helensburgh. See also notes of a farewell address to a few of his parishioners, *NofS* volume 2.

[9] The copy of the 1861 edition used in this study contains some handwritten notes from Campbell's widow confirming that there are two sermons by Mr Erskine ('The righteousness of God in the heart of man' and 'God's welcome to the returning sinner'), another two by A. J. Scott, ('On the natural adaptation of meekness and quietness of spirit to win unbelievers' and 'God's searching eye welcome to the believer'), and 'the rest by J. McL. C'.

[10] *FofT*. In the Preface, Donald Campbell similarly confirms his father's authorship of all but four of the *Fragments*.

Campbell the Preacher

and Expositions felt at the time to be very precious'.[11] Although this second set of sermon fragments is not as substantial as the Row sermons it is also of continuing interest because it offers access to Campbell's thinking during the quarter of a century following his deposition. In the preface to the 1898 edition of *Fragments of Truth* his son, Donald, indicates that 'some of the addresses, especially those on "Reconciliation,"...contain many of the elements of the teaching which was afterwards fully expounded in his great work on the Atonement.'[12] It is likely that these addresses contain the heart of what Campbell ventured to teach his Glasgow congregation about atonement during 1847.[13] Even if that cannot be proved conclusively, it remains the case that these sermons help to build a picture of Campbell's thought during the period between his removal from the Church of Scotland and the publication of *The Nature of the Atonement*.

Along with the 1898 edition of *Fragments of Truth* is bound another book published anonymously, called *Bible Readings*.[14] Daniel P. Thimell has suggested that 'internal evidence strongly supports Campbell's authorship of Bible Readings as well.'[15] If this was the case then it would mean that a further twenty five addresses would need to be taken into account. However, it seems most unlikely that these talks derive from Campbell because Lesson VIII begins with the speaker anticipating that the congregation will ask the question, 'Does *she* mean to say that God is not angry with sin, – does not punish it?'[16] Although it is possible that this is a printer's error, the concluding exhortation to 'let us women remember this',[17] leaves little room for doubt. The material recorded in *Bible Readings* seems to arise from a situation where a woman was addressing a women's group. One possibility is that these talks may come from Miss Jane Gourlay, who was credited with

---

[11] *FofTE*, iv.
[12] *FofT*, Preface.
[13] *Memorials*, 1.207. In a letter to Thomas Erskine written on 18th June 1847, Campbell explained that he had 'ventured to attempt to teach my people on the subject of the atonement.' Cf., 1.168, 1.207.
[14] *Bible Readings*, (Edinburgh: David Douglas, 1864).
[15] Thimell, in *Christ In Our Place*, Hart and Thimell, (eds.), footnote 190.
[16] *Bible Readings*, 43.
[17] *Ibid.*, 49. Similarly the illustration used on 51-52 about a doctor operating on a lady suffering from cancer to remove her breast, is very difficult to imagine on the lips of a nineteenth century male preacher.

recording and editing the sermons in *Fragments of Truth*.[18] If that was the case then perhaps these *Bible Readings* might help to reveal something of the way in which Campbell's ideas were absorbed and used by others. However, in the absence of further information it is not possible to reach such a conclusion with any degree of confidence. For the purposes of this study, therefore, the material in *Bible Readings* will not be taken into consideration. Nevertheless the Glasgow *Fragments* and the Row sermons together represent a resource of over a hundred sermons and talks, which provides sufficient material to examine the consistency of Campbell's thought.

The Glasgow *Fragments* are a valuable resource because, as his son explains, 'the teaching here recorded belongs to a time intermediate between his ministry at Row and the writing of his books.'[19] Taking into account the various editions of these *Fragments* it is possible to identify three layers of material spanning over twenty years, with the Row sermons supplying another earlier layer. Examination of material drawn from these different periods of his life helps to establish the degree of consistency in his teaching.

Having identified the key elements of *The Nature of the Atonement* in chapter 2 it is necessary now to examine the assertion that these core ideas can also be found in the addresses contained in *Fragments of Truth*. The first set of *Fragments* to be considered will be the group which were added in 1861. After this the sermons common to the 1843 and 1861 editions will be examined, and then the talks unique to the 1843 edition will be explored. After investigating the extent to which key elements of Campbell's soteriology can be found in these addresses, consideration of the Row sermons will indicate how similar elements can be found in his earlier preaching. If common themes are present in all of these strata it supports Campbell's claim that his main theological emphases were already in place at an early stage of his ministry.

---

[18] *FofT*. In the Preface, Donald Campbell says 'All who knew Miss Jane Gourlay will remember her with true regard; and they will understand with what zeal and energy and love she threw herself into the work of preserving for others the teaching which she found so valuable to herself.'
[19] *Ibid.*, Preface.

The Glasgow *Fragments* and *The Nature of the Atonement*

Fragments Added in 1861

Within this group of sermons Donald Campbell claims that four addresses on Reconciliation[20] probably dating from 1847, contain some of his father's key thoughts about atonement, and these will be considered in greater detail than the others. The terminology employed is not precisely the same as in *The Nature of the Atonement*, but there are clear similarities of thought.

These talks explore different aspects of 2 Corinthians 5:17-21, with the first one concentrating on the call to be reconciled.[21] At the outset Campbell argues that the call to be reconciled implies that men and women are in a state of alienation from God; and he suggests that this alienation has external and internal forms. In the external events of life people are challenged to submit to God's authority gladly, but may react with anything but cheerfulness. In addition, God claims the supreme rule within our inner life. Often this claim is resisted because 'you are seeking to be gods to yourselves, and are thus rejecting the true God.'[22]

Campbell secondly considers the nature of the external and internal change involved in reconciliation. Where the external events of providence were once met with resentment, the change brought about by reconciliation with God is that all events are welcomed as coming from the loving hands of God. 'While the result of our "being reconciled to God" is a thankful acquiescence in all His dealings, they are still felt according to their nature – some cause us to rejoice, others to weep; but however various our emotions, still in the deepest part of our being we are in peace, for there the unshaken confidence abides that "He doeth all things well."'[23] If it is difficult to submit gladly to such external events it is even more difficult to submit to God's inner rule which He has every right to demand.

Thirdly Campbell asserts that such a reconciliation with God is eminently desirable, for without it we are spiritually dead and unable to be what God intended us to be. 'We are intended to the children of God, led by His Spirit, having no will but His. So long as God claims this supremacy in man's heart, there can be

---

[20] *FofT*, Chapters 17-20.
[21] *Ibid.*, Chapter 17 'Reconciliation'.
[22] *Ibid.*, 17.199.
[23] *Ibid.*, 17.201.

no peace for man but in yielding it.'[24] Campbell is clear that human beings are not able to save themselves and their only hope is in divine mercy, for 'to make return possible, there must be on the part of God free unconditional forgiveness. Man must be met on the threshold with the assurance that all his past sin is blotted out, all his transgressions covered.'[25] The basis for reconciliation lies, therefore, not in human repentance, but in the fact that God has made Christ to be sin, or to be a sin-offering for us.

The invitation to be reconciled is an invitation to share in the divine nature. 'If I, who have consciously resisted God's Spirit — I, who have been as a god unto myself — pleasing my own-self, am called on to give up this independent life and to accept my own place as a creature, if I yield to this call, and am thus reconciled to God, you can understand how I thus become a partaker of the Divine nature, and how my spirit in thus yielding itself has become righteous.'[26] Such an emphasis upon becoming partakers in the divine nature anticipates the clear statement in *The Nature of the Atonement* regarding Christ's 'participation in humanity, and our participation in the divine nature through Him.'[27]

Gratitude for what Christ has done may inspire a person to want to live for God, but gratitude alone is insufficient to overcome the conflict within and produce a life of holiness. It is clear that this change has been brought about because Christ was 'made sin for us' or 'a sin-offering'; but what was it in this sacrifice that brings about reconciliation? Campbell addresses the nature of sacrifice, and the nature of Christ's sufferings when he says,

> We must ask, "What *was* it that God accepted? What was there well-pleasing to Him in the death of His Son? What is the essential excellence in this sacrifice? The true answer is that of the apostle, — It is "the condemnation of sin in the flesh." The suffering is *in its own nature*, a condemnation of the fleshly life. If we could see the inward nature of the sufferings of the Saviour, we should see the condemnation of sin as its very essence. It is important that we discern clearly that the flesh is condemned. — the old man nailed to the tree, — not so much

---

[24] *Ibid.*, 17.204.
[25] *Ibid.*, 17.206.
[26] *Ibid.*, 17.208.
[27] *Nature*, 321 (259).

by the *fact* of Christ's sufferings, as by *the inward condition of His Spirit* in suffering.[28]

This effective condemnation of sin was possible because Christ never succumbed to temptation.[29] His resisting temptation and his offering of himself to God was through the power of the Holy Spirit.

> If, farther, we see the sacrifice of Christ to have been offered *through the Eternal Spirit* — if we see that Christ's condemnation of sin was in the strength of the Eternal Life — and that this life was in Him as Man — as being a partaker of humanity — then we not only know the fact, but we are invited to partake in it, and we see the possibility of doing so; *Life* is given in Christ through partaking in His death. Thus we become righteous, and we are enabled to receive Christ to reign in our hearts; we are enabled to condemn sin in the Spirit of Sonship; the Life of Christ becomes our life, and His righteousness is fulfilled in us.[30]

So in this talk, written perhaps in 1847, we see Campbell identifying the condemnation of sin as an important dimension of the sacrifice of Christ. This idea is explored more fully in *The Nature of the Atonement* where Christ's dealing with humanity on the part of God, within the Retrospective aspect of atonement, involves a similar condemnation of sin. Christ concurs with the Father's diagnosis and condemnation of sin, and by his life of obedience on earth he exposes and condemns the sinful behaviour of people. Another element of Campbell's presentation in *The Nature of the Atonement* which is prefigured here is his emphasis upon Christ offering his atoning sacrifice 'through the Eternal Spirit'.[31]

It is because Christ was a partaker in humanity that human beings can be invited to partake in his condemnation of sin and to partake in the life of Christ. In this way Campbell paves the way for a closing exhortation for his hearers to be reconciled to God. This means welcoming the Spirit of adoption who teaches God's children to cry 'Abba, Father', and to come as children

---

[28] *FofT*, 17.211-2.
[29] *Ibid.*, 17.212 'In the Son of God there was a living condemnation of sin, inasmuch as He never gave place to sin. If He had ever yielded to sin, there would have been no condemnation of sin in his sufferings.'
[30] *Ibid.*, 17.213.
[31] Heb. 9:14. Cf., *Nature*, 105, 152, 156, 169, 256. (110, 142, 144, 153, 213).

into their Father's presence. Thus reconciled to God, believers will be better able

> to welcome all God's providential dealings, — to receive them *all* as parts of His great plan, the *soul* of which is that you become partakers of Christ's life through partaking in His death — *all* as discipline, aiding the development within you of His life. In the school of Christ you will discern the divine fitness of all the events that are appointed for you to cherish this life; you will be reconciled to them all, not only because they all come from God but because you are yourselves in the light of His purpose in sending them — thus you will be not only willing, but *able* in all things to give thanks.[32]

In Campbell's stress upon the work of the Spirit of adoption, there is the basis of what he later calls the 'prospective aspect of atonement', because his prospective language is another way of describing the divine purpose 'that we should receive the adoption of sons.'[33]

At the beginning of his second address on reconciliation[34] Campbell draws attention to the coinherence of christology and soteriology.[35] Although the doctrine of incarnation is difficult to comprehend,[36] without this complex doctrine no concept of atonement will be coherent.[37] God Himself in the person of the

---

[32] *FofT*, 17.214-5.

[33] See also, *FofT*, 9.100, '…for the very purpose of all that Christ did, and suffered, and *was* on earth, is to bring us into the adoption of children, and to make us heirs of God and *joint heirs* with Jesus Christ — that is, to make us partakers of the nature of God, and participators in all that Christ inherits as the Son of God.'

[34] *Ibid.*, 18 'Reconciliation: Christ the Reconciler.'

[35] *Ibid.*, 18.216. 'There is much to make us pause, and to fill our minds with awe, in the character of the work which is here brought before us; — God taking the human nature into union with the Divine, — God manifesting Himself in the flesh.'

[36] *Ibid.*, 18.218. 'Although the mind may not distinctly apprehend the *ground* on which the death of Christ brings life to the sinner, yet the greatness, the excellent dignity of Him who died, makes it easy to believe that His death is adequate to the purpose it was intended to effect.'

[37] *Ibid.*, 18.216-7 'The subject of the incarnation can only be apprehended by faith; it is altogether beyond the sphere of the intellect. That the Divine should be united with the human! — if in some aspects we seem to comprehend it, in others it is wholly beyond your grasp. But the impossibility of fully grasping it ought not be an objection to the doctrine.'

Man Christ Jesus has entered into such a union with human nature

> that it is scarcely figurative to speak of the blood of God as the ransom. The blood is human, but the person is divine; it is a man who dies, but it is God who has made the atonement. And thus it is only they who acknowledge the Divinity of our Lord who can ever fully and freely believe in the atonement. No other conception of Christ, however exalted, can bridge over the difficulty. The distance between the Creator and any creature must ever be infinite; whatever steps may be taken to lessen it are but an apparent filling up of the interval; the distance is still infinite, it can be no more![38]

God has not inflicted punishment upon some innocent victim, but has taken the load upon himself.

> Whilst we conceive Christ to be a mere creature, we cannot get over the injustice of an innocent and holy being suffering for the guilty; but the character of the transaction is wholly changed when we see that He, against whom the offence was committed, Himself became the ransom — that it was not on another He laid the load — that it was not a holy and exalted creature who was sacrificed for one vile and low, but the Creator who put Himself in the place of the creature, the Sovereign Judge who vindicated by His own sufferings the honour of His own law.
>
> Besides, had the sacrifice been made by any but God Himself, it would infer that we owe to a creature an obligation infinitely higher than we owe to God, inasmuch as redemption is unquestionably a greater blessing than creation, and we must give to Christ a place in our hearts which ought to belong to none but Jehovah.[39]

Campbell advances an *a posteriori* approach which stresses that 'the distinctive character of Christianity is, that it requires us to see light in God's light. It is not satisfied with our accepting facts as true, but requires us to see in the light of God the meaning of the facts.'[40] For Campbell, truth is not ultimately proved by quoting verses from the Bible because truth has an authority of its own which the believing conscience recognises.[41]

---

[38] *Ibid.*, 18.218-9.
[39] *Ibid.*, 18.219.
[40] *Ibid.*, 18.219-220.
[41] *Ibid.*, 18.221. 'So it is with the truths of Revelation; whilst we believe them on the simple testimony of the Bible, we are not using the Bible as God

He contrasts the sacrifice of Christ with the sacrifices of the old dispensation which could not take away sin. The good news is that 'it is possible for the blood of Christ to take away sin, because it possesses a virtue in itself adequate to the end.'[42] The blood of Christ is effective because it is somehow able to cleanse the conscience and thus bring the human conscience into harmony with the will of God. Within this sermon Campbell appears to be content simply to affirm the effectiveness of the blood of Christ, without clearly explaining how Christ's sacrifice brings about such a transformation of the human conscience. For further clues to Campbell's understanding of the atoning element in Christ's death it is necessary to turn to the next sermon in this short series, which will be examined in due course.

Before moving on to Campbell's next address it is worth noting that his discomfort with any notion of God inflicting punishment upon the Son is already visible within this second reflection upon reconciliation. He is not at this stage describing his work as a moral and spiritual approach to atonement, but his dissatisfaction with penal and legal approaches is evident. Similarly there is the insistence, visible in *The Nature of the Atonement*, that soteriology must be viewed in the light of what God has done in Christ, rather than being determined by a set of legal presuppositions. He makes explicit the assumption that any doctrine of atonement assumes the divinity of Christ, and this assumption undergirds everything he says here, and all he later writes in *The Nature of the Atonement*.[43]

---

would have us. The Scriptures are intended to do for man what Euclid does for the mathematical student – they lead him into the light of truth; but this light *when seen* is believed in, not on the authority of the book, but on its own authority; *the truth is seen to be true.*'

[42] Ibid., 18.222.

[43] In recognising that atonement rests upon the divinity of Christ Campbell was standing in a long and honoured tradition. For example, in his arguments with the Arians, Athanasius insisted that Christ had to be God in order to accomplish salvation. Anything or anyone less than God would have been unable to deal with sin and recreate a fallen universe. *St. Athanasius: Select Works and Letters: Nicene and Post-Nicene Fathers of the Christian Church*, second series, vol.4. (eds.), P. Schaff and H. Wace, (Edinburgh: T & T Clark, 1891), 385. *Contra Arianos* II, 67, 'Mankind then is perfected in Him and restored, as it was made at the beginning, nay, with greater grace...And this has been done, since the own Word of God Himself, who is from the Father, has put on the flesh and become man. For if, being a creature, He had become man, man had remained just what he

In his next examination of this topic,[44] Campbell challenges the notion that justification simply prepares the way for sanctification by removing a legal barrier. For him, justification involves a real transformation of the human spirit as the conscience is washed clean by the blood of Christ. It is within this sermon that he begins to shed light on the issue, left unresolved in the previous address, about what made Christ's sacrifice more effective than the blood of bulls and goats. At the heart of his understanding of sacrifice it would appear to be the case that, taking the dignity of the person for granted, it is the element of *obedience* which makes the sacrifice efficacious.

> The blood of bulls and goats could not take away sin, the blood of Christ could. What does this mean? The voluntary shedding of His blood indicated the entire surrender of His will by the Son to the Father. It was this doing of the will of God that made the sacrifice a reality; it was this which constituted the essence of the atonement, this made the blood of Christ a sanctifying thing, able to accomplish the salvation of man. On this, and not on the dignity of the sacrifice, however, much weight may be elsewhere laid upon that doctrine, when other aspects of truth are to be brought out, – on this doing of the Divine will by Him who is the Head and Root of the race, the apostle here rests, as that which made Christ the Mediator of a better covenant.[45]

Such a stress upon *'doing of the will of God'* anticipates the approach expounded in *The Nature of the Atonement* where Campbell claims that the key to atonement can be found in the phrase from Psalm 40, 'Lo, I come to do Thy will, O God.' Another way of depicting this reality is to see *'doing of the will of God'* as the outward expression of a person's inner zeal for God. The close relationship of these two elements in Campbell's thought is indicated by the way he similarly attributes atoning

---

was, not joined to God; for how had a work been joined to the Creator by a work? Or what succour had come from like to like, when one as well as other needed it? And how, were the Word a creature, had He power to undo God's sentence, and to remit sin'

[44] *FofT* Chapter 19 'Reconciliation: The Conscience Purged'.

[45] *Ibid.*, 19.230. Cf., 19.237-8 'The *essence* of Christ's sacrifice is contained in the words, "Lo. I come *to do thy will*, O Lord;" and the *essence of Christianity* is also in *doing the will of God,* in so apprehending the Divine character as to resign not our circumstances merely, but ourselves, our own spirits, to God; this deepest reconciliation could only be through the shedding of blood.'

power to zeal for God. In *The Nature of the Atonement* he argues that it was 'his zeal for God' which gave an atoning dimension to the dramatic actions of Phinehas recorded in Numbers 25:10-13.[46] Similarly he argues that it is Christ's 'perfect zeal for the Father's honour' which gives his suffering the power to atone.[47]

Campbell was not alone in identifying the atoning power of godly zeal because John Owen had pointed to Christ's *'unspeakable zeal* for, and *ardency of affection unto, the glory of God'* and concluded that 'these were the coals which with a vehement flame, as it were, consumed the sacrifice.'[48] The inherent connection between godly zeal and obedience means that obedience is a major atoning element within Owen's approach.

> It was not, then, [by] the outward suffering of a violent and bloody death, which was inflicted on him by the most horrible wickedness that ever human nature brake forth into, that God was atoned, Acts ii. 23; nor yet was it merely his enduring the penalty of the law that was the means of our deliverance; but the voluntary giving up of himself to be a sacrifice in these holy acts of obedience was that upon which, in an especial manner, God was reconciled unto us.[49]

The extent of Campbell's familiarity with Calvin's works remains uncertain, but this is another place where Campbell could have demonstrated the orthodoxy of his proposals by referring to the work of Calvin. The significance of the obedience of Christ for soteriology is expressed clearly in the *Institutes* where Calvin says, 'Now someone asks, How has Christ abolished sin, banished the separation between us and God, and acquired righteousness to render God favourable and kindly toward us? To this we can in general reply that he has achieved this for us by the whole course of his obedience.'[50]

---

[46] *Nature*, 103f (108-09).

[47] *Ibid.*, 113 (115-6).

[48] J. Owen, *The Works of John Owen*, vol. III, (ed.), W. H. Goold, (London: Banner of Truth, 1965), 177-8.

[49] *Ibid.*, 180.

[50] Calvin, *Institutes*, II. xvi. 5. Cf. II. xvi. 12. 'As if he could atone for our sins in any other way than by obeying the Father!' E. David Willis, *Calvin's Catholic Christology: The Function of the so-called Extra Calvinisticum in Calvin's Theology*, (Leiden: E. J. Brill, 1966), 85. 'What is saving in Christ's teaching, miracles, and death is not simply that they occurred, but that they occurred voluntarily. The heart of the reconstituting act is the free obedience of the Second Adam which displaces the willful disobedience of

Integral to his understanding of *'The Nature of the Atonement'* is the sense that the Cross of Christ provides an example for believers to follow.[51] The biblical call to take up the cross implies that believers are to adopt Christ's attitude towards sin and suffering. For 'every one who is a partaker of *Christ's* suffering is ceasing from sin. I trust you all see the close connexion between these passages and the one I am commenting on; how they all prove that those sufferings which formed the sacrifice of Christ for us, are also set before us as our example — that the Cross which gives confidence, is at the same time a cross to be borne.'[52] Whilst different language is employed in *The Nature of the Atonement*, Campbell is expressing similar sentiments when he represents Christ interceding with the Father, praying that his confession, and hence his attitude to sin, will be 'reproduced in us'.[53]

Taking up the cross is not some form of human good works because for Campbell it is clear 'that we can only follow his steps by being filled with His Spirit.'[54] Through the cross God intends to cleanse the conscience of sinful human beings. There is no sense here that the cross is needed to persuade an otherwise reluctant God to be merciful. The truth about the cross is that 'its end is to reconcile us to God, not God to us.'[55] In his earliest sermons, as well as in his later publications, Campbell is always keen to show that the cross is not needed to make God love us. The problem that needs to be tackled resides in people, and not in the God whose love motivates every aspect of atonement.

It is true that a sacrifice was needed to vindicate God's character and honour, but this insight must be complemented by the realization that the sacrifice of Christ also involved a condemnation of sin. 'It was the condemnation of sin *in the flesh* that made Christ's offering of himself an acceptable sacrifice. He gave up willingly unto death that which had sinned — that which was evil. His doing so, as the Head of the race, enables each one of us to do the same. Thus is God's character, as the

---

the first Adam, and frees the members of the Second Adam for new obedience in place of their inherited disobedience.'

[51] 1 Peter 2:21 'Christ suffered for you, leaving you an example, that you should follow in his steps.'
[52] *FofT*, 19.233.
[53] *Nature*, 153 (142).
[54] *FofT*, 19.233.
[55] *Ibid.*, 19.234.

righteous Lawgiver, vindicated, by the righteousness of the law being fulfilled in us.'[56]

Such a condemnation of sin assumes Christ's full identification with humanity because it was not enough for God to condemn sin from the outside. It is Christ, as man, who condemns sin from within the situation itself.

> Connect the language in Hebrews concerning the sacrifice of Christ, "Lo, I come to do thy will, O God" with this declaration — that when He came, He came to condemn sin in the flesh. He took our flesh, He became our brother, that is, He came into the condition in which alone He could condemn sin in the flesh as one connected with it. There is no real difficulty in holiness condemning sin; but Christ as God could only condemn sin as a thing outside of Himself — apart from Himself, with which He had nothing to do; Christ, as man, condemning sin is the same thing as His offering up of Himself a sacrifice. Man, in whose own flesh the sin is, cannot condemn sin in the flesh without giving up himself. This was Christ's work; He yielded His will as a continual sacrifice, saying, "Not my will but thine be done"; thus He continually condemned sin in the flesh.[57]

In addition to the linguistic links between *Fragments of Truth* and *The Nature of the Atonement* it is also relevant to notice that this stress upon Christ needing to be fully identified with humanity in order to 'condemn' its sin effectively, is strongly represented in the earlier Row sermons. Whether it was an individual, or a universe full of people, an atonement of this nature would be required to vindicate God's character, and to transform the individual concerned, so that she or he would identify fully with God's condemnation of sin.

In the fourth address on this topic[58] Campbell once again employs Psalm 40 as a way of getting to the heart of atonement and reconciliation.[59] In *The Nature of the Atonement* Campbell claimed that the atonement was the natural development of the incarnation, and he anticipates that idea by saying that 'the

---

[56] *Ibid.*, 19.235.
[57] *Ibid.*, 19.239-240.
[58] *Ibid.*, 20 'Reconciliation: The Atonement'
[59] *Ibid.*, 20.241 'nothing is to be believed concerning the atonement which is not a following out of our Saviour's own words, "Lo, I come to do thy will, O God,"' Cf., 20.242 'When we ask what are the elements contained in the atonement, we have *First*, Christ's declaration "Lo, I come to do thy will, O God," as the key word to the whole.'

atonement must either be regarded as *distinct* from the incarnation and example of Christ, or as identical with them. It is impossible to view it as *distinct*, without ascribing to the character of our Lord a sort of duality which we cannot but shrink from.'[60]

Christ had come to do God's will and his cry, 'it is finished', declared that he had succeeded in doing what he set out to do. The will of God that Christ has come to fulfil is an expression of the love which is at the heart of all that God is and does.

> This Will of God is *Love*. His name is *Love*, His righteousness is Love. Therefore He who came to do His will in humanity, came to show forth love. Love was the law of His being, and by reference to this *Love*, all questions with regard to His work are answered. Love moved Him to come to our earth, to lay down the glory He had at the right hand of the Father, and love determined all that He felt and did in humanity. Thus love is the great principle which is to guide us into the knowledge of the nature of His work.[61]

In his earliest preaching Campbell had argued passionately for the unlimited extent of God's love. By the time he wrote *The Nature of the Atonement* he did not feel that he needed to argue this case over again, but it is clear that God's love is the foundation for all that he proposes in both *Fragments of Truth*[62] and *The Nature of the Atonement*. The suffering which Christ endured was not inflicted upon him by an angry God, but arose naturally and inevitably out of his deep love for sinful human beings. So

> The natural consequence of a love which made Christ identify Himself with sinners was, that He should feel the pressure of human sin as a pressure on His own spirit. We know how deeply one human being may suffer in the suffering of another, and those who know what real love is, know that the pain of sympathy with a beloved object is often harder to endure than any suffering merely personal; the suffering of a mother, for instance, in that of her child. But in spiritual

---

[60] *Ibid.*, 20.241-2.
[61] *Ibid.*, 20. 242-3.
[62] See for example, *Ibid.*, 16.190-1 'Man may shut out the light — may reject the life, but the grace of God *hath*, in Christ, *appeared unto all men;* and the sole reason why any of the sons of Adam perish is — as shall yet, by the assembled universe, be seen and known — that they *would* not come to Jesus that they might have life.'

beings, physical suffering must always be regarded as secondary in comparison with mental suffering. To realize the sin of one with whom we are identified by love is greater suffering than any physical pain we could endure for him, and the intensity of suffering will be in proportion as the nature of him who endures it is alien from the sin. If we realized true brotherhood aright we should know this by our own experience. But in proportion as sympathy with the sin is allowed to mingle with sympathy for the sinner, the suffering will diminish. Thus the holy and loving Saviour suffered because men kept not His Father's law; it was love that made the suffering so intense, as well as love that was content to bear it.[63]

Another point of contact with *The Nature of the Atonement* can be seen when Campbell explains that by demonstrating God's love, Christ attracted opposition and suffering, and in persevering on this path he was made perfect through suffering.[64]

It was not the amount of physical suffering, it was His infinite love for those who inflicted it — His grief that they should so hate holiness, so reject Him, the Holy One, that made the suffering so bitter; it was His infinite love that made the suffering infinite, and that same infinite love was the strength in which it was endured. He endured the cross, despising the shame, for the joy that was set before Him. What joy? The joy of bringing many sons to glory.[65]

Campbell is convinced that Christ's sufferings cannot be seen as something inflicted by God the Father. As he sees it, the battle is not with God's wrath but with the power of the flesh.[66] If this is the case then why does Isaiah 53 say that 'it pleased the Lord to bruise him'? The sacrifice of Christ is pleasing to God because it is a perfect sacrifice of love which fully reflects in humanity the love of God.[67] Campbell believes that Jesus was conscious of

---

[63] *Ibid.,* 20.243-5

[64] *Ibid.,* 20.246 ,'what men call death was the *perfecting* of the work, but it was *only* the perfecting of that self-sacrifice which had gone on daily.' Cf., Chapter 2. *Made Perfect through Suffering.*

[65] *Ibid.,* 20.247.

[66] *Ibid.,* 20.247-8

[67] *Ibid.,* 20.248, 'What are the elements in this sacrifice of self in which God takes delight? It is dying to the creature as a step towards living to the Creator. It is dying to man's favour and to self, in order to live in God's

being the beloved Son in whom God was well pleased, at every point of his life and even in the darkest moments of his passion. Campbell was convinced that at no stage was God's displeasure against human sin personally transferred to Christ. So while there was real suffering it arose as a natural consequence of the incarnation of the love of God and not by the Father inflicting penal suffering upon the loving Son.[68] Once again he is arguing that the atonement develops naturally from the incarnation. It is not that the Son is subject to an outer necessity but rather that there is an inner inevitability of suffering when divine holiness and love condescend to become incarnate in a fallen world.[69]

This examination lends support to Donald Campbell's claim that these four talks anticipate *The Nature of the Atonement* in a number of ways. Although they lack the retrospective and prospective terminology of the later work, nevertheless similar ideas are clearly present and Campbell regularly appeals to some of the same biblical passages. Further support for his son's claim can be found in other sermons from this 'time intermediate between his ministry at Row and the writing of his books.'[70]

In his later work Campbell takes care to argue that there is a 'fixed and necessary character of salvation' which is rooted in the consistent character of God.[71] This concern is mirrored in

---

favour and for others. The *dying* is welcome because of the life that comes from it, the *satisfaction* is in the result.'

[68] Ibid., 20.249 'I believe that although Christ truly tasted death for every man, he was, all the while, *conscious* that He was Himself accepted of God. I cannot believe otherwise without giving up what is natural in the constitution of things. I am jealous of admitting any artificial element into the atonement, and feel that we glorify God more truly when we see all the Redeemer's suffering as arising naturally out of His union with fallen humanity — as the *necessary* consequence of Holy Love coming into contact with unholiness and enmity.'

[69] Hans Urs von Balthasar, *Mysterium Paschale*, (Edinburgh: T & T Clark, 1990), 22-3, 'he who says Incarnation, also says Cross. And this is so for two reasons. The Son of God took human nature in its fallen condition, and with it, therefore, the worm in its entrails — mortality, fallenness, self-estrangement, death — which sin introduced into the world....The second reason...has to do not with the man assumed but with the Logos assuming: to become man is for him, in a most hidden yet very real sense, already humiliation — yes, indeed, as many would say, a deeper humiliation than the going to the Cross itself.'

[70] *FofT*, Preface.

[71] See *Nature*, chapter 8.

another of the Fragments based on Romans 8:28-30.[72] In this sermon Campbell argues that God's goodness is not limited only to those that love him. However, on the basis of Romans 8 he affirms that it is only to those who love him that the promise, to bring good out of every circumstance, really applies. This division does not reflect any reduction of God's love for all but reflects the fixed and necessary nature of things within a moral universe.

> It is of importance to perceive that this arises out of the nature of things. Men suffer loss from not realizing this with regard to all the laws of God's kingdom. They are not arbitrary enactments. So long as men do not discern the connexion between sin and misery to be an eternal and unchangeable connexion, fixed in the very nature of things, so long as they suppose it to be a merely arbitrary one, and that God might, if He so pleased, give them blessedness though they continue sinners, so long they may flatter themselves with the idea that He may dispense with the laws He has made.[73]

Also present within this set of *Fragments* is the conviction present in *The Nature of the Atonement* and in the Row sermons that Christ is the mediator who reveals the truth about both God and humanity. Reflecting upon John 14: 8-10, Campbell depicts Jesus as the one who performs this dual revelatory role.

> They apparently suggest that we are to look to Jesus, not so much to know what He is in himself as man, as to know, by contemplating Him, what God is. But, in truth, the two are one. Jesus in one aspect is *God toward man*; if we would know what God is, we must look at Him; in another aspect He is *man toward God*; if we would know what humanity is — what God created man to be — we must look at Him. He is at once the true and full revelation of God, and the manifestation of man as God intends man to be. He is the Mediator because of this oneness.[74]

In dealing with God on behalf of human beings Christ, as portrayed by Campbell in *The Nature of the Atonement* is the one who made 'a perfect confession of our sins.'[75] The coherence of such an idea has been considered already but it is important to

---

[72] *FofT*, 21. 'Conformity to the Son, the good promised to them that love God.'
[73] *Ibid.*, 21.252f.
[74] *Ibid.*, 10.103-4.
[75] *Nature*, 117 (118).

see signs of this idea in other parts of Campbell's work. In a further reflection upon Romans 8:28-30 he asserts that although 'Christ had no personal history of sin such as we have; He was holy, yet when He took our nature on Him, He felt the pressure of the circumstances we had brought upon ourselves; He confessed our sins, He bore our sorrows...'[76] As will be shown later in this chapter the seeds of this idea can be located much earlier during his period at Row.[77]

An important dimension of the prospective aspect of *The Nature of the Atonement* is the intercession of Jesus as the Great High Priest.[78] This note is sounded clearly in the Row sermons and is present in a talk about 'The purged conscience' where Campbell says of Jesus that 'He is the High Priest of redeemed humanity.'[79] The High Priest's prayer that his confession will be 'reproduced in us' has sometimes been seen as proof of Campbell's 'exemplarism'. In his second study on Romans 8:28-30, Campbell leaves his hearers and readers in no doubt, that when it comes to salvation the initiative is firmly in divine hands.

> I have deep sympathy with those whose minds are most occupied with God's part in the work of man's salvation. It is an evil thing to suppose that man may save himself, if he will and when he will; — to make man's will the power whereby he is to be saved; or to think of faith in any way but as the gift of God, inwrought by the operation of His Holy Spirit... "Work out your own salvation with fear and trembling, because it is God who worketh in you." We work out our salvation when we yield to God's Spirit instead of following our own spirit, when we lay hold of His strength, and welcome His power to save.[80]

In this way Campbell demonstrates an evangelical understanding of repentance, because he avoids the introspection and legalism embodied in the 'Practical Syllogism', and makes clear that salvation is based entirely upon the grace of God.

---

[76] *FofT*, 22.264.
[77] Cf., *S&L* 2.28.238 / *NofS*, 2.23.8.
[78] *Nature*, 143, 150f., 160, 167, 168, 172 (136, 141f., 147, 151, 152, 155).
[79] *FofT*, 15.176.
[80] *Ibid.*, 22.271-2.

Fragments Common to the 1843 and the 1861/1898 Editions

Turning to another layer of material we discover the objective nature of atonement being emphasized in a sermon 'On Regeneration' which contrasts new birth with the natural birth of a child. Whereas the baby has no choice but to be born, when it comes to being born again this is, to some extent, dependent upon the will and choice of the individual. He seems to be aware of the criticism that this might diminish God's role in regeneration and is at pains to point out that human beings cannot regenerate themselves. In two footnotes he defends himself against misinterpretation by saying

> Not that the will of man is the primary cause of regeneration; but that man may either resist or co-operate with the will of God, which would have all men to be saved, and which striveth in all men, against the darkness and corruption of their fallen nature. In confirmation of this, compare John i.11,12, and John iii,19...We have not to beget life within ourselves — it is *given* to us. We have only to yield to it. Life and death are put before us. Life in Christ — death in following the old Adam. We are called to *choose* Life that we may live.[81]

The objective nature of the atonement is underlined from another angle when Campbell reflects upon the way in which Christ can be seen as our brother. In the introduction he added to *The Nature of the Atonement* in 1868, Campbell expressed Christ's identification with humanity in terms of 'perfect Brotherhood towards men'.[82] This imprecise christological terminology is rooted in Hebrews 2 which portrays Jesus Christ as the one who has been made like his brothers in every way.[83] In the first of the Fragments this idea is visible in Campbell's assertion that, whether people like it or not, Christ has established a real connection with them by virtue of his becoming our brother.

> Have you every felt your mind arrested by the simple fact, that Jesus Christ the Son of God, is the Son of Man? That He, who is the Eternal Word, who dwelt from eternity in the bosom of the Father, was made flesh, became the Son of Man, was born your brother? Have you ever felt the difference between a race thus connected with the Lord Jehovah and all

---

[81] *Ibid.*, 13. Footnotes on pages 133 & 134.
[82] *Nature*, xvii (19).
[83] Heb. 2:17, and 2:11-2.

other created things? Have you ever felt the difference between being merely created by God, and being thus related to Him? It is manifest that every part of the history of such a race must, in the eye of God, be connected with this great event, — God made flesh.[84]

Campbell affirms without explanation that God has thus established a real connection with the human race. As by birth I am related to the other members of my family, so Jesus is related to the whole human family by sharing in our human birth. Something fixed and objective has taken place because 'whatever Christ is to us He is by birth; we cannot make or change the relation. He is our Brother.'[85]

In a sermon on 2 Corinthians 1:3-7[86] Campbell suggests that while Jesus experiences the same sorts of sufferings as others he received those sufferings in a different way.

Now, how does Jesus receive the suffering? First, — He receives it as the righteous reward of sin, the wages of sin which is death. He does not rebel or kick against it, therefore, but says, "Thou art righteous, O Lord, because Thou hast judged thus." And this righteousness of feeling in Christ, this willingness that transgression shall meet with its due reward, even when He himself stands in the transgressor's room, is well-pleasing in the sight of Him who loveth righteousness; and, therefore, He gives this beloved Son to taste in His heart, even in the midst of sorrow the joy of this oneness of mind with Himself. This is one of the ways in which God comforts Christ.[87]

Although expressed in different language, what is being described here is Christ making a perfect confession of sin, offering *'a perfect Amen in humanity to the judgement of God on the sin of man'*.[88] In this sermon there is also a rejection of a penal interpretation of Christ's sufferings because Christ endures the pain of the cross in the conviction that such suffering is not an arbitrary punishment but the only way to destroy sin and take it out of circulation.[89]

---

[84] *FofT*, 1.3-4.
[85] *Ibid.*, 1.13.
[86] *Ibid.*, 26. 'The Consolations of Christ'
[87] *Ibid.*, 26.298-9.
[88] *Nature*, 117 (118).
[89] *FofT*, 26.298 'Christ receives suffering as the wise and perfect remedy, appointed by a tender father, for the recovery of His children from an

Fragments Unique to the 1843 Edition

James Goodloe understandably suggests that the nine sermons 'which did not get carried into the 1861 edition must have been thought to have had less immediate significance than the others.'[90] The preface to the third edition in 1861 expressed the hope that perhaps they could be included in a second volume of addresses; but such a volume never materialised. While they may not be theological classics this group of sermons possibly takes us closest to the beginnings of Campbell's ministry in Glasgow. One address for the New Year alludes to the fact that 'in this place we have now for nearly a year meditated together, and received instruction on divine things.'[91] This seems to refer to January 1834, which marked a year since he had started his ministry at the Lyceum Hall in Glasgow in January 1833.[92] It is not surprising to find that the ex-pastor of Row remarked that the first principle he had proclaimed was the love of God for all and not just for the elect.

> You have had set before you the character of God as *Love*, and your attention has been directed to the manifestation of that love to *man*, — not to the elect, or to the redeemed, but to man — to that humanity which God created, and which He would not lose; which He intended to be in His own image; from which men are fallen, it is true, but to which they are more than restored in the Lord Jesus Christ.[93]

The outworking of this love is to create an objective atonement because 'the Gospel, or "God's spell" which in our old Saxon is the meaning of the word — God's spell is the only spell — the only power strong enough to free man from evil, by

---

otherwise incurable disease; and in this view, also, He does not rebel against it, but says, "The cup that my Father hath given me shall I not drink it?" He recognises the purpose of love in the suffering, and therefore will have nothing to do with the deceitful baits of the tempter, whose desire is to make that purpose void, and who snatches from us the bitter but salutary draught, that he may substitute for it a sweetened cup of poison.'

[90] Goodloe, 'Transformation of the Religious Consciousness', 76.
[91] *FofE*, 19.277.
[92] Another possible date would be January 1838, which would be the first new year after the congregation had moved into their new premises in Blackfriars Street. However as the opening services for the new building took place on 17 September 1837 it seems less likely that, after four months, Campbell would say that they had been meeting there for 'nearly a year.'
[93] *Ibid.*, 19.281.

Campbell the Preacher

bringing him into harmony with the law of his being.'[94] Such an objective restoration of the divine image in humanity echoes Irenaeus' teaching 'that what we had lost in Adam, that is, the being in the image and likeness of God,...we should regain in Christ Jesus.'[95]

In *The Nature of the Atonement*, Campbell sees salvation originating in the Fatherliness of God.[96] The longstanding nature of this idea within Campbell's thought is evident in his claim, in a sermon on 2 Timothy 1:8-10,[97] that creation itself only makes sense in the light of a Father's love.

> The nearest idea, perhaps, that we can form of the thought of God's heart in creation, is through that shadowing forth of it which is in the paternal heart, which not only delights in seeking the good, and itself constituting the happiness of the objects of its affection, but longs for offspring on whom this love may rest, with an intenseness which only they who have felt it can fully conceive. Such a feeling as this in the heart of God can alone account for the creation of man at all.[98]

The divine purpose for human beings is revealed in Christ by processes of refraction and reflection. The light of God's purpose has been refracted through the person of Christ to reveal what God is like. The light which shone through Christ also shone upon him, and in the light reflected from Christ, God's idea for humanity comes to light.[99] So here in another layer of Campbell's sermons we recognise the idea of Christ revealing the truth about God and humanity.

Campbell's key to the atonement reappears in these sermons as well. So in an exposition of Romans 12.1-2,[100] he reflects on Psalm 40 with its emphasis upon doing the will of God. He is aware of those Old Testament passages which remind Israel that without the inner attitude of obedience all their sacrifices are an empty sham. Although all people are called to demonstrate an attitude of obedience to God it is with the coming of the Messiah

---

[94] *Ibid.*, 18.269. Cf., 18.273 'It is by the infusion of this divine life, that we are delivered from the power of the flesh and its evil workings.'
[95] Irenaeus, *Adversus Haereses*, III. xviii.1, in Henry Bettenson, (ed.), *Documents of the Christian Church*, (Oxford: OUP, 1963²), 30.
[96] *Nature*, 295-7 (241-2).
[97] *FofE*, 12 'The Purpose of God for Man Revealed in Christ Jesus.'
[98] *Ibid.*, 12.170.
[99] *Ibid.*, 12.172-3.
[100] *Ibid.*, 15. 'Renewal of heart, the only source of real transformation of character.'

that the ideal begins to be realised. 'Assuredly Christ is the speaker, yet when He says, "I delight to do thy will," it is as *man* that He speaks.'[101] This emphasis upon Christ offering obedience as man is theologically important for it points to a victory over sin which is at the same time both divine and human. The victory of obedience over sin had to be accomplished within a truly human context and not simply imposed divinely from outside.[102] By emphasizing the saving significance of Christ's obedience 'as *man*' Campbell anticipates Barth's depiction of 'Jesus Christ, the Servant as Lord.'[103] Within Barth's portrayal it is Jesus as the true man, the royal man, who brings humanity to exaltation and salvation through his obedience to God's will. According to Barth

> Jesus is the man in whose human being and thinking and willing and speaking and acting there takes place the grateful affirmation of the grace of God addressed to the human race and the whole created cosmos — an affirmation which we all owe but none of us makes. He is the man who (like us in His creatureliness and fleshliness, at all points our Brother) does not break but keeps the covenant of God with His people in the action of His life...But the action of His life as it begins with the commencement of His being as man is one long invasion and conquest of this opposition and tension. And as this invader and conqueror He is the man who is faithful both to God and therefore also to Himself, the man who is

---

[101] *Ibid.*, 15.224.

[102] The need for this victory to be accomplished under genuinely human conditions is the basis of Colin Gunton's assessment that Aulén's portrayal of the victory accomplished by *Christus Victor* overlooked the fact 'that the victory charted in the New Testament is as much human as divine.' Endorsing G. B. Caird's observation 'that the victory is achieved by obedience' he goes on to suggest that 'it is the refusal to succumb to temptation that is Jesus' victory.' There are firm biblical grounds for interpreting the cross as a victory providing that it is remembered that 'the victory is at once human and divine — a divine victory only because it is a human one — and although the synoptic gospels do not explicitly describe the ministry of Jesus as a victory, they clearly see it as in part a conflict between the authority of God represented by Jesus and that which would deny it.' Gunton, *Actuality of Atonement*, 579.

[103] K. Barth, *Church Dogmatics*, vol. IV, part 2, (Edinburgh: T & T Clark, 1958), 3-377.

reconciled with God, the true man, and in relation to all the rest the new man.'[104]

In expounding 1 John 1:1 – 2:11, Campbell defines true confession as 'putting away the old life, ceasing to justify it, consenting to the sentence of God upon it.'[105] The person of Christ is not directly in view but when he goes on to talk in *The Nature of the Atonement* about Christ making a perfect confession, it will be a confession consenting to the sentence of God upon the sinful humanity he had identified himself with.

The evidence examined thus far indicates that key elements of Campbell's mature theology can be detected in sermons from the different stages of his ministerial career in Glasgow. On its own, however, this evidence is not enough to prove that Campbell was a consistent thinker. It might be argued that it is not surprising to find such elements in sermons which are fairly close in time to the period when Campbell was writing *The Nature of the Atonement*. If it can be shown that similar elements are present within the much earlier Row sermons then this would give weight to the argument that the basic theological approach remained consistent over a considerable period of time.

The Row Sermons and *The Nature of the Atonement*

The sermons from the final period of Campbell's ministry at Row, 1829-1831, inevitably cover an untidy bundle of topics and do not provide a systematic treatment of key doctrines. At many points the reader is made aware of the passions stirred up by the disciplinary proceedings designed to stop the 'Row heresy' in its tracks. However, in the midst of all of this material it is possible to detect many of the key themes which Campbell would continue to explore throughout his ministry.

The Whole Counsel of God

In an undated sermon considering 'The whole counsel of God'[106] Campbell sets out to explain the complete counsel of God which he has not withheld from his hearers. For ministers the temptation exists to hold back some uncomfortable truths, but he is certain that he has given them the truth and nothing

---

[104] *Ibid.*, 30. Cf., 51.
[105] *FofE*, 9.155.
[106] *S&L*, 1.18.

but the truth. Although he does not identify numbered 'points' to help his congregation follow his sermon, there are eight topics which he draws particular attention to. Clearly he felt that this summed up much of his teaching and it, therefore, seems to be an appropriate place to begin the process of considering which elements from this period were carried through into his later ministry.

It comes as no surprise that the first topic he highlights is the conviction that God is love. 'God has been declared in scripture to be love. This has been declared to you — not as a form of speech — of words without a reality of meaning, but as the real truth concerning God — that God is love — that the motive of God's actions is love — that the reason why God has not ceased to be alone in the universe is because God is love — and the original of every plan in the mind of God is this, that God is love.'[107] He takes some time to argue that every event in providence speaks of God's love. Such love not only reveals the character of God but if He lavishes such care on people then this gives dignity and value to human beings.[108]

This perspective on humanity must be taken along with the second main theme of his preaching which is that 'you are sinners.'[109] In a recent review of the re-issue of *The Nature of the Atonement*, Dean Turbeville provocatively asserts that 'much of what presently troubles the peace and purity of the church can be found in its nascent form in Campbell's writing.'[110] One of the 'errors' he alleges is present in Campbell's thinking is a 'denial of the radical depravity of the human soul.' The evidence presented in the previous chapter refutes such a superficial analysis of a complex piece of writing. His sermons demonstrate that Campbell the preacher was in no doubt about the radical depravity of human beings. The depth of this alienation is such that sinful people shrink from the message that God is love in order to escape 'from the consciousness of utter baseness, and

---

[107] *Ibid.*, 1.18.418.
[108] *Ibid.*, 1.18.424 'We are as nothing when compared with God; but we are of exceeding great importance, if our importance is to be marked by the feeling of God concerning us. We are of no value in the sense in which men put on themselves a value which gratifies pride — we are utterly nothing in this respect — but we are very precious if our value is to be measured by God's care of us, and by God's feeling for us.'
[109] *Ibid.*, 1.18.428
[110] Dean Turbeville, 'Review of *The Nature of the Atonement*, by J. McLeod Campbell, Eerdmans, Grand Rapids, 1996', *Interpretation* 52 (1998) 98-9.

Campbell the Preacher

ingratitude, and sin.'[111] In our natural state, he argues, 'we are naturally perfectly deaf to the voice of God.'[112] The preacher charged with the heavy responsibility to declare the whole counsel of God needs 'to declare that in you there dwelleth no good thing — it is to declare that the whole natural man is a mass of iniquity...that man in his natural state is altogether condemned of God.'[113] This bleak diagnosis is repeated in another sermon where he says that each child of Adam is one 'whose nature is corrupted and depraved, whose whole being is a state of rebellion against God.'[114] Far from having an over optimistic view of human nature, Campbell's diagnosis tends to be rather sober and gloomy. Whilst Turbeville's attack is aimed at *The Nature of the Atonement* in particular, it represents a grossly distorted caricature of Campbell's approach.

Campbell's sober description of human depravity is mercifully not the end of the story, because the good news is that Christ died for all. The minister who was being called to account, for preaching the universal extent of the atonement, wasted no opportunity to proclaim this part of his credo.[115] The argument he follows at this point is very similar to the approach expressed twenty five years later in *The Nature of the Atonement*,[116] for he argues that Christ's death for the elect alone is insufficient to prove that God is love.

> If there are some whom God does love, and others whom God does not love — if the manifestation of God in Christ be the expression of a love which embraces only some men, then, if

---

[111] *S&L*, 1.18.419.
[112] *Ibid.*, 1.18.419.
[113] *Ibid.*, 1.18.428.
[114] *EG*, 13. 'It means that I — a child of Adam, born under sin, under the power of iniquity, whose nature is corrupted and depraved, whose whole being is a state of rebellion against God — am called to be not only different from, but to be just the opposite of, what I am.' Similarly see *NofS* 2.Valedictory Address 'You all know that I have fully and openly set forth this truth, that you are born in sin and that our nature is corrupted and that we grow up under a load of sinful flesh which is enmity against God.'
[115] See e.g., *GT*, 8.16. '"I bring you good tidings of great joy which shall be *to all people.*" And God would have you understand that this universality is part of the *goodness* of the good news — for God would have you feel that unless it were for all, it would not be enough to comfort you.'
[116] *Nature*, 56 (74). 'I am unable to see any way out here, or any escape from the conclusion that the doctrine of an atonement for the elect only, destroys the claim of the work of Christ to be what fully reveals and illustrates the great foundation of all religion, that God is love.'

you would attempt to prove from Christ's having died for the elect that God is love, I might equally prove from the supposition of God's having created others for misery and damnation that God is hatred; and the proof would be just as strong that God was hatred from the one, as that he was love from the other.[117]

Although he does not talk about the 'prospective aspect of the atonement' at this stage of his ministry, the same perspective is present in the next element of the whole counsel of God he has been proclaiming. He reminds his hearers that he has consistently taught them 'that it is the desire of God concerning men that we should be heirs of God — that we should be the children of God — that we should be sons and daughters of the Most High.'[118] There is a consistency of both thought and language over the years, because in 1856 he wrote about 'what it was the desire of the divine love that we should become.'[119] The purpose of Christ's sufferings was not simply to remove sin and guilt but to lead to our participation in eternal life. In other words the divine purpose is 'that we should receive the adoption of sons.'[120]

Campbell next draws attention to a topic which plays a less visibly prominent role within *The Nature of the Atonement*. In his preaching he has regularly outlined 'as the true condition of the Christian, that he has the Spirit of the living God in him — that he is and knows himself to be an heir of God — and that now having the place of a son, he is hereafter to be manifested as a son, and is to reign a king upon this earth.'[121] Such language raises questions about the role of the Spirit in Campbell's theology as a whole. His involvement in the Gareloch pentecost has been noted earlier,[122] and the conviction that Christ 'has the Spirit for you' is a frequent theme in the Row sermons. However, as Campbell resisted invitations to join the Catholic Apostolic Church which emerged partly out of Edward Irving's charismatic ministry,[123] it might be asked whether the Spirit diminished in importance in Campbell's thinking as the years passed. Such a conclusion is inaccurate, however, because the

---

[117] *S&L* 1.18.430.
[118] *Ibid.*, 1.18.432.
[119] *Nature*, 130 (127)
[120] *Ibid.*, 132 (128), where Campbell is referring to Galatians 4:5.
[121] *S&L*, 1.18.433.
[122] See Chapter 1. Factors contributing to his dismissal.
[123] *Memorials*, 1.115-125; and 2.153-4.

wider Campbell corpus illustrates that there continued to be a definite pneumatological dimension to his thinking. Thus in *Thoughts on Revelation*, published in 1862, he asserted the activity of the Spirit in the work of revelation and salvation. For 'if Christianity cannot be realised in us apart from our relation to the Father and the Son, no more can it apart from our relation to the Holy Spirit.'[124] Within the second edition of *Christ the Bread of Life*, published near the end of his life in 1869, he stressed the 'action of the Holy Spirit on the spirits of the faithful' during communion.[125] Such evidence, drawn from the different strata of Campbell's work, further confirms the basic coherence of his theological approach, and indicates that he did not withdraw from an orthodox trinitarian understanding of the work of the Spirit. As chapter 7 will show, Campbell advocated a 'classical trinitarian Spirit christology' which did not merge the identities of the Risen Christ and the Holy Spirit.[126] This implies that a proper recognition of the work of the Spirit is essential to an adequate understanding of *The Nature of the Atonement*, even if Campbell does not make this explicit within the book itself.

Next on Campbell's list is a topic which does not play a prominent role in his later published work for he explains that he has not shunned to declare 'the future prospect of the wicked.'[127] In part he is defending himself against those critics who argued that his stress on God's universal love must lead inevitably to universalism, but he is also here implying 'the fixed and necessary character of salvation'[128] God has provided everything necessary for life and godliness for all without compromising his holy intolerance of sin. Through the gift of his Son he has made it possible not only for people to be forgiven but also for them to be transformed, to be made holy. Those who choose not to be made holy must therefore perish, because the distinction between good and evil remains in God's character, and in God's dealing with people. So if there is to be condemnation at a future judgement it will arise, 'not from lack of love in God, but from sin in man.'[129] This is similar to his later stress upon the way in which wrath originates in the divine

---

[124] *TR*, 136. See also 59, 77, 79-80, 82-5, 95, 118-120, 130, 141, 192-4.
[125] *Bread2*, 173.
[126] See Chapter 7. *The Son who gives the Spirit*.
[127] *S&L*, 1.18.433.
[128] *Nature*, 166 (151).
[129] *S&L*, 1.18.435.

love.[130] Talk of future judgement may be less evident in *The Nature of the Atonement*, but it shares with these sermons this underlying sense that there is a fixed and necessary character to the way in which God's universe operates.

Eschatology and pneumatology combine in the penultimate theme he identifies in this sermon. As a foretaste of his future kingdom God has provided 'an earnest of the inheritance' which consists of the gifts of the Holy Spirit.

> I refer to what I have taught you on the subject of the gifts of the Spirit, and the power of the Holy Ghost, as the Spirit of Christ dwelling in the members of the body of Christ, which was manifested in the early history of the New Testament church — but has usually ceased in the church for so long a period. I have not shunned to declare to you that it was never the purpose of God to recal (*sic*) these gifts — that they are an earnest of the inheritance; and that, having been an earnest of the inheritance, they are, just like the inheritance itself, a thing for all — a thing for every period.[131]

Campbell claims that he was stating 'these doctrines much in the order in which they have been pressed on your attention.'[132] It would appear from his comments in April 1830 that he had adopted this teaching some time late in 1827 or early in 1828.[133] In the final section of this sermon he identifies convictions which he had come to at a later date, but which now formed the bedrock of his preaching.

> The last subject with which I have occupied your attention, is that which, properly speaking, is the foundation of every thing else, I mean the subject of our Lord's humanity — the subject of our Lord's having taken our nature, just as we have it — flesh and blood, just as it exists in you and me. Though this is the last in the order in which I have myself been

---

[130] *Nature*, 127 (125).
[131] *S&L*, 1.18.435.
[132] *Ibid.*, 1.18.435-6.
[133] Newell, 'A. J. Scott and His Circle', 37, 77-9, 92. Newell quotes from a letter Campbell wrote to Chalmers on 28 April 1830 (New College MS, CHA. 4.134.21). 'Personally it has been my faith in this department of truth for two years and upwards that the gifts enjoyed by the first Christians were *not* characteristic of *that time but of this present dispensation* and therefore possessed in right of God's gift by the church *all along and on until the second coming of Christ, however,* through lack of faith in that right, they have in point of fact been unsought and unenjoyed.'

instructed, yet it is the foundation truth of all — the foundation of all the rest.'[134]

This doctrine will be examined more fully in chapter 4, but at this point it is appropriate to note that he sees connections between the 'subject of our Lord's humanity' and his role as the High Priest and as the coming judge. The link with judgement here is that by virtue of Christ's coming in our flesh he has effectively condemned sin. Here we encounter an idea which is widespread both in the Row sermons, and in *The Nature of the Atonement*, that by his total obedience to God, under fully human conditions, Christ has effectively condemned human sin.[135] His obedience exposes the fact that men and women choose to disobey God. By assuming a fully human nature and by offering perfect obedience to God, Christ has shown that temptation can be overcome by the power of the Holy Spirit.

Campbell repeats this idea on a number of other occasions such as the sermon entitled 'The confidence of hope', where he says that

> Christ condemned sin, not only by being the opposite of sin, but by giving himself as a sin-offering to God — by submitting to feel and experience the wrath and curse of God, due to us for sin — by submitting to feel the curse that was upon us. Now, this was more than merely proving to us that there was no excuse for our sin; it proved to us the righteousness of God's curse upon sin.[136]

Christ as 'The Great Confessor'

In his dealing with men and women on behalf of God, Christ's unity with God expressed itself in this condemnation of sin; and in his dealing with God on behalf of humanity his sharing the divine perspective on our sin took the form of a perfect confession of our sins.[137] This retrospective aspect of atonement comes to the surface in a striking form in a sermon on 'Confession and Forgiveness' where Campbell portrays Christ as 'the great confessor' of the world's sin.

---

[134] *S&L*, 1.18.437.
[135] *Ibid.*, 1.18.438.
[136] *Ibid.*, 1.13.303. 'The confidence of hope' preached at Row on 13 April 1831.
[137] *Nature*, 116-7 (118).

Now how was Christ in the world? As the great confessor of its sin. He was in the world as condemning sin in the flesh. Above all he died and suffered – he expressed his Amen to God's righteous sentence upon sin. Now this is to have the mind of Christ, that we should confess the sin that is in mankind as Christ confessed it. There is this difference between Christ and us, that Christ, being perfectly holy had not personal sin to confess. But we have the mind of Christ concerning sin when we see our sin as Christ sees it and feel about it as Christ felt and confess our sin as Christ for us confessed it. Now this is the thing that gives boldness, in a day of judgement that when God comes to destroy sin there is not a feeling in the heart of the person whom God is about to justify that runs counter to God's judgement: but every feeling in his heart says Amen to God's judgement – he feels that it is most proper and desirable that all other happenings should be put an end to.[138]

This extract is rich with striking anticipations of what Campbell would later have to say about both the retrospective and prospective aspects of atonement. Michael Jinkins observes that 'this is the only place in Campbell's early recorded sermons in which he specifically uses the phrase which would become so characteristic for him in later years.'[139] Whilst Christ is not described as the 'great confessor' of human sin in any other of the Row sermons, the idea embodied in that phrase is visible in many places. Within this sermon the retrospective aspect of atonement, involving Christ dealing as High Priest with God on behalf of humanity, is also expressed when Campbell depicts Christ expressing 'his Amen to God's righteous sentence upon sin'. This idea is evident in several other sermons,[140] and it is clear that both in terms of ideas and language there is a clear anticipation of what Campbell would later write for publication in *The Nature of the Atonement*.[141] From this early stage in his ministry, Christ's confession of human sin is viewed as a key element in his understanding of atonement.

---

[138] *S&L* 2.28.238 and *NofS* 2.24.8. Cf., *FofT*, 22.264.
[139] Jinkins, *Atonement and the Character of God*, footnote on 270.
[140] See e.g., *S&L* 2.20.25 'Christ, in whom there was continually dwelling the truth of God's love, in the Psalms, *always* says Amen to God's future judgements.' *NofS* 3.29.5 'This state of mind before God which I have now described as the *confessing of sin*, and as *the commending of righteousness* is the *Amen of the heart to God's judgement of evil* and *to God's judgement of good*.'
[141] *Nature*, 117 (118).

The prospective dimension is also apparent here, because as well as describing how the sinless High Priest vicariously confesses the sins of others, there is the clear intention that Christ's confession, and his attitude to sin, will take root in human hearts, so that people are similarly able to say 'Amen to God's judgement' on sin. The fact that this emphasis can be detected in other sermons from this period,[142] tends to indicate that the stress upon Christ's confession being 'reproduced in us'[143] had been thought through by the young preacher of Row long before the publication of *The Nature of the Atonement*.

The Sufferings of Christ

In *The Nature of the Atonement* Campbell would argue that if atonement is seen in its own light then it will be necessary to move from a penal to a moral interpretation of the sufferings of Christ. The mature author and the young preacher both use similar language to express unease with strictly penal understandings of the cross. The youthful preacher highlights the issues in the following way.

> Is it because of the amount of pain and of agony endured? That, alas! is the feeling that many have about the cross of Christ; but I ask you, is it the existence of the mere pain that God has built so much upon? Is it the existence of mere pain and agony, call it ever so great — and it was great, it was infinite! — but is it the existence of pain in the human nature of Christ that a God of love builds all this upon? It is impossible. It cannot be. What was it then? It was the righteousness of the sacrifice — the holiness of the blood — the purity of all the groans, and of all the tears, and of all the pain which Christ endured — it was because, in that sacrifice, God's eternal law of love was magnified and made honourable — because sin was condemned in our flesh —

---

[142] *GT*, 2.5 'It is this discovery of the character of God, that He so loved me while I was at enmity against Him, that works love in me to Him, and puts me in a condition to share in His condemnation of sin, and makes me hate the evil thing in me that He hates...' *NofS* 2.16.8 'When the Christian confesses his sins, he is not confessing them simply as *facts* but *as things which he feels*. And in respect of which he shares in God's feelings. My recognition of the righteousness of God's condemnation of sin is in the confession of sin. When it is really confession, and saying, "Forgive me", it is as pure a thing as the joy of the Lord.'
[143] *Nature*, 153 (142).

because the feelings with which the eternal God regards sin were then expressed in the groans and agonies of Jesus — it was therefore that God could make it the foundation of all these things — because in it, God's love to sinners — because in it, God's hatred of sin, — were brought out and expressed; and the Eternal Word did declare the Eternal Father, in that he became flesh, and gave his flesh and his blood — gave himself to death for the life of the world — and thus God was manifested.[144]

When the mature author came to consider this theme the basic framework remained the same, but the wisdom of years enabled him to encapsulate it rather more succinctly![145]

An Objective Love

At each stage in his career Campbell was keen to insist that the atonement was not needed to make God love people, but was the outworking of the prior love of God.[146] He makes this clear in a sermon entitled 'Christ's Invitation and Promise'[147] where he says, 'Carry this along with you, and let no man deceive you, and do not imagine that Christ, the Son, came to change the Father; he came to reveal the Father — he did not come to make God kind, but to show us God's kindness.'[148] It is this prevenient love which generates a response.

In a sermon on 'Humility and contrition'[149] Campbell argues that God is pleased when He sees people 'sharing in his own condemnation of sin.'[150] However, he is clear that salvation is

---

[144] *S&L*, 1.18.306-7.

[145] *Nature*, 102 (107) 'The sufferings of Christ in making His soul an offering for sin being what they were, was it the pain as pain, and as a penal affliction, or was it the pain as a condition and form of holiness and love under the pressure of our sin and its consequent misery, that is presented to our faith as the essence of the sacrifice and its atoning virtue?

[146] See e.g., *Ibid.*, 17.

[147] *S&L*, 2.22.

[148] *Ibid.*, 2.22.76. Cf., *NofS* 1.4.3 'The love of God is not excited, is not produced by anything in the creature but is the origin of creation and the origin of redemption. It came forth even whilst we were dead in trespasses and sins.' *NofS* 3.34.4 'The work of God in Christ was not to make God a kind or loving Father: but to reveal to us a Father's heart and to recall us to the bosom of a Father's love.'

[149] *S&L*, 1.5.

[150] *Ibid.*, 1.5.90.

not dependent upon human humility and contrition, for it is the salvation accomplished by Christ, which enables us to discern our sinfulness and share in God's condemnation of it. The divine love which originates salvation is much more than an inspiring example because the person who rejoices in God knows that 'this love has not been a powerless love, has not been merely a great love but an effectual love; a love that hath provided all that he needeth, for he knows that Christ hath the Spirit for him.'[151]

In a sermon on Titus 2:11-14[152] he makes it clear that he is not advocating any kind of exemplarism. When the Bible calls upon people to be holy,

> It is not calling upon you to imitate Christ as you would imitate a man such as I am. It is not saying, 'ere is the example of perfection: walk ye after this example and be ye perfect.' There is this great difference, that it is Christ in you that is to make you what Christ was...if his holiness was through the Eternal Spirit — then it is quite clear that we need the same Spirit in order to our being holy; so when our Lord shows us holiness in our condition, he is not saying, 'ou may be holy if you please in your own strength' but he teaches us that there is none good but God, and that you may be holy if you walk in the Spirit — you may be holy if God dwell in you, and work in you.[153]

By denying any innate human ability to save ourselves, and by saying that new life is only possible when God dwells within human nature, Campbell is declaring the need for an objective intervention by God. The only hope for corrupt human beings is for God to bring about a new creation which will enable them to live in this new way.

Christ the Revealer

In *The Nature of the Atonement* Campbell sees the Son of God as the one who reveals the truth about God and human beings made in God's image.[154] This note was sounded many years previously, in what is probably the earliest of his sermons to be

---

[151] *Ibid.*, 1.5.102.
[152] *NofS*, 3.31.
[153] *Ibid.*, 3.31.4-5.
[154] *Nature*, 138 (132).

recorded, where the first truth to be confessed concerned the nature of the God-man.[155]

> Jesus Christ, in his person and being as God-man, and in his history, both in his humiliation and in his exaltation, is the revelation of God and of man; discovering what God is, and what man is, and what God is to man, and what man is to God; so that to him that believeth on Christ the truth is known on these subjects.'[156]

Thus appears another doctrinal area where it is evident that Campbell held consistent views over a long period of time.

Conclusion

This survey supports the claim that Campbell's key theological ideas were already present in his early preaching by demonstrating that there are significant points of contact between *The Nature of the Atonement* and the sermons from his ministry in Glasgow. In addition it has become evident that many of his core ideas are visible within the Row sermons, preached twenty five years before the publication of his best known book.

The repetition of common themes in the Row sermons, the Glasgow *Fragments* and in *The Nature of the Atonement* points towards the conclusion that there is a consistency of thought that persists over at least a quarter of a century. It is also possible to notice the ways in which those common themes were worked on over the years. It seems reasonable to conclude with Drummond and Bulloch that during the period between his deposition and the writing of *The Nature of the Atonement*, 'his thought had developed greatly, but it had not substantially altered.'[157] If his theology had not 'substantially altered,' then surely the larger Campbell *corpus* needs to be taken into account in any consideration of his theology. In particular it implies that *The Nature of the Atonement* should not be read in isolation from the rest of his work. Failure to appreciate the wider theological context provided by his sermons has contributed to distorted and inaccurate assessments of Campbell's theology; and by

---

[155] *GT*, 5 'Confessing Christ.' Essay delivered to a clerical society in Glasgow, early in December 1828.
[156] *Ibid.*, 5.3.
[157] Drummond and Bulloch, *The Scottish Church*, 208.

examining the content of his preaching this study seeks to contribute to the necessary reappraisal of his theology.

Chapter 4

The Flesh of Christ Differed Not in One Particle from Mine

Over 60 years ago Eugene Bewkes suggested that Campbell 'did not have any well thought out Christology to support his faith doctrine until some years after the Row episode. But when he did arrive at it, it made more clear the fact that he had very early grasped the fundamental elements of Christian faith.'[1] The claim that Campbell did not have a coherent christology during his eventful ministry at Row is called into question by the fact that a pastoral admonition was circulated, early in 1833, warning congregations about his erroneous teaching on various topics, including the humanity of the Lord.[2] If, amongst other things, the Presbytery of Lorn felt it necessary to warn people against aspects of Campbell's christology, then this implies that his approach was sufficiently well thought out to be recognised and criticised. This suspicion is quickly confirmed by an examination of the Row sermons which reveals that they contain a significant amount of christological material which Bewkes' assessment overlooks.

The material examined in this chapter will demonstrate that, from the earliest stages of his ministry, Campbell had a coherent christology. Statements about the humanity of Christ are woven into sermons on a variety of topics. In order to interpret these statements accurately and in context, it will be necessary to provide a brief exposition of the themes being addressed in particular sermons. Far from being a peripheral aspect of his theology, Campbell argues that this topic represents the core of the gospel he preached. Indeed he claims that the subject of our Lord's humanity functions as the foundation of 'the whole counsel of God' which he has not shirked from declaring to his parishioners.[3] Without compromising belief in the eternal nature

---

[1] Eugene Garrett Bewkes, *Legacy of a Christian mind*, 56.
[2] For further details see, Chapter 1. *Campbell's Orthodoxy is Called into Question.*
[3] *S&L*, 1.18. 413-441. See also Chapter 3. *The Whole Counsel of God*

of the divine Son, he affirms that the Son has assumed our nature in order to redeem it. This emphasis upon the Son assuming fallen human nature, which undergirds his soteriology, surfaces in a number of his early sermons.

The Subject of the Lord's Humanity

Christ Assumes our Sinful, Fallen Nature

The idea that Christ assumes *fallen* human nature is stated explicitly in a sermon based on Psalm 26.[4] There is an unconscious affirmation of Christ's pre-existence in Campbell's treatment of this text as he reminds his hearers that 'it is a Psalm of Christ.'[5] Viewed in this way the psalmist's plea, 'Judge me, O Lord' sheds light on the inner life of Christ as well as the life of faith. Such a prayer is appropriate on the lips of Christ because he offered total love and obedience to God at all times. Christ's sinlessness is assumed because he alone could look into his heart and say with conviction, 'I have never sinned.'[6] In stark contrast to this, our personal history involves not only being in the flesh but actively 'sowing to the flesh.' As Campbell draws out the differences between Christ's personal history and ours, he reveals a christology which maintains belief in the eternal divine nature of the Son while affirming that the Son has assumed the 'sinful, fallen nature of man'.

> What is Christ's personal history? That being God he became man – that being the second person in the Godhead he took the sinful fallen nature of man, and was found in form and fashion as a man – that he became a man, being still God, though he now had taken unto himself the nature of man – that as a man he did continually choose the good and reject the evil, and fulfilled all righteousness – and that that perfect holiness, which he had before he became man, was continued in his becoming man, and was never sullied through his becoming man: but that he was mighty to bring glory continually to the Father, and that he always presented himself a living sacrifice, holy and acceptable to God, so that having been without sin, when he came he continued without sin when he took our nature – he was without sin and did

---

[4] *NofS*, 2.21, preached at Row on 10th April 1831.
[5] *Ibid.*, 2.21.1.
[6] *Ibid.*, 2.21.2.

fulfil the righteous law of his Father. Then he did preserve the place in his Father's sight which he had before, of being the beloved Son in whom the Father was well pleased. As he was of one mind with the Father before he came into this world, so he continued of one mind with the Father during all the time of his sojourning upon this earth and he continues to be of one mind with the Father in that state in which he is now in our nature exalted to the right hand of God. This is his personal history.[7]

Campbell's language is imprecise but the heart of his message is clear. He is speaking about the second person of the triune God who did not assume some perfect version of human nature, but the 'sinful, fallen human nature' common to all. Whilst this assumption of fallen human nature represents divine humility, it is not a *kenosis* which empties him of deity for 'he became man, being still God'. Talk of Christ assuming not just 'fallen' but 'sinful' human nature immediately raises questions about the sinlessness of Christ. However, Campbell is in no doubt that within the context of fallen human nature Christ maintained his perfect holiness and was without sin. Whilst he does not here explicitly mention the work of the Holy Spirit, it is clear from his sermons in general that it is by the power of the Spirit that Christ is able to maintain this perfect holiness. Similarly it is the power of the Spirit of Christ which enables people to have the mind of Christ and to obey God. The righteous action of Christ has fulfilled the law on our behalf, and forgiveness is found in being included in the representative figure of Christ. 'This is the fact that through the work of God in Christ, through our being included under Christ, as our head, in his having fulfilled the law as our head, we are now in the condition that God is not imputing sin to any one of us.'[8]

In seeking to emphasize that Christ did not overcome temptation using divine advantages unavailable to others, Campbell stresses that it was 'as a man' that Christ continually chose good rather than evil. He makes the same point in a different way, in the next sermon to be considered here, when he asserts that 'it was not *as* God' that Christ resisted temptation.[9] The danger of such language is that it could give the impression that Christ alternated between operating 'as a man' and 'as God', or that the divine and human natures of

---

[7] *Ibid.*, 2.21.4.
[8] *Ibid.*, 2.21.4.
[9] *S&L*, 2.23.108; *NofS*, 1.8.7. Appendix 4.

Christ were able to operate independently of each other. Taken in isolation such phrases could lead to a Nestorian dualism which would undermine the dogma of two natures in the one person of Jesus Christ. However, when these expressions are placed within the larger context of Campbell's sermons it becomes clear that he does not fall into the trap of christological dualism. The unity of Christ's person is clearly conveyed when he affirms that 'Christ is a man while he is God,'[10] and when he urges his hearers to remember that Christ 'did not cease to be God…when he became man.'[11]

If such dangers can be guarded against, then something important can be affirmed by referring to what Christ does 'as a man'. In his consideration of impassibility Thomas Weinandy employs similar language arguing that 'within the Incarnation the Son of God never does anything as God. If he did, he would be acting as God *in a man*…All that Jesus did as the Son of God was done *as a man*…He may have raised Lazarus from the dead by his divine power or, better, by the power of the Holy Spirit, but it was, nonetheless, as a man that he did so.'[12] These comments are part of a philosophically complex account of incarnation and impassibility which is far removed from the language employed by the young preacher from Row. However, they illustrate that it is possible to speak of what the Son of God does 'as a man' without necessarily ending up with a dualistic understanding of the person of Christ.

From this sermon it emerges that for Campbell 'the subject of the Lord's humanity' meant that the Son of God assumed sinful, fallen human nature, and this impression is confirmed by material embedded in other sermons.

The Flesh of Christ Differed Not in One Particle from Mine

In a sermon[13] preached before the dispensation of the Lord's Supper, Campbell considers what is involved in the life of faith. At the outset he claims that there are two kinds of life which people may experience. On the one hand there is the life in the flesh where the hopes and aspirations arise from the nature inherited from our human parents. On the other there is a life

---

[10] *NofS*, 2.22.5.
[11] *S&L*, 1.13.300.
[12] Thomas G. Weinandy, *Does God Suffer?*, (Edinburgh: T & T Clark, 2000), 205.
[13] *S&L*, 2.23 and *NofS*, 1.8. Appendix 4.

which is inspired by the Holy Spirit. He sees this life embodied in the apostle Paul who had discovered that life in the Spirit was possible only as believers are crucified with Christ.

For Christ, crucifixion was the inevitable consequence of the incarnation, for 'He took our nature and it was under the curse because of sin; and so he came under the curse for us, and died under the operation of that curse in which he had voluntarily put himself.'[14] It is important to remember that 'when he speaks of being crucified with Christ, you are not to suppose that it is only the closing scene of the life of Jesus that is referred to; but that Christ through his whole life was crucifying the flesh. It was accounted of by him as a dead thing, because of sin; and he ever presented himself, through the eternal Spirit, without spot to God.'[15] Throughout his life Christ was engaged in a battle against the flesh, and in the power of the Spirit he ever was able to offer his flesh in perfect obedience to God. His crucifixion was not imposed upon him, but was his own voluntary deed.

Christ died as the head and representative of the human race. This representative role means that all are included in his death and resurrection and it implies that believers are intended to live a new life relying on the same Spirit who was at work in the process whereby Christ constantly crucified the flesh. True life involves crucifying the flesh, and refusing to allow natural human desires to dominate life. This is not some masochistic recipe for a miserable existence, because one kind of life is being replaced by the fuller life of the Spirit which flows from Christ. Campbell claims that in the case of the apostle Paul, and in the case of the Christian believer now, there is a real presence of Christ within the believer and within the church.

> As truly as Christ is in glory, so truly is he in every Christian. As truly as Christ is now at the right of the Majesty on high, so truly is he now present, in the Spirit, in every child of God. And he lives by Christ in him – not Christ thought of – not Christ contemplated, but Christ, the living Christ, at the right hand of God, actually as truly present in his body, as my blood is, at this moment, in my hand. Just as my hands and feet have in them the same blood that is in my heart, and it is all one blood, so the members of Christ's body have in them one Spirit, and that is Christ's Spirit; that Spirit which is now

---

[14] *S&L*, 2.23.94; *NofS*, 1.8.2. Appendix 4.
[15] *S&L*, 2.23.95; *NofS*, 1.8.2. Appendix 4. Cf., Calvin, *Institutes*, III. viii. 1, 'while he dwelt on earth he was not only tried by a perpetual cross but his whole life was nothing but a sort of perpetual cross'.

dwelling in the glorified head Christ Jesus, and which comes down upon them from this High Priest, as the oil poured on the head of Aaron ran down to the skirts of his garments.[16]

Such comments are further evidence of Campbell's place within a strongly Reformed tradition, for they echo the emphasis of Calvin in his comments about the sacraments. Although the body of Christ may be spatially present in heaven, he argues that there is a real participation in that body by 'the secret working of the Spirit, which unites Christ himself to us.'[17]

As Jesus presented himself spotless to God in the power of the Spirit, believers are also called to surrender themselves to God. It is entirely legitimate, Campbell argues, to portray Christ as an example for what it means for us to crucify the flesh and its desires, because the human nature of Christ was not different in kind from ours. The Son's assumption of fallen human nature is expressed strikingly when Campbell states that 'The flesh of Christ differed not in one particle from mine; but Christ did present his flesh, which was even my flesh, without spot to God through the eternal Spirit.'[18]

To say that 'the flesh of Christ differed not in one particle from mine' does not imply, as the pastoral admonition later suggested, that Campbell believed 'that our Lord's holiness was not immaculate.' Whilst Christ had assumed sinful flesh, and had therefore been open to genuine temptation, at every point he resisted those temptations and maintained an immaculate holiness. However, it is theoretically and practically very important to remember that when Christ resisted the temptations to sin he did so, not by virtue of being God, but as a human being living in constant dependence upon the power of the Spirit.

> Men will say Christ is God. Yes he is God; but it was not *as God* he did those things...If it was because he was God that he was what he was, and not through his humbling himself, and continually receiving the Spirit from the Father, then he was no example to me.[19]

---

[16] S&L, 2.23.102; NofS, 1.8.5. Appendix 4.
[17] Calvin, *Institutes,* IV. xvii. 31, 12.
[18] S&L, 2.23.109; NofS, 1.8.7. Appendix 4.
[19] S&L, 2.23.108; NofS, 1.8.7. Appendix 4. See also GT, 3.3. 'Christ emptied himself, doing nothing, not even his miracles as God, but all as the loving, confiding dependant upon his Father, that the Father might be glorified in the Son.'

Some of the issues relating to talk about what Christ does 'as God' have already been addressed. There is a pastoral aim at this point because Campbell wants his hearers to see that if Christ had relied upon special powers and privileges, which were his by right as the eternal Son of God, then he could not be a practical example to human beings who lack such resources. By assuming the same flesh as fallen humanity he serves as a prototype for the life of faith which crucifies the desires of the flesh in the power of the life-giving Spirit. Campbell is able to affirm the humanity of Christ fully because he understands the incarnation within a trinitarian framework, which allows the work of the Spirit to be fully acknowledged. The incarnate Son continually receives the Spirit from the Father, and the Spirit enables the Son to resist temptation and to crucify the flesh.[20] The Holy Spirit makes it possible for the Son to offer this flesh 'without spot to God'[21] as a perfect atoning sacrifice, and in due course this leads to the ascended Christ pouring out the Spirit upon believers, to enable them to live for God.

At this point Campbell appears to suggest that there is a distinction between the divine and human in terms of their respective capacities for suffering. Some of his comments here indicate that he is still working with the traditional concept of an impassible God.

> The capacity of sorrow and suffering which Jesus had did not come from the Holy Ghost in him; for the Holy Ghost could not suffer. It was his soul, his human soul, which he made an offering for sin, and not the Spirit of God: but it was by the Spirit of God that he did so. And the mystery is, that the capacity of intelligence is all from man, as Christ finds him: but that the feelings are all through Christ in him.[22]

It is not immediately clear what Campbell intends by the comment that 'the capacity of intelligence is all from man.' In using this kind of language was he perhaps warding off any suggestions that the Son of God had assumed an incomplete human nature which was lacking a mind or intelligence?[23] This

---

[20] For a fuller treatment of this theme see Chapter 7. *Campbell's Trinitarian Christology*.

[21] *S&L*, 2.23.103; *NofS*, 1.8.5. Appendix 4.

[22] *Ibid.*,

[23] Gregory of Nazianzus 'If any one has put his trust in him as a man without a human mind, he is himself devoid of mind, and unworthy of salvation. For what he has not assumed he has not healed; it is what is

stress upon the full humanity of Christ does not threaten the unity of Christ's person because it is affirmed alongside the conviction that the character, or personality, of the Eternal Word remains constant before, during and after the Incarnation.[24]

Anticipating to some extent his insistence in *The Nature of the Atonement* that the sufferings of Christ are not a measure of what God can inflict, but rather reveal what God feels about sin, Campbell sees the sufferings of the man Christ Jesus as the manifestation of what God feels. This comes across clearly in a sermon on 1 John 3:3 preached at Row on 30 January 1831, where he is also trying to maintain his belief in a God who, by definition, cannot suffer pain.

> Would that we saw the sight that God sees when those whom he so loved as that he gave his Son to die for them, are hating him, and hating one another. God cannot suffer pain because he is God. But when God became man, that man who was God did suffer pain – and the soul of Christ was poured forth, a sacrifice for sin, and in his agony was expressed what God *always* feels…All that Christ's agony then expressed, God is feeling always towards sin.[25]

Although his presuppositions will not allow him to think of God experiencing pain directly, the language he uses depicts a God who steps into real human emotions, and uses them to reveal the truth about himself, which is the truth about how he feels.

> Therefore, be not kept back by this; but understand that it was human tears which Christ shed. They were such tears as never man shed, because they were wholly shed through the Holy Ghost; and he spake such words as never man uttered, because uttered through the Holy Ghost…This is what causes that we should see the glory of God in the face of Jesus Christ – that, in very truth, the very and eternal God did come into human feelings, and human emotions; and then was God manifested in the flesh.[26]

---

united to his Deity that also saved,' in Bettenson, *Documents of the Christian Church*, 45.

[24] See for example *S&L*, 1.14.342; and 1.14.346. See Chapter 4. *He took Sinful Flesh*.

[25] *NofS*, 2.18.10.

[26] *S&L*, 2.23.103-104; *NofS*, 1.8.5-6. Appendix 4.

Campbell's colourful language, in a sermon preached at Row on 17 April 1831 goes so far as to claim that the human feelings of Jesus reveal the actual feelings of God.

> 'his is the way in which you are to love God, by knowing that God is revealed to you in Christ Jesus. The infinite God – the invisible God – the originator of all things – you cannot search out, you cannot understand or know. No man knoweth the Father but the Son, and he to whom the Son revealeth him. But God in Christ you may know for Christ is a man while he is God and the human feelings of Christ express the very feelings of God, and the heart of Christ is the heart of God.[27]

In addition to emphasizing the unity of Christ's person, Campbell implies a kind of communication of attributes when he claims that 'the human feelings of Christ express the very feelings of God'. However, the way in which Campbell links Christ's human feelings with the 'very feelings of God' sits rather uneasily alongside his comments that 'the Holy Ghost could not suffer',[28] and that 'God cannot suffer pain because he is God'.[29] Such statements affirm divine impassibility and imply that the sufferings of Christ were restricted to his human nature. Comments like these echo patristic debates on the same theme with theologians such as Athanasius, seeking to affirm that the Son was ` with the Father whilst holding to the axiom of God's impassibility. He attempted to resolve the tension between these views by attributing the sufferings of Christ to the human flesh assumed by the Logos. However, that tension is still apparent, when Athanasius asserts that 'verily it is strange that He it was Who suffered and yet suffered not. Suffered, because His own Body suffered, and He was in it, which thus suffered; suffered not, because the Word, being by Nature God, is impassible.'[30]

---

[27] *NofS* 2.22.5. See also, *S&L*, 2.24.131 'Christ was man – he was God, but he was also man; he had a human heart and soul; human feelings, and thoughts; human joys and sorrows; many experiences that were painful; many experiences that were joyful;' *S&L*, 2.26.194, 'in him the Father is revealed; he has declared the Father's name. To know Christ is to know God... in him the fulness of God is revealed in a body; because in him there is manifested, in the shape of a man's mind and feelings, the very heart and mind of God.'

[28] *S&L* 2.23.103; *NofS*, 1.8.5. Appendix 4.

[29] *NofS*, 22.18.10.

[30] *Letter to Epictetus*, 6, in *St. Athanasius: Select Works and Letters*, 572. Cf., *Orationes contra Arianos*, iii.34. Cf., Gregory of Nazianzus 'the only Son...in

Although Athanasius was thus able to affirm that the Logos was fully God, his comments suggest a certain tension between God's inner nature and the God revealed in the economy of salvation.

Similar language is employed by Thomas Weinandy in his vigorous defence of divine impassibility, where he argues that 'the Son of God did not suffer as God in a man, for to do so would mean that he was not a man. The Son of God suffered as a man.'[31] He is keen to avoid any idea of the Son suffering in his divine nature believing that 'if the Son of God experienced suffering in his divine nature, then it would be God suffering as God *in a man*. But the incarnation which demands that the Son of God actually exists as a man and not just dwells in a man, equally demands that the Son of God suffers *as a man* and not just suffers divinely in a man.'[32] Great care is being taken here to keep faith with the Chalcedonian principle that the characteristics of the divine and the human natures in Christ were preserved, coming together to form one person. However, demarcating the boundary between the divine and human in Christ in such detail could make it more difficult to affirm the unity of the one person.

Alan Torrance argues instead that such attempts to cordon the divine nature off from suffering 'occurred by virtue of the attempt to define the God of revelation by way of a methodology formed *in advance* of the content of the revelation. And it was this which led to a notion of divine impassibility which was ultimately incompatible with the God of the incarnation.'[33] In contrast when the divine revelation in Christ sets the agenda for theology then 'it should become quite clear...that we cannot sidestep the question of God's identification with the sufferings of Christ by appealing to the two natures of Christ and defining the divine nature in

---

his flesh passible, in his Deity impassible', in Bettenson, *Documents of the Christian Church*, 45.

[31] Weinandy, *Does God Suffer?*, 205.

[32] *Ibid.*, 204. Weinandy provides a stimulating and interesting defence of impassibility, but it is surprising, that he does not engage with Luther's *theologia crucis*, which provides much of the inspiration behind Moltmann's approach. I am not sure that he has refuted the challenges to impassibility which arise from an *a posteriori* approach which begins explicitly from what God has done in Christ.

[33] Alan Torrance, 'Does God Suffer? Incarnation and Impassibility', in *Christ In Our Place*, Hart and Thimell, (eds.), 356.

accordance with a "metaphysical" conception of divine substance. A blithe assertion that the suffering relates only…to Christ's human nature would be unacceptable.'[34]

Aspects of both approaches are evident in Campbell's sermons as he affirms both divine impassibility and the reality of Christ's suffering. As his orthodoxy was being questioned by so many critics it would have been theological suicide for Campbell explicitly to challenge notions of divine impassibility. Probably he had no desire to question divine impassibility, but whether he realised it or not, he was undermining traditional concepts of impassibility by proclaiming that 'the human feelings of Christ express the very feelings of God.' For if the sorrow and suffering that were part of Christ's experience correspond to something within the nature of God, then this implies a capacity for feeling and pain within the Godhead which classical images of an impassible God would find difficult to entertain. Campbell remained faithful to the tradition at this point, but the general tenor of his theology probably points in a different direction.

His desire to do theology in the light of the gospel[35] bears some resemblance to Luther's approach, who believed that 'he is worth calling a theologian who understands the visible and hinder parts of God to mean the passion and the cross.'[36] If Campbell had followed Luther's dictum *Crux probat omnia* to its conclusion it would have led him eventually to challenge the axiom of impassibility. Christologically this would have been helpful because traditional notions of impassibility can make it difficult to affirm a significant degree of unity between the divine and human natures. If there is such a profound distinction between the two natures, and between the immanent and economic trinities, then what confidence can there be that what appears in the human nature of the God-man is a reliable guide to his divine nature? If such a gap exists between these two natures, then how could Campbell ever be sure that a God who elects some, does not lurk menacingly behind the God revealed in the incarnation of Christ?

Having emphasised the Son's complete identification with fallen humanity, Campbell is also keen to underline that Christ was and is fully the Son of God. For 'Christ was the Son of God

---

[34] Ibid., 365.
[35] See Chapter 2. *The Priority of Revelation*.
[36] Martin Luther, 'The Heidelberg Disputation, Thesis XX,' *Library of Christian Classics*, volume XVI, (London: SCM Press, 1962), 278, 290.

from eternity: Christ was the Son of God when in the flesh: Christ was the Son of God when he was manifested as such, by being raised from the dead.'[37]

God's love for human beings is displayed in the fact that in union with the eternal Son, believers become sons of God. Salvation is not simply the announcement of pardon but a profound transformation which involves 'the mystery of our participating in the nature of God, without our being God.'[38] There is nothing automatic about this because human beings cannot make themselves God's children, but in his grace God makes this possible by his Spirit.

> And it is no fiction, no idle speech to call us sons: it is a plain literal fact, that as I am the son of Adam, so also am I the son of God; while I am not God, but a different person; and so through the second Adam it comes to pass, that men have the divine nature; not a likeness of it, but the very thing itself. The believer has the divine nature in him because he has the divine Spirit in him, at the very time that he is not God but a creature; and this is the way God brings out the greatest depth of his love.[39]

The apostle Paul lived by faith in the Son of God, and faith remains the door to life. People become partakers of the divine nature not by waiting and wondering if God loves them. God's truth is conveyed when the gospel is preached and when that gospel is received the Spirit is received. The good news that Christ loved all and gave himself for all is the bread of life and the person who believes this will be fully alive.[40]

Campbell is not surprised that the preaching of a gospel that Christ died for *some* rather than for *all*, does not have the same capacity for bringing life. Whatever opposition may come, he is convinced of the importance of proclaiming the good news that Jesus is that Son of God who loved every human being. The Christ who died and rose again for all, is the one who has the Spirit and eternal life for all. At the heart of his message is the mystery of God coming into fallen human flesh in the incarnation. The mystery of God coming into the fallen flesh of the believer. The mystery of Christ in the members of his body. This eternal life is received by faith and must be lived by faith,

---

[37] *S&L*, 2.23.107, *NofS*, 1.8.7. Appendix 4.
[38] *S&L*, 2.23.105; *NofS*, 1.8.6. Appendix 4.
[39] *S&L*, 2.23.106, *NofS*, 1.8.6. Appendix 4.
[40] *S&L*, 2.23.112, *NofS*, 1.8.9. Appendix 4.

through a constant dependence upon Christ. The sermon concludes with a passionate plea to those who have not yet believed to respond to the gospel before the day when God will come forth in judgement.

By affirming that the flesh assumed by Christ 'differed not in one particle from mine' this sermon supplies further evidence of Campbell's belief that Christ had assumed fallen human nature. It also alerts us to the importance of pneumatology for a right understanding of christology, because Campbell's portrayal of Christ's humanity relies upon a recognition of the vital role of the Holy Spirit in the whole process of incarnation. Alongside this emphasis upon the subject of the Lord's humanity it is clear that he believed in the eternal divine nature of the Son of God. His conviction that 'God cannot suffer pain because he is God' tends to suggest that Campbell believed that he was operating within the traditional boundaries for christology established by the Council of Chalcedon.

He took Sinful Flesh

In a sermon on Romans 8:1-4,[41] Campbell opens with an affirmation of God's desire to bring sons and daughters to glory. Although he is conscious that the preaching of 'the holiness of a doctrine' may incur opposition, Campbell sets out to consider the ways in which God's love has been manifested in Christ. In the opening sections of the sermon he counters those who argued that his ideas about universal pardon implied universalism. Such an implication is not necessary and is ruled out by the apostle Paul's teaching in the first few verses of Romans 8. The good news that 'there is therefore now no condemnation' for those who are in Christ Jesus carries with it a sober realization that a condemnation exists for those outside of Christ who are not walking in the way of the Spirit. A judgement and a condemnation continue to exist after the work of God in Christ because God always holds people accountable for the way in which they use the gifts he entrusts to them. 'God then in giving you his unspeakable gift, has not ceased to be your God and your Judge.'[42]

Campbell moves on to argue that the double-sided command to love God with our whole heart and to love our neighbour as

---

[41] *S&L*, 1.14. Sermon on Romans 8:1-4 'The condemnation of unbelief, and sin condemned in the flesh of Christ.'
[42] *Ibid.*, 1.14.335.

ourselves is what lies at the very heart of the law. True happiness for human beings, therefore, is found in fulfilling the royal law of love. God's work in Christ does not suspend the operation of the law or break the link between happiness and love. Rather than abrogating the law, God has come in Christ to create a way whereby sinful people can be made holy and loving, because it is only in living in love and righteousness that people can find true happiness. 'Therefore it is the object of God that the righteousness of the law might be fulfilled in us, by our being made holy, and by our having in us the love which is the fulfilling of the law.'[43]

This provides the basis for the next stage of the argument which ties in with Romans 8:3. The law could issue the command, but it could not enable people to love God and their neighbours. This, according to Campbell, is what is implied in saying that the law was 'weak'. 'The defect was not in the law, but in the flesh,'[44] because sin resided in the flesh and generated hatred rather than love. It was under these circumstances that God intervened, sending his son in the likeness of sinful flesh. The references to Romans 8:3 indicate that talk about Christ assuming 'sinful flesh' was not some theological novelty, but a reiteration of the Apostle Paul's perspective on the incarnation.[45]

> He was found in *form and fashion as a man*, that is, he *took sinful flesh*. Christ took our flesh, *just as it was, in that condition which made the law to be weak*....Now, creatures in flesh and blood could not love God, because the law was weak through the sin that was in their flesh; and to *remove this hindrance to* THEIR *loving God, God sent his own Son in the likeness of sinful flesh*...I am not stating to you just now, simply that Christ took human nature, but that he took *our* nature, *just as we have it* – just as those had it in whose case it was that the law was weak through the flesh – *he took that very flesh which made the law weak.*[46]

By virtue of assuming sinful flesh Christ is able to condemn sin, and to offer himself as an expiatory sacrifice. This work of

---

[43] *Ibid.*, 1.14.340.
[44] *Ibid.*, 1.14.340.
[45] John A. T. Robinson, *The Body: A Study in Pauline Theology*, (London: SCM Press, 1952), 37-8. 'The first act in the drama of redemption is the self-identification of the Son of God *to the limit*, yet without sin, with the body of the flesh in its fallen state.'
[46] *S&L*, 1.14.341-2.

condemning sin does not involve constant criticism of people's behaviour, but is a process of revelation which brings the truth about human sinfulness out into the open. Through a constant reliance upon the power of the Holy Spirit, the one who has assumed sinful flesh shows that sin is not an inevitable or necessary condition for human beings. By consistently acting in a loving and holy fashion he reveals the sinful way in which others behave. This process of revealing the sorry truth about the human condition is only possible because Christ was divine, holy and sinless.

> (The) Eternal Word, having come into our nature perfectly holy, in love, as God is love, continued *with the same character, not in the least changed by the fact of his having taken flesh*, but that he was, in flesh, precisely the same moral being that he was before he took it — that, in our nature, he was just as holy as he was before he assumed it, or as he is now in his glorified body. The law, then, in Christ's case, was fulfilled, in that though the flesh had power to prevent every other being who had it, from fulfilling the law, in Christ's case it was wholly overcome — not that he had not the same nature and tendency, but that in him there was no sin, and he was sinless in our body of sin and death. He was sinless in condemning sin in the flesh.[47]

When Christ 'took sinful flesh' this involved a complete identification with humanity because he shared 'the same nature and tendency', and this presumably means the same tendency to sin. However in spite of having this same vulnerability to temptation, 'in him there was no sin'. Instead of sowing to the flesh Christ resisted temptation by the power of the Spirit, and so was sinless, even though he lived in the context of our sinful flesh.

To some his language about Christ having 'the same nature and tendency' might give the impression that there was something sinful within the nature of the one 'who knew no sin',[48] but it is clear that Campbell was convinced that exposure to authentic temptation did not lead to actual sin in Christ's case. Part of the difficulty may be that biblical language about the likeness of sinful flesh is sometimes taken out of context, and judged on the basis of extra-biblical definitions of 'original sin'

---

[47] *Ibid.*, 1.14.342.
[48] 2 Corinthians 5:21.

or 'total depravity'.[49] Viewed within the parameters of Pauline theology it is possible to affirm Christ's identity with sinful, fallen nature without compromising the sinlessness of Christ. So for example James Dunn argues that for Paul *sarx* is not evil.

> Flesh is not evil, it is simply weak and corruptible. It signifies man in his weakness and corruptibility, his belonging to the world. In particular it is that dimension of the human personality through which sin attacks, which sin uses as its instrument (Rom. 7:5, 14, 18,25) – thus *sarx harmatias*. That is to say, *sarx harmatias* does not signify *guilty* man, but man in his *fallenness* – man subject to temptation, to human appetites and desires, to corruption and death.[50]

Campbell states clearly that the Eternal Word, who has taken our nature, continues 'with the same character', because he is the 'the same moral being' throughout the incarnation.[51] This personal continuity is expressed in similar language later in the sermon when Campbell speaks of the Eternal Word as 'having still the personality which he had before he came'.[52] This emphasis serves the purpose of affirming that the Son of God who was holy before the Incarnation, continued at all times to be holy and sinless in spite of very real temptations. In this way Campbell would have been sure that his teaching avoided any sense 'that our Lord's holiness was not immaculate.'[53] This

---

[49] Donald Macleod views the subject from the perspective of the theology of the Westminster Confession arguing that, 'To be "fallen",...is to have sinned against God; and to be "fallen" is to be in a state of sinfulness, devoid of righteousness and "wholly defiled in all the faculties and parts of soul and body" (*Westminster Confession* VI.II). How can any of this apply to Jesus?...Fallen nature is sinful nature, dominated by "the flesh" (in the Pauline sense) and characterized by total depravity.' Donald Macleod, *The Person of Christ*, (Leicester: IVP, 1998), 228. Cf. Donald Macleod, 'The Doctrine of the Incarnation in Scottish Theology: Edward Irving', *Scottish Bulletin of Evangelical Theology* 9 (1991) 40-50.

[50] J. D. G. Dunn, 'Paul's understanding of the Death of Jesus as Sacrifice', in S. W. Sykes (ed.), *Sacrifice and Redemption*, 37.

[51] C. E. B. Cranfield suggests that Paul uses the word 'likeness' in Romans 8:3 both to signify that 'the Son of God assumed the selfsame fallen human nature that is ours' and to indicate that 'fallen human nature was never the whole of Him – He never ceased to be the eternal Son of God.' C. E. B. Cranfield, *Romans: A Shorter Commentary*, (Edinburgh: T & T Clark, 1985), 177.

[52] *S&L*, 1.14.346.

[53] *Memorials* 1.105.

emphasis upon the 'same character' at work before, during and after the incarnation indicates that he did not think of the person of Christ in a dualistic manner. His comments are compatible with the orthodox insistence that 'the distinction of natures being in no way annulled by the union, but rather the characteristics of each nature being preserved and coming together to form one person and subsistence, not parted or separated into two persons, but one and the same Son and Only-begotten God the Word, Lord Jesus Christ.'[54]

Reflecting upon the Chalcedonian Definition, John McIntyre suggests that 'it would almost certainly appear that it is the *hypostasis* of the divine nature of the Logos who is the subject of the incarnational situation...This much is clear: there is no question of there being a second *hypostasis* or person.'[55] If it is the case that the Eternal Word has 'still the personality which he had before he came', then within Campbell's approach it is the Eternal Word who is the active subject of the incarnational situation, and there is no question of there being a second independent person within the constitution of the God-man. This avoids any danger of dualism but perhaps raises questions about the extent to which the real humanity of Christ might be overshadowed by such an emphasis. Within the Chalcedonian tradition these issues had been catered for by use of the concepts of *anhypostasia* and *enhypostasia*, although the adequacy of these categories continues to be a matter of some debate.[56] While Campbell does not use such technical terms in his early sermons, his comments could be interpreted within that kind of framework. If his stress upon the Eternal Word continuing throughout the incarnation 'with the same character' as before runs the risk of minimising the reality of Christ's humanity, then this weakness is one which is already embedded within the two-nature tradition he inherited.

By his assumption of sinful flesh the Son of God has provided a complete condemnation of sin and this process of revealing the true nature of sin reaches its climax on the cross. On its own,

---

[54] 'The Definition of Chalcedon, 451', in Bettenson, *Documents of the Christian Church*, 51.

[55] John McIntyre, *The Shape of Christology*, (Edinburgh: T & T Clark, 1998²), 95.

[56] Carl E. Braaten, 'The Person of Jesus Christ', in *Christian Dogmatics, Volume 2*, (eds.), Carl E. Braaten and Robert W. Jenson, (Philadelphia: Fortress Press, 1984), 506. K. Barth, *Church Dogmatics*, vol. IV, part 2, 49ff. Cf., McIntyre, *The Shape of Christology*, 94-103.

an act which revealed the existence and extent of human sinfulness would shed light on the human condition but it would not necessarily deliver people from their bondage to sin. Therefore, it was necessary that Christ should provide not just a condemnation of sin but also a sacrifice to take away sin. This we see taking place 'when we see Christ coming into our nature, and taking it up, and presenting it holy to God, and doing this as a sacrifice for sin.'[57] It is interesting to note that Campbell is content to describe this sacrifice as being 'expiatory' and as 'propitiatory'. Similar language reappears at certain places in *The Nature of the Atonement* but it is clear that he is not thinking of a propitiatory sacrifice which involves Christ enduring punishment, because this sacrifice involves the offering of a human nature which has been perfected and presented holy to God. Christ was always the Son who could approach his Father with confidence, and his sacrifice is needed so that others can approach God with a comparable confidence. It is when Christ is seen as the head, the representative, that people can draw close to God in and through him.

The way in which Christ maintained his sinless obedience and offered himself holy to God was through the Holy Spirit. Christ's experience of the Spirit is once again set in a Trinitarian context because Jesus

> continually put trust in his Father for the Spirit, and did continually receive from the Father, the Spirit without measure. Having still the personality which he had before he came – in that he was the Eternal Word – when he found himself loaded with his flesh, he did not use strength, or might, or power, as God, to destroy his flesh, or to cast it from him; but, having humbled himself to be a servant, recognizing that his flesh was evil, he did trust to his father, and, continually receiving the Spirit from the Father, thus presented his blood without spot to God.[58]

In this way Christ not only reveals the truth about God's love but also reveals the potential within human beings. By consistently crucifying the flesh and offering it up holy to God, the Son of God demonstrates that it is possible for human beings to glorify God. Whilst some may feel that it is worthless to speculate about how Christ maintained his sinless obedience, Campbell argues that it is important because the divine

---

[57] *S&L*, 1.14.344.
[58] *Ibid.*, 1.14.346.

intention was for Christ to 'tread a path of holiness, and that we should tread in his footsteps.'[59] He denies any charge of falling into Socinian errors about the person of Christ, because there is no doubt in his mind that Christ is God.

For Campbell a right understanding of Christ's assumption of a humanity like ours was essential because only such a saviour who fully identified with us in our weakness would be able to accomplish the salvation which fallen human beings need. Only a saviour who became 'bone of my bone, flesh of my flesh' is able to function as a sympathetic and effective High Priest. The Captain of salvation does not only sympathise with believers because he is the one who supplies the Holy Spirit to his people. The strategic difference at this point is that whereas 'Christ received the Spirit directly from the Father, you receive it through Christ.'[60] Hence all that is needed for salvation, for life and godliness, is available, in Christ. All of which leads Campbell to call upon his hearers to rely not on their own efforts but on the gift of God in Christ which includes the gift of the Spirit who supplies the power needed to condemn the flesh and to live in accord with the Spirit. He reminds his congregation of the dimension of judgement inherent in the death which faces everyone. The solemn sign of death is a reminder of God's judgement upon sin, and seen against such a bleak background, the work of God in Christ should not be seen as taking away God's condemnation of sin but rather as 'the bestowing in Christ of the gift of a new life.'[61] With this note of warning Campbell encourages his hearers to crucify the flesh and glorify God in the power of the Spirit.

The picture emerging from these sermons is of one Christ in two natures. Although Campbell invests most energy in affirming that Christ has come in 'sinful flesh' this is not at the expense of the divine nature of the Son. He maintains the union of the two natures in the one person of Christ without explaining precisely how this takes place. The rooting of this perspective on the person of Christ in Romans 8:3 is one which reappears in a number of other sermons.

---

[59] *Ibid.*, 1.14.348.
[60] *Ibid.*, 1.14.350.
[61] *Ibid.*, 1.14.355.

In the Likeness of Sinful Flesh

In the second of three sermons based on Titus 2:11-14,[62] Campbell sets out to consider what the grace of God teaches about denying ungodliness and about the future hope. In fact he spends so much time on the first of these topics that he does not get around to the future hope until the next sermon. He is convinced that true wisdom consists in beginning to see things as God sees them, and this wisdom is to be found in Christ alone. In grace and love the Son of God has come into the human condition to transform it.

> The grace of God is that love which moved the eternal Son of God to come forth from the bosom of the Father and take our nature and become bone of our bone, and flesh of our flesh, and inasmuch as the children are partakers of flesh and blood, in like manner to take part of the same in order that he might be a sacrifice for sin, in order that he might bring into our condition the light of the eternal love, and holiness and goodness of God, and might reveal by that light, what our darkness was, and that having thus brought in light, he should be raised from the dead that he might be the author of eternal salvation to as many as obey him.[63]

In pointing to Christ's total identification with humanity he repeats the arguments used in other sermons. Christ has identified fully with human beings by assuming their fallen flesh, and by his actions in our flesh he teaches us the truth about sin. Christ condemns sin, not by strident criticism but by revealing that it is not necessary for people's lives to be dominated by sin.

> Christ came in our nature – in our very nature – that he came into that very world in which we are, and enjoyed no privilege, no distinction to screen him from the power of the world, or from the oppression of the world – that he was exposed to all the attacks of Satan, and enjoyed no advantage to keep Satan from coming to deceive him, and attempting to destroy him.[64]

The human predicament, portrayed in Romans chapter 7, is of people struggling unsuccessfully to overcome sin. This sorry state is brought to an end by Christ, by virtue of his coming 'in

---

[62] *NofS*, 3.31. Appendix 5.
[63] *Ibid.*, 3.31.2. Appendix 5.
[64] *Ibid.*, 3.31.2. Appendix 5.

the likeness of sinful flesh'. For Campbell the reference in Romans 8:3 to the Son coming 'in the likeness of sinful flesh' does not mean that Christ came into something 'like' sinful flesh, that was actually slightly different from it. He interprets this phrase to mean that Christ assumed a flesh which was the same as ours, and this interpretation is endorsed by contemporary biblical scholarship.[65] Campbell sees these words as biblical proof for a real participation by Christ in our human nature and condition.

> You are not to suppose that this means in appearance merely...Likeness of man means participation in manhood. It means taking that which is humanity — and the likeness of sinful flesh means that he took that flesh which we have for the purpose of condemning sin in it.[66]

This total act of identification not only has the negative effect of condemning sin by bringing it out into the open, because it also has the more positive purpose of revealing the truth about human life as God intended it. Hence 'when I see before me the man Christ Jesus, denying ungodliness I see what I ought to be. I see what I am called to be. When I see him denying all worldly lusts I see, I say, what I ought to be, and what I am called to be.'[67]

In addition to revealing what people are intended to be, Christ shows that it is possible for people to live as God intended. He does not simply offer us an example of perfection and leave us with the impossible task of trying to follow that example. The one who constantly received the Spirit from his Father has, since the resurrection, become 'the second Adam, the quickening Spirit' who pours out the Spirit upon his people. It is the power of this Spirit which makes it possible for people to live a new kind of life freed from the power of sin.

---

[65] See for example, J. D. G. Dunn, 'Paul's understanding of the Death of Jesus', 37. '*Homoioma*...does not distinguish Jesus from sinful flesh or distance him from fallen man, as is often suggested; rather it is Paul's way of expressing Jesus' *complete identity* with the flesh of sin, with man in his fallenness.' Cf., C. K, Barrett, *A Commentary on The Epistle to the Romans*, (London: A & C Black, 1971), 156. 'We are probably justified...in deducing that Christ took precisely the same fallen nature that we ourselves have, and that he remained sinless because he constantly overcame a proclivity to sin.'
[66] *NofS*, 3.31.3. Appendix 5.
[67] *Ibid.*, 3.31.3. Appendix 5.

Christ having condemned sin in the flesh — having presented himself without spot to God, through the Eternal Spirit, did this as a sacrifice for sin, and so put away our sin, and so we have our sin forgiven through the shedding of his blood, and he being exalted to the right hand of God, in reward of his holiness and righteousness, has received from the Father this high place, that now he is the second Adam, the quickening Spirit — that now he has the Holy Spirit for us to dwell in us by the Spirit that, through his Spirit in us, we might be what he was.[68]

What emerges here is an emphasis which will be explored more fully during the exploration, in Chapter 5 of Christ's priestly office. In his glorified humanity, Christ stands in heaven as the second Adam to whom God the Father has entrusted the Holy Spirit.[69] Describing the risen Christ as 'the quickening Spirit' does not imply a merging of Christ and the Spirit but highlights Christ as the one who pours out the Spirit on believers.[70]

Further confirmation that Christ assumed our fallen human flesh is found by Campbell in the gospel encounter where Jesus responded to a man's praise with the rebuke 'why callest thou me good?'[71] In this way Campbell senses that Jesus was trying to get the man to see that there was nothing naturally good in his human nature, because human nature has no independent ability to do good. The goodness which the man had perceived to be at work in the person of Jesus could not therefore be the outworking of any inherent human goodness, but could only be the result of the Spirit's work within him. As there is no one good but God, the only way for a person to be truly good is for the holiness and love of God to enter into their human nature.

---

[68] *Ibid.*, 3.31.4. Appendix 5.
[69] Weinandy, *Does God Suffer?*, 236. 'If it is not the Son of God as the risen man who makes present the eschatological Spirit, then it would mean that it was not as man that he obtained our salvation. If the Son of God, as the risen man, does not send forth the Spirit, then what he did as man, in his suffering and death, was not the means by which he obtained his risen lordship so as to be empowered and authorized to send forth the Spirit. As it was as man that the Son died on our behalf reconciling us to the Father, so it is now as the risen man that the Son makes available the fruit of his human suffering and death in the new life of the Holy Spirit.'
[70] See Chapter 7. *The Son who Gives the Spirit.*
[71] Mk. 10:18.

Repeatedly he presses home the message that the call to be holy is not out of the question in this life. Christ has shown what is possible and the ascended Christ supplies the Spirit who makes a new kind of life possible. In this way the grace of God teaches what sin is and how sin can be overcome. The grace of God not only warns against wrong but encourages people to fulfil the royal law of love. His battle with those who would limit the scope of atonement surfaces here as he argues that it is impossible to teach me to fulfil the law by loving all men if God himself does not love all people. For 'how can the grace of God teach me to love all men unless God, God himself, loves all men? How can the Spirit of Christ teach me to love all men unless Christ himself loves all men?'[72]

He Did Not Cease to be God

In a sermon entitled 'The confidence of hope'[73] Campbell stresses again that at no point during the incarnation did Christ ever cease being God. One of his reasons for drawing attention to this fact is that if there was any sense in which Christ had ceased, even temporarily, to be God then he would no longer be in a position to function as a genuine revelation of God. It is vital to 'remember that he did not cease to be God (for he could not cease to be God), when he became man....(In) taking to himself the form of a servant, he did not cease to be in reality God; – that humbling himself as he did, he did not cease to be in reality God. If we lose sight of this, we will not be able to pass from the sight of Christ, to the knowledge of God.'[74]

The now familiar emphasis upon Christ being 'in our nature' occurs as Campbell proclaims that 'God dwelling in my nature' means in practice that God is 'surrounded by my temptations'. Another way of underlining the full humanity of Christ is present as Campbell describes Christ as 'our brother'. By so fully sharing in our human condition Christ has condemned sin in the flesh and exposed it for the evil it is. By living in the human environment and by resisting temptation 'He therefore proved that there was no necessity for our being sinners, and that it was from ourselves – of our own free choice, that we were sinners; and so he condemned sin in the flesh.'[75] Human

---

[72] *NofS*, 3.31.8. Appendix 5.
[73] *S&L*, 1.13.
[74] *Ibid.*, 1.13.300.
[75] *Ibid.*, 1.13.302.

beings cannot shirk responsibility for their sin and blame it on their circumstances, because in those self-same circumstances Christ has lived a life of perfect holiness. Once more he rejects the idea that Christ's resistance to temptation was due to Christ being God. Whilst Christ is truly God he overcame temptation by being constantly dependent on his Father and lived a life of perfect holiness through the power of the Holy Ghost.

To some hearers Campbell's argument that the incarnation has shown that there is 'no necessity for our being sinners' might raise fears about Pelagian error.[76] However, there is no sense here of people being able to make themselves good by their own effort. The argument that Christ has shown that it is possible not to sin fulfils a kind of legal function in justifying God's right to judge people for their sin. If the element of free choice was removed, then it would be unjust of God to hold people responsible for sin which was the inevitable result of genes or circumstances. In addition, his reflections on Christ's victory over temptation show that people are not simply being urged to follow the inspiring example of Christ, because the Holy Spirit is provided to make a holy life possible.[77] So he not only portrays Christ as the one who reveals the truth about God, but also as the one who reveals the truth about human life as God intended it. In addition to revealing 'what I ought to be', Christ shows that it is possible for people to live as God intended. The one who constantly received the Spirit from his Father has, since the resurrection, become the second Adam, the quickening Spirit who pours out the Spirit upon his people. It is the power of this Spirit which enables people to live a new kind of life freed from the power of sin.

This sermon is another place where key ideas about atonement can be detected, which would be written out for the press at a later date. Campbell rejects any idea that it was

---

[76] Pelagius in Bettenson, *Documents of the Christian Church*, 53. 'Everything good and everything evil, in respect of which we are either worthy of praise or of blame, is *done by us*, not *born with us*. We are not born in our full development, but with a capacity for good and evil; we are begotten as well without virtue as without vice, and before the activity of our own personal will there is nothing in man but what God has stored in him.'

[77] *S&L*, 1.13.303. 'If Christ did present himself through the eternal Spirit without spot to God – if Christ was holy through the Holy Ghost – and if it be the sure truth of God, that Christ has the Spirit for us, then you see here *(sic)* is a perfect provision as well as a perfect example for us, that we should follow in his step.'

merely the amount of pain and suffering which gave the sacrificial death its atoning power. His preference for a moral rather than a penal approach to atonement is visible as he speaks about 'the moral character of Christ's agony'.[78] Whilst the language differs from *The Nature of the Atonement*, the basic sentiments are similar. The agonies of Jesus in the flesh show that he is identifying with God's condemnation of sin, which is another way of saying that Jesus is offering *'a perfect Amen in humanity to the judgement of God on the sin of man.'*[79] He reminds his hearers that atonement was not needed to make God loving because 'the cross of Christ is to be seen just as the heart of God unveiled in its feelings towards man: in its movements towards every human being, continually, without ceasing, day or night – whether praying or withholding prayer – whether seeking his face, or going from him – this is the heart of God'.[80] What God has done in Christ provides the ground of confidence to the believer who can look forward to receiving a divine inheritance.

'He Became What We Are...'

In a sermon on 1 Peter 1:3-5, preached at Row on Sunday 16 May 1830,[81] Campbell explores aspects of the living hope arising from the resurrection of Jesus Christ. At the heart of his vision of hope is the idea, which he often returns to, that believers are 'partakers of the divine nature.'[82] This leads him to use *theosis* style language about the transformation brought about by the incarnation.

> This was the great object of God in taking human nature into union with his own nature, that through Christ, there might pass into those whose nature he took, the very nature of God – the Spirit of God. He became the Son of Man, that we might

---

[78] *Ibid.*, 1.13.306-7. 'Is it because of the amount of pain and of agony endured?...It is impossible. It cannot be...It was the righteousness of the sacrifice – the holiness of the blood – the *purity* of *all the groans,* and of *all the tears, and of all the pain which Christ endured* – it was because, in that sacrifice, God's eternal law of love was magnified and made honourable – because sin was condemned in our flesh – because the feelings with which the eternal God regards sin were then expressed in the groans and agonies of Jesus.'
[79] *Nature,* 117 (118).
[80] *S&L*, 1.13.320.
[81] *NofS*, 2.13. Appendix 6.
[82] 2 Peter 1:4.

become the sons of God, and the one is just as literal as the other; and as truly as Christ became the Son of Man, so every one on whom Christ's work is accomplished, actually receives the divine nature, and is in that literal sense the son of God.[83]

A two-nature christology is in view when he speaks about God 'taking human nature into union with his own nature' in the event of the incarnation. This union of the divine and human has profound implications for humanity because by entering into such a union with fallen human nature, the Son of God has purified and recreated that nature. In the person of Christ humanity has been recreated and a new humanity has been born.[84] The glorified humanity of the Son in heaven is the hope set before believers now. Therefore salvation is much more than a legal imputation of righteousness which may or may not make a difference to the way that people live. Campbell offers a much larger picture of salvation because he proclaims a 'physical' doctrine of redemption which is summed up in his declaration that 'He became the Son of Man, that we might become the sons of God.'[85] Whilst he does not in any place justify his teaching by reference to the Church Fathers there are unconscious echoes here of the Athanasian emphasis that the only one competent to re-create fallen humanity was the one who had been involved in its creation at the beginning.[86]

Alongside this high view of the person of Christ, Campbell still makes time to remind his hearers of the subject of the Lord's humanity. He finds another way to affirm the reality of Christ's human nature by explaining how the incarnate Christ had to undergo a process of development. This is not idle speculation into the hidden years about which the gospels say so little, but provides a basis for the preacher to challenge his hearers. If Christ remained faithful to God in the midst of the bustle of everyday life then there is no reason why the demands of day to day living should excuse people from the call to holy living.[87]

---

[83] *NofS*, 2.13.2. Appendix 6.
[84] Cf. Ephesians 2:14.
[85] Cf., *St. Athanasius: Select Works and Letters*, 65 *De Incarnatione*, §54, 'For He was made man that we might be made God'.'
[86] *Ibid*, 40 *De Incarnatione*, §7, 'For being the Word of the Father, and above all, He alone of natural fitness was both able to recreate everything, and worthy to suffer on behalf of all and to be ambassador for all with the Father'.
[87] *NofS*, 2.13.13-14. Appendix 6.

The Union of Creature with the Creator

A fascinating summary of the christology found within the Row sermons is located in a short preface, which Campbell wrote to go along with two of his published sermons. In the space of a few lines the essential orthodoxy of his position is confirmed, because he states that,

> the second person of the Deity took into personal subsistence with himself, the very flesh of the Virgin Mary; and not a better flesh, an immortal flesh, an incorruptible flesh: that by the union of creature with the Creator, the whole of mankind, and all the animals, and the inert matter itself of this globe, are interested in the work of redemption, and are to take their eternal standing of happiness or misery on that basis.[88]

He clearly endorses the eternal divine nature of 'the second person of the Deity' whilst taking care to underline that the flesh assumed is real human flesh. Although he does not here make use of the 'sinful flesh' language of Romans 8:3, there can be little doubt that he is affirming that the Eternal Word has assumed fallen, rather than unfallen, nature.

The 'physical' understanding of redemption is strikingly expressed in the claim that the union of creature with the Creator means that all people and animals, and the 'inert matter itself of this globe' are implicated in the redemption accomplished by Christ. One of the implications of this statement is the recognition that redemption takes place not just at the cross but in the entire event of incarnation, crucifixion and resurrection. Campbell's language seems fully compatible with T. F. Torrance's claim that 'the work of atoning salvation does *not* take place *outside* of Christ, as something external to him, but takes place *within* him, *within* the incarnate constitution of his Person as Mediator.'[89] If Christ was simply to accomplish the task of providing pardon then he would cease to be quite so important once that task had been completed. However if the crucial act takes place within his Person then in an active sense he is eternally the source of salvation.

There is no need for fearful speculation as to whether or not I am one of the elect, because the atoning exchange which has taken place in the person of the Mediator has redeeming

---

[88] *TS*, pp vi-vii. Appendix 1.
[89] T. F. Torrance, *The Trinitarian Faith*, (Edinburgh, T and T Clark, 1988), 155.

implications for all people and all things.⁹⁰ Campbell's inclusion of animals and 'the inert matter itself of this globe' within the scope of redemption, connects with a number of sermons which have an eschatological vision of believers reigning as kings and priests in a new heaven and a new earth. Even though the whole created order has been transformed by what has taken place in Christ, there are reminders here that Campbell is not endorsing universalism. The 'eternal standing of happiness or misery' is also dependent upon human response to the gift of salvation which is embodied in Christ.

This summary of Campbell's theology and the material from the Row sermons tends to suggest that Campbell's view of salvation is much broader than the individualistic exemplarist approach he is sometimes accused of holding. It also suggests that an orthodox and evangelical understanding of the person of Christ undergirds his preaching and his theology.

Glasgow *Fragments*

The *Fragments* dating from Campbell's ministry in Glasgow are not such a rich resource for this topic, and some of the relevant material has already been examined.⁹¹ However, one of the earlier *Fragments* provides useful confirmation of Campbell's perspective on the subject of the Lord's humanity.

Jesus can Touch the Deep Stream of Pollution in Our Flesh

Reflecting on Galatians 5:14-18, Campbell considers that 'man's soul is the theatre of a conflict between two powers, which try to draw him in two different directions.'⁹² In this battle with the power of the flesh, human will-power is not sufficient to resist the reign of our fallen nature. 'There is, deep in every heart, a fountain of pollution and darkness, deeper than we can fathom – deep as hell itself, and of the very essence of hell; for hell consists in a spirit that has no peace, being in rebellion against

---

⁹⁰ *Ibid.*, 183. 'Since he is the eternal Word of God by whom and through whom all things that are made are made, and in whom the whole universe of visible and invisible realities coheres and hangs together, and since in him divine and human natures are inseparably united, then the secret of every man, whether he believes it or not, is bound up with Jesus for it is in him that human contingent existence has been grounded and secured.'
⁹¹ See Chapter 3. *Fragments* added in 1861.
⁹² *FofE*, 18.267.

God, and having no resting-place either in God or man, because it has no trust.'[93]

If human nature in general is in such a sorry state, does that also imply that Christ assumed a human nature like ours afflicted by this 'fountain of pollution and darkness'? If there is an 'evil fire of enmity'[94] at work within the flesh, does this mean that there was an evil fire of enmity at work within the human nature assumed by Christ? If 'every child of Adam has this flesh working in him'[95] then this is the only kind of flesh available for Christ to assume.

Campbell is not embarrassed to link Christ with such impurity because he is convinced that the power of Christ's purity is more contagious and powerful than the evil power at work in human existence. 'It is said, no one can touch pitch and not be defiled; but Jesus can touch the deep stream of pollution in our flesh, and yet not be defiled by it. His purity can come in contact with our pollution, and cleanse it.'[96] Jesus is portrayed as the good physician who is able to supply the remedy to our fallen condition, and he 'is ever willing to impart His Spirit, as the power of holiness, the power of love to us.'[97] In Campbell's eyes the sinlessness of Christ is not compromised by this stream of pollution in human flesh, because Christ never submitted to its demands. The principle at work appears to be 'what is not assumed is not healed', because it is only as the divine physician assumes such diseased flesh that he is able to redeem it by the power of the Spirit.

At this point it is appropriate to relate Campbell's approach to some recent discussion about what is implied by talking about Christ assuming fallen human nature. Kelly M. Kapic observes that 'there is disagreement among those holding to the fallen position whether Jesus had an inner propensity to sin (i.e. concupiscence), some affirming and others denying'[98]. So whilst

---

[93] *Ibid.*, 18.269.
[94] *Ibid.*, 18.270.
[95] *Ibid.*, 18.274.
[96] *Ibid.*, 18.275.
[97] *Ibid.*, 18.275. Cf. 18.270 'The wells of salvation furnish a living spring of water, by which this evil fire of enmity may be quenched: the divine altar furnishes a fire by which this stubble may be consumed.' 18.273 'It is by the infusion of this divine life, that we are delivered from the power of the flesh and its evil workings.'
[98] Kelly M. Kapic, 'The Son's Assumption of a Human Nature: A Call for Clarity', *International Journal of Systematic Theology* 3 (2001) 165.

Thomas Weinandy is adamant that 'our salvation is unconditionally dependent upon the Son's assuming a humanity disfigured by sin and freely acting as a son of Adam', he is also keen to point out that he neither 'sinned personally' nor 'had an inner propensity to sin'.[99]

> While Jesus assumed our fallen condition and thus could be tempted, yet...he was filled with the Spirit from conception, thereby freeing him from the morally corrupting effects of original sin. Even though the New Testament does not make any distinction between temptations that arise from 'outside' and those that originate from 'within' a person (cf. Jas 1:1-3), the received tradition seems to demand that Jesus' temptations could not have arisen from within him since he did not share our concupiscence, i.e., our propensity to sin.[100]

Questions arise here about the precise nature of 'concupiscence' and whether this is indeed synonymous with a propensity to sin. If 'concupiscence' is seen as immoderate or sinful desire, then the presence of concupiscence within the human constitution of Christ would be equivalent, in some traditions, to saying that Christ was a sinner. However, it may also be possible to see our human propensity to sin in a different light as pointing to the way in which the temptation to sin arises not simply from external factors but from sources within human nature which need to be healed. Weinandy's obvious hesitations about ascribing to Christ an 'inner propensity to sin' introduce a degree of ambiguity into his account of the person of Christ. For if Christ did not experience and overcome this propensity to sin, which is the source of those temptations originating from 'within a person', then a lingering doubt must surely remain that a damaged part of human nature remains unassumed and thus unhealed.

The language employed by Campbell in this *Fragment* from his early ministry in Glasgow points in a different direction. For it is hard to read his assertion that 'Jesus can touch the deep stream of pollution in our flesh, and yet not be defiled by it',[101]

---

[99] Thomas G. Weinandy, *In the Likeness of Sinful Flesh: An Essay on the Humanity of Christ*, (Edinburgh: T & T Clark, 1993), 18-9.

[100] *Ibid.*, 49. Weinandy refers to Aquinas who claimed that 'the Son assumed a humanity that sin tainted, but did not assume original sin and he did not sin himself. Thus Jesus did not inherit interior moral concupiscence or the "*fomes*" of sin.'

[101] *FofE*, 18.270, 275.

without concluding that Campbell believed that Christ had assumed a fallen human nature complete with its propensity to sin, but that he remained sinless by constant dependence upon the Holy Spirit. His preaching only makes sense on the assumption that Christ has faced and overcome this inner propensity to sin. For only if Christ has resisted the full force of external and internal temptation, being holy in our nature by the power of the Spirit, is he able to prove that there is 'no necessity for our having sinned against God.'[102] The incarnation functions as the just foundation of divine judgement against human sinfulness by demonstrating that sin is neither automatic nor inevitable. It is not just that the divine Son enters a world scarred by the fall and has to work within a creation groaning in travail, but it is also the case that the battle between good and evil rages within the human nature he has assumed. This does not mean, as his critics suggested, 'that our Lord's holiness was not immaculate'[103] because at no point did he ever yield to this inner propensity to sin. It is such a complete identification with fallen humanity which makes plausible the idea of Christ making a perfect confession of our sins.

Campbell's Christology

To some extent there is nothing remarkable about the christology that is scattered throughout Campbell's sermons. He does not offer a clear, systematic account of christology, and within such a collection of sermons it would be surprising if he did. Although he could have expressed his convictions more precisely (and succinctly) his core convictions are evident and it is clear that his christological beliefs were essentially orthodox. On the basis of his sermons there can be little doubt that he would happily 'acknowledge one and the same Son, our Lord Jesus Christ, at once complete in Godhead and complete in manhood, truly God and truly man, consisting also of a reasonable soul and body; of one substance with the Father as regards his Godhead, and at the same time of one substance with us as regards his manhood; like us in all respects, apart from sin.'[104]

---

[102] *S&L*, 2.30.286.
[103] *Memorials*, 1.105. Letter written on the 19 January 1833.
[104] 'The Definition of Chalcedon', in Bettenson, *Documents of the Christian Church*, 51.

What makes his approach of interest is the way in which he seeks to take seriously the subject of the Lord's humanity. While orthodox belief affirmed in theory that the Son was truly man, in practice this dimension of christology was neglected by many writers. Against that background of comparative neglect Campbell's treatment of the theme is noteworthy. In a variety of ways he emphasises that Christ assumed our 'sinful, fallen nature', taking into personal subsistence with himself not some 'better flesh', but our 'sinful flesh'. In the climate of suspicion surrounding his trial it is perhaps not surprising that his critics in the Presbytery of Lorn assumed that Campbell's perspective 'on the subject of the Lord's humanity' inevitably implied 'that our Lord's holiness was not immaculate'. He believed that such an idea 'might justly be mentioned with abhorrence',[105] for he was convinced that the incarnate Son was sinless, overcoming temptation, 'as a man', through constant dependence upon the power of the Holy Spirit. The work of the Spirit is crucial not only in resisting temptation but to the christology as a whole. Christology and pneumatology coinhere at this point and Campbell is able to avoid a docetic presentation of Christ by giving adequate space to the role of the Spirit in the whole process of incarnation.[106]

Campbell's christology is moulded by soteriological concerns because he is convinced that the only one competent to be a saviour for fallen humanity is one who has fully shared in the human condition. The union of the creature with the Creator in the person of the mediator provides the basis for a view of salvation which embraces the transformation of all creation. Taken as a whole there appears to be sufficient grounds for rejecting Bewkes' contention that Campbell 'did not have any well thought out Christology' during his ministry at Row.

The Sources of Campbell's Christology

It is possible, even probable, that the immediate source of these ideas is to be found in the teaching of Edward Irving who had been teaching about Christ 'taking up fallen humanity' over a number of years. It was in March 1827 that Irving was first suspected of heresy for preaching that Christ had assumed fallen humanity in order to redeem it. During the following year he published a study of christology entitled *The Doctrine of the*

---

[105] *Memorials*, 1. 105. Letter written on the 19 January 1833.
[106] This is further explored in Chapter 7. *Campbell's Trinitarian Christology*.

Incarnation opened in six sermons. In the context of the friendship which developed between Campbell and Irving in 1828 it would have been surprising if Campbell was not aware of his friend's views about the person of Christ. After Irving's visit to Row, in June 1828, Campbell stated that Irving's 'peculiar views were new' to him,[107] and it is likely that these 'peculiar views' concerned the subject of the Lord's humanity.[108] This would fit in with Campbell's statement that, although the subject of the Lord's humanity was the foundation of the gospel he preached, he only became aware of this theme some time after reaching firm conclusions about other key aspects of his theology.[109] Campbell's core convictions about assurance and universal atonement were firmly in place well before Irving arrived in Row in the summer of 1828, and it may be that this aspect of Irving's teaching about Christ's humanity was embraced by Campbell as something which provided further undergirding for his own approach.

Another possible influence on Campbell at this point may have been Thomas Erskine of Linlathen with whom he was in regular contact for over forty years. The extent to which Campbell may have developed some of Erskine's soteriological ideas has already been considered;[110] and it is interesting to note that in outlining the moral character of the atonement in 1831, Erskine made clear his conviction that Christ had assumed fallen human nature. In his comments about both soteriology and christology he uses language similar to that employed by Campbell.

> It was a fallen nature; a nature which had fallen by sin, and which, in consequence of this lay under condemnation. He came into it as a new head, that He might take it out of the fall, and redeem it from sin and lift it up to God, and this could be effected only by His bearing the condemnation, and thus manifesting, through sorrow and death, the character of God, and the character of man's rebellion; manifesting God's abhorrence of sin, and the full sympathy of the new Head of the nature in that abhorrence, and thus eating out the taint of

---

[107] *Reminiscences*, 28.
[108] For further information on their friendship see Chapter 1. *Factors Contributing to his Dismissal*
[109] *S&L*, 1.18.437. 'Though this is the last in the order in which I have myself been instructed, yet it is the foundation truth of all – the foundation of all the rest.'
[110] See Chapter 2. *Conclusion*.

the fall, and making honourable way for the inpouring of the new life into the rebellious body…[111]

While Campbell had already been proclaiming that Christ has assumed fallen human nature before Erskine's book was published, his friendship with Erskine would have meant that he was aware of Erskine's key ideas before they appeared in print. However, in spite of this friendship, Campbell was convinced that he and Erskine had arrived at similar conclusions independently of each other.[112] Their reaching similar conclusions need not imply slavish dependency, but could equally have arisen from their independent reflection upon similar biblical and theological materials. Both of them were aware of Irving's writings and both relied heavily upon biblical language and imagery.

Noting that Erskine 'never formally acknowledged any debt to Irving' in relation to his christological thinking, Horrocks assembles evidence supporting the claim that the mystical writings of William Law 'arguably remain a potential alternative source for Erskine's christology.'[113] However, he concedes that the question, 'to what extent Erskine, rather than Irving, influenced John McLeod Campbell in his own doctrine of fallen human nature remains open.'[114] Campbell's close personal contacts with Irving during 1828 probably tip the scales of influence in Irving's direction; but even if Erskine is not seen as the main influence on Campbell, he clearly functioned as another valuable witness to this truth.

Moving back further in time, part of the inspiration behind the approach adopted by Irving, Erskine and Campbell may lie in the work of the Puritan writer, John Owen, who developed a

---

[111] Extract from *The Brazen Serpent or Life coming through Death*, included in Hanna, (ed.), *Letters of Thomas Erskine*, 547-8.

[112] Hanna, (ed.), *Letters of Thomas Erskine*, 103-4. 'Mr. Scott was with Mr. Campbell in the summer of 1828, and there met Mr. Erskine. It was quite unique the triple friendship which had thus a common birthtime and birthplace; one particular feature marking it in each case. "That historical independence," Dr. Campbell wrote a year or two before his death, "which we mark when two minds, working apart and without any interchange of thought, arrive at the same conclusions, is always an interesting and striking fact when it occurs; and it did occur as to Scott and myself; and also as to Mr. Erskine and me, and I believe too as to Mr. Erskine and Scott."' Cf., R. H. Story, *Memoir of the Life of the Rev. Robert Story*, 152.

[113] Horrocks, *Laws of the Spiritual Order*, 188, 192.

[114] *Ibid.*, 192.

christology which acknowledged the mutual importance of the full humanity of Christ and the work of the Spirit.[115] Alan Spence suggests that Owen's approach can be summarised by saying that 'the Holy Spirit renewed the image of God in the human nature which the eternal Son had assumed into personal union with himself.'[116] The humanity of the Son is genuine because the Spirit formed or made the body of our Lord Jesus Christ 'of the substance of the blessed Virgin'. Salvation would not be possible without the full humanity of Christ, 'for if he had not been made like us in all things, sin only excepted, if he had not been partaker of our nature, there had been no foundation for the imputing that unto us which he did, suffered and wrought, Rom. viii.3,4. And hence these things are accounted unto us, and cannot be so unto angels, whose nature he did not take upon him.'[117]

Through this emphasis upon the actings of the Spirit upon the human nature of the Son, Owen pioneered a way of affirming the full humanity of Christ within the context of an incarnational approach. However, in Owen's case it would not be possible to describe the flesh which the Son assumed, 'into subsistence with himself', as the 'sinful, fallen nature of man'. The import of Owen's language is that it was unfallen nature which Christ assumed, because 'his nature, therefore, as miraculously created in the manner described, was absolutely innocent, spotless, and free from sin, as was Adam in the day wherein he was created.'[118]

From *The Nature of the Atonement* it is clear that Campbell was aware of some aspects of Owen's work about atonement, but the extent to which he was aware of Owen's portrayal of Jesus as a man sharing our nature, inspired by the Holy Spirit, remains uncertain. Clearly Owen's theology could not be appealed to as evidence to support Campbell's teaching about Christ assuming 'sinful flesh', but it could offer sound Reformed support for his

---

[115] *Works of John Owen*, vol. III, 159-188. J. Owen, *The Works of John Owen*, vol. I (ed.), W. H. Goold, (London: Banner of Truth, 1965), 169-178. Cf., Alan Spence, 'Christ's Humanity and Ours: John Owen', in Christoph Schwöbel and Colin Gunton, (eds.), *Persons, Divine and Human*, (Edinburgh: T & T Clark, 1991) 74-97. Alan Spence, 'Incarnation and Inspiration: John Owen and the Coherence of Christology', unpublished PhD, King's College, University of London (1989).
[116] Alan Spence, *Incarnation and Inspiration*, 144.
[117] *Works of John Owen*, vol. III, 164.
[118] *Ibid.*, 168.

emphasis upon the work of the Spirit upon the human nature of Christ.

A Distinguished Line of Thinkers

Geoffrey Wainwright observes that 'in the history of theology there is a narrow but distinguished line of thinkers who insist that the humanity which Christ assumed was not a humanity as it still was "before the fall" nor yet a humanity as it will be in the definitive kingdom, but precisely a *fallen* humanity – though he himself remained without personal sin and was raised in glory at his resurrection.'[119] As samples of this 'distinguished line' of theologians Wainwright mentions Gregory Nazianzus,[120] Karl Barth[121] and Hans Urs von Balthasar;[122] and it is not difficult to identify some others who merit inclusion in this distinguished line of thinkers.

In the course of affirming that 'the nature which God assumed in Christ is identical with our nature as we see it in the light of the Fall', Karl Barth acknowledges the pioneering work of Edward Irving in promoting this doctrine.[123] It addition to including Irving in this 'distinguished line' there may also be a case for adding the name of Jonathan Edwards to the list. As with the case of Owen the extent of Campbell's knowledge of Edwards' work is a matter of debate, but he could have found support for his understanding of the person of Christ in Edwards' statement that 'He did not take the human nature on him in its first, most perfect and vigorous state, but in that feeble forlorn state which it is in since the fall…'[124]

Campbell's occasional references to Calvin during his trial, and the absence of direct references to Calvin in *The Nature of the Atonement* have already been noted. Though he did not do so,

---

[119] Geoffrey Wainwright, *For Our Salvation: Two Approaches to the Work of Christ*, (Grand Rapids: Eerdmans, 1997), 150-1.
[120] 'For what was not assumed, was not healed.'
[121] K. Barth, *Church Dogmatics*, vol. IV, part 1, 258. Cf. *Church Dogmatics*, vol. I, part 2, 40 and 151ff; vol. IV, part 1, 130f; vol. IV, part 2, 27.
[122] von Balthasar, *Mysterium Paschale*, 22. 'The Son of God took human form in its fallen condition, and with it, therefore, the worm in its entrails – mortality, fallenness, self-estrangement, death – which sin introduced into the world.'
[123] *Church Dogmatics*, vol. I, part 2, 147-159.
[124] Jonathan Edwards, 'Sermon on Luke 22:44' in *Edwards' Works*, vol.2, (London: Banner of Truth), 866.

Campbell might have adduced the support of Calvin for his interpretation of the humanity of Christ.[125]

In an examination of the background to Irving's doctrine of human nature, David Dorries[126] advances evidence to support the contention that some of the Church Fathers, such as Irenaeus[127] and Athanasius[128] endorsed the view that Christ assumed human nature under the condition of the fall. Similar material is also considered by Thomas Weinandy, whose study of patristic, medieval and contemporary writers leads him to conclude, that 'the christological tradition definitely confirms that the Eternal Son assumed a humanity which bore the birthmark of Adam. He became man in the likeness of sinful flesh.'[129] Weinandy is aware that there is a degree of ambiguity and tension in patristic christology at this point. On the one hand the principle, that what is not assumed is not healed, leads to an emphasis upon the Son assuming flesh like ours in order to be an effective Saviour. But on the other hand stress upon the

---

[125] Calvin, *Institutes*, IV. xvi. 18. 'For, to wipe out the guilt of the disobedience which had been committed in our flesh, he took that very flesh that in it, for our sake, and in our stead, he might achieve perfect obedience. Thus, he was conceived of the Holy Spirit in order that, in the flesh taken, fully imbued with the holiness of the Spirit, he might impart that holiness to us.' Cf., II. xii. 3. See also David W. Dorries, 'Nineteenth Century British Christological Controversy, centring upon Edward Irving's Doctrine of Christ's Human Nature', unpublished PhD, University of Aberdeen (1987), 288, who argues that 'for Calvin, Christ's incarnate nature was identical to the nature of fallen mankind.'

[126] Dorries, 'Nineteenth Century British Christological Controversy'.

[127] Henry Bettenson, (ed.), *The Early Church Fathers: A selection from the writings of the Fathers from St. Clement of Rome to St. Athanasius*, (Oxford: Oxford University Press, 1956), 77. Irenaeus, *Adversus Haereses*, V.praef. 'Our Lord Jesus Christ, the word of God, of his boundless love, became what we are that he might make us what he himself is.' *Ibid.*, 79, *Adversus Haereses*, III. xviii.6-7 'For he who was to destroy sin and redeem man from guilt had to enter into the very condition of man, who had been dragged into slavery, and was held by death, in order that death might be slain by man, and man should go forth from the bondage of death.'

[128] *St. Athanasius: Select Works and Letters*, 331, *Contra Arianos*, I.43 'The Saviour, humbled Himself in taking "our body of humiliation", and took a servant's form, putting on the flesh which was enslaved to sin.' *Ibid*, 386, *Contra Arianos*, II.70. 'For therefore did He assume the body originate and human, that having renewed it as its Framer, He might deify it in Himself'

[129] Weinandy, *In the Likeness of Sinful Flesh*, 70. See also Weinandy, *Does God Suffer?*, 211ff.

obedience of the Son, who makes himself a perfect offering for sin, tends to underline his dissimilarity to us. At this point it is not necessary to resolve that ambiguity, but to observe that there appears to be growing agreement that the idea of Christ assuming fallen human nature is not a theological novelty, but is rather a doctrine with deep roots in the Christian tradition. It would appear to be the case that the 'distinguished line of thinkers' who advocated this doctrine is much less 'narrow' than some have thought. The evidence surveyed here suggests that, by virtue of his clear teaching that Christ assumed fallen human nature, the name of John McLeod Campbell also deserves to be added to this 'distinguished line of thinkers.'

The Significance of the Subject of the Lord's Humanity

Some writers have failed to notice this dimension of Campbell's thought, perhaps due to lack of familiarity with the Row sermons, which quickly went out of print. He never wrote out this Christology 'for the press' and so did not develop these ideas in a systematic fashion. A few writers[130] have noticed his emphasis upon Christ assuming our sinful, fallen nature, but its implications for understanding the rest of Campbell's theology have not been adequately explored.

This study suggests that Campbell's teaching about Christ assuming fallen human nature is significant, in part, because it sheds new light on the controversial proposal in *The Nature of the Atonement* that Christ made 'a perfect confession of our sins.'[131] For if the Son of God has identified with human beings to the extent of assuming our sinful, fallen nature, then he is in a better position to make a real and meaningful confession of human sinfulness. Such a confession would not be a fiction, as some critics suggest, but could be a genuine confession of the sin which is part of the warp and weft of human existence. Recognition of Christ assuming sinful, fallen human nature does not answer all the questions related to the idea of Christ offering

---

[130] See for example the thorough work of Faris, 'The Nature of Theological Inquiry' 113-9. He notes on page 117 that 'for McLeod Campbell it is obviously an important matter to hold that the flesh which Christ took upon himself was *our sinful flesh*, the flesh of all mankind, because it was this flesh that Christ had taken up and made holy. The fact that Christ did this for us, as our head and representative is our only plea before God.'
[131] *Nature*, 117 (118).

a perfect confession but it provides a basis for countering some of the major criticisms of Campbell's approach.

It has to be conceded that Campbell does not in *The Nature of the Atonement* make clear this presupposition about Christ assuming fallen human nature. If this element was absent from his mature theology this would seriously challenge the thesis that his early christology influences and illuminates his soteriology.

However, the lack of explicit references to this theme in *The Nature of the Atonement* does not in itself prove that Campbell drew back from his earlier understanding of Christ's humanity. Silence on this matter might simply indicate that this belief was something he took for granted, assuming there was no need to justify it. Ultimately it is not necessary to rely on such an argument from silence, because the language Campbell uses in *The Nature of the Atonement* contains clear echoes of the expressions used in the Row sermons to emphasise Christ's total identification with fallen humanity. So when he refers to the Son of God 'in our nature',[132] the language is reminiscent of many early sermons where it clearly refers to Christ coming into our fallen human nature.[133] Another parallel is evident in his references to Romans 8:3, a verse which he frequently used in his early preaching, to support his conviction that Christ assumed sinful flesh.[134]

These connections make it unlikely that he jettisoned these convictions about the subject of the Lord's humanity on being evicted from the manse at Row in 1831. It seems much more probable that these core convictions about Christ coming 'in the likeness of sinful flesh', continued to shape his thinking as he prepared his thoughts about atonement for publication. This suggests that the idea, that 'the flesh of Christ differed not in one particle from mine,' can be regarded as a key to a more accurate interpretation and evaluation of *The Nature of the Atonement*. Perhaps if Campbell had made this idea more explicit in his later work, it would have saved him from considerable misunderstanding and misrepresentation. Having embarked on the task of re-assessing Campbell's soteriology in

---

[132] *Nature*, 59 (76).

[133] The phrase 'God in our nature' features regularly in the early sermons. See for example, *NofS*, 1.2.4,12; 1.4.4,6,8; 1.6.7,11; 1.8.9.

[134] See Chapter 4. *He took Sinful Flesh* and *In the Likeness of Sinful Flesh*.

chapter 2, further reflections upon the soteriological significance of his christology will be advanced in the concluding chapter.[135]

Thomas Weinandy asserts that while this notion of Christ assuming our sinful humanity 'lay dormant within the church's theological tradition, it is...absolutely essential for a complete understanding of the Incarnation and for founding...an adequate and comprehensive soteriology.'[136] The material considered in this chapter points to the conclusion that this notion is, similarly, a vital prerequisite for an accurate understanding of Campbell's portrayal of the person and work of Christ.

---

[135] See Chapter 7. *The Soteriological Significance of Campbell's Christology*.
[136] Weinandy, *Does God Suffer?*, 212.

Chapter 5

Christ's Twofold Office

Since Calvin's time, the idea of Christ's threefold office has provided many theologians with a useful framework for exploring the coinherent themes of the person and work of Christ. Whilst Calvin is credited with popularising the threefold office as a category of systematic theology it would be wrong to imagine that he created this formula out of nothing. Suggestions of Christ's threefold office can be found in earlier writers such as Eusebius and Chrysostom,[1] and in the work of other sixteenth century writers such as Erasmus, Andreas Osiander and Martin Bucer.[2]

In earlier versions of the *Institutes*, Calvin had followed the more widespread practice of speaking about Christ's twofold office as Priest and King. In the 1545 edition of the *Institutes* Calvin adds that Christ 'was also installed in the office of the chief prophet', and in the 1545 *Catechism of the Church of Geneva* the full threefold office is clearly expressed. Here it is stated that the name of Christ 'signifies that he is anointed by his Father to be King, Priest and Prophet'.[3] The move to describing Christ's threefold office is completed in the final edition of the *Institutes* where a chapter is devoted to indicating how Christ fulfils the three offices.[4]

J. F. Jansen has suggested that a major reason for this development towards the idea of Christ's threefold office can be found in the need to provide theological justification for the reformed understanding of Christian ministry. He claims that 'Calvin is anxious to find an adequate biblical foundation for the church's ministry that will preserve the principle of the priesthood of all believers while yet safeguarding the ministerial order against a Roman denial of its authenticity and an

---

[1] John Frederick Jansen, *Calvin's Doctrine of the Work of Christ*, (London: James Clarke, 1956), 29-32.
[2] Geoffrey Wainwright, *For Our Salvation*, 99-120.
[3] Calvin, *Calvin: Theological Treatises*, (ed.), J. K. S. Reid, (London: SCM Press, 1954), 95.
[4] Calvin, *Institutes*, II. xv.

Anabaptist repudiation of church orders.'5 If it is the case that Calvin's teaching about Christ as prophet functioned as a theoretical base for his understanding of ministry, then there may be grounds for suggesting that Christ's prophetic office did not play as significant a role within Calvin's thinking about the person and work of Christ as the offices of Priest and King.

Jansen's study of Calvin's understanding of the work of Christ points to the conclusion that 'while the doctrine of the three offices historically may derive its popularity from Calvin, it is not an adequate or true expression of his own theology. In this instance the earlier and simpler formulation is the better expression of Calvin's Christology.'6 A recognition of the essential twofold structure of Calvin's understanding of Christ's work leads James B. Torrance to assert that within Calvin's writings the prophetic office 'is clearly subordinated to the twofold office of King and Priest.'7

Whilst this assessment of Calvin may be open to debate, within the sermons of John McLeod Campbell the emphasis is clearly much more upon the twofold office of Christ as King and as Priest. His awareness of Christ's prophetic office surfaces in his reminiscences where he recalls that in 'Diets of Catechising' he 'chiefly dwelt on the offices of Christ as a Prophet, a Priest and a King.'8 However, within his preaching the stress falls upon the twofold office, because in these early sermons it is noticeable that Campbell does not portray Christ as prophet, except where he is referring to biblical passages which explicitly describe Jesus as a prophet.9 On one occasion he implies that the

---

5 Jansen, *Calvin's Doctrine*, 45-46. Similarly Wainwright, *For Our Salvation*, 104, says that 'while the pairing of royal and priestly offices had been a commonplace in the Middle Ages, it has been suggested by George Williams that "the conceptualization of Christ as Prophet, Priest and King in Strasbourg and also elsewhere among Protestants" was connected with "the contemporary enhancement of the status of the university-trained teacher (*magister/Meister/Lehrer*) among them": the new pastor-teachers were claiming an authority coordinate with the civil magistracy, were relativizing the sacerdotal view of ecclesiastical ministry, and at the same time were encountering Christocratically the pretension of some radical separatists to a direct authority from the Holy Spirit.'
6 Jansen, *Calvin's Doctrine*, 106.
7 James B. Torrance, 'Vicarious Humanity and Priesthood of Christ', 82.
8 *Reminiscences*, 127.
9 In two sermons, *S&L*, 2.35.427, and *NofS*, 3.32.4, Campbell quotes from Lk. 24:19 where those on the road to Emmaus speak of Jesus of Nazareth as a prophet mighty in word and deed.

category of prophet is not an adequate description of who Jesus was, because 'Christ is not merely a prophet to instruct us what it is concerning God we are to believe, and trust to.'[10] While Campbell does not offer an explanation for this comparative neglect of the prophetic office, the contrasting ecclesiological contexts of Calvin and Campbell may offer some reasons for their varying treatments of this theme.

If it is correct to suggest that part of Calvin's motivation for including the prophetic office in the later editions of his work, was to legitimise his understanding of Christian ministry, then this stands in contrast to Campbell who does not appear to have had the same apologetic need to portray Christ as prophet. Having been dismissed from the official ministry of the Kirk, he did not spend time and energy developing an alternative view of ministry. For Calvin the prophetic office of Christ also served the purpose of guaranteeing that 'the perfect doctrine he has brought has made an end to all prophecies.'[11] Although Campbell was concerned to underline the finality of the revelation brought by Jesus Christ, for him it was Christ in his being as the Son of God, rather than as the final prophet, who played the decisive role in divine revelation. The truth about God was to be found in the Incarnate Son who said 'Anyone who has seen me, has seen the Father.'[12]

Whilst the prophetic office of Christ plays no significant role within Campbell's preaching and theology, there is sufficient material about Christ as priest and king to justify talk about Campbell's understanding of Christ's twofold office. Although Campbell does not use that terminology, his portrayal of Christ as the High Priest and as the King can conveniently be described in that way. This chapter concentrates mainly upon material contained in the Row sermons which illustrates Christ's twofold office, and it advances the aims of this study by contributing to a fuller picture of Campbell's understanding of Christ's person and work.

In his study of the threefold office Geoffrey Wainwright[13] identifies five historic uses of the triad of prophet, priest and king. He argues that 'the five uses may be styled (1) the christological, (2) the baptismal, (3) the soteriological, (4) the

---

[10] *NofS*, 2.23.1.
[11] Calvin, *Institutes*, II. xv. 2.
[12] Jn. 14:9. Cf., Heb. 1:1-2 which declares the Son's priority above the prophets.
[13] Wainwright, *For Our Salvation*, 109.

ministerial, and (5) the ecclesiological. Naturally, there is overlap among them.' Within this analysis, 'the baptismal' use refers to the experience of the baptised who, by virtue of their baptism share in the royal, priestly and kingly dignity of Christ. Wainwright places this 'baptismal' category second in his list because this experience of grace comes directly from the person of Christ. However, there is a case for arguing that it would be much more appropriate to place 'the baptismal' category after 'the soteriological', because the Christian experience of grace flows from both the person and work of Christ. In distinguishing between the 'baptismal' and the 'ecclesiological' uses of this phrase, Wainwright may be seeking to draw attention to both the nature of individual Christian experience and the corporate experience of the church. Clearly there is considerable overlap between the two, and for the purposes of this study it seems appropriate to combine them. Whilst the ministerial and the ecclesiological uses of this triad are not prominent within Campbell's thinking and preaching, the first three of Wainwright's categories combine to provide a helpful basis for examining and evaluating Campbell's understanding of Christ's twofold office as priest and as king. The following examination of Campbell's teaching about Christ as Priest and King will seek to consider its 'christological', 'soteriological' and 'baptismal' dimensions, and it will also seek to indicate some of the areas where Campbell's approach resembles Calvin's.

The Priestly Office

Before considering Campbell's understanding of the priesthood of Christ it will be helpful to look briefly at Calvin's portrayal of Christ's priestly office where these 'christological', 'soteriological' and 'baptismal' dimensions are clearly evident. In the work of accomplishing salvation Christ the priest is the one who appeases God's wrath 'by the sacrifice of his death'. Soteriology is undergirded by christology because the only-begotten Son alone was able to offer an adequate satisfaction for our sins. This brings benefits to the baptised because the one who is both priest and sacrifice 'is an everlasting intercessor: through his pleading we obtain favour'. So 'now, Christ plays the priestly role, not only to render the Father favourable and propitious toward us by an eternal law of reconciliation, but also to receive us as his companions in this great office [Rev. 1:6]. For we who are defiled in ourselves, yet are priests in him, offer ourselves and our all to God, and freely enter the heavenly sanctuary that the sacrifices of prayers and praise that we bring may be acceptable and sweet-smelling before God.'[14]

Similar aspects of Christ's priestly work can also be detected within Campbell's sermons, even if it is presented in a much less systematic way. Perhaps the most significant sermon relating to this theme is one based on Hebrews 10:31.[15]

An High Priest over the House of God

In this sermon Campbell wants his hearers to be aware that while God is 'infinite love, yet we are taught that he will destroy the wicked.'[16] The author[17] of the letter to the Hebrews writes to warn his readers against turning back from God. Having been illuminated, they have encountered opposition and have endured it joyfully. The hope of a better future had spurred them on to persevere. In Jesus they had 'an High Priest over the house of God' and knowing this enabled them to draw near to God. The hearers of the sermon, like the readers of the letter before them, are faced with a choice between drawing near to God or 'trampling under foot the Son of God.'

From Campbell's perspective it is the light of the atonement which illuminates people's lives. The battle about the extent of the atonement is clearly visible as he observes 'that some have held, and do hold and teach, that Christ did not die for all: but that he only died for a certain portion of the human race. This is a widespread error in our land and the root of it is not understanding what the atonement is.'[18]

He rejects a penal approach to atonement believing that it misses the point of genuine atonement.[19] During Old Testament times various sins rendered people unfit for worship, but the shedding of sacrificial blood removed that uncleanness and made it possible for people to worship God. Seeing the worship in the Temple as 'typical' of the Christian's relationship with God he believes that 'the great object of the sacrifice of Christ was to put us in a condition to worship God.'[20] The object of atonement, therefore, is not the negative purpose of avoiding

---

[14] Calvin, *Institutes*, II. xv. 6. See also IV. xix. 28, IV. xix. 30.
[15] *NofS*, 3.36. Appendix 7.
[16] Ibid., 3.36.1. Appendix 7.
[17] Campbell assumes that the Apostle Paul wrote the letter to the Hebrews.
[18] *NofS*, 3.36.6. Appendix 7.
[19] Ibid., 3.36.6-7. Appendix 7.
[20] Ibid., 3.36.8. Appendix 7.

punishment, but much more positively to enable people to come and worship God in spirit and in truth. The apostle could encourage his readers to draw near to God because of his convictions about the High Priestly work of Christ. It is against this background that Campbell provides a theologically rich vision of the person and work of the High Priest.

The Spirit of Christ comes to me from the risen Christ — the second Adam — the quickening Spirit — and I am entering into the Holiest by a living way when the Spirit of Christ, coming from the risen man Christ Jesus, is entering into me and when I am thus joined with him and am conscious of the holy presence of God through having the Spirit of him, who is in the holy presence of God, and when I am conscious of fellowship with the holiness of God, through having this Spirit of him who has fellowship in the holiness of God...

...(Through) the rent veil of the flesh of Christ we have a way into the Holiest. He is there in the immediate presence of God in unbroken communion with God and his Spirit in us to connect us with this, and thus we are called to sit in heavenly places in Christ Jesus...The High Priest is in the Holy of Holies and we having the High Priest over the house of God are connected with his presence in the Holy of Holies. In the service of the temple, while the high priest was alone within the veil, the people were without, but in truth both were engaged in one act of worship, and so it is now: for the members of Jesus all participate in the worship which their great High Priest is rendering to the Father within the veil. There is but one Spirit and the Spirit in which Jesus within the veil is honouring, worshipping and glorifying the Father is the same Spirit which is in all the members, so that it is one great work of giving glory to God through the living Head Christ Jesus.[21]

Viewed from a 'christological' perspective this passage yields several important insights into the nature of Christ. The one who occupies the office of High Priest over the house of God is described as the 'risen Christ', as 'the second Adam', and as 'the quickening Spirit' who pours out the Holy Spirit upon his people. This High Priest 'is receiving continually of the fullness of the Godhead' and he is uniquely equipped to be 'a real Mediator between God and man' because he is also our 'Brother'. This stress upon Christ as our brother, as the one who has fully identified with us in our humanity, is one of the

---

[21] *Ibid.*, 3.36.10-11. Appendix 7.

christological points which Campbell underlines when he refers to Jesus as the High Priest in a number of other sermons.[22] Campbell's depiction of Christ as the High Priest stands or falls upon the conviction, highlighed in chapter 4, that Christ has fully identified himself with fallen humanity. In the contemporary words of Morna Hooker, 'it is only someone who is "one of us" who can be our high priest'.[23]

The High Priestly language employed here also serves to illustrate a number of 'soteriological' themes. This Priest has offered an adequate sacrifice for sins because he *'presented himself through the Eternal Spirit, without spot to God.'* By thus entering the very presence of God, the High Priest achieves salvation by bringing believers into the Holiest place. The 'soteriological' and the 'baptismal' dimensions overlap as Campbell describes how believers are truly involved in the worship of heaven in the person of the High Priest. 'In the service of the temple, while the high priest was alone within the veil, the people were without, but in truth *both were engaged in one act of worship, and so it is now: for the members of Jesus all participate in the worship which their great High Priest is rendering to the Father within the veil.'*[24] There were sound historical precedents within the Reformed tradition for such an approach, because in his *Commentary on Hebrews* Calvin had spoken of all Israel going 'into the sanctuary together in the person of the one man.' This prefigures the priestly ministry of Christ and implies 'that our High Priest has entered heaven, because He has done so not only for Himself, but also for us.'[25]

The 'baptismal' dimension is clearly in view because this High Priest provides the Holy Spirit who enables believers to participate in 'the mind of God, the holiness of God' and to 'sit in heavenly places in Christ Jesus'. Campbell's stress upon the

---

[22] E.g., *S&L*, 1.16.390 'That precious foundation-truth that Christ is bone of your bone and flesh of your flesh — that he came in your very nature, and partook of it, just as you possess it — that truth which is the well-spring of every one who welcomes Jesus Christ as the high-priest touched with the feeling of our infirmities' Cf., *NofS*, 3.34.7-8. Appendix 8.

[23] Morna D. Hooker, *Not Ashamed of the Gospel: New Testament Interpretations of the Death of Christ*, (Carlisle: Paternoster, 1994), 113. H. Thielicke, *The Evangelical Faith, Volume 2: The Doctrine of God and of Christ*, (Edinburgh: T & T Clark, 1977), 366.

[24] *NofS*, 3.36.11. Appendix 7.

[25] Commentary on Heb. 6:19. J. Calvin, *The Epistle of Paul the Apostle to the Hebrews and the First and Second Epistles of St. Peter*, (Grand Rapids: Eerdmans, 1963), 87.

Spirit enabling Christians to 'participate in the worship which their great High Priest is rendering to the Father within the veil' is consonant with Calvin's conviction that Christ receives 'us as his companions in this great office' of priesthood so that we 'are priests in him'.[26] The continuing worship which Christ is offering within the veil similarly resonates with Calvin's teaching about Christ appearing 'before the Father's face as our constant advocate and intercessor.'[27]

Whilst this vision of the ascended Christ acting as the great High Priest should encourage people to respond to the opportunity to draw near to God, Campbell laments that some 'men are turning up their Bibles to see if they can find texts that will help them to say that God really does not love them.'[28] The debate about assurance being of the essence of faith surfaces in the concluding sections of the sermon as he urges people to draw near to God.

In addition to some of the familiar elements of Campbell's theology, this sermon adds to an understanding of his christology by offering a comprehensive picture of Christ as the great High Priest. Christologically, it underlines Christ's assumption of our fallen humanity as a necessary precondition for him to function as the High Priest. Soteriologically, it points to the one who is both priest and sacrificial victim. The representative character of the High Priest's work suggests that salvation transforms people by drawing them into the presence of God and by enabling them to participate in Christ's ongoing priestly work.

Past and Present Dimensions of Christ's Priestly Ministry

The emerging picture of Christ's priestly work is enhanced by another sermon based on Hebrews chapter 2.[29] In this sermon Campbell begins with a running commentary on the whole chapter, and affirms 'that Christ connected himself with all mankind by the ties of brotherhood when he became man.'[30] It is again underlined that this full identification with human beings in their fallen predicament is an essential component of Christ's High Priestly work. Although the preacher's language

---

[26] Calvin, *Institutes*, II. xv. 6.
[27] *Ibid.*, II. xvi. 16.
[28] *NofS*, 3.36.11. Appendix 7.
[29] *NofS*, 3.34. Appendix 8.
[30] *Ibid.*, 3.34.4. Appendix 8.

lacks precision, the principle that 'what he has not assumed he has not healed',[31] would appear to be at work here. Campbell implies that salvation is only possible if Christ has indeed 'been in the very nature in which I am'.

> Two things are contemplated in Christ's work of reconciling sinners to God: *first, the work of Christ in his own person, when he dwelt in the flesh, and the work of Christ now, as our High Priest entered within the veil.*...In both these it behoved him to be made like unto his brethren...because if he had not been my brother, that is, dwelt in my flesh, and been in the very nature in which I am, he could not have done that which he has done — he could (not)[32] have glorified God in that very nature in which God has been dishonoured.'

In thinking about Christ's suffering Campbell resists any idea that God was punishing Christ upon the cross. Anticipating the approach which would be expressed later in *The Nature of the Atonement*, he considers the kind of sorrows that God could see with satisfaction. 'What are the sorrows over which God can rejoice? The sorrows of holiness in a world of sin — the groans and sighs of the righteous One in the midst of the disobedience of the Father's law.'[33] While Christ has fully identified with human beings he remains free from sin, and because his moral vision is not obscured by sin, he sees sin for what it truly is and feels profound pain over the ways in which men and women flout the laws of God.

The 'christological', 'soteriological' and 'baptismal' elements are again interwoven in Campbell's depiction of the person and work of the High Priest. His full humanity is necessary equipment for the task of being a merciful and faithful high priest. Once more Christ is seen as the High Priest who presents himself as a sacrifice to God. This vision of the High Priest has a directly pastoral application because the High Priest is the one who is engaged in a constant ministry of intercession. 'The intercession of Christ is not a form....*This intercession is in his presenting, in his holy and glorified human nature the very same petitions which we present on earth* — his having it in his heart, not as a thought: but as a sentiment and as a feeling, *so that my prayer in the Spirit is Christ's own personal prayer. When I beseech God to give, Christ beseeches God to give. He is desirous to get the*

---

[31] Gregory of Nazianzus.
[32] 'not' added to the text.
[33] *NofS*, 3.34.7. Appendix 8.

thing.'[34] Viewed from this perspective prayer does not depend upon our human ability to pray but is much more about being caught up into Christ's continual intercession.

Christ's High Priestly work has not come to an end, because *'He is still reconciling men to God. This he does as the channel of our prayers, and as the channel of God's answers — as our merciful High Priest — as thus for ever bringing us nearer and nearer to God.'*[35] His priesthood did not come to an end with the sacrifice of himself upon the cross but it continues now and for ever. By virtue of his experience in our flesh, the great High Priest knows all that human beings have to face and is willing and able to help people to resist temptation and to live in the way that pleases God.

This sermon confirms the emerging picture of Christ as High Priest in Campbell's preaching and underlines the constant intercession of the High Priest which undergirds all human attempts to pray. Michael Jinkins argues that a theology of prayer can be deduced from Campbell's portrayal of Christ's priestly office.

> Christ is the only true worshipper...perfectly praying to God in our humanity *on our behalf*. The way to true prayer is to pray 'in the name of Christ,' with 'the mind of Christ'...(We) only pray truly when our prayers participate in the prayer which Christ continually offers to God on our behalf. To pray in the name of Jesus is to pray *after* Christ, or in accordance with the mind of Christ, trusting the Spirit of God to join our prayer to Christ's own, and to open our ears to Christ's prayer for us, to what it is that Christ wants us to pray. The essential quality of this prayer (and this is the key to understanding the true nature of prayer) is the utter dependence upon God, the Father, which we have seen in the self-giving life of Christ.[36]

Jinkins outlines an attractive view of prayer which focuses more attention upon the continuing priestly activity of Christ than upon human efforts to pray. His account is based on a plausible reading of clues contained in a variety of Campbell's books and sermons, but he expresses things much more systematically and concisely than Campbell himself would have done. However attractive this portrayal of prayer may be, there does not appear

---

[34] *Ibid.,* 3.34.7-8. Appendix 8.
[35] *Ibid.,* 3.34.8. Appendix 8.
[36] Michael Jinkins, *Love is of the Essence: An Introduction to the Theology of John McLeod Campbell,* (Saint Andrew Press: Edinburgh, 1993), 19-20.

to be sufficient material to justify Jinkins' bold assertion that 'few dogmatic theologians have worked out with such care a theology of prayer as McLeod Campbell has.'[37] It is more accurate to say that an interesting theology of prayer is latent within Campbell's preaching and writing, and that any adequate Christian understanding of prayer will need to include the priestly dimensions highlighted by Campbell.

In addition to these two sermons which explicitly address Christ's priestly office, there are other references to his priestly work scattered through a number of the Row sermons. In a sermon about 'Confessing Christ'[38] Campbell sees Christ's presence at God's right hand as our advocate, as the guarantee that we have been forgiven. 'So that if any man ask me, how do I know that my sin is forgiven, my answer is because Christ is at the right hand of God for me — because he is my high priest over the house of God — because he is my advocate, and my intercessor with the Father.'[39] At the heart of this priestly function is the notion of representation, because 'he is there not as an individual, but as the Saviour — as the Head — as the representative of those for whose salvation he came; and his very presence there is that which is to inspire us with confidence in drawing near to God.'[40] As High Priest, Christ does not represent his people in some distant manner because there is an intimate connection between Christ and the members of his body. So 'just as my hands and feet have in them the same blood that is in my heart, and it is all one blood, so the members of Christ's body have in them one Spirit, and that is Christ's Spirit; that Spirit which is now dwelling in the glorified head Christ Jesus, and which comes down upon them from this High Priest, as the oil poured on the head of Aaron ran down the skirts of his garments.'[41] In using such language Campbell is intensifying the notion of representation and interpreting it to mean a real participation in the risen life of Christ. By virtue of his resurrection and ascension Christ is exalted as the great High Priest who pours out his Spirit on his people. This is the foundation for the frequent affirmation that 'Christ has the Holy

---

[37] Ibid., 18.
[38] S&L, 2.33.
[39] Ibid., 2.33.372.
[40] Ibid., 2.33.372.
[41] S&L, 2.23.102 and NofS, 1.8.5. Appendix 4.

Spirit for us', and that it is the Spirit who enables people to draw near to God.[42]

These selections indicate that Campbell had a clear understanding of Christ's priestly office, and there is evidence to suggest that he maintained this emphasis throughout his ministry. This priestly perspective is also present in at least one of the sermons from the Glasgow phase of his ministry,[43] and in his most significant book, *The Nature of the Atonement*. At a number of places there Campbell explicitly describes Christ as the High Priest;[44] and in devoting a chapter to 'The intercession which was an element in the atonement considered as prayer'[45] it is clear that Campbell is relying upon the language and imagery of Christ as the great High Priest. If the 'retrospective' and 'prospective' understanding of atonement which Campbell develops is to be in any way plausible, then it needs to be undergirded by a clear sense of Christ representing men and women in his capacity as the great High Priest.

The Royal Office

> The Lord Jesus Christ is sole king and rightful possessor of this earth; and that all kings, magistrates, rulers, judges, bishops, ministers, and persons in authority, of every class and degree, are his delegates, and consequently bound to use the power intrusted to them for the propagation of His truth.[46]

Alongside Campbell's understanding of Christ's priestly office it is also relevant to consider his portrayal of Christ's royal office. It is once again appropriate to set this in the context of Reformed theology by referring to Calvin's treatment of this theme. For Calvin, the kingly office of Christ has a practical application to the life of the baptised because 'God surely promises here that through the hand of his Son he will be the eternal protector and

---

[42] *NofS*, 3.25.5. In other sermons Campbell uses the phrases, 'Christ has the Spirit for you', 'He has the Holy Spirit for you', and 'He has the Spirit for you'. See *NofS* 1.5.3,4; 1.7.10,14; 1.8.9, (Appendix 4); 1.10.5; 2.13.14, (Appendix 6), 2.20.12; 2.24.10; 3.25.5; 3.30.8; 3.31.5; 3.35.3,6,11.
[43] *FofT*, 15.176-7 'The Lord Jesus Christ is revealed to us as the Head of this spiritual worship. He is the High Priest of redeemed humanity.'
[44] See for example *Nature*, 143, 156-7, 160, 167, 168, 172, (135-6, 144-6, 147, 151, 152, 155)
[45] *Ibid.*, chapter 9.
[46] *TS*, vi-vii.

defender of his church.'[47] In the battle against evil Christ has won a royal victory, because 'the cross, which was full of shame, had been changed into a triumphal chariot.'[48] As the risen victorious king, Christ is armed with such eternal power 'that the perpetuity of the church is secure in his protection.'[49] This protection is guaranteed because God has appointed his Son eternal King by immutable decree.[50] At this point it is worth noting J. F. Jansen's observation that Calvin does not attempt to fix any time in the life of Christ when He began to reign, for the kingdom comes in Him, He is king — He does not become king. Accordingly, Calvin avoids the tendency of later protestant dogmatics which confined the kingly office to the state of exaltation.'[51] It appears to be the case that Calvin does not explicitly explain when Christ was anointed to reign as King. Although his baptism is a 'visible symbol' of the sacred anointing which marks him out as the promised King,[52] this anointing did not begin at that moment, because 'we must bear in mind that Christ came endowed with the Holy Spirit in a special way'.[53]

The royal office of Christ has direct bearing on matters of salvation because 'Christ enriches his people with all things necessary for the eternal salvation of souls and fortifies them with courage to stand unconquerable against all the assaults of spiritual enemies.'[54] God has entrusted all power to the Son, so that through the Son he can 'nourish, and sustain us, keep us in his care, and help us.' As their king and pastor the Son rules over his people but another vital dimension of his royal power is that he will bring about judgement upon the ungodly. The Last Judgement 'may also be properly considered the last act of his reign.'[55] Campbell's debt to the Reformed tradition is again evident as a number of these themes reappear in the glimpses of Christ's royal office which surface in his Row sermons.

---

[47] Calvin, *Institutes*, II. xv. 3.
[48] *Ibid.*, II. xvi. 6.
[49] *Ibid.*, II. xv. 3.
[50] *Ibid.*, II. xv. 3.
[51] Jansen, *Calvin's Doctrine*, 86.
[52] Calvin, *Institutes*, II. xv. 5.
[53] *Ibid.*, III. i. 2.
[54] *Ibid.*, II. xv. 4.
[55] *Ibid.*, II. xv. 5.

'One from Among thy Brethren'

The priestly and kingly offices both play a part in a sermon on Deuteronomy 17:14-15 which explores the topic of 'Our King, Our Brother.'[56] In this sermon Campbell perceives that the Old Testament insistence that Israel must select one of their brothers to be the king, is an idea which finds ultimate fulfilment in the Lord Jesus Christ 'being set up as king'. Viewed in this way the kingly office does not highlight a transcendent distinction between Christ and people, but emphasises rather that the king is a brother who shares with us in 'having a common nature'.[57] 'The idea of brother, is that of one who is of the same root, the same stock – it is the conception of one who has in his veins the same blood which circulates in ours – one who is bone of our bone and flesh of our flesh – one who inherits that nature and being which we have, and who is no stranger to what is in us, because he himself has that which is in us.'[58]

Campbell reiterates 'the great truth which is the foundation of our religion, that Christ took our very nature – that he was made in the likeness of sinful flesh – that he became bone of our bone, and flesh of our flesh, and became, in very truth, our very brother; so that there is nothing in the whole of human nature with which he has not the acquaintance of one who took that nature upon himself.'[59] However, in passing he takes care to explain that what took place in the incarnation did not add to God's reservoir of knowledge. For it is not 'that God has not that acquaintance, that understanding, of our condition, as God, which is possessed by Christ as our brother'.[60] If this had been the case it would imply that God's knowledge before the incarnation was in some way imperfect and incomplete, and this would call into question His perfection and deity. Whilst the incarnation did not bring any 'new' knowledge to God it served

---

[56] *S&L*, 2.30. Campbell had appealed to this text as part of his defence before the Presbytery of Dumbarton in September 1830. See *Proceedings*, 16.
[57] *S&L*, 2.30.279.
[58] *Ibid.*, 2.30.279. His friend, the Rev'd Robert Story, used similar language at the Presbytery of Dumbarton on 21 September 1830. 'I will never cease to teach what I know many around me teach, that there is a connexion between every man and Christ…there is a connexion between Christ and every person of Adam's race, which does not exist between him and other races of beings.' *Proceedings*, p xxxii.
[59] *Ibid.*, 2.30.279.
[60] *Ibid.*, 2.30.279.

to demonstrate certain truths to human beings which they could not otherwise understand.[61]

It is evident from Campbell's comments that he did not believe that Christ had a superior kind of human nature which made it easier for him to resist temptation. 'Corrupted as the flesh is', it was in that situation that Christ crucified the flesh in the power of the Spirit. Christologically this implies that Christ assumed a human nature which was fully subject to the temptations of sinning, but that through constant dependence on the power of the Spirit, those temptations were always resisted. This creates the impression that Campbell is portraying a Christ who was *able not to sin*, rather than one who, due to his divine nature, was *not able to sin*.[62] The implication for the life of the baptised is that the incarnate Christ has shown that being in the flesh does not make sin inevitable. For 'the acquaintance with us which Christ has is, in fact, the knowledge that we are without excuse in sinning. It is the experimental knowledge that, corrupted as the flesh is, it puts the person who has the flesh under no necessity for sinning against God'[63]

---

[61] *Ibid.*, 2.30.279, 'we could not know or understand the knowledge which God has of us, had we not been taught it in Christ, who is God, and who is our brother.'

[62] Donald Macleod, *The Person of Christ*, 229-230, argues that while *able not to sin* was true of the First Adam, of the Last Adam we must say that he was *not able to sin*. He claims that 'it does not follow, however, that when Christ was tempted he was always aware, at the human level, that the Tempter could never conquer him...It would certainly be unwise to conclude that at every single point Jesus was in full possession of the whole truth about himself.' Such comments indicate difficulties rather than resolving them, for if Jesus was *not able to sin* his conflict was not the same as that faced by human beings. P. T. Forsyth, *The Person and Place of Jesus Christ*, (London: Hodder & Stoughton, 1910), 301, reflects that Jesus 'knew he came sinless out of each crisis; did he know he never could be anything else? How could he? Would it have been moral conflict if he had known this?' Forsyth is conscious that any notion of Jesus having a 'foregone immunity' to temptation, even if he was unaware of it, would place Jesus in a very different situation from the rest of humanity. One way forward, Forsyth suggests, is to see that the freedom to sin is not the hallmark of true humanity, because from Jesus we see rather that true humanity consists in the freedom not to sin. Part of the difficulty may be the assumption that we know in advance what divine nature and human nature are like, and then seek to force Jesus Christ into those categories.

[63] *S&L*, 2.30.285-286. See also 292 'we...should see this brother as our king, and should know that power belongeth to him to execute judgement.'

Christ's full identification with fallen humanity is a common feature of Campbell's portrayal of both the kingly and priestly offices of Christ.[64] While this clearly offers grounds for encouragement, it also brings the disturbing realisation that the one who will judge, is the one 'who has himself proved the fact of there being no necessity for our having sinned against God.'[65] Campbell argues that it would be potentially misleading to talk about Christ as our brother unless this is allied to the recognition that our brother is also 'our King'. 'There is, indeed, in the word "brother," viewed apart from the word "king," only a partial expression of the character of God.'[66] The compassionate, sympathetic connotations of the word 'brother' need to be held together with the authority associated with a king who expects his subjects to obey his commands. So for a more accurate view of God, and a more adequate understanding of Christian life, the firm authority of a king needs to be combined with the compassionate actions of a brother.[67]

Since Campbell's day attitudes to royalty have changed dramatically, and where monarchs still exist in Europe they have neither the authority to command obedience nor the power to enforce it. The youthful preacher from Row, however, had no such doubts about the authority and power of Christ the king. The message of unquestioning submission to Christ's authority sits uneasily with the contemporary suspicion of all kinds of authority, but for Campbell submission to Christ was not bondage but rather the route to blessing.[68]

The good news for believers is that the heavenly king protects and strengthens his people in their daily conflict with evil, for 'in Christ, as king, there is the provision for strength, as well as the provision for authority. Our king is one who has power, not merely to be used against us if we refuse him to reign over us, but to be used for us in our submitting to him. He is a king to minister to our need, to supply the wants of the poor and needy.'[69] Whilst Campbell does not make it explicit here, his sermons in general make clear that it is by the power of the

---

[64] *Ibid.*, 2.30.291.
[65] *Ibid.*, 2.30.286.
[66] *Ibid.*, 2.30.288. Cf., 2.30.291.
[67] *Ibid.*, 2.30.292-3.
[68] *Ibid.*, 2.30.296. 'Any other place than that of conscious dependance on God is unnatural to a creature as such; and blessed be God, to choose any other place is to refuse true blessedness.'
[69] *Ibid.*, 2.30.293. Cf. Calvin, *Institutes*, II. xv. 4.

Spirit that the King enables believers to fight the good fight of faith.

The kingship of Christ also has to do with questions about peace in the government of the universe. The knowledge of having 'a brother as a King,' brings peace to believers in the midst of a troubled world, because 'we see the character of him who governs, and can say that all must be well.'[70]

In addition there is an eschatological dimension to the way in which Campbell portrays Christ's kingly office in this sermon. So he urges his hearers 'to stand in awe of Christ – to fear the great and terrible day of the Lord your God, and to remember that your brother is your king.'[71] At the same time he wants the congregation to realise that the future will bring a kind of beatific vision as they encounter the King in all his heavenly glory.

> To have intercourse with him as a high Priest, touched with a feeling of our infirmities, is a high condition; yet it is the full realization of his being God, and the intercourse with him as God, in the kingdom that is to be revealed, that I regard as the highest condition of the creature; because, indeed, it is the right – the perfect condition.[72]

This sermon provides a good entry point into Campbell's thinking about the kingly office of Christ. In common with his portrayal of Christ as High Priest there is a strong emphasis on the real humanity of the King. The one who is both brother and king expects obedience and has the power to defend his people. The day is coming when his authority will be manifested before all and the eternal vision of the divine king will bring fullness of joy.

The Promised King

In a sermon on John 3:1-6 entitled 'The Kingdom of God'[73] Campbell portrays Nicodemus as one who was looking for the kingdom. This leads him into a reflection upon the Old Testament promise of a King or Messiah which comes to fulfilment in the angel's promise to Mary of the one who would reign over the house of Jacob for ever, whose kingdom will

---

[70] *S&L*, 2.30.297.
[71] *Ibid.*, 2.30.299.
[72] *Ibid.*, 2.30.297.
[73] *Ibid.*, 2.35.

never end.⁷⁴ Even the mistaken belief that the kingdom would appear instantly is seen as evidence for the widespread expectation in Israel for a promised king and a coming kingdom. A biblical basis for the christological claim that Jesus Christ is the promised king is partly provided by Psalm 2:6⁷⁵, because 'in this, the setting up of Christ, as a king over the earth, is distinctly announced.'⁷⁶ Alongside this Campbell refers to Isaiah 55:3, which is a text he refers to in a number of sermons.⁷⁷ For 'Jesus is here set forth as a witness, a leader and a commander. A witness is one to represent, to reveal God: a leader and commander is one to reign over men in God's name.'⁷⁸

Having considered God's establishment of such a king, Campbell moves to consider Revelation chapter 5, where the kingdom is entrusted to the Lord Jesus Christ, and this prompts him to ask why Christ receives it? He concludes that God entrusts the kingdom to Christ because he was worthy to receive it, and this worthiness resides in his love for righteousness and his hatred of wickedness. To some extent there is a contrast between Calvin's avoidance of identifying the time when Christ began to reign, and Campbell's suggestion that the time of Christ's being set up as a king was clearly the time of his resurrection.⁷⁹ Referring to Acts 13:32ff he argues 'that it was in raising him up from the dead, to his own right hand, that God fulfilled the promise made to the fathers, in that, he gave them the promised king.'⁸⁰ Christ was shown fit to be a king because he loved God with all his heart and because he loved all his neighbours as himself. Campbell does not miss the opportunity to stress that Christ loves all and has died for all.

---

⁷⁴ Lk. 1:30-34.
⁷⁵ 'Yet have I set my king upon my holy hill of Zion.'
⁷⁶ *S&L*, 2.35.430.
⁷⁷ Calvin uses this passage as he introduces his comments on the threefold office of Christ. Calvin, *Institutes*, II. xv. 1.
⁷⁸ *S&L*, 2.35.430.
⁷⁹ It would be unwise to exaggerate the differences between Campbell and Calvin at this point. In *NofS*, 1.7.7., Campbell argues that 'as God' the inheritance of the kingdom belonged to the Son 'from the first, but it was that he might possess it by right and title *as a man* that he was born and died and rose again: as he himself says that he came to be a King — that he was born to be a King.'
⁸⁰ *S&L*, 2.35.434.

God gave him the kingdom, because he loved God with all his heart, and thus proved himself fit to be trusted with it; so we are asked to bow the knee and give our hearts to him, because he loves each of us as he loves himself. No other king could make the heart bow. The heart can only bow to love – 'We love him *because* he first loved us'.[81]

Christ's love for God and for all his neighbours was shown by *his death* and by his *dying life* because the life of Christ was 'a continual death', by which he means a constant crucifying of the flesh in the power of the Spirit. If his death reveals the deadly nature of sin then his resurrection demonstrates the power of the Spirit to overcome sin. 'It is…in believing, that Christ died for us, and rose for us, and in seeing ourselves risen with Christ, we receive the Spirit.'[82]

All of this provides Campbell with a basis for urging his hearers to submit their lives to the rule of Christ, and this invitation is reinforced by a solemn warning that judgement will be the last act of his reign.

> (The) Judge standeth at the door…the day of grace now weareth to the evening, and…the dawn of the judgement morning is about to break upon us…(The) love of the righteous king has been proclaimed through many channels — through his word and sacraments — through the consciences of men and the Spirit speaking in their consciences…God has never left himself without a witness in the world, or in the heart; *every where* there has been a witness for God: and therefore, were Christ to come at this moment, it would be most righteous that every one who is not giving glory to God, should be overwhelmed with everlasting destruction.[83]

It is clear from this passage, and from a number of other sermons, that Campbell shares with Calvin the conviction that future judgement is an essential dimension of the work of the eternal King.[84] This conviction has firm biblical roots because the ideal king portrayed in the Old Testament is one who intervenes to ensure that justice prevails, especially for the weak

---

[81] *Ibid.*, 2.35.438.
[82] *Ibid.*, 2.35.447.
[83] *Ibid.*, 2.35.450.
[84] E.g., *NofS*, 1.5.3. 'God will yet reveal Christ as Judge and as King'.

The Enthronement of Christ and its Consequences

Campbell employs very similar arguments in a sermon based on Titus 2:11-14 which explores the hope of the appearing of the great God and our Saviour Jesus Christ.[87] From the outset he makes clear that the focus of Christian hope is not what happens to believers at death, but is the larger hope for the second coming of Christ. He also wishes to avoid any idea that the Gospel is primarily about Christ averting divine wrath away from sinners. On this occasion his concern is not so much to challenge punitive images of God, but to challenge individualistic views of salvation by insisting that the gospel of the kingdom is primarily about submitting to the righteous government of God.[88] In this way the affirmation that Christ is the messiah-king, is directly linked to the experience of Christian believers. These 'christological' and 'baptismal' emphases are similarly combined as he explains that submitting to this King means surrendering to the one who is able to deliver from the power of evil.[89]

Employing the same arguments and biblical references used in the sermon on John 3:1-6,[90] he continues to speak of the resurrection as the time of Christ's enthronement as the promised king, and affirms that God gave him the kingdom as a reward for righteousness. Affirming that Christ was enthroned as King after his resurrection, in no way detracts from Campbell's conviction that the Son was eternally divine. However he is keen to point out that the Son's exaltation was not the resumption of pre-existent glory but a reward for his obedient fulfilment of God's plan of salvation.

> You are not to suppose that Christ is exalted as King because he is God. Christ is as God blessed for ever; from eternity to eternity: but the kingdom foretold in prophecy was to be given to the King, as a reward of his righteousness....So that

---

[85] Ps. 72:1-4, 8-14.
[86] Is. 9:7, 11:2-5.
[87] *NofS*, 3.32. Appendix 9.
[88] *Ibid.*, 3.32.2. Appendix 9.
[89] *Ibid.*, 3.32.2. Appendix 9.
[90] See Chapter 5. *The promised King;* Sermon on Jn. 3:1-6. 'The kingdom of God.' *S&L*, 2.35.

Christ is exalted as a King because of his worthiness, because of his deserving, because he wrought for it and won it.[91]

The Jews and the first disciples were not mistaken in expecting the coming King to inherit a visible kingdom, 'but their great mistake was in imagining that this kingdom should be without our Lord's sufferings, death and resurrection.'[92] The symbolic description of Christ presented in Revelation 5:6 leaves Campbell in 'no doubt that this Lamb is Christ *after* his resurrection, because it is Christ having seven horns and seven eyes which are the seven Spirits of God — having the fullness of the Spirit as the risen Saviour — as the second Adam, the quickening Spirit.'[93]

Sensing that his congregation do not need to be convinced about the full divinity of the Son he pours his energies into alerting them to the idea that it is the exalted and glorified *man*, Christ Jesus, who has ascended to the throne. For 'we are clearly taught that Christ receives the kingdom because of his worthiness, because he was the man with clean hands and a pure heart, because he was the man who loved righteousness and hated wickedness: because he was the man, in short, with whom God was well pleased; and that Christ is exalted a King not because he is God: but because he is the righteous man, the Holy One of God.'[94]

Lest any fail to see the soteriological significance of this Campbell explains that the worthiness 'for the sake of which Christ was exalted as King'[95] was his atoning work when he laid down his life out of love for a fallen race. As the one closest to the Father's heart the Son alone knew that the Father most desired to create a way to bring sinful humanity back from its fallen state.

> Christ, from love to his Father, condescended to become man, to take our nature — to become a man of sorrows — to suffer and die and rise again, that he might be the Mediator between God and us, and that we might through him return to God. Thus Christ proved his love to the Father, by giving himself

---

[91] *NofS*, 3.32.5-6. Appendix 9.
[92] *Ibid.*, 3.32.4. Appendix 9.
[93] *Ibid.*, 3.32.5. Appendix 9.
[94] *Ibid.*, 3.32.6. Appendix 9.
[95] *Ibid.*, 3.32.7. Appendix 9.

up to the death, to gratify the desire of his Father's heart, that men should be brought back to God.[96]

In the midst of the preacher's many words a trinitarian theology is clearly visible. Within the life of the triune God the eternal Son, out of love for the Father, freely condescends 'to become man', and he lays down his life 'in the expectation that his Father would raise him up, and that he would receive from the Father power to be a quickening Spirit.'[97] By identifying Christ as the one who pours out the Spirit on believers, such language preserves the trinitarian identities of Christ and the Spirit.

Although undated, this sermon was preached some time before Campbell's deposition in May 1831. Something of the social unrest that preceded the passing of the Reform Act in 1832[98] seems to be in view when Campbell contrasts human desires for fairer forms of government with Christ's kingly rule.

> It is of God that we should desire a righteous government …but it is of the devil that we should desire that we should do it ourselves apart from God. And understand that this is God's plan to give us a righteous government and a righteous King, and to place us under that King, but that the King is set up of God because he is good and that the subjects are expected to rejoice in his sceptre because he loved them and gave himself for them.[99]

At this point the emphasis is not so much upon the way in which Christ the King reigns over his people now, but rather upon the hope for the future when Christ's invisible reign will become visible to all. He invites his hearers to turn their attention to 'the fact that this earth is to be the scene of the manifest kingdom of Christ – that here he is to reign.'[100] The 'baptismal' dimension of the kingly office is also apparent as Campbell underlines the way in which believers will share in the visible reign of Christ the King.[101]

---

[96] *Ibid.*, 3.32.8. Appendix 9.
[97] *Ibid.*, 3.32.7. Appendix 9. See Chapter 7. *The Son who Gives the Spirit.*
[98] Burleigh, *A Church History of Scotland*, 334. 'After two years of violent agitation throughout the country the Reform Bill passed into law on 4 June 1832. Many good people believed that a deadly blow had been struck at the well-being and constitutional stability of the nation.'
[99] *NofS*, 3.32.9. Appendix 9.
[100] *Ibid.*, 3.32.10. Appendix 9.
[101] *Ibid.*, 3.32.11. Appendix 9.

Campbell interprets current political and social uncertainties as signs that the eternal King will soon appear to carry out his work of judgement.[102] This eschatological perspective prompts him to urge people, as Jesus urged Nicodemus, to be born again in order to enter the kingdom. Such personal transformation is needed if they are to rejoice when the King of glory appears.

This sermon repeats Campbell's insistence that Christ's enthronement follows his death and resurrection and highlights some of the eschatological dimensions of Christ's kingly office. He portrays Christ not simply as the personal saviour of individuals but as the King whose reign will one day be visible to all. The sermon works within a trinitarian framework which affirms the eternal nature of the Son. Another feature which is of significance for this study of Campbell's understanding of the person of Christ is the claim that it is the man Christ Jesus who is enthroned in heaven. This idea is expressed in much greater detail in his sermon on 'The Parable of the Sower', and consideration of that sermon further assists the process of understanding Campbell's christology

'Man, as God, Reigning in Glory'

For his farewell sermon to his parishioners at Row, Campbell chose to preach from Luke 8 on 'The Parable of the Sower.[103] Taking his cue from the text that 'the seed is the word of God,'[104] he interprets this in Johannine fashion affirming that 'the Word truly is the Lord Jesus Christ'. The statement that 'the seed is the word' teaches 'that the seed is Christ — God manifested in the flesh — the Word manifested in the flesh'; in other words 'the revelation of God in a crucified and glorified Lord Jesus Christ.'[105]

A major section of the sermon takes a retrospective look at the 'history' of Christ and this provides valuable insights into the christology undergirding Campbell's theology.

> Christ's history is this, that having been the eternal Son of God — one of the persons in the Godhead — one with the Father and the Eternal Spirit, and having dwelt in the bosom of the Father before the worlds were, that by him the worlds were

---

[102] *Ibid.*, 3.32.12. Appendix 9.
[103] *S&L*, 2.29. Sermon preached at Helensburgh on 15 August 1831.
[104] Luke 8:11.
[105] *S&L*, 2.29.248-9.

made — that by him all things were created, and so that, first, his being God was revealed in his being the Creator; his history, further, is, that when God's creature, man, fell from the state in which he was created by sinning against God, that then Christ, the eternal Word, who had revealed the Father, in his mighty power, and wisdom, and goodness, as a Creator, came forth to reveal the heart of God as a Redeemer; and for this end that he became man...and being found in form and fashion as a man, he revealed God by the way in which he acted as a man; he revealed God by the testimony which he bore to his Father's character, by trusting the Father, and by trusting him for what was good.[106]

It is evident from this that Campbell's approach is built upon the assumption of an orthodox trinitarian theology, where one of the eternal persons of the Godhead willingly decides to become man in order to save human beings. Alongside the presupposition that the Son was fully divine, is held the affirmation that the Son became fully human, identifying with human beings as 'our very brother'. What also comes to the surface here is the notion, which would reappear in *The Nature of the Atonement*, that Jesus' attitude of trust performs the function of revealing the truth about the trustworthy God.

Although Campbell does not in this sermon use the title 'King' it is clear that the kingly office is in view as he begins to consider 'Christ's present place', because the man, Jesus of Nazareth now 'reigns and rules over all upon his Father's throne.' Campbell senses that whilst it would come as no surprise to his hearers to think of God upon the throne, the idea of the man, Jesus, reigning in heaven is a matter of *'deep, deep interest'*.

The man Christ Jesus, our brother, bone of our bone, and flesh of our flesh, is, at this moment upon the throne of Almighty God. And observe he is there, not because he is God, for that was his eternal glory; but he is there in his human nature — he is, in his humanity, exalted to that high place...It is on the one hand, a deep and glorious mystery, to see God upon the earth as a man; and, on the other hand, it is a deep and glorious mystery to see a man upon the throne of God....be not satisfied with holding it as a doctrine that Christ is God; but seek to understand, and realize, to your own minds, that the

---

[106] *Ibid.*, 2.29.249-250. Campbell provides a very similar summary on page 252.

very person who was upon this earth; Jesus of Nazareth, that very person who was crucified on the cross — that very person who was laid in the grave, is now reigning in the glory of God, on the throne of God.[107]

The 'deep and glorious mystery' of the man Christ Jesus reigning on the throne of Almighty God is significant for a number of reasons. It is another piece of evidence which shows that Campbell's approach to christology stands strongly in the Calvinist tradition. At a number of places in his discussion of the Lord's Supper,[108] Calvin argues strongly against Lutheran ideas about the ubiquity of Christ's risen body, stressing that the ascension implies that the body of Christ is located in heaven and is not ubiquitously present on the altars of the churches.[109] For Calvin neither the ascension, nor his understanding of the communication of attributes, lead him to believe that the human nature of Christ becomes somehow eclipsed by the divine nature, because 'from Scripture we plainly infer that the one person of Christ so consists of two natures that each nevertheless retains unimpaired its own distinctive character.'[110]

It is interesting to read Campbell's theology in the light of some current debates about this topic. Douglas Farrow, for instance, argues that the comparative neglect of the ascension by some theologians tends towards a form of eschatological docetism, whereby the humanity of the ascended Christ disappears from view. When the ascension is interpreted mainly as a support for the idea of the universal presence of Christ, 'is there not a marked tendency towards the de-humanization of Jesus, and thus towards that confusion between him and the Spirit that is so prevalent today?'[111]

In stark contrast to such statements Robert Jenson responds to questions about the presence of Christ's risen body by pointing to the Church as the 'body' where Christ is graciously present in the sacraments. He argues that

> sacrament and church are *truly* Christ's body for us, because Christ himself takes these same things for the object as which

---

[107] *Ibid.*, 2.29.253-4.
[108] Calvin, *Institutes*, IV. xvii.
[109] *Ibid.*, IV. xvii. 26. '...the Holy Spirit teaches that the body of Christ from the time of his resurrection was finite, and is contained in heaven even to the Last Day.' Cf., IV. xvii. 12.
[110] *Ibid.*, IV. xvii. 30. Cf., II. xiv. 1.
[111] Douglas Farrow, *Ascension and Ecclesia*, (Edinburgh: T & T Clark, 1999), 12.

he is available to himself. For the proposition that the church is a human body of the risen Jesus to be ontically and straightforwardly true, all that is required is that Jesus indeed be the Logos of God, so that his self-understanding determines what is real.[112]

In adopting such an approach Jenson, as a Lutheran, demonstrates that he stands in a very different tradition from Calvin and from Campbell. He merges the identity of the risen Christ with the identity of the Church to such an extent that there is a danger of the distinct human nature of Christ disappearing from view. T. F. Torrance would counsel against such a move believing that,

> in the doctrine of the Church as the Body of Christ everything turns upon the fact of the resurrection of Jesus Christ in Body and His ascension in the fulness of His Humanity...Are we to take the humanity of the risen Jesus seriously or not? Or are we to teach a docetic view of the risen and ascended Jesus?...(Today) we have to do battle for the Humanity of the risen Jesus ascended to the right hand of God the Father Almighty....
>
> To demythologise the ascension...is to dehumanise Christ, and to dehumanise Christ is to make the Gospel of no relevance to humanity, but to turn it into an inhospitable and inhuman abstraction.[113]

A further drawback of Jenson's approach is that it is a form of realized eschatology which leaves no need for a future coming of Christ.[114] Campbell, by contrast, follows Calvin in seeing the ascension as preparing the way for the parousia rather than removing the need for it to happen.

---

[112] Robert W. Jenson, *Systematic Theology: Volume 1: The Triune God*, (New York: Oxford University Press, 1997), 206.

[113] Thomas F. Torrance, *Royal Priesthood: A Theology of Ordained Ministry*, (Edinburgh, T and T Clark, 1993²), 43-44.

[114] Farrow, *Ascension and Ecclesia*, 176 '...the doctrine of Christ's return, not to mention the resurrection of the flesh and the judgement of this world, is effectively overthrown, since he has not so much gone from us as diffused himself in our midst.' See also Douglas Farrow, 'Confessing Christ Coming', in C. R. Seitz (ed.), *Nicene Christianity: The Future for a New Ecumenism*, (Grand Rapids: Brazos, 2001 /Carlisle: Paternoster, 2001), 133-148. Calvin, *Institutes*, IV. xvii. 29. 'But how weak and fragile that hope would be, if this very flesh of ours had not been truly raised in Christ, and had not entered into the Kingdom of Heaven.'

In this farewell sermon Campbell moves on to consider all that Christ Jesus has done, and is doing, for our sakes. There is a hint that he believes that the divine and the human nature of the one person of Christ each retains unimpaired its own distinctive character, when he writes of Christ that 'as God he could know no change, as God he could receive no increase.'[115] All that Christ has done is for our benefit and the result of the work of Christ is that God has given us, in Christ Jesus 'all things pertaining to life and to godliness.'[116] This gift includes forgiveness and a full revelation of God. It contains the gift of the Spirit who supplies power to know and enjoy God. God also provides hope for the future, which is bound up in the recognition that Christ will come as the judge of the living and the dead.

The preacher moves on to reflect upon the different ways in which people respond to the seed of the word and challenges his audience to invite Christ the king to reign in their hearts. The sermon ends with a note of foreboding because Campbell senses that the coming of the Lord is fast approaching and he regrets not having preached more often on such eschatological themes.

This sermon yields further evidence of the Reformed roots of Campbell's christology. One of the features which places him clearly in the Calvinist rather than the Lutheran tradition, is his testimony to the glorified humanity of the ascended Christ. The one who sits upon the throne of God in heaven fulfils the kingly office without abandoning his, or our, humanity.

Conclusion

As Campbell's sermons clearly portray Christ fulfilling the offices of Priest and King, it seems appropriate to summarize this aspect of his theology in terms of 'Christ's Twofold Office'. Although these emphases are combined in some sermons Campbell does not make the link explicit. It is surprising that while he draws heavily upon the Epistle to the Hebrews he does not make more use of the figure of Melchizedek who combines both offices in his person as the 'king of Salem' and 'priest of the most high God'.[117] Campbell's Reformed heritage is evident in these Row sermons with their clear echoes of Calvin's presentation of Christ's role as Priest and King. His

---

[115] *S&L*, 2.29.255.
[116] 2 Pet. 1:3.
[117] Heb. 7:1.

understanding of the glorified humanity of Christ in heaven, places Campbell firmly in the tradition of Calvin's christology rather than that of Luther's. His evangelical convictions are visible in the way that he challenges people to submit to the reign of the Christ. This call to conversion gains urgency from the conviction that the coming King is the one who will be judge of all.

Within his portrayal of Christ's priestly and kingly offices there is a striking emphasis upon the humanity of Christ and this is affirmed without in any way compromising orthodox belief that the one person in two natures was also fully divine. Campbell sees no need to argue the case for Christ's divinity, but preaches the full humanity of Christ with the enthusiasm of someone who has discovered a neglected treasure.

Before moving on to consider his trinitarian Christology in the final chapter, it is appropriate to ask if Campbell loses anything of theological significance by choosing to omit Christ's prophetic office? The conscious or unconscious avoidance of the *munus propheticum* certainly does not lead Campbell to neglect the eschatological dimension of faith because he has a vivid sense that Christ would return as King and Judge. The 'christological', 'soteriological' and 'baptismal' dimensions of Christ's twofold office come together in his eschatological vision of the redeemed becoming kings and priests, reigning on earth and offering praises to God.[118]

In a radical revision of the threefold office, Karl Barth asserts that the prophetic office was sometimes neglected, and at other times seen simply as a way of representing Jesus 'as the supreme teacher and example of perfect divine and human love.'[119] To counter such distortions Barth re-interprets the prophetic office under the headings of 'Jesus Christ the Guarantor' or 'Jesus Christ the Witness'. He seeks to avoid thinking of revelation merely as information which Christ communicates, in order to present the one 'who is Himself the material content of the atonement.'[120] Within his simpler framework Campbell does not fall into the trap of portraying Christ as the 'supreme teacher and example'. For him Christ does not just teach people about 'the way' back to God, because he himself, in his own person, is 'the way'. If he only teaches

---

[118] *NofS*, 1.6.7. Cf., *NofS*, 1.1.12; 1.7.4; 1.10.6; 2.13.9; 2.14.5; 2.17.7; 3.27.7; 3.32.6,11; 3.34.1-2; 3.
[119] *Church Dogmatics*, vol. IV, part 1, 137-8.
[120] *Ibid.*, 137.

about the way, then his importance diminishes once he has communicated the information; but if he himself is the way, then he remains eternally important.

Campbell's comparative 'neglect' of the prophetic dimensions of Christ's ministry stands in contrast to current scholarly interest in viewing Jesus as a prophetic figure. Setting Jesus in the context of first-century Judaism, N. T. Wright portrays him as 'an eschatological prophet/Messiah, announcing the kingdom and dying in order to bring it about.'[121] It is not possible here to engage in a detailed discussion of the issues raised either by Wright's approach, or by the less conservative approaches favoured by members of the 'Jesus Seminar'. Whatever conclusions are reached about such approaches, the contemporary interest in viewing Jesus as a Jewish prophet, highlights the importance of the prophetic office as a category for understanding the person and work of Christ.

Current studies draw attention to prophetic dimensions of the life and ministry of Jesus which are largely absent from Campbell's reading of the Gospels. Whilst it is clear that he affirmed the full humanity of Christ, the consequence of neglecting these prophetic dimensions, is that Campbell presents a rather general view of Christ's humanity which lacks much of the controversy and complexity present in the gospel accounts. This is another point where the coinherence of christology and soteriology is apparent. For the absence of a prophetic perspective means that Campbell depicts an uncontroversial Jesus, and that makes it harder to understand why the Roman and Jewish authorities bothered to crucify such an uncontroversial figure. Soteriologically this might imply that the neglect of the prophetic office is more problematic than Christ's perfect confession of our sins.

---

[121] N. T. Wright, *Jesus and the Victory of God*, (London: SPCK, 1996), 660.

Chapter 6

Romanism, Revelation and Real Presence

After twenty years of comparative obscurity Campbell came to the attention of a wider public with the publication, in 1851, of *Christ the Bread of Life*.[1] This small book is significant not only because it opens a window onto Campbell's understanding of the Eucharist, but also because of what it contributes to the emerging picture of his theology as a whole. Along with the first and second editions of *Christ the Bread of Life*, the Row Sermons, dating from the period 1828-31, are another valuable source of information about Campbell's understanding of Communion. As the material from these sources spans a period of about forty years, the subject of communion provides another way of testing the thesis that Campbell was a consistent thinker.

The theological position he established early in his ministry involved a decisive move away from the key tenets of the federal Calvinism favoured by Evangelicals in the Kirk. However, this reappraisal of Campbell's thought argues that such a move away from federal Calvinism should be seen as a theological journey within evangelicalism rather than a way of leaving it behind. Such an evangelical evaluation of Campbell's approach finds further support in *Christ the Bread of Life*, where he presents a robust challenge to Roman Catholic teaching about transubstantiation. In common with many nineteenth century evangelicals, he viewed with concern the growing size and influence of the Roman Catholic Church in Britain. His polemical intentions are made explicit in the book's full title which explains that Campbell is offering '*An attempt to give an profitable direction to the present occupation of thought with Romanism.*'

---

[1] *Bread1.*

'The Present Occupation of Thought with Romanism'

At the end of the eighteenth century there were probably around thirty thousand Roman Catholics living in Scotland.[2] During the first half of the nineteenth century that situation changed dramatically as the Roman Catholic Church in Scotland, in common with England, experienced noticeable growth so that by 1840 the figure had risen to ninety thousand. This growth was largely due to the influx of Irish Catholic immigrants, whose numbers increased further in the 1840s as a result of famine in Ireland.[3] Living and working in Glasgow, Campbell would have had first hand knowledge of the significant growth of urban Catholicism.

On a political level the Emancipation Act of 1829 removed restrictions on Roman Catholics playing active roles in civic and political life. John Wolffe argues that as a result of these political changes 'Roman Catholics now felt that they could look forward to a continued increase in strength and influence. In retrospect Emancipation was the beginning of a sustained period of Roman Catholic growth and consolidation in mid-nineteenth century Britain. There was a corresponding hardening in anti-Catholicism among evangelicals.'[4]

Campbell's links with Edward Irving [5] make it likely that he was also sympathetic to Irving's suspicion of Catholicism.[6] The Albury Park conferences on eschatology argued for a move from post-millennialism to a pre-millennial approach which 'tended to treat as axiomatic identifications between Rome and the

---

[2] John Wolffe, *God and Greater Britain: Religion and National Life in Britain and Ireland 1843-1945*, (London: Routledge, 1994), 31.

[3] John Wolffe, *The Protestant Crusade in Great Britain 1829-1860*, (Oxford: Clarendon Press, 1991), 16. See also Wolffe, *God and Greater Britain*, 34. 'From the early nineteenth century the growing industrial and urban centres of the central belt began to attract Roman Catholic migrants from the Highlands as well as from Ireland: one calculation indicates that between 1755 and 1851 the proportion of Roman Catholics in the population of Inverness-shire fell from 19 per cent to 11.2 per cent, while in Lanarkshire it rose from nothing to 12.5 per cent.'

[4] Wolffe, *The Protestant Crusade*, 44.

[5] See Chapter 1. *Factors Contributing to his Dismissal*.

[6] *Ibid.*, 31. In 1826 Irving 'addressed the Continental Society on the subject of "Babylon foredoomed", arguing that, although the Roman Church would be destroyed by Christ at the second coming, in the meantime it would grow in strength. Protestants had a responsibility to cry out against Rome and to be instruments in God's hands for saving an elect remnant.'

mystic Babylon and between Antichrist and the papacy.'[7] Such a linkage would have helped to stir up anti-Catholic feelings which, Wolffe argues, were already deeply rooted in British culture.

Through his network of friends,[8] and through his own reading, Campbell would also have been aware of events south of the border where the activities of the Oxford Movement[9] were stirring up a renewal of interest in Catholic principles. Whilst Keble, Newman and Pusey had initially set out to promote a Catholic revival within the Established Church, there was widespread suspicion that the Oxford Movement was travelling quickly towards Romanism. In a letter written to offer sympathy over the death of Campbell's father in January 1843, A. J. Scott, living in London, ventured the opinion that 'Puseyism, or rather Popery in the Church of England, waxes madder and madder. It is more and more plain to me that the disease is in the system of the English Church itself, and that the way is preparing for its downfall.'[10]

---

[7] Wolffe, *The Protestant Crusade*, 31-2. See also 113-7.

[8] While staying with his friend A.J. Scott at Woolwich in 1838 Campbell was introduced to F. D. Maurice (*Memorials* 1.147), and he kept in touch with Maurice over a number of years. In 1845 he was introduced to the well known Evangelical minister, the Revd Edward Bickersteth. (Cf. *Memorials* 1.167.) Peter B. Nockles, *The Oxford Movement in Context: Anglican High Churchmanship1760-857*, (Cambridge: Cambridge University Press, 1994), 110-1, states that Bickersteth supported the Tractarian proposal to produce a *Library of the Fathers*. Such contacts would have made it possible for Campbell to be well informed about significant developments within the Church of England.

[9] Keble's sermon on *National Apostasy* in 1833 is usually viewed as the beginning of the Oxford Movement. Newman's conversion to Roman Catholicism in 1845 is normally seen as the end of this period of Catholic revival in the Church of England. A detailed work which puts the Oxford Movement in its historical and theological context is, Nockles, *The Oxford Movement in Context*. See also, Owen Chadwick, *The Spirit of the Oxford Movement: Tractarian Essays*, (Cambridge: Cambridge University Press, 1990). W. Church, *The Oxford Movement: Twelve Years: 1833-1845*, introduction by G. F. A. Best, (Chicago: University of Chicago Press, 1970). Alec R. Vidler, *The Church in an Age of Revolution*, (Harmondsworth: Penguin, 1961), 45-55 and 157-168. B. G. Worrall, *The Making of the Modern Church: Christianity in England since 1800* (London: SPCK, 1993²), 15-35 and 159-182.

[10] *Memorials* 1. 171-2.

The fear of a Romeward trend appeared well founded as some notable Tractarians converted to Catholicism. Something of the passion of this period is conveyed in Alex Vidler's description of the situation in 1850. 'When the Oxford movement began to issue in secessions to Rome, above all in Newman's secession, there was a sense of horror about what might be going to happen next, and what did happen next was, in the words of *The Times* newspaper, "an audacious and conspicuous display of pretensions to resume the absolute spiritual domination of this island which Rome has never abandoned."' [11]

The audacious step was the famous 'Papal Aggression' of 1850, when Pope Pius IX set up a Roman Catholic hierarchy of Bishops for England and Wales and appointed Cardinal Nicholas Wiseman (1802-65), as Archbishop of Westminster. The deep-seated British suspicion of the Roman Catholic Church was not slow to surface, and in a letter to *The Times* the Prime Minister of the day, Lord John Russell, described the new hierarchy as ' a pretension of supremacy over the realm of England, and a claim to sole and undivided sway, which is inconsistent with the Queen's supremacy, with the rights of our bishops and clergy, and with the spiritual independence of the nation, as asserted even in Roman Catholic times.'[12] In this letter, addressed to the Bishop of Durham, the Prime Minister was not only critical of Rome, however, because he observed that Anglican clerics had 'been the most forward in leading their flocks, step by step to the very verge of the precipice.'[13]

Campbell's hesitations about Catholic doctrine had been evident as early as 1830, when he warned communicants at Row that it was 'a lie of Satan, that the bread becomes the body of Christ, or that the wine becomes the blood of Christ.'[14] With the visible growth of Catholicism over the next twenty years, the so-called 'papal aggression' of 1850, and with the Cardinal Archbishop in Westminster openly praying for the conversion of England to Roman Catholicism,[15] it is not surprising to find

---

[11] Vidler, *Church in an Age of Revolution*, 161.
[12] Letter to *The Times* on 7th November 1850, cited by Wolffe, *God and Greater Britain*, 112.
[13] Vidler, *Church in an Age of Revolution*, 161-2.
[14] *NofS* 1.9.2.
[15] Wolffe, *God and Greater Britain*, 113. 'Meanwhile, swelled by the influx of immigrants from an Ireland in the grip of famine, the Roman Catholic Church in England, Scotland and Wales appeared to be growing fast and

Campbell writing in 1851 about 'the present occupation of thought with Romanism.'

In the second edition of *Christ the Bread of Life*,[16] published in 1869, Campbell identifies the infallibility of the Church and transubstantiation as the two key errors of contemporary Catholicism.[17] His brief response in the preface[18] to comments about infallibility made by Cardinal Wiseman and by Dr Newman, would be enough to confirm his knowledge of developments in England. In addition, his correspondence indicates his firsthand knowledge about these dramatic developments. For in June 1852, whilst staying in London, he wrote to his brother to explain that he had had a third lengthy meeting with Henry Manning, a Tractarian convert to Catholicism, who was later to become Cardinal Manning. After a discussion lasting two and a half hours, Manning promised to visit when he came to Glasgow; but Campbell suspected that this was 'more from the hope of impressing than from being impressed.'[19] No further meetings are recorded, but this encounter indicates that Campbell made real efforts to be well informed about the Roman Catholic position. Whereas *Christ the Bread of Life* contains Campbell's response to what he perceives to be the error of transubstantiation, his response to issues relating to infallibility is found in *Thoughts on Revelation*.[20]

It is against this background that Campbell's reflections upon *Christ the Bread of Life* are to be seen. He does not enter into a scholarly examination of transubstantiation but offers some explorations of this theme drawing particularly upon John 6:27-58 and 4:1-34. The 1851 edition had only two chapters and contained neither an introduction nor a conclusion. His first attempt at writing for the press was not a runaway success and the following year Campbell confessed that he had 'been from time to time not a little cast down by the small measure of

---

presenting an increasingly serious challenge to Protestantism, especially in north-west England and south-west Scotland.'

[16] *Bread2*.

[17] *Ibid.*, 1. 'THE INFALLIBILITY OF THE CHURCH and TRANSUBSTANTIATION are to Protestants the most repulsive aspects of the teaching of the Church of Rome. — Yet they are also her great attractions to those who pass over to her from Protestantism; and once accepted, form her strongest hold upon them.'

[18] *Ibid.*, 2.

[19] *Memorials*, 242-3.

[20] *TR*.

acceptance which my book has met with, in a land where so many know and love Him of whom it speaks.'[21] After the hard work of writing and revision he found it painful to think that the problem might lie in 'the style in which it is written', but it is not surprising that some readers were rather daunted by his complicated sentences and lengthy paragraphs.[22] Part of the difficulty may also be that so much of the time is dedicated to explaining what he does not believe about the Lord's Supper, that very little space remains for a more positive exposition of this ordinance.

In the 1869 edition he sought to clarify his position by revising existing material and by adding some new material. His friend Thomas Erskine had previously complained about 'the abruptness of the commencement,'[23] and Campbell tried to remedy this by writing a new preface and by adding some fresh material to the beginning of chapter 1. With some justification he could say 'that the subject is now approached easily and naturally.'[24] The new third chapter, which sets out to explore 'the development of the Mass to the Lord's Supper', not only continues his critique of transubstantiation but also supplies some hints about Campbell's own understanding of the Lord's Supper. With this additional material, and some improvements in its written style, the 1869 edition provides clearer access to Campbell's thinking on this topic, and the following evaluation will concentrate on the second edition.

Christ the Bread of Life

According to Campbell the table prepared for God's people in the presence of their enemies[25] refers to that spiritual table, the food on which is that bread of life which has come down from

---

[21] *Memorials*, 1.240. Letter to Erskine of Linlathen, 31 March 1852.

[22] His son, Donald, observes that 'it was hardly to be expected that a book which developed this line of thought in a train of close argument, should obtain a wide popularity. It did not furnish a readily available weapon for warfare with Rome, but demanded a higher standard of religion than the disputants commonly attained. But the book was read and pondered by many thoughtful men in England and Scotland, especially by many clergymen; and those who studied it found in it the fruitful gems of many thoughts.' *Memorials*, 1.213.

[23] *Memorials*, 2.226.

[24] *Memorials*, 2.227.

[25] Ps. 23:5.

heaven.'[26] Reflection upon this leads him to conclude that Christ has always been the Bread of Life sustaining the faithful. 'For the meat that endures unto Eternal Life has ever been the same, — *Christ the Bread of Life*, the same yesterday, to-day, and for ever. This is the testimony of God, that God has given to us Eternal Life and that this life is in His Son.'[27] It is worth noting here that by adapting the language of Hebrews 13:8, Campbell was implicitly claiming that Christ is the pre-existent, eternal Son of God who fully shares in the eternal nature of God.

The language of a meal, employed in Psalm 23, vividly conveys the notion that faith involves an active participation in the Eternal Life which is in the Son of God. 'And the form of the language has reference to the manner of that participation, viz., our eating His flesh and drinking His blood.'[28] In these opening remarks Campbell asserts his conviction that the life of faith involves a feeding on Christ as the Bread of Life.[29]

Exposing the Errors

The main intention of the book's first section, however, is to expose what he perceives to be the errors surrounding the Roman Catholic view of transubstantiation. His attention moves quickly on to John 6: 27-58 where Jesus urges upon his hearers the importance of eating the flesh of the Son of Man and drinking his blood. For Campbell, the Church of Rome falls into error at this point by linking this passage directly to the Lord's Supper. In so doing it demonstrates a misunderstanding of the true nature of that ordinance which, properly understood, sets forth in *act* what the biblical passage sets forth in *word*.

> *They both declare the manner of the life which is by the faith of the Son of God*, using our experience of the conscious process of eating and drinking to illustrate the self-appropriating movements of the will in receiving and in feeding upon the spiritual food which is our Lord's broken body and shed blood; thus helping us to conceive of the intimacy of our union with Christ, and of the literal truth of the expression

---

[26] *Bread2*, 12.
[27] *Ibid.*, 11.
[28] *Bread2*, 13.
[29] *Ibid.*, 17.

'partaking in Him', through our knowledge of what the food which we eat is to the body which it nourishes.[30]

Campbell is convinced that if the words 'I am the bread of life' are interpreted as pointing directly to the Lord's Supper, then this would set them apart from all the other 'I am' sayings in John's Gospel. He argues that it is better to read the saying about the bread of life alongside Christ's equally important claims to be the light of the world (John 8:12), and the true vine (John 15:1-5). He claims that all these sayings perform a similar function in bearing witness to the nature of faith. Employing a variety of images the evangelist identifies Christ as the only source of eternal life, and reveals that the life of faith involves an intimate relationship of dependence upon him. Campbell contends that the other 'I am' sayings lose something of their revelatory character if the bread of life saying is interpreted in isolation as referring to the eucharist. He plausibly argues that these sayings deserve to be seen in parallel, but goes too far in asserting that everything breaks down if John 6 is seen as pointing to the eucharist. It would not be difficult to produce a list of Protestant commentators who do not see John 6 as primarily referring to the eucharist, or a comparable list of Catholic writers for whom the eucharistic dimension is dominant. However, even if it was conceded that the primary purpose of the 'I am' sayings is to point to the nature of Christ and the nature of the salvation he brings, this would not necessarily rule out the possibility that these images could carry other messages as well. Campbell himself prefers to interpret the language about the body and blood of Christ in a symbolic rather than a literal fashion. It is surprising, therefore, that he is not willing to acknowledge the ways in which symbols and symbolic language tend to communicate different levels of meaning. At one level the bread of life discourse can be seen in parallel with similar passages, as an affirmation of the nature of Christ and his salvation, and of the intimate connection between the believer and Christ. At another level, however, it may also convey an implicit message about the way in which this Christ

---

[30] *Ibid.*, 19. Cf. Calvin, *Institutes*, IV. xiv. 17. 'Therefore, let it be regarded as a settled principle that the sacraments have the same office as the Word of God: to offer and set forth Christ to us, and in him the treasures of heavenly grace.' In Book IV. xiv. 6, Calvin refers to Augustine who 'calls a sacrament "a visible word" for the reason that it represents God's promises as painted in a picture and sets them before our sight, portrayed graphically and in the manner of images.'

is encountered and experienced in the eucharist. On the grounds of biblical hermeneutics alone Campbell's case is not entirely convincing.

A more serious concern for Campbell is his conviction that the Roman Catholic approach to the Lord's Supper brings about a radical change of focus. For Campbell, eating the flesh and drinking the blood of Christ is symbolic language describing the believer's direct participation in the life of Christ. This relationship begins to change when it is believed that the bread and the wine literally become the body and blood of Christ. When this happens the Lord's Supper ceases to be an ordinance setting forth the truth in symbolic actions, and becomes in itself 'the medium of our participation in Christ.'[31] The process, whether it is understood as transubstantiation or consubstantiation, is shrouded in mystery and this leads Campbell to conclude that faith in Christ is being replaced by faith in a mystery.

> Say to me, "You must believe that *literally* this is Christ's body," or say to me, "You must believe that *mystically* this is Christ's body," the important fact remains, that what I am required to exercise is, a faith about the bread and the wine as the medium in which I receive Christ, and *not* a faith that simply contemplates Christ, and realizes that He is my life.[32]

Although Campbell concurs with a common Protestant argument that transubstantiation 'contradicts our senses', he does not feel that our bodily senses are 'our highest faculties of perception.'[33] For him transubstantiation fails when it is assessed by the spiritual faculties with which God has endowed human beings.

> When partaking of the Lord's Supper, I by my bodily senses, take cognisance of the bread and wine, and know what they are, as I consciously partake of them; while in my spiritual nature, I deal with the spiritual realities which they symbolize, and discern the Lord's body broken for me, His blood shed for the remission of my sins, which I thankfully receive, and consciously feed upon, as the spiritual food of the Divine Life. The two conjoined processes are quite distinct. They are both experienced realities. In neither is there any mystery.[34]

---

[31] *Bread2*, 22.
[32] *Ibid.*, 25-6.
[33] *Ibid.*, 28-9.
[34] *Ibid.*, 30.

The Self-Evidencing Light of Revelation

Alongside this he repeatedly emphasizes that participation in Eternal life is a 'conscious experience',[35] and he encourages his readers to draw upon their experience of spiritual life in assessing the truth of the doctrine of transubstantiation. He is convinced, on the basis of his own experience, that a belief in bread and wine being literally or mystically transformed cannot nourish faith in the way that is possible through 'the direct faith of Christ'.[36] This is an important aspect of the approach adopted throughout *Christ the Bread of Life* and it is a place where Campbell is vulnerable to the criticism that he is building too much upon the experience of the individual. Similarly, at the end of the third section of the book, he talks about evaluating the Mass by 'the light of Christianity'. He explains what this method involves when he says that 'I appeal rather to Christian consciousness than merely to the authority of texts of Scripture.'[37] This kind of emphasis leads James C. Goodloe to assert that 'Campbell's understanding of Christian experience is the authority which has grown to dominate his theology. By the analysis of Christian consciousness is scripture interpreted, doctrine examined and recast, practice evaluated and reformed.'[38] If this assessment is correct then Campbell's concept of Christian consciousness would appear to be taking precedence over the authority of scripture. If individual Christian consciousness is the final arbiter then it would become very difficult to assess whether one person's experience was more or less authentic than another's.

In the preface to the second edition, Campbell expresses his unease about an infallible church claiming the right 'to interpret with authority' the 'sure understanding of Scripture.'[39] He acknowledges that it might be possible to 'substitute the right of private judgement' in biblical interpretation, but senses that this would still leave the individual at the mercy of conflicting interpretations of Scripture. He seeks to replace both the authority of an infallible church and the anarchy of private

---

[35] *Ibid.*, 34. 'Is not the movement of your own being in which you appropriate them a *conscious* movement? Is not the participation in the Eternal Life which results — the being spiritually quickened, also a conscious experience?

[36] *Ibid.*, 35.

[37] *Ibid.*, 183.

[38] Goodloe, 'Transformation of the Religious Consciousness', 148.

[39] *Bread2*, 2-3.

judgement, with his own view of Revelation.[40] His response to the claim of infallibility is to direct 'faith to the living God as Himself the teacher who gives us certain knowledge of Himself.'[41] However, Campbell would not see this as some abstract philosophy of Christian consciousness, because it is rooted in his reflections upon the words of Jesus in John chapter 6. For there at the heart of the bread of life discourse, Jesus says 'It is written in the Prophets "They shall all be taught of God"',[42] which Campbell tends to interpret in terms of God's ability to speak to people's consciences in a direct fashion in and through the power of the Holy Spirit.

Campbell is arguing that to insist that God must always reveal himself through an infallible church, or through an infallible book, would be to impose limits upon divine freedom and power. The God who created men and women in his own image is able to speak in a direct and compelling way to the human conscience. This leads him to argue that while 'the Romanist looks to the Church to interpret the Scriptures that he may certainly know the meaning of what he reads; the man of God expects and waits upon the teaching of God and so expects to understand that which he reads. For in God's light alone does the individual human spirit see light clearly. Spiritual light as natural light is its own witness.'[43] In reaction against a resurgent brand of Roman Catholicism it is understandable that Campbell should try to find an alternative approach to revelation and authority. It is equally understandable that some will feel that he moved to a position where revelation is somewhat at the whim of the individual. Campbell himself would not accept such a conclusion because he had a clear sense that revelation involved divine initiative. If the Word who became flesh is 'the true light that gives light to every man'[44] then God has taken the initiative and human beings are called to yield to the voice of God within their consciences. The Bible itself contains many stories of God communicating directly to people without the help of the institution of the Church, and without having to read from a book. These considerations suggest that Campbell can legitimately claim that it is wrong to insist that God must always reveal himself through the Church or the Bible.

---

[40] *TR*.
[41] *Bread2*, 4.
[42] Jn. 6:45 which refers back to Is. 54:13.
[43] *Bread2*, 143.
[44] Jn. 1: 9.

However, the way in which he frames his comments does not remove the danger of the anarchy of private judgement. One way in which it would be possible to guard against this danger would be to argue for a divine consistency which holds together these different forms of revelation. A sovereign God is undoubtedly free to communicate to people in many and various ways, but if he is the constant character Christians believe God to be, then these other forms of revelation will not be at variance with the revelation of God in Christ which the Bible witnesses to.

This is another point where Campbell's debt to the Reformed tradition is visible. His emphasis upon believers being taught directly by God contains echoes of Calvin's earlier stress upon 'the secret testimony of the Spirit',[45] who bears witness to the truth of scriptural doctrine. 'Scripture indeed is self-authenticated; hence, it is not right to subject it to proof and reasoning. And the certainty it deserves with us, it attains by the testimony of the Spirit.'[46] Whilst Campbell follows Calvin's example in linking John 6:45 with Isaiah 54:13,[47] he developed the idea of people being taught by God in a rather different way. For Calvin this direct teaching or discipling was reserved for the elect alone, and those who are unteachable show, in that way, that they are reprobate.[48] By contrast Campbell affirms the idea of God teaching people directly without in any way interpreting this as an outworking of Calvin's double decree. With such ideas present in the tradition Campbell would have had some grounds for claiming that his stress upon God communicating 'certain knowledge of Himself', was a contemporary version of Calvin's teaching about 'the secret testimony of the Spirit'. However, for whatever reasons, he did not choose to support his argument by appealing to the Reformed tradition at this point, and his presentation is probably weakened by this omission.

Furthermore, his concept of revelation would be more adequate if he could have found a way to acknowledge the role of the wider Church in discerning between authentic and inauthentic interpretations of Scripture. Remembering his

---

[45] Calvin, *Institutes* I. vii. 4.
[46] *Ibid.*, I vii. 5. See also I. vii. 1; III. i. 1,3; III. ii. 15, 33-6.
[47] Cf. *Ibid.*, I. vii. 5; II. ii. 20; III. ii. 6; III. xxii. 20; and III. xxiv. 4.
[48] *Ibid.*, III. xxiv. 14. 'And Christ, quoting Isaiah's prophecy, "They shall all be taught by God" [Jn. 6:45; Is.54:13], means only that the Jews are reprobate and alien to the church because they are unteachable.'

personal context it is difficult to see how he could concede a positive role in the process of interpretation to the wider church. On the one hand he reacted in a typically Protestant fashion to Roman Catholic claims to have infallible access to revelation. On the other hand, the way in which the Church of Scotland removed him from its ministry must have left him feeling that the Scriptures did not, in practice, function as the ultimate authority within the Kirk.[49] The result is that the corporate, ecclesial dimension of biblical interpretation and revelation tends to be neglected and this is a vulnerable spot in Campbell's understanding of revelation.

To some extent Campbell's emphasis upon the importance of Christianity as a 'conscious experience' represents a restatement, or a development, of his earlier stress upon assurance being of the essence of faith. It has been shown earlier[50] that there are grounds for claiming that Campbell was being faithful to the tradition of Calvin in declaring that assurance is of the essence of faith. If genuine Christian faith embodies an assurance that the individual is the object of God's love, then this implies that at some basic level Christian faith must be a 'conscious experience'. It is also relevant to remember that Christian consciousness for Campbell is not an abstract philosophical concept, because it is the filial consciousness of being a child of the divine father. This consciousness does not mean whatever the individual wants it to mean, because it has taken form and shape in the human experience of the incarnate Son of God. Although it is not always clearly explained, it is the reality of the God-man which provides the blueprint for the 'conscious experience' which Campbell is referring to. Criteria for assessing 'conscious experience' are provided by the person and work of Christ.

The Priority of Revelation

The centrality of the revelation embodied in Christ is evident in the third section where he seeks to assess the claim of the Mass

---

[49] In the proceedings against Campbell, the Rev. Mr. Gregor of Bonhill explained that 'We are far from appealing to the word of God on this ground; it is by the Confession of Faith that we must stand; by it we hold our livings…. and the parish has a right to have the Scriptures interpreted according to the Confession of Faith.' *Proceedings*, p xxix.
[50] Chapter 1. *Assurance of the Essence of Faith.*

to be a sacrifice for sin.⁵¹ Whilst he does not 'wish to be understood as depreciating that appeal to reason which is more usual',⁵² he is adamant that the Atonement is 'the proper light to which to take the claim of the Mass to be a sacrifice for sin,' and that this is none other than 'the light of Christianity'.⁵³ He neither denigrates reason nor retreats into an irrational supernaturalism, because as he perceives it there is no ultimate conflict between revelation and reason.⁵⁴ Nevertheless, although there is no conflict between them, Campbell is in no doubt that ultimately revelation takes precedence over reason. So, 'in a question affecting religion a Christian man writing for Christians will naturally take the subject to the light of Christianity as at once the highest light and that which is specially appropriate, and as having the advantage of being ground common to himself and to those he addresses.'⁵⁵ In a post-Enlightenment context where the human faculty of reason was so often seen as 'our last judge and guide in everything';⁵⁶ there is a sense here in which Campbell is striking a blow against the infallibility of human reason which is much more significant than his tilt against the infallibility of Rome. In a small way he was anticipating the approach of twentieth century writers such as Karl Barth, within which Christian self-description, shaped by the biblical narrative, takes priority over the claims of reason. Within such an approach, reason continues to play an important part, but it is not permitted to play a foundational role. Rather it is what God himself has freely chosen to do which establishes the ground rules of debate and of theology. Campbell is feeling towards that kind of position when he explains that spiritual error begins 'in not studying the Incarnation in the light of the love which has come forth in the Incarnation.'⁵⁷

---

⁵¹ *Bread2*, 180-3.
⁵² *Ibid.*, 182.
⁵³ *Ibid.*, 181.
⁵⁴ *Ibid.*, 182-3. For example he argues that a failure to honour 'the just demands of reason' would be an admission that 'divine light can contradict itself'. It is this contradiction between revelation and reason that Campbell feels unable to concede.
⁵⁵ *Ibid.*, 183.
⁵⁶ John Locke, *Essay Concerning Human Understanding, Volume II*, (New York: Dover, 1959), 438.
⁵⁷ *Bread2*, 170. Cf., 169. 'The love that is in the Incarnation is only known perfectly in the light of its accomplished purpose; while on the other hand it is the meditation of the Incarnation as the coming forth of divine love

As his argument against the Mass continues Campbell readily admits that the belief that God condescends to permit worshippers to eat and drink 'material substances invested with an overawing Divinity',[58] is one that generates a great depth of religious experience. He is not convinced, however, that this profound sense of wonder and obligation can be accurately described as 'Christian' experience,[59] in part because he perceives that as the belief that Christ is in the bread and wine increases, interest in the truth revealed by Christ decreases. Thus he argues that 'there is abundant historical evidence, that in proportion as the food of life is believed to be received in the bread and wine, it is less and less sought through belief of the truth.'[60] In passing, Campbell expresses concern that there are so few good examples of, what he sees as, genuine Christian life and experience, with the result that people mistakenly applaud sincerity even when it is sincerely wrong.[61]

The Trinitarian Nature of Prayer and Worship

Campbell notes the unease of the Protestant reformers with the eucharistic offering of Christ in the Mass, but reflects that this wrong emphasis develops naturally from the prior belief in transubstantiation. There is an inner necessity about this because what is received in worship from God provides the raw material of what is offered back to God in worship. Error in one area must lead inevitably to error in the other, because 'feeding upon Christ, and worshipping God through Christ, are so related that what we understand to be the first of these will always determine our conception of the other also.'[62] A similar dynamic is at work in Campbell's understanding of prayer and worship, because it is only when the spiritual truth about *Christ the Bread of Life* is discerned that the believer is able to worship God in spirit and in truth. Here in embryo we come across

---

that prepares us for understanding this its purpose, enabling us at the same time to understand all that this purpose has involved...'
[58] *Ibid.*, 40.
[59] *Ibid.*, 41. 'Now here are elements of an experience which, while it has no claim to be called Christian experience or fellowship in the life of Christ, may yet too easily be accepted as religion, and earnest and solemn religion too, even where Christian experience is not unknown.'
[60] *Ibid.*, 43.
[61] *Ibid.*, 67-74.
[62] *Ibid.*, 50.

Campbell's trinitarian[63] view of worship where believers participate in the Son's communion with the Father in the power of the Spirit. Viewed from this perspective worship is totally gift because 'what we receive from God, in Christ, as Eternal Life, is what, being fed upon, and so becoming our own actual life, we offer to God in worship. Our life ascends to God in worship. And it is its being the Divine nature — its being the Eternal Life, that is the secret of the acceptableness of the worship, and of the sureness of the response to it.'[64]

> It is the Eternal Life which comes to us through the Son, ascending from us through the Son — the Son in us honouring the Father — the worship of Sonship — as such grateful to the Father, who seeketh such worship...In such worship there is a continual living presentation of Christ to the Father — a continual drawing upon the delight of the Father in the Son — the outgoing of a confidence that, whatever is asked in Christ's name — in the light of His name — in the faith of the Father's acknowledgment of that name — will be received. The praises rendered — the desires cherished — the prayers offered — are all within the circle of the life of Christ, and ascend with the assurance of partaking in the favour which pertains to that life — which rests upon Him who is that life.[65]

Although the high priestly christology outlined in the previous chapter is not mentioned at this point, the ongoing priestly ministry of Christ undergirds the participative, trinitarian understanding of worship which Campbell is expressing.[66]

---

[63] James B. Torrance contrasts 'unitarian' and 'trinitarian' views of worship. Within the 'unitarian' view the emphasis falls upon what we the worshippers do; whereas a trinitarian approach to worship emphasizes the 'gift of participating through the Spirit in the incarnate Son's communion with the Father.' James B. Torrance, *Worship, Community and the Triune God of Grace*, (Carlisle: Paternoster, 1996), 1-31.

[64] Bread2, 52.

[65] Ibid., 130-1

[66] Graham Redding, 'Significance of the Priesthood of Christ', 179. 'Deeply imbedded in this description of Christian worship, and worthy of note, is a strong appreciation of the continuous nature of Christ's offering to the Father. His offering is not confined to the offering of his life at Calvary 2000 years ago. Rather, it is deemed to continue in heaven. Christ is the one, true worshipper in whom, with whom and through whom, and by the Spirit, the Church's own meagre offerings of praise and thanksgiving are joined, perfected and offered to the Father. In highlighting this important aspect of Christian worship McLeod Campbell goes beyond Calvin, the

After such a sustained piece of anti-Catholic polemic, Campbell injects a small piece of ecumenical balance by suggesting that for some Protestant groups there is a similar danger of the celebration of the Lord's Supper becoming a substitute for the everyday experience of living by faith. He refers to 'a comfort experienced through partaking of the Lord's Supper which does not flow from the exercise of faith in Christ, but from a vague persuasion of benefit derived from the ordinance itself because of some assumed virtue in it to promote man's peace with God.'[67] Thus he pleads with Protestant readers to examine themselves to see if their comfort derives from participating in the ordinance, or from direct faith in Christ.'[68] The critique of Protestant attitudes is much briefer than his attack on transubstantiation, but in his arguments with both constituencies he has the one aim of proclaiming the importance of a direct faith in Christ and a real participation in the life of Christ by the Spirit. After exposing these perceived errors Campbell turns to the task of outlining a more adequate perspective on Christ as the Bread of Life.

Advancing an Alternative Approach

Having outlined his reasons for rejecting mainly, Roman Catholic interpretations of Christ as the Bread of Life, Campbell seeks to develop a more adequate approach. The heart of the approach advocated in the second and third sections of the book is found by reading John chapter 4 alongside the bread of life discourse in chapter 6. In John 4:34 Jesus says 'my meat is to do the will of him that sent me, and to finish his work', and Campbell senses that this indicates that in the spiritual life, the process of eating and drinking refers to doing the will of God. The parallelism between Christ's experience and ours

> implies that, as doing the will of the Father was His meat, doing His will is our meat...For it appears to me a statement that has its light in itself, that, as spiritual beings, it is by movements of the will that we appropriate spiritual food. Such movements are acts of spiritual eating and drinking, issuing in the consubstantiating of our spirits with that which

---

Scottish Reformers and the Westminster tradition, who...failed to develop a proper understanding of the nature of Christ's *eternal* offering and its implications for worship and prayer.'
[67] *Bread2*, 56.
[68] *Ibid.*, 61-4.

being received into the will is received into us, into what is, in the most intimate sense, our proper selves, so affecting what we are.[69]

Although Campbell is clearly uncomfortable with a literal interpretation of John chapter 6 which leads in the direction of transubstantiation, his own language is dramatic and literal in another way. For him, the language of eating points to a literal sharing in the very life of Christ. When he borrows the vocabulary of consubstantiation he refers not to a process involving bread and wine, but to a process transforming human beings from within by the Spirit of the Son of God.

In the material added to the 1869 edition he wants to make sure that his readers notice two key things. 'First, that our feeding upon Christ in those movements of the will in which we call Him Lord in the spirit is the inmost aspect of the life of faith. Second, that this calling of Jesus Lord in the Spirit is the due development in us of the Incarnation as the coming of the Eternal Son into humanity saying to the Father, "Lo I come to do thy will, thy law is in my heart."'[70] The language here is both deliberate and significant, and it is another reminder of the consistency in Campbell's thinking over the years. The familiar words from Psalm 40, are used in some of the Glasgow *Fragments*, and in *The Nature of the Atonement*, as a clue to the meaning of the incarnation and the atonement. There is also another kind of consistency at work here, because Campbell wants to stress the connections between Christ's experience and the experience of the believer. The way in which he speaks here about the Eternal Son coming 'into humanity' is further unconscious testimony to the essential orthodoxy of his understanding of the person of Christ.

He wants to underline that salvation is not simply a change in our legal standing before God, but is a profound transformation as we are made partakers of a divine nature. If the Son of God came to do the will of God, that indicates that the divine purpose is to make people like Christ who will also want to do the will of God. A change in legal standing before God will not on its own inspire or enable people to do the will of God. The only way in which sinful people will want to do the will of God is if the Spirit of God indwells them and empowers them to share in the mind and outlook of Christ. The only way in which

---

[69] *Ibid.*, 89-90.
[70] *Ibid.*, 171.

this spiritual life can be sustained is by feeding on Christ; is by those movements of the will whereby we yield to Christ as Lord.

Throughout the second section of the book Campbell is also engaging in dialogue with aspects of his native Protestant tradition. He is forced to concede that his interpretation of feeding on Christ is not prominent in many of the devotional classics which his contemporaries would be familiar with. Part of the explanation he advances is that these valiant Christians were more concerned to write about Christ, than about the mechanics of feeding upon Christ. More contentiously he argues that the failure to recognize these spiritual truths indicates, even in some outstanding Christians, 'a departure from the simplicity that is in Christ in their conceptions of justification by faith and of the way in which faith excludes boasting.'[71] He gladly recognizes that the Reformed emphasis upon justification and sanctification indicates that justification should lead to changed lives, but he feels that these should not be seen as two distinct stages in the spiritual life. Campbell prefers to see one process whereby God justifies people by making them holy. 'Two things have been spoken of where there is but one thing, laborious efforts at harmony made where identify should be recognised; and a complexity embarrassing to the spirit has been introduced instead of the simplicity that is in Christ'.[72]

Whilst he does not in this book employ the contrast between the filial and the penal approaches, which is such a feature of *The Nature of the Atonement*, that fundamental rejection of penal approaches is never far beneath the surface. From Campbell's perspective, views of atonement which do not involve a direct participation in the life of Christ, are regarded as 'superficial and inadequate'. For 'that view of the work of Christ and of the merits of Christ I regard as superficial and inadequate, which, as to the work of Christ, permits us to cherish peace on the ground that the work has been performed apart from the recognition of that call to spiritual perfection in it which that work addresses to us.'[73]

Campbell wishes to move away from any sense that salvation is an external thing which Christ obtains on our behalf and then presents to us. If this was the full story then Christ could tend to fade from view as more and more attention was focused upon

---

[71] *Ibid.*, 97-8.
[72] *Ibid.*, 103.
[73] *Ibid.*, 116. Cf., 115-121.

the priceless gift he supplied. Protestant readers would not have been surprised to find Campbell claiming that the doctrine of transubstantiation tended to divert attention from Christ and redirect it onto the bread and the wine of the Mass. Those same readers must have been shocked to find that Campbell suspected that some Protestants were guilty of a similar kind of error. In Campbell's eyes the doctrine of transubstantiation was in danger of distracting people into wondering about the mysterious way in which the bread and wine became the body and blood of Christ. He felt that complicated systems of doctrine could pose equally dangerous distractions for some Protestants.

> An intellectual substitute for the life of Christ is not less fatal than a material substitute. The mental operation of reference to Christ's work assumed to be imputed to us is no more able to supply the place of receiving Christ as our life than the physical operation of feeding upon the material substance assumed to be transubstantiated into the body and blood of the Lord: and the mental pleading of Christ's merits in prayer is no more able to supply the place of praying in the Spirit of Christ than the physical act of offering up the eucharistic offering. The physical substitute for the life of faith assumes a physical mystery. Does not the intellectual substitute assume a moral mystery? The former is without witness in the conscience and is taken upon trust in the way of implicit faith. Is this not true of the latter also?[74]

Advocates of the views Campbell criticises could offer robust responses to his argument because he does not, in *Christ the Bread of Life*, engage in a detailed debate with other writers. However, the lack of scholarly detail in his comments does not imply that Campbell has nothing important to say. What he is struggling, and sometimes failing, to communicate is a trinitarian construal of the life of faith, where salvation is not just provided by Christ but is in fact located in Christ.

> In fellowship with Him as the truth and the life is the Lord known as the way. No man cometh unto the Father but by Him, inasmuch as humanity cannot attain to God but in the Eternal Life given in the Son of God. No other conscious condition of humanity is nearness to God, but that which is presented to us in the humanity of Christ. For not as a mere permission to come — a personal liberty and warrant to come — are we to conceive of our access to God in Christ, but as a

---

[74] *Ibid.*, 138-9.

spiritual power to draw near to God in newness of life; as the Apostle says of Jew and Gentile, 'Through him we both have access by one spirit unto the Father' [75]

One of the assumptions undergirding this approach is the affirmation of both the humanity and divinity of Jesus Christ. In the humanity of Christ we can see an experience of nearness to God and this experience indicates the experience of eternal life which God intends for his children. It is not, however, sufficient to see Christ in his humanity as an example, because while an example may inspire, it may not necessarily impart the power that is needed for people to follow that example. It is that combination of humanity and divinity in Christ which both inspires and enables people to experience Eternal Life.

> Our Lord not only speaks with divine authority: He speaks, so to express myself, with human authority also. His humanity pronounces to our humanity as the fixed and certain law of the wellbeing of all humanity that which it is itself through its connection with His Divinity. The comfort to us of faith in our Lord's humanity depends on our faith in His Divinity; for the interest to us of the Eternal Life seen in His humanity depends on His power to impart it to us — to sustain it in us.[76]

The language lacks precision but Campbell's approach assumes and requires an orthodox christology which does justice to both the humanity and divinity of Christ.[77]

So by the end of the second section of *Christ the Bread of Life*, which was where the first edition ended in 1851, the reader is left with a portrayal of life in Christ, but is not supplied with a coherent theology of the Lord's Supper. Campbell's conviction that the doctrine of transubstantiation is erroneous has been repeatedly stated, but most readers of the first edition would still be left wondering about his own understanding of the Lord's Supper.

---

[75] *Ibid.*, 119-120.

[76] *Ibid.*, 87-8.

[77] T. F. Torrance, *The Trinitarian Faith*, 149. 'Here we see again the soteriological significance of the Nicene *homoousion*: if Jesus Christ the incarnate Son is not true God from true God, then we are not saved, for it is only God who can save; but if Jesus Christ is not truly man, then salvation does not touch our human existence and condition.'

From Simplicity to Mystery — the 'Development of the Mass of Romanism from the Sacred Institution of the Lord's Supper'[78]

Some aspects of Campbell's theology of the Lord's Supper surface in the new third section, written for the 1869 edition of the book. These comments shed some light on his understanding of the eucharist, but they play only a supporting role in a chapter dedicated to tracing the development of the doctrine of transubstantiation. His attempt to trace this development suffers from the weakness, apparent earlier in the book, that he does not provide detailed historical justification for his assertions about the stages leading to a full-blown doctrine of transubstantiation.

Assuming a simplicity of faith and experience in the early church, Campbell senses that things began to change imperceptibly when thanksgivings for encountering Christ in the Lord's Supper, became thanksgivings for the ordinance itself.[79] He concedes that some of the language used by the early Church might give the impression of a real presence in the bread and the wine. This does not unnerve him however, because Campbell somehow knows that this was not the meaning intended by either the early Church or by Jesus. This being the case, 'no use of such language by the early Christians can prove more than our Lord's own words, prove I mean that if our Lord in speaking of the bread and wine as His body and His blood is not accepted as implying that the bread and the wine then in His hands were actually His body and His blood, neither can similar words used by the early Church be regarded as having more than a symbolic import.'[80]

At this point Campbell naturally assumes the validity of the reflections upon John chapter 6 which he has sketched out earlier in the book. Nevertheless, it still feels inadequate that he makes such a bold analysis of the understanding of Christ, and of the early Church, without offering any biblical or historical evidence to support it. At several stages in this chapter, as in the rest of the book, the reader is often left wondering about the evidence for Campbell's confident claims. Acknowledging that weakness it is necessary to follow through the development which Campbell perceives, from the simplicity of the Lord's

---

[78] *Bread2*, 144.
[79] *Ibid.*, 151.
[80] *Ibid.*, 152-3.

Supper as understood by Jesus to the mystery of transubstantiation.

He regrets that 'it did come to pass that the symbols were in the course of time confounded with and then substituted for what they symbolised. That quickening and strengthening of the life of faith which was experienced in the worthy partaking of the Lord's Supper came in time to be regarded as a grace received through the bread and the wine: until at last these came to be regarded as special mediums of life to be partaken in, in order by so doing to receive the life put into them.'[81] He speculates that this state of mind 'may have passed through the gradually deepening shades of assumed mystical presence by which we see Transubstantiation arrived at now'[82] and that this implied nothing less than the creation of a new faith.

As Campbell sees it this new faith is characterised by mystery and darkness. In contrast to this he is convinced that revelation brings light and 'if the divine light be the divine love, the demand which Revelation makes on the heart should take precedence of that which is made on the understanding.'[83] Sadly he concludes that revelation was too quickly viewed as demanding an intellectual response rather than a response from the heart. This led, in his view, to an insistence on an intellectual submission to orthodoxy by an authoritarian church.[84] From this perspective the incarnation becomes a mystery which needs intellectual scrutiny rather than serving as an indication that God invites people to participate in the divine life.

Although Campbell is aware that it would be helpful to examine in detail the claim that the Mass is a sacrifice for sin, he does not address this issue in the book. His correspondence from this period indicates that he had spent considerable time thinking and writing about the 'Eucharistic Sacrifice', but that he had reluctantly decided not to publish this in the 1869 edition.[85] It is tempting to wonder if, this missing material might

---

[81] *Ibid.*, 153-4.
[82] *Ibid.*, 154.
[83] *Ibid.*, 160.
[84] *Ibid.*, 160-1.
[85] *Memorials* 2.227. In a letter to Erskine of Linlathen, Campbell states that 'the aspect of the mass as "the sacrifice on the cross continued" is to Romanists even more important than that which I have considered; and the hope of being helpful to them caused me to write a good deal which I proposed to give in a supplemental note. I was not, however, able to satisfy myself with the effectiveness of my statement; and I found that I must

help fill in some of the gaps in Campbell's argument, but it is just as likely that it would share the characteristics, and weaknesses, of the other sections in *Christ the Bread of Life*.

At an earlier stage in the book, Campbell expresses his intention to provide a fair representation of the Roman Catholic point of view. Indeed he hopes 'that any intelligent Romanist would have no hesitation in recognizing the fairness of my representation.'[86] Later he is at pains to point out that his concern to identify error does not mean that all those believing this error had missed out on eternal life. For 'to trace an error, even so great an error as this to its root, though that root be a wrong conception of the glory of God in the Incarnation is not to deny the possession of a living Christianity to all in whom this error has been found.'[87] So, as he reflects on church history he thanks 'God for contradictions between what men have believed and what men have been.'[88] With an eirenic spirit he explains that living Christianity can be detected not only in the lives of people in the midst of Catholicism, but also in the experience of those who are set in the midst of the error of Calvinism.[89] Judged by the standards of the nineteenth century Campbell seeks to be moderate and respectful in the language he uses, and he is even handed to the extent that he is willing to criticise Protestants as well as Roman Catholics. The intention to be fair to his opponents may be genuine, but his analysis of Roman Catholicism remains rather general and superficial.

'Feeding upon Christ' — Campbell on Communion

Having listened to Campbell's comments, about what he perceives to be the errors in the doctrine of transubstantiation, it is also appropriate to consider the clues Campbell gives about his own understanding of the Lord's Supper. He asserts that at

---

desist from writing.' In a footnote his son explains that this was 'on account of the state of his health.' Cf. Letter to his Eldest Son, *Memorials*, 221f.

[86] *Bread2*, 54.
[87] *Ibid.*, 178.
[88] *Ibid.*, 179.
[89] *Ibid.*, 179. 'when can it be more intensely felt in the light that God is love than when the Calvinism of Leighton is seen in combination with a spiritual life which makes his words to come nearer than any other to the words of the Holy Apostles of our Lord, in their power to feed spiritual life in us.'

the heart of faith there is a feeding upon Christ which involves those movements of the will whereby we call him Lord in the Spirit. Viewed from this perspective the Lord's Supper can be seen in its true light 'as an abiding witness-bearing to our relation to Christ as our life.'[90] The abiding witness of the Lord's Supper is summed up in Galatians 2:20 where the apostle Paul writes about being crucified with Christ. This paves the way for the most significant reference to Campbell's view of the Lord's Supper that can be found within the second edition of *Christ the Bread of Life*, which therefore deserves to be considered at length. Campbell argues that the Lord's Supper is not identical to the feeding which is at the heart of the life of faith.

> Nevertheless, rightly engaged in, it is itself a high exercise of the faith of which it is the confession — a feeding upon Christ as well as a declaration that we live by feeding on Him; yet this with a special character of its own. Our ordinary feeding upon Christ has its ever-varying aspect determined by the special demands on faith which successively arise in God's ordering of our circumstances, but at the Communion Table we are, as it were, upon the mount of the Lord, above the region in which the daily battle of the life of faith has to be fought: though in the light in which the excellence of that conflict and its high issues are clearly seen and calmly realised, as they cannot be in the fight itself. With all its elements present to our spirits we seal our faith by that special act of personal appropriation of the unsearchable riches which we have in Christ of which the eating the bread and drinking the wine, the symbols of the Lord's body and blood, is the divinely chosen expression. To this there is nothing parallel as a confession of Christ except the receiving of Baptism by conscious believers or that highest Godward movement of our spirits on this side of the veil, the faith in death which says 'Lord Jesus, receive my spirit.'[91]

For Campbell, the Lord's Supper is a 'high exercise' of faith; a 'feeding upon Christ'; a 'declaration' that we live by feeding on Christ; something which has its own 'special character'. Communion is a moment of special intensity within the life of faith and during that experience 'we seal our faith by that special act of personal appropriation' which consists of eating and drinking the symbols of the Lord's body and blood. It

---

[90] *Ibid.*, 145.
[91] *Ibid.*, 146-7.

appears from this that the active faith of the communicant is a very important dimension within Campbell's understanding of the Lord's Supper. The emphasis on the faith of the individual is reinforced by the way in which he draws a parallel with the faith involved in believers' baptism and in the willing surrender to God in the act of dying. Throughout this book Campbell has underlined the importance of conscious experience of Christ, and of the acts of will which are essential to feeding on Christ. While he rightly encourages Christians to approach the Lord's Supper with faith, he may be in danger of so emphasising acts of will, and the faith of the individual communicant, that the efficacy of communion becomes overly dependent upon the worthiness of the recipient. If this were to happen then there would be a risk that an understanding of the eucharist as God's gift might be obscured by too great a stress upon the worthiness of the recipients.

Campbell notes that some early Christian liturgies contain a prayer for the Holy Spirit to 'make the bread the body, and the wine the blood of Christ.'[92] He believes that the intention of the *epiclesis* can be reconciled with his conviction that the bread and wine are, and remain, only symbols. 'Thus the Holy Spirit makes the bread to be to us the body and the wine the blood of Christ *according to the Lord's meaning in so speaking of them.*'[93] What comes to the surface again in this sort of statement is Campbell's confidence that he has rightly understood what Christ intended in his talk about his body and blood. He freely acknowledges that he is interpreting the *epiclesis* on the basis of the concepts of faith and Christian experience outlined earlier in his book. When viewed from this perspective it becomes clear to him that the focus of the Spirit's activity is upon people, rather than upon the material elements used in the Lord's Supper. For 'the prayer contemplates not an action of the Holy Spirit on the bread and the wine, making them to be the body and blood of Christ, but an action of the Holy Spirit on the spirits of the faithful making the bread to them the body and the blood of Christ, i.e. making the eating of the bread and the drinking of the wine to be to them the occasion of that spiritual feeding on Christ, and communion in His body and blood, apart from which the outward act of communion would be an empty shell.'[94] Campbell is aware that some Christians came to

---

[92] *Ibid.*, 172.
[93] *Ibid.*, 173.
[94] *Ibid.*, 173.

interpret things in a less symbolic, more literal fashion, but for him such a move marked a departure from the symbolic simplicity found in both Jesus and the early Church.

The Real Presence of Christ

Although there do not appear to be any significant references to the Lord's Supper in the sermons from his ministry in Glasgow there is relevant material in his earliest sermons. This material helps justify Campbell's claim that what he wrote for the press 'was all present substantially very early in his preaching.' On Sunday 4 July 1830, Campbell concluded a sermon on 1 Corinthians 15:21-6 and 57-8 by reminding his hearers that in three weeks time they would be sharing in the Lord's Supper. From his explanation it appears that eating and drinking at the Lord's Supper overlaps with that feeding upon Christ which should be the everyday experience of the believer.

> For what is it you declare, when you eat the bread at the Lord's table? The meaning of the action is that you are dead to the world, and alive to God in Christ Jesus…and that now, until Christ comes to bring in the kingdom — until he appears the second time without sin unto salvation, you are feeding on the broken body and shed blood of Christ: on that which reveals the world's evil, and the Lord's righteousness, and delivers from the power of sin, and brings out life, the power of the world to come…It is not words that can at all be a preparation, it is when a man asks you, 'What do you mean by eating?' that you should be able to say, 'I am finding the bread of life — because I am finding in it that love, and holiness and power to overcome the world, and power to live to the glory of God, and I thus do what he bids me…The Spirit coming to me is the actual presence of Christ in me. It is not a notion but the Holy Ghost — the Spirit of Christ in me…And eating the flesh and drinking the blood of Christ is walking in the Spirit of Christ.'[95]

If the Spirit 'is the actual presence of Christ in me,' then one aspect of 'real presence' is that the Spirit who empowered Jesus is truly present within the believer. The powerful presence of the Spirit mediates the real presence of Christ to the believing soul.

---

[95] *NofS*, 1.11.9-10.

Before the celebration of Communion on Sunday 25 July 1830, Campbell preached on Galatians 2:20[96] announcing, that it was the preaching of the gospel which was the bread of life, which is able to produce in his hearers the love of God.

> Christ, the Son of God, loved each of you, and gave himself for each of you; and thus there is life for each of you: and I come to you with this bread of life, and set the bread of life before you…God has given me an instrument for producing this love in you, for he has told me to tell every child of Adam this good news, Christ loved you, and gave himself for you — Christ tasted death for you, and for you he arose from the dead — your flesh he took, and your flesh he crucified. He rose and has now the Spirit for you. This news is the bread of life.[97]

In preparation for Communion Campbell issues the solemn warning to those who are about to participate in ordinance of the Lord's Supper.[98] The statement after the 'Fencing of the Tables' is full of words and themes resonant with Calvin's *Institutes* and which point forward to what he would later publish in *Christ the Bread of Life*. What they are about to participate in is not some dull routine because the truth is that the Lord is 'giving you his broken body and shed blood — giving you the word in the shape of bread and wine — giving you in the form of this manifest ordinance that same thing which is set forth in the truth of the preached Gospel.'[99] Hence he underlines that word and sacrament, word and act, are united in proclaiming the same message.[100]

Having stressed the importance of the Word of God, Campbell once again shows his Reformed instincts by underlining the vital role of the Holy Spirit in drawing the believer into a conscious participation in the risen life of Christ.

> And as with the word of truth there goeth forth the Spirit of truth, so with this sign of truth — with this seal of truth — with this visible bodily substance expressive of truth — there

---

[96] *S&L* 2.23, *NofS*, 1.8. See Appendix 4. See also Chapter 4. *The Flesh of Christ Differed Not in One Particle from Mine.*
[97] *S&L* 2.23.112, *NofS* 1.8.9. See Appendix 4.
[98] *NofS*, 1.9.1. See Appendix 10.
[99] *NofS*, 1.9.2. See Appendix 10.
[100] Calvin, *Institutes* IV. xiv. 17. 'Therefore, let it be regarded as a settled principle that the sacraments have the same office as the Word of God: to offer and set forth Christ to us, and in him the treasures of heavenly grace.'

goeth forth the Spirit of Christ — the Holy Ghost — so that those who receive it worthily, as those who truly receive the word of life, do thereby actually receive the Spirit which is the truth that is in these symbols. .....in very truth, the worthy communicant is through the Holy Ghost coming through the risen body of Jesus — coming to him through the glorified humanity — made to experience in this ordinance, the power of Christ's resurrection, and to have fellowship in Christ's sufferings, so that he is actually feeding on the body and blood of Christ by the Spirit. Thus does he substantially receive Christ into his soul through the Holy Ghost. It is the recognising the Spirit there, which shows us how the unworthy communicant, not discerning the Lord's body, is rejecting the Spirit, and Christ in the Spirit.[101]

The theology expressed here is similar to the position Campbell articulated in 1869 when he wrote about the 'action of the Holy Spirit on the spirits of the faithful making the bread to them the body and the blood of Christ.'[102] So from the beginning to the end of his forty year ministry it is clear that he believed that the Holy Spirit played a vital role in enabling people to feed on Christ. It is apparent that he did not view Communion solely as a bare remembrance of Christ, but along with Calvin viewed the Lord's Supper as an opportunity for a real encounter with the ascended Lord, as the secret power of the Spirit lifts the believer up into a direct communion with Christ.[103] So another dimension of Campbell's understanding of real presence is that believers are mysteriously lifted by the Spirit into the real presence of the ascended Christ.

Woven into his comments about the positive role of the Word and the Spirit, Campbell issues a stark warning against transubstantiation.[104] Having warned his congregation about the true nature of the Lord's Supper Campbell addresses the communicants directly and explains, 'That eternal truth in Christ is now put into the form of this bread and wine — that true glory is now in these things to those that will receive them by faith; and through them, as through a glass, are to look in the face of Christ and see the glory of God, and worship God in the Spirit.'[105]

---

[101] *NofS*, 1.9.2. See Appendix 10.
[102] *Bread2*, 173.
[103] Calvin, *Institutes* IV. xiv. 9; IV. xiv. 17; IV. xvii. 10, 12, 18, 26, 31, 33.
[104] *NofS*, 1.9.2. See Appendix 10.
[105] *NofS*, 1.9.3. See Appendix 10.

At 'the close of the dispensation of the Holy Sacrament' Campbell speaks to various groups within the congregation. Along with the warnings he issues to those who may have participated in the Lord's Supper in an unworthy fashion, he exhorts those who have discerned the Lord's body at his table to go on from there and to learn to rely on Christ at all times. Whatever they have experienced of God in Communion is continually true of him because God is not confined to his ordinances.[106] Such an emphasis on the importance of a continual experience of God echoes Calvin who explained that 'the Sacrament does not cause Christ to begin to be the bread of life; but when it reminds us that he was made the bread of life, which we continually eat, and which gives us relish and savour of that bread, it causes us to feel the power of that bread.'[107]

In addition to this series of sermons relating to the celebration of the Lord's Supper at Row in July 1830 there are a number of other references which help to shed light on his understanding of Christ as the Bread of Life. Thus, in a sermon based on Psalm 34, Campbell asserts that the believer feeds on 'the bread of *eternal life*' which 'is the bread of the divine *life.*' God takes delight in the love that is embodied in Christ and in eating bread and wine believers participate in the same love.

> Is it not in Christ that he is eternally well-pleased? What does infinite love feed on but the infinite love that is embodied in Christ? And are we not to feed on the same holiness and truth? Is not his body broken — is not his blood shed for us? Except ye eat the flesh — except ye drink the blood of the Son of God, ye have no life in you. And what is that flesh? What is that blood? Is not the love of God, the holiness and the truth of God, contained in that flesh and blood?...In Christ we find our feast; and there man meets with God; and there man tastes of the fatness of God's house; and there man drinks of God's pleasures — there that same thing which rejoiceth the heart of God, rejoiceth the heart of man, and so we indeed drink of God's pleasures. It is a truth — it is no delusion — no speculation — no refinement — in sober truth, it is eating the flesh and drinking the blood of Christ, who is the well-beloved of the Father, in whom the Father is eternally well pleased.[108]

---

[106] *NofS*, 1.9.5. See Appendix 10.
[107] Calvin, *Institutes* IV. xiv. 5.
[108] *S&L* 2.20.22-3. *NofS*, 2.19.7.

The overlap between what is experienced in the Lord's Supper, and what is to be experienced continually, means that on a number of non-sacramental occasions Campbell can speak about Christ as the Bread of Life in a variety of other ways. In a sermon entitled 'The Children's Bread', he states that 'The provision which God has made for this purpose is the provision of *light*; a revelation of the condition in which we are, considered in reference to God; a revelation of the character of God in his aspect towards us; and this light is the children's bread, the food which nourishes eternal life.'[109] But this is not some mystical alternative to Christ because for Campbell 'Christ is this light. There is contained in him the light in which God sees and condemns the sin of the world; and so manifested, as to cause us in like manner to see, and in like manner to condemn. This light entering into us, we become the children of God. And this is the glory of God in such adoption, that it is through the revelation of his own character that he accomplishes the work. It is the knowledge of what the Father is, that brings back the erring child.'[110]

On another occasion he speaks about the forgiveness of God as the bread upon which God's people are to feed.[111] In a tract dating from his early years in Glasgow he stated that 'the bread of life is Christ's obedience. The bread of life is He who came not to do his own will, but the will of him that sent him and *He that sent Him was with Him.*'[112] Whilst preaching about the Lord's Prayer Campbell employs similar language, but applies it to the Holy Spirit, who is portrayed as the daily bread which the heavenly Father gives to his children.[113] While this is rather untidy it is far from being incoherent, because for Campbell, participating in the life of Christ means experiencing the power of the Spirit of Christ. If salvation is complete in Christ, then feeding on Christ will involve all these other things as well. The central ideas remain the same when Campbell gets around to writing *Christ the Bread of Life*, but he is more cautious and disciplined in the way he expresses things.

---

[109] *GT*, 1.
[110] *Ibid.*, 2.
[111] *NofS* 3.33.6
[112] John McLeod Campbell, *On keeping a Conscience void of offence towards God and towards Man, while considering what claims to be of God*, Tract 1, (Greenock: Greenock Intelligencer, May 1834), 6.
[113] *NofS*, 3.26.8.

Conclusion

While there are good grounds for claiming that *The Nature of the Atonement* is a classic treatment of soteriology, there are few grounds for regarding *Christ the Bread of Life* as a classic treatment of the Lord's Supper. Whilst his discomfort with transubstantiation is everywhere apparent, there is only a brief exposition of Campbell's view of this sacrament. However, this examination of Campbell's thinking about Communion lends further weight to the assertion that over a forty year period there is a consistency in his theological approach. The evidence drawn from the Row sermons, and from the first and second editions of *Christ the Bread of Life*, all supports the claim that Campbell's theology did not substantially change over the years.

One area of continuity is Campbell's emphasis upon the work of the Spirit in Communion. This is visible both within some early sermons and in the second edition of *Christ the Bread of Life*, published just a few years before his death. As time passed, charismatic gifts may have become less important for Campbell, but it is clear that the Spirit continued to play a vital role in his thinking. Closely related to this is a trinitarian framework for prayer and worship, with believers participating in the Son's communion with the Father in the power of the Spirit.

The priestly christology evident in the early sermons and in *The Nature of the Atonement* is once again apparent. The eternal Son is the one through whom we receive eternal life and through whom we offer our worship to God. Only one who is fully human and fully divine is qualified to function as such a priestly mediator. Jesus Christ is both 'the revealer of the Father'[114] and the one who reveals the truth about human life because 'He knew in Himself what humanity can be when filled with the life which was in Him.'[115]

Campbell's polemical attitude towards Roman Catholicism does not prove that he was an evangelical at heart, because Protestants from many backgrounds would have harboured similar sentiments. Although his explicit concerns about Catholicism do not guarantee his evangelical credentials, they are at least consistent with the claim that he held evangelical convictions. The clear echoes of Calvin's approach to the

---

[114] *Ibid.*, 184.
[115] *Ibid.*, 184.

sacraments in Campbell's preaching and writing are further pointers of the evangelical, Reformed nature of his theology.

Having surveyed material from various stages of Campbell's career, the final stage of this reappraisal of his theology outlines his trinitarian christology and draws attention to the implications of this for an accurate interpretation of his soteriology.

Chapter 7

Perfect Sonship Towards God: Campbell's Trinitarian Christology

This exploration of material from different stages of Campbell's ministry has provided the foundation for a reassessment of his theology. While recent interpreters of Campbell develop different perspectives on his soteriology they are united in concluding that he has little to add to our understanding of christology. This perceived weakness is expressed most vigorously by Leanne Van Dyk who senses that attempts to reconstruct his christology are unlikely to succeed.

> Campbell does not, in *The Nature of the Atonement* or anywhere else, suggest a precise and conceptually rigorous account of the relationship between Christ and human persons or other issues in Christology. He does not, for instance, attempt to specify the nature of Christ's person, how Christ is human and divine, the coherence of Chalcedon, or his theological affinities to either an Alexandrian or an Antiochan form of Christological expression. The interpreter of Campbell has only to rely on the evidence of the text and what can reasonably or plausibly be deduced from the rather peculiar and idiosyncratic Christological expressions Campbell uses…
>
> …Campbell does not typically use the language of 'human nature' and 'divine nature', preferring instead terms that emphasize the relationship of sonship to the Father and brotherhood to humanity. It is a (*sic*) unproductive exercise to scrutinize Campbell's terminology for precise Christological expressions.[1]

Both George Tuttle and James Goodloe reach similar conclusions, but this rather pessimistic assessment of Campbell's christology arises largely from a neglect of material in his sermons. It is surprising that Van Dyk's detailed study of Campbell's soteriology contains no references whatsoever to either the Row sermons or the Glasgow Fragments. Tuttle offers

---

[1] Van Dyk, *Desire of Divine Love*, 123-4.

a clear exposition of Campbell's thought and shows an awareness of material contained in the Sermons and Lectures collection. However, he does not draw upon the Notes of Sermons volumes and mainly uses material from the sermons to illustrate the development of Campbell's thought during his trial. Michael Jinkins similarly draws only upon Sermons and Lectures to deepen his understanding of Campbell's theology, but he does not draw attention to the christological significance of the material. Goodloe offers the most thorough study of the sermons thus far, but his enthusiasm for seeing Campbell as a theologian dominated by his understanding of Christian experience, blinds him to other facets of his theology. On the basis of the sermons it is difficult to see how he arrives at the misleading conclusion that 'Campbell neither questions the doctrine of the incarnation nor offers any consideration of Christology.'[2]

Although Campbell did not provide 'a precise and conceptually rigorous account' of the key issues which Van Dyk mentions, the evidence has demonstrated that his sermons contain the heart of the christology which undergirded his soteriology. So whilst Campbell never sets out to prove his orthodoxy by reference to the Chalcedonian definition, this study identified a number of points where his theology is consistent with it. He did not explain in detail how it is possible for Christ to be fully divine and fully human, but we have shown that his preaching is undergirded by just such an orthodox confession. It is correct to observe that Campbell does not talk about 'human nature' and 'divine nature' within *The Nature of the Atonement*, but his preaching provides a complementary perspective with sermons stressing that 'Christ came in human nature',[3] by which he means that Christ assumed fallen human nature. When he affirms that believers become 'partakers of a divine nature', this presumably implies the divinity of the one who enables such a participation in the divine nature.[4] It is clear that the sermons contain sufficient material to suggest that the search for Campbell's christology need not be 'an unproductive exercise.'

Close examination of material from the Row sermons and from the Glasgow *Fragments* has helped to identify some of

---

[2] Goodloe, *Extent and Nature of the Atonement*, 10.
[3] See for example, *NofS*, 1.7.7. Cf., *NofS*, 1.6.8; 1.8.7; 1.11.5; 2.13.2; 2.23.2; 3.27.4, 8; 3.31.3, 6; 3.34.4; 3.35.5.
[4] *NofS*, 1.3.4; 1.8.6.

those key christological themes. In his teaching about Christ assuming fallen human nature, and in his portrayal of Christ as the King and High Priest, Campbell concentrates on the full humanity of the incarnate Christ and the glorified humanity of the ascended Christ. As a preacher he is keen to point to the practical implications for Christian living in the knowledge that Jesus Christ was fully human. However this emphasis upon the humanity of Christ was not at the expense of an orthodox belief in the full divinity of Christ. The priestly soteriology which Campbell expresses most clearly in *The Nature of the Atonement* requires a high priest who is both true God from true God and fully human. In order to represent God fully to human beings the High Priest needs to be fully divine, and to save fallen humanity, the great High Priest also needs to represent fallen humanity fully.[5] It is this need to be 'in all things...made like unto his brethren'[6] which necessitates his assuming human nature as it is since the fall. This understanding of Christ's person is not explained systematically in the language of a two nature christology, but is expressed in terms of 'perfect sonship towards God and perfect Brotherhood towards men.'[7] Having concentrated in earlier chapters upon the human end of the *homoousion* it is necessary now to complete the picture by considering the divine dimension.

Campbell's Trinitarian Christology

In *The Nature of the Atonement* Campbell is unapologetic that he did not resolve various theological mysteries before embarking on his exploration of atonement. He believed that it was essential to interpret the atonement in its own light,[8] in order to understand all other doctrines in the light of what God has done in accomplishing atonement in and through Christ. At times the language he uses echoes Melanchthon's dictum that 'to know Christ is to know his benefits', because he argues that Christ's relationship with human beings 'is indeed a mystery as to its *nature* and *manner*, and to be known to us only in its *results*.'[9] Such comments do not, however, imply that Campbell's thinking is so dominated by his understanding of Christian

---

[5] T. F. Torrance, *The Trinitarian Faith*, 149.
[6] Heb. 2:17.
[7] *Nature*, xvii (19)
[8] Chapter 2. *The Priority of Revelation.*
[9] *Nature*, 322(259).

experience that christology is subordinated to soteriology, but suggest instead that reflection upon Christian experience leads the believer to recognize the divinity of the Saviour.[10] The more he reflects upon *The Nature of the Atonement*, the more convinced Campbell becomes that if Christ saves he must be divine. Hence he argues that 'the faith of the atonement, and the faith that we have eternal life in Christ, is more easy to us when it rests on the faith of the divinity of Christ. Indeed, apart from that previous faith, the faith of what the gospel reveals Christ to be to us would be to me impossible. I cannot believe in one as my life, of whom I am not warranted to think as God.'[11] This affirmation of the divinity of Christ is set within a trinitarian framework, because he states that 'the ultimate mystery which our faith receives' involves 'believing in God the Father, the Son, and the Holy Spirit.' He implies that the economic trinity is a reliable guide to the immanent trinity when he explains that our human responsibility is to study what has been revealed of the trinity '*in its manifestation in connection with man*.'[12] It is appropriate now to explore trinitarian dimensions of christology by considering how Campbell portrays the Son in relation to the Father and the Spirit

The Son who Reveals the Father

In a Row sermon, based on Matthew 11:20-30,[13] the young preacher reflects upon the one who offers rest. The one who issues this invitation has the power to provide the salvation which people need, because the Father has delivered all power into the hands of the Son. 'While Jesus is God, he is also man. He needed not power to be delivered to him as God *He ever had*

---

[10] *Nature*, 322-3 (259-260). 'The divine perfection of sonship in humanity, presented in Christ to our faith, is, in respect of its perfection, what leads us up to the mystery of the divinity of Christ as truly as His power to quicken and sustain sonship in spirit and in truth in us does.' Cf. Forsyth, *The Person and Place of Jesus Christ*, 9. 'All Christology exists in the evangelical faith of the layman who has in Jesus Christ the pardon of his sins and everlasting life....It is the evangelical experience of every saved soul that is the real foundation of Christological belief anywhere.'

[11] *Nature*, 324.(260) Cf., Forsyth, *The Person and Place of Jesus Christ*, 86-7 'No half-God could redeem the soul which it took the whole God to create...If it is an eternal salvation, and the gates of hell cannot prevail against it, he who gives it is an eternal saviour.'

[12] *Nature*, 323 (260).

[13] *S&L*, 2.22. 'Christ's invitation and promise'.

it as God but he *received it as man.*'[14] His reflections upon Matthew 11:27 move on to focus on the Son who reveals the Father, for 'the Scriptures tell us plainly that Christ came to reveal God.'[15] This emphasis is also evident years later in *The Nature of the Atonement* where Campbell insists that it is 'the Son who alone reveals the Father.'[16] It surfaces again in *Thoughts on Revelation* where his comments on Matthew 11:27 further illustrate the trinitarian shape of his theology. For he argues that 'these words reveal the Divine circle into which we have to be taken up, that the love of God may accomplish its desire in us. We are to know the Son by the teaching of the Father: we are to know the Father by the teaching of the Son. The Father drawing us to the Son, the Son revealing the Father; these are Divine actings in the Holy Spirit.'[17]

This process of declaring the Father's name, or manifesting the Father's character, reveals that when it comes to love there is no difference or division between the Father and the Son. So 'do not imagine that Christ, the Son, came to change the Father: he came to reveal the Father he did not come to make God kind, but to show us God's kindness.'[18] In thus revealing the Father's love, the Son not only manifests his own love but also makes clear his unity with the Father. The eternal loving relationship between the Father and the Son is reflected in another early sermon which indicates that the motivation behind the Incarnation was partly the Son's desire to express his love for the Father. 'Christ, from love to his Father, condescended to become man, to take our nature to become a man of sorrows to suffer and die and rise again, that he might be the Mediator between God and us, and that we might through him return to God. Thus Christ proved his love to the Father, by giving himself up to the death, to gratify the desire of his Father's heart, that men should be brought back to God.'[19]

In his introductory remarks before a Communion Service in July 1830 Campbell reassures his hearers that the one who makes this perfect revelation of the Father must also be fully divine. If the revealer was less than divine then there would be a real danger of idolatry. Believers need not fear idolatry in giving

---

[14] *S&L*, 2.22.73.
[15] *S&L*, 2.22.75.
[16] *Nature*, 296 (241)
[17] *TR*, 139.
[18] *S&L*, 2.22.76.
[19] *NofS*, 3.32.8.

their hearts to Christ because he is the Son of the Father, the King of Glory.[20] It is clear from references to passages such as John 3:16[21] that Campbell viewed the Son as the Father's gift to a needy world, and that Jesus Christ was the beloved Son in whom the divine Father was well pleased.[22]

When Campbell published his ideas about atonement in 1856 a central emphasis was the revealed truth that 'God is the Father of our spirits.'[23] He believed that this awareness that God is our Father and that we are his offspring, is built into the fabric of human existence and is the plain message of the Bible.[24] Perhaps one of his most significant reflections on the Father-Son relationship appears in the final paragraph of the Introduction which Campbell added to the second edition of *The Nature of the Atonement* in 1867. After referring to John 14:9 and 14:6, he states that 'we see the Father when we see the Son, not merely because of identity of will and character in the Father and the Son, but because a father as such is known only in his relation to a son.'[25] While he does not explore this further, his language points in the direction of a relational ontology whereby the Father is not seen in isolation but is always spoken of in the context of his relationship to the Son, just as the Son is constantly portrayed as the eternal Son of the Father.

In a sermon based on Psalm 89:14-17, Campbell affirms that in the suffering of the just for the unjust, as a substitute for sinful people there was 'a perfect oneness between the Father and the Son'.[26] Within the context of the sermon this perfect oneness refers to the Father and Son being one in their love for sinful humanity. The Son neither suffers because He is more tender-hearted than the Father, nor does He suffer in order to persuade the Father to show tenderness to sinners. Whilst Campbell does not employ the language of nature or substance, it seems reasonable to suggest that such 'a perfect oneness' in

---

[20] *NofS*, 1.9.3. Appendix 10.
[21] See for example *NofS*, 2.20.10.
[22] For example, *Nature*, 145, 297, 301-2 (137, 242, 245-6). See also *NofS*, 1.9.9, 3.32.6-7.
[23] *Nature*, chapter XV.
[24] *Nature*, 295 (241).
[25] *Nature*, xl (34). See also 145 (137) 'the Son alone could reveal the Father for, indeed, manifested sonship can alone reveal fatherliness, being that in which the desire of that fatherliness is fulfilled, which therefore reveals that desire by fulfilling it.'
[26] *NofS*, 3.27.4.

will and purpose arises out of a deeper oneness because the Son is *homoousios* with the Father.

The Son who Receives the Spirit

Within this intimate Father Son relationship the Spirit is the Father's gift to the Son. Within the humble context of the incarnation the Son 'continually put trust in his Father for the Spirit, and did continually receive from the Father, the Spirit without measure.'[27] Such a continual giving and receiving of the Spirit was needed to enable the Son to overcome the tendencies towards sin which were inherent within the fallen human nature he had assumed. In the language of the young preacher of Row the struggle to resist temptation is described as 'condemning sin in the flesh' or 'crucifying the flesh'. So 'having humbled himself to be a servant, recognizing that this flesh was evil, he did trust to his father, (*sic*) and, continually receiving the Spirit from the Father, thus presented his blood without spot to God.'[28] This dynamic was evident to the disciples who could see that in the midst of his trials Jesus 'went to his Father in prayer, and that he received the Spirit of peace'.[29]

This process of crucifying the flesh in the power of the Spirit continued throughout Christ's life and came to a climax on the cross where Christ offered himself without spot to God, 'through the eternal Spirit'.[30] Campbell uses this phrase frequently as he expounds his priestly understanding of atonement both in *The Nature of the Atonement*,[31] and in his preaching.

One of the Glasgow sermon fragments, which appeared in the 1861 edition of *Fragments of Truth*, considers Hebrews 9:14 under the heading, *The Purged Conscience*.[32] For Campbell the blood of Christ was not intended simply to calm the conscience but to transform it. The blood of Christ is seen not just as a past event but as symbolising the present power of God which can transform sinners into children of God who gladly serve the

---

[27] *S&L*, 1.14.346. Cf., *S&L*, 2.23.108; *NofS*, 1.8.7. Appendix 4.
[28] *S&L*, 1.14.346. Cf., *S&L*, 2.23.95; *NofS*, 1.8.2. Appendix 4.
[29] *NofS*, 3.26.1.
[30] Heb. 9:14.
[31] *Nature*, 105, 136, 143, 147, 152, 156, 169, 256 (110, 131, 136, 138,142, 144, 153, 213).
[32] *FofT*, 15. If this dates from the same time as *Fragments* 17-20, then it may have been written around 1847. See Chapter 3. *The Glasgow Sermons.*

living God in spirit and in truth. What gives Christ's blood such transforming power is that it was offered *through the Eternal Spirit*. As Campbell seeks to explain how this 'works' he offers some enigmatic clues about his understanding of the relationship between the Son and the Spirit.

> The true description of this offering of Himself is, that it was *through the Eternal Spirit*. Mark this, I beseech you. Consider what it means. The blood of Christ, shed to purge your conscience, is brought before us in connexion with the state of His own inward spirit towards His Father; and the pureness of the offering, its being *without spot*, is ascribed to the *Eternal Spirit*, through whom He offered Himself; and He is *thus* set before us as made a High Priest after the power of an endless life, and not after the law of a carnal commandment.[33]

Taken in isolation such language about 'the state of' Christ's 'own inward spirit towards His Father' might suggest that Hebrews 9:14 was referring to the Son's inner attitude rather than to a specific work of the Holy Spirit. The overall impression, however, seems to point in a more personal and trinitarian direction because he portrays the person of the Son freely offering himself up to the Father in and through the power of the Holy Spirit.

> This sacrifice of self this death to redeem them that were under the power of death, was the mind of the Spirit of God, and *so* was the fulfilling of the will of God; for "God so loved the world, that He gave His Son." Those whose eyes are opened by the Eternal Spirit to see the mind of the Father revealed in the death of the Son, *must* have their conscience purged from that slavish dread of God which prompts to the performance of dead works. They who spiritually discern that it was *through the Eternal Spirit* that Christ offered Himself, *cannot* but discern His thoughts towards man to be thoughts of peace and not of evil; they are thus set free from all necessity of *doing something to change the mind of God*, and can walk at liberty, delighting themselves in God's commandments, which they love.[34]

Campbell's comments are tantalizingly brief, but perhaps unconsciously he is expressing a form of trinitarian *perichoresis*, which a later writer defines as a 'unique unity in which the three persons live by virtue of their mutual relationships.'[35] If the Son's sacrifice 'through the Eternal Spirit' involves fulfilling the

---

[33] *FofT*, 15.178.
[34] *FofT*, 15.179.
[35] J. Moltmann, *History and the Triune God*, (London: SCM Press, 1991) 59.

mind of the Spirit; and if this is virtually synonymous with fulfilling the will and purpose of God (the Father); then Father, Son and Spirit are together mutually implicated in the work of redemption. Partly these comments embody Campbell's desire to negate any suggestion that the Son was more loving than the Father, but they may also hold a deeper significance. If Father, Son and Holy Spirit are so united in love and saving purpose then it seems plausible to suggest that this unity of action arises from the essential unity of the triune God. Whilst the preacher's aim at this point is to enable his congregation to experience personal transformation, rather than to offer precise doctrinal definitions, the basis for his appeal would appear to be a trinitarian understanding of the being of God.

This stress upon Christ offering himself to God 'through the Eternal Spirit' surfaces regularly in the Row sermons.[36] In one sermon[37] Campbell considers the judgement of God from a variety of perspectives. He argues that the God who forgave sinners in Nineveh, when they repented in response to the message of coming judgement, would also have forgiven the evil generation living before the Flood if they had shown repentance. Judgement day is coming but the good news is that God has provided 'a space for repentance, and that he has himself made provision for us that we should repent.'[38] For parishioners in Row the coming judgement presents a particular challenge because God will hold them responsible for their response to the truth which has been clearly declared from the pulpit. The summary of truth which Campbell offers contains themes which have been considered in earlier chapters. Reminding them that Christ died for everyone, he explains that Christ did not take the nature of man as before the fall, but assumed our fallen nature, maintaining holiness at all times by dependence upon the Holy Spirit. Central to Christian faith is the narrative of Christ 'taking the nature which you have, just as you have it, and in that nature glorifying God, and being the Holy One of God you have been taught that this was through the eternal Spirit through the eternal Spirit he offered himself without spot to God.'[39]

---

[36] See e.g., *S&L*, 1.13.303; 2.23.95 & 109; (*NofS*, 1.8.2 & 7); *NofS*, 3.25.10; 3.30.8; 3.31.3-6; 3.36.10.
[37] *NofS*, 3.25. Sermon on 2 Peter 3:15 'The long-suffering of our Lord is salvation.'
[38] *NofS*, 3.25.4.
[39] *NofS*, 3.25.10.

Similar language is employed in a Row sermon based on Titus 2:11-14,[40] where the preacher refers to Christ offering himself to God 'through the eternal Spirit' no less than nine times. He seeks to persuade the congregation that the grace of God has appeared in order to bring salvation and to teach people to resist temptation and to live in a righteous way. Naturally the basis for such an appeal is found in the example of Christ who assumed our flesh, exposed himself to the assaults of Satan and resisted temptation through the power of the Holy Spirit. In life and in death, Christ offers himself spotlessly to God through the eternal Spirit. A life of holiness is not an impossible ideal because it is made possible for believers by the power of that same Spirit.

> Christ condemned sin in the flesh by being in our condition, and perfectly holy in it. He has cleared God of all these in it he presented human nature, his own blood without spot to God through the Eternal Spirit, and thereby has taught us what sin is, and that it is not of God, and that there is no excuse for it, and that there is power in the Spirit of God to give us perfect deliverance from the bondage of sin.[41]

There were good precedents within the Reformed tradition for seeing Christ's offering himself 'through the eternal Spirit' as a key part of atonement. Rejecting the idea that the 'eternal Spirit' being referred to is the divine nature of the Son, John Owen had insisted that the person of the Holy Spirit was in view and that 'the Lord Christ offered up himself unto God as a sacrifice by the eternal Spirit.' Amongst the graces imparted to the incarnate Son by the Spirit, his *'unspeakable zeal'* and his *'ardency of affection unto the glory of God'* helped to make his sacrifice effective.[42]

In this context it is interesting to notice how Jürgen Moltmann also finds Hebrews 9:14 suggestive as he seeks to develop a contemporary theology of the cross,. He asserts that 'the surrender through the Father and the offering of the Son take place "through the Spirit". The Holy Spirit is therefore the link in the separation. He is the link joining the bond between the Father and the Son, with their separation.'[43] Within Moltmann's

---

[40] *NofS*, 3.31. Appendix 5. Cf., Chapter 4. *In the Likeness of Sinful Flesh.*
[41] *NofS*, 3.31.3. Appendix 5.
[42] *Works of John Owen*, vol. III, 176-180.
[43] J. Moltmann, *The Trinity and the Kingdom of God*, (London: SCM Press, 1981), 82-3.

later theology the Holy Spirit plays an increasingly significant, and an increasingly personal, role. Within these earlier comments, however, the Spirit appears in a less clearly personal light, as the bond of love uniting Father and Son at the cross.

Returning to Campbell's approach there appear to be fewer grounds for suggesting that the Spirit plays a less than fully personal role within the life of the triune God. The Father's gift of the Spirit to the Son is seen in the way that the Son continually receives the Spirit from the Father to empower his life and ministry. The Son is enabled to offer the perfect sacrifice of himself 'through the Eternal Spirit'. Latent within these comments is a theology which both distinguishes the person of the Son from the person of the Holy Spirit whilst affirming their triune unity.

The Son who Gives the Spirit

Another dimension of the Spirit as the Father's gift to the Son consists in the way in which the ascended Christ receives the Spirit in order that he might communicate the Holy Spirit to others. So, for example, in the sermon 'Confessing Christ'[44] Campbell contrasts the experience of the incarnate Son of Man with the experience of the risen Son of God. 'As the Son of Man he had not yet received the Spirit, excepting for himself: as the Son of God ascended up on high, he received the Holy Ghost for us. The Christ whom we are called on to confess is the risen Saviour, who has the Holy Ghost for us.'[45] This new phase of the Father's giving to the Son means that Christ gives the Spirit to believers to make new life possible. So when Campbell thinks of the ascended Christ fulfilling his kingly and priestly offices he celebrates that Christ 'has the Holy Spirit for you'.[46] He expresses this dimension of the Son's ministry in the language of 1 Corinthians 15:45 by describing the risen Christ as 'a quickening Spirit'. 'He laid down his life, not in uncertainty, but in order that he might take it up again, which shows us that our Lord would not have thought of making an atonement for our sins, if he had not the prospect of being exalted and of receiving

---

[44] *S&L*, 2.33. For discussion of this sermon see, Chapter 5. *Past and Present Dimensions of Christ's Priestly Ministry.*
[45] *S&L*, 2.33.370. See also *NofS*, 1.2.12; 1.9.10; 2.16.6; 3.28.8 and 3.31.5.
[46] See e.g. *S&L*, 2.33.372, 374,375; *NofS*, 1.5.4; 1.7.14; 1.10.5; 3.31.4; *EG*, 20; 'Address to a few Parishoners of Row, delivered at Helensburgh in August 1831', 4, contained in *NofS* vol. 2.

the Spirit for us. So when he laid down his life he did so in the faith, and expectation that his Father would raise him up; and that he would receive from his Father power to be a quickening Spirit.'[47]

To talk of Christ as 'a quickening Spirit' might appear to run the risk of confusing the identities of the risen Christ and the Spirit. In this context Ralph Del Colle identifies two contrasting approaches, which he labels: a 'revisionary trinitarian Spirit christology', and a 'classical trinitarian Spirit christology'.[48] By 'revisionary trinitarian' he has in mind approaches which seek to revise classical trinitarian and christological doctrine. So for example whilst Geoffrey Lampe[49] recognised a trinitarian pattern in Christian experience he believed that this need not lead to an affirmation of distinct hypostatic identities for the Son and the Spirit within the Godhead. In contrast Del Colle advocates a model of Spirit-christology which 'seeks to articulate the relationship between the "person" of the Holy Spirit and that of the Son in the incarnation and work of redemption... while at the same time preserving the integrity of the doctrine of the trinity.'[50] Although the christologies he explores are much more complex than anything found in Campbell's preaching or theology, this reappraisal shows that Campbell belongs much more within the classical trinitarian family of approaches. For whilst the Spirit plays an important role in Campbell's portrayal of the person of Christ, this does not lead to a merging of the identities of the Risen Christ and the Holy Spirit. His place within the trinitarian tradition, more specifically the Western version of that tradition, comes across when he asserts that the life of sonship becomes possible 'after the risen Saviour had sent upon His Church the promise of the Father, that in the power of the Holy Ghost proceeding from the

---

[47] *NofS*, 3.32.7. See also *NofS*, 2.17.9; 2.20.11.
[48] Ralph Del Colle, 'Schleiermacher and Spirit Christology: Unexplored Horizons of *The Christian Faith*', *International Journal of Systematic Theology* 1 (1999) 286-307. See also Ralph Del Colle, *Christ and the Spirit: Spirit Christology in Trinitarian Perspective*, (Oxford: Oxford University Press, 1994).
[49] Geoffrey Lampe, *God as Spirit*, (London: SCM Press, 1977). For Del Colle's treatment of Lampe's position see *Christ and the Spirit*, chapter 5.
[50] Del Colle, *Christ and the Spirit*, 4-5.

Father and the Son, they might be the sons of God in spirit and in truth.'[51]

Three Phases of Imparting the Spirit to the Son

It is interesting to notice what Campbell omits as well as what he includes in his thoughts about the relation between the Son and the Spirit. On the basis of the New Testament evidence, Tom Smail suggests that it is possible to identify three main phases in the imparting of the Spirit to the Son.[52] Firstly, 'The regenerative coming of the Spirit at Jesus' conception', then secondly, 'The Spirit comes to Jesus at his baptism to anoint him as Messiah', and thirdly 'The Spirit transfigures Jesus at his resurrection.' In identifying different phases of the imparting of the Spirit to the incarnate Son, Smail stresses that this does not mean 'that he had more of the Spirit, in a quantitative sense at one time than at another. He had all of the Spirit from the start, but the Spirit in him responded creatively to the ever changing and developing demands that his life and his death made upon him at every point.' This arises from the way in which 'the life of the Son in his interaction with the Father and the Spirit is not lived in the still immobility of static perfection but in the dynamic of constant interchange and mutual giving.'[53]

Campbell's reflections upon Christ being made 'a quickening spirit' at his resurrection, correspond to what Smail identifies as the third phase of the imparting of the Spirit to the Son. It could perhaps be argued that Campbell's emphasis upon the incarnate Son continually receiving the Spirit from the Father assumes the activity of the Spirit in the conception and the baptism of the Son, but he never explicitly makes this connection. Although the Holy Spirit figures prominently in Campbell's preaching it is surprising that he does not appear to mention the Spirit's role in either the Son's conception or baptism. The one exception is a sermon where Campbell responds to the perceived criticism that he is indulging in unhelpful speculation by concentrating upon

---

[51] TR, 137. See also 136. "If Christianity cannot be realised in us apart from our relation to the Father and the Son, no more can it apart from our relation to the Holy Spirit.'

[52] T. Smail, *The Giving Gift*, (London: Hodder & Stoughton, 1988), 99-107. Compare the detailed way in which John Owen had identified eleven aspects of the Spirit's work in relation to the Son. *Works of John Owen*, vol. III, 159-188.

[53] Smail, *The Giving Gift*, 96-7.

the way in which Christ maintained his holiness during his life and ministry. The way in which he rhetorically frames his critics' question implies that he believed that Christ was preserved in a sinless condition from conception onwards by the work of the Holy Spirit.[54] Even at this point the emphasis falls upon the work of the Spirit after Christ's conception rather than offering any insight into the Spirit's role in the conception itself. His lack of attention to this topic stands in stark contrast to the detailed and vigorous way in which his friend Edward Irving explores these themes.[55] For Irving the Spirit literally plays the vital role in the conception of Christ. Inspired by Luke 1:35 he affirms that 'the Holy Ghost was the author of His bodily life, the quickener of that substance which He took from fallen humanity.'[56] At an earlier point in the tradition John Owen offered a meticulous exposition of the *'framing, forming, and miraculous conception of the body of Christ in the womb of the blessed Virgin'* which 'was the peculiar and especial work of the Holy Ghost.'[57] Owen is concerned to show that the forming of the body of Christ was not the result of a creative act of the Son but that it was the work of the Spirit. He appears to assume that if the Son created a body for himself that this would create a human nature different in kind from the nature of those he came to save. By stressing the continuous working of the Spirit upon the human nature of Christ from before his conception, Owen creates space for the full humanity of the incarnate Son. Campbell's silence at this point is unhelpful because a failure to think systematically and consistently about the Spirit's role in Christ's conception potentially undermines the affirmation of the full humanity of Christ which is such an important dimension of Campbell's christology.

It is similarly surprising that Campbell does not, in any of the surviving sermons, appear to reflect upon the significance of the pouring out of the Spirit in the baptism of Jesus. Once again this contrasts starkly with the approach adopted by Irving who

---

[54] *NofS*, 3.31.6. 'For they say, "If you hold that Christ's human nature was always holy, from his conception till his death, why lead people into speculation about how it was holy?"'
[55] G. Carlyle, (ed.), *The Collected Writings of Edward Irving in Five Volumes*, (London: Alexander Strahan, 1865) Volume 5, Section III, 'The Method is by taking up the fallen humanity', 114-146.
[56] *Ibid.*, 126.
[57] *Works of John Owen*, vol. III, 162.

views the baptism as Christ's anointing to the prophetic office,[58] equipping him with the prophetic power and wisdom needed to preach good news to the poor and to engage in conflict with the powers of evil. Irving argues that the impartation of the Spirit at Christ's conception empowered him to keep the law, whilst the baptism of the Holy Ghost which Christ received at his baptism with water empowered him 'to live the life above the law which His Church…was to live until His second coming.'[59] At his baptism Christ received the Spirit who enabled him to preach, to heal and to deliver people from evil. 'Thus' claims Irving, Christ 'shewed us an example that we should follow His steps; and hereby He became the great prototype of a Christian.'[60]

By regularly proclaiming that 'Christ has the Spirit for you', Campbell was, at least implicitly, affirming that Christ's experience of the Spirit was the prototype for Christian experience. An obvious way of providing some biblical support for this approach would be to link Christian experience to Christ's baptismal experience in the river Jordan. However there is no evidence that Campbell tried to help his congregation to make such a connection. Reflection upon Christ's baptism could also have given the minister of Row an opportunity to explore aspects of Christ's prophetic office, but as noted previously the prophetic office does not figure in Campbell's depiction of the person of Christ.

Campbell's preaching accords a prominent place to the Spirit who is active in Jesus Christ and available to believers through Christ. Whilst his language assumes a dynamic interchange within the Trinity, whereby the Father is constantly giving the Spirit as his gift to the Son, this assumption is not given adequate biblical or theological foundation. Compared with the work of either his contemporary, Edward Irving, or the Puritan, John Owen, the christology advanced by Campbell is poorly developed, but there are sufficient hints to suggest that he was employing similar presuppositions. The understanding of the person of Christ which emerges from Campbell's sermons is probably inspired by Irving's more detailed work. As Campbell

---

[58] *Collected Writings of Edward Irving*, Volume 5, 129. '…the occasion of His baptism; which if I err not, was His anointing to the prophetical office.' Owen views Christ's baptism in a similar way. 'And this collation of extraordinary gifts for the discharge of his prophetical office was at his baptism, Matt. iii.17.' *Works of John Owen*, vol. III, 171f.
[59] *Collected Writings of Edward Irving*, Volume 5, 132.
[60] *Ibid.*, 133.

was not attempting to write a systematic theology, his preaching sought to underline some of the practical implications of the approach which Irving had developed in a more rigorous fashion.

When material from Campbell's early sermons and his mature theology is used to put flesh on the bones of his christology, the end result is not a spirit-christology which merges the identities of the Son and the Spirit, but a classical trinitarian understanding of the person of Christ. Study of the Row sermons and the Glasgow *Fragments* advances research into Campbell's theology in new directions by drawing attention to its pneumatological and trinitarian dimensions.

In the light of this it is necessary to raise some critical questions about Leanne Van Dyk's somewhat confusing comments about the role of the Holy Spirit in Campbell's theology. On the one hand she argues that within his theology the Spirit's role in redemption is largely unexamined, and that Campbell's preoccupation with the relationship between the Father and the Son means 'that the Spirit's participation in the divine life is rendered superfluous.' This leads her to suggest that a 'fuller development of the person of the Holy Spirit would have strengthened Campbell's Trinity doctrine.'[61] However, on the other hand she also claims that 'a fully developed Spirit doctrine is latent, or potential, in Campbell's work'. So whilst the Spirit's shadowy role is not fully developed nevertheless she detects 'a vital sense in *The Nature of the Atonement* both of Trinitarian intimacy and cooperation in divine acts ad intra as well as purposeful, salvific divine activity ad extra.[62]

Van Dyk's comments are the understandable result of reading *The Nature of the Atonement* in isolation from the sermons. For it is only when his sermons are taken into consideration that it becomes possible to affirm with confidence that a coherent doctrine of the Spirit is not just latent, but present in Campbell's thought. His claim that what he had 'written for the press was all present substantially very early in my preaching,'[63] suggests a consistency in his thinking over the years, which is supported by the evidence outlined earlier. It seems reasonable to conclude that while his enthusiasm for some charismatic experiences may have waned in the years following the Gareloch pentecost, he did not withdraw from his fundamental convictions about the

---

[61] Van Dyk, *Desire of Divine Love*, 169.
[62] Ibid., 170.
[63] *Memorials* 2.159.

Spirit's role in the person and work of Christ. This is confirmed, linguistically and theologically, by the way in which he appeals to Hebrews 9:14 in the Row sermons, in the Glasgow Fragments, in *The Nature of the Atonement*, and later in *Thoughts on Revelation*.[64] Thus when Campbell's preaching is permitted to assist in the process of interpreting his theology there are much firmer grounds for affirming a clear doctrine of the Spirit than Van Dyk suspects.

In a similar way the material brought to light in this study supplies the evidence, which Van Dyk was unable to provide, to support her contention that 'Campbell's theology is a Trinitarian theology.'[65] It also points to the conclusion that her suggestion that the search for Campbell's christology is likely to be an 'unproductive exercise' is unduly pessimistic.

The christology which emerges from this study also challenges James Goodloe's negative conclusions about Campbell's christology. In addition to asserting that Campbell does not offer 'any consideration of Christology', he goes on to claim that his understanding of the consciousness of being a child of God leads him to impose 'upon the Scriptures a unified depiction of Christ as the perfect son and perfect elder brother, the unity of which depiction is not supported by the Scriptures themselves.'[66] Such an assessment seems to ignore those biblical passages, where the Father speaks of his beloved Son in whom he is well pleased, which could plausibly provide a scriptural basis for viewing Christ as the perfect Son of the Father. It also overlooks Hebrews 2:17, which Campbell was fond of using, which speaks of the one who in all things was 'made like unto his brethren.' The portrayal of the divinity and humanity of Christ which surfaces particularly in Campbell's sermons is a more complex depiction of Christ than the one Goodloe appears to be operating with.

Reflecting on Campbell's preaching and theology points to the conclusion that a coherent christology is visible even though it remains systematically undeveloped. In his preaching, and presumably in his later theology, Campbell is operating with a classical trinitarian understanding of the person of Christ. His emphasis upon the continuing glorified humanity of Christ places him in the Calvinist, rather than the Lutheran, tradition in his approach to christological issues. In line with Owen and

---

[64] *TR*, 130.
[65] Van Dyk, *Desire of Divine Love*, 170.
[66] Goodloe, *Extent and Nature of the Atonement*, 10, 66.

Irving he allows space for Christ to assume full humanity by attributing Christ's victory over evil and temptation to the activity of the Spirit who is continually given by the Father to the Son. This permits a christology which leaves space for Christ's full humanity and for a genuine process of human development.[67] However, while Campbell lays the foundation for a christology affirming the full humanity of Christ, he does not give his hearers or readers much of an impression about what the human Jesus was actually like. In the midst of proclaiming that Christ assumed fallen human nature and continually received the Spirit, Campbell pays insufficient attention to the controversial life of the historical Jesus. The resultant christology does not fall into the trap of docetism but offers a rather general and slightly impersonal picture of Christ. The human Christ portrayed by Campbell is a rather more comfortable character than the one who emerges from the pages of the Synoptic Gospels. Humanly speaking it is perhaps more difficult to see why the Jewish and Roman authorities would have bothered to crucify such a figure.

The Soteriological Significance of Campbell's Christology

By examining materials from different stages in his life it has been shown that Campbell was justified in claiming that what he wrote for the press was 'all present substantially very early in my preaching.'[68] Acknowledging this consistency in his thinking means that it is necessary to take the wider corpus of material into consideration in order to get an accurate impression of his theology. More particularly it underlines the need to interpret *The Nature of the Atonement* in the light of the christology evident in his early preaching.

To some extent there was little controversial in Campbell's christology because he was clearly operating within a trinitarian, two-nature framework. What calls out for attention is his affirmation that Christ assumed fallen human nature, an emphasis which attracted some criticism in the months following his trial. Such thinking is not, as his critics supposed, further evidence of his heretical views, but rather a sign that he belongs to a 'distinguished line of thinkers'[69] in the tradition who adhered to such a view. The significance of his emphasis

---

[67] *NofS*, 2.13.13-14. Appendix 6.
[68] *Memorials* 2.159.
[69] Geoffrey Wainwright, *For Our Salvation*, 150.

upon the Son coming 'in the likeness of sinful flesh' is that it contributes to a more positive evaluation of his theology in general, and sheds fresh light on his soteriology in particular. This study has suggested that this insight enables a more positive assessment of Campbell's much debated suggestion about Christ offering 'a perfect confession of our sins', [70] and it is necessary now to support that claim.

'A Perfect Confession of Our Sins'?

The evaluation of *The Nature of the Atonement* advanced in Chapter 2, argues that some assessments of Campbell's soteriology give a distorted impression of his work by focusing exclusively upon comments about Christ's perfect confession, whilst overlooking other important aspects of the priestly model of atonement which Campbell develops. A proper recognition of these other elements suggests that Campbell's approach may be more 'objective' and coherent than his critics have allowed. However, even if a more sympathetic view of his soteriology can be conceded, the question still remains as to whether notions of a 'perfect confession' or a 'perfect repentance' are weak links within his argument.

The idea that Christ has offered a perfect confession for our sins may be questioned from a number of angles. Part of the discomfort with the notion of Christ engaging in an act of representative confession may arise from the contemporary emphasis upon the autonomy of the individual which is one of the legacies of the Enlightenment. If the individual's needs are of paramount importance then it is harder to envisage how any one could possibly represent all and act on behalf of all. Individualism reacts against the idea that someone can act on my behalf without asking my permission first. However, even in an individualistic age, some representative figures are in a position where their actions have significant implications for others. It is clear, for example, that the decision of the President of the USA to declare war on Iraq, has direct and serious implications for millions of people in many countries. At that political level it is clear that the words and actions of representative people do have a major impact upon the lives of the people they represent, whether they approve of this or not.

If it could be shown that similar forms of representative action do not operate within the moral realm, then that would

---

[70] *Nature,* 117 (118).

certainly undermine Campbell's soteriology. However, it would also call into question other models of atonement because all of them appear to operate on the assumption that the atoning actions of a representative or a substitute can have beneficial implications for others. Within Campbell's preaching and theology, Christ by becoming human has made himself our brother; and this process of identification with human beings in their plight makes it possible for Christ to be viewed as a representative of others.

In seeing Christ as our representative, Campbell was utilizing biblical concepts because figures such as the King and the High Priest in Israel functioned as representatives of the people. However, simply identifying Christ as our representative does not solve all the problems because at the very point where Campbell portrays Christ as making a perfect representative confession of our sins, he explains that this act of perfect contrition includes all the major elements of repentance 'excepting the personal consciousness of sin'.[71] To some extent such language might be seen as challenging the idea that Christ had assumed a fallen nature with a propensity to sin, because by some definitions such a propensity would bring with it a personal consciousness of sin.

Within the context of Campbell's thinking it seems more likely that this phrase is a vigorous way of protecting the doctrine of Christ's sinlessness. It is another way of expressing his conviction that Christ was 'holy in our nature' and that he never yielded to temptation and was not guilty of committing sin. Such language need not exclude the possibility that his human nature was capable of sinning and vulnerable to genuine temptations. If it was the case that the fallen nature he had assumed had an inner propensity to sin, then this would mean that the incarnate Son would be intensely aware of the reality of temptation. His lack of personal sin and guilt need not lessen his personal awareness of sin in the sense that a moral vision undiminished by personal sin would enable him to be more keenly aware of the sins committed by others. It is this total act of identification with sinful humanity which makes plausible the idea of Christ bearing the burden of their sins and offering a perfect confession of those sins to God. Something similar is present a century later where Karl Barth depicts the Son as assuming not only our fallen nature but the sin and guilt which come with it, because '…it is our familiar humanity out and out,

---

[71] *Nature*, 118 (118).

namely, not only with its natural problems, but with the guilt lying upon it of which it has to repent, with the judgement of God hanging over it, with the death to which it is liable.'[72] If Christ has taken responsibility for the guilt lying upon fallen humanity then it is appropriate for him to confess this guilt to the Father.

But does such a confession atone? As early as the work of Athanasius there is the conviction that repentance alone is insufficient to undo the corruption introduced by sin. For 'had it been a case of trespass only, and not of a subsequent corruption, repentance would have been well enough; but when once transgression had begun men came under the power of the corruption proper to their nature and were bereft of the grace which belonged to them as creatures in the Image of God. No, repentance could not meet the case.'[73]

If Campbell was arguing that a representative prayer of confession offered by Christ was sufficient, on its own, to deal with the sins of the world then the weakness of his proposal would be further exposed by Athanasius' comments. It may not, however, be so easy to dismiss Campbell's idea when it is remembered that Christ's perfect confession is but one part of a larger priestly model of atonement. In addition it is also important to notice that when he talks about Christ's perfect confession or repentance he is using these words in a very specific way. As the Son has confessed the Father's love to sinful people so he now confesses the sins of the people to the Father. This is an act of confession which confesses that human nature is sinful and that such a sinful nature rightly attracts the judgement and wrath of God. There is a sense in which Campbell's language is fully consistent with that used by Athanasius because it can readily be interpreted in terms of Christ confessing to the Father that human nature is so riddled with sin that the only way for God to deal with this flesh is by putting it to death and recreating it. If Christ assumed sinful human nature with its inner propensity to sin and has direct personal experience of 'the deep stream of pollution in our flesh,'[74] then although he is not personally guilty of sin he would be in a position to confess that human flesh needs more than just the verdict of 'not guilty'. Such fallen flesh needs to be

---

[72] *Church Dogmatics* vol. I: part 2 40.
[73] Athanasius, *The Incarnation of the Word of God: Being the Treatise of St. Athanasius, De Incarnatione Verbi Dei*, (London: Geoffrey Bles, 1944), § 7, 33.
[74] *FofE*, 18.275.

redeemed and recreated and this is what is accomplished in the representative person of Christ through his death and resurrection.

Such a view of Christ functioning as the representative of fallen humanity, and putting sinful flesh to death so that a new humanity could be born, is expressed by the young minister of Row in terms of our dying and rising with Christ.

> When Christ gave his flesh to death, willingly and freely, he did it not as an individual, but as our head and representative; as having taken on him our sins and borne our griefs; as having come into the place of taking the load and burden of our race upon him, so that, in this sense, all died when Christ died; and that as, in the judgement of God, Christ did not suffer as a private person, but as a head and representative, so also, all rose when Christ rose: he rose not as a private person, but as a Head. In this sense we are included both in the death and resurrection of Christ, and so we are not under the law but under grace not debtors to the flesh to live after it, but to the Spirit which the living Saviour received for us, that we should live after the Spirit.[75]

These reflections suggest that Campbell's approach does not collapse around the idea of Christ offering a perfect confession of sin. By setting these proposals in the larger context provided by the sermons from his ministries in Row and in Glasgow, it is possible to offer an alternative reading of these disputed comments. When Christ's confession is interpreted in the light of his coming in the likeness of sinful flesh, and within its context as part of a wider representative, priestly model of atonement, then there are grounds for suggesting that the idea has a much greater degree of coherence than its critics have usually allowed. While Campbell only occasionally describes Christ as a substitute,[76] it is clear that he is much more comfortable with seeing Christ as our head and representative, the second Adam[77] who rescues humanity through his death and resurrection. His unease about the language of substitution should not be taken to mean that he is peddling a subjective, exemplarist approach to the work of Christ. There is something profoundly objective about the way in which Christ the representative confesses human sin and absorbs divine wrath

---

[75] S&L 2.23.95f., NofS 1.8.2.
[76] NofS, 2.27.3,8.
[77] NofS 2.14.7.

and judgement by accepting the death which is the rightful wages of sin. Reading Campbell's soteriology against the wider context of his preaching and theology suggests that amidst the clumsiness of his written style, he has nevertheless opened up significant perspectives upon the work of Christ. His doctrine of atonement has its own set of limitations, but they are not the limitations suggested by most of his critics.

As intimated in the treatment of Christ's Twofold Office, the shortcomings of Campbell's approach are not so much to do with Christ making a perfect confession of sin, but are probably related to the absence of the prophetic office from his portrayal of the person and work of Christ. This absence seems all the more noticeable in the light of contemporary New Testament scholarship which is very interested in the prophetic dimension of the ministry of Jesus. So for example, N. T. Wright depicts Jesus as the eschatological prophet of the kingdom who takes upon himself at the cross the judgement which will lead to the re-birth of the people of God.[78] To view Jesus in this way allows an understanding of Christ absorbing divine judgement at the cross which does not conjure up the vindictive pictures of God which Campbell rightly rebelled against. It also enables a more realistic understanding of the complex religious and political forces which combined to crucify Jesus. It would be inappropriate to criticize Campbell for being unaware of perspectives brought to light by more recent scholarship, but the inclusion of these sorts of insights would have enabled him both to affirm his priestly approach to atonement and to create a more human and more plausible account of the death of Jesus.

Conclusion

This study argues that the theology of John McLeod Campbell deserves to be re-evaluated, and it begins that process by examining several aspects of his theology. A key part of this reappraisal of his work has involved drawing upon a significant number of Campbell's sermons which have been overlooked for many years.

A weakness of recent studies of Campbell's theology is their failure to pay serious attention to the role of the Spirit in his theology. As this has partly been due to a failure to take seriously his participation in the Gareloch pentecost, it has been

---

[78] N. T. Wright, *The Challenge of Jesus*, (London: SPCK, 2000). E.g. Chapter 4 'The Crucified Messiah'.

important to provide an account of his involvement in this controversial episode. Allied to this there is a general tendency to overlook, or to be unaware of, the prominent pneumatological dimension in his preaching. Through an exposition of some of the material in the sermons this study has shown that a retrieval of Campbell's teaching on the work of the Holy Spirit contributes to a fuller understanding of his trinitarian christology and assists interpretation of the priestly model of atonement expressed in *The Nature of the Atonement*.

It is not only in the field of pneumatology that a neglect of Campbell's sermons has contributed to incomplete and inaccurate construals of his theology. His preaching was profoundly theological, and within these sermons it is not difficult to detect the contours of his christology. Whilst Campbell did not provide a systematic account of every aspect of christology, the evidence of the Row sermons and the Glasgow *Fragments* suggests that he had a well-thought out trinitarian understanding of the person of Christ from the early stages of his ministry.

The foundational element in Campbell's preaching was the conviction that 'the flesh of Christ differed not in one particle from mine; but Christ did present his flesh, which was even my flesh, without spot to God through the eternal Spirit.'[79] Campbell shared this belief that Christ had assumed sinful fallen nature with his friends Edward Irving and Thomas Erskine, and this conviction attracted a degree of criticism in the period after his dismissal from the ministry of the Kirk. The discovery of this element in Campbell's thinking is significant because it contributes to a fresh reading of his much debated comments about Christ making a perfect confession of sin.

Campbell's priestly approach to soteriology has often been misunderstood because people have concentrated upon the issue of Christ's perfect confession and have overlooked the other aspects of this model of atonement. His soteriology has sometimes been caricatured as subjective and exemplarist, and such stereotypes have been challenged here by providing a fresh reading of *The Nature of the Atonement*. The material which emerges from Campbell's preaching about the work of the Spirit and the humanity of Christ, contributes to a re-reading of his soteriology. Campbell's understanding of the work of Christ turns out to be more objective and more plausible than many of his critics suggest. The close reading of the text offered here

---

[79] *S&L*, 2.23.109; *NofS*, 1.8.7.

supports the claim that *The Nature of the Atonement* can be regarded as a 'classic' treatment of this doctrine, and will hopefully stimulate others to take another look at Campbell's thinking for themselves.

James Goodloe's recent work tends to depict Campbell as a Scottish Schleiermacher whose theology is dominated by his understanding of Christian experience. This leads him to portray Campbell as being in 'the mainstream of nineteenth-century liberal Protestantism.'[80] Whilst Campbell's questioning was initially provoked by reflection upon his parishioners' experience, his determination to understand the atonement in its own light indicates an *a posteriori* approach to the theological task in which the revelation of what God has done in Christ, rather than our experience, takes priority.

In common with other recent studies Goodloe shows no awareness of the influence of Romanticism upon Evangelicals during the first half of the nineteenth-century. Similarly he takes no account of Campbell's role in the outbreak of charismatic phenomena around the Gareloch. A more adequate portrayal of Campbell takes this broader historical context into account and sees him as a leading exponent of radical evangelicalism in Scotland. When the larger picture, shaped by both his preaching and theology, is taken into consideration it becomes clear that Campbell's theological pilgrimage represents a journey within evangelicalism rather than a departure from the evangelical fold.

In 1971, Bernard Reardon suggested that 'John McLeod Campbell's is the outstanding name in Scottish theology in the last century.'[81] Such a statement would be difficult to prove conclusively, but this exploration of his life and thought suggests that there are good grounds for affirming that John McLeod Campbell is an outstanding name in nineteenth-century theology who continues to merit serious study.

---

[80] Goodloe, 'Transformation of the Religious Consciousness', 196.
[81] Bernard M. G. Reardon, *From Coleridge to Gore: A Century of Religious Thought in Britain*, (London: Longman, 1971), 404.

Appendix 1

Extract from a Preface written by John McLeod Campbell to Accompany the Publication of *Two Sermons* in 1830

The doctrines necessary to the full display of THE TRUTH are, that love is an essential attribute in Godhead, and manifested to all his creatures; while hatred is a property only of a sinful creature: in opposition to the false doctrine that God loves only a part of his creatures, and hates the remainder: that the second person of the Deity took into personal subsistence with himself, the very flesh of the Virgin Mary; and not a better flesh, an immortal flesh, an incorruptible flesh: that by the union of creature with the Creator, the whole of mankind, and all the animals, and the inert matter itself of this globe, are interested in the work of redemption, and are to take their eternal standing of happiness or misery on that basis: that the person of the Holy Ghost dwells in the church, which is the mystical body of Christ, and is ever present to manifest and put forth all power, wherever men by faith call for the exercise of his gifts: that the Lord Jesus Christ is sole king and rightful possessor of this earth; and that all kings, magistrates, rulers, judges, bishops, ministers, and persons in authority, of every class and degree, are his delegates, and consequently bound to use the power intrusted to them for the propagation of His truth.[1]

---

[1] John McLeod Campbell, *Two Sermons*, (London: John Hatchard & Son, 1830), vi-vii.

Appendix 2

Extract of a Letter from the Rev. John McLeod Campbell, Minister of Row

In September 1825 I was placed in the Parish of Row. I cannot say that there was anything then to mark my Theological Creed. As to Church politics I was distinguished, to my own mind, among the young Ministers, my contemporaries, by a deep conviction of the practical evils, which had arisen from party feelings, and by determined purpose to hold personally a perfect neutrality. As to pastoral feeling I was then conscious to a single and strong desire to be the instrument of good to the flock over which I had been appointed overseer: but beyond the purpose of entire devotedness, this desire took no distinct form, nor had I any theory or view, peculiar to myself, as to the reason of the want of living religion, to the prevalence of which my eyes now in a measure opened. As to personal religion I can, in looking back, trace the elements of that which I have since felt certain is vital godliness, and know that the apprehensions of a goodwill in God towards me, expressed by the gift of Christ, and of the desire of that goodwill as being personal holiness, and of my need of strength through the Holy Ghost, in order to the accomplishment in me of that desire on the part of God, were indistinctly, but truly in my mind, mingled with erroneous views of the relative places of *seriousness* and true holiness, and of the importance of religion as distinct from its intrinsic excellence: while as to doctrinal views the fact of an atonement, and the necessity of regeneration, were the only points, which had any distinct prominency as realities, in my mind. I cannot now say that I had any distinct weighing of the question, whether Christ had died for all, or only for the elect, or of any of the other questions on the subject which have so engrossed my attention. As to election I was content to hold it simply as a matter of fact, and to excuse myself for not considering it much, by regarding it as a mystery, and I believe in point of fact that I was practically and in real feeling unfettered by it, in declaring to my fellow sinners so much of God's love as I then knew myself.

Appendix 2

Two circumstances in the character of the labours on which I immediately entered, appear to me to have had an important influence in leading to subsequent results. The one was my having been led to form the resolution, and act upon it, of using no assistance in my preparations for the Pulpit, but the Bible. I never read any sermons on the texts which I selected, before beginning to write myself: *nor did I consult any commentary, unless in seeking to ascertain the precise translation of the original.* I think I took for granted (because of my ignorance of God, and inexperience in the faithfulness of that word, 'He giveth liberally and upbraideth not') that I would, at no distant date, run out of matter, and exhaust my resources, in which case, but in which case alone, I purposed availing myself in some shape, of the labours of others, though not of course in the way of plagiarism. But having been led, whenever I had difficulty of any kind in my preparation for the pulpit, to go to God in prayer, instead of feeling that I had run out of topics, or illustrations, I found the preparation for each successive Sabbath occupy less time than that for the previous one, until at last it was a very common thing with me to write out fully, two discourses of from 35 to 40 minutes reading, each on the Saturday. The other circumstance was my, immediately on my induction, proceeding to visit my Parish, with the resolution, which I was also in a great measure enabled to act upon, of giving the character of ministerial visits to all my intercourse with my people, and avoiding the error of making religious discourse the topic only at seasons set apart for the purpose. This practice thus adopted had a powerful influence in increasing in my own mind, the feeling that religion was a thing truly of all times, and of all seasons, and it contained a demand on my people, which in the way in which it wrought upon them, soon made it apparent how much it was the fact that though willing, so to speak, to give a *little* of their time to God, that they might with the less disturbance from conscience *enjoy themselves* in the *rest* of it, they had not yet been taught to count all things loss for the excellency of the knowledge of the love of God in Christ Jesus. These two circumstances — my exclusive study of the word of God, and my exclusive intercourse as the Servant of God with men, increased rapidly my acquaintance with the extent of the demand for personal religion on the part of God, and with the little measure of compliance with these on the part of men, and rendered my meditations, chiefly researches into the reasonableness of the former, and the consequent sin in not meeting them, and the various devices of Satan, by which men were enabled to live at peace in an evil way; and my discourses contained the exposition of the discoveries on these subjects, which were daily making to me, along with such personal warnings, and practical exhortations to my people, as these discoveries suggested. The first doctrinal and practical subject on which I remember to have felt that much light was given me, was *Repentance*. I was led to see how much of that little repentance which was to be found, was merely regret for the personal evil consequences of having exposed one's self to the wrath of God; and how large a proportion of the confessions of sin, with which even the most serious were acquainted, were more truly speaking confessions of folly and imprudence, and not of guilt; and how much of the acknowledgement, as to the superiority of religion to irreligion, was rather the acknowledgement of the greater *importance of eternal interests*, as compared with *temporal interests*, and not the acknowledgement of the intrinsic excellence and beauty of holiness and love, and the intrinsic deformity and hatefulness of sin and selfishness.

At the time when this subject was opened up to me, I remember that the hollowness and hypocrisy of the professions made of repentance in men's approaches to God — their hollowness and hypocrisy *as seen by him* appeared to me most awful, and not the less awful, though through the error in which they were on the subject, men felt a measure of consciousness of sincerity, and took to themselves the comfort of thinking that they were complying with God's call upon them to repent.

A similar mocking of God, I was at that time, and in connection with the same subject, made to see, in those *verbal* tributes of admiration to God, as just, holy and good, which men offer in their prayers. not because their hearts are full of his excellence, and enamoured of his beauty, but because they think it will please him, and recommend themselves to him. At this time I laboured hard to make these distinctions visible to my people, and to give them a true standard by which to measure themselves, and tests by which to detect the deceptions of their own hearts. I did not at that time, however, see any great fruit of these labours, and was often subjected to the pain of hearing persons, whose demeanour indicated that they were not now creatures in Christ Jesus, expressing the strongest approbation of sermons which it appeared to me, were peculiarly fitted to disturb their false peace. And I found the higher I raised the standard, I only the more stimulated the efforts of a self-righteous and self-deceiving spirit to personate, in the way of acting as in a dramatic exhibition, the character of excellence held forth.

Meditating with prayer, on this painful ministerial experience, I was gradually taught to see that *so long as the individual is uncertain of being the object of love to his God, and is still without any sure hold of his personal* safety, in the prospect of eternity, it is in vain to attempt to induce him to serve God under the power of any purer motive than the desire to win God's love for himself, and so to secure his own happiness: consequently, however high the standard, correspondence with it was sought under the influence of unmingled selfishness, making every apparent success a deeper deception. And thus I was gradually led to entertain the doctrine commonly expressed by the words, 'Assurance of Faith', having first seen the want of it precluded singleness of heart and eye in the service of God — and then having found in studying the Epistles to the first Christian Churches, that its existence, in those disciples, was *in them* taken for granted, and in every practical exhortation was presupposed, I accordingly began to urge on my people, that in order to their being free to serve God — in order to their being in a condition to act purely, under the influence of love to them, and delight in what he is, their first step in religion would require to be, *resting assured of his love in Christ to them as individuals*, and of their individually having eternal life given to them in Christ.

I think this was the character of my preaching in the latter part of the year 1826, but I cannot easily fix, and in the summer of 1827, I think, it first was that I understood that offence was taken with what I taught. This however, for some time, amounted merely to the complaint that I 'carried the subject of Assurance too far', and no one ventured then, to advance the charge of heresy. It was at the same time also that I first enjoyed the happiness of seeing many awakened from their false security, and not a few to delight themselves in the Lord: and what my pressing of high attainments, as the fruits of faith, had been *unable* to accomplish, I now found produced by the earnest demand for *the true faith itself*. Towards the end of 1827, at the time when my summer parishioners all returned home, the report carried up to Glasgow of what they had been hearing at Row, produced a considerable sensation there, in what is called 'the religious world'. In consequence of this, a Minister of Glasgow selected as the subject of an Essay in a Theological Society, 'The Assurance of Faith'. Knowing that many misapprehensions of what I had taught on the subject reached my brethren, I felt it my duty to attend: and hear this Essay read: and if the opportunity was given (for I was not then a member of the Society) to reply or explain, as it might appear right. The Essay was exceedingly temperate, but full of what I knew to be false principles. I was asked, and gladly accepted the invitation to speak: and after they had all spoken, and very courteously, I was again permitted to reply. I went away thankful for the indulgence which I had experienced, and full of expectation as to the result of their meditating on what I had been enabled to say.

The following week I preached a public Sermon, on a week day, for one of the Glasgow Charitable Institutions, and I remember, in order to preclude the charge of Antinomianism, while at the same time, as affording the opportunity of setting forth the practical importance of the Assurance of Faith, I selected as my text, John, Chapter 17, verse 17, 'Sanctify them through thy truth.'

Most of the Ministers of Glasgow were present, and from this occasion I date the opposition of my brethren. I had fondly hoped that the explanations given in the Clerical Society, would have removed prejudices, and commended the truth. They however had calculated on my being changed by what had come from them, and in consequence, were much offended to hear me, so shortly after, state so fully what they had condemned, and for many Sabbaths most of the Ministers of Glasgow were preaching with pointed reference, (and with a view of confutation) to what I taught. There was as yet, however, no organised opposition in the Parish of Row.

The controversy in which I was constantly engaged, in almost all my intercourse with my brethren, *obliged me to examine narrowly the foundation furnished, by the communications made in the Gospel, for the Assurance of Faith.* This led *directly to the closer consideration of the extent of the Atonement,* and of the circumstances in which mankind had been placed by the shedding of the blood of Christ. And it soon appeared to me manifest, that unless Christ had died *for all,* and unless the Gospel announced him as *the gift of God to every human being,* so that there remained nothing to be done to give the individual a title to rejoice in Christ as his Saviour, there was no foundation in the record of God for the Assurance which I demanded, and which I saw to be essential to true holiness. The next step therefore was my teaching as the subject matter of the Gospel, universal Atonement and pardon through the blood of Christ.

It may appear strange to one unacquainted with these matters, that those who had been hitherto most satisfied with my teaching on the subject of Assurance, viz. some sects that urge this subject much, now became opposed to me, and strangely held, that if I regarded the Atonement as universal, I deprived the individual Christian of *all* Assurance, while those who objected to the urgency with which I pressed personal Assurance, now held that doctrine to become still more dangerous when connected with that of universal pardon.

Such opposition made more and more apparent to me the want of true religion in the land. I was made to mourn over many whose strong confidence, along with their outward propriety of conduct, had made me hope well of them, when I saw by their opposition to the universality of the Atonement, that their Assurance had been very much its own basis — that their faith had not been the belief of a record of God, true whether believed or not; but had been the assumption of a fact, for which they had no other proof but that they assumed it. And that instead of resting on the character of God as revealed in Christ, they looked upon the death of Christ as so much suffering — the purchase money of heaven to a certain number to whom it infallibly secured heaven. And I was made to mourn over the opposition to the doctrine of universal pardon, taking as it did such forms as, 'If all are forgiven, then we need not repent, or be sorry for our sins, or think of a future judgement, and we may do what we please.' For it was thus apparent, *beyond all my previous fears, that what men called repentance, was not a real sorrow for sin, but merely something offered in exchange for safety*: and I was shocked to hear men avow, that if they were certain that their heavenly Father forgave them their sin, they would feel it unnecessary to grieve because they had offended him, and instead of being led to repentance by the knowledge of this his goodness, would be encouraged by it to sin yet more and more. It was however rather as what others would be likely to say, than as what they would say themselves, that men uttered such things; but it was manifest that, though speaking in the *third* person, they spoke of *themselves*.

While I was labouring to remove objections, the bringing of which made such painful discoveries, it became more and more apparent to me that men objected because they wished to object — that they hated the light and only sought to excuse themselves by denying that it was light — to excuse themselves to themselves — I mean, to find apologies of a specious kind for rejecting a doctrine which they felt was searching; and I was struck to find thus illustrated, our Saviour's declaration that, while it was for righteousness sake that his followers would be hated, the form in which that hatred would manifest itself would be speaking evil of them falsely. No man will admit a thing to be *holy* and at the same time object to it. He must first call it, and find some excuse for calling it, *unholy*, and then he can condemn it. (See Isaiah, Chapter 66, verse 5; John, Chapter 16, verse 2). And thus while rejoicing at being taught of God the secret of the prevailing ungodliness — that *it was the simple unbelief of God's manifested character in Christ;* and while urging the faith of forgiving love, as that which purifieth, I found myself charged with Antinomianism, and in the setting forth doctrines leading to licentiousness; and, as if to stamp the character of the opposition awakened, it first took an active form in the Parish, in the person of some individuals of much practical ungodliness.

Written to his brother in India, 1st January 1831.

Appendix 3

Libel, &c.

MR JOHN MACLEOD CAMPBELL, Minister of the Gospel at Row, You are indicted and accused this seventh day of September, eighteen hundred and thirty, by the subscribers, heads of families, and inhabitants of the said parish, That albeit the doctrine of universal atonement and pardon through the death of Christ, as also the doctrine that assurance is of the essence of faith, and necessary to salvation, are contrary to the Holy Scriptures and to the Confession of Faith approven by the General Assemblies of the Church of Scotland, and ratified by law in the year sixteen hundred and ninety; and were moreover condemned by the fifth Act of the General Assembly held in the year seventeen hundred and twenty, as being directly opposed to the word of God, and to the Confession of Faith and Catechisms of the Church of Scotland: Yet true it is and of verity, that you the said Mr John M'Leod Campbell hold and have repeatedly promulgated and expressed the foresaid doctrines from the pulpit or other place or places from which you delivered discourses, as also in conversation, in your addresses to communicants at the celebration of the Lord's Supper, and in your ministerial visitations of families within your parish: In so far as on various occasions during the course of the last twelve months, you the said Mr John M'Leod Campbell have declared that God has forgiven the sins of all mankind whether they believe it or not: That in consequence of the death of Christ, the sins of every individual of the human race are forgiven: That it is sinful and absurd to pray for an interest in Christ, because all mankind have an interest in Christ already: And that no man is a Christian unless he is positively assured of his own salvation: And more particularly:

First, You the said Mr John M'Leod Campbell, in a sermon preached by you in the Floating Chapel at Greenock on the twenty-eighth day of April, eighteen hundred and thirty, or on one or other of the days of that month or of March immediately preceding, or May immediately following, used the following expressions, or at least expressions of a similar import and tendency, *videlicet*. 'Before I can say to any man fear God and give him glory, I must know that his condemnation is taken away, and his sins forgiven;' And again, 'It is a fact at this moment of every person present that his sins are put away, and if I did not know this, I could not say to you fear God and give him glory, because it would be an impossibility:' And again, 'I could not conceive any thing I could ask of God which be has not told me that he has already given me:' And again, 'Christ's right to judge men is that he has redeemed them:' And again, 'judgment pre-supposes our forgiveness.' And again, 'It is as persons who have been forgiven that we shall be judged:' And again, 'We cannot repent and give God glory unless we now have forgiveness:' And again, 'There could be no judgment to come, unless there had been pardon to come.'

Secondly, You the said Mr John M'Leod Campbell in a sermon preached by you at Row, on the eighth day of July eighteen hundred and thirty, in presence of the Presbytery of Dumbarton, being the day on which the said Presbytery held a parochial visitation of the parish of Row, or on one or other of the days of that month, or of June immediately preceding, or of August immediately following, used the following expressions, or at least expressions of a similar import and, tendency, *videlicet*; 'That he alone bore the character of peace-maker who knew that Christ died for every human being:' And again in speaking of the love of God, you said, 'That that love to every individual of Adam's family was equal or according to the agonies of the Son. of God:' And again, in speaking of the words in the fifth chapter of Matthew's Gospel, 'Blessed are they that mourn,' you. said,. 'that the causes of this mourning were not within the believer, his sins having been taken away, but they existed outwardly in the unbelief and sinfulness of the world.'

Thirdly, You the said Mr John M'Leod Campbell, in a Sermon preached by you in the School-house at: Helensburgh, on one of the days of the month of October eighteen hundred and twenty-nine, used the following expression or expressions of a similar import and tendency, *videlicet:* 'That it was a gross error in the modern preachers of evangelical doctrines to maintain that the reason why men were not, cured was that they did not seek an interest in Christ or come to him, because according to his idea an interest in Christ was the privilege of all men indiscriminately, and that the reason why men were not happy in the enjoyment of it was, that they would not allow themselves to be persuaded that they were continually in a state of reconciliation:' And again, 'That the only cause why a man should at any time be sorrowful, was regret or dissatisfaction at himself, for not believing himself to be in a state of favour with God:' And again, 'That by the death of Christ, all mankind were put into a state of pardon, or in that state in which God was not imputing their sins to them, and that the continued belief of this fact was all that was necessary to constitute the faith of the gospel.'

Fourthly, You the said Mr John M'Leod Campbell, in the sermon preached by you as aforesaid on the eighth day of July eighteen hundred and thirty, in presence of the Presbytery of Dumbarton, being the day on which the Presbytery held a parochial visitation of the parish of Row, or on one or other of the days of that month, or of June immediately preceding, or of August immediately following, used the following expressions, or at least expressions of a similar import and tendency, *videlicet* 'That it was an indispensable feature in the character of a Christian, that he should know that God has had mercy on him, and has for given him.'

Fifthly, You the said Mr John M'Leod Campbell in the sermon preached by you as aforesaid, in the school-house at Helensburgh, on one of the days of the month of October eighteen hundred and twenty-nine, used the following expressions, or expressions of a similar, import and tendency, *videlicet*, 'That men allowing themselves to remain in doubt with respect to the simple fact of their having been individually restored to a state of favour with God, was the cause of all their misery, and that this was really the unbelief which the gospel condemns, it was giving the lie to God.'

Sixthly, You the said Mr John M'Leod Campbell at the dispensation of the Lord's Supper at Row, in the month of July eighteen hundred and thirty, in fencing the tables, debarred from the Lord's Supper, 'all who had not a personal assurance of their own salvation.'

Seventhly, You the said Mr John M'Leod Campbell, in a sermon preached by you in the parish church of Row, on the fourth day of July eighteen hundred and thirty, or on one or other of the days of that month, or of June immediately preceding, or August immediately following, used the following expressions, or expressions of a similar import and tendency, *videlicet*, 'All men are both under the curse and under grace at the same time.' And on the same occasion, you said that the doctrine of the Church of Scotland regarding election 'tended to fatalism.'

Eighthly, You the said Mr John M'Leod Campbell, at a parochial examination at Easterton, in the parish of Row, in the autumn of eighteen hundred and twenty-nine, when explaining the nature of faith from the question in the Shorter Catechism, 'What is faith in Jesus Christ,' observed, That none could receive and rest upon Christ for salvation, who had not an assurance of their own salvation;' or words to that effect.

Ninthly, You the said Mr John M'Leod Campbell, in a sermon preached by you at Row on the fourth day of July eighteen hundred and thirty, or on one or other of the days of that month, or of June immediately preceding, or August immediately following, used the following expressions, or expressions of a similar import and tendency, *videlicet*, 'That every man is in this state, that while he has in him death in Adam, he has life given him by Christ,' – 'That the curse in Adam extended only to the death of the body, and takes effect upon all — the blessing of life in Christ is co-extensive with the curse, and belongs to all upon whom the curse has passed — that if Christ had not died, mankind would not have risen, nor would they have gone to hell to eternal punishment, but to Hades.'

Tenthly, You the said Mr John M'Leod Campbell, in the sermon preached by you as aforesaid, in the Floating Chapel at Greenock, on the said twenty-eighth day of April eighteen hundred and thirty, or on one or other of the days of that month, or of March immediately preceding, or May immediately, following, used the following expressions, or expressions of a similar import or tendency, *videlicet*, 'Now, inasmuch as it is true concerning you, that in the first place, the work of God in Christ has put away your sins, so that it is the fact, that your sins are at this moment not imputed to you inasmuch as it is true, in the second place, that the character of God, the real name of God, what he truly is, is revealed in this very work of God in Christ, so that no person can see that work and be ignorant of God; — and inasmuch as it is true, in the third place, that Christ has the Holy Ghost for you, that in the Spirit you may behold and enter into and dwell in the light of God's glory in the face of Jesus Christ; inasmuch as these things are true, you observe, that sinners as you are, that deserving of condemnation, and by nature under condemnation as you are, that notwithstanding all the evil of your circumstances as these have arisen from the fall; your new circumstances which have arisen from the work of God in Christ, are such that it is perfectly reasonable to say to you, 'fear God and give him glory.' You are actually in a condition to meet this demand; you are precisely in circumstances in which to receive this

Appendix 3

command; there is no one thing you can name that creates the least obstacle, why you should not at this moment 'fear God and give him glory:'" And again, 'Now let me not be misunderstood, I am not saying that God has no right to judge his creatures, I am not saying that the judgment recorded 'in the day thou eatest thereof thou shalt surely die,' is not a righteous judgment. But this I say, that the principle upon which Christ judges the earth, is that Christ has redeemed us. — Not that the judgment suspends the pardon — not that the judgment makes the pardon conditional — not that it makes it uncertain till the judgment is come; — but that the judgment pre-supposes our forgiveness, that it has a reference to our forgiveness, that it is as those who have been forgiven that we judged shall be:' And again, 'If we look at the actual condition of men, we would say, here is the darkness of total ignorance of the mercy that is in God-of the might that is in God for us. — Here are people who do not know that Christ died for them — who do not know that Christ has the Spirit for them — who do not know that the Bible says that their sins are remitted — here are people who conceive that they are giving God glory in saying there is no proof of these facts. This is the real darkness in which men are living.' All which or part thereof being found proved by the said Reverend Presbytery of Dumbarton, before which your Case is to be heard, it ought to be found and declared that you are unfit and unworthy to remain a minister of the Church of Scotland; and you ought to be forthwith deposed from the office of the holy ministry, and from the pastoral charge of the said church and parish of Row, and the said church ought to be declared vacant. According to the Laws of the Church of Scotland, and the usage observed in the like cases.

(Signed)
    GEORGE M'LELLAN, Farmer, Bolernick
    PETER TURNER, Farmer, Bolernick
    A. LENNOX, Surgeon, Helensburgh.
    ALEX. M'DOUGAL, Grocer, Row.
    JOHN M'KINLAY, Greenfield, Row.
    JOHN THOMSON, Spirit-dealer, Helensburgh.
    PARLAN M'FARLANE, Farmer, Farlane.
    ALEX M'LEOD, Feuar, Helensburgh.

List of Witnesses — to be adduced for proving the foregoing Libel.
Reverend Patrick Brewster, one of the Ministers of the Abbey Parish of Paisley.
Peter M'Leod, Clothier in Helensburgh.
Robert M'Farlane, Farmer in Greenfield, lying between the Parish Church of Row and Gare-Lochhead.
John M'Farlane, Feuar in Helensburgh.
Peter Bain, Teacher at Gare-Lochhead, near Helensburgh.
James Bain, Student of Divinity, residing in Easterton, near Helensburgh.
James Brown, Parochial Teacher in Row.
Reverend William Cunningham, residing in Greenock.
Frederick Hope Pattison, sometime residing in Glasgow, now in Helensburgh.
Archibald Patterson, sometime manufacturer in Glasgow, now residing in Helensburgh.
Reverend John Arthur, residing in Helensburgh.
Reverend Robert Crawford, assistant to the Reverend Mr Archibald Wilson, Minister of Cardross.
Reverend Doctor Robert Burns, one of the Ministers of Paisley.
Alexander Munro, now or lately Tutor in the family of Lord John Campbell, Ardincaple House, near Helensburgh.
William Stewart, Surgeon in Glasgow.
Robert Baillie Lusk, Bookseller in Greenock.
James Dunn, Anchorage Office in Greenock.

   (Signed)
                    George M'Lellan, Farmer, Bolernick.
                    Peter Turner, Farmer. Bolernick.
                    A. Lennox, Surgeon, Helensburgh
                    Alex. M'Dougal, Grocer, Row.
                    John M'Kinlay, Greenfield, Row.
                    John Thomson, Spirit-dealer, Helensburgh.
                    Parlan M'Farlane, Farmer, Farlane.
                    Alex. M'Leod, Feuar, Helensburgh.

Which Libel the Presbytery having duly considered, did, and hereby do, agreeably to the Form of Process, appoint the Clerk to make out a complete extract thereof, to be served upon said Mr John M'Leod Campbell: — and further appoint the

Appendix 3

Presbytery Officer to go to the Manse of Row and serve the same upon Mr Campbell, or leave it at his dwelling-house, together with the List of Witnesses and a Copy of the Productions in aid of Proof, on or before Friday the tenth current, and summon him to appear before the Presbytery at their next Meeting, on Tuesday, the twenty-first current, at twelve o'clock noon. And the Officer is to return to the Presbytery on that day an Execution of the said Summons, signed by himself and two witnesses to the delivery thereof.

Extracted from the Records of the Presbytery of Dumbarton, on this and the preceding twenty-two pages, by
　　　　　　　　　　　　　　WILLIAM JAFFRAY, *Pby. Clk*

Appendix 4

Notes of Sermons 1.8

Sermon on Galatians 2:20 'The Life of the Christian', preached at Row on Sunday 25 July 1830

My dear hearers, I desire now to set before you the Christian as a living man — as a living member of the body of Christ; and, in illustrating the statement which the apostle here makes, we shall first have our attention engaged with the actual condition of the Christian, and then with that out of which his being in that condition arises. First, he is one who says of himself, that he is crucified with Christ, yet that he lives, and that it is not he, but Christ who lives in him: and second, the manner of this life is, that it is by the faith of the Son of God, who loved him, and gave himself for him. The condition itself, you observe, is that he is crucified with Christ; that yet he lives; but that it is not he that lives, but Christ that lives in him — this is his condition; and the history, or explanation, of his being in this condition is, that he lives by the faith of that Son of God who loved him, and gave himself for him.

I would, first, shortly explain to you the meaning of the word life, as it is used in the word of God, in reference to this subject. There is a life which is to the flesh, and a life which is to the Spirit: and I trust you will be enabled to understand me while I place before your minds the creatures who may either be in the one condition or in the other; and show you what is said of a man when it is said that he lives, and when it is said that he lives to the flesh, and when it is said that he lives to the Spirit. When I see a human being before me, I see a being who is a distinct person, who has a consciousness of existence, and who is in a condition of being conscious of feelings of joy or sorrow, of some kind or other. He is alive, in this sense, that he is conscious of life, that he is feeling that there are certain things affecting him, that there are certain things giving him pleasure, and certain things giving him pain — this is to be a living man, in the general sense of the word of life.

Now, when I inquire how this person comes to have feelings of pleasure or pain from any source, I have my attention directed to his nature, to his capacities of pleasure or pain and I

Appendix 4

find that he has pleasure or pain through some capacity of feeling, or of understanding, which he possesses. If I inquire what this capacity is, I will find, according to the scriptural distinction, that it is one of two things, either the flesh or the Spirit; that the capacity which a man naturally has of feeling interest in any thing is the flesh — the carnal mind — the nature which every man has when he comes into the world — the nature which he received from his parents, that which is born of the flesh being flesh; and when I inquire into his life, I find the history of it to be that he is conscious of feelings, of joys and of sorrows, of hopes and of fears, of various kinds of interest, all of which he has through the flesh.

But I understand from the word of God, that it is not only the flesh that can give a man the capacity of feeling, or of hoping, or of fearing; but that there are capacities of feeling, possibilities of being made joyful or sorrowful, which arise from having the Spirit. And by the Spirit I am taught to know something quite distinct from the flesh, something which is altogether another thing from the flesh, and which gives a person who possesses it a capacity of a particular kind, just as the flesh gives a capacity of a particular kind. Now, to say that a man lives, is to say that he has feelings in the flesh, or in the Spirit. But to say that a man lives to the flesh, is to say that if you consider this man's feelings, you will trace them to the nature he had when he came into the world; and to say that a man lives to the Spirit, is to say, that if you consider this man's feelings, you will trace them to the spiritual nature, to a new nature received since he came into the world.

I wish you to see this, for it will enable you to understand what I am to state afterwards, that a man, viewed as a man, may have no capacity of feeling and enjoyment but the natural capacity, which he has through the flesh; but that there is another capacity, which is in the Spirit, which he may also have; that to live is to be conscious of feelings, that to live in the flesh is to have feelings entirely the result of what the flesh is, and to live in the Spirit is to have feelings the result of that which the Spirit is. The man is carnal when his hopes and fears are referred to the flesh; and spiritual when they are referred to the Spirit.

The account which the apostle gives of himself here, is, that he is crucified with Christ. This expression has reference to the flesh of Christ; for it was crucified: he was put to death in the flesh. He was quickened in the Spirit, but put to death in or by the flesh — it was through having the flesh that he died. He took our nature and it was under the curse because of sin; and so he came under the curse for us, and died under the operation of that curse in which he had voluntarily put himself.

The apostle is not stating the fact that Christ was crucified; but the fact that he, himself, was crucified with Christ. When he speaks of being crucified with Christ, you are not to suppose that it is only the closing scene of the life of Jesus that is referred to; but that Christ through his whole life was crucifying the flesh. It was accounted of by him as a dead thing, because of sin; and he ever presented himself, through the eternal Spirit, without spot to God. This expression, while it refers to the closing scene of his life, includes all that went before. To say that Christ was crucified, is to say that Christ's flesh was given up to death; and to say this is to say that it was so by the voluntary deed of Christ himself, and not of necessity; to say that Christ's flesh was given up to death, or was crucified, is to say, that Christ consigned his own flesh, by his own voluntary deed, to death — that Christ accounted of it as a thing that was sentenced to die — that Christ was willing it should die. We are not speaking of it merely as a thing done to him, outwardly, by others, but done to him, inwardly, in every day of his existence in the flesh; and we are to consider him as one who looked on his flesh as a death-doomed substance, because of sin, and therefore rejecting every movement of it, and treating it as a thing which had no claim on him that he should please it.

The statement here, however, is that Paul was crucified with Christ. This properly refers not to the condition which was the *object* of faith, but to the condition which was the *effect* of faith. When Christ gave his flesh to death, willingly and freely, he did it not as an individual, but as our head and representative; as having taken on him our sins and borne our griefs; as having come into the place of taking the load and burden of our race upon him, so that, in this sense, all died when Christ died; and that as, in the judgement of God, Christ did not suffer as a private person, but as a head and representative, so also, all rose when Christ rose: he rose not as a private person, but as a Head. In this sense we are included both in the death and resurrection of Christ, and so we are not under the law but under grace — not debtors to the flesh to live after it, but to the Spirit which the living Saviour received for us, that we should live after the Spirit. This is the condition of us all; but the apostle is not here stating this, which was the object of his faith, that Christ died and rose for him; but he speaks of himself as acquiescing in the deed of God in thus dealing with him. As in Christ he had passed through death, so did he, himself, see, and recognise, and feel in his heart, that it was most righteous that his flesh should die. It is as if he had said, I am not only content that Christ should die, as my representative, and to recognise the sufferings of Christ as the channel of forgiveness to me; but there is a far deeper thing, even to be myself contented with the condemnation of my flesh, which took place in Christ, when God, by the sacrifice of Christ, condemned sin in the flesh – contented to see my flesh as condemned in Christ, and crucified. Thus I can look back on the whole history of Christ's dealing with the flesh; I can consider all his denyings of it, his treating of it as a thing that was dead, and had no claim on him that he should sow to it, and I can say Christ was righteous in this; and I can put my flesh on that footing, in reference to myself; and I have fellowship in his crucifixion of the flesh; I share in his surrender of the flesh, in his recognition of the doom of death as a just doom upon the flesh and, every moment of my being, I see that this flesh is a death-doomed thing, which has no claim to indulgence, or that I should treat it as a thing to which I should live. I am crucified with Christ; I am dead to the flesh; I live not in the flesh; and my body, in respect of life, is a dead thing to me. If you conceive a man linked to a dead body, you will see, in that case, that none of his feelings could come through that body – no emotion of any kind – no pleasure – no pain, nothing whatever could come through this dead mass. In such a case the body would be dead, not because I wished it to be dead, but because it was actually dead; but in this case the body is not actually dead – it is still alive – it is capable of every enjoyment of which human nature is capable, but it is counted dead by me. I treat it as a dead thing; I will not take its advice, nor be influenced by its longings. This is the meaning of the expression. It is a man's seeing the meaning of Christ's treatment of the flesh – a man's seeing this to be done by him as our head and representative, and to be the declaration of what the flesh is; it is a man's putting his seal to this deed of Christ, and recognising the righteousness of God in it; and, in like manner, condemning sin in his own flesh; and accounting his flesh as a thing to which he is dead, and which is dead to him.

'Nevertheless, I live.' What is the meaning of this? If the flesh is crucified, it requires some explanation to show how there should be any life at all. Take any person, now present, and let his flesh be crucified; he would then have no enjoyment of any kind. Let his flesh be accounted dead – let it be crucified, and rejected as a channel of pleasure, or of feeling, or of interest, and the man would become like a blank sheet of paper, without choice, feeling, or interests of any kind. Therefore, the apostle, having declared he was crucified with Christ, that his flesh was dead, and that he would not sow to it, tells us that although, in respect of his flesh, he was as a dead man, as one who had nothing to connect him with external things, yet that he did live — 'Nevertheless', says he, 'I live.' That is, although I have no share in the joys of the flesh, although I treat is as a dead thing, I am not, on that account, without joys, sympathies, or feelings. Although I am dead to the hopes and fears, joys and sorrows, which come through the flesh, I yet have a life, though not a carnal life; I have feelings, though not carnal feelings; I have sorrows, though not carnal sorrows; I am as a dead man, in respect to this flesh; but, in another respect, I am still a living man.

This is what is declared in saying, 'Nevertheless I live.' It is just saying, you might suppose, (and it is what people often do feel), that crucifying the flesh would make life a blank, a dull and dead thing. They think they could give up a part of the flesh; but if you would have them kill the whole, they ask, 'What pleasure could we then taste?' But the apostle says his whole flesh is given up — it is crucified — it is dead — so I am a blank on that side; but still I am not therefore a blank, for I live. Mark this, you who look upon religion as if it were a choosing some of the workings of the flesh, and refusing others — as if it were a selection from among the feelings of the natural man, or a cherishing the amiable, and rejecting the unworthy — you who feel as if we were making religion a dark, gloomy, and dead thing, when we refuse to make such exceptions: know that while the apostle crucified the flesh — while he was dead with Christ, yet he was alive. And, therefore, I would call on you to inquire what new life is to be got; not how much of the old life you will be allowed to keep. Nothing will be allowed to be kept. Yet look not on this as a matter of gloom, or of despair: for Paul says he has another life — a new consciousness — a new capacity of enjoyment — a new way of feeling, of hoping, and of fearing. Consider that he who said he was crucified with Christ, yet said, 'Nevertheless I live.'

And what was this life? He says, 'Yet not I but Christ liveth in me.' What is the meaning of saying, 'Yet not I', after saying, 'I live'? The meaning is this, that his old life was altogether his own, and there was no person concerned with him in it, so to speak; but his new life was not his own, but another person was concerned in it, and that was Christ. It is just in this way — seeing myself as a natural man, I might say, 'I live — I live in the flesh'; viewing myself as crucified with Christ I say, 'I am dead; my flesh is not a thing on which I look as if it had any interest in me at all': but when I say, 'Nevertheless I live', I am not saying, 'I have got a new nature connected with me on the same principle as my old nature was.' Conceive of a person with one arm cut off, or who has, for some reason, been taught not to use this arm: he might say, 'Yet I am not helpless, for I have another arm'; and his connection with what he had would be of the same nature as his connection with what was taken away. But if, instead of using his other arm in place of the arm taken from him, he is told of another person who has an arm of strength, which his will is to act upon, and by which he is to do all things; then he might say, 'I am not helpless'; and if he should say, 'For I have got another arm', he will correct himself and say, 'Yet not I but this other person for me.' So the life which I have as a natural man, was derived from my parents; but having received it, it is mine; it is my own independent of them. Now if I got the Spirit of Christ in such a way as that it would be mine, apart from Christ, then would the new life be mine, just as the old was. But this is not the case; for the new nature, which I receive, never is mine, in the same sense in which the old nature was mine; though it is as truly mine — as truly within my reach — as truly at my command, what I am to call my own — what I may be reasonably called upon to sow to — to live in — to dwell in, as if it were. Still it is not mine at all, in one sense; and therefore the apostle after having said, 'I live', says immediately, 'Yet not I'. As if he had said, 'You are not to suppose this new life is like my old life; or that it is as if I have got some new sense, as when a blind man get his sight; but it is Christ who liveth in me. This new power of interest — this new capacity of feeling — this new power of understanding which is in the spirit, is not mine *properly*, but belongs to Christ and when I am exercising it, it is not I but Christ in me.' It must be a great mystery to the natural man, that another should live in me; but it is the fact that this new life is not like the first: good is it for us that it is not; for the first we had in our own keeping and we lost it, but the second is secure, though ours, for it is hid with Christ in God. It is a great mystery that men, who have all their lives been accustomed to live without reference to another being, are made to know that that nature is to be crucified, and that there is a new nature to be received from another being.

My dear hearers, I know well that this way of speaking must appear to many of you altogether mystical and incomprehensible; but you must be taught it, for it is the mystery of God manifested in the flesh; and this mystery you must be made to enter into, and to share in, if you would see the kingdom of God; for 'except a man be born from above he cannot enter into the kingdom of God.' Except a man receive this new life — except he be brought into the condition of saying, 'Nevertheless I live, yet not I, but Christ liveth in me', he cannot be a partaker of the kingdom of Christ and of God. Therefore, however mysterious and away from the common run of things it may appear to you, and however unlike it is to any thing you have been taught in the world, yet it is a lesson you must learn, otherwise you will have neither part nor lot in the kingdom of God. Therefore, however strange it may appear to you, you must attend to it; and you must not make light of these things, saying, 'This is not common sense, this is not a reasonable thing, we cannot understand this.' I tell you that common sense cannot make you understand a thing which is supernatural. Attend to it. look to it, and see it. This is what Paul says, yea, what every child of God says, 'I am crucified with Christ; nevertheless I live; yet not I, (let no man that hears me think it is I: it is not I), but Christ liveth in me', and I exhibit this mighty work of God — this great mystery, the Son of God taking me up, and joining himself to me, through the Spirit: I present this mystery of having a nature properly my own, which I received from my parents, and another nature, which is also mine by the gift of God, which is mine in Christ, and which I receive continually from Christ, and the actings of which in me, are not my actings but Christ's. I present this mystery of one person, thinking through the power of another person, and feeling through the capacity of another — this mystery of another who is distinct from me, and yet united to me; and by whose power I think, and feel, and understand. This is the mystery of God in us. None but the Creator could say, 'I dwell in the creature'. This is the great mystery of godliness: and this is the mystery, which, however unlike what common sense would have us to expect, is the real history of the condition of every child of God.

'I live, yet not I, but Christ liveth in me.' I trust you understand what I have been saying, whether you receive it or not — that the apostle, in respect of his flesh, in respect of that nature which he had received from his parents, accounted it as a dead thing; and did not set himself to the work of indulging it in part, and restraining it in part, determining what indulgence of the flesh was innocent, and not to be called sin; but that he accounted the whole flesh a thing accursed of God, and so to be crucified. And at the same time, while this was the case, he lived — had enjoyments, feelings, and interests, though not of the flesh. It was not a *doctrine* in him — it was not *an opinion,* which was Christ in him — I beseech you understand this. It was that *Christ himself* was there. As truly as Christ is in glory, so truly is he in every Christian. As truly as Christ is now at the right of the Majesty on high, so truly is he now present, in the Spirit, in every child of God. And he lives by Christ in him — not Christ thought of — not Christ contemplated, but Christ, the living Christ, at the right hand of God, actually as truly present in his body, as my blood is, at this moment, in my hand. Just as my hands and feet have in them the same blood that is in my heart, and it is all one blood, so the members of Christ's body have in them one Spirit, and that is Christ's Spirit; that Spirit which is now dwelling in the glorified head Christ Jesus, and which comes down upon them from this High Priest, as the oil poured on the head of Aaron ran down to the skirts of his garments.

Now, what is the manner of this life — 'Christ liveth in me; and the life which I now live in the flesh'? My dear hearers, I must explain this expression before going further. I have just told you that the flesh was dead, and yet he says there that this life is in the flesh. Here is a still further mystery, that my flesh is not *actually* dead — that my flesh is a thing which I, in no respect, feed and cherish, and yet that I live in my flesh. I have the emotions, and the feelings: and I am not feeling as if I were disembodied, but that I live this life in the flesh. Jesus, through the Spirit, presented himself without spot to God: and I, through the Spirit, am made to yield my members as instruments of righteousness: that is, the killing of my flesh is not ceasing to use it; but using it in another manner, and employing it according to the will of God. Thus did Christ present his flesh without spot. It was the fact that he presented this flesh without spot to God; while, *in itself,* it was still the same flesh, just as he took it, yet it was *always presented,* through the Spirit, without spot to God; Therefore is it said, 'The life which I live in the flesh.' There will be another state of the body, in which there will not be the carnality that now is; but the statement here is not that the person goes out of the body, and lives in another state; but that the Spirit of God makes him live, even in the flesh, to the glory of God. The capacity of sorrow and suffering which Jesus had did not come from the Holy Ghost in him; for the Holy Ghost could not suffer. It was his soul, his human soul, which he made an offering for sin, and not the Spirit of God: but it was by the Spirit of God that he did so. And the mystery is, that the capacity of intelligence is all from man, as Christ finds him: but that the feelings are all through Christ in him. Dare not to say, 'These matters are dark, therefore I need not study them': and remember, it is not to the wise and the learned I speak, but to every babe that hears me; because the difficulty which the most learned man has to understand these things, is just the same difficulty that the most unlearned man has. Spiritual things are to the natural man foolishness. The brightest and most shining light, according to what the world calls light, the most learned and most distinguished of this world's scholars, is on a perfect level with that boy before me, as to understanding these matters. It requires that you should see far and deep: but it is with other eyes than you naturally use; eyes which the learned and philosophic mind needs to receive just as much as you — it is spiritual discernment — the teaching of the Holy Ghost. Therefore, be not kept back by this; but understand that it was human tears which Christ shed. They were such tears as never man shed, because they were wholly shed through the Holy Ghost; and he spake such words as never man uttered, because uttered through the Holy Ghost. And so, in regard to the members of Christ's body, they may laugh or sing for joy, or they may be in sorrow: and outwardly you would see but tears or smiles, but inwardly the thing is holy — holiness put into human feeling — thoughts, feelings and emotions, that were holiness to the Lord. And thus it is that I yield my members instruments of righteousness unto God; and, through the Spirit, I present my body a living sacrifice, holy and acceptable unto God. I do not say the flesh is changed in itself; but it is presented holy. God is bringing a clean thing out of an unclean — light out of darkness — love out of enmity. It now feels the opposite of what if felt before. This is in the expression, 'I live in the flesh'. This is what causes that we should see the glory of God in the face of Jesus Christ — that, in very truth, the very and eternal God did come into human feelings, and human emotions; and then was God manifested in the flesh.

It may be inquired, why it was necessary that Christ should die, having had holy flesh — having made it holy continually by the Spirit? But in the death of Christ we have this answer, that although the flesh was always presented holy to God, yet it was a continual victory. If the flesh had not been continually constrained by the Spirit — if it had been natural to it, so to speak, in itself to be thus holy, then there would be no explanation of its death: but if its holiness was from the Holy Ghost, and not from its own nature, then Christ gave the Father glory when he died — he declared by his death that his holiness was not of the flesh but of the Spirit. If any creature had said this flesh is different from other flesh, and this is the reason why this man is different from other men, the death of Christ would have proved him to be mistaken. The flesh was the same, but it was holy through the Spirit; and it was given up to death to prove what flesh is in itself; and so it is appointed unto all men once to die.

'The life which I now live in the flesh, *I live.*' Thus he takes it home after all. After having attributed his life to Christ, he takes it back to himself — it is Christ, and it is I. It is here that you behold the astonishing condescending love of God. When I say to the people, 'You can do no good thing', and yet command them to do good, they feel as if it were inconsistent and unreasonable, because they do not know that it is God that is to do it in them. The apostle does not give us to understand that when Christ wrought in him it was like another man working in him, or that he was, so to speak, idle — as if his will had nothing to do with it — as if his inclination was in no respect concerned in it; but after he has said it was Christ in him that lived, still he connects himself with it, and comes back to this, that he, Paul, lived though it was Christ in him that lived. Christ, the living head, acts in living members, not in dead members; and therefore they, in acting, can say that *they* act while he acts — they feel while he feels in them. This great mystery is the mystery of our participating in the nature of God, without our being God.

My dear friends, I know that some of you are startled when I say that a Christian has the mind of God — that he has the joy, the peace of God — that he sees as God sees, and feels as God feels. I beseech you now to see the explanation of this, and that I am quite right in saying it, and that I might not only say that the Christian sees and feels as God sees and feels, but, in one sense, I might say, it is God in him that sees and feels, for it is the Spirit of God in him: and this is the way in which God can make me share in God's joys, and still be but a man; by the Spirit of Christ in me he gives me to share in his own feelings and joys; and this is the great mystery, and this is God's manner of love. 'Behold what manner of love the Father hath bestowed on us, that we should be called the sons of God.' What *manner* of love, not what *amount* of love. And it is no fiction, no idle speech to call us sons: it is a plain literal fact, that as I am the son of Adam, so also am I the son of God; while I am not God, but a different person; and so through the second Adam it comes to pass, that men have the divine nature; not a likeness of it, but the very thing itself. The believer has the divine nature in him because he has the divine Spirit in him, at the very time that he is not God but a creature; and this is the way God brings out the greatest depth of his love. It is a wonderful and glorious thing to see God making creatures, and giving them various capacities of pleasure, various sources of enjoyment; but it is a far higher — a far deeper — a far more glorious thing, to conceive of God as setting his eyes on you and me, and saying, 'I shall let them into the secrets of my own heart; I shall make them conscious of the very joys of God.' Men will say, it is great presumption to expect this. Is it presumptuous to say that God will do a thing that is full of love — that because it is a far higher love therefore it is not likely God will do it? I answer, the higher it is the more worthy of God. And surely if it is a thing to the praise and glory of God that he makes creatures for happiness, it is still more for the glory of God that he will not grudge them his own happiness . They never can be literally God: power belongs to God alone: but they can receive, and God gives them to receive, the Spirit — the heart — the feeling — the enjoyments of God. This is what is implied when it is said, 'Behold what manner of love the Father hath bestowed upon us, that we should be called the sons of God.'

My hearers, I beseech you observe this; and see that it is altogether because of their low notions of dignity and greatness, that men can ever think it dignity in God to deny us his nature, or to keep us at a distance from him. This is the little mock dignity of human pride: it is like the pomp and state of an eastern monarch, who keeps himself above his subjects, by throwing them at a great distance. This is not true dignity; this is not the dignity of love, whose greatness is that it will come down and dwell with the lowly. The high and lofty One, who inhabiteth eternity, yet dwelleth with the humble and contrite spirit. and it is the glory of God, that God will dwell with men who are meek — that he will call them his people; yea, make them his children, heirs of God, and joint heirs with Christ.

I do live with a new life in the flesh. It was in the flesh, observe. It was not, 'Perhaps God will meet my labours on earth with some distinction hereafter'; but in the flesh, he lived the life of Christ. Christ was the Son of God from eternity: Christ was the Son of God when in the flesh: Christ was the Son of God when he was manifested as such, by being raised from the dead. And just as truly was he the Son of God, when in our flesh, as before; just as truly as after our flesh in him was glorified. And so the Christian is the son of God from that very moment in which Christ enters him — from that moment in which the Spirit of God is in him — from that moment in which he becomes a living member of the body of Christ; and it is in telling out what God has done for him, and in giving praises to the Lord, that he confesses that he is a child of God — that the Spirit of God is in him — that Christ is in him.

O my friends, do you think this the work of a man? Do you think it any praise to me that Christ should conquer my flesh in me? Certainly not. How then is it presumption? Is it taking praise to myself to ascribe this work to Christ? I would have you know yourselves. If you look at what a man obtains by dint of human exertion — if you look at the wealth and the learning which he acquires from the exercise of his natural powers, and if I were to say that I am a son of God, in that sense, this would be to say that I have *acquired* a great deal, I have *reached* a great way, I have made great exertions, and great attainments; but if a babe may be a son of God, then it is no praise to me to say, 'I am a son of God'; it is merely saying, 'I yield myself up to the Holy Ghost, to be possessed by God'. I beseech you, let the tendency which so prevails among men, to separate between themselves and Christ, and so lose the whole benefit of the declaration that he left us an example that we should follow his steps — let this tendency be met, counteracted, and overcome by the words of Paul. Men will say Christ is God. Yet he is God; but it was not *as God* he did those things. He laid aside his glory; he humbled himself; he was contented to take the place of a servant. If he had done them as God then he had been no example to me; but if as man then he was an example. If it was because he was God that he was what he was, and not through his humbling himself, and continually receiving the Spirit from the Father, then he was no example to me. But he was an example, because he took my very flesh, just as I have it, and received from the Father the very Spirit which he himself is willing to give to me. Let no man, from false jealousy for the glory of the Redeemer, refer his perfect and spotless holiness to a wrong cause, thinking that he is jealous for God when he talks of the human nature of Christ as *in itself* different from ours. The flesh of Christ differed not in one particle from mine; but Christ did present his flesh, which was even my flesh, without spot to God *through the eternal Spirit*. If any man forget this, and that he came down for the very purpose that he should be within our reach, and that we should look him in the face, and know him as our brother — if any man is losing sight of this (and this false jealousy for Christ is Satan transforming himself into an angel of light) he is putting Christ as far off from us as God would have been without the incarnation. Look to Paul. He said, 'I am crucified with Christ.' He did not say, 'I have this sinful nature, and Christ had it not'; but he says, 'And now I am crucified with him.' He did not say, 'I need not expect to follow his footsteps', but he says, 'I do follow his footsteps; and not I myself but Christ takes the burden of it.'

This is what I desire to press most especially upon your attention; that we are taught here that the holiness which is in the child of God, is the work of Christ Jesus, as truly as his personal holiness was; and, that where the Spirit of the Lord is, there, and there alone there is liberty; and that Christ in us does that for us, which he did in his own person. O! this is a great mystery — the secret of all strength — of all liberty — of all victory over the world, the flesh and the devil — the secret which will correct that delusive and false feeling, as if I was to be contented with some low standard of holiness suited to my circumstances; and lay aside Christ, as if he were not a proper standard for me.

But how is it that Christ comes into any one? This is the most important inquiry: how comes any one to be able to say, 'I am crucified with Christ, nevertheless I live'? This is Paul's account of the matter. 'The life which I live in the flesh, I live *by the faith of the Son of God.*'

I would take this opportunity of putting faith and good works on their proper footing. Paul had this life by faith in the love of Christ. People expect to get their life, that is, their enjoyment of the things of God, by looking to their good works. That is not God's plan. You must get the life through faith, and the life will be fruitful of good works. Every work that springs not from faith is a dead work. Paul had a life by which to do good works. He had the flesh, and this he did not use, but crucified it. He did not take it, as people think they can take their flesh, and, by restraining it, do something with it to please God. He did not take his natural man, and get the Spirit of God in consequence of the good use he made of the natural man. This is the feeling of many; they think if they exert themselves, then God will help them. This was not the apostle's way: he never thought of using his natural strength. He crucified himself — he crucified the flesh; and laid it aside, and accounted it as dead; and he lived by the faith of the Son of God.

'The life which I live', says he, 'I live by the faith of the Son of God.' The question we now consider is, how the power of the Son of God comes to be power in me. The answer is, it is by faith: the Spirit is received through faith: it is in receiving the truth concerning the Son of God, that Christ dwells in our hearts by faith.

My dear hearers, observe that the life which the apostle had, and which wrought in him all manner of godliness, was a life which was not his own, but the life of Christ in him; and this life of Christ came into him by faith; that is, it was in believing the record concerning the Son of God that the life came into him. The truth is in the blood, and the life is in the truth. There are three that bear witness, the Spirit, the water and the blood. The Spirit is the Holy Ghost — the water is the water of baptism — and the blood is the blood of Christ; all testifying to one thing.

See how this mystery ends. It ends in this, Believe and thou shalt be saved — Believe and live: and however deeply mysterious in itself, yet in itself it has this simplicity. All we have to do with men to bring them into this life, is not to teach them how to perform some deep, dark, mysterious, inexplicable labour, or piece of work; but just to tell them to believe this, the declaration of the gospel, that Christ sanctified himself for us, that through the faith of the truth we might be sanctified; and that the eternal God is now unveiled in the work of Christ, so that he can enter into a man; and we are all told that Christ is given to us, and in Christ the Spirit; so that we have given us a right and a power to share in his nature; and we are called on to receive this truth — to welcome this living word which became flesh — to receive his flesh and blood — to receive God in our nature, by the Spirit in us. So that it is not a thing for man to say, 'I shall sit down and wait, and if God choose to enter into me, well, and if not I cannot help it.' This is the truth, the Lord hath put life into a truth, and put the truth forth in a word; and that word is the preached gospel; and that gospel is preached to me, and when I receive it, I receive the Spirit; and yield myself to be dwelt in of the living God. 'The life which I live, I live by the faith of the Son of God.'

But, my hearers, it is God's truth that will produce life, and nothing else. If any of you be a father, and your son ask you for bread will you give him a stone, and if he ask a fish will you give him a serpent? That is the manner, not of a father, but of the devil, and of every one who listens to his teaching. To give a hungry soul that is without the new life — a soul that has no power in it to serve God — to give it a doctrine in which there is no life, this is to give it a stone — this is to give it a serpent. God has put life into his own truth; and his truth is life because it is the truth of God. But it is not every one that says to Jesus, 'Lord! Lord!' who has the life — it is not every one that takes up a notion of Christ; but the man who has the faith of the Son of God, *the* Son of God — not a Son of God of man's contrivance — not a Saviour of man's invention, but *that* 'Son of God who loved me, and gave himself for me' — this is the Son of God.

Christ, the Son of God, loved each of you, and gave himself for each of you; and thus there is life for each of you: and I come to you with this bread of life, and set the bread of life before you, by telling you this and if I did not tell you this, I would be giving you, not bread but a stone; not a fish but a serpent. And God forbid that I should give you any word but the word of life; or that I should call on you to love God, and not give you the materials for loving God. God has given me an instrument for producing this love in you, for he has told me to tell every child of Adam this good news, Christ loved you, and gave himself for you — Christ tasted death for you, and for you he arose from the dead — your flesh he took, and your flesh he crucified. He rose and has now the Spirit for you. This news is the bread of life. And show me the man that believes it, and has not life, and then I will give it all up. Show me the man that *believes in his heart*, that the eternal Son of God died for him, and that he has forgiveness through the blood of Christ, and that Christ has the Holy Spirit for him — show me the man who believes this and is not alive, and *then* I will say there is no life in this truth. But if you merely show me men who say, as many do, that Christ died for some, but they cannot tell for whom, and say *they* are dead, I do not wonder at it, for they have no quickening knowledge: but show me the man who, in his heart, has apprehended Christ as his Lord and Saviour, who is seeing him wounded for *his own* transgressions, and bruised for his iniquities, and as having received gifts for him — who is understanding that the Spirit, which Christ has, he has for him, and that the kingdom which Christ is to establish here, is a kingdom in which he is to share — show me the man who is in the faith of this, and then you will show me a living man. And therefore, that you might know the secret of his victory over the flesh, Paul explains the mystery, and says that he who dwelt in him was the Son of God, who loved him, and gave himself for him — who loved *him*, I repeat, and gave himself *for him*. Therefore, because of his love

Appendix 4 309

to you all, will we, unto the death, testify, that the Son of God loved *you*, and gave himself *for you* — therefore, because there is no other name that can save you, will we testify of this name, that you may be saved — and therefore, while we have a being, will we thus testify that you may live and not die; that you may repent and not perish; that you may taste of the liberty of the children of God — of being heirs of God, and joint heirs with Christ; that you may say, 'Now are we the sons of God; we are crucified with Christ; nevertheless we live'; and that you may thus feel and speak and so be in the sight of God that God may have joy over you, and see in you that which he wishes to see; that the world may be benefited by you; that the whole earth may have your cry ascending over it; and that the day of the Lord may thus be hastened, and the glory of the Lord made to cover the earth — therefore will we thus preach that the devil may be utterly cast out of this earth, and have no possession but of those who choose to give glory to him. Thus will we use this foolishness of preaching, that Satan's kingdom may tremble — this will we proclaim this doctrine of pardon to all, as a support and a strength for all — thus will we take these truths to conflict with the powers of darkness, and to overcome them. And we know that Satan will spread his lies, and stir up his adherents; yet will we not regard these things: none of these things will move us; but we will confess that Jesus is that Son of God who loved every human being — who tasted death for every human being — who rose again for every human being — who has the Spirit for every human being — in whom there is this eternal life for every one of you, that you may live to God and not die.

My dear hearers, there is so much before us of the duty of this day, that I cannot longer dwell on this subject: but I would just shortly remind you of what I have said. I have shown you what is meant by saying that a man has life, viz. that he is a conscious, thinking being, capable of enjoyments, and what two kinds of life this living man may have, a life in the flesh or a life in the Spirit; and then I showed you the state of the apostle, that his was not a life in the flesh, but in the Spirit and how it came to be so — what his own account of it was — that he was crucified with Christ, etc., and I set before you, in plain words, the mystery of God in the flesh. I know that no man will receive it unless taught of the Spirit of God; but let no one therefore feel as if, that being the case, I might as well have been silent; but rather learn from it where to get the capacity to understand this mystery of God, Christ in your flesh — Christ in the members of his body. And I have shown you how we become living members of the body of Christ; that it is by faith — just by faith — that the life comes in by believing the truth; and it is by the faith of the Son of God, who loved you, and gave himself for you.

I entreat those who know this love, to remember what manner of love it is — to remember that the open door, through which the life-blood flows, is faith. I entreat them to remember that, as the life is received by faith, so it is lived by faith. I not only become alive by faith, but I live by faith. I would again remind every child of God that it is not only true that their first feeling of life was through faith, but that every pulse of a true life that has ever been in them, has been the pulse of faith — that all that is not of faith is sin: so saith the apostle, 'That which is not of faith is sin.' Therefore I warn you that you are called to abide in Christ, that Christ may abide in you: you are called to believe in Christ: and this is the work of God, at first and all along, that you believe in him — that while the light is shining, you walk in the light — that you be continually knowing it and realising it: and that you judge nothing according to the flesh; but that you give yourselves up to the Lord, that he may instruct you and guide you continually. Know that if you abound in love, you will abound in giving glory to God; that if you be strong in faith all things are possible to him that believeth; and that the removal of mountains is a strong expression, indicating that I can do, by Christ in me, all that Christ in himself could do. My dear hearers, it is the might of Christ, not only for health to the soul, but for health to the body, that we may be going about, in the power of Christ, continually doing good.

I would now speak to those who have not Christ in them. O, my dear hearers, it is awful, it is very awful to believe that Christ died for every one, and that Christ rose again for every one: and though the devil may deny it as he chooses, and make use of the mists that rise from the world, and the flesh, to darken this truth, nevertheless, as the clouds cannot extinguish the sun, so these mists will not extinguish the light of the glorious Sun of Righteousness. It is, indeed, an awful thing that this is the truth, that you are all bought with blood — that you are all redeemed to God by the blood of his Son — that he has set you apart for the service of God — that God has given you, in Christ, all things pertaining to life and godliness — that there is, at this moment, no one thing in your condition, no one barrier whatever, between you and rejoicing in God. Your sin is put away as a condemning and forbidding thing; and also, in respect of its power to keep you back, for you have liberty and strength in Christ. There is power in the Spirit for you to overcome and you have the Spirit in Christ: and I say to every one of you, 'Look unto God, and give him glory and rejoice.' I come unto you saying only what the word of God demands of me that I should say; and therefore is it an awful thing that you will not give glory to God. It is an awful thing that you will deny the Lord that bought you. It is an awful thing that you will allow that he rose again, but will not say that he rose for you — that you will acknowledge that he has the Spirit, but not that he has it for you. Is it not awful, that when God has bestowed every thing upon you for life, you will still remain dead, because you will not believe? O! God will be a righteous judge and the cobwebs of your own sophistries and delusions, by which you try to fence yourselves about, and say, 'How can we be sure that Christ died *for us?*' — these shall all be swept away by the besom of destruction. Your refuge of lies cannot stand. The covering is narrower than that a man can wrap himself in it; and when the dark, and cloudy, and stormy night of God's judgement has come upon you, then will you know what you have been trusting to, and what you have been rejecting in this day of grace, mercy and remission of sins. It is possible for you to go on in such a day, and to say peace, peace, while there is no peace: because Christ has put away your sin, therefore is it possible for you to live as you are doing: but when God has come forth in judgement — when he will arise out of his place, to punish the inhabitants of the earth for their iniquity — when God comes to see what trees are bringing forth fruit, after he has so long time been digging about them and dunging them — when Christ shall say of them that rejected him, 'They were borne with and spared through me; for when I said, suffer it this year yet, I got the year for which I asked: I have digged about it, and dunged it, and it is not my fault if it be not fruitful': then will the husbandman come forth as the treader of the wine-press of the fierceness of the wrath of Almighty God. No man can tell how soon the Son of God may come forth to tread the wine-press — to pour forth his fury on your poor miserable souls.

O! may the Lord give you *now* to know and to feel these things. And O, let not my warning voice, which is not my voice, but the voice of the Holy Ghost, speaking by my lips, let not my voice be heard in vain. Repent! Repent! and give God glory that ye perish not. Turn to the Lord! Seek him, while he may be found; call upon him, while he is near.

Amen.

Appendix 5

Notes of Sermons 3.31

Sermon on Titus 2:11-14 (Second Sermon on the Text)

I shall not now press upon your attention what is the grace of God which hath appeared, even the love of God which has been revealed in the work of Christ: or that it is grace to all men, even love manifested on the part of God to all men, to every man, or that it is grace bringing salvation to us, love which has placed man in a condition in which he may rejoice in God, and be saved from all iniquity. I desire now to illustrate, as God may speak by me, what the grace of God teaches, both as to what is to be our present condition, that is, that we should 'deny ungodliness, and worldly lusts, live soberly, righteously and godly in this present world', and as to the hope, in regard to the future which it would impart to us, that we should be 'looking for that blessed hope, and the glorious appearing of the great God and our Saviour Jesus Christ.'

My dear friends, the grace of God is here represented as teaching: that is, we are here regarded as persons who are to receive wisdom from the knowledge of the grace which has appeared — we are to be enlightened by it and to know what it is we are called to, through the understanding of this grace. There is no true wisdom that is not from Christ. Christ is made of God to us wisdom and although there be many called wise according to this world's wisdom, yet are there are none truly wise but those who have their wisdom from Christ, for 'the wisdom of the world is foolishness with God', and that which men call knowledge, and that which men boast of as knowledge is of no account in the judgement of God. God calls the wisdom of the world foolishness. Look to the word of God as to the matters in the 1st Epistle to the Corinthians, chapter 1, verse 17, where we are taught God's estimate of man's wisdom: verses 17-21, 'For Christ sent me not to baptise but to preach the Gospel: not with wisdom of words; lest the cross of Christ should be made of none effect. For the preaching of the cross is to them that perish foolishness, but unto us which are saved it is the power of God. For it is written, 'I will destroy the wisdom of the wise, and will bring to nothing the understanding of the prudent. Where is the wise? Where is the scribe? Where is the disputer of this world? Hath not God made foolish the wisdom of this world? For after that, in the wisdom of God, the world by wisdom knew not God it pleased God by the foolishness of preaching to save them that believe.' And again at the 25th verse, 'Because the foolishness of God is wiser than men, and the weakness of God is stronger than men.' Then at the 30th verse, 'But of him are ye in Christ Jesus who of God is made unto us wisdom.' Now my dear hearers, I seek to press this matter upon you that it is all a delusion to feel as if there were any true wisdom that is not received from Christ; it is all a delusion to feel as if man's talents, and man's observation and man's enquiry, could attain unto wisdom. There is no true wisdom but in seeing things as God sees them, for God alone sees things as they truly are, and we never see things as God sees them until we see them by the light of Christ, and so it is the grace of God in Christ Jesus that is to be our wisdom: and we are not to think ourselves able to understand or judge of anything truly, until we understand the grace of God and are able to bring the light of God to bear upon that thing. Now, the grace of God is kindness and love to man and the love which God has shown to you is that which is to instruct you, for it shows you the mind of God regarding you, and how God desires to bless you: and so in understanding the goodness or goodwill or grace of God you know your true character — your true interests, and how these interests are to be secured and so it is by understanding that purpose of love which was in the heart of God, and which has come forth in the gift of Christ, that your darkness, as to your own condition, is to be removed and that you are to be brought into the light of love. Understand that the word of God is not a thing to be believed by you as if believing it were something which gives you a claim upon God: or some condition upon which God would give you salvation. Know that the word comes to you as light, and comes to you in darkness to instruct you concerning God and to make you to know truly both God and yourselves. And so the wise are those who judge of all things by that light — not the wise of this world — not the learned of this world: but the man, however illiterate, however ignorant of this world's systems, who has judged of things by the light of the cross of Christ — that is the truly wise man. And my dear friends, you may well understand how grace should teach you how the things done of God, for your good, being understood in God's own light and God's own knowledge, should truly instruct you as to your own condition and so make you wise.

I must here dwell for a little upon the character of the grace of God, before I go on to consider what it teaches. I do not now stop to consider its extent, as embracing all, or its completeness as bringing entire and full salvation: but I desire you to understand what the grace of God in itself is. The grace of God is that love which moved the eternal Son of God to come forth from the bosom of the Father and take our nature and become bone of our bone, and flesh of our flesh, and inasmuch as the children are partakers of flesh and blood, in like manner to take part of the same in order that he might be a sacrifice for sin, in order that he might bring into our condition the light of the eternal love, and holiness and goodness of God, and might reveal by that light, what our darkness was, and that having thus brought in light, he should be raised from the dead that he might be the author of eternal salvation to as many as obey him.

Now mark the manner in which Christ gives light. If I were to see you under the influence of some man who was deceiving and misleading you whilst I knew that he was a deceiver, and I were to come among you and place myself in your condition, wherein you were exposed to his deceptions and that every lie that he addressed to you, I met with a denial, and every deception he attempted to practise upon you I exposed. I would thus be bringing to you precious and important light, unveiling to you the delusions under which you were labouring, exposing the deceiver in his true character, and calling on you to understand your true condition. And further, if I were to receive power, in regard to you, to enable you through me, to see these delusions, and reject them, then were I such a deliverer as you needed. Now, I entreat of you to understand that man, being born into this fallen flesh, and evil world, and exposed to all the devices of Satan, the Lord Jesus came and placed himself in like condition, was born into our flesh, was born into our world — was born into a condition in which he was exposed to all the attacks of Satan — that this was the condition into which he came, and that he placed himself precisely in our circumstances, he condescended to teach us what the evil of our state was and to expose to us all the devices of the enemy.

My dear friends, here is the great importance (one part of it at least for it is not all) that there is in seeing that Christ came in our nature — in our very nature — that he came into that very world in which we are, and enjoyed no privilege, no distinction to screen him from the power of the world, or from the

Appendix 5

oppression of the world — that he was exposed to all the attacks of Satan, and enjoyed no advantage to keep Satan from coming to deceive him, and attempting to destroy him. He came into the very condition in which we were in order that he might teach and enlighten us, and make us to know the evil. Therefore is it said that he came to condemn sin in the flesh. If you look to the Epistle to the Romans, chapter 7, you will see this matter clearly set forth. At the close of the 7th chapter we have a passage which is connected with the subject, and which passage, because it has often been misapplied, I would very shortly notice: 7:21-24, 'I find then a law, that when I would do good, evil is present with me. For I delight in the law of God, after the inward man. But I see another law in my members, warring against the law of my mind, and bringing me into captivity to the law of sin which is in my members. O wretched man that I am! Who shall deliver me from the body of this death?' These words, my friends, express the condition of man as needing a Saviour — they express the condition of man as under captivity to the law of sin and as utterly helpless and they, as in bondage, constrained to cry, 'O wretched man that I am! Who shall deliver me from the body of this death?' The apostle is here stating what man, what every man is, apart from Christ, and he is doing this in order to commend the Gospel to us, in order that we may rightly esteem the gift of Christ. The error to which I refer is the error of supposing that in these words the apostle is stating his experience as a Christian man. He is not doing this. That would be to say that the experience of a Christian man is being in captivity to the law of sin and death: for here he says. 'O wretched man that I am! Who shall deliver me from the body of this death?' Now we know that those whom the Son makes free are free indeed, and we know that when the Jews said, 'We are Abraham's seed, and never were in bondage to any man', our Lord taught them saying, 'Whosoever committeth sin is the servant of sin', showing that the liberty which he promised was deliverance from the power of sin, and every word of God tends to show us that in Christ we have a victory over sin, and therefore to suppose that the apostle is here expressing the experience of a Christian is to suppose that the experience of a Christian is that of being under the law of, and in captivity to, sin and death. But he is stating what man is in himself in order to commend Christ, and therefore adds, 'I thank God through Jesus Christ our Lord', showing us that while saying, 'O wretched man that I am! Who shall deliver me from the body of this death?' he does not speak as saying, 'I am not delivered', but as showing what he would be but for Christ, and so goes on to thank God. Now we find in the 3rd verse of the 8th chapter he ascribes this deliverance to God. 'For what the law could not do, in that it was weak through the flesh, God sending his own Son in the likeness of sinful flesh, and for sin, condemned sin in the flesh.' We are here taught that in our evil state, in order to grant us deliverance, God sent forth his own Son in the likeness of sinful flesh, that he might condemn sin in the flesh. In the likeness of the flesh of sin — that is the literal translation of the words, as it is elsewhere said in the likeness of man. You are not to suppose that this means in appearance merely, as some heretics have taught that our Lord had not a true body, but only the likeness of man, and not the reality of man. Likeness of man means participation in manhood. It means taking that which is humanity — and the likeness of sinful flesh means that he took that flesh which we have for the purpose of condemning sin in it. We are in this flesh — we are sowing to this flesh, and we are reaping corruption — we are all of us carried away as by a flood — our iniquities like the wind have carried us away — the Lord Jesus came, and entered into our condition — entered into our flesh — took our flesh, that he might condemn sin in the flesh — and he condescended to be partaker of our nature, that he might prove to us what the evil is of sowing to the flesh, and our Lord condemned sin in the flesh by walking in the Spirit; and so it is said, 'He through the Eternal Spirit offered up himself without spot to God.' Now, I feel it exceedingly important, in regard to the teaching power of the grace of God, that you should understand not merely that God loves you all: but that you might understand that the kindness of Christ, in coming to be your Saviour, was his coming to take your nature, was his condescending to put himself in your precise condition, and to have experience of your trials and of your difficulties, and that it was his doing all this under the power of the love which he had to you, so that Christ's love brought him forth from the bosom of the Father — brought him down into our nature, making him to take part in the same. Forasmuch as the children are partakers of the flesh and blood, he also himself likewise took part of the same — constrained himself to dwell in this flesh — in this world — constrained himself to dwell exposed to the assaults of Satan, in order that he being holy in our flesh — in order that he presenting it without spot to God through the Eternal Spirit, in order that he rejecting all temptation, and being holy in thought and feeling, in word and action, while we were in all these respects sinful, might show us the reality of our sin and what it is with which we are chargeable, and what our evil is in our sowing to the flesh, and sinning against God. My dear friends, it is in this way that we shall know the teaching power of the grace of God. It is when we see that our Lord was in our condition — was exposed to our temptations and experienced all our trials, and when we see the holy One of God, from his first being as a man, until his death on the cross, moving in perfect holiness in the midst of these very circumstances in which the children of men have all sinned against God — it is then that the beam of light comes in upon this darkness of man, and truly shows man what his sin is, and just as I would be condemning another by doing the opposite of what he did in the same circumstances, so Christ condemned sin in the flesh by being in our condition, and perfectly holy in it. He has cleared God of all these in it — he presented human nature, his own blood without spot to God through the Eternal Spirit, and thereby has taught us what sin is, and that it is not of God, and that there is no excuse for it, and that there is power in the Spirit of God to give us perfect deliverance from the bondage of sin.

Now my dear friends, it is the grace of God which teaches us to deny ungodliness and worldly lusts and how is this? Because we see Christ denying ungodliness and worldly lusts. It is when we see Christ, perfectly holy, not contaminated by sin, but pure and spotless, and see him as really in our very nature (and if we see him not as a real man, we are taught nothing) we are taught to deny ungodliness and worldly lusts. O it is a powerful teaching: if man would take it as God gives it. Here is a man who is also God — here is God in human nature — how did he speak, feel and act? That is just the same with asking, 'How should I speak, feel and act?' When I see before me the man Christ Jesus, denying ungodliness I see what I ought to be. I see what I am called to be. When I see him denying all worldly lusts I see, I say, what I ought to be, and what I am called to be. Seeing him living soberly and righteously and godly, in this world, I see myself called to live in it soberly and righteously and godly. My dear friends, it is the mind of God — it is the character of God that is revealed to us — that eternal life which was with the Father has been revealed to us. And why? That we might partake of it — that we might share in that eternal life. Look to the language in the first Epistle general of John — there he speaks in the beginning of the first chapter concerning the Lord, 'That which was from the beginning, which we have heard, which we have seen with our eyes, which we have looked upon, and our hands have handled of the word of life.'

He here dwells upon that personal acquaintance with Christ which they had as having intercourse with him, as hearing his words, as seeing him with their eyes and handling him with their hands — it is that intimate acquaintance which they had with Christ in the days of his flesh. Now, he says that the life was manifested that they had seen it and that he declared unto them that eternal life which was with the Father, and with his Son Jesus Christ. We then see that the apostles were sent forth to declare that the eternal life of God was manifested in the man Christ Jesus, that this eternal life they had seen and known in Christ, and that they were, through the knowledge of it, brought into a condition of sharing in it, of having fellowship with the Father and with the Son, and that they preached the Gospel in order to bring other men into the like condition, that others also might have fellowship with the Father and with the Son. It is just the same with saying that which was the life of God always — that which was his from eternity has been revealed as the life of the man Christ Jesus; and we are called to know that to be our own life — to have it as our own life; and we are in the condition of having fellowship with the Father and with the Son: because we share in the life of the Father and of the Son: and our object in teaching you is to bring you into the like fellowship.

Now, my dear friends, observe that this is the true character of the teaching grace of God in the man Christ Jesus, who is God manifested in the flesh, who is the heart and mind of God revealed in the man Christ Jesus — who is the holiness and love of God revealed in the man Christ Jesus, and we are made to look to all this in order that we should partake in it. It is just that word, 'Be ye holy, for I am holy; be ye perfect as your Father in heaven is perfect.' This is the counsel of God, to show Christ, God in our nature, that we may feel ourselves called to be like God — it is to have in us the mind of God as revealed in the man Christ Jesus. Now my dear friends, you must at once feel that if we realise to ourselves that Jesus is our very brother, that he came in our very condition — that he partook of our very nature; just as we have it, and lived in the world in which we are living and was exposed to the attacks of Satan, to which we are exposed, and in all this was perfectly holy, and perfectly pure before his God and Father, you can understand how the kindness and love which was expressed in condescending to come into our condition, in order to show us God, is a light to teach us to be what he was — to have the same mind which was in Jesus. But my dear friends, it is not only that the Lord Jesus as man is what we ought to be — it is that he as man has thus, in our circumstances, and in our very nature, shown it as a thing possible in our condition, and then that he is able to make us what he was himself. It is not calling upon you to imitate Christ as you would imitate a man such as I am. It is not saying, 'Here is the example of perfection: walk ye after this example and be ye perfect.' There is this great difference, that it is Christ in you that is to make you what Christ was. Christ having condemned sin in the flesh — having presented himself without spot to God, through the Eternal Spirit, did this as a sacrifice for sin, and so put away our sin, and so we have our sin forgiven through the shedding of his blood, and he being exalted to the right hand of God, in reward of his holiness and righteousness, has received from the Father this high place, that now he is the second Adam, the quickening Spirit — that now he has the Holy Spirit for us to dwell in us by the Spirit that, through his Spirit in us, we might be what he was. The apostle says that the law of the Spirit of life in Christ Jesus had made him free from the law of sin and death: and we are taught that it is the Spirit of life, given to us in Christ, that gives us deliverance from the law of sin and death, for Christ was holy through the Eternal Spirit: therefore when the man came to him and said, 'Good Master, what must I do that I may inherit eternal life?' Christ said, 'Why callest thou me good? There is none good but one, that is God.' Our Lord then said, 'Do not call me good.' And why? Not because he was not good — not because he was not holy — for it is always testified that he was the holy one of God. Why then object to the man calling him good? Because he would have the man to see that the goodness was not his as man: but through the Spirit of the Father in him; that there is none good but one, that is God; and that as he had come to be a servant, and as he had taken on him the form of a servant, so his goodness was not his but it was of his Father; and said the Father who dwelt in him, he did the works. Now then, if Christ was not holy through anything in his flesh — if he was not holy through any circumstance in his creature nature — if his holiness was through the Eternal Spirit — then it is quite clear that we need the same Spirit in order to our being holy; so when our Lord shows us holiness in our condition, he is not saying, 'You may be holy if you please in your own strength': but he teaches us that there is none good but God, and that you may be holy if you walk in the Spirit — you may be holy if God dwell in you, and work in you. But Christ not only tells us that through the Spirit of God in us, we may be holy: but he has received the

Spirit for us: and the grace of God, that teaches to deny ungodliness and worldly lusts, is that grace that Christ, having presented himself without spot to God, has been called to the right hand of God as the quickening Spirit, that he has the Spirit for us, and that as he lived by the Father, so we are called to live by him; and so he says, 'As the living Father hath sent me, and I live by the Father, even so he that eateth me shall live by me.' Now therefore it is that the grace of God not only shows us holiness in Christ: but shows us Christ as the fountain of holiness to us — as having power over all flesh to give us eternal life.

My dear friends, this then is the grace of God that brings salvation — this is the grace that shows us what sin is — that shows us what holiness is — not that speaks about it: but *shows* it as a living thing: and it shows us living holiness in Jesus Christ — and while it calls us to have the mind of Christ it shows us that we have in him the Spirit that we may be holy and without blame before God in love.

My dear friends, I feel that these are things which no man can understand unless he bend to the lowly condition of looking to God for the Spirit — that they are to the natural man foolishness: but that they can be and are spiritually discerned; and therefore I solemnly call on you in the name of God not to be tempted of Satan to let this word out of your minds. O I beseech you, let not the wicked one come and take away the good seed. You have heard it said that in order that you should know what sin is and be delivered from the power of sin, the Lord came into your nature and was holy in your nature and then ascended up on high and received for you the same Spirit which he had formerly for himself, and that now you are called to see in him, both what you ought to be, and what you may be, and that there is no reason why you should not, for God has given you Christ.

Now my dear friends, do not think that you can ever be taught to deny ungodliness by any lower Gospel than this. It is in vain to expect that men will deny ungodliness by being told to do so. In order to my denying ungodliness I must know what ungodliness is and I must see that I have power to deny it. And you might as well ask a man to fly in the air, who had no wings to fly with, as ask a man to be holy who had not provision for his being holy Men have come to feel as if holiness were a thing out of the question in this life — men have come to feel as if deliverance from the power of sin was more than we could expect — as if the most we could expect was forgiveness.

My dear friends, this is a lie of the devil, for Christ came to teach us to deny ungodliness and worldly lusts: and it is a vain thing to expect that people will deny that which they do not see themselves in a condition to deny — it is in vain to expect that people will deny that ungodliness which they see no power to conquer. I therefore would have you to know that when God speaks of Christ as a Head, and when he says that the grace of God in Christ teaches men to deny all sin, he is giving us to know that our sin is not only condemned and forgiven, (as I set forth last Lord's day), through the blood of Christ, but that we have in Christ power to walk with God, and that therefore it teaches us to deny ungodliness and worldly lusts. I wish you would understand how vain it is to try to induce any man to attempt that which he feels to be hopeless. But men speak of sin as if it were a hopeless thing to expect to be holy in this life — as if our being in this nature made it impossible for us to be holy, as if the flesh, which is fallen in Adam, made it impossible for us to be holy. If this is so why are we called to be holy? If this is the case why is it said that the name of Christ is Jesus, *because he shall save his people from their sins?* O be not deceived in this, for no man will ever in sober earnest propose to be holy, who does not see himself in a condition to be so. Know therefore that the grace of God which teaches you to deny ungodliness and worldly lusts, is that love of God which is expressed in the Lord Jesus, and that he has through the Eternal Spirit presented human nature without spot to God, and in it he has power, namely, the Spirit for others, to enable them through this Spirit dwelling in them to be holy before God.

My dear friends, I have dwelt largely on this, because I have been made to feel it is a word especially needed in this present time, when men either deny that Christ has come in our very nature or say that it is not a question of very much importance, for they say, 'If you hold that Christ's human nature was always holy, from his conception till his death, why lead people into speculation about how it was holy?' I will tell you why. Because I am sent to teach you repentance, because I am sent to teach you to be holy and because I know no other way in which you can be holy but through the Spirit of Christ: and because I know of no other way in which you can be made to look to Christ to present you holy, but by seeing how his human nature was presented holy. As long as you do not know that this human nature has, through the Eternal Spirit, been presented holy, you are not in a condition to be holy, you feel an insupportable difficulty in thinking of your own nature. All objections to the truth of God arise from the love of sin. The scoffers who deny the Lord's coming are those 'who walk after their own lusts', and so those who deny any part of God's truth are those who are indulging in sin, and this is the reason why men appear as if they were jealous for the glory of Christ, when in point of fact they are objecting to the way in which Christ's holiness is explained: because it tells clearly that if Christ presented his own nature without spot to God, through the Spirit, Christ has power through his Spirit to make them holy and therefore they are hindered from casting the blame of their own unholiness upon their condition: those who are ignorant of this truth as to the manner of Christ's holiness suffer great loss on the subject of Christ's work. They admit that Christ was wholly righteous, but they lose the good of that admission in two ways: first, they look on Christ's righteousness as something to supersede the necessity for their being righteous, as if it were something that was to cast over them an appearance of righteousness when they were not righteous: not seeing that the intention of God in all the work of Christ is our sanctification. And then as on the one hand they feel that they may trust to Christ's righteousness and not be righteous, so on the other hand they feel that our being holy is out of the question. Thus on the one hand, making real personal righteousness unnecessary, and on the other impossible, they find an easy way of meeting the charges of sin which the conscience brings against them. I beseech you that you would, in the strength of God's Spirit, look through this delusion; and know that the truth of God is that Christ presented himself without spot to God through the Eternal Spirit, condemning sin in the flesh and that Christ is now exalted as our living Head, that that which he did in his own person he may do in us, and that we through the faith of Christ and through the Spirit of Christ may walk with God in newness of life. Understand this and you will know that the grace of God teaches you, actively teaches you to deny ungodliness and worldly lusts.

What is ungodliness? My dear friends, I must explain these things briefly. Our time will not allow me to enlarge: but I trust to be enabled to state them simply. You observe that there are first things to be denied; and then things we are to possess: that is, we are found in a certain condition, which is under the power of ungodliness and worldly lusts, and we are to be brought into another condition, namely, to live soberly, righteously and godly. We are to be changed: you see, by the grace of God — to cease to be what we are, and then to become the very opposite of what we are — we are to deny ungodliness. Ungodliness is our living without God in the world. It is that pleasure men have in forgetting God. It is a real truth of God that men have a satisfaction in getting quit of the thought of the living God — that it is a relief for men in flesh and blood to put away from them the feeling of the presence of the living God. This is true even of you who are confessing the importance of religion and pleasing God. And in point of fact every false religion is a contrivance for getting quit of God — every false religion is something which enables men to have peace away from God. True religion is being brought to delight in God himself — false religion is the having something to which I trust as giving me a ground of peace before God, while I am not walking with God: to all, false religion is ungodliness; every form of error — every superstition — every false doctrine — every observance of man by which men have some peace to their consciences, while they are not giving glory to God is a contrivance of the devil's to keep quiet the conscience and to keep men comfortable in their ungodliness. And why do they listen to the devil, and why take part with these lies? Because they love to being their own masters — because the feeling of moving always under the eye of God — the feeling of always being called to say, 'Not my will, but thine be done' — the feeling that I have no liberty to choose for myself in anything, but am in everything to allow God to choose for me, this is unwelcome to flesh and blood, and so men easily fall a prey to Satan, because he offers them something with which to get peace without yielding to God, and so religion with men in general is an excuse for ungodliness — it is giving to God a certain portion of their time, it may be of their worldly substance, as a substitute for their hearts. God says, 'My son give me thy heart.' Men say, 'I will give anything but my heart. I will give my time. I will give my money. I will even give my thoughts, but my heart I must reserve for myself. My heart I reserve for the things that gratify the flesh.' Satan comes to men and says, 'You need not give your heart.' He says, 'Go to church and that will do' or, 'Feed the poor and that will do' or, 'Show respect for religion and that will do — and your heart you may give to the world, and the things opposed to God.' Or he says, 'Confess that you ought to do so and so, and that will do.' O this is common with those who are called religious people. They are saying, 'We ought to love and serve God', and this they think will do. They take the words of Paul and say, 'Wretched man that I am! Who shall deliver me from the body of this death?' and they forget what follows that he thanks God for deliverance through Jesus Christ his Lord, and leaving this out of view they say that they are like the apostle, that they are not conquerors — only this they can say that their cry is, 'O wretched man!', as if this were the experience of a child of God; and so Satan makes them think that the confessing that they ought to love God will do for the absence of love to God. This is one of the many ways that Satan teaches you to excuse yourselves for being ungodly. It does not matter whether as a Mahometan you go on pilgrimage to Mecca, or as a Papist you give money to endow a monastery, or as a Protestant you speak much of the errors of Papacy, and go about in religious societies creating a bustle about the diffusion of religious knowledge or, as a secluded retired person you sit moping in darkness and ignorance of God, saying you can find no peace, and think these things will please God — I say it matters not which of all these things the man is doing, for these are just various ways by which men contrive to quiet their consciences away from God. But the grace of God teaches you to deny ungodliness, that is, to deny the root of all these errors. And what is the root of them? Your unwillingness to feed upon God — your unwillingness to rejoice in God himself. These are the various ways in which Satan gives you something to gratify your corrupted and depraved appetites, and you desire to be at peace, not in God. How does the peace of God teach you to deny this? In the first place, because it is *grace*. What can make a man ashamed of ungodliness like the grace of God? What can make a man ashamed of refusing his heart to God like the knowledge that God loves him? What can make a man ashamed of having trusted in every refuge of lies and having refused to trust God like the knowledge that God loves him? It is the grace of God that teaches you to deny ungodliness. But this is not all. The grace of God is the condescension of Jesus to be our brother and in our nature to do the Father's will, and so the grace of God teaches to deny ungodliness, because it teaches you that Christ denied ungodliness, because it shows you the living example of Jesus, not seeking glory to himself, but always giving the glory to his Father. And so the grace of God teaches you to deny ungodliness, and you are made to feel that you should not choose that which Christ did not choose, that you should not set your heart on that on which Christ did not set his heart. But further the grace of God teaches you to deny ungodliness because it shows you that you have the Spirit of Christ given to you that you may not live in the flesh: because the grace of God calls you to crucify the flesh and walk in the Spirit. It also teaches you to deny worldly lusts. There is a difference between these and the former. Worldly lusts are the desire of those things which are in the world around us and by which Satan feeds the flesh. Ungodliness is the desire of being as a god to myself. I might be ungodly without being capable of any enjoyment from this world. The devil is ungodly though he has not our flesh through which to enjoy the world. Now there are these two things in man. There is the positive unwillingness to have God to reign over him, and the positive liking for those things that are in the world about him. Now the grace of God, while it makes us willing to have God to reign over us teaches us to deny worldly lusts, because we are made to see these things in their true character when we see them as those which Christ rejected. Satan came to Christ and showed him all the kingdoms of the earth and their glory, and said, 'All these things will I give thee if thou fall down and worship me: for they are mine and I give them to whom I will.' Satan has here testified that he would give to Christ the full enjoyment of the things of this world but the Lord rejected this temptation; and those who know the grace of God are taught to reject the like temptation.

My dear friends, I press on you that the Scriptures say, 'Love not the world: if any man love the world the love of the Father is not in him', and thus the grace of God which teaches me what the Father is, and teaches how worthy he is of all love and homage, must teach me to deny that which is against his will — to deny worldly lusts. My dear friends, what has the world to offer? The world has nothing to offer that is truly good. It has everything to offer that is pleasing to the flesh — to the natural heart of man: but nothing truly good. The person who is taught by the grace of God is taught to deny worldly lusts because he is taught to deny himself. He is taught to deny his own flesh: he sees his flesh condemned in the death of Christ and so he looks upon it as dead through the body of Christ and sees himself as crucified with Christ, and as the world can only come to me through my flesh, if I hold my flesh as a dead thing, and refuse to feed it, and to cherish it, then I deny worldly lusts. But the grace of God teaches me not to be a blank — not to be a nothing, but to be filled with that which is good: to be sober, righteous and godly. It is a great delusion to think to recommend religion to man by the indulgences which it will allow them. Men are always seeking a religion which will allow them to carry two worlds along with them and, men say, even with great show of wisdom: but with real folly. You may be religious, and pious enough although you should take the enjoyment of the innocent pleasures of this life and so they seek for an enjoyment out of

God, which they may have along with the enjoyment that is in God, forgetting that God has taught us that no man can serve two masters. But my dear friends, I would have you to know that you are not to recommend religion in this way. You are not to say that religion will add to your pleasure and not take away many pleasures[1], at least of those you have. You are always to recommend religion as complete in itself, as giving something sufficient to fill up every blank. Men say this is discouraging and is giving a gloomy view of religion. Yes, to the man who would feed the flesh: but not to the man who will believe that he can be happy without feeding the flesh — who can believe that if he takes the things of God, through the Spirit of God he will be happy. I say religion is nothing but gloom and darkness to the flesh, but religion has no gloom, no darkness, but all brightness, all joy to the spiritual eye. And therefore I commend religion by saying, 'Here is a pearl of great price: sell all and have it.' I don't say you may keep a part and yet have it: but I tell you that it is worth the sacrifice that you may well sell all and be content with it only.

'To live soberly, righteously and godly.' My dear friends, I must very shortly mention what these are. To live soberly — this does not mean merely not to be drunk; it manifestly means that condition in which he who possesses is as if he possessed not, because the fashion of this world passeth away — it means the state of perfect liberty to serve God in which we are, if we look on our present condition as that of strangers and pilgrims, who have no continuing city. The sober minded man is unmoved by the things now around him; he is dwelling in the light of that which is coming, and is free to obey the voice of his God. To live soberly then is to live as Christ lived, who pleased not himself, who was content to have his Father as his portion: and sought no portion in a present world. *To live righteously* is to be utterly fulfilling the will of God in regard to all. A man is righteous who fulfils the law of God, and Christ came a sacrifice for sin, to condemn sin in the flesh, that the righteousness of the law might be fulfilled in us, who walk not after the flesh, but after the Spirit. Therefore a man is living righteously who is fulfilling the law to man. And what is the law? 'Thou shalt love thy neighbour as thyself.' 'Give no man anything but to love one another.' The grace of God teaches us true righteousness, for it teaches us to love all men, because the grace of God shows that God loves all men. It is in vain for those who deny that God

---

[1] 'pleasures' added to the text.

loves all men, that Christ died for all men, to say that the grace of God will teach us to love all men. How can the grace of God teach me to love all men unless God, God himself, loves all men? How can the Spirit of Christ teach me to love all men unless Christ himself loves all men? O that you would understand that unless the Spirit of Christ is the Spirit of him who loves all men, the Spirit of Christ cannot make you or me to love all men; and this is righteousness to owe no man anything but to love one another. And the grace of God teaches us to live godly, that is, it teaches us love to God — not merely not to seek happiness away from God: but to seek happiness *in* God — in living to God. The grace of God shows me not only what it is to love God and rejoice in God but it shows me that in Christ which can enable me to love and rejoice in God, and so to live godly in this present evil world. I would only say one word on this part of the passage, and that is that it contains the complete contradiction of the lie of Satan, that holiness is not for this world. It is not said that the grace of God teaches me to live soberly, righteously and godly when I go to another world, but that it teaches me to do so in this present world, as if the apostle was made by the Holy Ghost to guard us especially from the delusion of feeling as if holiness were among the future things: and not of the things to which we are now called.

I have already detained you so long as not to allow me to press this much. It may be that the Lord will enable me to speak more to your consciences on a future occasion. But in the meantime I solemnly leave this doctrine with you in the name of the Lord, that the Lord your God has revealed his love to you, by giving you Jesus Christ, in whom you have the condemnation of sin, in whom you have the manifestation of holiness, in whom you have the forgiveness of sin, in whom you have power to be holy, and that God, not by empty words, but by placing you in this condition, here teaches you to deny ungodliness and worldly lusts, and to live soberly, righteously and godly in this present world. The Lord bless his word.

Amen.

Appendix 6

Notes of Sermons 2.13

Sermon on 1 Peter 1:3-5

> *Blessed be the God and Father of our Lord Jesus Christ, who according to his abundant mercy, hath begotten us again unto a lively hope, by the resurrection of Jesus Christ from the dead, to an inheritance incorruptible, and undefiled and that fadeth not away, reserved in heaven for you, who are kept through the power of God, through faith unto salvation, ready to be revealed in the last time.*

My dear hearers, I have more than once directed your attention to the circumstance that the resurrection and not the death of Christ, we find in the writings of the apostles, regarded as the cause of joy and rejoicing — that the resurrection and not the death of Christ was announced as the good news. Paul says, 'I declare unto you glad tidings how that the promise made unto the fathers, God fulfilled the same unto us their children, *in that he has raised up* his Son Jesus again from the dead', and the preaching of the apostles was that 'with great power they bore testimony to the resurrection of the Lord Jesus.' At the same time there is in the death of Christ that which gives its value to the resurrection of Christ, and there is in the death of Christ that which is essential to the resurrection of Christ. I mean not merely to say that one could not have risen again who had not died for that is perfectly obvious, but that one could not have risen again, who had not died *as Christ died*. It is the resurrection of our Lord as the accomplished thing and not the death of our Lord, as that which was preparatory to his resurrection upon which the apostles fix attention I desire at present to occupy your thought, with the view of the resurrection that is given to us in this passage — that by the resurrection of Christ from the dead we are begotten unto a lively hope, that is, that the resurrection of Christ from the dead is the instrument of begetting in us a living hope of an inheritance which is described as 'incorruptible and undefiled and that fadeth not away' and of which we are told that it is reserved in heaven for those who are kept by the power of God through faith unto salvation, 'ready to be revealed in the last time.' There is first the recognition of God's abundant mercy in this work spoken of. Then there is the work itself which is the begetting in us a lively hope; then there is the instrument by which the hope is produced, the resurrection of Christ from the dead, and then this object of it, the inheritance incorruptible and undefiled, and then this circumstance in respect of it that it is reserved for us in heaven and then last of all the circumstances of the people for whom it is reserved. I shall go over these in succession. We shall pass over the abundant mercy of God, and look to the hope. Let us consider the first, what is meant by a lively or living hope. Life you know, in the words of the Holy Ghost, is opposed to death and as that which is distinctive of the children of God expresses spiritual, not animal life; a living hope, or a hope the desire of which is a life, and is a life because it is a hope which is the cause of spiritual life. It is not of animal life, for that would be no distinction, all having that life but it is of spiritual life that this word is spoken. And what I have now to explain to you is the meaning of the expression 'a living hope'. You must recall what has been often said to you about what life is. The spiritual life in man is one with the life that is in God. In regard to the promises of God, they are said to have been given that by them we might become partakers of a divine nature. There is but one spiritual life, that eternal life, which was with the Father before the world was. And nothing else is intended to be expressed than that a man becomes a partaker of that life which is God's own life — not a life of God's giving simply: but a life which is one with the life of God. In the same way when it is said that we are made partakers of a divine nature this does not mean that we receive a nature which is the gift of God — but a nature which is God's own nature. Spiritual life then is the life of God — it is the character of God's own existence — of God's own blessedness; and to say of any creature that it has received spiritual life, is to say that it is alive with the life of God. This is the life of God in the soul of man. It is the same as to say of any creature who is partaker of the divine nature — that it is partaking of God's own nature. Any who know what it is that is meant by Christ dwelling in us by the Spirit will see that these are no figures, merely intended to express something great or excellent — but that they are to be taken literally; and that it is true that the man who has received a divine nature has God in him, and therefore may be literally said to have a divine nature. It is not his likeness to God but it's being the very truth that the Spirit of God is in him; and so when any man is said to partake in spiritual life, it is not meant that he has received some happiness of a very high character — some blessedness of a very high order, but that *literally* and *truly,* if you know what his blessedness is, you know what God's blessedness is, and so also with joy and peace. Now I wish to press this upon you, and to fix in your minds that these are not metaphors — that these are not expressions used to set forth something else than their plain meaning indicates: but that they are just to be taken literally as they are, and that this was the great object of God in taking human nature into union with his own nature, that through Christ, there might pass into those whose nature he took, the very nature of God — the Spirit of God. He became the Son of Man, that we might become the sons of God, and the one is just as literal as the other; and as truly as Christ became the Son of Man, so every one on whom Christ's work is accomplished, actually receives the divine nature, and is in that literal sense the son of God.

Now what we have to consider is how a hope should be a life — and how a person should be alive in tasting God's own blessedness. Hope is an expectation of a future thing. There is no uncertainty implied in the word Hope — it merely indicates the futurity of the object of our attention and not a doubt of the reality of its coming to pass. 'We hope for that we see not, and with patience we wait for it.' It is owing to the circumstances in which we are placed, that every human hope — every hope springing from our connection with one another, rests on uncertain grounds; and in cherishing such hope I am obliged to rest merely on probable evidence. This is the reason why hope in the ordinary acceptation of it, seems to imply uncertainty — but this does not apply to the religious hope, for hope of this last kind has just as good a reason for being *certain,* as all expectations from man have for being *uncertain.* A person whose hope rests upon God's promises must cherish it with undoubting confidence, as it is a matter of course, that the person whose hope is resting upon man's promises must still have doubts mixed with his hopes. The person who has a living hope, is a person who is expecting some future thing; and I have to explain how this expectation is in the man a *present life* — or how being in the condition of looking forward to something that is yet to be done, I should be in the condition of now sharing in the mind of God. It is because what is past and present is an unfinished manifestation of God; and because unless I see that in which it results, I have not the complete manifestation of God; but if I see not only what hath been and what is, but also what shall be, then I have the entire and complete discovery of God's whole plan. I have an acquaintance with God's full character, and this knowledge of what God is to do, is the means of enabling me to understand what God has done, and is doing. This is a life to me, because the way in which I come to share in God's feelings is by being made acquainted with them – because the love that is in God hath been made life for us, and because the mind that is in God hath been set forth in action to us; and because it is the way in which a creature can really become acquainted with the mind of its God – that that mind should be revealed in the doings of God. This is the reason why this hope is a life, because the expectation of what God is yet to do is the means of letting me know what God has done; and is now doing. This is the way in which God lets me into the secret of his counsel.

I am anxious that you should apprehend this. And observe how it is, that God imparts life to us. It is just by making himself known. There is no other way in which I can come to have the mind of God in me but just by the knowledge of God – and therefore the Spirit which worketh life and which sustains in me a divine life, is said to be truth. And it is written 'the Spirit is truth', and the character of his actual working is that 'he takes of the things that are Christ's and *shows* them to us.' This is true because it is by knowing God, that I am to be made sharer in the mind and feeling of God. If you settle this point, that it is not by any labour or deed of mine, that I am to be made a partaker of a divine nature – that my labours do not in any respect change me – they merely show me *what I am* – that it is not therefore my any exertion I shall ever be changed – but that the only instrument which can change me is making me to know the living God. If you settle this in you minds you will see how a hope should be a life: because it is the case that I must know God in order to be like him, and that it is by knowing what God does, that I am to know what God is – then if I have not the future part of God's plan before me I cannot know anything of God at all, if I don't know what he is seeking to effect; I must be ignorant not only of that future: but incapable of rightly knowing the past or present: therefore is it that inasmuch as God himself is always resting on the prospect that is before us, and towards which all things are working – inasmuch as it is the end and not the means that is the great thing to engage attention — so it is by the hope of the future — by the expectation of what he is to do, that I am now to be made alive, and partaker of a divine nature.

My dear friends, if you would examine the matter, you would find that your present death which you call life, is a state of feeling which is itself cherished by hope — that the difference between the Christian and the man who is not a Christian in not in respect of one's living by faith and hope, and the other not — but in this that the faith and hope of the one rests on what God has spoken; while the faith and hope of the other, rest upon the word of man. Now your character can be traced every moment to the character of your hope. There is not one person upon earth in whom there is not expectation of some kind or other; and his present character may be gathered from the character of his expectation — his plans refer to that which he is expecting, and therefore his doings must have the same reference. But not only so his language, thoughts, and feelings, all take their character from his hope. Let me have a control over a man's hope, and then I will have a command over that man's character, and I may make him what I please. Thus God proceeds with us: he would make us live in a spiritual life, by giving us a spiritual hope and this hope is begun in us 'by the resurrection of Christ from the dead.'

My dear hearers, it is from not seeing the exceeding importance of the future — it is from not knowing that it is the character of the expectation which people are cherishing, which decides their present tone and character of mind, that men put so readily from them the consideration of what God has declared to us concerning the future. When we hear men say, 'it is of no importance to enquire what God's future dealing will be — what we have to do with God's commands — his present will!', and when we hear them treating the setting forth of God's plan as if it were speculation, an unnecessary occupying of men's thoughts — when we find this the language of men, we are led to consider what it is, in them, which leads them thus to make light of that to which God attaches so much importance and we find that their reason is that they think such things not practical, and when we enquire what they mean by practical teaching, we find that their notion of what is practical is derived from the idea that our calling is a calling to do certain things — to perform certain duties not knowing that our calling is to cherish certain feelings, and to possess a certain character. If the place assigned to us was that of servants, if we were only on the footing of having a rule given us, and called on to walk

Appendix 6 333

according to that rule, then it were of no importance to us whatever to know what God's plan was — it were enough to know what God bids us do, and our part would be to adhere strictly to the rules prescribed to us. It is quite enough that the man employed as a servant knows the work assigned to him, though he has not the least notion how the thing is to look when all is done — though he has not the least notion of what is the mind of his employer. But this is not our calling; we are not called merely to do a piece of work for God; but to be in the condition of being sons — heirs of God — and joint heirs with Christ — in the condition of being persons who know, and enter into, and are delighted with their Father's plan. If a man's son were to be put into the condition of an hired servant and kept in ignorance of what his father's plan was, he could in no respect enter into his father's plan nor anticipate what it was to be when finished: so if I am not in the knowledge of the great plan of God — of what he is working to accomplish — I am not in the condition of a child — I am not in the condition of sharing in the mind of God, while he is working. But if I do know God's plan, from seeing the end he has in view — if he has shown me his plan and told me, 'I mean to do this and that — and to do this now in order that I may do that hereafter'; then I have it in my mind while the thing is going on, and I know the use of everything, and I share in the feeling of my Father who has appointed that this work is to be done. This is the reason why the knowledge of the future is essential to be known, if we are to be the children of God, and to share in God's feelings, and enter into God' designs.

'We are begotten unto a lively hope,' that is, there is produced in us the expectation of the future, and that expectation is one which is a present life — through which we now share in the feelings of God. This is accomplished in us by the resurrection of Jesus Christ from the dead. You will observe here the resurrection of Jesus Christ from the dead, is not the cause of our now having a living hope in the way of necessarily producing it — but is the instrument which God employs for producing it. The *fact* of Christ's being raised does not produce a living hope in us, but that fact known by us does so. So God begets us unto a living hope by making us to know the resurrection of Christ. I have shown you already that the hope which is to make me alive with the spiritual life, must be the expectation of what God is to do. Now when I know the resurrection — what is implied in it, and all the consequences of it, then I am in that knowledge of the future which is a present life in me.

I shall shortly state what the resurrection means, and then consider the incorruptible inheritance to the hope of which it call us.

The resurrection of Christ from the dead is what we are now to consider. What is implied in Christ's resurrection? We find that 'as in Adam all die, so in Christ all shall be made alive.' We find it plainly stated in the word of God that it is through the resurrection of Christ from the dead that our bodies shall be raised — that if God had not raised up Christ, then the dead rise not — that if God raised up Christ, then the dead shall be raised. Thus, our attention is fixed on the resurrection of Christ as what implies the resurrection of the human race — because Christ has arisen, therefore all men shall be raised. This is the first thing implied in it, and this is the case, *because* Christ died for all men — as our head and representative: and in thus having died for all men he hath, *in regard to every man,* overcome him that hath the power of death, that is, the devil. If Christ had not died for all men then none but those for whom he had died, would be raised; because the devil had a right to keep the rest in their graves. In Adam all die, and this doom was not taken off men through any fickleness or change in God — as if God could say one thing today, and another tomorrow — the law of God changeth not, and the doom therefore is never recalled, and the devil was in right of the law, and because of the unchangeableness of God's own government, entitled to plead that none of these should rise from their grave. The accuser of the brethren was entitled to make this plea, and it could not be rejected for, however wicked in himself, if he lay hold of any part of God's truth by that he shall stand. The devil was entitled to plead the permanence of the death of every man unless that were done which made it quite consistent with the unchangeableness of that law that they should be released. Therefore it follows that no man can be raised from the dead, unless the power of the devil in respect of that man had been overcome. Now this was the case when Christ tasted death for every man. It was righteous in God when Christ came forward as head and representative of the human race; and in our nature magnified the law of God — it was then righteous in God to reward life to him, and that he should be the Prince of Life: and he thus came and overcame him who had the power of death; that is, the devil and therefore the resurrection of Christ implies that of all men.

Now my dear friends, to know how the resurrection of all men should be connected with this living hope, you must consider that if there was no resurrection — if the death which came through sin was just the permanent thing and man rested in that state, there could have been no lively hope. There was no possibility whatever of the prospect of God's plan being a present life to me, if I was to continue under the doom of the law. To tell me what God was going to do could not quicken me — it could be no present life to me — I could not be called to sympathise in that which was to be (while I was to be silent and in darkness at the time) when that plan was to have its accomplishment. Therefore the delivering us from this bondage was essential to its being possible that I should (under the doom of death) ever receive a life giving hope.

But the mere prospect that I am to be raised, is not information enough to be in me a living hope, and therefore we must consider what more is implied in the resurrection of Christ. Now the resurrection of Christ, while it implies the resurrection of all, does not imply the resurrection of all at the same time. See 1 Corinthians 15: 17-26. We learn from the passage first of all that 'as in Adam all die, even so in Christ shall all be made alive.' But further we learn that it is not the counsel of God that all should be raised at the same time, but every man in his own order. We learn that there is an order — a succession — that Christ is the first who is raised — this is the first part of the succession of resurrection: then follows the resurrection of Christ's people, at his coming, only Christ's people observe. And then comes the end, afterwards, at a future period. The apostle does not say what time is to intervene between Christ's own resurrection and that of Christ's people; nor what time is to intervene between their resurrection and the end. But it is said that this end comes when he shall have put down all rule, and authority and power and we read concerning it that the last enemy that is destroyed is death. Now the destruction of death is just in this, that there shall be no one of the human race in their graves, and the last enemy being destroyed which is death, is the same thing which is referred to in Revelation 20: 14, where it is declared that death and hell are cast into the lake of fire. This is the second death. This is the subjugation of death. It is the completion of the word 'that as in Adam all die, so in Christ shall all be made alive.'

I do not enter further into the proof of the fact: but I wish to show the connection between the manner of the resurrection and the lively hope. It is the knowledge of this concerning the resurrection that first Christ is raised, then those who are Christ's, and then cometh the end. Now the way in which this is a present life is in the plan of God which is contained in the plan of judgement — of division — of dealing with some of those who are raised differently from others. The fruit of the death of Christ which is a life to all, without this, would not have been a prospect which would have been a present life. But while all are raised through the resurrection , yet all are not raised at the same time or in the same circumstances, but there is a distinction — and it is this distinction — which gives its living power to the resurrection. Now this distinction is the millennial kingdom of Christ as enjoyed by these and the escape from death which is also partaken of by those who are partakers of the first resurrection.

These two things are to be taken into account in order to know the life-giving power of this hope, both the reward and the punishment, the joy and the sorrow, the kingdom to be possessed by the saints and the second death to be endured by God's enemies. The difference between a resurrection considered simply and this plan of God is that the former has no power in it to commend that which is good or to put reproach on that which is evil — it has no power in it to elevate the souls of those who are on God's side — neither any power to mark the evil history of those who are not on God's side. But when we know that while all are to be raised — that the resurrection of every human being will be a record through eternity that Christ died for him — that thus there will be a seal of that truth which cannot be broken — a stamp which cannot be done away with, we have at the same time the distinction which justifies God in raising the dead at all, and that which makes the knowledge of the resurrection to be life to us. I merely mention that because more is implied in the resurrection of Christ, which I must state before going on to the character of the inheritance. The resurrection of Christ implies further, the redemption of the earth. This redemption is not to be separated from the difference of the resurrection of people who have been upon the earth. The difference of dealing with some from that of others is necessarily contained in this redemption. And this is a further part of the truth contained in the resurrection of Christ, which makes the knowledge of it to beget in man a living hope, and it is this, that Christ is to cast out Satan — it is that the earth is to be redeemed from the curse which came upon it at the fall — it is that it is precious in the sight of God as a thing bought with the blood of Jesus, and not to be cast away — not to be consumed — but only to be baptised with fire and purified — it is that this earth, on which Christ trod, which furnished the substance of his body when he was here below — that this earth into which he was received when he was laid in the grave, and which a season possessed his body, though his body saw no corruption in it, shall not be cast away as a vile and useless thing: but inasmuch as it came under a curse, by no fault of its own: but just as a manifestation of God's hatred of sin, so it is to be redeemed from that state, and will harmonise with the high place of those who shall be on it. This then is the prospect that God is to show what he can do in glorifying this earth and making it beautiful. Beware of that awful delusion of Satan which would teach you to make light of any part of God's creation as if it were evil. It is a strange contradiction that men will have their hearts chained to the earth — that men will look upon it as their home — and still feel as if they were taking from the spirituality of religion when you talk of reigning on the earth. What do you see in this earth? A high beauty — the traces of its great Creator — it has still on it the marks of the handiwork of a mighty parent though under a blot and curse. And do you not feel that such a beauty is about it, though the curse in upon it, and do you not see that it is in the mighty wisdom and power of God to make this earth a thing worthy of its God and Redeemer; yea to make it the palace of the universe — the highest thing among material creation. Just as the nature of man which had been possessed of Satan, and dwelt in as the dwelling place of every vile and unclean thing, has been sanctified and purified through its being taken by the Lord Jesus Christ, who is now raised and so the earth itself shall in like manner be glorified of God. Now this is contained in the resurrection — that he hath bought and redeemed the earth and will in due time, make it to be worthy of him, whose it is — who hath bought it — while in comparison it was a waste and howling wilderness, and will make it a glorious habitation. Now out of these things the breaking down of the resurrecion of Christ and making it the resurrection of various classes in succession, along with the glorifying of the earth — out of these arise the outward circumstances referred to in the verse, that we are begotten 'to an inheritance incorruptible, undefiled, and that fadeth not away, reserved in heaven for you.'

Let us first consider what is expressed by saying of the inheritance that it is incorruptible, etc. Three things are here expressed. The one is that it is not liable to change — it is incorruptible — the other is that it is pure , it is undefiled, and the third is that it is permanent, it fadeth not away. By being not liable to change is meant — not liable to have any mixture of evil produced in it. To say it is incorruptible is equivalent to saying nothing can mar its beauty — nothing can mingle with it to lesson its perfection. The epithet 'undefiled' expresses the pure state in which it is and 'fading not away' expresses its permanence — that there is no end of it; but none of these things expresses what the inheritance itself is. They are fitted to reveal it as having a glory in it, but do not declare what the thing itself is. I shall shortly state to you what is the outward situation of it, and its inward excellence. The former is the condition which those are seen occupying who are partaking in it. The inheritance includes the situation of the person as inhabiting the glorified earth- it includes his situation as a rightful possessor of it. It is not merely that he dwells in it; observe: but that he is the owner of it, the person whose property it is, for it is not merely that we are to see the earth in its beauty, but as our own — as our own property — as that in which we have an inheritance. It further expresses the condition of the person as having this inheritance, for a high purpose, to reign upon it, not simply as an estate But as a kingdom — a possession over which to reign: and last of all it includes the capacity for reigning as well as a kingdom over which to reign, without which it would not be a blessed prospect. Now this is the hope that is here referred to, as the outward description of the inheritance. The prospect before the heir of inheritance is that a time is coming when upon this earth in its glorified state, he shall be a king — when he shall have a *rule,* and when *that rule* he shall be in the capacity to exercise, being himself in the possession of a glorified humanity, being made like the Lord Jesus himself in his present glory.

But this does not yet let you into the blessedness of the inheritance. These are the outward things, but it does not let you into the character of it. My dear hearers, I am anxious to save you from going away with a beautiful picture — with something to fill the imagination, and which may lay open a glory, on which the mind may rest, and in the prospect of which you may delight and which may be the source of joy to any one who can take a lively conception of it.

Spiritual things can only be spiritually discerned. This outward thing possesses its high value, to the true Christian, in the inward state of being connected with these outward things. It is then we shall call him Father in the true unbroken sense of adoption and be as children with the full unclouded brightness of his glory reflected in our character — it is then that we shall have been brought to the full enjoyment of God, and of our place before God, and this is the true joy of the person looking forward — and it is in feeding on this, and not in feeding on the beauties of the thing, that it becomes a present life.

Now, what is the complete hope? It is, that in due time, we shall thus be raised spiritual bodies — we shall thus possess the earth in it glorified state as a possession, and kingdom, and shall reign over it — we shall be full of the mind of God, and have that mind in us so that there shall be no limitation — no break — nothing to mar the harmony and beauty of thoughts and feelings — we shall be just the perfect reflection of the mind of God. As a polished mirror reflects the surface of the sun shining on it, with equal brightness will the moral beauty of God be reflected by the child of God. Now this perfection of beauty — this untainted holiness — this love which is just this very love which is just the very love of God himself, is the prospect possessed by me, this going forth from me — this giving value to all I see about me — this making me to reign in righteousness — this is the true glory that is the prospect of every child of God. It is not the outward pomp or beauty, but this invisible spiritual thing, that is the life of it all and yet it is the truth, that these outward things have in them a beauty and loveliness, a holy beauty and loveliness; because there is no one that can know that God is God, and what is meant in that statement who will not delight in the prospect of seeing the works of God thus perfectly praise him and none can know how every evil thing is a mark of God's curse upon sin, who will not delight in the prospect when every evil will be taken away — and there will be a fitness in all the influences given to us, and in the very constitution of our own spiritual bodies — a perfect fitness to sustain in us, this holy oneness of thought and feeling with God.

Now, it is in respect of this character of our future condition that the inheritance is said to be incorruptible, undefiled and that fadeth not away, Incorruptible is expressive of this, that there shall no more be an evil — those who have passed through death, in the resurrection, have got into a state in which there is no such thing as a fall. In one sense there is no such thing as a fall to Christians now — that is, that they shall not fall away utterly — but there is a falling away in that they are continually coming short of the glory of God. Now it is the feeling of a child of God when dwelling in the light of God. O that this were to continue! Alas! a day or an our may see us in a very different state of feeling from what we are in at this moment. Now it is in respect of the unchangeableness of it that it is said to be incorruptible — they will be as pillars in the temple of God and go no more out. — they shall be a part and so essential a part of the edifice that unless the whole building fall to pieces they are not to be moved, they shall have a permanent unchanging place there, and nothing that hurteth, or defileth, or maketh a lie shall be found in God's holy house. O to think of an incorruptible inheritance on whose beauty no taint can come — whose holiness never can be stained by sin — to think there is prospect of entering into a state where I shall have full fruition of God's being — that in entering upon it, I shall never depart out of it, and that I shall never have to say there, 'O that it were with me as in times past.' There is no such voice there, no such lamentation — no cry that God would again visit us with the light of his countenance for it is an unbroken, unchanging thing, seeing that the inheritance is incorruptible.

'It is undefiled.' This is expressive of its own absolute purity — it is not merely excellence; but a perfection in excellence. The highest state to which any person is brought while in this body of sin and death is short of the meaning to the word undefiled, and even those seasons of closest communion with God which are remembered with greatest delight, and desired back again with most earnest language even these are still not undefiled. There was no perfection in them, there was never upon this earth and in this nature of ours perfection: but in the Lord Jesus. In the members of his body even in their best state, there is an approximation to it; but still it is at a great distance. Now the word is used here as if addressed to their experience — as if has said you would now rejoice if you were continually dwelling in the light of God if it were the fact concerning you that these approaches to God — these near communions with God, which you sometimes experience were enjoyed without an interruption through the whole of your time, thoughts and feelings. Now you have continually to lament because of the corruption that corrupteth you and mars your enjoyment of God but you are to look forward to a time when there shall be no interruption. But ii is not merely that there shall be no interruption — no evil to mar it; and to bring it down from its high place but that the place itself shall not be merely a high place, but, what is a far higher thing, it is an inheritance undefiled and that fadeth not away. Would that we better knew the meaning of the word eternity 'that fadeth not away.' Oh! the comparison of time and eternity which people make is a most frivolous thing, that the pleasures of sin are short, and those of heaven long: but let a person be made to know and to love in the joy of the Lord, then such a person would be continually occupied with the reality of the difference between time and eternity. So long as a person is not in possession of the secret that in the keeping of God's commands there is great reward to press on him the comparative value to time and eternity is merely to work on his selfishness: but in the way of actual personal experience, when a person feels the happiness that there is in serving God; then that person may safely, and in a way healthful to his soul, have his attention occupied with it, and therefore it is that we have our attention so often directed to it. It was the saying of an old servant of God, in a former period of the Church, that if the wicked in hell could but anticipate a time, however distant, when they would cease to be in its burnings it would be some alleviation of their misery. Leave only a ray of hope, and it would so far raise him up: and if the blessed in glory could anticipate a time however distant, when they might cease to be in glory — if they had not the certainty that it would abide, it would mar the joy of heaven and in proportion as the joy is real and intense will it be the case, that the prospect of losing it would be fit to destroy it for the present. It is a blessed thing to know that that which is true joy shall be eternal — that the inheritance is not to go away because it is in itself so worthy of God, that it shall continue.

But I have to explain the word 'reserved in heaven for you.' I wish to connect this with the chapter we read in another portion of the word of God, John 14: 1,2,3,9. This refers to Christ's coming again, and it is then that we receive the place which he has gone to prepare for us. See 2 Corinthians 5. Look back to the 14th verse of the previous chapter and you will see the connection which I mean. 'Knowing that he which raised up the Lord Jesus shall raise us up also by Jesus and shall present us with you.' Now you will observe that it is from the fact that he who raised up Christ would raise them up by Christ that he infers that our light afflictions would last but for a moment and work out for us a 'far more and exceeding and eternal weight of glory while we look not' (verse 18) 'at the things which are seen but at the things which are not seen.' He is evidently not speaking of the things now visible but of the objects of hope. What he is looking forward to, is the future state of things. Therefore at the beginning of the 5th chapter it is said, 'For we know that if our earthly house of this tabernacle be dissolved, we have a building of God, an house not made with hands, eternal in the heavens.' Now this is expressive of something which is kept for us, and yet it is connected with this prospect of our being raised with Christ. Connect this with the expression that he goes to prepare a place for us and will come again and receive us to himself: and connect this also with the expression in the Epistle to the Hebrews, 10:33,34. 'Partly, whilst ye were made a gazing-stock, both by reproaches and afflictions, and partly whilst ye became companions of them that were so used. For ye had compassion of me in my bonds, and took joyfully the spoiling of your goods, knowing in yourselves that ye have in heaven a better and an enduring substance.' Here he is speaking of the prospect which sustains them in their afflictions. If you take these passages in connection with that in our text, that his inheritance is reserved in heaven for you, you will see that we are taught to connect this prospect with something that is now ours in heaven, and yet that in prospect itself is not one which is accomplished at the time of our death, but when Christ returns again. Several passages refer to the same thing, which I cannot now take time to consider, but state the doctrine contained in them all, that Christ has entered into the holy place for us — that all that which is ours in prospect is ours now: because of the presence of Christ in the holy place — that our inheritance is in him, and he is now preparing a place for us — and this is the condition of things that will take place at his coming, when the New Jerusalem shall come down from God out of heaven, and when we who are of this Jerusalem shall be in it as kings and priests to God on this earth. The New Jerusalem, consisting of the body of Christ — the temple of God — consisting of living stones which is by that time completed — this is the house of God not made with hands. All this is expressive of a future thing, to be revealed, which is now secured to us, and prepared for us in heaven. Now there is a mystery in this which requires much spiritual discernment to enter into — the mystery that is in the fact that this society — this New Jerusalem , this living temple — this bride adorned for her husband is the living mass of the Church. All this will be revealed in due time: but in the present state of things this is given to us to know that the present state is one of preparation for the future — that the future prospect is the inheritance — that it has not yet come; because the inheritance is not yet delivered from the bondage of Satan, and because that which we now receive is but a foretaste or earnest until the redemption of the purchased possession, but that Christ is our head in the holy place — that he has entered personally upon it all — that he is now upon the throne of his Father, and we shall enter upon it when he comes, and shall give to us to sit down upon his throne, as he overcome and is now seated on his Father's throne. This is the meaning of this expression, that it is 'reserved in heaven for you.' It is not *heaven*, you observe, but it is this inheritance which is reserved *in heaven* — it is not a thing we are to enter upon the enjoyment of when we die, but that it is reserved in heaven and which is ready to be revealed in the last time.

I cannot now enter more fully into this doctrine of the inheritance being reserved for us in heaven; that is to say the right and title to reign as kings on this earth, and all the other things connected with our so reigning which are now in the person of our Head, and which we shall be endowed with when his kingdom is come; but I go on to consider shortly the description of those who have this prospect. 'They are kept by the power of God unto salvation' They are kept for a purpose, which is 'salvation.' They are kept for this purpose 'through faith' — they are thus kept 'by the power of God.' The expression 'salvation' is used repeatedly in a way that may appear a contradiction. We are said to be saved when we believe, and yet we are said to be waiting for salvation — we are spoken of as saved and yet salvation is spoken of as future, and Christ is said to 'appear the second time without sin *unto salvation.*' Now I wish to explain shortly the meaning of this language and in what sense it is true of the Christian that he has salvation now while it is notwithstanding a future thing. Observe, you must take this view of the condition of man that a mighty conflict is gong on between Christ and Satan — that men are by nature on the side of Satan and that in conversion they come to be on the side of Christ — that the condition of security or safety, in respect of eternity, is in being on the side of Christ and therefore it is that when a person is converted he is indeed a saved person; but in respect of a Christian's progress there is struggle still to be endured. There is enmity still to be subdued and contended against — from these he has to be delivered — this deliverance is a future thing. In this way it is true, that the person who believes is saved because he is absolutely safe. 'My Father who gave them to me is greater than them all and none is able to pluck them out of my Father's hand.' It is true that the man who is a child of God, that his eternal state is now decided and that through eternity he is to occupy the place of a child of God in the universe. Further he is saved even now in respect of his entering on all the rights and privileges of a child of God. They were given to him by God, and he by faith enters upon the possession of them. In the same sense he is now saved — still further he is saved now in respect of receiving an earnest of the inheritance (verse 9) 'receiving the end of your faith, even the salvation of your souls' in which he refers to those of whom he says, 'whom having not seen ye love ....' This rejoicing in God by the Holy Ghost — of present rejoicing in God through Christ he calls 'receiving the end of their faith', and then it was a receiving of salvation, in that it was the actual enjoyment of the earnest of their inheritance. The believer is saved because he has passed from that region which is appointed unto eternal burnings, and has come into that household appointed for eternal glory. He is saved in that he has an earnest of the inheritance, which he is already possessing in the Holy ghost — in that he is now in the Spirit rejoicing in God. through Jesus Christ, and is this living in the foretaste of this inheritance. In all these respects it may be truly said of him that he is saved. And yet there is a sense in which salvation is a future thing to the believer, for while thus absolutely saved, while he has these prospects for the future, he is still dwelling in this body of sin and death where Satan has his dominion and power — he is still exposed to all the assaults of the enemy, and still afflicted and tried by all the trials to which the children of God upon earth are exposed so that they now suffer a very grievous and sore trial — they are in a state from which deliverance is to be desired and longed for — in respect of which it is only the prospect of its not continuing that can make them endure it. Their joy is a joy that springs from the hope of that future state which is to succeed and in their struggles they are carried through by the power of this hope. To say of such a man that he is still to be saved is just to say to him, that there is an end to be put to this his conflict — that there is a conclusion of this his warfare — that these his trials and sorrows will at a future period, which is not far distant, all have passed away; and Christ who is to save him, who is actually to deliver him from that which remaineth, is to accomplish this at the last time, and it is in this sense that we are kept through the power of God unto salvation. It is the deliverance of the members of Christ's body from the possession of the devil, that is the thing unto which we are kept.

Now my dear hearers, I desire to press on your attention here, the nature of this future salvation. It is deliverance from the state of things which the natural heart loveth. It is a prospect which is only a joyful prospect to one who hath been begotten to a living hope and all its attraction depends on the present holiness of the person who cherishes it. It is not to the sense of weariness, the sense of fatigue in the struggle, that the deliverance is held out to us as a joyful prospect. Do not mistake

Appendix 6

me: as if I meant to say that there is any sin in looking forward to a time when all this war and fighting shall come to an end. On the contrary I say it is a thing for which we ought to be thankful, and for which to give God glory — but this is but a very little matter. The great thing in respect of which the Christian groans is his present want of conformity to the mind of God, and it is in respect of this that the prospect is such a blessed prospect. We are happy in it. It is just as if it had been said there are the children of men, and among them some whom God is reserving for some better thing than that which is now going on towards them — some who are, in point of feeling and experience, separated from the common state and condition of others, and kept for a purpose, set apart for a purpose. Now it is this separation — this taking out of the world — it is in respect of this that the work 'kept' is used. We are 'kept by the power of God unto salvation.' It is that they are the Lord's portion, and that the object for keeping them is their salvation.

My dear brethren, it would give you a very awful and solemn view of your condition to see you as *kept*, as thus hedged in and to see the mighty object of God in so keeping you is even salvation. The salvation comes with the reign of righteousness — with the great deliverance; and the thing for which God is keeping you is this salvation. Now the keeping you is the keeping you prepared for this salvation — to keep you for this salvation is to keep you with your lamps burning and your loins girt — it is to keep you unspotted from the world. This is what is accomplished in the keeping: but I would fix your attention on your thus being kept. it fixes your attention on an evil from which you are kept. It shows you enemies. It turns your thoughts to causes which are likely to hinder your salvation. It gives meaning to the words 'to watch and pray.' God is keeping you — God is preserving you from evil in order that when he comes you may be ready to welcome him — that when he comes it may be worthy of him to put honour and glory on you. That is God's keeping of you.

You are kept thus by the *power of God through faith*. The power of God is expressive of the might of the Holy Ghost. Faith is expressive of the state in which the man is thus kept. A man in the exercise of belief — a man in the condition of believing is kept. Faith is therefore expressive of the condition of the man who is kept. Now this teaches you that it is by being in the exercise of faith that you are in safe keeping: or in other words it presses upon you to work the work of faith. The condition of separateness from the world, is the condition of having the faith of the love of God in you — you are taught by these words that you are not kept by something that is outside of you as it were; but that you are kept by a state *in* you — that the keeping of you is through having you in this condition of mind. It is calculated to produce sloth and indifference, to conceive of the keeping, as of a kind of security and safety apart from the man's condition. To conceive of us as kept in such a way is to conceive that we are still kept whether we are believing or not believing. It is not by putting something *around you* that God keeps you from the evil, but by sustaining this faith in you. We are kept by faith. Now this is by the power of God. What is it to have the right apprehension of this? These words have been used not in order that you might say, 'then it is God's business and not mine.' 'Kept by the power' is not intended to express this — but that my continuing in the condition of faith is through my continuing to depend on the strength of the Holy Ghost. It is not that all this is the work of another in such a way as inducing me to leave the responsibility of the faith upon that other. There could only be an evil meaning in this. But the real truth of God on the subject is that inasmuch as it is the power of God that is to keep me I am not to go about to watch, or to pray, or to live in the exercise of faith *in my own strength;* but in continual dependence on the strength of God. It is information given me for my instruction, not for the purpose of making me feel as if I had nothing to do with it; but to teach that this is the strength in which you are to live in faith. You are to live on the continual dependence on the might of God. This is the meaning of these words, 'We are kept by the power of God through faith unto salvation ready to be revealed in the last time.

Its being revealed in the last time, I don't enter on further: but I see its importance so as to warrant me to press upon you that the hopes of the first Christians were directed to this last time. It was not the prospect of death — it was not the prospect of happiness when they died — not the prospect of going to God when they left this life, that was their joyful prospect, or the source of their consolation or strength — but this inheritance reserved in heaven for them — which even they who have departed are looking forward to, and have not yet entered on the enjoyment of. What they have received they don't look on as the rest — the resting point on which their hope builds. But it is the inheritance that is reserved in heaven to be revealed when the last time is come.

Now my dear hearers, I trust that in going over this passage at home, and in taking the different expressions used, that you may be enabled of the Holy Ghost to recall what I have placed before you. I have explained how the life is imparted to us through hope. I have shown you what the origin of this hope is, or how it comes to be that these are future things, that will now make us to enter into the joy of the Lord. I have considered shortly the character of this hope both as to the external circumstances in which the Christian expects to be placed, and as to the internal state in which he will be found. I have considered the character of the inheritance 'incorruptible'. I have shortly explained what is meant by its being reserved — also the present condition of those who have the earnest of the inheritance, that it is the condition of being kept through faith, by the power of God, and I have explained the meaning of saying that salvation is come, and yet is to come. Now my dear friends, I desire to press on you shortly, in conclusion, that there is no other prospect of happiness held out to you but that contained in the word of God, that this inheritance is incorruptible, undefiled, and fadeth not away — that there are no conditions of happiness, through eternity stated but one. In the present day which is a day of grace, it is not the minister of religion alone that can invite you to come, and taste, and be happy — the votaries of sinful pleasure can do the same. Those who are occupied with this world's pursuits who are ambitious of this world's honour, may say, 'Come with us', and will tell you truth in saying that with them there is a certain kind of pleasure to be found. At present it is a comparison of different pleasures. At present I may say, 'You will be happy if you know and love and serve and honour him.' But I say though in the present time God has permitted that there should be many enjoyments, which have arisen necessarily out of this being a day of grace (for not otherwise would it be a day of grace) yet it is not so to be judged of, but that the time is coming when God will indicate his own love of holiness and hatred of sin, by strictly acting on the principle of confining all happiness to the holy — of conferring every state of blessedness on the holy — a time is coming in which God will mark his condemnation of sins, by giving nothing but misery to the wicked. Therefore you are shut up into this, that if you won't be contented with the food eaten in the house of God — the fatness of God's house — there will be no other food for you.

Know ye what he is saying now to you. There will be no pardon for you in the day of judgement. That would then serve no purpose. It is not mercy *then* you need, but (inasmuch as God's judgement will be strictly on the principle of giving to men according as their works are) what you need for salvation *now,* is that blood which purges the conscience from dead works to serve the living God. Were you to know that it is not some outward deed that can fit you for the judgement — that will make the day of judgement a peaceful day to you: but that it is a present sense of forgiveness that alone can put you into that condition, this would show you the vanity there is in every expectation of future mercy. Now this may show you how very far from any understanding of the truth of God these people are who conceive that to think of sharing in God's feeling is altogether extravagant and presumptuous. There is no righteousness but one. There is none good but one, that is God — there is none righteous, absolutely righteous, but God. There is no righteousness in any creature, but that which is in a creature through the Spirit of God in that creature. And it is having the mind of God in us that can alone make us righteous. Therefore as God has declared that he will judge the world in righteousness, and will separate according to the strict rule of righteousness that which will prepare you for judgement must be something that will make you righteous in the present day — something that will give you the mind of God — the heart of God — the feelings of God. I will speak more distinctly to those among you who can understand it, and then to those among you to whom it sounds like strange doctrine.

I would say to those of you who see it — to those who know that God intends, most strictly to adhere to his plan of separating between the good and the evil — and those whose prospect on the day of judgement is that, as Christ was so are we in this world — we being different from it, as he was different from it. I say to those who know that this is their present consolation in respect of the future judgement, I beseech you enter more into the mind of God. It is a *very* great evil, when any thoughts or feeling possess the mind which interferes with the work of God, and I have been perceiving so much of late how little there is of the work of faith of the real acting of faith, even in those who are the children of God, that I press in on you that you realise that God's keeping of you unto salvation is inseparable from your living in the faith of God. The faith by which you are to be kept is not a statement concerning God. It is living in the sight of God, as the present living God, and as such having intercourse with him now; just *present intercourse.* I wish you to see the difference between thinking about God, and having communion with God — between knowing and being able to declare about God, and being delighted to meditate on what you know about God, and having real *intercourse* with God as *the living God*. This is the condition in which you are to be through eternity. This is the condition of seeing his face — this is the perfection — the *seeing* him continually in the *sight* of it. The present life of the Christian is just through the discerning now, as a present living thing, the forgiveness that is in God. This is that faith that keeps you, and I beseech you know that you are not to be ashamed before Christ when he shall appear — and that it is only the person who is looking to him by faith, and seeing him in faith, who will welcome him when he appears. Now there are many whose ideas of a future judgement are confused and indistinct — who think it will be a dealing with people upon some mixed principle; partly merciful, and partly punishing — who say that they trust to the merits of Christ and do the best they can to please God — that they will be dealt with according to the condition in which they are then found. No man could be satisfied with his own present condition who did not know *certainly* that he was on the same side with God in this great controversy if he knew that God will divide men according as they are or are not upon his side. It is the artifice of Satan to get the whole subject into a mist so that people do not see what is before them — do not see what they are doing. But the kingdom of light is sustained in a different way. God will judge the world in righteousness. It is the seeing distinctly that when God raised all, he does by this do nothing more than prove that Christ died for all, and that all are responsible for that gift — but that when he does raise them he will deal with them as they have dealt with him. Now just think what an awful thing it is to think of the character of God's inheritance, which is incorruptible, etc. — of that state of things, of which it is said that all shall be like Christ Jesus, and to suppose that the great mass of people — that people who are ordinarily professing Christians are real Christians. What is the bent of your thoughts? What is the point on which your thoughts are directed — the things which move your fears or anxiety? What makes you rejoice? I ask you to consider these things, and consider whether you can say these are things which made Jesus rejoice or weep. If your joys be not those which are his — if your sorrows be not those which are his sorrows, how can you be said to suffer with him, and to be prepared to reign with him or to have the same mind with Christ so as to be acknowledged to be the sons of God by a resurrection from the dead? If the Spirit of him who raised up Jesus dwell in you then he shall quicken you: and just as the resurrection of Christ himself was the token of his holiness and the manifestation that he was the Son of God, so is the resurrection of every member of the body of Christ. The distinguishing resurrection which belongs only to the character of the sons of God — in like manner such a token that Christians are partakers of the divine nature. Consider what was one of the great reasons why Christ placed himself in your very circumstances. Was it not that you might see what you ought to be — was in not to set you an example that you should follow his steps? I ask you this. There is too much separation between Christ and us — there is too much of a feeling as if the present world required a certain degree of violation of the will of God, and as if our present condition rendered it impossible to do the will of God. What have you been learning from Christ when he dwelt in this body of sin and death? Did not he need food and clothing? Did not he endure cold and hunger? Did not he, when a helpless infant, depend on the care of parents to rear him, and the kindness of friends? Was he not in every respect like his brethren? Did he ever use the almighty power of God to save himself from any one thing to which he was subjected? Never! Never! Why then did he thus become altogether a son of man, and throw himself altogether into the condition in which you are placed but just to show you that the necessity of providing food and clothing, is no apology for ceasing to give God glory? Let none say that because he has a family to provide for, it is some excuse for his not being constantly filled with the glory of God. There is nothing in the condition of man to prevent it, for in the very circumstances in which you are called upon to glorify God, in these did Jesus Christ glorify God. It is an awful thing to think how Christ is kept at a distance from us — how instead of having fellowship with him, we are just dwelling in cold and indistinct notions of him, as having done *something* for us — and that is all. This is never the meaning of God. This is what Satan has done. While God has taken our nature, people have adopted false notions of Christ's dignity, and false notions of the work of Christ which have assisted them in putting all the light that in contained in the work of Christ so far them that in point of fact men's ordinary views of Christ leave them as ignorant of what is to glorify God in this body of sin and death, as if they had never heard of Christ at all. But understand that the resurrection of Christ from the dead by the Spirit of holiness to the glory of God the Father, is what is to work in you. Now the power of Christ the risen Saviour is in seeing what he has done and what he is doing, that discovery of God which put you in a condition to reject the devises of the evil one and he has the strength for you to walk in this light: because he has the Spirit for you. Therefore do not say this is too much to expect from human nature — from flesh and blood such as we are, though this may be hereafter. Don't be cheated with such words, for we expect nothing from human nature, but sin — absolute sin: but what we expect is that you should *in the might of Christ*, glorify God on this earth.

I just part with you with this one other thing that the Lord God of Hosts speaks to you by living witnesses by the members of the body of Christ — by those who can tell that they have found life, and that which was said is life to them, and that this aggravates your condemnation if you reject. O! it is very extraordinary that if two shall come and speak to you and set forth a doctrine, one will say, 'this doctrine I have found a new life to me', and the other shall say, 'I cannot venture to say certainly I am a child of God' — that you will prefer the word of the latter to that of the former — that you will prefer the word of the latter to the word which comes accompanied with professed experience of its power. There is nothing that is more a condemning thing than this. It is utterly unreasonable, for the reasonable thing were surely to feel that the person who could not tell you that he had found life was not in a condition to speak to you and that the person who said that he had found life for himself in Christ was the person whom you should believe.

I add no more. I beseech you by the mercies of God that you put not lightly from you the words spoken and any to whom the thing may appear mysterious, let him ask the teaching of God remembering who hath said 'if you being evil give good gifts unto your children, how much more will your heavenly Father give good things — even the Holy Ghost, to them that ask him', and this is the work of the Holy Ghost to take the things of Christ and reveal them to you.

Amen.

Appendix 7

Notes of Sermons 3.36

Sermon on Hebrews 10:31 'It is a fearful thing to fall into the hands of the living God'

My dear hearers, it is needful above all things that we have the fear of God, and the reverence of God, as God, as the one living and true God — as he to whom alone power doth appertain, in whose favour there is life, in whose wrath there is death — it is needful that we feel and know assuredly that we have to do with God and with God alone — it is needful that we know that it is not necessary for us to please men: but to please one, even God — that having his approbation, being what he desires to see us, all is well with us — that not having his approbation, being in that condition which he condemneth all is evil with us, and there is no power that can come between us and the putting forth of his vengeance, that none can stay his hand, that none can pluck us out of his power, or come between us and the outpouring of his wrath. It is needful that we feel that not only do we depend upon God; but that God is he who is jealous — that he is a jealous God; and will by no means give his glory to another — that he will not suffer any to prosper who set themselves against him, and that while God is love: yea, infinite love, yet we are taught that he will destroy the wicked — that to them there shall be no peace, and that without holiness none can be saved. It is a fearful thing, therefore, to fall into the hands of the living God. It is a fearful thing to meet him in the manifestation of his wrath. It is a fearful thing that it concerns God's glory that we should be destroyed when we stand thus before God — that it is a thing in which the righteousness of his government is involved that we should be destroyed — then shall we find that it is in the heart of God to destroy — that it is in his heart to pour forth the fierceness of his sore displeasure. O then let us tremble when we think of him who alone is omnipotent, to whom alone power appertaineth — and when we come to listen to a word which he has spoken, O! let us look to him that we may be enabled to feel *whose* word it is, that we may give it all reverence, and bow before it as the word of Almighty God.

There is an awful and soul destroying weakness in our apprehensions of God when we see him, not as the God of judgement — when we dream of him as if all tenderness — mercy — forbearance — and as if he could not find it in his heart to destroy the wicked. My dear friends, let us not be deceived. Our God is love, yet our God hath appointed a day in which he shall judge the world in righteousness, and in which the wicked shall be destroyed from before him and cast into utter darkness, where is weeping and gnashing of teeth. O then let us desire to be enabled of God to feel how terrible a thing it is to fall into the hands of the living God. Most men live in such a mixture of doubt concerning God — partly thinking of him as stern and just, and partly thinking of him as merciful, so that they are kept back from God on the one hand by the fear of his terror, and on the other hand, prevented from feeling the importance of being in the state in which God desires to see them by the apprehension they have of his mercy. They have such notions of God's awful power, and of his opposition to sin, as keeps them far away from him, and yet they have such notions of his tenderness, pity and compassion; as prevents them from feeling that they really are exposed to destruction.

My dear friends, live not in this state of mist and darkness. Understand God truly — understand his terrors — understand what the awful power of God is which will come forth to destroy you — and understand God truly — understand his love — understand his grace for it has appeared. Know God in his indignation against sin, and know him in his love to your souls, that you may, by apprehending God truly, be preserved from this perishing because you neither treat God's love with the trust it deserves, nor the wrath against sin with the fear it should awaken. 'It is a fearful thing to fall into the hands of the living God.' This word, as it meets us here, was spoken to those whom the Holy Ghost was exhorting by the apostle Paul, that they should live according to that which God had made known of himself to them — that they should walk with God in Christ, in newness of life — and while speaking to them as those who had seen the love of God in Christ, he still feels it necessary to remind them of the terrors of the Lord, and how fearful a thing it is to fall into the hands of the living God.

But he says, 'Call to remembrance the former days in which, after ye were illuminated, ye endured a great fight of afflictions; Partly, whilst ye were made a gazingstock both by reproaches and afflictions, and partly, whilst ye became companions to them that were so used.' We find here that in seeking to save them from the sin of departing from the Lord, and refusing to walk with their God, he would have them call to remembrance the former days in which after they were illuminated, they had suffered persecution. Thus we see that their having suffered after they were illuminated — that their having endured afflictions at that time, is a thing which he feels it good to bring to their remembrance, that they may still be steadfast and immovable, always abounding in the work of the Lord: for he says, 'Ye have in heaven a better and an enduring substance.' He is here reminding them of what they had been called to endure after they had been brought to know the Lord — he is reminding them of the spirit in which they had endured it, and of the source of that spirit — he is reminding them that they had suffered being enlightened — that they took joyfully the spoiling of their goods. They did so knowing in themselves that they had in heaven a better and an enduring portion.

We are here taught, first of all, that these persons who had been illuminated were subjected to afflictions — that they had suffered a great fight of afflictions — that these consisted partly in their being made a gazingstock by reproaches and afflictions, and partly in their being made companions of them who were so used. We see from this that that receiving the light of the gospel had brought these men into a condition of being made gazingstocks, of being the objects of reproach, of enduring affliction — that is, of suffering at the hands of men. We see that when they were brought into the light of the truth of God, then they were made objects of reproach to the world which was still in darkness. The world knew them not, because it knew him[1] not and that world that knew not Christ when he came, and saw not that he was God manifest in the flesh — that world that saw no glory to God in him, that saw not the mind of God in him — that same world is incapable of recognising the Spirit of Christ in the converted — in those in whom is the Spirit of Christ, and as it hated Christ, so it hated those in whom was found the mind of Christ and so we find that these persons when they had been enlightened, were in consequence of this change, brought into the condition of suffering reproach and afflictions — of suffering both personally, as individuals, and as being companions of those who were so used. He reminds them of what they had thus suffered, and marks that these sufferings had been the consequence of their having been so enlightened. But he reminds them at the same time, that they had taken

---

[1] 'them' in the text.

joyfully the spoiling of their goods, that they had submitted to it joyfully, with gladness, and with thanksgiving unto God. They were enabled to endure privation and not only so; but to rejoice in the midst of it. Mark this — they had taken joyfully — not patiently merely — but they had taken *joyfully* the spoiling of their goods. They took joyfully the spoiling of their goods knowing in themselves that they had in heaven a better substance.

This is another consequence of their being illuminated to which I entreat your attention. Having been illuminated they became subjects of reproach and affliction — having been illuminated they were enabled to bear these joyfully — having been illuminated they knew in themselves, that they had in heaven a better and an enduring substance. Here, observe first, the *knowledge* — they *knew* — that they had this — they were enabled joyfully to give up that which was torn from them because of the certainty with which they contemplated another portion. Their knowledge that they had another portion was what enabled them to bear joyfully — it was not the vague uncertain hope that they might receive it, but the knowledge that *they had it*. And then they knew it not in the way of taking the opinion of men for it: but each personally knew for himself that in heaven he had a better and an enduring substance

Again, they knew that it was *a better substance*. They made a comparison between that which was taken and that which was secured to them. They saw them opposed to each other. They not only knew that they had another substance but they saw the substance which they were losing to be inferior to the substance which they were securing. I entreat of you to mark this. The spoiling of their goods they took joyfully because they knew in themselves that they had in heaven a *better*, and an enduring substance. They were content to give up that which the world would take away because they knew that they had a better portion in heaven. They knew also that it was *an enduring substance* — not only a better, but an enduring substance — a substance which would last for ever. Thus were they enabled to take joyfully the spoiling of their goods.

Now, the apostle referring them to these things calls on them not to cast away their confidence, which hath great recompense of reward. He declares to them that it is a fearful thing to fall into the hands of the living God and then he says, 'Cast not away *therefore* your confidence which hath great recompense of reward.' He thus teaches that it was on thus keeping their confidence that they would not fall into the hands of the living

God — that they would escape the wrath to come — that they would enjoy great reward: and therefore he calls on them to hold fast this their confidence, and that they may do so he reminds them of what they had already endured, and of the way in which they had been enabled to endure it.

My dear friends, what I seek to be enabled to set forth to you from this passage is the character of the life to which we are called through the Gospel, and the source of strength we have for living that life. We are here taught that these persons were under affliction in consequence of having been illuminated, and that they took them joyfully, and that the secret of their doing so was their knowing that they had in heaven a better and an enduring substance.

Let us now look to that into which the knowledge of which they had been introduced, and see what it was in regard to which they were illuminated, when their being enlightened brought such consequences upon them. It was something that made them a gazingstock — it was something that made them objects of reproach to the world — it was something therefore that put them in opposition to the world — it was something that made them appear fools in the eyes of the world — something that not only made them appear fools in the eyes of the world, but stirred up the enmity of the world against them, for there is this great difference between what men feel when they say in sober earnest, of any that are mad, and what they feel in regard to those whom they account mad because they know not their character, and know not their motives, they being under the guidance of the Spirit of God. We never see what is commonly called madness stirring up enmity: we see it always awakening pity There is no man in his sober senses who will feel enmity to another because that other is mad: and however extravagantly and wildly that other may speak, yet the man who is in his sober senses will feel nothing but pity and compassion for the madman. A person who would take offence at what a madman said would be thought altogether unreasonable. But when men speak of the followers of Jesus as mad, it is not in that spirit in which they treat real madness: but it is with enmity and condemnation. At the very time that they call them mad they blame them as much, in that which displeases them, as if they recognised that they were not mad: but were in the exercise of all their senses, and so were responsible for what they did. I desire you therefore to feel that the thing which is here referred to, is the experience of these people when they were reproached, and made a gazingstock, is

Appendix 7 357

this treatment of the world in calling men mad, and yet not really believing that they are mad but, in the spirit of enmity and hatred, condemning them at the very time that they call them mad. This was what these Christians were made to experience, through being illuminated.

They suffered also the spoiling of their goods: which shows us how those who accounted them foolish followed up their estimate of them by condemning them and treating them as persons who were altogether responsible for what they did, by inflicting suffering upon them and as it were punishing them for their madness. So we find that they had suffered not only reproach but also loss of goods — their worldly substance was taken from them because of the profession they had come to make.

Let us consider what it is which they were in the knowledge of and through the knowledge of which they had been brought into this state. We find the apostle here warning them against an evil expressed in the previous verse (29). 'Of how much sorer punishment suppose ye, shall he be thought worthy, who hath trodden under foot the Son of God, and hath counted the blood of the covenant, wherewith he was sanctified, an unholy thing and hath done despite unto the Spirit of grace', and we find that to which he was urging them, and that which he was desiring they should persevere in, is expressed at the 19th verse: 'Having therefore, brethren, boldness to enter into the holiest by the blood of Jesus, By a new and living way which he hath consecrated for us, through the veil, that is to say his flesh; And *having* an High Priest over the house of God; Let us draw near with a true heart in full assurance of faith, having our hearts sprinkled from an evil conscience and our bodies washed with pure water. Let us hold fast the profession of our faith without wavering (for he is faithful that promised).'

Now my dear friends, I go back to these verses to show you that when the apostle was considering and calling on them to consider the awfulness of falling into the hands of the living God and when urging them to call to mind the former days, had their experience in them and when he calls on them not to cast away this confidence which had great recompense of reward — that he was warning them against the sin of treading under foot the Son of God, counting the blood of the covenant wherewith they were sanctified, an unholy thing and doing despite unto the Spirit of grace. This was the sin against which he was warning them, and he was urging them to this that they 'having boldness to enter into the holiest by the blood of Jesus, by the new and living way which he had consecrated for us through the veil, that is to say his flesh and having an High Priest over the house of God', should 'draw near with a true heart in full assurance of faith', and inasmuch as he is telling them to hold fast we are clearly taught that, that which they had and which he desired they should continually have, is this drawing near to God with a true heart in full assurance of faith, having their hearts sprinkled from an evil conscience, and their bodies washed with pure water, that this is what he desired they should abide in — that this is the state in which he recognises them as being, and that this is that in which he desires them to abide while, on the other hand that which he is fearful of their falling into is that which is expressed in the 29th verse. We are thus taught that when illuminated they were brought into the condition of knowing that they had boldness or liberty to enter into the Holiest by the blood of Jesus — that he was to them a new and living way consecrated for them through the veil of his flesh — that he was to them an High Priest over the house of God, and that in consequence of their knowing this, they were drawing near with a true heart in full assurance of faith, having their hearts sprinkled from an evil conscience and their bodies washed with pure water. This we are taught was the condition into which they were brought in being illuminated. This is the condition their being in, which exposed them to the scoffs, the reproaches and the afflictions that are here referred to, and this is the condition in which they were sustained, this being the knowledge in them that they had in heaven a better, even an enduring substance.

We may see also clearly that inasmuch as their drawing near to God in full assurance of faith, having their hearts sprinkled from an evil conscience and holding fast the profession of their faith — inasmuch as this brought upon them afflictions and scoffings, that they knew the only way by which they could escape these, would be the trampling under foot the Son of God, the counting the blood of the covenant, wherewith they were sanctified, an unholy thing, and the doing despite to the Spirit of grace. And we may also see, that inasmuch as the state in which they held fast their confidence, which had a great recompense of reward was this drawing near to God with a true heart in full assurance of faith, so that state in which they were exposed to fall into the hands of the living God, of that God who had said, 'Vengeance belongeth unto me. I will recompense', was the state of treading under foot the Son of God, counting the blood of the covenant, wherewith we are sanctified, an unholy thing and doing despite to the Spirit of grace. And we are thus taught that there are two states, in one or other of which we must be found, and that if we are in one of these we please God and offend man, and if in the other we may please man but expose ourselves to the wrath of God. These are the two states or conditions — on the one hand, the state of approaching God in that new and living way which has been consecrated by the flesh of Christ, having our hearts sprinkled from an evil conscience, and this is the condition in which we are well-pleasing in the sight of God, and exposed to the enmity of man — the other condition is our treading under foot the Son of God, counting the blood of the covenant, wherewith we are sanctified, an unholy thing, and doing despite to the Spirit of grace — and this is the condition in which we may obtain the favour and esteem of men: but in which we shall certainly be exposed to the vengeance of God.

We are further being taught that the person who is submitted to suffer at men's hands: and who is committing his way to the Lord, will be enabled to submit joyfully and to suffer with thanksgiving and praises on his lips — that the person who makes the choice of that condition in which he is meeting the will of God, and opposing the will of men will certainly be called to suffer and to make sacrifices. but that he will be enabled to rejoice in the midst of the sacrifices he is called to make.

Now my dear friends, I desire to set before you the light that is here spoken of, which we have in the previous part of this chapter, and in the preceding chapter and, after considering which, the apostle proceeds to urge them to the confidence which is well-pleasing in the sight of God. In order that you may see these two conditions truly — that you may feel that you must either be in the one or the other and that you may see how being in the one you are pleasing to God and exposing yourselves to the enmity of man, and in being in the other you are pleasing man and exposing yourselves to the wrath of God. Mark I entreat you, that it was after they were illuminated, after they had received the light of the truth that they endured. I ask you to mark this that you may feel the importance of truth — that you may feel that we are saved by knowledge, 'This is eternal life, to know thee the only true God, and Jesus Christ whom thou hast sent.' Men speak often as if it were not knowledge that made the difference between the saved and the lost. Yea men often say that they know enough if they would but practice what they know. They often speak as if it were not increase of light that was needful for them: but only to act more upon the light which they have. Now my dear friends, I feel it of exceeding great importance that you should know that men perish for lack of knowledge, and that by knowledge men are saved. Those who perish for lack of knowledge have had a knowledge which has left them without excuse if they perish, because it ought to have led them on to know more. And those who thus go down to destruction because of their ignorance still have known that which made their ignorance without excuse. Therefore is it said, 'This is the condemnation that light has come into the world, and men loved the darkness rather than light', in which we are taught that men have contemplated the darkness, and that men have contemplated the light, and here is there, that measure of knowledge possessed which left them without excuse, or not knowing more. But I entreat you to understand that there is a knowledge of God in the knowing of which is life — that there is a light which being in us is life. Now this light is that which these men had received to whom this Epistle is addressed. This light is that to which reference is made when it said, 'after ye were illuminated', and the light is that which is contained in the passage which the apostle concludes by saying, 'Having therefore brethren boldness', etc. He is there gathering a conclusion. He says, '*Therefore* brethren', from what he has been previously setting before them as the light of which we speak.

And what is it? It is the atonement — it is the change that has been made in our condition through the atonement — it is the new situation in which we have been placed through the work of God in Christ. That is the light, for he goes on to speak of the access to God through Christ as the thing which he had been declaring to them. Therefore the light is the truth concerning the work of Christ — the atonement.

I desire now to be enabled to set before you the *atonement and to show you what the atonement is.* In this chapter (the 10th) and in the previous chapter we have references to the Mosaic dispensation, to the service under the laws, to the sacrifices offered in the temple, and these are here employed to instruct us in the atonement. My dear friends, I would say to you before going further that I see ignorance of the atonement to be the great *root* error of men at the present time, and to be the source of many other errors. You are not ignorant that it is a thing which some have held, and do hold and teach, that Christ did not die for all: but that he only died for a certain portion of the human race. This is a widespread error in our land and the root

Appendix 7

of it is not understanding what the atonement is, and those who hold this error, this false doctrine, do not attempt to prove their doctrine so much by any quotation from the word of God: which they profess to find expressing it, as from the view they have of the atonement. They look on the atonement as the suffering of the Son of God for man — as the suffering of that punishment which men would have had to endure throughout eternity if he had not suffered for them, and they look upon it as a substitution of suffering on the part of one being, instead of suffering which was to be endured by other beings, and in this way they come to the conclusion that it cannot be that any should experience the wrath of God for whom Christ has suffered: because they say that this would be inflicting punishment twice for the same sin, which would be injustice. The meaning of all this is, that the atonement is just a provision or saving men from misery, and is intended therefore to deliver those for whom it was made, from being cast into hell by their intended suffering being endured by another. But in all this there is an entire ignorance of the nature and object of atonement. In the 9th and 10th chapters of this Epistle we find that the Holy Ghost by the apostle Paul is connecting together that which took place in the service of the temple, and that which takes place under the Gospel dispensation. We find that he makes the sacrifices of the temple typical of the atonement, of the sacrifice of Christ and that he thus teaches us, through the intention of these sacrifices in that service, what was the object of the sacrifice of Christ. Now what do we find to be the character of that service? We find first of all a temple — a place honoured by the peculiar manifestation of the presence of God. We then find man called to worship towards this temple, and to join there in the service of God, and we find them taught to look on partaking in this service as the great object of desire. We find then certain things producing what is called uncleanness, and so disqualifying *for partaking* in the service, and we find that they were taught to look on the being unclean, and on a condition of not being permitted to participate in the service, as in itself an evil thing and that the evil was that they were disqualified for the service. We find also a provision made for removing this disqualification, for taking away this uncleanness — and that the value of this provision was that it did take away this uncleanness; and this provision was the shedding of blood. We find that those who did not partake in the sprinkling of blood, instead of receiving any benefit from the blood that was shed were stoned to death, because of their despising the ordinance of God. Now these things were all types. But of what were they types? They were the types of that to which we are called. What is our calling? If you look to the 12th chapter of this Epistle you will see what our calling is, and what the things were of which they were typical. Chapter 12:22-24, 'But ye are come unto mount Zion, and unto the city of the living God, the heavenly Jerusalem, and to an innumerable company of angels. To the general assembly and Church of the firstborn, which are written in heaven and to God the Judge of all, and to the spirits of just men made perfect. And to Jesus the Mediator of the new covenant, and to the blood of sprinkling that speaketh better things than that of Abel.' I enter not minutely into this passage, but I call on you to understand that the temple service at Jerusalem, and the assembling of the people there to worship was typical of the worship of the true God to which we are now called, and the high privilege of joining in the temple worship was typical of the high condition of really worshipping God in the spirit and of being united to all those of God's creatures who are giving glory to God, and when God taught the Jews to look upon it as the one desirable thing that they should partake in the worship of the temple he was thereby shadowing forth this truth that we should see it as the one desirable condition that we should be joining in the worship of the living God — that we should be joined to that innumerable company which are singing the high praises of God. Now as the worship was typical of this, and as this was what was taught in teaching them to value the worship of the temple, so the uncleanness which disqualified for the temple worship set forth to us that the great evil of the condition of sin is its disqualifying us for and excluding us from the worship of God. Ceremonial uncleanness under the Old Testament dispensation was a typical thing — it was just a thing which God had appointed as an ordinance: but the uncleanness of sin is a reality. And we are taught by that uncleanness which disqualifies for joining in the service of the temple that the great evil of sin is that it puts us at a distance from God, and keeps us outside of the glorious company in whose hearts are the praises of God the Most High God. And accordingly when we find that the shedding of blood was for the remission of sin, that is, for the taking away of this uncleanness, we are taught that the great object of an atonement was the taking away of our real uncleanness, and the putting us truly into a condition to worship God. Now my dear friends, mark this well. There can be no shadow of doubt that the great benefit which the Jewish people derived from these sacrifices was this, that by these sacrifices they were in a condition, notwithstanding of their uncleanness, to have their uncleanness taken away and to draw near and join in the worship of God. This was the benefit derived from these sacrifices and it is therefore manifest that the great object of the sacrifice of Christ was to put us in a condition to worship God.

Now if men had understood that an atonement or propitiation for sin has for its object to bring men into this blessedness and that this is the end which God had in view, they would have had no difficulty in seeing how this should have been done for those who yet are lost — there would have been no difficulty in conceiving that men should perish ultimately for whom the atonement was made. For in seeing this they would see that to bring men to worship him was the great object of desire to God and that through the precious blood of Christ they have been placed in a condition wherein to worship God — and so dear to the heart of God was this that to bring it about he spared not his own Son: but gave him up to the death for them — and when we see further, that those who despised the provision which God made under the Old dispensation for their joining in the worship of the earthly sanctuary, were stoned to death, we are taught to expect that when God has made provision for men in order that they may worship him and give him glory, God will punish those who despise this provision, and refuse to give glory to God.

Now my dear friends, I have said this to meet, and desiring that it may be used of God to remove, that misconception on the subject of atonement in which I know many of the people are — and I beseech *of you to lay aside all previous impressions and systems, and to come in simplicity of heart, looking to God to enable you truly to understand* this 9th and this 10th chapter of the Epistle to the Hebrews, and see whether they do not manifest that the object of the shedding that blood might have our consciences purged from dead works to serve the living God.

Now this was the light wherewith they had been enlightened — the light that God in his love had, through the atonement, placed them in a condition to give glory to God — the light that God had appointed a time in which he would judge men in righteousness, according to the provision he had thus made for giving him glory and that at that time those who had refused to give God glory would be cast into utter darkness, and those who had given God glory would receive the reward of the inheritance. This being the light they had received we find the apostle urging them to walk in this light, and inasmuch as I know that the declaring unto men that all have their sin put away through the shedding of that blood they all have remission of sin, has been a stumbling block to some, because they have conceived that the remission of sin meant man's deliverance from the wrath to come, I entreat of you to look to the language of the Holy Ghost in this 10th chapter, and to see that all along, from the beginning of it, he is proving that the sacrifice of Christ has put away sin — that the Holy Ghost himself says, 'Their sins and their iniquities will I remember no more', and that there is no more offering for sins, because sins are remitted, which is as much as saying, 'There is no sacrifice for sin because there is no sin now to make atonement for', by which he does not teach the non-existence of sin, as if there were no such thing as sin, but by which he does teach that sin as a thing needing atonement has been finished or put away, that is, that sin as a ground of distrust or fear, in drawing near to God has been taken out of the way — that sin as a thing standing between man and the worshipping of God has been taken away through the blood of Christ and that whereas once the curse of God's law stood between God and man as a sinner, and so shut man out from God, now there is no such thing, but in place of this there is the Lord Jesus Christ who is the way, the truth and the life. I entreat of you to observe that the apostle is just reasoning as if we must feel and know certainly that the one thing needful for us is to be in a condition to worship God — that the one great evil of our state, as sinners, is that by nature we are not in a condition to draw near to God with boldness and therefore that the great thing to be accomplished is to take that which hindered out of the way. In the shedding of the blood of Christ we have that done for us, which God saw to be the great thing we needed. And that this really is what we are here taught is manifest because, having considered the remission, or putting away of sin by the shedding of the blood of Christ, so that really there was no more atonement needed, he says, 'Having therefore boldness (or liberty) to enter into the Holiest by the blood of Jesus.' Here he declares that we have liberty of entering into the Holiest because of this blood — in and through this blood we have this liberty. I entreat of you to see that he does not say, 'We have this liberty because we believe — because we have repented — because we are changed beings.' We have liberty to enter into the Holiest by the blood of Jesus — we have a new and living way, consecrated for us through his flesh — we have an High Priest over the house of God — and this is our condition because of nothing but the work of God in Christ.

Appendix 7

'Therefore let us draw near with a true heart, in full assurance of faith, having our hearts sprinkled from an evil conscience.' I beseech you to see that he does not so speak to them upon any ground that distinguished them from other people, but that he is simply referring to that light which had come to them in the Gospel, that light which he is now again setting forth to them — that light which he is causing to shine upon them through the consideration of the Old Testament dispensation, and that light was that they had liberty to enter into the Holiest by the blood of Jesus — that they had consecrated for them a living way through the flesh of Christ — that they had in Christ an High Priest over the house of God.

But what is it to have liberty to enter into the Holiest? Liberty to enter into the Holiest is liberty to enter into the personal presence of the Holy God — to enter into the heart of the Holy God, and to dwell with him who cannot look upon sin but with abhorrence. Liberty to enter into the Holiest is to be in this condition, that there is nothing to hinder me from entering into the true presence of God — nothing to hinder me from standing in his presence — from having communion with him, from showing myself before him without fear — without distrust — without uncertainty as to how I shall be received. This you see is the forgiveness — this is the remission — this is the pardon of God. And although it is true that I have sinned — although it is true that I have broken God's law; yet no man has a better right[2] to come near to God than I in that right which is given *to me* in the gift of Christ. This is the liberty — a liberty to come near and enter into the Holiest.

My dear friends, entering into the Holiest is not going from one place to another — going into the Holiest is not like going from one room into another: but from one state of mind and feeling concerning God[3] into another. Going into the Holiest is going from a state of darkness and ignorance and distance and distrust and fear into the state of consciously being in communion with God — understanding God — understanding his holiness — dwelling and rejoicing in the light of his holiness. My dear friends, you must understand that our having access into the Holiest by the blood of Jesus is a thing which is one with our being in a condition to have our hearts sprinkled from an evil conscience. I say I do not avail myself of that access into the Holiest which I have by the blood of Christ unless I am in

---

[2] 'right' added to the text
[3] 'God' added to the text.

very truth coming near into real communion with God, and entering into the holiness of God, and having fellowship with God in his holiness and his truth and his righteousness and his love — entering in and dwelling with God. I am not otherwise entering into the Holiest. This is what we have given us in the blood of Christ. We have liberty to enter into the Holiest by the blood of Christ — by a new and living way which he has consecrated for us through his flesh.

My dear friends, this liberty which the apostle gathers from all he had previously said — this liberty is liberty to enter in by a new living way, to enter in by the rent veil of the flesh of Christ into the holiness of God. I enter into it in the Spirit of Christ. *The Spirit of Christ comes to me from the risen Christ — the second Adam — the quickening Spirit — and I am entering into the Holiest by a living way when the Spirit of Christ, coming from the risen man Christ Jesus, is entering into me and when I am thus joined with him and am conscious of the holy presence of God through having the Spirit of him, who is in the holy presence of God, and when I am conscious of fellowship with the holiness of God, through having this Spirit of him who has fellowship in the holiness of God.*

My dear friends, our Lord and Brother is a real Mediator between God and man, and a Mediator is one in whom we can come near to God — he is one in whom God and man can meet together. The mind of God, the holiness of God, all the glory of God, is in Christ, accessible to us because he is dwelling in the presence of the Father, and is receiving continually of the fullness of the Godhead, and through him we have participation of this his Spirit coming into us, and we join and share in it by his Spirit in us.

If I were standing above you and beholding the glorious assembly around the throne, while you were shut out from this vision, if there was a connection between you and me so that I could make you conscious of what I saw, understood and felt; in this way you might through me, be seeing all that is above, though not with your own eyes. Thus it is that through the rent veil of the flesh of Christ we have a way into the Holiest. He is there in the immediate presence of God in unbroken communion with God and his Spirit in us to connect us with this, and thus we are called to sit in heavenly places in Christ Jesus. *Thus it is we have a new and living way which he has consecrated for us through the veil, that is, through his flesh — and he having presented himself through the eternal Spirit, without spot to God, we are now in this condition, that in him we have this continual access to the enjoyment of God, through coming near to and actually living nearest to the living God. For Jesus is a High Priest over the house of God.* The High Priest is in the Holy of Holies and we having the High Priest over the house of God are connected with his presence in the Holy of Holies. In the service of the temple, while the high priest was alone within the veil, the people were without, but in truth *both were engaged in one act of worship, and so it is now: for the members of Jesus all participate in the worship which their great High Priest is rendering to the Father within the veil. There is but one Spirit and the Spirit in which Jesus within the veil is honouring, worshipping, and glorifying the Father* is the same Spirit which is in all the members, so that it is one great work of giving glory to God through the living Head Christ Jesus. It is upon this ground, because these things were so, that the apostle exhorts them to draw near to God with a true heart, in full assurance of faith, having their hearts sprinkled from an evil conscience. Draw near with a single honest heart — with an eye looking one way. The reason why they could be thus honest was because they might look God in the face. It is elsewhere said, 'We all with open face beholding as in a glass the glory of the Lord.' He requires this true heart because, he says, ye have no excuse for double dealing in this matter — ye have no excuse for any want of sincerity — for any want of singleness of purpose. Your God has put away your sin, so ye have no inducement to try to make it less than it is. What makes the heart doubt in this matter of sin? It is our feeling as if it stood between us and God, and so in desiring to please him we have a continual desire to make it less than it is and so cheat ourselves for the sake of peace and not to look on the length and breadth of our guilt. But when we know that our sin is put away, when he who teaches us this, and in the name of God makes this known to us, may well call on us to have true hearts. I say to you now. Have true hearts because your sin is put away. Now deal honestly in the matter, because this great guilt is not imputed. Now look on it as it is seeing it has been atoned for, and is no longer a hindrance to keep you back from God. Therefore says the apostle, 'Draw near with a true heart, in full assurance of faith, that is, in the fullness of faith — in the plenitude of faith — and in saying this he is urging them to come in the fullness of the faith of the thing that is spoken, not giving it a partial reception, but receiving it fully, truly and largely: as if he were to say, 'Give up your hearts to it and let this doctrine of the grace of God be, in you, matter of a full large and plentiful belief. Let it not be a partial thing but let your souls just be filled with this truth.' And why so? Because this is the welcome that the truth should meet with — because this is the way to meet it with undoubting. O it is an awful thing to see that when God's love is proclaimed men are looking about for excuses for doubting it. Men are turning up their Bibles to see if they can find texts that will help them to say that God really does not love them. What a reception is this to give such a truth. God sends forth a word full of love and tenderness, full of grace to perishing sinners, revealing to them that he has placed them in a condition to draw near to him, and rejoice in him, and instead of meeting with a free unconstrained welcome, they look upon it with a suspicious eye, with a slow hesitating look as if it were the most unwelcome news. But the apostle exhorts to draw near in full assurance of faith, to draw near in the full undoubting confidence of these things, 'Having their hearts sprinkled from an evil conscience.' What is an evil conscience and what is it to be sprinkled from it? An evil conscience is a conscience reproaching us before God, a conscience in which we feel that our will is not the same with God's — that we are in a state of opposition to God, according to that word, 'If I regard iniquity in my heart the Lord will not hear me.' The evil conscience is the conscience that is troubled and distrustful in the presence of God. How were they to be delivered from this? They were to have their hearts *sprinkled* from an evil conscience. Through faith in the remission of their sins, through the blood of Christ, they were to be delivered from this evil conscience, through understanding this blood of Christ, and were to be brought to have a real holy trust in God. This does not merely express that there can be no peace towards God: but in being brought to be of one mind with God. O let not Satan teach you to think that that state of personal distrust which many call humility is pleasing to God. Do not let Satan teach you to think that God can be pleased with you without your being in the condition of children towards him. Is not God a Father? And who can have a Father's heart and not desire his children to have confidence in him as a Father? O be not deceived. This, and this alone, is pleasing to God, that we should trust in him with undoubting confidence, that we should have free communion with him, that we should delight in coming very near to him, and that all our intercourse with him should be the intercourse of children with a Father. This is altogether pleasing to God, and it is a 'confidence which has great recompense of reward', and so those who know in themselves that they have in heaven a better substance than what men can take from them — an enduring substance — they have the Spirit of adoption — they

Appendix 7

have in them the proof that there awaits them a better substance which will correspond with their high place of being children of God. This state, while it pleases God, displeases men. The Hebrew converts were exposed to afflictions, just for this reason, that no man in his unenlightened, natural state, has this Spirit of adoption — that every man in this state is desirous to be at peace with his own mind as to his condition: that when any man therefore is changed, and receives the Spirit of adoption, and professes to have confidence in God through Christ and to rejoice in God as his Father through Christ and testifies to others that this his confidence is just because he has access to the Holiest by the blood of Christ, then that man becomes a living proof to every man who has not the same confidence. Every man who sees his neighbour thus feeling is placed in this condition, that either he must confess that he himself is sinning against God in not being in the same state, or that he must keep up the notion in his own mind that his neighbour is under a delusion. And so when men arise who really give God glory and who really rejoice in God through Christ, and are not ashamed to profess certainly that they have the adoption of sons in Christ, and who do not hesitate to tell other men that God has given them the like access, they immediately become a condemnation to all that ignorance of God, to all that distrust of God which is around them in the world and those who see and hear them must either come and join them, or must feel in their presence a continual discomfort, and must take every way to convince themselves that they are not true men. I desire to press on you that there is but one other state of mind — that you must either be in the state here described as having great recompense of reward, or you must be 'treading under foot the Son of God, counting the blood of the covenant an unholy thing and doing despite unto the Spirit of grace.' Know that this is just the other state. It is the state of every man who is despising that which God has given him, that he might draw near to God with full assurance of faith. He is not so drawing near to God, he does not know the fullness of faith, he is ignorant of that which is here required. And how is he ignorant? By despising that gift of God which is Christ Jesus through which we must go to all. Now this is the other state, and this is the state which pleases men. Men like exceedingly to see any, who have an outward appearance of godliness, doubtful and distrustful. Men are conscious of their own want of confidence towards God and they feel delight when they can say, 'There is a good man and he has not that assurance.' They are pleased when they see each other thus treading under foot the Son of God, denying that it is a sanctifying thing. This is what men like to hear. They have no objections to hear what any may say about a freeness or fullness in Christ — about an offer to all — about the reality of giving to Christ's blood the glory that belongs to it and saying that in it we have access to God, which we truly have. This men like to hear and if he who thus speaks calls it presumption to have this undoubting confidence in God, then while he is thus treading under foot the Son of God, men will be pleased with his word because they soothe them and repress their rising convictions. And men do despite to the Spirit of grace when they speak of the Spirit in a way that is an excuse for their not walking with God — when instead of knowing that the Holy Spirit has come near to us all, and seeketh to make us all strong for God, and for holiness. Men say we can do nothing without the Spirit, not in the way of saying, 'We can do everything *with* the Spirit', but excusing themselves for doing nothing. What is this but doing despite to the Spirit? Is not this denying the Spirit's willingness to be strong in them? Is not this denying the Spirit's willingness to enable me to walk with God? Is not this denying that he is the Holy Spirit? Is not this doing despite to the Spirit of grace and this men like? Men like to hear others speak of the Spirit which God has given us in Christ in a way which puts holiness far from them instead of seeing that he brings holiness near to them, and leaves them without excuse if they do not walk with God in newness of life. And men are pleased when we do despite to the Spirit of grace: but if men are pleased God is not so. What will God say when he sees all this provision, which he has made for our being holy, cast away as a useless thing? What is it for God to see us, to whom he has given all things pertaining to life and godliness living as if he had not given us Christ? O if those who 'despised Moses' law died without mercy under two or three witnesses, of how much sorer punishment suppose ye shall he be thought worthy who hath trodden under foot the Son of God, and hath counted the blood of the covenant, wherewith he was sanctified, an unholy thing, and hath done despite unto the Spirit of grace? For we know him that hath said, Vengeance belongeth unto me. I will recompense, saith the Lord. And again, The Lord shall judge his people. It is a fearful to fall into the hands of the living God.'

God bless his word.

Amen.

Appendix 8

Notes of Sermons 3.34

Sermon on Hebrews 2 'Therefore we ought...'

The first thing in this chapter to which I draw your attention is the inference which the apostle makes from the character of the Gospel in the 2nd and 3rd verses: 'For if the word spoken by angels was stedfast and every transgression and disobedience received a just recompence of reward: how shall we escape if we neglect so great salvation; which at first began to be spoken by the Lord and was confirmed unto us by them that heard him?' in which you see clearly that the apostle, instead of inferring from the greatness of the salvation that was in Christ Jesus, that those for whom this Saviour had been provided were saved because of the gift of God to them, rather gathers and would have us to understand, that just in proportion to the greatness of that salvation is the greatness of the condemnation to which we are exposed if we come short of the grace of God. Instead of contrasting the law and the Gospel, as men are often contrasting them, as if the Gospel were something which, instead of regarding man as under responsibility as the law does, takes him out of the condition of responsibility in the judgement of God, you see that the apostle regards the law given by Moses and the grace and truth which came by Jesus Christ, as in this respect just alike, and to be viewed as talents received from God with the difference that the latter is a far greater talent than the former. But they are on the same footing in this respect that God holds every person responsible for every gift that he has bestowed upon them. And therefore if the gift of God bestowed upon them was stedfast, that is, if it had the stability of God's word — if it had the stability of God's counsel — if it was a thing which God himself sanctioned with the awful sanction of his judgements — 'if the word spoken by angels was stedfast, and every transgression and disobedience' of that word 'received a just recompence or reward: how shall we escape if we neglect so great salvation?' How shall we escape to whom God has spoken by his Son from heaven — how shall we escape who have come into this world in the day of God's fullest dispensation — the day of God's largest discovery of his grace?

How shall we escape if such mighty means have been contrived of God for our deliverance, and if, after they have been provided we are, through our own fault, not delivered? How shall we escape if we neglect so great salvation — that is, if by our neglect the thing come to nought — how shall we escape so great salvation, the greatness of which is contained in this, that it was at first spoken by the Lord himself when he was upon this earth — that it was at first spoken by the Son of God when he was dwelling in our flesh — and was afterwards confirmed to those who did not hear it from his own lips, by those who actually had so heard it — was afterwards confirmed by those that heard him, to whom God gave witness by signs and wonders, by diverse miracles and gifts of the Holy Ghost, according to his own will? Carry with you from these verses this fact that instead of your being delivered from your responsibility to God, by the fact that Christ died and rose again and has given you all things pertaining to life and godliness, you are in truth only under responsibility for a greater gift and liable to a greater condemnation, if the gift of God has been bestowed upon you in vain.

The next subject embraced in this chapter is the place of men. 'For unto the angels hath he not put in subjection the world to come whereof we speak. But one in a certain place testifies saying, What is man that thou art mindful of him? or the son of man, that thou visitest him?' Now the world to come, as the words are used by the apostle, always means, not the world that now is in another place, but the world that is not yet. It is common for people to think that this refers to the spiritual world, the invisible world — the world in which Christ now is — the world in which we believe the spirits of just men made perfect to be — that is not a world to come — that is, a world already existing as truly as *this* world exists — but there is a world which is to come — a world which literally and truly is *to come* — a world that is not yet — a world that is coming. And what is that world? Not the spiritual state of things which is not, but that state of things which shall be after the present dispensation has come to a close, and after Christ has come to reign on the earth — the dispensation of judgement, the reign of righteousness — that is the world *to come.*

Now the apostle here says that the world to come, that glorious world which is about to be revealed, is not put under the angels, but is put under man, those who are to reign as kings and priests with Christ. It is of the greatness of the salvation that the apostle is speaking. And if you see that this greatness consists, not merely in the greatness of the evil from which you are delivered, but in the glory and excellency of the good things to which you are entitled if you partake of it, then you will see how the place of kings and priests being given, not to angels but to us, magnifies the salvation. He is showing how great a gift God has freely bestowed upon us and how great a gift therefore we cast from us if we receive it not as God bestows it. We, says he, speak of a world to come. Now this world to come which we hold forth to your hope — this world to come, concerning which we say that those who believe shall be there kings and priests — this world to come, the glory of which we hold forth to you that your hearts may be filled, and that you may overcome — that you may obtain a victory over the present evil world, is not put under the subjection of angels. And why does he state this? In order to make us feel that it is put under subjection to us.

But one in a certain place testified saying, 'What is man?' Now he is going to state how God deals with man — and he goes to the Psalm in which this question is put, 'What is man that thou are mindful of him, or the son of man that thou visitest him? Thou madest him a little' — that is, for a little while, according to the translation in the margin — 'Thou madest him a little while lower than the angels: thou crownest him with glory and honour, and didst set him over the works of thy hands.' Here are two conditions of man spoken of. It is asked, 'What is the son of man that thou visitest him?' And then the character of God's mindfulness — the manner of God's visiting is expressed in his making him inferior to angels only for a little and afterwards in his crowning him with glory and with honour. It is further said, 'Thou hast put all things in subjection under his feet', that is, thou hast given him the highest place — thou hast given him the place nearest to thyself, and over thy works. 'For in that he put all in subjection under him he left nothing that is not put under him. But now we see not all things put under him. But we see Jesus who, as a man, 'was made a little lower than the angels, for the suffering of death' — we see him now 'crowned with glory and honour, that he by the grace of God should taste death for every man.'

No doubt, says the apostle's reasoning, you do not now see that word fulfilled in regard to man that all things are put in subjection under him: but in the world to come it shall be so. Nay though this dominion is not yet possessed by men for whom it is waiting it is given them already in Christ. He for a little while humbled himself and came into a condition lower than angels, while in the days of his flesh: but he is now crowned with glory and honour, and this is a source of confidence to us because it is true that by the grace of God he tasted death for every man. If he had tasted death only for himself and then received glory and honour it would have had no connection at all with this prospect of mankind. But if he tasted death for every man and if, after having thus taken the burden of all mankind upon himself and tasted the curse, he is exalted and crowned with glory and honour, then we are to see that, he having done this for every man, every man is now in a condition that, except he neglect the great salvation which was first spoken by the Lord and afterwards confirmed by those who heard him, he will in due time have that word fulfilled to him, that for a little time only will he be inferior to the angels, and that ultimately he will be crowned with glory and with honour.

Observe the amount of his teaching. The apostle says, 'Give heed to the things which ye have heard, and let it not slip from your mind; for if that word spoken by God's messengers — if that word was itself a word which God could acknowledge, and the contempt of which God punished, how much more reason have we to expect God's wrath if we neglect that great salvation; the greatness of which was manifested, first, in that it was spoken first by the Lord from heaven; second, in that this word was accompanied by signs and wonders and diverse miracles, and gifts of the Holy Ghost; and third, that the prospect which it holds out to man is that he should be higher than God's other works and should have all things put under his feet, and be crowned with glory and honour. So great is the salvation — and in proportion to the greatness of the thing placed before you for your reception that you may enjoy it and give God glory on account of it, will be the indignation and wrath poured forth on you if you neglect so great salvation. I beseech you to see the connection that is here made between the greatness of the salvation and the prospect of being raised to that high place and the fact that Christ tasted death for every man 'that he by the grace of God should taste death for every man.'

Having thus mentioned the death of Christ, the apostle considers the importance of setting before them the glory of God in the way of conferring the blessing — that is the glory that God has in our receiving life through the death of Christ. My dear friends, those facts which you have been accustomed to hear as facts from your childhood, very often pass before your minds without exciting the least surprise or calling from you the least consideration; just because you are familiar with them, they pass lightly over you as if you had never heard them before; there are many of them such as would fill you with astonishment, and cause you to wonder, and to ask, 'Can these things be true?' Among these facts is this that the Son of God tasted death — that he who was Lord of all became obedient unto death — that he did so being infinite — being righteous — being the Holy One of God — having no sin in himself — that in these circumstances he tasted death. Now the apostle here considers that he cannot expect those whom he addresses to listen with real faith to anything he says, unless the glory of God appears in what he says, and therefore having reminded them that the Son of God had tasted death for every man, he considers that the glory of God was contained in this truth and so expresses it. 'For *it became him* for whom are all things and by whom are all things in bringing many sons unto glory, to make the Captain of their salvation perfect through suffering.' It became him — that is, it was worthy of his character — it was a thing in no respect out of keeping or inconsistent with God's holiness, righteousness or love, that this holy and righteous being should taste of death — it became God to make the Captain of salvation perfect through suffering. There is glory to God in it.

O my dear friends, do not think that you are to consider that there is glory to God in it, because you are told that God did it. This is not enough to give God joy in you. God wishes you to understand it to be to his glory. *He desires to hear from you the voice of an intelligent praise. He desires from you the acknowledgement of hearts that enter into his counsel:* and therefore the apostle does not simply say, 'He of whom are all things had made the Captain of your salvation perfect through suffering.' He does not say, 'You have nothing to do with the character of God, manifested in doing it — it is enough for you that God does it.' He does not so treat those of whom Christ said, 'I call you not servants but friends.' I wish you to understand that Christ would have us to know what our Lord doeth. And so Christ's apostle, Paul, in speaking of the doings of Jehovah thinks it altogether right that he should not merely state what God did, but the glory of God in doing it, and he claims faith for it because it was becoming in God, and altogether worthy of him. And this is the high place to which we are raised, that we are called to sit in judgement, and see God's glory and to see the difference between that which is to his glory — and that which is not — and to give a preference to that in which he is glorified. 'Therefore', said the apostle, *'it became him* for whom are all things, and by whom are all things, in bringing many sons unto glory, to make the Captain of their salvation perfect through suffering.'

Now my dear friends, what I wish you further to observe here is, that the apostle not only states the fact that it was worthy of God, as a reason why they should with confidence rest upon it, but he tells the object which God had in view. We must see God's motives in order to give God glory. The motive here was the bringing sons and daughters to glory. It was not that God was to have pleasure, and enjoyment in the agony of his own Son. It was not that the holy and loving Father could have pleasure and enjoyment in a certain quantity of suffering to be endured by the Son of his love: but it was the thing dear to his heart to bring sons and daughters to glory, and that in bringing them to glory the greatness of the thing which he contemplated was such as altogether to justify the making 'the Captain of our salvation perfect through suffering.'

It is here said that it became God to make for us a perfect Captain, and to make him perfect through suffering. We are here taught that God did not present us with a Captain of our salvation who was to be by a word of power made perfectly what we needed, but that he made the Captain of our salvation perfect through suffering: and when the Lord Jesus said, 'It is finished', concerning the work which he wrought, he then declared the Captain of salvation is perfected. Thus we find that the Captain of our salvation is not made perfect *by a word of power but* by a *process of suffering*. This is the thing which the apostle feels requires explanation — how it should be by suffering he was to be made perfect. Observe for what he was to be made perfect. He was not to be a mere sufferer, but a deliverer — a Captain — a Head — a Guide — one who is to lead others — one who is to engage in some mighty conflict — as a leader, and fit to succour those who adhered to him and fought under his banners, and to make them also perfect. Why is he so made perfect? 'For both he that sanctifieth, and they who are sanctified are all of one, for which cause he is not ashamed to call them brethren, saying, I will declare thy name unto my brethren, in the midst of the Church will I sing praises unto thee.' Now observe, he is not here speaking of that oneness with Christ which is the effect of our receiving Christ's nature, but of that oneness with Christ *which is the effect of Christ's taking on our nature*. There is a oneness with Christ which is common to all men: because Christ has taken human nature, but there is a oneness which is peculiar to the people of God because they have received Christ's nature. Here he refers to that oneness which comes through his having taken our human nature. 'It became him for whom are all things, and by whom are all things, in bringing many sons unto glory to make the Captain of their salvation perfect through suffering.' Then he connects the sufferings with the oneness, 'For both he that sanctifieth and they who are sanctified are all of one.' But he who sanctifieth, that is, he who ministers the Spirit to us for our sanctification and we who are sanctified, that is, we who receive the Spirit are all of one mass — have all one substance — have all one nature.

'For which cause he is not ashamed to call them brethren.' Because he has come into our nature — because he has come to place himself on the level of humanity, and to look upon himself as one of us — and to make common cause with us, therefore he is not ashamed to call us brethren, saying, 'I will declare thy name unto my brethren, in the midst of the Church will I sing praise unto thee' — saying, 'I thy child will declare thy name unto them — my kindred according to the flesh — I will teach them their Father's name and character. I have declared thy name and will declare it.' This is clearly connected with a most important truth that God is our Father — that God as our Creator is our Father. And therefore the prodigal son, while in the far country, remembered his father's house and his home in the father's house — and before he went away he had received a portion of goods as a son — and in squandering the portion that belonged to him, he squandered a son's portion. This shows us that in squandering the gifts of God as our Creator we are squandering gifts given to children. And therefore when we come to think of God and to know God in Christ and to know that, when God comes forth to meet us returning prodigals it is not then that a Father's heart is excited in God towards us: but that from the first moment of our existence the heart of God towards us has been the heart of a Father and his gifts to us, the gifts of a Father's love, and therefore the work of God in Christ was not to make God a kind or loving Father: but to reveal to us a Father's heart and to recall us to the bosom of a Father's love. I am exceedingly anxious to break down the false idea that the word 'brother', when we are told to love the brethren and to lay down our lives for the brethren, means believers or Christians, or those who are only our brethren according to the Spirit. It means our brethren, the children of men — it means that we are to call every man our neighbour and our brother, in that Christ connected himself with all mankind by the ties of brotherhood when he became a man.

'I will declare thy name unto my brethren, in the midst of the Church will I sing praise unto thee: and again I will put my trust in him. And again, Behold I and the children which God hath given me.' Here we are carried forward to the result of his declaring God's name. Those who believe this name of God so declared are given to him for children — born again — not of flesh and blood: but of the Spirit of God — quickened by the second Adam.

'Forasmuch then as the children are partakers of flesh and blood, he also humbled himself likewise and took part in the same, that through death he might destroy him that had the power of death, that is, the devil. And deliver them who through fear of death were all their lifetime subject to bondage.'

In this passage the apostle begins to explain the *necessity that there was for Christ,* taking our nature and becoming bone of our bone — flesh of our flesh — yea, our very brother. 'Forasmuch then as the children are partakers of flesh and blood, he also himself likewise took part of the same flesh and blood' — he took what they had. Those who were in this condition, and to whom he was to declare his Father's name and to reconcile us to God — they were in their condition of being partakers of flesh and blood and therefore he took part of the same. He became *their very brother:* not *in name but in reality,* that is, just as they had it, he took it, otherwise the thing could not possibly serve the purpose. His flesh was not different from theirs, but it was theirs. And therefore it is said that *he was made in the likeness of sinful flesh — in the likeness of flesh as it is in us sinners.* 'Forasmuch then as the children are partakers of flesh and blood he also himself likewise took part of the same' — placed himself literally in their condition in respect of flesh and blood. Why? 'That through death he might destroy him that had the power of death, that is, the devil. And deliver them who through fear of death were all their lifetime subject to bondage.'

You will observe that there are two objects proposed: first, that through death he might destroy death and the devil. Flesh and blood were under the sentence of death, and Christ, to come within the reach of death, took flesh and blood — he took flesh and blood that he might come in contact with death, and might through death destroy the devil.

My dear friends, have you ever considered that word, that the devil has the power of death — have you ever considered that word that death is in the hands of the devil and that death came by sin, so death was in the hands of the devil? I ask you to consider the fact. I ask you merely to see that while death comes ultimately from God, as all things ultimately do, it comes through the devil — that sickness, disease and all the manifestations of death are a part of the power of death which is in the hands of the devil, and that as he has received the power, so has all the manifestation of death in its original appointment been through him. In itself and apart from the work of Christ, while it is the sentence of God that awards death to man, it is through the devil that it comes. The devil had the power of death. Let no man draw back from these plain words. Christ found death under the power of the devil and came into our nature and so came in contact with the devil (as it were) who had this power, that he might destroy this power of the devil and might wrest the power of death out of the devil's hands. Christ actually did so, for he declares in the vision which John had of him in the Isle of Patmos, that he had the keys of death and hell. How had he the keys? They belonged to the devil originally. Christ had them because he destroyed him that had the power of death, that is, the devil.

We are to understand from this that while the devil had the power of death according to the law of God, when man sinned, still, in respect of the work of Christ, he has never been permitted to exercise it, but at Christ's discretion. Christ overcame him; and now though he does exercise the power, yet it is by permission — it is not as one who does it necessarily and of right but as one who does it according to a licence received from Christ.

But Christ came to destroy him that had the power of death, that is, the devil. Now the destruction of the devil in this consists in taking from him the power *of death*. The death of Christ was the great instrument by which he received power to execute this judgement, and do this great thing. *Through death* he destroyed him that had the power of death. To understand this you must know how the devil came to have the power of death. It was in consequence of the unchangeableness of God's law and the fixedness of God's dispensation in creating man, and putting him under a law of life.

The devil had the power of death in this that he could *ever plead the unchangeableness of God against man. He was the accuser of the brethren.* He had power in such a way as a man has power who knows that I am obnoxious to a law, and that that law must be put in force, and that if the judge were disposed to allow me to escape punishment, he could plead that in that case the law would be violated. Now God never changes the word which proceeds from his mouth. How then was this evil of our condition to be remedied? It was to be remedied in this way — that one should come into the nature in which we were, and which was under the power of death, and in that nature should give glory to God — in that nature should be holy and righteous — in that nature should be worthy and that he should as the righteous One receive life. And so he justified God in the curse which he had pronounced upon sin and declared the name and character of the Father in that work which he did on earth; and then it was a righteous thing that this righteousness of Christ — this obedience of the second Adam, should have power to prevail over the disobedience of the first Adam, and that the grace of God should reign through righteousness unto eternal life. And thus Christ by the power of that sacrifice of his own blood which he offered to God broke the power of the devil and established for ever a reason why men should now be taken from under his power and placed under the power of Christ and why the keys of death and hell should be entrusted to the righteous Lord. Thus then, Christ destroyed him that had the power of death, that is, the devil, and he did so through death.

I cannot now detain you during the time that would be needful to illustrate this fully: but at your leisure meditate on the fact that Christ overcame through death. Why not in some other way? Why did he not come and fulfil the law, and without tasting of death, destroy him that had the power of death, that is, the devil? O it was that God would have his character fully manifested, and his law fully executed, and in it Christ did manifest God's character and vindicate the righteousness of the curse pronounced upon sin, and therefore he could receive the keys of death and hell. I do not enter further on this at present, but I ask your own prayerful meditation upon this passage It was written for your profit and it is not so written unless you may understand it. Be not carried away with the delusion of thinking that it is a humility or deference to God that you should read such passages, and pass lightly over them, and not understand what they mean: but know that they are written for your instruction: and that you are not instructed by them so long as you do not understand: and you are to understand them by looking to God for his Spirit to enable you to comprehend them.

'That he might destroy him that had the power of death, that is, the devil and deliver them who, through fear of death, were all their lifetime subject to bondage.' Now who were these? Who were the people who through fear of death were all their lifetime subject to bondage? They were just the children of men.

It was not some men but all men were subject to this bondage. The object of Christ then was to deliver those who were subject to this bondage, that is, the human race. And I wish you to mark well what we meet in every part of the word, the recognition of the fact that *literally Christ tasted death for every man*. I ask who are they are that are subject to this bondage? Every one might answer, the children of men. Christ died, for this is the description of those for whose deliverance he came. They were, through fear of death, all their lifetime subject to bondage.

Now my dear friends, the bondage to which we have been all our lifetime subject is a very varied bondage: but there is obviously one thing in it, which we always meet in it wherever we look, and it is that death is a cause of fear and terror and is felt to be an evil. I believe we have been very much in error in looking on the fear of death just as the fear of hell and of future misery. I believe that the great object of fearful anticipation is a thing that is full of wrath and evil — not the death that is the effect of the fall: but the second death that comes through rejecting the Gospel of Christ. But whatever the thing is — whatever is the extent or power of the terror that is connected with our being appointed to death, from that we are intended to be delivered in consequence of Christ's having overcome the devil, and wrested the power of death out of his hands.

Mark here how very reasonable a thing it is for me, for every minister of Christ, to call upon you to be delivered from the fear of death. Mark how reasonable it is for me to call on every man to be no longer in that bondage. Mark how reasonable it is for me to say to every man, 'Are you now prepared to die? Could you at this moment welcome death?' For here it is declared that Christ came to deliver men from the bondage under which they were through the fear of death, by overcoming him that had the power of death, that is, the devil, by causing men to know that death was now in the hands of Jesus Christ — that death was now in the hands of their Saviour — in the hands of him who so loved them as to give himself to die for them, and therefore they are now entering into his wishes, consigning themselves to be delivered from the fear of death. I as a messenger of Christ maintain that it is reasonable to make this one test of having become one of the followers of this Captain of salvation, that a man should be ready at every moment to welcome death — that a man should be ready for death, as coming from the hands of his Redeemer.

'For he took not on him the nature of angels, but he took on him the seed of Abraham. Wherefore in all things it behoved him to be made like unto his brethren, that he might be a merciful and faithful High Priest in things pertaining to God, to make reconciliation for the sins of the people. For in that he himself hath suffered, being tempted, he is able to succour them that are tempted.'

My dear friends, it arises very much from our erroneous views of salvation that we do not feel at once the necessity that is here expressed. The apostle says, *'It behoved him in all things to be made like unto his brethren,* that he might be a merciful and faithful High Priest in things pertaining to God, *to make reconciliation* for the sins of the people.' It behoved him to be our brother that he might make reconciliation for our sins, and might be a merciful and faithful High Priest in things pertaining to God. Two things are contemplated in Christ's work of reconciling sinners to God: *first, the work of Christ in his own person, when he dwelt in the flesh, and the work of Christ now, as our High Priest entered within the veil.* In both these it behoved him to be made like unto his brethren. It behoved him to be made like unto his brethren in this respect because if he had not been my brother, that is, dwelt in my flesh, and been in the very nature in which I am, he could not have done that which he has done — he could not[1] have glorified God in that very nature in which God has been dishonoured. *It is not the mere excellence of Christ's obedience that makes Christ's obedience a ground of remission for us — but that Christ in our very nature — in that very world in which we are surrounded by those very temptations through which we have sinned against God — in these very circumstances did glorufy God.* But there is more than this in it. The Captain of our salvation was made perfect through suffering: because *by being in our very nature he was not only in a condition which had been unholy: but to shed tears and taste of sorrows which God could see with satisfaction.* What are the sorrows over which God can rejoice? The sorrows of holiness in a world of sin — the groans and sighs of the righteous One in the midst of the disobedience of the Father's law. God who condemns all disobedience has no pleasure in any sorrow that is a carnal sorrow: but he has pleasure when he sees a creature affected by that which is evil in his state, and made to grieve over it.

O let us not think it a light matter whether we are or are not grieved because of the sins without us as well as those within us. Let us not fancy that we are just to do our duty. That was not the manner of Christ. He did not come into the world and tell

---

[1] 'not' added to text.

his message and then left it: but with all the tenderness of God in his heart, and that a human heart, he was ever affected with the spectacle of sin, according to the tenderness and holiness of his feeling — and this was a thing acceptable to God. Thus in giving himself up to be grieved and agonised by the sins of man, he was offering acceptable service — not that God has pleasure in sighs and groans and tears as such: but that God had pleasure over those sighs and tears which were awakened by the contemplation of sin, and that the blood shed, and the life wasted and worn out, and this groaning over this sinful world were all to the glory of God. O beware of hard-heartedness in a world where every good man must be broken-hearted — continually meeting with spectacles that will move him to tears — but be like that Man of sorrows who sorrowed as a pattern, and as an example, as well as a High Priest, and who has, in this, set before us that to which we are to be conformed. *It behoved him then to be our brother — to have the sympathies of humanity that he might present to God such sorrows, such tears, such grief and pain, as were altogether to the praise and glory of God.*

But my dear friends, it was not merely to weep over us that Christ needed to have our nature — but it was needful that he should taste the curse. He tasted the curse of God — he tasted of the evil of this condition into which we had come through sin, and all this power of the flesh to make him cry out, 'My God, my God, why hast thou forsaken me?' This is a deep part of our Lord's experience: but one which we should seek to enter into. We should seek to understand what a testimony is here borne to the powerlessness of the flesh, and that there Christ is showing forth what the flesh is in itself. It behoved him to be made like unto his brethren in order that he might die — in order that he might experience the curse of God through sin.

These are some of the particulars of our Lord's oneness of nature with us, as connected with his being a sacrifice for our sins. But he presented himself a sacrifice, and having done so he was ever a High Priest — he was a merciful and faithful High Priest for us in things pertaining to God. Why should a High Priest be merciful and faithful? Why should he who stands between us and God be merciful and faithful? Because the real character of *Christ's mediation and intercession* is that he is one with us, and feels with us — and it is our groans in him that the Father hears and it is through him that we receive the supplies of God's grace. A High Priest must be merciful in order that he be one who will come with our cries for mercy, and *in presenting them to the Father will himself ask the thing*. The intercession of

Christ is not a form. It is not like a man putting his name to a paper to give it authority, without thinking of what he is doing. *This intercession is in his presenting, in his holy and glorified human nature the very same petitions which we present on earth* – his having it in his heart, not as a thought: but as a sentiment and as a feeling, *so that my prayer in the Spirit is Christ's own personal prayer. When I beseech God to give, Christ beseeches God to give. He is desirous to get the thing.*

O my dear friends, observe that you have not a friend in Christ who gives merely because he has promised, and who says, 'If you come to me when you want a thing I will go and intercede with the King.' *But Christ's heart beats responsive to our heart – his feelings beat responsive to ours, and in presenting our requests he is presenting his own.* This is the reason why it behoved him *to be a merciful High Priest.*

Observe the commencement of the following chapter. 'Wherefore holy brethren, partakers of the heavenly calling, consider the Apostle and High Priest of our profession, Christ Jesus. Who was faithful to him that appointed him, as also Moses was faithful in all his house.' His faithfulness is that he will honestly and faithfully and truly administer to us the gifts which he receives from the Father for us. This mercy *assures me that he will present my petition,* not coldly, and indifferently: but with all the longings of the heart of the Son of God, whose longings the Father ever attends to, and his faithfulness assures me that that gift of power, that gift of every good thing which he received from the Father, he will dispense to me truly and faithfully. We are unfaithful in that we do not trust him, but he is faithful in that every expectation that is ever cherished in his name he makes good, and no man was ever yet disappointed who trusted in the faithfulness of our faithful High Priest.

'To make reconciliation for the sins of the people.' Here view this as connected with his continued acting still. *He is still reconciling men to God. This he does as the channel of our prayers, and as the channel of God's answers – as our merciful High Priest – as thus for ever bringing us nearer and nearer to God.*

Now observe here, 'For in that he himself hath suffered, being tempted, he is able to succour them that are tempted.' O my dear friends, recollect that word of the Lord to the children of Israel. 'Be ye kind to strangers, *for* ye were strangers in the land of Egypt and ye know the heart of a stranger.' Now Christ knows our hearts just as the children of Israel were to know the hearts of strangers: having been strangers in Egypt, they were to know the hearts of strangers. Christ having been a stranger and

Appendix 8

pilgrim on this earth knows the heart of every one who takes up his cross and follows him. He knows our hearts — we who account ourselves strangers with him — we who separate ourselves from the world which lieth under the wicked one — we who look not for our comfort or consolation from things that now are — we have a High Priest who knows all our feelings because he has felt them all. You know, even in regard to human things, if there is a person who is experiencing some sore trial — who has lost some dearly beloved friend — the compassion of his thoughts, and the sharer of his heart that such a person, meeting with another similarly circumstanced, feels that there is a bond of friendship between them and how apt we are to say of the young and inexperienced that they know not and cannot sympathise with our feelings. *But our High Priest knows all for he has been in our very condition.* If we have to contend with the suggestions of the devil, who seeks to lead us captive at his will; then let us remember that the devil tempted Christ, and sought to lead him away, and that he did address to the Son of God all forms of temptations — that if we are encompassed by men who will scoff and laugh at us if we follow after godliness — who will call us fools and madmen if we love the Lord our God, let us remember that we follow Christ who was scoffed at, and laughed at, and made the drunkard's song — who when he passed by was pointed at. Read the Psalms that you may know what Christ experienced, when on earth, and you will see how sorely he felt these things, and find him coming to God his Father with them. You may say he was the Son of God and how could he feel them? Yes! but he was the Son of man and therefore he did feel them. Observe how in the 22nd Psalm, 6th verse, he says, 'I am a worm.' He is coming with his complaints to God: he found no man's heart to sympathise with him. And what are his complaints? Listen to him complaining — hear praying and saying, 'I am a worm and no man, a reproach to the people. All they that see me laugh me to scorn: they shoot out the lips, they shake the head.' This Psalm is proved to be our Lord's, by his using the first verse of it when extended on the cross, 'My God, my God, why hast thou forsaken me?' Also by what is written in the 8th verse, 'He trusted in the Lord that he would deliver him, let him deliver him, seeing he delighted in him', and again in the 16th verse, 'They pierced my hands and my feet.' In this Psalm we see Jesus showing that he had a heart to be affected by the laughing and scorning of wicked men — here he shows that he had a human heart. Therefore if we be so tried of men, we have a High Priest who was by these feelings tempted to please men, and to cease to be faithful to them: but who still told them the truth, and they hated him for it. Again, are we tempted of the flesh? So was Christ. He took all its temptations — its weakness, its wearinesses, he took our bodies, being liable to cold and hunger. As we are so was Christ. He sat on the well-side *weary* when he asked the woman of Samaria to give him water to quench his thirst. And if we would be inclined to sit down in fatigue, and take our rest and forget our Father's work, let us remember that though thus weary, yet he preached to the people, his meat and his drink being to do the will of him that sent him, and often after spending whole days in preaching he passed whole nights in prayer. There is an awful temptation in the flesh to seek our ease and comfort: but we have here no rest. I do not enter further into this at present. Our time does not permit me. God may enable me to do so on a future occasion. But meanwhile, while God says, 'Be ye holy for I am holy', and points your attention to Christ as he in whose strength you are to obey his commands, that that Lord Jesus, to whom your thoughts are directed is one who knows all the difficulties that stand in the way of your being holy, having been exposed to them himself, and having overcome them all and who did so in the strength of the Holy Ghost and therefore he knows your condition and what you need, and will afford you help. May God give you to feel your need of such a High Priest and to prove him, and to see how faithful and how merciful he is.

Amen.

Appendix 9

Notes of Sermons 3.32

Sermon on Titus 2:11-14 (Third Sermon on the text)

My dear friends, I have already illustrated, as God has spoken by me, the truth that the grace of God has appeared and that it has appeared bringing salvation to all men, and that this grace of God teacheth us, 'That denying ungodliness and worldly lusts, we should live soberly and righteously and godly, in this present world.' The portion of the passage I have read which contains the immediate subject on which I desire, in the strength of God, to speak to you at this time, is that which follows, 'Looking for that blessed hope, and the glorious appearing of the great God and our Saviour Jesus Christ.' I said that it was my desire to set before you the grace of God — to set before you what the grace of God teacheth us at the present time — and to set before you what that hope is, into the enjoyment of which we are introduced by the faith of that grace. Now this hope is the 'looking for that blessed hope, and the glorious appearing of the great God and our Saviour Jesus Christ'. I desire that you may distinctly apprehend what the subject is on which I am now to discourse to you. It is this, that the hope set before us in the Gospel, the hope to the cherishing of which we are called by the grace of God, is the hope of the appearing of the great God and our Saviour Jesus Christ — that it is not according to the mind of God that his people should rest their expectation on any nearer event, on any event than the second coming of the Lord — that it is not according to the mind of God that his people should have their attention fixed on the day of their death, and the prospect of happiness when they go hence — that it is not the counsel of God — that their having been led to make their hope rest upon the time of their own death, and not on the coming of the Lord, is an evil thing, not according to God's will, and which Satan has made use of for much injury to the Church of Christ.

My dear friends, I desire that you may distinctly understand that I do not teach you that there is no interest to be felt in the day of our death, and that I do not teach you that there is no blessedness entered on by the saints of God when they die;

unquestionably they do enter upon a blessedness: and they cease from the severe toil and trouble of the present time. But what I teach is this that the Church of Christ is to be divided, as men have divided that Church into the Church Militant and the Church Triumphant, into the Church now struggling on earth, and the Church now rejoicing in glory: but that whether on earth, striving against sin or now giving God glory in heavenly places in Christ Jesus, the Church of Christ is an expectant Church until Christ comes — that the event, upon which the eye of the saints of God, as still in the body is to be fixed, is the coming of the Lord, and that the event upon which the eye of faith, in those who are not in the body, is at this moment fixed, is the coming of the Lord, and that there is no other hope but one hope for the living saints and for the departed saints, even the hope of the reign of righteousness: and that there is but one hope for all saints: that it is not that each has a hope for himself, of the blessedness to be tasted when he dies; but that every saint from the beginning downwards has looked to one point — has cherished one expectation that all who have died in the light of the truth of God in the matter, have died in the hope of the truth of this glory — that all who have lived in the light of the truth of God in the matter are living in the hope of the truth of this glory — and that one thing which God has looked forward to from the beginning, even the reign of righteousness, is set forth to the Church, in all ages, as the object of her faithful, her believing, her expecting, her longing desires.

My dear friends, this is a very wide subject, and is a subject with which, I grieve, to know and feel the great proportion of the people are comparatively unacquainted, and therefore it is not in one discourse that I could possibly expect to set forth fully to you the truth of God in the matter: but I believe I shall now be enabled of the Lord to open up this subject to you, so as that you may go on with the word of God and thereby be introduced into the fullness of the light of the truth regarding it.

The first thing connected with this subject on which I fix your attention is that the Gospel is always called the Gospel of the kingdom, the good news of the kingdom. The good news is always represented as tidings concerning a King, and the Saviour is always spoken of in prophecy, and was expected by the Old Testament saints, and by the New Testament Church at first as a King. The truth and the error that are opposed to each other in this matter are these. The error is looking upon the Gospel as good news concerning the way at which a person may come to be at peace with God and as nothing more than this, and so looking on the Saviour as one whose recommendation to me is that, through him, I may personally have peace with God. Now this is a part of the truth but a very small part, and which has been allowed to occupy men's thoughts to the exclusion of the greater part of the truth. The truth is that I am to look on the Gospel as information concerning a righteous government, concerning a reign of righteousness concerning a state of things which is set forth as a kingdom, bound together by having a King, and in which there are many interested, and this a righteous kingdom and that it is good news to me: because it calls me to share in the hope of this kingdom now and to share in its blessings hereafter. The error looks at Christ as if he were to come between me and the wrath of God: instead of seeing him as a righteous King under whose government I shall have peace: and under whose sceptre I shall serve God without fear in righteousness and holiness. Now I would turn your attention to some of the words of God on this subject and first to that which we read in the first chapter of the Gospel of Luke. I refer to these passages for the purpose of showing that it was a King that was expected, and that it was through the righteous character of his kingdom that a blessing was expected to be enjoyed. I would first refer to the word of the angel to Mary at the 30th verse. 'And behold thou shalt conceive in thy womb and bring forth a Son and shall call his name Jesus. He shall be great and shall be called the Son of the highest and the Lord God shall give unto him the throne of his father David. And he shall reign over the house of Jacob for ever and of his kingdom there shall be no end.'

Now you will observe the whole substance of the Gospel, contained in this word, is that the coming Messiah was to be a King for ever, and to reign over the house of Jacob, and to do so without end. Now in the latter part of this chapter at the 68th verse we find the father of the forerunner of our Lord setting forth the Gospel in these words, 'Blessed be the Lord God of Israel, for he hath visited and redeemed his people. And hath raised up an horn of salvation for us in the house of his servant David, as he spake by the mouth of his holy prophets which hath been since the world began. That we should be saved from our enemies and from the hand of all that hate us. To perform the mercies promised to our fathers and to redeem his holy covenant. The oath which he swore to our father Abraham that he would grant unto us that we, being delivered out of the hand of our enemies, might serve him without fear. In holiness and righteousness before him all the days of our life.'

What I mark here is that the blessing promised here is the being protected by this King, the enjoying peace and security under his sway and the being kept by him in a condition to serve him without fear in righteousness and holiness all the days of our life. I trust you are enabled to see in what this differs from that with which I am contrasting it. The view I am seeking to remove is the apprehension of the Messiah just as one to come between me and the wrath of God and of the blessing to be received through the Messiah just as a security from wrath and enjoyment of happiness, whereas we are here taught that the true apprehension of the Messiah is that of a righteous King to reign over me in righteousness, and to bring me, not from God who is my friend: but from the devil and the devil's servants, who are my enemies and to keep me in a condition to serve God without fear in righteousness and holiness. Now this view of the coming Messiah was in substance what the Jews had, that is, they looked for a King and a kingdom and protection by this King from their enemies, and a state of security and peace and prosperity as a people of God. We know that their views were very carnal. We know that they little understood what it is to be God's enemies, and God's friends, and what it is to enjoy the blessedness of serving God without fear: but we must beware lest in objecting to that which was false in the views of the Jews we reject that which is true and therefore we must carefully consider the mention which is made in the word of God of their expectations, and the kind of reproof they received from Christ and what he said to put them right in that in which they were wrong.

The first thing to which I would call your attention to show you wherein they were wrong and wherein they were right is a passage in the Gospel of John, the 3rd chapter. In the early part of this chapter we have the record of a conversation between our Lord and Nicodemus, a ruler of the Jews, who came to him by night, having seen the miracles he had wrought, and being convinced he must be a teacher sent from God. Now the moment Nicodemus presents himself to Jesus as a disciple, and says, 'Teach me, for thou art a teacher sent from God', the first thing our Lord says is, 'Except a man be born again, he cannot enter into the *kingdom of God.*' He does not tell him that there was a kingdom: he takes this for granted; he knew that Nicodemus was looking for a kingdom, and in this Nicodemus knew more than most professing Christians in this land, for he was expecting a King and a kingdom. But wherein was he in the dark? He did not know that in order to the enjoyment of that kingdom, he himself must be a changed man. He did not know that a man must be born again in order to enter into that kingdom. What I wish you to see is that our Lord did not say to Nicodemus, 'You are wrong in expecting a kingdom.' No, he said, 'You are right in expecting a kingdom, but you are ignorant as to your own unfitness for that kingdom. You must be born again before you can enter into it.' This then was one great error in which they were. They saw not the need which men had to be changed in order to enter into the kingdom.

My dear friends, I trust you see what I am now seeking to prove to you, that inasmuch as Christ did not reprove the Jews for expecting a kingdom, they were right in expecting it — inasmuch as Christ did reprove them for their ignorance concerning the character of his kingdom, they were in that matter wrong and inasmuch as Christ was at pains to show them what the preparation for the kingdom was, he established their expectation of a kingdom, while they were ignorant as to what it was to be prepared for it.

Look to the 9th chapter of Matthew — our Lord entering on his public ministry, 'opened his mouth and taught them saying, 'Blessed are the poor in spirit, for theirs is the kingdom of heaven." Now my dear friends, this is precisely what he said to Nicodemus. He said to Nicodemus, 'Except a man be born again, he cannot enter into the kingdom of God.' He said to the multitude, 'Blessed are the poor in spirit, for theirs is the kingdom of heaven.' We are not by nature poor in spirit. No man but a regenerate man, one born of the Spirit, is poor in spirit. and so to say that he must be born again and that he must be poor in spirit, was in truth to say the same thing. After this there follow several verses down to the 12th verse, in all which our Lord speaks as in the prospect of the kingdom, and is instructing a multitude who were looking for the kingdom, what was the necessary preparation for sharing in its glory. Every one of the blessings is promised in reference to the kingdom. It is the kingdom that is coming that the poor in spirit are to possess — it is the kingdom that is coming that the mourners in Zion are to be comforted — it is in the kingdom that is coming that the meek shall inherit the earth — it is in the kingdom that is coming that those who hunger and thirst after righteousness shall be abundantly satisfied with the righteous reign and the righteous glory of their God — it is in the kingdom that is coming that those who are merciful shall be revealed as those who have received, and enjoyed the mercy of God, and shall enter upon that kingdom of glory, which come to them of the free grace and goodness of God — it is in the kingdom that is coming the pure in heart, who now see God by faith, shall see him face to face for it is said, 'when he shall appear we shall be like him, for we shall see him as he is' — it is in the kingdom that is coming that the peacemakers shall be called the sons of God, that is the time when the children of God shall be revealed as such, and that is the time when those who are persecuted for righteousness sake shall be exalted: for those who now confess Christ before men shall then receive the reward of the inheritance. Now you see that our Lord did not discourage them as to the expectation of a kingdom, but taught them how to prepare for it.

Another error in which the Jews were, was their not understanding that he himself had to suffer before he entered into glory — we find even the disciples under the influence of this mistake, and so in that discourse with Nicodemus our Lord told him that, 'as Moses lifted up the serpent in the wilderness: even so must the Son of Man be lifted up', showing that this must be in order to man's salvation, and in order to his being exalted as King: but still there is not one word spoken to discourage him from expecting a kingdom. And accordingly, when two of the disciples had this request made in their behalf, by the mother, that one might sit on his right hand and the other on his left in his kingdom, he did not deny that there was such a kingdom: but he said this place asked for them was awaiting those for whom it was prepared of his Father, not encouraging them in their ambitious expectations, but at the same time confirming them in their expectation of a kingdom.

But the passage to which I specially turn your attention is the 19th chapter of Luke, where we are told that the Jews were under a strong impression that the kingdom would immediately appear. At the 9th verse our Lord speaks thus to Zacchaeus, 'This day is salvation come to this house.' The people saw by this that he was claiming the character of the Messiah, and at the 11th verse we read, 'And as they heard these things he added, and spake a parable, because he was nigh to Jerusalem and because they thought that the kingdom of God should immediately appear.'

Now you observe that the parable is spoken because they thought that, being near to Jerusalem, he was just going into it to take possession of it and that of course the kingdom should *immediately* appear. Now what did he say? 'He said therefore, a certain nobleman went into a far country to receive for himself a kingdom and to return.' Here it is quite manifest that our Lord was only correcting the mistake of thinking that the kingdom should *immediately* appear. He did not teach them that it was a mistake to think that it was a mistake to think that the kingdom should appear: but that it was a mistake to think that it would *immediately* appear, and therefore he taught them that the nobleman, that is himself, was to go into a far country to receive for himself a kingdom and to return, confirming them in the expectation that the kingdom should appear: but correcting them in the false impression that it should appear immediately. The same thing he taught Nicodemus by saying, 'The Son of Man must be lifted up', is here taught by saying that the nobleman should go into a far country to receive a kingdom and return. And we still find in the close of this Gospel of Luke the same expectation of a kingdom in the minds of the disciples. We read in the 24th chapter of two of them, who were walking and to whom the Lord joined himself: but they did not know him, and our Lord asked them, 'What manner of communications are these that ye have one to another, as ye walk and are sad? And the one of them, whose name was Cleopas, answering said unto him, Art thou only a stranger in Jerusalem and hast not known the things which are come to pass there in these days? And he said unto them, What things? And they said unto him, Concerning Jesus of Nazareth, which was a prophet mighty in word and deed before God and all the people. And how the chief priests and our rulers delivered him to be condemned to death and have crucified him. But we trusted that it had been he which should have redeemed Israel.' This was as much as to say, 'We are beginning to fear lest we have been mistaken. We trusted that it had been he who should redeem Israel.' They had been looking for a deliverer and our Lord, to whom they had been looking as the deliverer, suffered death, and so they could not see how he could be the promised deliverer. Then he said to them at the 26th verse, 'O fools and slow of heart to believe all that the prophets have spoken. Ought not Christ to have suffered these things, and to enter into glory?' showing them that they had been ignorant of the Scriptures. He goes on to explain to them Moses and the prophets, and the Psalms, showing that they ought to have known from the Scriptures that, before he could enter into his glory, before he could be exalted as a King, he must first suffer these things: but he never hinted that they were wrong as to their expectation of a kingdom. So in Acts 3:3 we are told that he was with them forty days, teaching them of the things pertaining to the kingdom of God. This is what he, our Lord, when he was risen from the dead, before he ascended up to his Father, was employed in teaching his disciples further the things concerning the kingdom of God. Now we would surely think[1] that if they had been formerly mistaken in looking for a visible kingdom, that they would now have corrected their error: but they were in no mistake for we find at the 6th verse that, when he was about to part with them, they asked him saying, 'Lord, wilt thou at this time restore the kingdom to Israel?' showing that they still expected this. Instead of saying that they were mistaken in expecting such a kingdom our Lord says: 'It is not for you to know the time or the seasons', that is, 'you are right in expecting that I will do it, and I shall do it in due time: but it is not for you to know when I am to do it.'

I trust that I have been enabled to show you that the expectation cherished was that of a King and a kingdom — that the expectation was that of a visible kingdom, that the disciples and the Jews were daily, in the time of our Saviour, looking for that kingdom; but their great mistake was in imagining that this kingdom should be without our Lord's sufferings, death and resurrection — that they were corrected in this but in such a way as to give them no reason to lay aside their expectation of a kingdom, and of a visible kingdom: but teaching them that they were wrong in expecting it before the Lord's death and resurrection.

The next point to which I would turn your attention is that regarding which we are instructed in a passage in the Revelations 5th chapter, which I desire first of all to connect with what we have read in the 19th chapter of Luke, in which our Lord said that the nobleman went into a far country to *receive a kingdom* and to return. In the 3rd chapter of John he said that the Son of Man must be lifted up, and in the last chapter of Luke, he told his disciples that he must first suffer and then enter into his glory. Now this 5th chapter of Revelations contains the record concerning the kingdom. You can have no doubt that going to the far country was going to his Father, out of this visible world into the invisible and that this was what took place in his death, resurrection and ascension. Now we find in the 5th chapter of Revelations, a book in the hand of God upon the throne, 'written within and on the backside, sealed with seven seals.' This book my dear friends, is the book containing the deeds of the inheritance, the title to the kingdom, and when it is said that this book was in the hand of him who

---

[1] 'think' added to text.

sat upon the throne and that a strong angel proclaimed with a loud voice, 'Who is worthy to open the book and loose the seals thereof?' the question is, 'Who is worthy to receive the kingdom? Who is worthy to be exalted as King?'

We find at the 6th verse these words, 'And I beheld, and lo, in the midst of the throne, and of the four beasts, and in the midst of the elders, stood a Lamb as it had been slain, having seven horns and seven eyes, which are the seven Spirits of God sent forth into all the earth. And he came and took the book out of the right hand of him that sat upon the throne.' There can be no doubt that this Lamb is Christ *after* his resurrection, because it is Christ having seven horns and seven eyes which are the seven Spirits of God — having the fullness of the Spirit as the risen Saviour — as the second Adam, the quickening Spirit. Here we see the nobleman in the far country receiving the book of the inheritance — receiving that which gave him a kingdom. That it was in his resurrection that our Lord was set up as King you will see from Acts 13:32-34, 'We declare unto you glad tidings, how that the promise which was made unto the fathers, God hath fulfilled the same unto us their children, in that he hath raised up Jesus again; as it is also written in the second Psalm, Thou art my Son, this day have I begotten thee, And as concerning that he raised him up from the dead, now no more to return to corruption, he said on this wise, I will give you the sure mercies of David.' Here the words, 'Thou art my Son, this day have I begotten thee', and the words. 'I will give you the sure mercies of David', are connected with the resurrection of our Lord, and with his being raised up of the Father to his own right hand — not simply with his resurrection: but with his being raised up of the Father — that God raised him up.

Now if you look to the portions of the Old Testament from which the apostle makes these quotations, you will see that they both refer to the setting him up as King. The first is a quotation from the 2nd Psalm, 6th verse, 'Yet have I set my king upon my holy hill of Zion.' This is the setting up of Christ as King and it is added, 'I will declare the decree, the Lord has said to me, Thou art my Son, this day have I begotten thee.' So that this is the decree of the setting up of Christ as King upon Zion, 'Thou art my Son, this day have I begotten thee.' And the other passage is a quotation from the 55th of Isaiah, in which we find the sure mercies of David thus spoken of at the 3rd verse, 'Incline thine ear, and come to me: hear, and your souls shall live and I will make an everlasting covenant with you, even the sure mercies of David. Behold I have given him for a witness to the people, a leader and commander to the people': so that the setting up of the Lord as King is thus connected with his going into a far country to receive the kingdom.

The next subject connected with the kingdom to which I turn your attention is the ground or the principle, upon which God proceeds in the exalting of Christ. You are not to suppose that Christ is exalted as King because he is God. Christ is as God blessed for ever; from eternity to eternity: but the kingdom foretold in prophecy was to be given to the King, as a reward of his righteousness. Therefore we find in the 5th of Revelations, that the question is, 'Who is *worthy* to open the book and to loose the seals thereof?' as if it were said: 'The kingdom will be given to him who is worthy of it.' And it is added, 'No man was found worthy to open the book', and then it is said, 'The Lion of the tribe of Judah has *prevailed'* , that is, has proved himself worthy 'to open the book' and then when Christ receives the book, the song that is sung, at the 9th verse is, 'Thou art worthy to take the book, and to open the seals thereof', and again at the 12th verse, 'Worthy is the Lamb that was slain to receive power and riches and wisdom and strength and honour and glory and blessing.' So that Christ is exalted as a King because of his worthiness, because of his deserving, because he wrought for it and won it.

In the 24th Psalm the same thing is taught us, as to him who is to be exalted as God's King: 'The earth is the Lord's and the fullness thereof.' This is the kingdom that is going to be disposed of: it is said expressly that it belongs to God, 'for he founded it on the seas and established it upon the floods.' Then the question comes, 'Who shall ascend into the hill of God the Lord and who shall stand in his holy place?' that is, 'Who shall be King?' for in the 2nd Psalm it is, 'I have set my king upon my holy hill of Zion.' And the question is, 'Who shall sit upon my holy hill of Zion? Who shall ascend into the hill of the Lord?' The answer is, 'He that hath clean hands and a pure heart', showing us that it was to be obtained through righteousness: and that the question here is, 'Who shall be King?' still more clearly appears from what follows, at the 8th verse, 'Who is this King of glory?' the enquiry is, 'Who is this King of glory?' The answer is that he is 'the Lord, strong and mighty', in short, the man Christ Jesus. Who is the Lord, strong and mighty? The man Christ Jesus is the God-man. Again, in the 40th Psalm[2] you have the same thing taught you. 'My heart is inditing a good matter: I

---

[2] 45th Psalm

speak of the things which I have made *touching the King*: my tongue is the pen of a ready writer.' Now observe what is said of the King, 'Thou art fairer than the children of men.' You will recollect in the 5th chapter of Revelation that *no man* was found worthy to open the book; but Christ was found worthy to open it. This is just what is said here, 'Thou art fairer than the children of men.' None of them were found beautiful in God's sight, because they were all corrupted and transgressors from the womb: but Jesus was fairer than the children of men. God said, 'This is my beloved Son in whom I am well pleased.' And so it is that the King is described in the first place as fairer than the sons of men, and then again at the 7th verse what this fairness was is clearly set forth, 'Thou lovest righteousness and hateth wickedness, therefore God, thy God, hath anointed thee with the oil of gladness above thy fellows', that is, above thy brethren, the children of men, so that Christ is here represented — the King, about whom the Psalm says that he is fairer than the children of men. He is represented as anointed with the oil of gladness above his fellows, *because* he loved righteousness and hated wickedness — showing us that the oil of gladness was poured upon him: because he loved righteousness, because he was the man with the clean hands, and a pure heart: because he was the man who was worthy to open the book. In the 89th Psalm at the 19th verse we find the same doctrine is taught as to the setting up of this King, 'Then thou speakest in vision to thy Holy One and saidst, I have laid help upon one that is mighty. I have exalted *one chosen out of the people*', that is, one taken from amongst his fellows, chosen out of the people. 'I have found David my servant: with my holy oil have I anointed him.'

I do not quote more to illustrate this but I beseech you to mark that, whilst it is taught us that Christ is exalted as a King in his resurrection, and whilst it is taught that this is the *good news*, that God in doing this, fulfilled the promise he made to the fathers: we are clearly taught that Christ receives the kingdom because of his worthiness, because he was the man with clean hands and a pure heart, because he was the man who loved righteousness and hated wickedness: because he was the man, in short, with whom God was well pleased; and that Christ is exalted a King not because he is God: but because he is the righteous man, the Holy One of God.

My dear friends, I would still further direct your attention to the nature of this worthiness — to that in which our Lord showed that he loved righteousness and hated wickedness — to that by which he proved he was fit to receive the kingdom. You will find it in that same 5th chapter of the Revelations, at the 9th and 10th verses, 'And they sung a new song, saying, 'Thou art worthy to take the book and to open the seals thereof: for thou wast slain and hast redeemed us to God by thy blood, out of every kindred and tongue and people and nation. And hast made us unto our God, kings and priests: and we shall reign on the earth.' And again at the 12th verse, 'Saying with a loud voice, Worthy is the Lamb that was slain to receive power and riches and wisdom and strength and honour and glory and blessing.' What I wish you to re-mark here is that Christ is proved to be the worthy One — to be the One fit to be exalted, because he was the Lamb that was slain, because he laid down his life for men, because he fulfilled the law of God which is, 'Thou shalt love the Lord thy God with all thy heart, soul, mind and strength, and thy neighbour as thyself.'

My dear hearers, it was in laying down his life, that he might take it up again, that our Lord proved this. He tells us, 'I lay down my life that I may take it up again — therefore my Father loveth me.' He came to do his Father's will, 'Then said I, in the volume of the book it is written of me, I come to do thy will O God.' And God raised him in testimony that he was altogether well pleased with him, and this is the thing in which he pleased God, that he laid down his life[3] that he might take it up again, and therefore the Father loved him.

My dear friends, it is not immediately connected with this subject, at least it is such a subject in itself, as to require to be treated separately, but I must here direct your attention to that worthiness that was in Christ. because of which he was exalted as King — that you may understand the whole of this subject, and the Gospel of the forgiveness of sins in his blood and feel fearful lest those to whom this subject is (in a great measure) new, may be disposed to hear it lightly: because they do not at once see its connection with the atonement, and with the gift of the Spirit through the risen Saviour. I desire therefore, for a moment, to direct your attention to the fact that that worthiness for the sake of which Christ was exalted as King, is his work for men; and therefore it is the same worthiness which made him lovely in God's eyes, and made God give him the throne that ought to make him lovely in our eyes, and make us give him the throne and rejoice to see him as King. It was the part of God to deal with Christ after this manner; because of his righteousness to give him the kingdom as God can give, that is, by exalting

---

[3] 'his life' added to text.

him as King — it is our part to give him the kingdom as we can give it, that is, by taking him as our King: by exalting him, by obeying him, by taking him as our King to reign over us.

Now my dear friends, know that the very thing which makes God exalt Christ as King, is the very thing which is to enable us to take him as our King, that it is the very same work of Christ by which he pleased God, so that God gave him the kingdom that should win our hearts, and cause us to be the willing subjects of his kingdom. And what is that work? We are told by himself, 'I laid down my life that I may take it up again, therefore my Father loveth me.' View it in this way — Christ pleased the Father, and fulfilled that word, 'Thou shalt love the Lord thy God with all thy heart, soul, mind and strength'; therefore he was worthy to be made God's King upon Zion. Christ fulfilled the law in that he loved the Lord his God with his whole heart, soul, mind and strength; and his neighbour as himself; therefore was he worthy to be our King: and Christ showed that he loved his God, by laying down his life that he might take it up again, and showed that he loved every man as himself by laying down his life for them: and therefore when we see Christ laying down his life, that he might take it up again, we see him fulfilling the law of love to God, and the law of love to man, and worthy to be exalted of God as a King, and worthy to be exalted and honoured by men as their King.

My dear friends, I desire in a single word to show you how Christ's laying down his life, that he might take it up again, was fulfilling the law, 'Thou shalt love the Lord thy God with all thy heart, soul, mind and strength. What was the effect of Christ's laying down his life that he might take it up again? By laying down his life he made atonement for the sins of the world, he put away sin by the sacrifice of himself. By laying down his life he therefore placed all men in this condition that sin was not imputed to them. Again by taking it up again he received the Spirit for all men, he became the fountain of eternal life to all men: he became one in whom they had power to live unto God. Thus, then, he changed the condition of mankind by laying down his life and taking it up again, that is, by laying down his life, he put away our sins, by taking it up again he gave us a new life as our risen head. And he laid down his life, not in uncertainty, but in order that he might take it up again, which shows us that our Lord would not have thought of making an atonement for our sins, if he had not the prospect of being exalted and of receiving the Spirit for us. So when he laid down his life he did so in the faith, and expectation that his Father would raise him up; and that he would receive from his Father power to be a quickening Spirit.

O see these two great things! And see their connection. He put away sin by his death that through his resurrection you might receive new life. This is that work of Christ which proved that he loved righteousness and hated iniquity, first that by this he showed his love to God. How can any deed show love to God, supreme love to God? No man can be profitable to God. Even Christ could not be profitable. Christ could not benefit his Father, for that would be taking from the infinite blessedness of God. Therefore understand how Christ could prove his love to the Father: just in this way, as I might prove my love to a man if I were to say, 'I see that there is something very near your heart — something on which your heart is set, and I am willing at the expense of my own life to accomplish what you wish.' By this I would show that I love this man better than my own life — by this I would show that I loved him with all my mind and with all my strength. Now this was the way in which Christ fulfilled the law. He loved God with his whole heart and soul and mind and strength, and he loved his neighbour as himself. He saw and knew how God loved men. He was not under the power of these lies of the devil which prevail among us, under which men are deceived into the belief that God does not love all men — that God only uses his creatures for his own glory — not loving, and not caring for them: but using them for the sake of something which *they call* God's glory. Christ was in no such mistake. He was in the bosom of God, and he knew all the longings and yearnings of the heart of God — and he saw how God grieved, because they were corrupted and rebellious, and offending against their Creator and their God and he knew that the desire nearest the heart of God was that they should be brought back from this evil state, that they should be brought to love and glorify God; and therefore Christ, from love to his Father, condescended to become man, to take our nature — to become a man of sorrows — to suffer and die and rise again, that he might be the Mediator between God and us, and that we might through him return to God. Thus Christ proved his love to the Father, by giving himself up to the death, to gratify the desire of his Father's heart, that men should be brought back to God. And so Christ pleased his Father when he said, John 12:24, 'Except a corn of wheat fall into the ground and die it abideth alone: but if it die it bringeth forth much fruit.' And when Christ was willing to die that he might bear much fruit — when Christ was willing *to die* that he might be the author of life to others, when Christ was willing to pour out his soul to death, that he might be the Author of Eternal life to as many as would obey him, in this did he please the Father.

O my dear friends, see the sweetness of this word and see the exceeding great consolation and the power that there is in the knowledge that he did not come to make God kind, he did not come to make God merciful, he did not come to turn the heart of God to men and take away the enmity of God's heart against man. He came forth to gratify the love of God to men, he came forth in order that God's wishes might be accomplished in the deliverance of man from his evil state, and so desirous was he that God's love should have its desire accomplished that he was content to pour forth his soul unto death, that having died for men and being raised again, he might be the channel of life to them and that through him men might glorify God.

Now my dear friends, you are not to feel as if, because Christ did all this from love to God, therefore it was not from love to men. There was no love in God to man that was not in Christ to man and so when Christ had spoken of the first commandment he tells us that the second is like to it. He knew it was like it – yea, he knew that love to God and love to man were inseparable and he knew in his own heart that when he loved the Lord his God with his whole heart and soul and mind and strength, then he also loved his neighbour as he loved himself and us, in the work he did for men, Christ showed that he loved God with all his heart and mind and strength, so he showed by the same work that he loved his neighbour as he loved himself

I would just say one word about the neighbour. My dear friends, I feel it a most important matter that none of you should feel as if you were outside of this – that you should feel that I am speaking of things concerning yourselves; and you are outside of it if you are not Christ's neighbours and you are inside of it if you are Christ's neighbours. Now, is it the case that to love my neighbours is to love every man? Is it the case that every man is my neighbour? My dear friends, we are taught that he is. We read of a man who came to our Lord and said, 'What is the great commandment?' And our Lord said that the first was love to God and that the second was like the first – the love of our neighbour. We are told that this man, being willing to justify himself, said 'But who is my neighbour?' He felt in his heart, 'If he means by my neighbour, my friends and those who show me kindness, then I think I can, in some measure, meet this requisition, but if he means those who have never showed me kindness – those who have wilfully showed me *unkindness* then I cannot say I love them.' Our Lord saw his heart and what was his answer? Did our Lord say to him, 'Your neighbour is your brother according to the flesh? Or your neighbour is the man who loves you and shows you kindness?' No. Our Lord spake a parable concerning a certain man, a Jew, who fell among thieves and was left by them in a sad plight, being robbed of his money and wounded by them. This man our Lord represents as passed by, by other Jews: but he represents one man, a Samaritan, passing that way, and coming and taking this wounded Jew, who had been so treated by the thieves and showing him the greatest kindness: and he asks, 'Which of these was this robbed and wounded man's neighbour — the man who passed by or the man who showed him kindness?' The man could not but feel that he who had showed him kindness, even the Samaritan was the neighbour. Now what did this teach? The Samaritans and the Jews *hated* each other. It you were to ask a Jew, who was the man of all others whom he hated the most, he would say, 'A Samaritan', and the Samaritans hated the Jews in like manner. And here our Lord chooses persons who were least of all expected to show kindness to each other, and yet says that these two men were neighbours. It is just as much as saying that every man is your neighbour, even a Samaritan. So that it is clear that in the eyes of Jesus; to love my neighbour as myself is to love every man as myself. And so we are taught that our Lord loved every man because he loved all as his neighbours, and as he showed his love by laying down his life , that he might take it up again, our Lord proved his love for every man by dying for every man.

But my dear friends, I wish you to mark this other word also, that he loved *his neighbour as himself.* How did Christ love himself? In this way that he desired that God should be glorified in him, that he desired that his soul might live and praise the Lord. 'Let my soul live and it shall praise thee.' This was Christ's love to himself, that he desired that he should live and praise God. Now this his desire was granted, for in his resurrection he received length of days that he should live for ever, and when our Lord procured eternal life for me, he loved me as he loved himself. And what life did he procure? Not a life of happiness away from God — not a life of safety, though we be sinners — not a life of security from God's wrath, though we abide in the bondage of corruption: but he purchased for me all that was needful for my living for ever to the glory of God. Christ desired that he might live for ever to the glory of his Father, and so he loved every one of us as he loved himself,

Appendix 9

desiring for every one of us what he desired for himself, even that we should live for ever, to the glory of God in a resurrection body. I have said this that you might understand that God exalts Christ as King, because God was pleased with him, that you may see why I should, in his being King, because he loved us, and gave himself for us, and the good news is that he is King who loved us and gave himself for us.

There are many principles of government which men speak of. There is one which is now much commended by men and which is a snare of Satan to deceive them greatly. Men are now taught to feel as if all government should spring from themselves and, as if this were the case, all would be well. My friends, that longing which many of you have in your hearts after a righteous government is a righteous longing, but the mistake which men commit is that they are looking for it not to God, but to themselves. It is of God that we should desire a righteous government — it is of God that we should desire that power should be used for the good of the governed — it is of God that we should desire that it should be no longer in the hands of oppressors: but it is of the devil that we should desire that we should do it ourselves apart from God. And understand that this is God's plan to give us a righteous government and a righteous King, and to place us under that King, but that the King is set up of God because he is good and that the subjects are expected to rejoice in his sceptre because he loved them and gave himself for them And I know that this is the good news of the kingdom that God has put all things in the hands of Christ for he is the Lamb that was slain, he it is who loved us and gave himself for us.

I cannot now enter into some other parts of the doctrine, as I had intended but thus far we have come, that the true apprehension of the Gospel is that it is the good news of a kingdom — that the true blessedness of Christ's kingdom is that he is a righteous King — that the true blessedness is to be through the reign of this righteous King — that Christ is exalted King because of his worthiness and that the worthiness which commended him to God and which is to commend him to our hearts, is that he is the Lamb which was slain — that he is the Saviour who laid down his life for us, that we might live unto God.

The next point to which I turn your attention is what we are to understand concerning the scene, the place of his kingdom. A kingdom may be either visible or invisible. An invisible kingdom is the obedience of many to one, in their hearts: but where outward circumstances do not accord with the will of that king. A visible kingdom is an outward state of things in which the king is manifestly acknowledged and honoured. 'The kingdom of God cometh not with observation, neither shall men say, lo here or lo there, for the kingdom of God is within you.' This refers to that invisible kingdom of God which is in every man who in his heart has received Christ to be his King. But although Christ may have among us many who have received him into their hearts and over whom he is now reigning as King, yet the kingdom of Christ is not a visible kingdom, because the outward state of things is according to the mind of the devil, and because the aspects of society, and the state of things among men is altogether contrary to the will of Christ. This then is the character of the present time, that now the kingdom of God cometh not with observation — that now is the visible kingdom of Satan — that now there is an outward state of things that is according to the mind of the devil, while there are many exceptions of individuals whose hearts are right with God. But we are taught to look forward to a time when Christ shall be manifested as King — when he shall reign visibly — when he shall appear as King, and the hope in our text, 'Looking for that blessed hope and the glorious appearing of the great God and our Saviour Jesus Christ', refers to this time when the coming of Christ will be an outward thing, and when the Lord will be revealed reigning as King.

The next point to which I turn your attention is the fact that this earth is to be the scene of the manifest kingdom of Christ — that here he is to reign. We have already seen in the 24th Psalm that it is concerning the earth that God is enquiring to whom he shall give it as a kingdom — it is the earth that is the Lord's and the fulness thereof. And we find the same thing taught us elsewhere — more especially we find that the earth is represented as the abode of righteousness in a future condition of it, as in the 3rd chapter of 2nd Peter and see that the apostle is there warning Christians against scoffers, who should come, 'walking after their own lusts and saying, Where is the promise of his coming? for since the fathers fell asleep, all things continue as they were from the beginning of the creation', that is, scoffers who, yielding to the desire of their own hearts and wishing to live in the gratification of the lusts of the natural man, are flattering themselves with the expectation that there will be no change — that things will go on as they have been going on, and that since the fathers fell asleep, all things continue as they were from the beginning of the creation, so they shall be. The apostle warns us against these men, and these men are charged with this, that they are ignorant that there were a heaven and an earth of old, before the flood, which were destroyed, and that the world that then was, being overflowed with water, perished and also forgetting that the heavens and the earth which are now, are reserved for fire against the day of judgement and perdition of ungodly men, and then he calls on Christians to remember that there were a new heaven and new earth wherein would dwell righteousness, for which they were to look, according to God's promise. Now, observe, we are thus taught to look for new heavens and a new earth, while we are taught that the new earth is the present earth in a new state, for we know that the earth that was before the flood is the same earth that exists now: but that a change came on it, and so they are distinguished and so it is the same earth that now exists, that shall be after the Lord comes: but a change is to come on it and therefore they are distinguished.

My dear friends, if you have difficulties as to this matter, I refer you to the 65th chapter of Isaiah: read it and see whether it is not manifest that it is in this very earth, in another state of it, that it is to be called that new earth; and that it is on this very earth where God has been dishonoured that God is to be honoured. I would further say to you, that Satan may not take advantage of you, if any of you find a difficulty through the word *new:* that this word is here used in some such way as when a converted man is called a new creature. I am called the same *person* as I was before conversion, yet am I a new man; so the earth will be the same globe of earth, but still so changed as to be justly called a new earth. And I have in connection with this expression 'the new earth' to say a word to those who feel as if it were some dishonour to Christ to say that he is to come and reign on this earth. They say, 'Do you think he is to come to this vile earth? Was it not enough that he was once humbled? Shall he again leave glory for it?' He will not be on the earth as it now is but it shall be changed, and you are not to judge of what this earth shall be when the curse is taken off and the power of God is put forth in beautifying and glorifying it, by what it now is. You might as well think to know what body a saint shall have at the resurrection, by looking at the body he has now. The saints shall dwell in bodies, but they shall be glorified bodies and Christ shall reign on earth: but it shall be this earth redeemed from the curse.

The next thing to which I turn your attention, and I do it just in a word, is the fact that we are not only called to honour Christ as a King: but to reign with Christ — we are not only called to rejoice in a kingdom by considering the character of the King, and the love he has to us: but to know that as we are now expected to cherish in ourselves the same love which Christ showed to us, so in the kingdom we are to partake in its glory and reign with Christ.

My dear friends, you must have observed in the 5th chapter of the Revelations that when the inheritance is given to Christ, immediately the saints say, 'Thou are worthy to take the book and to open the seals thereof, for thou wast slain, and hast redeemed us to God by thy blood out of every kindred and tongue and nation. And hast made us unto our God kings and priests and we shall reign in the earth.' The moment they saw the book in Christ's hands they said, 'We shall reign on the earth', that is, they saw that he had gotten the earth and knowing that they were heirs of God and joint heirs with Christ, they knew that as Christ was to reign, so they would reign. So a few chapters after, we find them wearying for the fulfilment of this word and we find that they are told to have patience, and to wait, showing that it is not at death that men get their reward, not till the number of their brethren who were to be put to death, as they were, should be accomplished. And so we are told, 20th chapter 4th verse, that when the number is accomplished they arise, 'And I saw thrones and they sat on them and judgement was given unto them and I saw the souls of them that were beheaded for the witness of Jesus and for the word of God, and which had not worshipped the beast, neither his image, neither had received his mark on their foreheads, or in their hands, and they lived and reigned with Christ a thousand years.' So my dear friends, I would have you to understand that we are taught to look at this kingdom as one in which the saints of God are to share: and this is connected with the subject of the second resurrection. And immediately after we are told of the resurrection of the just it is said, 'But the rest of the dead lived not again until the thousand years were finished. This is the first resurrection.' We find then that it is the purpose of God that the saints should share with Christ in the glory of the kingdom, and reign with him on earth — that this is to be during a thousand years — this being the first resurrection, and that the rest of the dead lived not, being still left to lie in their graves.

This is a subject which I may be enabled of God to bring before you on some other occasion and therefore I leave it at present, merely stating it. But before parting with you, I must, in the strength of God, seek to speak a word that may more personally touch yourselves — not that any word I have spoken this night is not a personal one: every word of truth concerns the God with whom we have to do, but still I desire to speak more personally in the way of applying to you the things which you have heard. And first of all I would solemnly and affectionately charge you, who have before known anything of these things and who have found any comfort in them, to go on unto perfection, and seek to know the counsel of God in them, fully, and not to be satisfied with the acknowledgement of the doctrine, for there is life eternal in every part of the truth of God: and therefore the man who does not find a doctrine needful to him, the man who does not find it food for him, who does not find that he eats it and that it is as marrow in his bones, does not know the doctrine truly. Therefore I would say to all to whom this doctrine has come merely as a thing admitted and who have not yet found a witness within them, testifying that it is true, I would say to every such man that the Spirit of God, longing for a reign of righteousness, cannot, like the dove, rest upon the waters but must return until the dry land appears beyond the flood of judgement which faith sees resting upon the earth: because *that* is the land wherein dwelleth righteousness — and you have not seen the matter truly unless you find that there is a craving in your hearts which this doctrine meets — a longing in your hearts which this doctrine gratifies. Understand then, that the person who really and truly apprehends this doctrine, finds it to be a real food and nourishment for his soul. He is hungering and thirsting after righteousness and he is carried forward to the reign of righteousness and he rejoices in hope till that righteous time and now he is upheld by the faith of it.

And now I would say to those who have believed in the remission of their sins through the blood of Christ, but who have not yet known the doctrine I have proved from the Scriptures: but who opposed it; I solemnly call on all such to remember that this word of God does not overturn any truth that they have already received. It is very painful to see how often the children of God are kept back by the flesh, although they are called to go on to perfection, although they are required to forget the things that are behind and to press forward to the things which are before, yet still is it the fact that they are often found enquiring whether what they know already is not enough and saying that they may be saved without knowing it. My dear friends, is this the language for a child of God? It is not language for a child of God to say, 'If I am saved, that is enough.' If you have been taught to love God — if you have been taught to delight in God's ways — then your question will be, 'How can I know more about God? How can I be carried further into the understanding of God's plan?' And so you will desire to understand his counsels. Therefore believe that there is something wrong — believe that there is some serving to the flesh when a person who knows God and trusts God in respect of his own eternal well-being is not hungering and thirsting after a fuller light and understanding of the truth of God. And when a man says, 'It is enough for me to look to the day of my death, and that is the great thing for me.' Know that he is not entering into the full liberty of a child of God, whose high calling is that he should be jealous for his Father's glory.

But I would now speak to those who are as ignorant of what Christ has done as they are of what Christ is yet to do. Alas! that there are such in every assembly of the people. Alas! that there is ground to fear that by far the greatest proportion of the people are in this situation, that they do not know what Christ has done already. And I solemnly call on such, by the consideration of his coming in judgement, by the consideration of his coming to enquire what the fruit has been of what he has already done, that they would take to heart their ignorance and seek to know the truth. I am speaking to those who have not known that Christ died for them. I am speaking to those who have not known yet that their sins have been forgiven through the shedding of Christ's blood. I am speaking to those who have not yet known that they have power in Christ to walk with God and I tell them that the Lord is coming to enquire and to divide and separate and he is coming to divide in this way that those who have been brought back to God, to rejoice in God and give him glory, by the knowledge of the name of Jesus, may be exalted in glory and that those who have not may be cast into outer darkness. My dear hearers, who are in this awful state, I ask you, 'Are you prepared to meet your God? What will you do when he appears? Where will you hide yourselves when the Judge makes bare his arm, and when his terrors are abroad upon the earth?' The Lord has long waited desiring to see the love, and the grace and the forgiveness that have been extended to you, working eternal life in you; and now he is soon to come to enquire and see what the fruit is. And how are you prepared to meet him? Are you prepared to meet your God? My dear hearers, this is a reasonable question, because we are called to be standing with our loins girt and our lamps burning, and we ourselves as men who wait for the coming of the Lord. And it would have been a reasonable question at any time since the Lord went away, because we are called to be always expecting his return, but it is peculiarly a reasonable question in proportion as the time wears on, in proportion as we are nearer and nearer the day of the Lord, and more especially as there are signs of judgement. And are there not signs? Are there not signs in the state of the nation? Are there not signs in the heavings of men's minds? Is there not a vague expectation now abroad, throughout all Christendom, of some great thing to happen? Men are looking for great things to come upon the earth. And things shall come; and the devil knowing that his time is short tells them to be active and much they may be able to accomplish. And why is this but just to prevent their listening to the voice of their God? And he gives them this and that delusive hope and says that would fulfil your longings and so they are satisfied. O be not satisfied with the devil's answer to the question, 'When will things be better?' Men ask this, and the devil answers, 'When you obtain certain things you are desiring.' But what is the Lord's answer? 'Things will be better when the reign of righteousness comes.' But are you prepared for such a change as this? You may think yourselves prepared for such a change as you are looking for: but are you prepared for the change that God wishes? Nicodemus thought that he was prepared. He looked forward to the kingdom, just as men look forward now to the political millennium, never of course thinking that they themselves need to be changed. If they can get new laws and a new constitution: that, they think is enough. But our Lord promises us nothing that will make us happy in this way: 'Except a man be born again, he cannot enter into the kingdom of heaven' — you cannot otherwise receive the good things that are in store. There must be an inward change in you. No outward change will do. And therefore let not the devil teach you that all the fault is in your circumstances. There are people who go about teaching this: but the fault is in yourselves. Now no man likes to hear this. People like to put the blame of the evil of their condition on anything rather than themselves. But God teaches us that the evil is in man, that God is going to change the inward condition: but that the inward change must be in order to prepare us for this and that except a man be born again he cannot perceive the blessedness which God has in store. I ask you, 'Are you born again? You are all flesh and blood — you have received this from your first father Adam, but are you born of the Spirit? Have you received the Spirit from the second Adam? Is the Spirit of Christ in you?' This is the question — for if the Spirit of Christ is not in you, you are not prepared for the kingdom — if the Spirit of Christ is not in you, you cannot welcome the reign of Christ. And let no man deceive you by making you think that you may be born again though you do not know it. This is not true for we are told that the Spirit bears witness with our spirit that we are the children of God, and that the Spirit is the Spirit of adoption whereby we cry, 'Abba, Father.' I therefore testify to you that except ye be born again you are not prepared for the coming glory, and I testify to you that except ye know that you are born again you are not born again; and that those who are having doubts, in darkness and in uncertainty, not knowing what it is to cry, 'Abba, Father', are not prepared for the kingdom of God.

My dear friends, the Lord give you to take this word home to yourselves, and grant that you may now be made of him to seek to know more fully the doctrine you have heard and that you be found in that condition in which you can rejoice before God that the King of glory shall appear and that you feel your awful need of that blessed hope and the expectation of the glorious appearing of the great God and our Saviour Jesus Christ.

Amen

Appendix 10

Notes of Sermons 1.9

Notes of Fencing of the Tables, Communion Service and Concluding Address 21 July 1830

We now proceed to the peculiar service of this day; and as is our custom, I proceed to read with you that portion of the word of God which is usually read as our authority — the institution of this ordinance as it is given to us by the apostle Paul, as he received it from the Lord. I Corinthians 11:23-29 inclusive. 'For I have received of the Lord that which also I delivered unto you, that the Lord Jesus, the same night in which he was betrayed, took bread: And when he had given thanks, he brake it, and said, Take, eat, this is my body, which is broken for you: this do in remembrance of me. After the same manner also he took the cup, when he had supped, saying, This cup is the new testament in my blood: this do ye, as often as ye drink it, in remembrance of me. For as often as ye eat this bread, and drink this cup, ye do show forth the Lord's death till he come.

Wherefore, whosoever shall eat this bread, and drink this cup of the Lord, unworthily, shall be guilty of the body and blood of the Lord. But let a man examine himself, and so let him eat of that bread and drink of that cup. For he that eateth and drinketh, unworthily, eateth and drinketh damnation to himself, not discerning the Lord's body.'

It is the practice in our Church at such a time as this to address to the people what is usually described as the Fencing of the Tables, and according to this practice I would now speak to you yet once more, as in one sense standing between you and the table, while in another sense the channel of your approach to it. At the same time, having already dwelt so much on this subject; and so much having been spoken by the other ministers of Christ with the object and tendency of saving you from sin in this matter, I do not feel it needful to detain you long. Yet when I say needful I do not say this in respect of *your* need, for should I measure the time I should occupy by the measure of your unpreparedness I should detain you very long indeed: but I speak in respect of the opportunity which in the present circumstances is given and which I feel to be limited by the necessary interference of other duties: I just remind you and every one proposing to communicate here, this day, that you stand to me in the relation of people to a pastor, and that I am here the Minister of Christ thus publicly to declare that none ought to come to the table, but those who have passed from death unto life — none but those who have in very truth become living members of the body of Christ — none but those in whom the Spirit of Christ dwelleth — and that it is an unwarranted approach which every one makes, who is not in a condition to take up the language of the text, 'I am crucified with Christ, nevertheless I live: yet not I, but Christ liveth in me, and the life which I now live in the flesh I live by the faith of the Son of God, who loved me and gave himself for me' — that none but those of whose feeling this is the expression — of the state of whose inward hearts this is the description — that these and none else ought to come to the table. All must admit that none but these have any right to sit down at the table of the Lord, and I would now therefore speak to those who are within the circle of those who have thus known the Lord, and call upon you to remember these words, 'Let a man examine himself and so let him eat of that bread and drink of that cup.'

And I call upon you to remember what I have already twice pressed upon you that these words were first spoken to those whom the apostle recognised as believers, and that the judgement, to which those to whom he was writing exposed themselves, was not a judgement which implied that they were not Christians: but a judgement within the Church: and that judgement they endured, they endured because they had come forward to the Lord's table, while at the time not abiding in Christ: I therefore beseech every one now purposing to come forward, every one who, looking inwardly, can say, 'Whereas I was blind, now I see' — I beseech every such person to remember the words, 'Let a man examine himself', and let him seek in the strength of the Holy Ghost to come forward as in the perfect light of a present life, and of a present salvation, not in the remembrance of a past knowledge — not doing the thing as a matter of course but knowing of a truth that our Lord is giving you his broken body and shed blood — giving you the word in the shape of bread and wine — giving you in the form of this manifest ordinance that same thing which is set forth in the truth of the preached Gospel. And as with the word of truth there goeth forth the Spirit of truth, so with this sign of truth — with this seal of truth — with this visible bodily substance expressive of truth — there goeth forth the Spirit of Christ — the

Holy Ghost — so that those who receive it worthily, as those who truly receive the word of life, do thereby actually receive the Spirit which is the truth that is in these symbols. I wish you to understand that although it be a lie of Satan, that the bread becomes the body of Christ, or that the wine becomes the blood of Christ — although it be a lie of Satan's, that the *actual* flesh and blood of him that was crucified, is in any sense in the bread, or with the bread: yet it is the truth of God of which these lies are the corruption and perversion — a truth of God which men often lose sight of by means of these lies — a truth of God which I would now recall to you, and by which I would ask you to be nourished and fed — that in very truth, the worthy communicant is through the Holy Ghost coming through the risen body of Jesus — coming to him through the glorified humanity — made to experience in this ordinance, the power of Christ's resurrection, and to have fellowship in Christ's sufferings, so that he is actually feeding on the body and blood of Christ by the Spirit. Thus does he substantially receive Christ into his soul through the Holy Ghost. It is the recognising the Spirit there, which shows us how the unworthy communicant, not discerning the Lord's body, is rejecting the Spirit, and Christ in the Spirit.

Now may it be given to you to know *that* strength, and power, and might which is to be received in faith; therefore come to it in the faith that ii is no mere sign or symbol; but an actual participation of God to which you are called. It is not a word spoken outwardly, 'Christ died for me'; but a thing done inwardly in the Spirit. It is a confessing Christ, not with reference to those who see the outward appearance merely, but a true confession. It is a part of the confession by which the Church makes known to principalities and powers the manifold wisdom of God. It is thus we may confess, to the whole universe, for we know not how far the movements of one mind are exposed to other minds who are not trammelled by flesh and blood. It may be to the whole — to all who delight in the works of God — to all in this universe who wish to know what is of God in the universe and what is of Satan. You therefore, who worthily communicate, are showing to all who thus distinguish the works of God in you — that you are brought back from the grasp of Satan — that you are delivered from the power of that strong one. It is a confession of that mighty work of God in you, in which angels and principalities and powers in heavenly places are desiring to see, the manifestation of the power and love of God. This, beloved in the Lord, is your high calling: thus it is you are to come and thus to give glory to God: and therefore is it that it is a vain mockery in every one to come to this table, who does not *thus* come to give glory to God. I therefore warn all who know not that Jesus died for *their* sins, rose again for their justification: and has the Spirit for *them,* that they come not to the table, and again warn those that so know these things that they come in the Spirit and not as a matter of course; that they do it not in a lifeless way, but by sowing to the Spirit, and giving God glory. The Elders will now bring forward the elements, meanwhile we shall sing to the praise of God.

My dear friends, we are showing forth the Lord's death till he come again when we are living by the power of a world to come, and having the *earnest* of the Spirit. Therefore may we with perfect truth sing in respect of this ordinance, that which is spoken chiefly and ultimately in reference to the kingdom which is yet to come. Sing then in the 24th Psalm.

Address to the Communicants

You have been testifying in the Spirit concerning the Lord of Hosts that he is the King of glory. I trust that you can now also testify in the Spirit — yea, that you are testifying in the Spirit, of the Man of sorrows — he who was acquainted with griefs — that he is the King of glory: and when I think how you must judge who are yourselves in the Spirit, made to shed holy tears, and to experience a godly sorrow; because men keep not the law of your God and when I think how the name of Jesus must have twined itself about your hearts, and that you know that every sorrow which he tasted, he tasted for you, that he might save you from that which he knew to be evil, although you loved it and thought it good; even from sin. I know and am assured that it is well for you that the Lord of Hosts is this King of glory. For had he who is your crucified Head been only a fellow creature; how should your hearts have been given to God? Would you not think of the creature as having done more for you than he that made you and would not this wean your hearts from your God? But God has in all things the glory in Christ and all things are done in Christ that God might have the glory. Be not therefore afraid of idolatry in giving your hearts to Christ. Fear not that the glory when given to the Son is taken from the Father, or that when given to the Father it is taken from the Son — but ever in the Son see the Father — let it be the glory of the Father that ever shines to you in the face of Jesus Christ, and let it be the Father's name that you know to be declared by him, so

Appendix 10

that the more you know of Jesus, the more you know of God. O! how hath grace much more abounded when sin did much abound, and how have the resources of the love and wisdom of God overcome the mighty devices of the devil. Truly it was a masterpiece of Satan to teach you a joy out of God — a joy in the flesh — to teach you to sow to the flesh, and so seal you up into rebellion: but this is the glory of Jesus, that he will teach you a joy in the Spirit, even while dwelling in the flesh — that he will show you such a loveliness in God, even when the world, the devil and the flesh are linked together to shut out God, as that Christ shall triumph in you, and present you to the Father living sacrifices. This is the glory which God has in every true communicant at this table, that though in the flesh only capable of hating God and your fellow-men — though in the flesh you have long hated God and man — though in the flesh capable of all sinful enjoyment away from your God: yet are you now in some measure tasting a joy, the opposite of the flesh — a joy in dwelling in love to God and your fellow creatures, and in this is the mighty victory in Christ. Surely then you may rejoice that it is God himself who has done and is doing it: therefore you should cast your crown at the feet of the Lamb, that through the Lamb you may give all the glory unto the Father, that God in all things may be glorified through Jesus Christ.

Communicants, I trust you know something (and I speak to those who do know something) of the broken body and shed blood of Christ — to those who know what it is to have their hearts broken — to those who know what it is through the Spirit to grieve — who know what it is through partaking of the power of Christ's resurrection and this receiving the Spirit of the risen Saviour — to have been made to enter into the fellowship of his sufferings, even the sufferings which he felt here in the days of his flesh. I now therefore proceed to administer to you these precious memorials — this precious setting forth of that glory which was in God before worlds were; which every deed of God has been showing forth, and which will not fully shine forth until that day come when the Son giveth up the kingdom unto the Father, that God may be all in all. That eternal truth in Christ is now put into the form of this bread and wine — that true glory is now in these things to those that will receive them by faith; and through them, as through a glass, are to look in the face of Christ and see the glory of God, and worship God in the Spirit.

The Lord Jesus, in that night in which he was betrayed took bread, and gave thanks which we shall now do after his example. Let us pray.

> O! Lord we will rejoice that it is our privilege in all things to give thanks — that as it was the privilege of the well-beloved of the Father on that night in which he was betrayed to give thanks, while in the knowledge of all the things that were coming upon him, because he lived in the faith of the glory which he now hath with the Father; so is it our privilege to give thanks when we are showing forth his death till he come again. It is not only when he comes revealed in glory that we shall shout praises to our God: but even now it is our privilege to give thanks: yea, in all things to give thanks, in showing forth the Lord's death to give thanks; in showing forth that we are dead to the world to give thanks — in showing forth that which is the symbol of our suffering at the hands of the world to give thanks. Now therefore, O! our God we give thee thanks because Jesus died; and rose again: we give thee thanks because he suffered the just for the unjust — we give thee thanks because we are called to feel the power of his resurrection; and the fellowship of his suffering: we give thee thanks because we are called to be not of the world, even as Christ was not of the world — because we are called to be set apart to the Lord our God — because we are not our own but bought with a price — because we are to see the flesh as dead, and to crucify it: and to see the Spirit only as life: and to live in the Spirit. O Lord we give thee thanks and praise and now glorify thyself in us — now glorify thyself in this ordinance — now bless this bread and this wine, so that they may feed the souls of thy people. O! let them enjoy the vision of him delivered and accepted — of him suffering and raised again. O! let them feel that it was *for them,* not merely in love to them, but that they might know their God and might join with him in condemning sin in the flesh, so should they also. O! Father, let this be the experience of every communicant this day. Let there be here broken hearts — joy in the Lord — separation from the world — strength — purposes of new obedience in the strength of Jesus. Let there be a true knowledge of the creature's nothingness, and of the might of him who has all power in heaven and in earth, and who is head over all things to his Church. O! Lord accept our thanksgiving. O! Lord answer us and bless us in Christ Jesus, our living Head.
>
> Amen!

Appendix 10

Our Lord took bread and having given thanks brake it, and gave it to his disciples, saying, Take, eat, this is my body which is broken for you; this do in remembrance of me. And after the same manner he took the cup, saying, This cup is the New Testament in my blood shed for the many for the remission of sins. Drink ye all of it. For as often as ye eat this bread and drink this cup ye do show forth the Lord's death till he come.

It is better to go to the house of mourning than to the house of mirth. Yet a little while and the world shall rejoice and ye shall be sorrowful; but your sorrow shall be turned into joy. The house of God is now the house of mourning, but it is they who mourn that shall be comforted and it is better to be in that house of mourning than in the house of feasting which the world now is. Let me remind you, blessed of the Lord, that sorrow endures only for this night of our Lord's absence; but joy will assuredly come in the morning for Jesus hath said that ye shall see him and then our sorrow shall be turned into joy. Far better is it to weep in that world in which Jesus wept than to rejoice in that which gave him no joy — but better still will it be to rejoice in that world where the Lord reigneth; and where tears are for ever wiped away from every eye. We are to thank and bless God that we are taught here to weep the tears of holiness but still more should we bless him for the prospect of the period when even holy tears are to be wiped away from our eyes. O! then at this table, once more spread for you, yea, in every moment and in every place, show forth the Lord's death till he come again. Let it be your ground of thanksgiving that you are now to weep where Jesus wept, and to be in entire fellowship with him in his sufferings until he come again, and then, when Christ, who is our life, shall appear, shall we appear with him in glory, for it is said of the members of his body, that they shall awake and sing, even they that dwell in the dust. Let it then be your prayer that you may attain to the resurrection from among the dead. And now keep yourselves by the power of the Holy Ghost given to you and walk with God in this adulterous and wicked generation, and give him glory, that in the day when he cometh, he may confess you in the presence of his Father. The Lord bless you and keep you and cause the light of his countenance to shine upon you.

Amen.

Address to the Parishioners of Row by their Pastor, the Rev. J. M. Campbell delivered at the close of the dispensation of the Holy Sacrament

My dear friends, I now desire to speak to you for a short time in the name of the Lord.

I desire to set before you what God would now have you to know of his present feeling towards you, and in meeting which you will meet the desires of your God: I desire that you may see yourselves as the Lord seeth you.

I would first speak to those who have this day met the Lord at his table: but have not given glory to God there, and lastly to those who have withheld their presence from the table of the Lord.

O! my dear hearers, did we know how God looks on us, did we know the kindlings of compassion in our God, how he regardeth us when we come to him, when we acknowledge his love, and receive him to reign in us, then would we know that there is nothing, yea nothing precious in the eyes of God in this wide world, that is not stamped with glory to him through Jesus Christ — then would we know that there is nothing in all the actings of the children of men, which he can contemplate with any delight: but that which is the working of the Spirit of Christ in them — then would we know that there is nothing to be seen here throughout all the desolate waste of human beings, polluted and debased as they are through sin, which the Lord can praise and which can refresh the heart of God, but that glory which is given to him in the Spirit.

I would now speak a word to those of whom it is true — of whom God knoweth that it is true — that they have this day discerned the Lord's body at his table — who have known God, who have realised a communion with God at his table, and I ask them to hear this word. God is not confined to his ordinances: but is above his ordinances, and whatever of God cometh forth to our hearts through faith in this ordinance or in the word of the preached Gospel, is in God continually — is in God wherever we are and in whatever way we are occupied. I beseech you let not any of you judge, what they have tasted in the Lord, in such a season as this to be something of which they shall say, 'We shall look back with thankfulness to what we have known of the Lord today, instead of feeling and knowing that all the ordinances of God are just as windows in a house intended to let in light upon us — are means to produce a glorious end, that they let in light from without and that if all the other parts of the building were away, then the light would be much more full. Yet it is not the mind of God nor is it the desire of God that you should live subject to ordinances — that you should be limited to them: but that in them God manifesteth what he is — that you, having met God in them and seen God in them, may enter into what he continually is — and so, having met him at his table, and said, 'Surely it is good to be in this place — surely the Lord is here' — you are now called upon to go forth and bear about with you continually the joy of the Lord and to remember that there is not an hour, nor a condition, nor a circumstance in which glory may not be given to God, as well as at his table — that it is not a thing to be experienced now and then; but that whatever you attain to there, you are called ever after to live up to it — and beyond it. It is the will of God, it is the glory of God that you should go on unto perfection — that you should go on from grace to grace — from strength to strength. You are not to treasure up the bright vision you have had of God this day, saying, 'I saw God last communion Sabbath', but you are ever to go about, beholding him, and saying, 'I have now seen him who is holy and true, as he truly is, so now let me through the Spirit dwell in this vision. Now let me sow to the Spirit — let me give glory to God by living *continually* in the vision of God.' This is one of the reasons why it is said, 'When they deliver you up, take no thought how or what ye shall speak for it shall be given you in that same hour what ye shall speak.' This is one of the reasons why ye are to take no thought for tomorrow, why we are to be living from moment to moment, by that fountain from which the same love is ever flowing.

It is not now and then we are to go to God, as if we were going to consult a friend but it is the will of God that we should continually live a life of dependence, and in doing this should lead a life of continual communion and fellowship with God in Christ. I therefore warn you, because I know you are exposed to snares in this matter — because I see there is no one thing a greater source of evil to those who know the Lord than this kind of limiting of God, as if it were not as easy for God to sustain you always, as for a single moment. It is not that God gets wearied of supporting your weakness. Can the everlasting arm grow weary or decay? Assuredly not. And seeing the strength given you is not the strength of flesh and blood, but of the eternal Spirit — seeing this life is not a dying life; but eternal life — I ask you, 'What is to fill up eternity — what is to prevent weariness in it? Do you think the Hosts in Glory ever cease from their praises?' They cease not day nor night to give glory to God. Take this then as a reproof — that God is everywhere, as at this table, and that the Spirit of the Lord is never straitened, and with regard to all sin — to all deadness and coldness, we can say with confidence, 'Are these the Lord's doings? Is his Spirit straitened?' I beseech those therefore who have this day had communion with God to be warned in this matter and to remember while they are mourning over the darkness and deadness about them — while they see also that there are so few who understand his love — to remember what is true concerning themselves. We know that as it is but an individual here and there who is giving any glory to God at all, so it is but as an hour here and there in the lives even of those few individuals in which God is glorified.

If you would seek to increase the glory that is given to God — if you would seek to reclaim the waste of human hearts about you that are led captive of Satan at his will, look on the many hours and seasons of your own time — look on the many emotions and feelings of your own hearts that are not redeemed to God. O redeem the time because the days are evil. To be living in the knowledge and love of God's excellence and praising God — this is what eternity is — that you should be in this state even now, is what God has made provision for in the gift of Christ.

But I do not doubt that there are some among those who know the Lord, and who have in times past rejoiced in him, who have not met the Lord this day at his table. I know well how Satan will seek to take advantage of this admission. But as I know there may be those here who are members of the body of Christ, and who have in times past given glory to God, who may this day have come to the Lord's table and have not seen the light of his countenance, and have been in darkness and deadness, I must speak for their sake. Dearly beloved I beseech you to justify God in this matter. God is not capricious, now showing you his face and then concealing it. It is awful dishonour to God thus to conceive of him. It is not then of God that you have been dead and dark, it is wholly of yourselves. There has been no hindrance: yea none whatever on the part of God. I do not say that this disappointment of expectation — this want of communion with God is *in no respect* a chastisement or a judgement. It may be a Fatherly chastisement, a correcting judgement but nevertheless these have been inflicted on you through the operation of your own unbelief.

Appendix 10

You have been sowing to the flesh, and so have become in a measure carnal. That is the real reason why you have thus sinned against God: therefore instead of becoming doubtful whether it was the Lord you met in times past because you met him not today, I beseech you, enquire what root of bitterness has sprung up within you — what is that in which you are grieving God's Spirit — what is that in which you have been sowing to the flesh — what is that which has hindered you from seeing God this day. Has it been the absence of a spirit of prayer — or what conformity to a world lying under the wicked one — what fear of bearing the reproach of God's people — what fear of standing up for God's honour — what fear of acknowledging God's work, when God maketh bare his arm to work mighty works? What of all these has it been that has come as a withering blast upon you that you have not been partaking this day in the joy of the Lord? It is better that you should have been made to feel that the Lord is *jealous*, very jealous — it is better that you should have been made to feel that the Lord is righteous: most righteous — and while he is ever forgiving, and ever inviting, and ever receiving back every one who comes to him, yet it is the case that no departure from God can pass without the expression of God's displeasure upon it. O I do feel that the children of God, in resting their attention on the assured faith of God's love — upon the necessity of rejoicing in Christ, as the only condition of giving glory to God, are exposed to the great delusion of being hindered from looking narrowly into their own hearts and their services to God. I beseech you, be not afraid to look at the worst of it. I beseech you do not mistake a continual habit of thinking of yourselves as the people of God for the *realising* of the love of God in the soul of man. There is no greater or more dangerous device of Satan than this, and it is not the less dangerous because it is only when men are taught to rejoice in God, that they are exposed to it; for it is the peculiar form of delusion that Satan makes use of in such a season as this. If God has not been seen by any one of his believing children I beseech him to consider what is the cause of separation. He will find it, not in any change of God — not in any diminution of the willingness of God to fill him with the Spirit, but he will find that he has been sowing to the flesh, and thus has been *deadening* and *darkening* his own soul: and I desire that he should find it out, and be humbled by it — and while I know there is a provision for continual joy in the Lord in whom we are to rejoice, yet do I know that as this joy exists in people, dwelling in flesh and blood, whose vision of God is ever obscured — whose conformity to God's mind is always limited, so must there arise out of this very fact that to know the history of the inward state of their hearts is to know the history of much darkness — of much sorrow — and of much grief. I dare not withhold one word of this, however Satan may lead some to wrest and abuse it because I know such things are; but I say not, 'They are shut out' — God has not withdrawn himself in *sovereignty,* as some will tell you: but *their iniquities* have raised a cloud between them and their God and their sins are causing him to hide his face from them. I beseech them to look the matter fully in the face, and if they have done iniquity in time past that they do so no more. It is only *in walking with God,* that we can have the sensible assurance of God's love. It is a very different thing to say that my walking with God is a proof to me that God loves me and to say that it is *in walking* with God that I shall know that God loves me. If a dear friend asks me to accompany him on a journey, in whose conversation I have continual expressions of his affection and love, it is not my walking with him that proves his love for me, but in walking with him I know his love. It is not my conversing with him that proves the warmth of his heart, but it is in conversing with him that *I know* it: and so it is in walking with God. I must have the revelation that God is love before I can walk with him, but in walking with him I am continually tasting it. I am continually trusting in him and finding him trustworthy. I am continually seeking him and finding him. I am continually putting up petitions which God is hearing and answering and thus I am getting into a personal intimacy with the eternal Jehovah, so that I can speak to him — as such a one as he is from personal experience, and I can say concerning his word, 'It tells me such and such things concerning his character. I believed it because it is the word of God. I went to God to find true whatever was said, and I found it all true.' And now I can say he answers my petitions — he bears my burdens — he lightens my darkness — he is contented to be my Lord and my God. I do not from all this gather the first proof that God loves me; but from this I gather personal experience that it was even as I was told. And every one who comes to God will say what the Eastern queen said of Solomon that the thousandth part was not told them of all the excellent love which they found in the heart of God. This is the true place of Christian experience: not to prove to me that Christ died for me — not to prove that God loves me — for, blessed be God, I have *his* word for that, and that is implied in the death of Christ; what I first knew by faith, I now know by experience —

what I knew before upon God's word, I now find by an intercourse with God and I can witness to the fullness of his love because that fullness hath come forth upon me. In thus walking with God I enjoy God. It is not saying my walking with God is a thing that entitles me to come to God: but it is just saying, 'If I don't come, I don't come'. This is obvious, you will say and yet this is all. How can I see the face I don't look at? How can I hear the voice I don't listen to? If I am looking another way I can never rejoice in that love, however tender — if I listen not to his voice: its tones, however tender, can never awaken my confidence. The secret of the Lord is with those that fear him — they who walk with him know the blessedness that there is in serving God.

Now I would say a few words to the children of God, according to the season. I believe that when God places his watchmen in Zion, it is the mind of God, that they should tell the hour of the night, and it is not only an eternal truth we have to declare, but in all times and circumstances our eyes are to be opened to see the present condition of the people, and speak accordingly. And therefore I would say to them that while I know that at all times the blessedness of man is in dwelling in the secret of the Lord, I know the time is fast approaching in which they will *peculiarly* need to know the way into that sweet hiding place. The time is fast approaching in which they will need to know what it is to escape from things seen and temporal to things unseen and eternal, from the things of man to the things of God.

My dear hearers! There are two operations which always produce and reproduce each other — where the light of God is shining in my heart, there it will produce enmity on the part of the world, and where this last is, it will, if rightly understood, increase the love of God. I wish you to know then that every one who is now believing that God loves this sinful world, and that this love embraces every child of Adam — that every one who knows and believes this truth is set up of God, as a light to the world, that he should spread the light of this truth. And I see in this truth the very principle that explains to me the enmity of the people of the world to the name of Jesus and I see in the setting forth of his name that which stirreth up enmity: and I therefore remind you this day of the peculiar meaning which Christ has in the ordination of the Supper. It is to show forth his death till he come. And what is the meaning of this? It is that the Church is now called to participate in his sufferings and death, even until he come. The expectations of men and the counsel of

God are directly opposed to each other, when men are expecting *during* the period of the communion of the broken body and shed blood of Jesus — the period of the Church's glory. We have now given us this consoling light to comfort us, that the world hated our Lord — that the world put Christ to death — that while he was delivered by the determinate counsel and foreknowledge of God, men slew him by wicked hands. Thus we have a short way of deciding the question as to whether the world will praise the worthy as to whether the world will now be given to the worthiest, that is, to those who live on the broken body and shed blood — to those who show forth the Lord's death till he come again. Let not the having sat at the table of the Lord be unproductive of wisdom to you in this respect. As surely as the world hated Christ because he was God manifested in the flesh, so truly do the people of this land, who are unrenewed, hate every one in whom the same mind is manifested. Therefore you need to know that this is your present employment, to show forth the Lord's death till he come again and that it is a very different thing to hear of the sacrifices which others have made, and to think of the glory that there was in suffering for his name's sake — that this is very different from the tasting of it *yourself*.

That which you think your strength will in this prove your weakness: for it is not the man of much nerve — it is not the man commonly said to possess firmness and courage that is fit to fight this battle, those things that may make a conqueror, and may lead a man to the highest rank in the army or to the first place in parliament, all these powers of the natural man are just so many things in the way of the spiritual man, are just so many things to be crucified. What may appear strange too — a person's fearlessness of his fellow-men is just in some circumstances the same with the fear of man; and mere human courage is thus just human fear, for it is merely fearing some men more than others — merely fearing shame more than death — it is merely fearing the reproach of men more than the judgement seat of God — or it may be merely fearing even his own self-reproach in the pride of his heart. In all these things there is strength in the natural man, yet it will never avail you anything in this matter. What is the comfort if one class of people run down, and another class praise him: and if all the people of his own time will refuse to give him praise, yet after his death, it is to be hoped, (as is sometimes said) that justice will be done to his memory? Are not these the considerations that have comforted statesmen? Are not these the considerations by which their solitude has been sweetened? Men have thus been living on human applause all the while; for when the men with whom they were living refused it, they still thought they had a right to it — they still wished to have it and expected it of those who were to follow.

Those who fight the Lord's battles must be contented to be in no respect accounted of — they must expect to be in no respect encouraged by the expectation of human praise. And if you make an exception that the children of God will praise you, whatever the world will say, beware of this for you may turn them into a world, and find in them a world, and may sow to the flesh in sowing to their approbation: you will neither be benefited by them, nor they by you — so long as you are anxious as to how they will think of you. All such motives as these, if you are influenced by them, are a poison to you, and taking away from you the strength in which you are to give glory to God. I beseech you therefore, be prepared for a time when you shall be as persons unknown, even to those that know God. It is not the fact that all that see the face of the Lord do see each other — it is not the fact that the misapprehension of the world is the only misapprehension the Christian must be contented to labour under. He must expect even his brethren to see him through a mist, and to be disappointed of their sympathy, their cheers, and approbation. The man of God must walk alone with God, he must be contented that the Lord knoweth.

And it is such a relief; yea it is such a relief to the natural man within us to fall back upon human countenances, and human sympathy, that we often deceive ourselves and think it brotherly love when we are just resting on the earthly sympathy of a fellow-worm. You are to be followers of him who was left alone, and you are like him to rejoice that you are not alone, *because the Father is with you,* that you may give true glory to God. O! I cannot but speak of it. It is such a glory to God to see a soul that has been, through the flesh, accessible to the praise of men, surrounded by hundreds and thousands of his fellow creatures, every one of whom he knows how to please and yet that he should be contented, yea peaceful and happy in doing with a single reference to God, that which he knows they will all misunderstand and misconceive. Here was the victory of Jesus. There was not a single heart that beat in sympathy with his heart, or entered into his sorrow, or bore his grief, in the day of his bitter grief — but his way was with the Lord, his judgement was with his God, his Father, who said, 'This is my beloved Son in whom I am well pleased: hear ye him.' This was the perfect glory of the Father, that in flesh and blood such a trust in God was manifested.

And this is what you are called to — and you are not called to it as he was, seeing he was called to trust the invisible God, the unmanifested God: but you are called to see God in him. God has come near to you in Christ; and here you have a human heart — a perfect sympathy — the heart of God in your nature — and to this you are ever carried. And if there be any other sympathy with you in the wide universe, whether on the sea of glass, or still on this earth, it is only the pulsation of the blood that flows from Christ to his members, that is to you of any account. Feed upon it then, as it is in him — rejoice in it; and remember you are thus to walk in the world, not hanging upon one another. O! then be strong in him, and mighty to overcome all the might of the enemy.

Now I desire to say a word to those who have sat at the table of the Lord this day: but who must be conscious, if there is any truth in what I teach, that they had no right to be there. My dear hearers, I know quite well what an unholy operation there often is in such continual reproving — and that there is a tendency in the mind of man to say, 'We will go forward whether he will or not. What is his opinion to us? We will do as others do.' I know that by every step you take against the light, you cause a stronger voice to be raised in your hearts against the truth. I know that you are multiplying hindrances to yourselves, because you are multiplying deeds, which if you do not repent at all you must deeply sorrow over. But I charge you in the name of God that you consider what you have done. You who have not seen that Christ died for you: nor that Christ is given to you, as a living Head — I call on you to consider what a different thing it is now to take advantage of the veil of the flesh which conceals God from you and you from your fellows, and covered by that veil to come forward and take your place at the table of the Lord, from what it will be to have that place, when it will not be you that will take it but Christ that will give it. The time is fast coming when the Shepherd shall separate the sheep from the goats. Now the goats go on the road with the sheep, and no man can say, 'Keep back': but the time is at hand when the great Shepherd shall take out of his kingdom everything that hurteth, and defileth, and that loveth and maketh a lie. Now the tares and the wheat grow together, and the word is, 'Suffer them to grow together till the harvest': but the harvest is near, very near at hand, when he shall come and separate the tares from

Appendix 10

the wheat — the wheat he will gather into his garners, but the tares shall he gather into bundles and burn them with fire unquenchable. O the wrath of the Lamb! The terrors of him who suffered for those whom he gathereth. O the awful vengeance of that despised Lord who is coming back again — the crucified one — he who is despised and a reproach, and who is now a byword with the people — he who was cast off, as the offscouring of all things: and who has been cast off again and again and again, since he left this world, in the persons of his people — who has through them been thus insulted — thus hated — thus rejected, generation after generation: by countries and parishes and individuals one after another! He is coming to judge; and his fan is in his hand, and he will thoroughly purge his floor, and gather his wheat into the granary but the chaff he will burn with unquenchable fire. My dearly beloved friends, whom I love, because I know that God loves you, yet of whom I feel your condition is very awful: just because of this love. I would now warn you in the name of the Lord that this is the day of grace — the day in which God is not imputing sin to you — that this is a day which is fast coming to a close, and the word is, 'Seek the Lord while he may be found and call upon him while he is near.' The day of the Lord hasteth — all the signs show it. The terror of the Lord shall then be upon you. And O what shall it be for you that you should be among those whose hearts fail them for fear, when you ought to be among those who are giving glory to God. Now those of you who sat at the table of the Lord and know not the Lord, while they ought to have been there to the glory of God — you have been there to the gratification of Satan. You have no excuse, because everything has been set before you by so many lips that even the most ignorant may know.

But others have not been at the table of the Lord, and to them I would speak. I feel that the people are exposed to the awful mistake of imagining when I speak thus of those who have come to that table, not knowing the Lord, that they may say, 'We won't go to the table; and then we may live as we please. If we come to it then much would be expected of us — but as for us we make no pretensions. There are those who make high professions, and it would be a shame for *them* to do what we may do safely enough.' This is the way people talk when they single out those who are esteemed good, and think more is expected from them, than from others. If you would know what is expected of you, you must just know what God has done for you. It is not what you are that is of any importance. It is what

God has done for you — not whether you have chosen to come under grace — not whether you have chosen to make vows. You may have done none of these things — you may have thought yourselves better in not doing these things — but the judgement of God is not according to your choice, but according to what God has done for you. And what is that? What is it that is true concerning the most thoughtless of you? What is it that is true of the drunkards and the swearers — of those who are altogether absorbed in this world's pursuits? What is it that is true of the scoffers, yea of *every one* among the people? Just this — that Christ has shed his blood for them and that Christ has received the Spirit for them; and the glory, which God demands from each of you, and in withholding which you expose yourselves to the wrath to come, is the glory due from those who have been so bought. It is not the place you choose to take; but the place God gives you that is the important question. It is that the Lord has suffered and died, the just for the unjust — that God has now made propitiation for your sins — that he ascended from the grave after having conquered the devil — that he ascended upon high, leading captivity captive — that he purchased your liberty — that he proclaimed, 'You are free' — that he has strength for you to glorify God, and therefore you are without excuse in not giving glory to God. It will not be the question on a day of judgement, did you make a profession or not, but, are you a child of Adam: and are you being a child of the first Adam included in the work of the second Adam? Did Christ die for you? Did Christ rise for you? Did Christ reveal himself in his word preached to you? Did Christ make known his grace to you? These are the questions, and according to them you will be judged. O to see the coldness, the apathy with which people will discuss the question whether Christ died for all, or only for some. People speak upon these subjects with the same listlessness and want of personal interest with which they debate upon politics, excepting when the thing is much pressed upon them and then the enmity of their hearts turns their indifference to hatred. Is it not fearful to think that this one important truth of God, by which you now stand here — through the effects of which it is that you are there to listen and I am here to speak and according to which you are to be judged, should be a matter of such little moment to you? O it is not your unbelief that will condemn you at last but the cause of your unbelief. Men ask if there is no sin to be punished but unbelief? Unbelief is just the expression of the state of the heart — the inward state of enmity to God out of which the unbelief springs which God punishes. You think it is a matter of ignorance or of knowledge. If you would see that it is a matter of hating or of loving God, then you would have some notion of the awfulness of it. And I now charge every one present who refuses to believe that Christ has taken away his sins — who refuses to believe that Christ died and rose for him — I charge every such man with refusing to believe this *because he hates the light, and loves the darkness,* and this darkness he loves because his deeds are evil. And he may say, if he please, 'I cannot believe that doctrine for, if true, people may do what they please: but the secret feeling of his heart is — if the doctrine be true, we must sacrifice our present joys — we must be holy, we cannot stand on this supposed neutral ground. And it is the holiness of the doctrine — I charge it upon you — it is because it gives no place to sin — it is because it places you continually in a condition in which you can have no apology for not rejoicing in God — it is because it places you between these two things, either to believe what is told you and give glory to God, or to refuse it and make God a liar, that you refuse to believe it.

And whatever face you may put upon it among one another, whatever that face be, it is the secret fact, and your hearts know it, *I say your hearts know it* — and you are not honest with your God in the matter and you cannot put your hands on your hearts before God at this moment — no man can do so — and say that he ever supposed a single word which I spoke to him in the name of God, to have been intended, or to have a tendency to encourage him to commit sin. You know well this is not what we labour for. It is to give glory to God — and whatever words you my use, this is lying at the bottom of your hearts — you are just smothering your consciences — you are just keeping down the voice of conscience. But the time is coming when you can still it no longer — the time is coming when Christ will say, 'That voice was my messenger' — and will say it so loud, that they that are in their grave shall hear it — will say it so loud, that the mountains shall remove because of it — will say it so loud, that the things which are made shall be shaken and removed, the elements shall melt with fervent heat at the voice of that same righteous truth of God — at the voice of that same testimony concerning God. And you will then be taught to know it and to recognise it, and will be compelled to say, 'That is what our ministers taught us, though we then heard and believed it not, now we hear it revealed in flames of fire, and by the Head himself.' O dear, dear souls, that are thus destroying yourselves, will ye not turn to God? Will you not suffer him to bless you? Will you not receive Christ to dwell with you? Will you not believe that in very truth he desires to make you temples of the living God? Listen! O listen and God give you to receive his word.

Amen!

Bibliography

Primary sources: Works by John McLeod Campbell

Notes and Recollections of Two Sermons, by the Rev. Mr. Campbell, delivered in the Parish Church of Row on Sunday, 6th September 1829, (Greenock: R. B. Lusk, 1829).

A Letter written as A Word in Season to His People, by the Rev. J. M. Campbell, Minister of Row, (Greenock: R. B. Lusk, 1830).

Good Tidings of Great Joy to All People, (Glasgow: Edward Khull, 1830).

Notes of a Sermon, preached in the Parish Church of Row, on Thursday, 8th July 1830; Being the day of the visitation of that Parish by the Presbytery of Dumbarton. By the Rev. J. M. Campbell, Minister of Row, (Greenock: R. B. Lusk, 1830).

Notes of Sermons, Number One, (Greenock: R. B. Lusk, 1830).

The Everlasting Gospel; Notes of a Sermon, by the Rev. J. M. Campbell, Minister of Row, Dumbartonshire; Preached in the Floating Chapel, at Greenock, 28th April, 1830, (Greenock: R. B. Lusk, 1830).

Tract IV: Peace That Is Not Peace, (Greenock: R. B. Lusk, 1830).

Tract V: Peace in the Knowledge of God, (Greenock: R. B. Lusk, 1830).

Tract XIII: The Gospel, Good News concerning the Son of God, (Greenock: R. B. Lusk, 1830).

Two Sermons, (London: John Hatchard & Son, 1830).

Notes of Sermons by the Rev. J. McL. Campbell, Taken in Short Hand, 3 vols., lithographic reproduction, (Paisley: J. Vallance, 1831 & 1832).

Sermons and Lectures, Taken in Short Hand, Vol. I, (Greenock: R. B. Lusk, 1831[3]).

Sermons and Lectures, Taken in Short Hand, Vol II, (Greenock: R. B. Lusk, 1832).

Speech delivered at the bar of the Very Reverend the Synod of Glasgow and Ayr, on Wednesday, the 13th April, 1831, (Greenock: R.B. Lusk, 1831).

The Whole Proceedings before the Presbytery of Dumbarton, and Synod of Glasgow and Ayr, in the case of the Rev. John M'Leod Campbell, Minister of Row, including the libel, answers to the libel, evidence, and speeches, (Greenock: R. B. Lusk, 1831).

The Whole Proceedings in the case of the Rev. John M'Leod Campbell, late minister of Row, before the Presbytery of Dumbarton, the Synod of Glasgow and Ayr, and the General Assembly of the Church of Scotland; including besides all the documents, the speeches in all the different church courts, (Greenock: R. B. Lusk, 1831).

On keeping a Conscience Void of Offence towards God and towards Man, while considering what claims to be of God, Tract 1, (Greenock: Greenock Intelligencer, May 1834); Tract 2, (Glasgow: Edward Khull, July 1834).

Fragments of Expositions of Scripture, (London: J. Wright & Co, 1843).

Christ the Bread of Life: An attempt to give a profitable direction to the present occupation of thought with Romanism, (Glasgow: Maurice Ogle and Son, 1851).

Fragments of Truth: Being the Exposition of Several Passages of Scripture, (Edinburgh: Edmonston and Douglas, 1861[3]).

Fragments of Truth: Being Expositions of Passages of Scripture chiefly from the teaching of John McLeod Campbell, D.D. (Edinburgh: David Douglas, 1898[4]).

Thoughts on Revelation, (London: Macmillan, 1862).

Christ the Bread of Life: An attempt to give a profitable direction to the present occupation of thought with Romanism, (London: Macmillan and Co., 1869[2]).

Good Tidings of Great Joy to All People, (London: James Nisbet & Co, 1873[2]).

Reminiscences and Reflections, Referring to his early ministry in the parish of Row, 1825-31, edited with Introduction by Donald Campbell (London: Macmillan, 1873).

Responsibility for the Gift of Eternal Life, (London: Macmillan, 1873).

Memorials of John McLeod Campbell, D.D., Being selections from his correspondence, 2 vols., (ed.), Donald Campbell, (London: Macmillan, 1877).

The Nature of the Atonement, (London: Macmillan, 1906⁶).

The Nature of the Atonement, with new Introduction by James B. Torrance, (Carberry: Handsel Press, 1996).

Other Primary Sources

Anonymous, *Bible Readings*, (Edinburgh: David Douglas, 1864).

— *Christianity and Calvinism. The Rev. J. M. Campbell of the Row, the Synod of Glasgow & Ayr, the Confession of Faith, and the Bible, (Second Edition)*, (Glasgow: James Hedderwick and Son, 1831).

Barclay, George, *Strictures on the 'Notes and Recollections of Two Sermons, by the Rev. Mr. Campbell; Delivered in the Parish Church of Row, on Sunday, 8th September, 1829.'*, (Glasgow: Maurice Ogle, 1830).

Brash, Thomas, *Thomas Carlyle's double-goer and his connection with the parish of Row: a lecture delivered to the guild of Park United Free Church, Helensburgh, on 15th February, 1904*, (Helensburgh: Macneur & Bryden, 1904).

Buchanan, James, *A Letter to Thomas Erskine, Esq., Advocate, containing remarks on his late work, entitled 'The Unconditional Freeness of the Gospel.' By a Minister of the Church of Scotland*, (Edinburgh: John Lindsay & Co., 1828).

Burns, Robert, *The Gairloch heresy tried; in a letter to the Rev. John M. Campbell, of Row; and a sermon preached at Helensburgh and at Port-Glasgow*, (Paisley: Alex. Gardner:, 1830³).

— *The Church Revived without the Aid of Unknown Tongues. A Sermon preached in the Scots Church, Swallow Street, on Sabbath the*

6th *November 1831, to which are now added a few prefatory remarks*, (London: A. Douglas, 1831).

Carlyle, G., (ed.), *The Collected Writings of Edward Irving in Five Volumes*, (London: Alexander Strahan, 1865) Volume 5.

Carlyle, Thomas, A lay Member of the Church of Scotland. *Letter to the Rev. Robert Burns, D.D. F.S.A. and the Rev. Willam Hamilton, D.D., Occasioned by Their Late Publication Entitled 'The Gairloch Heresy Tried,' and 'Remarks on Certain Opinions Recently Propagated, Respecting Universal Redemption,' &c*, (Greenock: R. B. Lusk, 1830).

— *Protestant Truths and Popish Errors: A Letter to the Author of 'The Gareloch Heresy Tried;' Occcasioned by His Reply to the Lay Member of the Church of Scotland: With a Postscript Addressed to the Rev. Dr. Hamilton, Strathblane*, (Greenock: R. B. Lusk, 1830).

Carlile, Warrand, *'Christ tempted in all points like as we are, yet without sin.' An article which appeared in No. IX of 'The Morning Watch' under the title ON THE HUMAN NATURE OF CHRIST*, (London: James Nisbet, 1831).

Erskine, Thomas, *On the Gifts of the Spirit*, (Greenock: R. B. Lusk, 1830).

— *The Doctrine of Election and its Connection with the General Tenor of Christianity*, (Edinburgh: David Douglas, 1878²).

Fisher, Edward, *The Marrow of Modern Divinity*, originally published in 1645 and 1649, edited by C. G. M'Crie, (Glasgow: David Bryce, 1902).

Knox, John, *The Works of John Knox, Volume II*, (ed.), David Laing, (Edinburgh: Woodrow Society, 1848).

— *The History of the Reformation of Religion in Scotland*, (ed.), Cuthbert Lennox, (London: Andrew Melrose, 1905).

Hanna, William, (ed.), *Memoirs of the Life and Writings of Thomas Chalmers, D.D. L.L.D.*, Volume III, (Edinburgh: Sutherland and Knox, 1851).

— *Letters of Thomas Erskine of Linlathen*, (Edinburgh: David Douglas, 1884).

'Report on the Death of The Rev. John McLeod Campbell, DD'., *Glasgow Herald*, February 29th, 1872.

Story, Robert Herbert, *The Risen Christ: A Sermon preached in Rosneath Church on the Lord's Day after the death of John McLeod Campbell, D.D.*, (Glasgow: James Maclehose, 1872).

— *Memoir of the Life of the Rev. Robert Story, Late Minister of Rosneath, Dumbartonshire. Including Passages of Scottish Religious and Ecclesiastical History During the Second Quarter of the Present Century*, (Cambridge: Macmillan, 1862).

Secondary Works: John McLeod Campbell and Scottish Theology

Anderson, Robert Alexander, *John McLeod Campbell: The Problem of Authority in Religion*, (Oxford: DPhil. Dissertation, 1978).

Bebbington, D. W., *Evangelicalism in Modern Britain: A history from the 1730s to the 1980s*, (London: Unwin Hyman, 1989).

— *Victorian Nonconformity*, (Bangor: Headstart History, 1992).

Bell, M. Charles, *Calvin and Scottish Theology: The Doctrine of Assurance*, (Edinburgh: Handsel Press, 1985).

Bewkes, Eugene Garrett, 'John McLeod Campbell, Theologian: His Theological Development and Trial, and a New Interpretation of His Theory of the Atonement', Unpublished PhD, University of Edinburgh (1924).

— *Legacy of a Christian mind; John M'Leod Campbell, Eminent Contributor to Theological Thought*, (Philadelphia: Judson Press, 1937).

Brown, Stewart J., *Thomas Chalmers and the Godly Commonwealth in Scotland*, (Oxford: Oxford University Press, 1982).

Burleigh, J. H. S., *A Church History of Scotland*, (London: Oxford University Press, 1960).

Chambers, D., 'Doctrinal attitudes in the Church of Scotland in the Pre-Disruption era: The age of John McLeod Campbell and Edward Irving', *Journal of Religious History*, 8 (1974) 159-182.

Cheyne, A. C., 'The Place of the Confession through three centuries', in Alasdair I. C. Heron (ed.), *The Westminster Confession in the Church today*, (Edinburgh: St. Andrew Press, 1982) 17-27.

— *Studies in Scottish Church History*, (Edinburgh: T&T Clark, 1999).

Church, R. W., *The Oxford Movement: Twelve Years: 1833-1845*, with an introduction by G. F. A. Best, (Chicago: University of Chicago Press, 1970).

Dale, R. W., *The Atonement: The Congregational Union Lecture for 1875*, (London: Congregational Union, 1909⁷).

Dallimore, Arnold, *The Life of Edward Irving: Fore-runner of the Charismatic Movement*, (Edinburgh: Banner of Truth, 1983).

Dorries, David W., 'Nineteenth Century British Christological Controversy, centring upon Edward Irving's Doctrine of Christ's human nature', Unpublished PhD, University of Aberdeen (1987).

Drummond, Andrew Langdale, *Edward Irving and his circle*, (London: James Clarke 1936).

Drummond, Andrew L. and Bulloch, James, *The Scottish Church 1688 - 1843: The Age of the Moderates*, (Edinburgh: Saint Andrew Press, 1973).

Faris, Donald Leonard, 'The Nature of Theological Inquiry as Raised by the Conflict of the Teaching of McLeod Campbell and Westminster Theology', Unpublished PhD, New College, University of Edinburgh (1967).

Flegg, Columba Graham, *'Gathered Under Apostles': A Study of the Catholic Apostolic Church*, (Oxford: Clarendon Press, 1992).

Gerrish, B. A., *Tradition and the Modern World: Reformed Theology in the Nineteenth Century*, (Chicago: University of Chicago Press, 1978).

Goodloe, James C., 'John McLeod Campbell, the Atonement and the Transformation of the Religious Consciousness', Unpublished PhD, University of Chicage (1987).

— *John McLeod Campbell: The Extent and Nature of the Atonement*, Studies in Reformed Theology and History (New Series 3), (Princeton Theological Seminary: Princeton, 1997).

— 'Redeeming the past by reproducing the atonement', *Scottish Journal of Theology* 45 (1992) 185-208.

Grass, Tim, "The Restoration of a congregation of Baptists': Baptists and Irvingism in Oxfordshire', *Baptist Quarterly* XXXVII (1998) 283-297.

Hart, Trevor A., 'Anselm of Canterbury and John McLeod Campbell: Where Opposites Meet?' *Evangelical Quarterly* 62 (1990) 311-333.

Helm, Paul, *Calvin and the Calvinists*, (Edinburgh: Banner of Truth, 1982).

— 'The logic of limited atonement', *Scottish Bulletin of Evangelical Theology* 3 (1985) 47-54.

Henderson, G. D., *The Burning Bush: Studies in Scottish Church History*, (Edinburgh: Saint Andrew Press, 1957).

Hilton, Boyd, *The Age of Atonement: The Influence of Evangelicalism on Social and Economic Thought, 1795-1865*, (Oxford: Clarendon Press, 1988).

Hopkins, Mark T. E., *Baptists, Congregationalists, and Theological Change: Some Late Nineteenth Century Leaders and Controversies*, (Oxford: DPhil. Dissertation, 1988).

— *Nonconformity's Romantic Generation: Evangelical and Liberal Theologies in Victorian England: Nonconformity's Romantic Generation*, (Carlisle: Paternoster, 2004).

Horrocks, Don, *Laws of the Spiritual Order: Innovation and Reconstruction in the Soteriology of Thomas Erskine of Linlathen*, (Carlisle: Paternoster, 2004).

Jinkins, Michael, 'John McLeod Campbell', in Donald K. McKim (ed.), *Encyclopedia of the Reformed Faith*, (Edinburgh: Saint Andrew Press, 1992) 55-56.

— *A Comparative Study in the Theology of Atonement in Jonathan Edwards and John McLeod Campbell: Atonement and the Character of God,* (San Francisco: Mellen Research University Press, 1993).

— *Love is of the Essence: An Introduction to the Theology of John McLeod Campbell,* (Saint Andrew Press: Edinburgh, 1993).

— 'John McLeod Campbell', in Trevor A. Hart (ed.), *The Dictionary of Historical Theology,* (Carlisle: Paternoster, 2000) 106-108.

Jinkins, M. and Stephen Breck Reid, 'John McLeod Campbell on Christ's Cry of Dereliction: A case study in Trinitarian Hermeneutics', *The Evangelical Quarterly* LXX (1998) 135-149.

Johnson, Christine, *Developments in the Roman Catholic Church in Scotland 1789-1829,* (Edinburgh: John Donald, 1983).

Kendall, R.T., *Calvin and English Calvinism to 1649,* (Oxford: Oxford University Press, 1979).

Kettler, Christian D., 'The vicarious representation of Christ in the theology of John McLeod Campbell and R. C. Moberly', *Scottish Journal of Theology,* 38 (1985) 529-543.

— *The Vicarious Humanity of Christ and the Reality of Salvation,* (New York: University Press of America, 1991).

Kinnear, Malcolm A., 'Marcus Dods, John McLeod Campbell and the Atonement', *Scottish Bulletin of Evangelical Theology,* 13 (1995) 4-14.

Leckie, J. H., 'John McLeod Campbell: The Development of His Thought. I', *The Expositor, Eighth Series* 21 (1921) 54-67.

— 'John McLeod Campbell: The Development of His Thought. II', *The Expositor, Eighth Series* 21 (1921) 107-120.

— 'The Teaching of John McLeod Campbell', *The Expositor, Eighth Series* 25 (1923) 370-386.

— 'John McLeod Campbell's 'The Nature of the Atonement'', *Expository Times,* 40 (1928-1929) 198-204.

Logan, John B., 'Thomas Erskine of Linlathen, lay Theologian of the 'Inner Light'', *Scottish Journal of Theology,* 37 (1984) 23-40.

MacGregor, Geddes, 'The Row Heresy', *Harvard Theological Review* 43 (1950) 281-301.

Macleod, Donald, 'The Doctrine of the Incarnation in Scottish Theology: Edward Irving', *Scottish Bulletin of Evangelical Theology* 9 (1991) 40-50.

Macquarrie, J., 'Campbell on Atonement', in *Thinking about God*, (London: SCM Press, 1975) 167-178.

McFarlane, Graham, 'Christology and the Spirit in the Teaching of Edward Irving', Unpublished PhD, King's College, London (1989).

— 'Strange News from Another Star: An Anthropological Insight from Edward Irving', in Christoph Schwöbel, and Colin E. Gunton (eds.), *Persons, Divine and Human*, (Edinburgh: T & T Clark, 1991) 98-119.

— *Christ and the Spirit: The Doctrine of the Incarnation according to Edward Irving*, (Carlisle: Paternoster, 1996).

McIntyre, John, *Prophet of penitence: our contemporary ancestor*, (Saint Andrew Press: Edinburgh, 1972).

Murray, Douglas M., 'John McLeod Campbell', *The Blackwell Dictionary of Evangelical Biography 1730 - 1860*, volume 1, (Oxford: Blackwell, 1995) 191.

Needham, N. R., *Thomas Erskine of Linlathen: his life and theology 1788-1837*, (Edinburgh: Rutherford House, 1990).

— 'John McLeod Campbell', in Nigel M. de S. Cameron, *et al.* (eds.), *Dictionary of Scottish Church History and Theology* (Edinburgh: T & T Clark, 1993) 129-130.

— 'Thomas Erskine', in *Dictionary of Scottish Church History and Theology* 302-303.

— 'Robert Story', in *Dictionary of Scottish Church History and Theology* 798.

— 'Thomas Erskine', *The Blackwell Dictionary of Evangelical Biography 1730 - 1860*, volume 1, (Oxford: Blackwell, 1995) 364-365.

Newell, J. Philip, *A. J. Scott and His Circle*, Unpublished PhD, University of Edinbugh (1981).

— 'Scottish intimations of modern Pentecostalism: A. J. Scott and the 1830 Clydeside Charismatics', *Pneuma* 4 (1982) 1-18.

— 'Alexander John Scott', in Nigel M. de S. Cameron, *et al.* (eds.), *Dictionary of Scottish Church History and Theology*, (Edinburgh: T & T Clark, 1993) 752-753.

Nockles, Peter B., *The Oxford Movement in Context: Anglican High Churchmanship 1760 - 1857*, (Cambridge: Cambridge University Press, 1994).

Oliphant, Mrs M.O.W., *The Life of Edward Irving*, (London: Hurst and Blackett, 1864[5]).

Redding, Graham, 'The Significance of the Priesthood of Christ for a Theology of Prayer in the Reformed tradition, with reference to T. F. and J. B. Torrance and the Eucharistic tradition of the Church of Scotland', Unpublished PhD, King's College, University of London (1999).

Sell, Alan P. F., *Defending and Declaring the Faith: Some Scottish Examples 1860-1920*, (Exeter: Paternoster, 1987).

Shanks, D. A., *The Life and Thought of John McLeod Campbell*, (Glasgow: PhD. Dissertation, 1957).

Spence, Alan, 'Incarnation and Inspiration: John Owen and the Coherence of Christology', Unpublished PhD, King's College, London (1989).

— 'Christ's Humanity and Ours: John Owen', in Christoph Schwöbel, and Colin E. Gunton (eds.), *Persons, Divine and Human,* (Edinburgh: T & T Clark, 1991) 74-97.

Strachan, C. Gordon, *The Pentecostal Theology of Edward Irving*, (London: Darton, Longman & Todd, 1973).

— 'Theological and Cultural Origins of the Nineteenth Century Pentecostal Movement', in Paul Elbert (ed.), *Essays of Apostolic Themes: Studies in Honor of Howard M. Ervin*, (Peabody: Hendrickson, 1985) 144-157.

Stunt, Timothy C. F., 'Alexander John Scott', *The Blackwell Dictionary of Evangelical Biography 1730 - 1860*, volume 2, (Oxford: Blackwell, 1995) 986-987.

— *From Awakening to Secession: Radical Evangelicals in Switzerland and Britain 1815-1835*, (Edinburgh: T & T Clark, 2000).

Thimell, Daniel P., 'Christ in Our place in the theology of John McLeod Campbell', in Trevor A. Hart and Daniel P. Thimell, (eds.), *Christ In Our Place: The Humanity of God in Christ for the Reconciliation of the World*, (Exeter: Paternoster Press, 1989) 182-206.

Torrance, James B., 'Covenant or Contract? A study of the theological background of worship in seventeenth-century Scotland', *Scottish Journal of Theology* 23 (1970) 51-76.

— 'The Contribution of McLeod Campbell to Scottish Theology', *Scottish Journal of Theology*, 26 (1973) 295-311.

— 'The Vicarious Humanity and Priesthood of Christ in the Theology of John Calvin', in W. H. Neuser (ed.), *Calvinus Ecclesiae Doctor: Die Referate des Congrès International de Recherches Calviniennes vom 25. bis 28. September, 1978 in Amsterdam*, (Kampen: J. H. Kok B.V., 1978) 69-84.

— 'The Covenant Concept in Scottish Theology and Politics and its Legacy', *Scottish Journal of Theology* 34 (1981) 225-243.

— 'The Vicarious Humanity of Christ', in T. F. Torrance (ed.), *The Incarnation*, (Edinburgh: Handsel Press, 1981) 127-147.

— 'Calvin and Puritanism in England and Scotland - Some basic concepts in the development of 'federal theology'', in *Calvinus Reformator - His contribution to Theology, Church and Society* (Potchefstroom: Potchefstroom University, 1982).

— 'Strengths and Weaknesses of the Westminster Theology', in Alasdair I. C. Heron (ed.), *The Westminster Confession in the Church Today* (Edinburgh: St. Andrew Press, 1982) 40-54.

— 'The Incarnation and Limited Atonement', *The Evangelical Quarterly* 55 (1984) 83-94.

— 'Interpreting the Word by the Light of Christ or the Light of Nature? Calvin, Calvinism, and Barth', in R. V. Schnucker (ed.),

Calviniana - Ideas and Influence of Jean Calvin, Volume X (1986) 255-267.

— 'The Concept of Federal Theology - Was Calvin a Federal Theologian?', in W. H. Neuser, (ed.), *Calvinus Sacrae Scriptura Professor: Calvin as Confessor of Holy Scripture* (Grand Rapids: Eerdmans, 1990) 15-40.

— *Worship, Community and the Triune God of Grace,* (Carlisle: Paternoster, 1996).

Torrance, Thomas F., *Theology in Reconciliation,* (London: Geoffrey Chapman, 1975).

— *The Incarnation: Ecumenical Studies in the Nicene-Constantinopolitan Creed A.D. 381* (Edinburgh: Handsel Press, 1981).

— *The Trinitarian Faith,* (Edinburgh: T & T Clark, 1988).

— *Royal Priesthood: A Theology of Ordained Ministry,* (Edinburgh: T & T Clark, 1993^2).

— 'From John Knox to John McLeod Campbell: A Reading of Scottish Theology', in David F. Wright and Gary D. Badcock (eds.), *Disruption to Diversity: Edinburgh Divinity 1846-1996,* (Edinburgh: T&T Clark, 1996) 1-28.

— *Scottish Theology from John Knox to John McLeod Campbell,* (Edinburgh: T & T Clark, 1996).

Turbeville, Dean, 'Review of *The Nature of the Atonement,* by J. McLeod Campbell. Eerdmans, Grand Rapids, 1996', *Interpretation* 52 (1998) 98-99.

Tuttle, George M., *John McLeod Campbell on Christian Atonement: So Rich a Soil,* (Edinburgh: Handsel Press, 1986).

— 'The place of John McLeod Campbell in British thought concerning the atonement', Unpublished PhD, Emmanuel College, Victoria, University of Toronto (1961)

Van Dyk, Leanne, *The Desire of Divine Love: John McLeod Campbell's Doctrine of the Atonement* (New York: P. Lang, 1995).

— 'Toward a New Typology of Reformed Doctrines of Atonement', in David Willis and Michael Welker (eds.), *Toward* the *Future of Reformed Theology: Tasks, Topics, Traditions,* (Grand Rapids: Eerdmans, 1999), 225-238.

Whitley, H. C., *Blinded Eagle: An Introduction to the Life and Teaching of Edward Irving,* (London: SCM Press, 1955).

Winslow, Donald F., *Thomas Erskine: Advocate for the Character of God,* (Lanham: University Press of America, 1993).

Wolffe, John, *The Protestant Crusade in Great Britain 1829 - 1860,* (Oxford: Clarendon Press, 1991).

— *God and Greater Britain: Religion and National Life in Britain and Ireland 1843-1945,* (London: Routledge, 1994).

— (ed.), *Evangelical Faith and Public Zeal,* (London: SPCK, 1995).

Worrall, B. G., *The Making of the Modern Church: Christianity in England since 1800,* (London: SPCK, 1993²).

Wright, D. F., 'Isabella Campbell', in Nigel M. de S. Cameron, *et al.* (eds.), *Dictionary of Scottish Church History and Theology,* (Edinburgh: T & T Clark, 1993) 128-129.

Wright D. F. and Gary D. Badcock (eds.), *Disruption to Diversity: Edinburgh Divinity 1846-1996,* (Edinburgh: T&T Clark, 1996).

Wright, Ronald Selby, *Fathers of the kirk; some leaders of the church in Scotland from the Reformation to the reunion,* (London: Oxford University Press, 1960).

Secondary Works: General

Athanasius, *The Incarnation of the Word of God: Being the Treatise of St. Athanasius, De Incarnatione Verbi Dei*, with an introduction by C. S. Lewis, (London: Geoffrey Bles, 1944).

— *St. Athanasius: Select Works and Letters: Nicene and Post-Nicene Fathers of the Christian Church*, second series, vol.4 (eds.), P. Schaff and H. Wace, (Edinburgh: T & T Clark, 1891).

Aulén, G., *Christus Victor: An Historical Study of the Three Main Types of the Idea of the Atonement*, trans. Herbert, A. G., (London: SPCK, 1931).

Balthasar, Hans Urs von, *Mysterium Paschale*, (Edinburgh: T & T Clark, 1990).

Barrett, C. K, *A Commentary on The Epistle to the Romans*, (London: A & C Black, 1971).

Barth, K., *Church Dogmatics, vol. I, part 2*, (Edinburgh: T & T Clark, 1956).

— *Church Dogmatics, vol. II, part 2*, (Edinburgh: T & T Clark, 1957).

— *Church Dogmatics, vol. IV, part 1*, (Edinburgh: T & T Clark, 1956).

— *Church Dogmatics, vol. IV, part 2*, (Edinburgh: T & T Clark, 1958).

Bettenson, Henry, (ed.), *Documents of the Christian Church*, (Oxford: Oxford University Press, 1963²).

— (ed.), *The Early Church Fathers: A selection from the writings of the Fathers from St. Clement of Rome to St. Athanasius*, (Oxford: Oxford University Press, 1956).

— (ed.), *The Later Church Fathers: A selection from the writings of the Fathers from St. Cyril of Jerusalem to St. Leo the Great*, (Oxford: Oxford University Press, 1970).

Braaten, Carl E., 'The Person of Jesus Christ', in *Christian Dogmatics, Volume 2*, Carl E. Braaten and Robert W. Jenson (eds.), (Philadelphia: Fortress Press, 1984) 465-569.

Braaten, Carl E. and Robert W. Jenson (eds.), *Christian Dogmatics*, 2 vols. (Philadelphia: Fortress Press, 1984).

Calvin, J., *Institutes of the Christian Religion*, (ed.), McNeill, J.T., (Philadelphia: Westminster Press, 1960).

— *Calvin: Commentaries*, (ed.), Haroutunian, J., (London: SCM Press, 1958).

— *Calvin: Theological Treatises*, (ed.), Reid, J. K. S., (London: SCM Press, 1954).

— *The Epistle of Paul the Apostle to the Hebrews and the First and Second Epistles of St. Peter*, (Grand Rapids: Eerdmans, 1963).

Cameron, George G., *The Scots Kirk in London*, (Oxford: Becket Publications, 1979).

Carey, George, *The Gate of Glory*, (London: Hodder & Stoughton, 1986).

Cave, Sydney, *The Doctrine of the Work of Christ*, (London: University of London & Hodder & Stoughton, 1937).

Chadwick, Owen, *The Spirit of the Oxford Movement: Tractarian Essays*, (Cambridge: Cambridge University Press, 1990).

Cross, F. L. and Livingstone, E. A., (eds.), *The Oxford Dictionary of the Christian Church*, (Oxford: Oxford University Press, 1997).

Cranfield, C. E. B., *Romans: A Shorter Commentary*, (Edinburgh: T & T Clark, 1985).

Del Colle, Ralph, *Christ and the Spirit: Spirit - Christology in Trinitarian Perspective*, (Oxford: Oxford University Press, 1994).

— 'Schleiermacher and Spirit Christology: Unexplored Horizons of *The Christian Faith*', *International Journal of Systematic Theology* 1 (1999) 286-307.

Dillistone, F. W., *The Christian Understanding of Atonement*, (Welwyn: James Nisbet, 1968).

Dragas, George Dion, 'The Eternal Son: An Essay on Christology in the Early Church with particular reference to St. Athanasius the Great', in Thomas F. Torrance (ed.), *The Incarnation: Ecumenical Studies in the Nicene-Constantinopolitan Creed A. D. 381* (Edinburgh: Handsel Press, 1981) 16-57.

— 'St. Athanasius on Christ's Sacrifice', in S. W. Sykes (ed.), *Sacrifice and Redemption: Durham Essays in Theology*, (Cambridge: Cambridge University Press, 1991) 73-100.

Driver, J., *Understanding the Atonement for the Mission of the Church*, (Scottdale: Herald Press, 1986).

Duff, Nancy J., 'Atonement and the Christian Life: Reformed Doctrine from a Feminist Perspective', *Interpretation* 53 (1999) 34-43.

Dunn, J. D. G., 'Paul's understanding of the Death of Jesus as Sacrifice', in S. W. Sykes (ed.), *Sacrifice and Redemption: Durham Essays in Theology*, (Cambridge: Cambridge University Press, 1991) 35-56.

— *Romans: Word Biblical Commentary*, (Milton Keynes: Word, 1991).

Farrow, Douglas, *Ascension and Ecclesia*, (Edinburgh: T & T Clark, 1999).

— 'Confessing Christ Coming', in C. R. Seitz (ed.), *Nicene Christianity: The Future for a New Ecumenism*, (Grand Rapids: Brazos, 2001 /Carlisle: Paternoster, 2001), pp133-148.

Fiddes, P. S., *Past Event and Present Salvation*, (London: Darton Longman and Todd, 1989).

Ford, David F., *Self and Salvation: Being Transform(ed.)*, (Cambridge: CUP, 1999).

Forsyth, P. T., *The Person and Place of Jesus Christ*, (London: Hodder & Stoughton, 1910).

— *The Work of Christ*, (London: Independent Press: 1938^2).

Fowl, Stephen E., (ed.), *The Theological Interpretation of Scripture: Classic and Contemporary Readings*, (Oxford: Blackwell, 1997).

Goldingay, J., (ed.), *Atonement Today* (London: SPCK, 1995).

Gorringe, T., *God's Just Vengeance: Crime, violence and the rhetoric of salvation*, (Cambridge: Cambridge University Press, 1996).

Grey, M., *Redeeming the dream: feminism, redemption and Christian Tradition* (London: SPCK, 1989).

Gunton, Colin E., *The Actuality of Atonement: A Study of Metaphor, Rationality and the Christian Tradition*, (Edinburgh: T & T Clark, 1988).

— 'Two Dogmas Revisited: Edward Irving's Christology', *Scottish Journal of Theology*, 41 (1988) 359-376.

— *Christ and Creation*, (Carlisle: Paternoster, 1992).

— *Theology Through the Theologians: Selected Essays 1972-1995*, (Edinburgh: T & T Clark, 1996).

— (ed.), *The Cambridge Companion to Christian Doctrine*, (Cambridge: Cambridge University Press, 1997).

— *Yesterday and Today: A Study of Continuities in Christology*, (London: SPCK, 1997²).

— 'A Rose by Any Other Name? From 'Christian Doctrine' to 'Systematic Theology'', *International Journal of Systematic Theology* 1 (1999) 4-23.

— 'Aspects of Salvation: Some Unscholastic Themes from Calvin's *Institutes*', *International Journal of Systematic Theology* 1 (1999) 253-265.

— *Intellect and Action: Elucidations on Christian Theology and the Life of Faith*, (Edinburgh: T & T Clark, 2000).

Heron, Alasdair I. C., 'Homoousios with the Father', in Thomas F. Torrance, (ed.), *The Incarnation: Ecumenical Studies in the Nicene-Constantinopolitan Creed A.D. 381* (Edinburgh: Handsel Press, 1981) 58-87.

— (ed.), *The Westminster Confession in the Church today*, (Edinburgh: St. Andrew Press, 1982).

Hooker, Morna D., *Not Ashamed of the Gospel: New Testament Interpretations of the Death of Christ*, (Carlisle: Paternoster, 1994).

Jansen, John Frederick, *Calvin's Doctrine of the Work of Christ*, (London: James Clarke, 1956).

Jenson, Robert W., *Systematic Theology: Volume 1: The Triune God*, (New York: Oxford University Press, 1997).

Jones, L. Gregory, *Embodying Forgiveness: A Theological Analysis*, (Grand Rapids: Eerdmans, 1995).

— 'Crafting Communities of Forgiveness', *Interpretation* 54 (2000) 121-134.

Kapic, Kelly M., 'The Son's assumption of a human nature: A call for clarity', Paper presented at the Society for the Study of Theology Conference, Oxford, April 2000.

LaCugna, Catherine Mowry, *God for us: The Trinity and Christian Life*, (New York: HarperSanFrancisco, 1991).

Mackintosh, H. R., *The Christian Experience of Forgiveness*, (London: Nisbet, 1927).

Macleod, Donald, *The Person of Christ*, (Leicester: IVP, 1998).

McFarland, Ian, 'Christ, Spirit and Atonement', *International Journal of Systematic Theology* 3 (2001) 83-93.

McGrath, A.E., *Luther's Theology of the Cross*, (Oxford: Blackwell, 1985).

McIntyre, J., *The Shape of Christology*, (Edinburgh: T & T Clark, 1998²).

— *The Shape of Soteriology: Studies in the Doctrine of the Death of Christ* (Edinburgh: T & T Clark, 1992).

Moberly, R. C., *Atonement and Personality*, (London: John Murray, 1901).

Moltmann, J., *The Crucified God: The Cross of Christ as the Foundation and Criticism of Christian Theology*, (London: SCM Press, 1974).

— *The Trinity and the Kingdom of God*, (London: SCM Press, 1981).

— *The Way of Jesus Christ*, (London: SCM Press, 1990).

— *History and the Triune God*, (London: SCM Press, 1991).

Morgan, R., and Barton, J., *Biblical Interpretation*, (Oxford: Oxford University Press, 1988).

Mozley, J. K., *The Doctrine of the Atonement*, (London: Duckworth, 1915).

Murray, Iain, *The Puritan Hope: A Study in Revival and the Interpretation of Prophecy*, (Edinburgh: Banner of Truth, 1971).

Norman, E. R., *Anti-Catholicism in Victorian England*, (London: George Allen and Unwin, 1968).

Owen, J., *The Works of John Owen*, vol. I, (ed.), W. H. Goold, (London: Banner of Truth, 1965).

— *The Works of John Owen*, vol. III, (ed.), W. H. Goold, (London: Banner of Truth, 1965).

Placher, William C., 'Christ Takes Our Place: Rethinking Atonement', *Interpretation* 53 (1999) 5-20.

Rahner, Karl, *Foundations of Christian Faith*, (London: Darton, Longman & Todd, 1976).

Reardon, Bernard M. G., *From Coleridge to Gore: A Century of Religious Thought in Britain*, (London: Longman, 1971).

— *Religion in the Age of Romanticism*, (Cambridge: Cambridge University Press, 1985).

Robinson, John A. T., *The Body: A Study in Pauline Theology*, (London: SCM Press, 1952).

Rowell, Geoffrey, *Hell and the Victorians*, (Oxford: Clarendon Press, 1974).

Schwöbel, Christoph, and Gunton, Colin E., (eds.), *Persons, Divine and Human*, (Edinburgh: T & T Clark, 1991).

Seitz, Christopher R., (ed.), *Nicene Christianity: The Future for a New Ecumenism*, (Grand Rapids: Brazos, 2001 /Carlisle: Paternoster, 2001).

Smail, T., *The Giving Gift: The Holy Spirit in Person*, (London: Hodder & Stoughton, 1988).

— *Once and For All: A Confession of the Cross*, (London: Darton, Longman & Todd, 1998).

—'The Holy Spirit in the Holy Trinity', in C. R. Seitz (ed.), *Nicene Christianity: The Future for a New Ecumenism*, (Grand Rapids: Brazos, 2001 / Carlisle: Paternoster, 2001), 149-165.

Steinmetz, David C., 'The Superiority of Pre-Critical Exegesis', in Stephen E. Fowl, (ed.), *The Theological Interpretation of Scripture: Classic and Contemporary Readings*, (Oxford: Blackwell, 1997), 26-38.

Stott, J. R. W., *The Cross of Christ*, (Leicester: IVP, 1986).

Sykes, Stephen W., (ed.), *Sacrifice and redemption: Durham Essays in Theology* (Cambridge: CUP, 1991).

— *The Story of Atonement*, (London: Darton, Longman & Todd, 1997).

Thielicke, H., *The Evangelical Faith, Volume 2: The Doctrine of God and of Christ*, (Edinburgh: T & T Clark, 1977).

Tidball, Derek J., *Who are the Evangelicals?*, (London: Marshall Pickering, 1994).

Torrance, Alan, 'Does God Suffer? Incarnation and Impassibility', in *Christ In Our Place: The Humanity of God in Christ for the Reconciliation of the World*, Trevor A. Hart and Daniel P. Thimell (eds.), (Exeter: Paternoster Press, 1989) 345-368.

Travis, Stephen H., 'Christ as Bearer of Divine Judgement in Paul's Thought about the Atonement', in J. Goldingay (ed.), *Atonement Today*, (London: SPCK, 1995) 21-38.

Vidler, A., *The Church in an Age of Revolution*, (Harmondsworth: Penguin, 1961).

Wainwright, Geoffrey, *For Our Salvation: Two Approaches to the Work of Christ*, (Grand Rapids: Eerdmans, 1997).

Wallace, Ronald, *The Atoning Death of Christ*, (London: Marshall Morgan and Scott, 1981).

Weinandy, Thomas G., *In the Likeness of Sinful Flesh: An Essay on the Humanity of Christ*, (Edinburgh: T & T Clark, 1993).

— *Does God Suffer?*, (Edinburgh: T & T Clark, 2000).

Willis, E. David, *Calvin's Catholic Christology: The Function of the so-called Extra Calvinisticum in Calvin's Theology*, (Leiden: E. J. Brill, 1966).

Wright, N. T., *Jesus and the Victory of God (Christian Origins and the Question of God: Volume 2)*, (London: SPCK, 1996).

— *The Challenge of Jesus*, (London: SPCK, 2000).

Young, David, *F. D. Maurice and Unitarianism*, (Oxford: Clarendon Press, 1992).

Young, Frances, *From Nicea to Chalcedon*, (London: SCM Press, 1983).

Index

Abelard, Peter 69
Albury Park Conference
   33n, 37m, 222
Anhypostasia 168
Anderson, R. A. 6
Anselm 2n, 67, 76
Antinomianism 9, 13-14, 18,
   30, 32, 284, 286
Arminianism 9, 18
Ascension 216-217, 264
Assurance of faith 7, 9, 12,
   14-15, 25-33, 52, 61, 109,
   111, 184, 199, 233, 283-
   285, 287-290, 352-370, 422
Athanasius 72-73, 107, 124n,
   160-161, 177n, 188, 274
Atonement 8-25, 30-31, 46-
   53, 54-113, 117-151, 176-
   179, 195-203, 212-214, 254-
   278, 279, 284-286, 287-291

Baldwin Brown, James 51
Barrett, C. K. 172n
Barth, Karl 57, 84, 138-139,
   168n, 187, 219, 273-274
Bebbington, David 33n, 34n,
   50, 52
Bell, Charles 13-15, 30n
Bernard of Clairvaux 69
Bewkes, Eugene 46, 87-88,
   152, 183
Bible Readings 117-118
Blackfriars Street Chapel 45-
   48, 136n
'Black Act', *see* Marrow
   controversy

Blood of Christ 9, 124-136,
   224, 228-229, 240, 246-247,
   249-250, 260-264, 284, 307-
   308, 321, 352-370, 407,
   413, 415
Boston, Thomas 13, 14, 16,
   67n
Bread of Life 163, 308
Burleigh, J. H. S. 32, 213

Calvin, John 4, 14, 28, 29, 80-
   81, 110-111, 126, 156-157,
   188n, 192-196, 198, 199,
   203-204, 207n, 209, 210,
   216-218, 228n, 232, 248-
   250, 252
Campbell, Dr. Donald 7, 30,
   44, 45n, 61
Campbell, Donald (Son) 9,
   116n, 117-119, 131, 226n
Campbell, Mary 35-36
Campbell, Isabella 35
Campbell, John McLeod
   Christ the Bread of Life 46,
      48, 53n, 143, 221-253
   Everlasting Gospel 115n
   Fragments of Exposition
      136-139, 150-151, 179-
      182, 238, 254-255, 269-
      270, 277
   Fragments of Truth 116-
      135, 146n, 150-151, 238,
      254-255, 260-262, 269-
      270, 277

Good Tidings 115, 141,
147n, 149-150, 157n,
251
Memorials 5n, 10n, 12n,
19n, 33-34n, 38n, 42-
43n, 45n, 47n, 49n, 52-
54n, 65n, 101n, 111-
112n, 114-115n, 117n,
142n, 167n, 182-183n,
223n, 225-226n, 243-
244n, 269n, 271n
Nature of the Atonement 1-
6, 18, 20, 25, 41, 46-49,
51, 54-113, 118-151, 159,
169, 176, 186-187, 189-
191, 200, 203, 215, 238-
239, 252, 254-260, 269-
270, 271-278
Notes of Sermons 47, 114-
116, 139-151, 152-191,
192-220, 247-251, 254-
278, 294-311, 312-327,
328-351, 352-370, 371-
386, 387-410, 411-430
Reminiscences 8-9n, 34n,
38, 41n, 49, 60-61n,
103n, 111n, 184n, 193
Sermons and Lectures 47,
114-116, 139-151, 152-
191, 192-220, 247-251,
254-278
Thoughts on Revelation 48,
143, 225, 230-235, 258,
266n, 270
Two Sermons 115n, 279
Carlyle, Thomas 52
Catholic Apostolic Church,
see London Mission
Catholicism, *see* Roman
Catholicism

Chalcedonian Definition
161, 168, 182, 255
Chalmers, Thomas 33n, 35,
110, 144n
Christology 1-6, 34, 41-44,
70-74, 79, 90-92, 134-135,
152-191, 192-220, 254-278
Church of Scotland 1, 8-15,
17, 30-44, 233
Coleridge, S. T. 52
Communion 221-253, 411-
430
Concupisence 181
Confession, *see* Perfect
confession
Covenant theology, *see*
Federal Calvinism
Cranfield, C. E. B. 167n
Cry of derelication 92-94

Deification, *see* Theosis
Del Colle, Ralph 265
Depravity 140-141
Dickson, David 13
Divinzation, *see* Theosis
Dorries, David 188
Double decree 21, 232
Dragas, G. D. 72-73
Dunn, James D. G. 167n,
172n
Durham, James 13

Edwards, Jonathan 67-68,
77, 80n, 110, 187
Election 9, 16, 20-22, 32, 68,
280, 289
Emancipation Act 222
Enhypostasia 168
Epiclesis 246
Erskine, Ebenezer 14

Index

Erskine, Ralph 14
Erskine, Thomas 18-19, 31, 36n, 37n, 38, 40, 54, 67n, 111-113, 116, 117n, 184-185, 226, 245n
Eucharist 221-253, 411-430
Evangelical Party 6, 31-41, 50-53, 110, 221, 280
Evangelicalism 50-53, 252-253, 278
Exemplarism, see Moral influence
Experience, role in theology 58-63
Expiation 80n

Faris, D. L. 7n, 108, 189n
Farrow, D 216-217
Federal theology 7, 20-21, 110, 221
Fencing of the Tables 248, 411-430
Fiddes, P. S. 70, 81
Fisher, Edward 14, 61n
Fleming, Dr. 30
Flesh of Christ 152-191
Forgiveness 28-30
Forsyth, P. T. 206n, 257n

Gareloch Pentecost 1, 6, 35-40, 278
General Assembly 13-14, 30-44, 97
Gerrish, B. 80, 110-111
Glasgow, Campbell's ministry 44-48
Glasgow University 7, 48
Goodloe, J. 4, 19-21, 50-51, 58-63, 136, 230, 254-255, 270, 278

Gorringe, T. 99
Graham, Dr. 37-38
Gregory of Nazianzuus 158n, 160n, 187, 200
Gunton, Colin E. 2n, 76n, 97-101, 138n

Hart, Trevor A. 51, 54n, 67, 83n
Helm, Paul, 14n, 30n
Heresy, see Row heresy
Hog, James 14
Holy Spirit 1, 18, 34-40, 95-96, 108, 121-122, 142-144, 179-183, 246-249, 251, 252-271, 352-370
Homoousion 71, 107n, 241n, 256, 260
Hopkins, Mark 51
Horrocks, Don 111-113, 185

Impassibility 158-164
Incarnation 83-84, 122, 131n, 191
Infallibility 225
Intercession of Christ 86-89, 196-203
Irenaeus 137
Irving, Edward 5, 27, 32-45, 52, 142, 167n, 183-189, 222, 267-271, 277

Jansen, J. F. 192-193, 204
Jenson, Robert 216-217
Jinkins, Michael 4n, 92n, 93, 146, 201-202, 255
Judgement 75, 91, 98, 104-106, 143-144, 203-214, 262

Kapic, Kelly 180
Kelsey, David 59-60
Kettler, Christian 71, 107,
Kilninver 7, 44

Libel 12, 287-293
London Mission 45, 142
Lord's Supper 221-253, 411-430
Luther, Martin 57, 67n, 162, 219

MacDonald, James and George 36-37
MacLean, Hugh Bailie, 42-43, 53n
Macleod, Norman 48-49
Macleod, Donald 167n, 206n
Macquarrie, John 46, 83, 102-104
Manning, Cardinal 225
Marrow controversy 12-17, 19n, 30-32
Martineau, James 19
Maurice, F. D. 223n
Melanchthon, Philip 256
Moderate Party 6, 31-41, 50, 280
Moltmann, J. 1, 94, 100, 261n, 263-264
Moral influence theory 54-55, 87-89, 133, 149
Murray, Iain 33n

Needham, Nicholas 37n, 39, 40, 41n, 111
Newell, Philip 27n, 35n, 42n, 144n
Newman, J. H. 225

Owen, John 25n, 67-68, 110, 126, 185-189, 263, 267n, 268, 270
Oxford Movement 223

'Papal Aggression' 224
Pastoral Admonition 43, 183
Penal approaches 25, 44, 90, 147
Perfect confession 55, 77, 81-84, 132-133, 135, 139, 145-147, 176, 189-191, 271-278
Perfect repentance 55, 77, 80, 84, 99n
Perichoresis 261
Person of Christ 1-6, 34, 41-44, 70-74, 79, 90-92, 134-135, 152-191, 192-220, 254-278
Phinehas 75-77, 126
Pneumatology 1, 18, 34-40, 95-96, 108, 121-122, 142-144, 179-183, 246-249, 251, 252-271, 352-370
Prayer 201-203, 235-237
Presbytery of Annan 43
Presbytery of Dumbarton 10-27, 205n
Presbytery of Lorn 8, 43, 152, 183
Priestly office 74-89, 133, 145-147, 170, 173, 192-203, 218-220, 255-256, 352-370, 371-386
Propitiation 15, 66, 363, 428
Prospective aspect of atonement 54-56, 73, 74, 79, 84-89, 85, 109, 112, 122, 131, 133, 146-147, 203
Pusey, E. B. 223

Index

Rahner, Karl 68-69, 100
Reconciliation 119-131
Redding, Graham 82, 236n
Reform Act 1832 213
Retrospective aspect of atonement 54, 55, 56, 73, 74-89, 95, 109, 112, 121, 131, 145, 146, 203, 214
Revelation 68-71, 73-74, 85, 104, 123-124, 132, 137, 149-150, 170-171, 175, 230-235, 257-260
Roman Catholicism 41, 53, 221-253
Romanticism 33n, 52-53, 278
Rosneath 27, 33, 35, 48-49
Royal office 203-220, 387-410
Rhu, *see* Row
Row 1, 7-44
Row heresy 1, 7-44, 116, 139
Rutherford, Samuel 16, 80

Schleiermacher, F. D. E. 59, 265n, 278
Scott, A. J. 33-35, 41-43, 51, 53n, 112, 116, 144n, 185n, 223
Scripture 102-103
Shairp, Principal 64-65
Sinlessness 153-174, 179-183, 206, 273
Smail, Tom 93-94, 101, 266
Spence, Alan 186
Story, Robert 27, 32, 33n, 205n

Story, Robert H. 27n, 36n, 49, 185n
Stott, J. R. W. 54n
Synod of Glasgow and Ayr 28-30, 37, 39

Theosis 72, 176-179, 279
Thimell, Daniel P. 9, 117-118
Torrance, Alan 161-162
Torrance, James B. 7n, 54n, 78, 80, 107n, 193, 236n
Torrance, Thomas F. 1, 13, 16n, 74n, 80, 107, 178, 217, 241n, 256n
Transubstantiation 225, 227-229, 242-244, 249
Travis, Stephen 105-106
Trinity 92-94, 169, 215, 235-237, 256-271
Turberville, Dean 140-141
Tuttle, George 2, 4n, 60, 101-102, 112-113, 254

Universal atonement 9, 15-17, 44
Universal pardon 9, 17-25
Universalism 17-19, 22, 25

Van Dyk, Leanne 4, 18n, 27n, 31, 72-74, 78-80, 88n, 93, 95, 107, 109, 254, 255, 269-270
Von Balthasar, Hans Urs 131n, 187
Vicarious humanity 107-108
Vicarious repentance, *see* Perfect repentance
Victory of Christ 96-97

Wainwright, Geoffrey 187, 192n, 194-195
Weinandy, Thomas 155, 161, 173, 181, 188, 191
Westminster Confession 7n, 17, 31, 42, 50, 110, 233n
Wolfe, John 222-223, 224n
Wiseman, Nicholas 224-225
Wrath 19, 23, 52, 60, 64, 65, 78-79, 81, 86, 90-92, 104, 105, 130, 143, 145, 195, 211, 274, 275, 282, 311, 352, 353, 356, 359, 361, 364, 374, 381, 389, 390, 402, 427, 428
Wright, N. T. 220, 276

Zeal 125-126

Studies in Evangelical History and Thought
(All titles uniform with this volume)
Dates in bold are of projected publication

Clyde Binfield
The Country a Little Thickened and Congested?
Nonconformity in Eastern England 1840–1885
Studies of Victorian religion and society often concentrate on cities, suburbs, and industrialisation. This study provides a contrast. Victorian Eastern England—Essex, Suffolk, Norfolk, Cambridgeshire, and Huntingdonshire—was rural, traditional, relatively unchanging. That is nonetheless a caricature which discounts the industry in Norwich and Ipswich (as well as in Haverhill, Stowmarket, and Leiston) and ignores the impact of London on Essex, of railways throughout the region, and of an ancient but changing university (Cambridge) on the county town which housed it. It also entirely ignores the political implications of such changes in a region noted for the variety of its religious Dissent since the seventeenth century. This book explores Victorian Eastern England and its Nonconformity. It brings to a wider readership a pioneering thesis which has made a major contribution to a fresh evolution of English religion and society.
***2005** / 1-84227-216-0 / approx. 274pp*

John Brencher
Martyn Lloyd-Jones (1899–1981) and Twentieth-Century Evangelicalism
This study critically demonstrates the significance of the life and ministry of Martyn Lloyd-Jones for post-war British evangelicalism and demonstrates that his preaching was his greatest influence on twentieth-century Christianity. The factors which shaped his view of the church are examined, as is the way his reformed evangelicalism led to a separatist ecclesiology which divided evangelicals.
2002 / 1-84227-051-6 / xvi + 268pp

Jonathan D. Burnham
A Story of Conflict
The Controversial Relationship between Benjamin Wills Newton and John Nelson Darby
Burnham explores the controversial relationship between the two principal leaders of the early Brethren movement. In many ways Newton and Darby were products of their times, and this study of their relationship provides insight not only into the dynamics of early Brethrenism, but also into the progress of nineteenth-century English and Irish evangelicalism.
2004 / 1-84227-191-1 / xxiv + 268pp

November 2004

J.N. Ian Dickson
Beyond Religious Discourse
*Sermons, Preaching and Evangelical Protestants in
Nineteenth-Century Irish Society*
Drawing extensively on primary sources, this pioneer work in modern religious history explores the training of preachers, the construction of sermons and how Irish evangelicalism and the wider movement in Great Britain and the United States shaped the preaching event. Evangelical preaching and politics, sectarianism, denominations, education, class, social reform, gender, and revival are examined to advance the argument that evangelical sermons and preaching went significantly beyond religious discourse. The result is a book for those with interests in Irish history, culture and belief, popular religion and society, evangelicalism, preaching and communication.
2005 / 1-84227-217-9 / approx. 324pp

Neil T.R. Dickson
Brethren in Scotland 1838–2000
A Social Study of an Evangelical Movement
The Brethren were remarkably pervasive throughout Scottish society. This study of the Open Brethren in Scotland places them in their social context and examines their growth, development and relationship to society.
2003 / 1-84227-113-X / xxviii + 510pp

Crawford Gribben and Timothy C.F. Stunt (eds)
Prisoners of Hope?
Aspects of Evangelical Millennialism in Britain and Ireland, 1800–1880
This volume of essays offers a comprehensive account of the impact of evangelical millennialism in nineteenth-century Britain and Ireland.
2004 / 1-84227-224-1 / xiv + 208pp

Khim Harris
Evangelicals and Education
*Evangelical Anglicans and Middle-Class Education
in Nineteenth-Century England*
This ground breaking study investigates the history of English public schools founded by nineteenth-century Evangelicals. It documents the rise of middle-class education and Evangelical societies such as the influential Church Association, and includes a useful biographical survey of prominent Evangelicals of the period.
2004 / 1-84227-250-0 / xviii + 422pp

November 2004

Mark Hopkins
Nonconformity's Romantic Generation
Evangelical and Liberal Theologies in Victorian England
A study of the theological development of key leaders of the Baptist and Congregational denominations at their period of greatest influence, including C.H. Spurgeon and R.W. Dale, and of the controversies in which those among them who embraced and rejected the liberal transformation of their evangelical heritage opposed each other.
2004 / 1-84227-150-4 / xvi + 284pp

Don Horrocks
Laws of the Spiritual Order
Innovation and Reconstruction in the Soteriology of Thomas Erskine of Linlathen
Don Horrocks argues that Thomas Erskine's unique historical and theological significance as a soteriological innovator has been neglected. This timely reassessment reveals Erskine as a creative, radical theologian of central and enduring importance in Scottish nineteenth-century theology, perhaps equivalent in significance to that of S.T. Coleridge in England.
2004 / 1-84227-192-X / xx + 362pp

Kenneth S. Jeffrey
When the Lord Walked the Land
The 1858–62 Revival in the North East of Scotland
Previous studies of revivals have tended to approach religious movements from either a broad, national or a strictly local level. This study of the multifaceted nature of the 1859 revival as it appeared in three distinct social contexts within a single region reveals the heterogeneous nature of simultaneous religious movements in the same vicinity.
2002 / 1-84227-057-5 / xxiv + 304pp

John Kenneth Lander
Itinerant Temples
Tent Methodism, 1814–1832
Tent preaching began in 1814 and the Tent Methodist sect resulted from disputes with Bristol Wesleyan Methodists in 1820. The movement spread to parts of Gloucestershire, Wiltshire, London and Liverpool, among other places. Its demise started in 1826 after which one leader returned to the Wesleyans and others became ministers in the Congregational and Baptist denominations.
2003 / 1-84227-151-2 / xx + 268pp

Donald M. Lewis
Lighten Their Darkness
The Evangelical Mission to Working-Class London, 1828–1860
This is a comprehensive and compelling study of the Church and the complexities of nineteenth-century London. Challenging our understanding of the culture in working London at this time, Lewis presents a well-structured and illustrated work that contributes substantially to the study of evangelicalism and mission in nineteenth-century Britain.
2001 / 1-84227-074-5 / xviii + 372pp

Herbert McGonigle
'Sufficient Saving Grace'
John Wesley's Evangelical Arminianism
A thorough investigation of the theological roots of John Wesley's evangelical Arminianism and how these convictions were hammered out in controversies on predestination, limited atonement and the perseverance of the saints.
2001 / 1-84227-045-1 / xvi + 350pp

Lisa S. Nolland
A Victorian Feminist Christian
Josephine Butler, the Prostitutes and God
Josephine Butler was an unlikely candidate for taking up the cause of prostitutes, as she did, with a fierce and self-disregarding passion. This book explores the particular mix of perspectives and experiences that came together to envision and empower her remarkable achievements. It highlights the vital role of her spirituality and the tragic loss of her daughter.
2004 / 1-84227-225-X / approx. 360pp

Ian M. Randall
Evangelical Experiences
A Study in the Spirituality of English Evangelicalism 1918–1939
This book makes a detailed historical examination of evangelical spirituality between the First and Second World Wars. It shows how patterns of devotion led to tensions and divisions. In a wide-ranging study, Anglican, Wesleyan, Reformed and Pentecostal-charismatic spiritualities are analysed.
1999 / 0-85364-919-7 / xii + 310pp

Ian M. Randall
Spirituality and Social Change
The Contribution of F.B. Meyer (1847–1929)
This is a fresh appraisal of F.B. Meyer (1847–1929), a leading Free Church minister. Having been deeply affected by holiness spirituality, Meyer became the Keswick Convention's foremost international speaker. He combined spirituality with effective evangelism and socio-political activity. This study shows Meyer's significant contribution to spiritual renewal and social change.
2003 / 1-84227-195-4 / xx + 184pp

James Robinson
Pentecostal Origins (1907–c.1925): A Regional Study
Early Pentecostalism in Ulster within its British Context
Harvey Cox describes Pentecostalism as 'the fascinating spiritual child of our time' that has the potential, at the global scale, to contribute to the 'reshaping of religion in the twenty-first century'. This study grounds such sentiments by examining at the local scale the origin, development and nature of Pentecostalism in the north of Ireland in its first twenty years. Illustrative, in a paradigmatic way, of how Pentecostalism became established within one region of the British Isles, it sets the story within the wider context of formative influences emanating from America, Europe and, in particular, other parts of the British Isles. As a synoptic regional study in Pentecostal history it is the first survey of its kind.
2005 / 1-84227-329-9 / approx. 424pp

Geoffrey Robson
Dark Satanic Mills?
Religion and Irreligion in Birmingham and the Black Country
This book analyses and interprets the nature and extent of popular Christian belief and practice in Birmingham and the Black Country during the first half of the nineteenth century, with particular reference to the impact of cholera epidemics and evangelism on church extension programmes.
2002 / 1-84227-102-4 / xiv + 294pp

Roger Shuff
Searching for the True Church
Brethren and Evangelicals in Mid-Twentieth-Century England
Roger Shuff holds that the influence of the Brethren movement on wider evangelical life in England in the twentieth century is often underrated. This book records and accounts for the fact that Brethren reached the peak of their strength at the time when evangelicalism was at it lowest ebb, immediately before World War II. However, the movement then moved into persistent decline as evangelicalism regained ground in the post war period. Accompanying this downward trend has been a sharp accentuation of the contrast between Brethren congregations who engage constructively with the non-Brethren scene and, at the other end of the spectrum, the isolationist group commonly referred to as 'Exclusive Brethren'.
2005 / 1-84227-254-3 / approx. 318pp

James H.S. Steven
Worship in the Spirit
Charismatic Worship in the Church of England
This book explores the nature and function of worship in six Church of England churches influenced by the Charismatic Movement, focusing on congregational singing and public prayer ministry. The theological adequacy of such ritual is discussed in relation to pneumatological and christological understandings in Christian worship.
2002 / 1-84227-103-2 / xvi + 238pp

Peter K. Stevenson
God in Our Nature
The Incarnational Theology of John McLeod Campbell
This radical reassessment of Campbell's thought arises from a comprehensive study of his preaching and theology. Previous accounts have overlooked both his sermons and his Christology. This study examines the distinctive Christology evident in his sermons and shows that it sheds new light on Campbell's much debated views about atonement.
2004 / 1-84227-218-7 / xxiv + 458pp

Martin Wellings
Evangelicals Embattled
Responses of Evangelicals in the Church of England to Ritualism, Darwinism and Theological Liberalism 1890–1930
In the closing years of the nineteenth century and the first decades of the twentieth century Anglican Evangelicals faced a series of challenges. In responding to Anglo-Catholicism, liberal theology, Darwinism and biblical criticism, the unity and identity of the Evangelical school were severely tested.
2003 / 1-84227-049-4 / xviii + 352pp

James Whisenant
A Fragile Unity
*Anti-Ritualism and the Division of Anglican Evangelicalism
in the Nineteenth Century*
This book deals with the ritualist controversy (approximately 1850–1900) from the perspective of its evangelical participants and considers the divisive effects it had on the party.
2003 / 1-84227-105-9 / xvi + 530pp

Haddon Willmer
Evangelicalism 1785–1835: An Essay (1962) and Reflections (2004)
Awarded the Hulsean Prize in the University of Cambridge in 1962, this interpretation of a classic period of English Evangelicalism, by a young church historian, is now supplemented by reflections on Evangelicalism from the vantage point of a retired Professor of Theology.
2005 / 1-84227-219-5

Linda Wilson
Constrained by Zeal
Female Spirituality amongst Nonconformists 1825–1875
Constrained by Zeal investigates the neglected area of Nonconformist female spirituality. Against the background of separate spheres, it analyses the experience of women from four denominations, and argues that the churches provided a 'third sphere' in which they could find opportunities for participation.
2000 / 0-85364-972-3 / xvi + 294pp

Paternoster
9 Holdom Avenue
Bletchley
Milton Keynes MK1 1QR
United Kingdom

Web: www.authenticmedia.co.uk/paternoster

November 2004

www.ingramcontent.com/pod-product-compliance
Lightning Source LLC
Chambersburg PA
CBHW052047290426
44111CB00011B/1648